THE AMERICAN MARKETPLACE

Demographics and Spending Patterns

THE AMERICAN MARKETPLACE

Demographics and Spending Patterns

10th EDITION

BY THE EDITORS OF NEW STRATEGIST PUBLICATIONS

New Strategist Publications, Inc.
Ithaca, New York

New Strategist Publications, Inc.
P.O. Box 242, Ithaca, New York 14851
800/848-0842; 607/273-0913
www.newstrategist.com

ISBN 978-1-935775-27-0 (hardcover)
ISBN 978-1-935775-28-7 (paper)

Printed in the United States of America

Table of Contents

Chapter 4. Housing Trends

Chapter 5. Income Trends

Chapter 6. Labor Force Trends

Chapter 10. Time Use Trends

Chapter 11. Wealth Trends

List of Tables

Chapter 4. Housing Trends

Chapter 5. Income Trends

Chapter 6. Labor Force Trends

Chapter 7. Living Arrangement Trends

Chapter 9. Spending Trends

Chapter 10. Time Use Trends

Chapter 11. Wealth Trends

List of Illustrations

Chapter 4. Housing Trends

Chapter 5. Income Trends

Chapter 6. Labor Force Trends

Chapter 10. Time Use Trends

Chapter 11. Wealth Trends

Introduction

Times have been tough. The United States is slowly recovering from the Great Recession, the most severe economic downturn since the Great Depression. Many Americans feel betrayed by the nation's financial institutions, politicians, and economic policymakers. Although turmoil seems to surround us, in fact there is one area of stability: demographics. In contrast to the volatility of economics, demographic change is slow and steady. For those looking for a way out of the woods, demographics offer a path. By understanding the demographic trends, businesses and policymakers can rediscover their customers and constituents. But if demographic insight is your goal, where do you start? Billions of statistics are only a mouse click away, creating a confusing cacophony of numbers. To find direction, start here, with the 10th edition of *The American Marketplace: Demographics and Spending Patterns*, a demographic reference tool that cuts through the statistical clutter and offers a roadmap out of the wilderness.

The American Marketplace reveals the latest demographic trends and tells the American story. It examines our changing lifestyles in rich detail, from 2010 census data by race and Hispanic origin to the percentage of homeowners who are underwater on their mortgage, from rising health insurance costs to declining homeownership rates, from what people think about gay marriage to how much the Great Recession reduced household wealth.

Now that the first decade of the 21st century is complete and we are limping into the second, the New Normal can no longer be denied. Businesses and governments must adapt to a socioeconomic reality that was unexpected and often less than what was once antici-pated. *The American Marketplace* reveals that reality—where we stand today and where we will be tomorrow.

The outsourcing of trend analysis

The first edition of *The American Marketplace* was published in 1992, before the Internet had a name. Today, the Internet is the repository of the government's massive demographic and socioeconomic databases. These are of great value to researchers with the time to search, download, and analyze information. For many, however, the job of understanding demographic trends has become increasingly difficult because the government no longer publishes much in the way of analysis. Essentially, the job of uncovering the trends has been outsourced to bloggers, market researchers, students, and library visitors, many of whom are overwhelmed by computer screens filled with numbers. In short, it has become more time consuming than ever to get no-nonsense answers to questions about demographic and socioeconomic trends.

In *The American Marketplace*, New Strategist has done the work for you. Our editors have spent hundreds of hours scouring government web sites, extracting numbers, creating tables that reveal trends, and producing indexes, percent distributions, and other calculations that provide context. *The American Marketplace* has the numbers and the stories behind them. Thumbing through its pages, you can gain more insight into the dynamics of the U.S. population than you could by spending all afternoon surfing databases on the Internet. By having *The American Marketplace* on your computer (with links to the Excel version of each table) or on your bookshelf, you can get the answers to your questions faster than you can online—no calculator required.

New to this edition of *American Marketplace* is 2010 census data on race and Hispanic origin for the nation, states, and metropolitan areas. The Attitudes chapter has new data from the 2010 General Social Survey. Also, this edition of *American Marketplace* has the latest data on the changing demographics of homeownership, based on the Census Bureau's 2010 Housing Vacancies and Homeownership Survey and the 2009 American Housing Survey. The Income chapter, with 2009 income statistics from the 2010 Current Population Survey, reveals the struggle of so many Americans to stay afloat. In the Labor Force chapter, 2010 labor force data show declining participation rates because of the economic downturn. The Time Use chapter reveals how Americans spent their time in 2009, with data from the American Time Use Survey. In the Spending chapter, the 2009 Consumer Expenditure Survey data reveal how households are adapting to the new economic reality. In the Wealth chapter, you will see what the Great Recession did to household wealth, with tables showing the decline between 2007 and 2009. It is not a pretty picture.

How to use this book

The American Marketplace is designed for easy use. It is divided into 11 chapters, organized alphabetically: Attitudes, Education, Health, Housing, Income, Labor Force, Living Arrangements, Population, Spending, Time Use, and Wealth.

Most of the tables in *American Marketplace* are based on data collected by the federal government, in particular the Census Bureau, the Bureau of Labor Statistics, the National Center for Education Statistics, the National Center for Health Statistics, and the Federal Reserve Board. The federal government continues to be the best, if not the only, source of up-to-date, reliable information on the changing characteristics of Americans. Although the government collected most of the data presented here, each table in *The American Marketplace* was handcrafted by New Strategist's demographers, individually compiled and created with calculations that reveal the stories behind the statistics.

Each chapter of *The American Marketplace* includes the demographic and lifestyle data that are important for understanding unfolding events in the United States. A page of text accompanies most of the tables, analyzing the data and highlighting the trends. If you want more statistical detail than the tables provide, you can plumb the original source of the data, listed at the bottom of each table. The book contains a comprehensive table list to help you locate the information you need. For a more detailed search, use the index at the back of the book. Also at the back of the book is the glossary, which defines the terms commonly used in the tables and text.

The American Marketplace is a reference tool that will help you cut through the clutter and track the trends. Use it and prosper.

CHAPTER 1

Attitude Trends

■ More Americans think life is exciting (52 percent) than pretty routine (43 percent).

■ Only 24 percent of people aged 18 to 44 say that most people can be trusted. Among people aged 65 or older, a much larger 44 percent trust others.

■ Thirty-six percent of Americans think their income is below average, up from 26 percent in 2000.

■ Only 23 percent of the public was satisfied with their financial situation in 2010, down from 31 percent in 2000.

■ The 56 percent majority of Americans believe in evolution. Belief is greatest among Asians (82 percent) and college graduates (65 percent).

■ Forty-three percent of the public believes sexual relations between adults of the same sex is not wrong at all, up from 29 percent in 2000. Forty-seven percent of Americans support the right of gays and lesbians to marry.

■ Nearly half of Americans get most of their news from television. The Internet is in second place, with 22 percent depending on it. Newspapers have fallen to third place, with 18 percent getting most of their news from the newspaper.

Happiness Has Declined

Marital happiness has not changed, however.

When asked how happy they are, only 29 percent of Americans said they were very happy in 2010, down from 34 percent in 2000. This is the smallest percentage ever recorded by the General Social Survey.

The share of Americans who say life is exciting (52 percent) now substantially tops the percentage who say it is pretty routine (43 percent). Younger generations are behind the growing feeling of excitement—53 to 55 percent of adults under age 65 say life is exciting compared with only 42 percent of people aged 65 or older.

Only 32 percent of the public agrees that most people can be trusted, down from 35 percent who felt that way 10 years earlier. Young adults are far less trusting than older Americans, with only 24 percent of 18-to-44-year-olds believing most people can be trusted compared with 44 percent of people aged 65 or older. Blacks and Hispanics are far less trusting than Asians or whites.

■ Millions of Americans are struggling to recover from the Great Recession, reducing their happiness.

Fewer than one in four younger adults trusts others

(percent of people aged 18 or older who think most people can be trusted, by age, 2010)

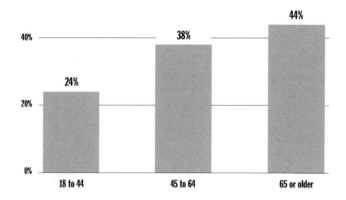

Table 1.1 General Happiness, 2000 and 2010

"Taken all together, how would you say things are these days—
would you say that you are very happy, pretty happy, or not too happy?"

(percent of people aged 18 or older responding, 2000 and 2010; and percent of people aged 18 or older responding by demographic characteristic, 2010)

	very happy	pretty happy	not too happy
TEN-YEAR TREND			
2010	28.8%	57.0%	14.2%
2000	33.9	56.4	9.6
2010 PROFILE			
Total people	**28.8**	**57.0**	**14.2**
Men	27.2	57.2	15.6
Women	30.1	56.9	13.0
Asian	14.8	64.1	21.1
Black	24.6	55.3	20.1
Hispanic	27.9	52.4	19.7
White	30.8	57.0	12.2
Aged 18 to 44	28.2	59.5	12.4
Aged 45 to 64	27.5	55.1	17.3
Aged 65 or older	32.8	54.5	12.8
Less than a bachelor's degree	26.6	56.9	16.5
Bachelor's degree or more	34.7	57.3	8.0

Note: Hispanics may be of any race.
Source: Survey Documentation and Analysis, Computer-assisted Survey Methods Program, University of California, Berkeley, General Social Surveys, 1972–2010 Cumulative Data Files, Internet site http://sda.berkeley.edu/cgi-bin32/hsda?harcsda+gss10; calculations by New Strategist

Table 1.2 Happiness of Marriage, 2000 and 2010

"Taking all things together, how would you describe your marriage?"

(percent of married people aged 18 or older responding, 2000 and 2010; and percent of married people aged 18 or older responding by demographic characteristic, 2010)

	very happy	pretty happy	not too happy
TEN-YEAR TREND			
2010	63.0%	34.3%	2.6%
2000	62.4	34.4	3.2
2010 PROFILE			
Total people	**63.0**	**34.3**	**2.6**
Men	62.2	34.6	3.1
Women	63.8	34.0	2.2
Asian	49.8	47.6	2.5
Black	54.7	41.9	3.4
Hispanic	50.5	47.2	2.3
White	64.9	32.6	2.5
Aged 18 to 44	65.0	32.7	2.3
Aged 45 to 64	63.0	34.1	2.9
Aged 65 or older	58.9	38.4	2.7
Less than a bachelor's degree	62.6	34.4	3.0
Bachelor's degree or more	63.9	34.2	1.9

Note: Hispanics may be of any race.
Source: Survey Documentation and Analysis, Computer-assisted Survey Methods Program, University of California, Berkeley, General Social Surveys, 1972–2010 Cumulative Data Files, Internet site http://sda.berkeley.edu/cgi-bin32/ hsda?harcsda+gss10; calculations by New Strategist

Table 1.3 Life Exciting or Dull, 2000 and 2010

"In general, do you find life exciting, pretty routine, or dull?"

(percent of people aged 18 or older responding, 2000 and 2010; and percent of people aged 18 or older responding by demographic characteristic, 2010)

	exciting	pretty routine	dull
TEN-YEAR TREND			
2010	52.1%	43.3%	4.6%
2000	46.6	49.1	4.3
2010 PROFILE			
Total people	**52.1**	**43.3**	**4.6**
Men	54.0	40.4	5.7
Women	50.4	45.9	3.7
Asian	51.4	45.2	3.4
Black	49.5	41.4	9.1
Hispanic	51.9	45.1	3.1
White	52.5	43.8	3.7
Aged 18 to 44	53.4	42.1	4.5
Aged 45 to 64	54.5	40.5	5.0
Aged 65 or older	42.5	53.2	4.3
Less than a bachelor's degree	46.7	47.6	5.7
Bachelor's degree or more	65.5	32.6	2.0

Note: Hispanics may be of any race.
Source: Survey Documentation and Analysis, Computer-assisted Survey Methods Program, University of California, Berkeley, General Social Surveys, 1972–2010 Cumulative Data Files, Internet site http://sda.berkeley.edu/cgi-bin32/ hsda?harcsda+gss10; calculations by New Strategist

Table 1.4 Trust in Others, 2000 and 2010

"Generally speaking, would you say that most people
can be trusted or that you can't be too careful in life?"

(percent of people aged 18 or older responding, 2000 and 2010; and percent of people aged 18 or older responding by demographic characteristic, 2010)

	can trust	cannot trust	depends
TEN-YEAR TREND			
2010	32.2%	62.5%	5.3%
2000	35.2	58.5	6.3
2010 PROFILE			
Total people	**32.2**	**62.5**	**5.3**
Men	35.6	58.0	6.4
Women	29.5	66.2	4.3
Asian	34.3	55.5	10.2
Black	12.7	81.2	6.0
Hispanic	13.5	84.9	1.6
White	37.6	57.3	5.1
Aged 18 to 44	23.8	71.1	5.1
Aged 45 to 64	38.2	56.6	5.2
Aged 65 or older	43.7	50.6	5.7
Less than a bachelor's degree	23.5	71.2	5.3
Bachelor's degree or more	55.5	39.3	5.2

Note: Hispanics may be of any race.
Source: Survey Documentation and Analysis, Computer-assisted Survey Methods Program, University of California, Berkeley, General Social Surveys, 1972–2010 Cumulative Data Files, Internet site http://sda.berkeley.edu/cgi-bin32/ hsda?harcsda+gss10; calculations by New Strategist

Most People Still Believe Hard Work Leads to Success

They are less likely to believe private enterprise will solve U.S. problems, however.

How do people get ahead? Nearly 70 percent of Americans say it is by hard work, and another one-fifth cite a combination of hard work and luck. Only 10 percent believe luck alone is the reason people get ahead. Women believe more strongly than men in hard work and Hispanics more than Asians, blacks, or whites.

The lifetime geographic mobility of Americans has changed little over the years. In both 2000 and 2010, about four out of ten people aged 18 or older said they live in the same place as they did at age 16. Educational attainment is an important predictor of mobility. People without a bachelor's degree are much more likely to have stayed put than those with a bachelor's degree.

A declining percentage of the public thinks private enterprise will solve our problems. The figure fell from 48 to 45 percent between 2000 and 2010. The percentage disagreeing with the notion that private enterprise will come to the rescue climbed from 15 to 28 percent during those years. The percentage of Americans who agree that we worry too much about the environment and too little about the economy grew from 38 to 42 percent between 2000 and 2010.

■ Anxiety about the Great Recession is causing some to reconsider their position on environmental issues.

Younger adults doubt private enterprise will solve problems

(percent of people aged 18 or older who agree that private enterprise will solve U.S. problems, 2010)

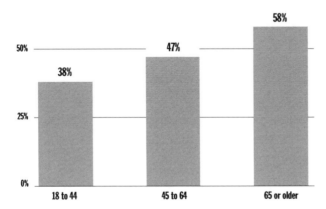

Table 1.5 How People Get Ahead, 2000 and 2010

"Some people say that people get ahead by their own hard work;
others say that lucky breaks or help from other people are more important.
Which do you think is most important?"

(percent of people aged 18 or older responding, 2000 and 2010; and percent of people aged 18 or older responding by demographic characteristic, 2010)

	hard work	both equally	luck
TEN-YEAR TREND			
2010	69.6%	20.4%	10.0%
2000	65.8	23.9	10.2
2010 PROFILE			
Total people	**69.6**	**20.4**	**10.0**
Men	66.5	20.7	12.8
Women	72.4	20.2	7.4
Asian	42.6	44.1	13.3
Black	64.8	21.0	14.2
Hispanic	84.0	9.3	6.7
White	71.5	19.8	8.7
Aged 18 to 44	70.1	18.8	11.2
Aged 45 to 64	70.3	21.1	8.7
Aged 65 or older	67.0	24.0	9.0
Less than a bachelor's degree	71.8	18.2	10.1
Bachelor's degree or more	64.3	26.1	9.6

Note: Hispanics may be of any race.
Source: Survey Documentation and Analysis, Computer-assisted Survey Methods Program, University of California, Berkeley, General Social Surveys, 1972–2010 Cumulative Data Files, Internet site http://sda.berkeley.edu/cgi-bin32/hsda?harcsda+gss10; calculations by New Strategist

Table 1.6 Geographic Mobility since Age 16, 2000 and 2010

"When you were 16 years old, were you living in this same (city / town / county)?"

(percent of people aged 18 or older responding, 2000 and 2010; and percent of people aged 18 or older responding by demographic characteristic, 2010)

	same city	same state, different city	outside state
TEN-YEAR TREND			
2010	39.4%	25.7%	34.9%
2000	39.9	26.0	34.1
2010 PROFILE			
Total people	**39.4**	**25.7**	**34.9**
Men	38.8	26.6	34.5
Women	39.8	24.9	35.3
Asian	35.2	16.8	48.0
Black	50.4	19.7	29.9
Hispanic	34.6	15.7	49.7
White	37.6	28.0	34.4
Aged 18 to 44	44.3	24.8	31.0
Aged 45 to 64	35.0	28.9	36.1
Aged 65 or older	34.8	21.8	43.3
Less than a bachelor's degree	44.6	24.0	31.3
Bachelor's degree or more	25.5	30.1	44.5

Note: Hispanics may be of any race.
Source: Survey Documentation and Analysis, Computer-assisted Survey Methods Program, University of California, Berkeley, General Social Surveys, 1972–2010 Cumulative Data Files, Internet site http://sda.berkeley.edu/cgi-bin32/hsda?harcsda+gss10; calculations by New Strategist

Table 1.7 Private Enterprise Will Solve Problems, 2000 and 2010

"Private enterprise will solve U.S. problems. Do you agree or disagree?"

(percent of people aged 18 or older responding, 2000 and 2010; and percent of people aged 18 or older responding by demographic characteristic, 2010)

	strongly agree	agree	neither agree nor disagree	disagree	strongly disagree
TEN-YEAR TREND					
2010	14.4%	30.2%	27.5%	22.8%	5.1%
2000	15.3	32.7	37.2	12.1	2.7
2010 PROFILE					
Total people	**14.4**	**30.2**	**27.5**	**22.8**	**5.1**
Men	21.5	33.9	19.7	20.4	4.5
Women	8.5	27.2	34.0	24.7	5.6
Asian	13.4	21.7	25.1	36.9	2.9
Black	8.2	15.4	24.7	40.3	11.3
Hispanic	8.4	29.3	35.8	20.0	6.4
White	15.8	33.6	27.8	18.9	3.9
Aged 18 to 44	11.1	26.9	34.3	23.4	4.3
Aged 45 to 64	16.6	30.5	22.4	23.0	7.5
Aged 65 or older	18.6	39.3	18.8	20.7	2.5
Less than a bachelor's degree	11.9	28.1	31.0	25.0	4.0
Bachelor's degree or more	20.5	35.5	18.8	17.2	8.0

Note: Hispanics may be of any race.
Source: Survey Documentation and Analysis, Computer-assisted Survey Methods Program, University of California, Berkeley, General Social Surveys, 1972–2010 Cumulative Data Files, Internet site http://sda.berkeley.edu/cgi-bin32/ hsda?harcsda+gss10; calculations by New Strategist

Table 1.8 Environment versus Economy, 2000 and 2010

"We worry too much about the environment, too little about the economy. Do you agree or disagree?"

(percent of people aged 18 or older responding, 2000 and 2010; and percent of people aged 18 or older responding by demographic characteristic, 2010)

	strongly agree	agree	neither agree nor disagree	disagree	strongly disagree
TEN-YEAR TREND					
2010	10.2%	32.3%	18.1%	31.7%	7.7%
2000	10.9	27.1	18.4	33.2	10.4
2010 PROFILE					
Total people	**10.2**	**32.3**	**18.1**	**31.7**	**7.7**
Men	10.0	33.1	18.9	29.8	8.2
Women	10.3	31.7	17.4	33.2	7.4
Asian	11.8	23.1	30.4	29.5	5.3
Black	21.3	40.4	11.4	23.5	3.3
Hispanic	8.6	40.3	20.6	23.8	6.7
White	8.0	30.6	18.9	33.7	8.9
Aged 18 to 44	8.6	31.5	20.1	33.0	6.8
Aged 45 to 64	10.7	30.3	17.1	32.5	9.3
Aged 65 or older	12.7	39.0	14.5	26.4	7.4
Less than a bachelor's degree	11.6	35.7	18.1	29.2	5.4
Bachelor's degree or more	6.2	23.4	17.8	38.4	14.2

Note: Hispanics may be of any race.
Source: Survey Documentation and Analysis, Computer-assisted Survey Methods Program, University of California, Berkeley, General Social Surveys, 1972–2010 Cumulative Data Files, Internet site http://sda.berkeley.edu/cgi-bin32/hsda?harcsda+gss10; calculations by New Strategist

Middle-Class Identification Has Declined

More are identifying themselves as members of the lower class.

The percentage of Americans who identify themselves as members of the lower class nearly doubled between 2000 and 2010, climbing from 4.5 to 8.2 percent. The percentage of those who identify themselves as members of the middle class fell from 46 to 42 percent during those years. Hispanics are least likely to put themselves in the middle class, at 25 percent.

A shrinking plurality of Americans believes their family income is average, the figure falling from 49 to 43 percent between 2000 and 2010. The percentage of those who say their family income is below average increased sharply, rising from 26 to 36 percent. Blacks, Hispanics, and people without a college diploma are most likely to say their incomes are below average.

The share of people who are satisfied with their financial situation has declined sharply in the past decade—falling from 31 percent in 2000 to 23 percent in 2010. The percentage who are not at all satisfied with their finances has climbed by 7 percentage points to 31 percent.

■ The growing number of Americans who feel like they are falling behind economically may lead to greater political turmoil in the years ahead.

Adults under age 65 are least satisfied with their financial situation

(percent of people aged 18 or older who are satisfied with their present financial situation, by age, 2010)

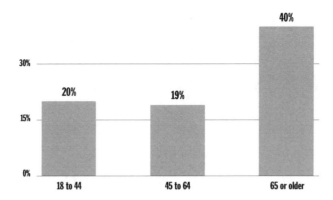

Table 1.9 Social Class Membership, 2000 and 2010

"If you were asked to use one of four names for your social class,
which would you say you belong in: the lower class,
the working class, the middle class, or the upper class?"

(percent of people aged 18 or older responding, 2000 and 2010; and percent of people aged 18 or older responding by demographic characteristic, 2010)

	lower	working	middle	upper
TEN-YEAR TREND				
2010	8.2%	46.8%	42.4%	2.5%
2000	4.5	45.6	46.0	3.9
2010 PROFILE				
Total people	**8.2**	**46.8**	**42.4**	**2.5**
Men	7.6	47.7	41.8	2.9
Women	8.7	46.1	42.9	2.2
Asian	7.2	42.5	48.9	1.3
Black	14.2	55.1	28.1	2.6
Hispanic	9.0	65.5	25.3	0.2
White	7.0	44.0	46.4	2.6
Aged 18 to 44	8.9	52.4	37.2	1.4
Aged 45 to 64	8.6	47.0	41.0	3.4
Aged 65 or older	5.0	31.1	60.0	3.8
Less than a bachelor's degree	10.8	55.2	32.6	1.4
Bachelor's degree or more	1.2	24.8	68.5	5.5

Note: Hispanics may be of any race.
Source: Survey Documentation and Analysis, Computer-assisted Survey Methods Program, University of California, Berkeley, General Social Surveys, 1972–2010 Cumulative Data Files, Internet site http://sda.berkeley.edu/cgi-bin32/hsda?harcsda+gss10; calculations by New Strategist

Table 1.10 Family Income Relative to Others, 2000 and 2010

"Compared with American families in general, would you say
your family income is far below average, below average,
average, above average, or far above average?"

(percent of people aged 18 or older responding, 2000 and 2010; and percent of people aged 18 or older responding by demographic characteristic, 2010)

	far below average	below average	average	above average	far above average
TEN-YEAR TREND					
2010	6.8%	28.8%	43.5%	18.4%	2.5%
2000	5.3	20.9	49.3	21.4	3.1
2010 PROFILE					
Total people	**6.8**	**28.8**	**43.5**	**18.4**	**2.5**
Men	4.9	30.0	42.4	20.2	2.5
Women	8.4	27.8	44.3	17.0	2.4
Asian	2.6	22.7	45.6	25.5	3.7
Black	10.9	36.0	45.3	7.6	0.2
Hispanic	7.9	37.9	47.4	5.3	1.5
White	6.0	26.8	42.8	21.5	2.9
Aged 18 to 44	7.7	28.8	45.8	15.5	2.2
Aged 45 to 64	7.6	31.3	37.5	20.2	3.4
Aged 65 or older	2.6	23.6	49.4	23.1	1.2
Less than a bachelor's degree	8.0	35.3	45.7	9.9	1.1
Bachelor's degree or more	3.8	11.8	37.6	40.9	5.9

Note: Hispanics may be of any race.
Source: Survey Documentation and Analysis, Computer-assisted Survey Methods Program, University of California, Berkeley, General Social Surveys, 1972–2010 Cumulative Data Files, Internet site http://sda.berkeley.edu/cgi-bin32/hsda?harcsda+gss10; calculations by New Strategist

Table 1.11 Satisfaction with Financial Situation, 2000 and 2010

"We are interested in how people are getting along financially
these days. So far as you and your family are concerned, would
you say that you are pretty well satisfied with your present
financial situation, more or less satisfied, or not satisfied at all?"

(percent of people aged 18 or older responding, 2000 and 2010; and percent of people aged 18 or older responding by demographic characteristic, 2010)

	satisfied	more or less satisfied	not at all satisfied
TEN-YEAR TREND			
2010	23.3%	45.2%	31.5%
2000	30.6	45.4	24.0
2010 PROFILE			
Total people	**23.3**	**45.2**	**31.5**
Men	23.5	45.4	31.1
Women	23.2	45.0	31.8
Asian	26.2	49.9	23.8
Black	17.0	38.9	44.1
Hispanic	11.0	57.2	31.8
White	25.4	45.5	29.1
Aged 18 to 44	20.4	46.4	33.2
Aged 45 to 64	19.5	45.0	35.5
Aged 65 or older	39.9	41.9	18.1
Less than a bachelor's degree	19.1	44.6	36.3
Bachelor's degree or more	34.5	46.7	18.8

Note: Hispanics may be of any race.
Source: Survey Documentation and Analysis, Computer-assisted Survey Methods Program, University of California, Berkeley, General Social Surveys, 1972–2010 Cumulative Data Files, Internet site http://sda.berkeley.edu/cgi-bin32/hsda?harcsda+gss10; calculations by New Strategist

Many Think Their Standard of Living Is Falling

Fewer Americans believe they are better off than their parents.

When comparing their own standard of living now with that of their parents when they were the same age, 59 percent of respondents say they are better off. The figure was a higher 67 percent 10 years ago. The oldest Americans are most likely to think they are better off than their parents were at the same age. Asians and Hispanics are more likely than blacks or whites to say they are doing better than their parents.

When asked whether they think they have a good chance of improving their present standard of living, only 58 percent of Americans agree. A decade earlier, fully 77 percent felt optimistic. By race and Hispanic origin, whites are least likely to feel like they will be able to get ahead. Only 53 percent of whites think they have a good chance of improving their standard of living.

Fifty-nine percent of parents believe their children will have a better standard of living when they reach their age. The share was a larger 69 percent 10 years earlier. Only 47 percent of parents aged 65 or older think their children will have a better standard of living when they reach their age compared with 67 percent of parents under age 45.

■ Americans who have the least are most likely to believe that things will get better.

Children will be better off

(percent of parents who think their children's standard of living will be better than theirs is today, by race and Hispanic origin, 2010)

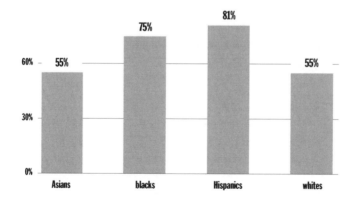

Table 1.12 Parents' Standard of Living, 2000 and 2010

"Compared to your parents when they were the age you are now, do you think your own standard of living now is much better, somewhat better, about the same, somewhat worse, or much worse than theirs was?"

(percent of people aged 18 or older responding, 2000 and 2010; and percent of people aged 18 or older responding by demographic characteristic, 2010)

	much better	somewhat better	about the same	somewhat worse	much worse
TEN-YEAR TREND					
2010	29.2%	29.7%	24.8%	12.1%	4.2%
2000	35.7	31.3	21.0	8.9	3.2
2010 PROFILE					
Total people	**29.2**	**29.7**	**24.8**	**12.1**	**4.2**
Men	27.6	30.0	26.3	12.1	4.1
Women	30.5	29.5	23.5	12.2	4.3
Asian	60.0	18.4	14.0	7.6	0.0
Black	29.8	28.6	25.6	8.9	7.1
Hispanic	35.4	37.7	14.5	7.0	5.4
White	27.3	30.1	26.2	12.8	3.6
Aged 18 to 44	26.8	30.1	26.4	13.2	3.5
Aged 45 to 64	27.7	27.2	24.9	14.3	5.8
Aged 65 or older	39.2	34.0	19.6	4.6	2.6
Less than a bachelor's degree	29.3	30.4	22.6	12.8	4.8
Bachelor's degree or more	28.9	27.9	30.3	10.4	2.5

Note: Hispanics may be of any race.
Source: Survey Documentation and Analysis, Computer-assisted Survey Methods Program, University of California, Berkeley, General Social Surveys, 1972–2010 Cumulative Data Files, Internet site http://sda.berkeley.edu/cgi-bin32/ hsda?harcsda+gss10; calculations by New Strategist

Table 1.13 Standard of Living Will Improve, 2000 and 2010

"The way things are in America, people like me and my family have a good chance of improving our standard of living. Do you agree or disagree?"

(percent of people aged 18 or older responding, 2000 and 2010; and percent of people aged 18 or older responding by demographic characteristic, 2010)

	strongly agree	agree	neither	disagree	strongly disagree
TEN-YEAR TREND					
2010	13.1%	44.9%	16.2%	21.6%	4.2%
2000	23.7	53.7	9.4	11.1	2.2
2010 PROFILE					
Total people	**13.1**	**44.9**	**16.2**	**21.6**	**4.2**
Men	14.0	47.4	14.1	19.1	5.4
Women	12.4	42.8	17.9	23.6	3.2
Asian	18.6	50.6	18.4	10.4	2.0
Black	25.6	50.5	9.9	11.6	2.4
Hispanic	20.0	56.3	11.7	9.4	2.6
White	9.5	43.6	17.3	24.9	4.7
Aged 18 to 44	17.1	44.9	16.9	18.0	3.1
Aged 45 to 64	10.5	42.0	16.1	25.6	5.9
Aged 65 or older	7.4	50.8	14.1	23.5	4.2
Less than a bachelor's degree	12.7	45.2	14.4	22.6	5.1
Bachelor's degree or more	14.3	44.0	21.0	18.7	2.0

Note: Hispanics may be of any race.
Source: Survey Documentation and Analysis, Computer-assisted Survey Methods Program, University of California, Berkeley, General Social Surveys, 1972–2010 Cumulative Data Files, Internet site http://sda.berkeley.edu/cgi-bin32/hsda?harcsda+gss10; calculations by New Strategist

Table 1.14 Children's Standard of Living, 2000 and 2010

"When your children are at the age you are now, do you think their standard of living will be much better, somewhat better, about the same, somewhat worse, or much worse than yours is now?"

(percent of people aged 18 or older with children responding, 2000 and 2010; and percent responding by demographic characteristic, 2010)

	much better	somewhat better	about the same	somewhat worse	much worse
TEN-YEAR TREND					
2010	27.4%	32.0%	20.6%	15.0%	5.1%
2000	32.9	35.6	19.2	8.6	3.7
2010 PROFILE					
Total people	**27.4**	**32.0**	**20.6**	**15.0**	**5.1**
Men	23.4	33.7	20.6	16.7	5.5
Women	30.5	30.5	20.6	13.6	4.7
Asian	15.9	39.3	31.1	11.4	2.1
Black	44.3	31.1	12.6	7.7	4.4
Hispanic	48.1	32.5	10.4	7.6	1.4
White	21.7	32.9	22.8	17.2	5.5
Aged 18 to 44	36.0	31.3	17.8	11.2	3.7
Aged 45 to 64	20.0	33.7	22.0	18.5	5.8
Aged 65 or older	17.0	30.3	25.9	19.2	7.7
Less than a bachelor's degree	31.6	32.8	17.2	13.1	5.4
Bachelor's degree or more	15.7	29.7	30.1	20.3	4.3

Note: Hispanics may be of any race.
Source: Survey Documentation and Analysis, Computer-assisted Survey Methods Program, University of California, Berkeley, General Social Surveys, 1972–2010 Cumulative Data Files, Internet site http://sda.berkeley.edu/cgi-bin32/hsda?harcsda+gss10; calculations by New Strategist

The Two-Child Family Is Most Popular

But larger families have grown in popularity.

In every demographic segment—by sex, race, age, or educational attainment—the plurality of Americans thinks two is the ideal number of children. A look at the 10-year trend confirms, however, that the two-child ideal has weakened during the past decade, falling from the preference of 52 percent of the public in 2000 to 48 percent in 2010. Meanwhile, the percentage of the public that prefers three children has been stable at 26 percent, and the percentage that prefer four or more children has grown from 10 to 12 percent during those years.

The great majority of the public believes children should have a good, hard spanking when they misbehave. Although the percentage of parents willing to spank has declined to 69 percent from 74 percent in 2000, even among the least-likely-to-spank demographic of Asian parents, three out of five acknowledge an occasional need for such punishment.

The percentage of people who believe it is better if the man is the breadwinner and the woman cares for the home (traditional sex roles) has fallen from 40 to 35 percent over the past decade. Only 31 percent of adults under age 45 prefer traditional sex roles compared with 48 percent of those aged 65 or older. Most people regardless of age do not think working harms a mother's relationship with her children.

Support for the view that government should help people pay their medical bills fell from 52 percent in 2000 to 47 percent in 2010.

■ Americans aged 65 or older, who are almost universally covered by government health insurance, are least likely to think the government should help people with their medical bills.

Even among the oldest Americans, a minority believes traditional sex roles are best

(percent of people aged 18 or older who think traditional sex roles are best, by age, 2010)

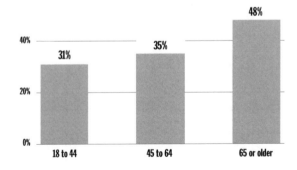

Table 1.15 Ideal Number of Children, 2000 and 2010

"What do you think is the ideal number of children for a family to have?"

(percent of people aged 18 or older responding, 2000 and 2010; and percent responding by demographic characteristic, 2010)

	none	one	two	three	four or more	as many as want
TEN-YEAR TREND						
2010	0.3%	2.5%	48.4%	26.3%	12.0%	10.5%
2000	1.2	3.5	52.3	25.8	10.0	7.2
2010 PROFILE						
Total people	**0.3**	**2.5**	**48.4**	**26.3**	**12.0**	**10.5**
Men	0.4	2.2	49.7	27.0	10.5	10.2
Women	0.2	2.7	47.5	25.8	13.1	10.7
Asian	0.0	1.9	56.7	32.0	9.4	0.0
Black	0.2	1.8	33.8	23.4	27.0	13.8
Hispanic	0.0	0.8	46.4	30.8	16.7	5.3
White	0.4	2.9	51.5	25.8	8.5	10.9
Aged 18 to 44	0.2	1.8	45.3	27.8	14.6	10.3
Aged 45 to 64	0.5	3.2	51.5	24.0	10.5	10.3
Aged 65 or older	0.2	3.0	51.7	26.3	8.0	10.8
Less than a bachelor's degree	0.3	2.2	47.3	26.6	14.1	9.5
Bachelor's degree or more	0.4	3.3	51.7	25.4	5.8	13.4

Note: Hispanics may be of any race.
Source: Survey Documentation and Analysis, Computer-assisted Survey Methods Program, University of California, Berkeley, General Social Surveys, 1972–2010 Cumulative Data Files, Internet site http://sda.berkeley.edu/cgi-bin32/ hsda?harcsda+gss10; calculations by New Strategist

Table 1.16 Spanking Children, 2000 and 2010

"Do you strongly agree, agree, disagree, or strongly disagree that it is sometimes necessary to discipline a child with a good, hard spanking?"

(percent of people aged 18 or older responding, 2000 and 2010; and percent responding by demographic characteristic, 2010)

	strongly agree	agree	disagree	strongly disagree
TEN-YEAR TREND				
2010	23.6%	45.4%	23.5%	7.5%
2000	31.9	42.5	18.1	7.6
2010 PROFILE				
Total people	**23.6**	**45.4**	**23.5**	**7.5**
Men	27.2	47.7	20.5	4.6
Women	20.8	43.6	25.8	9.8
Asian	27.6	33.1	31.0	8.3
Black	35.4	44.2	16.3	4.0
Hispanic	22.7	42.2	27.7	7.4
White	21.1	47.0	23.9	8.0
Aged 18 to 44	23.9	45.7	23.4	7.0
Aged 45 to 64	21.9	46.0	23.7	8.4
Aged 65 or older	25.7	43.4	23.6	7.3
Less than a bachelor's degree	25.9	45.4	23.1	5.6
Bachelor's degree or more	17.3	45.2	24.7	12.8

Note: Hispanics may be of any race.
Source: Survey Documentation and Analysis, Computer-assisted Survey Methods Program, University of California, Berkeley, General Social Surveys, 1972–2010 Cumulative Data Files, Internet site http://sda.berkeley.edu/cgi-bin32/hsda?harcsda+gss10; calculations by New Strategist

Table 1.17 Better for Man to Work, Woman to Tend Home, 2000 and 2010

"It is much better for everyone involved if the man is the achiever outside the home and the woman takes care of the home and family."

(percent of people aged 18 or older responding, 2000 and 2010; and percent responding by demographic characteristic, 2010)

	strongly agree	agree	disagree	strongly disagree
TEN-YEAR TREND				
2010	6.8%	28.6%	43.5%	21.2%
2000	11.1	28.9	40.7	19.3
2010 PROFILE				
Total people	**6.8**	**28.6**	**43.5**	**21.2**
Men	6.8	32.6	45.2	15.5
Women	6.9	25.4	42.1	25.6
Asian	2.8	18.4	60.5	18.4
Black	7.2	28.8	44.0	20.0
Hispanic	8.9	29.9	43.5	17.7
White	7.0	28.1	42.5	22.4
Aged 18 to 44	5.9	25.2	42.9	25.9
Aged 45 to 64	5.2	29.6	46.1	19.2
Aged 65 or older	12.8	35.7	40.0	11.5
Less than a bachelor's degree	8.1	32.3	42.2	17.4
Bachelor's degree or more	3.3	18.4	46.8	31.5

Note: Hispanics may be of any race.
Source: Survey Documentation and Analysis, Computer-assisted Survey Methods Program, University of California, Berkeley, General Social Surveys, 1972–2010 Cumulative Data Files, Internet site http://sda.berkeley.edu/cgi-bin32/hsda?harcsda+gss10; calculations by New Strategist

Table 1.18 Working Mother's Relationship with Children, 2000 and 2010

"Do you strongly agree, agree, disagree, or strongly disagree with
the statement: A working mother can establish just as warm and secure
a relationship with her children as a mother who does not work?"

(percent of people aged 18 or older responding, 2000 and 2010; and percent responding by demographic characteristic, 2010)

	strongly agree	agree	disagree	strongly disagree
TEN-YEAR TREND				
2010	28.8%	45.9%	20.1%	5.1%
2000	20.3	41.4	29.4	8.9
2010 PROFILE				
Total people	**28.8**	**45.9**	**20.1**	**5.1**
Men	20.0	48.5	25.7	5.8
Women	35.7	44.0	15.7	4.6
Asian	36.4	32.0	24.2	7.4
Black	28.3	47.7	15.2	8.8
Hispanic	27.3	44.3	23.5	4.9
White	29.0	46.3	20.6	4.1
Aged 18 to 44	31.5	45.6	18.5	4.4
Aged 45 to 64	28.3	46.4	19.5	5.7
Aged 65 or older	22.4	46.5	25.4	5.7
Less than a bachelor's degree	25.6	46.3	22.4	5.7
Bachelor's degree or more	37.8	45.1	13.7	3.5

Note: Hispanics may be of any race.
Source: Survey Documentation and Analysis, Computer-assisted Survey Methods Program, University of California, Berkeley, General Social Surveys, 1972–2010 Cumulative Data Files, Internet site http://sda.berkeley.edu/cgi-bin32/ hsda?harcsda+gss10; calculations by New Strategist

Table 1.19 Should Government Help the Sick, 2000 and 2010

"Some people think that it is the responsibility of the government in Washington to see to it that people have help in paying for doctors and hospital bills; they are at point 1. Others think that these matters are not the responsibility of the federal government and that people should take care of these things themselves; they are at point 5. Where would you place yourself on this scale?"

(percent of people aged 18 or older responding, 2000 and 2010; and percent responding by demographic characteristic, 2010)

	government should help 1	2	agree with both 3	4	people should help themselves 5
TEN-YEAR TREND					
2010	30.5%	16.4%	31.9%	11.1%	10.1%
2000	29.2	22.4	31.4	10.9	6.1
2010 PROFILE					
Total people	**30.5**	**16.4**	**31.9**	**11.1**	**10.1**
Men	29.6	14.9	29.7	13.3	12.6
Women	31.3	17.6	33.7	9.3	8.0
Asian	38.6	25.1	25.0	9.2	2.1
Black	53.1	15.7	26.9	1.9	2.4
Hispanic	38.6	16.6	36.1	5.3	3.4
White	24.7	16.9	32.9	13.1	12.5
Aged 18 to 44	32.6	18.4	31.5	11.2	6.3
Aged 45 to 64	31.1	15.8	30.0	11.3	11.7
Aged 65 or older	23.3	11.7	37.1	10.1	17.7
Less than a bachelor's degree	33.4	14.3	33.1	8.3	10.8
Bachelor's degree or more	22.9	21.8	28.8	18.3	8.1

Note: Hispanics may be of any race.
Source: Survey Documentation and Analysis, Computer-assisted Survey Methods Program, University of California, Berkeley, General Social Surveys, 1972–2010 Cumulative Data Files, Internet site http://sda.berkeley.edu/cgi-bin32/hsda?harcsda+gss10; calculations by New Strategist

Religion Is Important to Americans

Most consider themselves at least moderately religious.

Asked whether science makes our way of life change too fast, the 51 percent majority of Americans disagree. Not surprisingly, the college-educated are most likely to disagree (64 percent).

Most Americans now believe in evolution, a shift from years past. In all but one demographic segment, the majority believes in evolution. The only exception is among blacks, where only 42 percent believe human beings developed from earlier species of animals.

Americans are a religious people, with 58 percent identifying themselves as at least moderately religious. Interestingly, however, the share calling themselves not religious slightly surpasses the share calling themselves very religious, especially among adults under age 45. Religiosity is especially high among women, blacks, and the elderly. The same groups are most likely to see the Bible as the word of God. Only 47 percent of Americans describe themselves as Protestants, down from the 53 percent majority in 2000.

Only a minority of Americans approves of the Supreme Court decision barring local governments from requiring Bible readings in public schools. Support for the decision is greatest among college-educated Americans (58 percent) and smallest among blacks (38 percent).

■ Unique in the developed world, most Americans make room for religion in their lives.

Fewer than half of Americans are Protestants

(percent distribution of people aged 18 or older by religious preference, 2010)

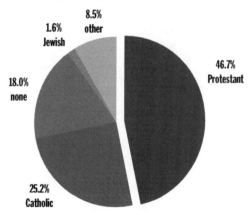

Table 1.20 Attitude toward Science, 2010

"Do you strongly agree, agree, disagree, or strongly disagree with the statement: Science makes our way of life change too fast?"

(percent of people aged 18 or older responding by demographic characteristic, 2010)

	strongly agree	agree	disagree	strongly disagree
Total people	**7.2%**	**41.5%**	**43.2%**	**8.1%**
Men	7.5	38.5	41.5	12.5
Women	6.8	44.2	44.6	4.4
Asian	23.5	38.6	23.5	14.4
Black	10.5	36.5	44.7	8.3
Hispanic	7.7	58.1	29.2	5.1
White	5.8	41.7	44.7	7.8
Aged 18 to 44	8.5	39.9	46.2	5.4
Aged 45 to 64	6.6	39.3	41.6	12.5
Aged 65 or older	4.7	51.4	38.7	5.2
Less than a bachelor's degree	7.9	46.4	40.3	5.4
Bachelor's degree or more	5.6	30.5	49.6	14.3

Note: Hispanics may be of any race.
Source: Survey Documentation and Analysis, Computer-assisted Survey Methods Program, University of California, Berkeley, General Social Surveys, 1972–2010 Cumulative Data Files, Internet site http://sda.berkeley.edu/cgi-bin32/ hsda?harcsda+gss10; calculations by New Strategist

Table 1.21 Attitude toward Evolution, 2010

"True or false: Human beings, as we know them today, developed from earlier species of animals?"

(percent of people aged 18 or older responding by demographic characteristic, 2010)

	true	false
Total people	**55.7%**	**44.3%**
Men	60.7	39.3
Women	51.3	48.7
Asian	82.1	17.9
Black	42.5	57.5
Hispanic	61.5	38.5
White	57.0	43.0
Aged 18 to 44	58.7	41.3
Aged 45 to 64	53.0	47.0
Aged 65 or older	52.7	47.3
Less than a bachelor's degree	51.6	48.4
Bachelor's degree or more	64.9	35.1

Note: Hispanics may be of any race.
Source: Survey Documentation and Analysis, Computer-assisted Survey Methods Program, University of California, Berkeley, General Social Surveys, 1972–2010 Cumulative Data Files, Internet site http://sda.berkeley.edu/cgi-bin32/hsda?harcsda+gss10; calculations by New Strategist

Table 1.22 Religious Preference, 2000 and 2010

"What is your religious preference?"

(percent of people aged 18 or older responding, 2000 and 2010; and percent responding by demographic characteristic, 2010)

	Protestant	Catholic	Jewish	Buddhism	Hinduism	Moslem/Islam	other	none
TEN-YEAR TREND								
2010	46.7%	25.2%	1.6%	0.9%	0.2%	0.6%	6.7%	18.0%
2000	52.7	25.4	2.2	0.6	0.4	0.6	4.0	14.1
2010 PROFILE								
Total people	**46.7**	**25.2**	**1.6**	**0.9**	**0.2**	**0.6**	**6.8**	**18.0**
Men	43.1	24.5	2.0	0.9	0.2	0.9	6.6	21.8
Women	46.7	25.8	1.3	1.0	0.1	0.4	9.9	14.8
Asian	15.9	17.2	3.6	18.2	4.0	2.6	2.7	35.8
Black	64.9	10.7	0.2	0.3	0.0	2.1	6.1	15.7
Hispanic	20.3	63.1	0.4	0.0	0.0	0.0	7.0	9.2
White	46.4	25.9	1.9	0.4	0.0	0.3	7.0	18.1
Aged 18 to 44	37.7	26.7	1.0	1.0	0.2	1.2	9.2	23.0
Aged 45 to 64	52.9	23.1	2.0	0.7	0.1	0.2	5.6	15.4
Aged 65 or older	59.1	25.4	2.6	1.4	0.0	0.0	2.1	9.4
Less than bachelor's degree	47.4	26.3	0.8	0.6	0.1	0.8	6.9	17.1
Bachelor's degree or more	44.8	22.5	3.8	1.9	0.3	0.3	6.0	20.4

Note: Hispanics may be of any race.
Source: Survey Documentation and Analysis, Computer-assisted Survey Methods Program, University of California, Berkeley, General Social Surveys, 1972–2010 Cumulative Data Files, Internet site http://sda.berkeley.edu/cgi-bin32/hsda?harcsda+gss10; calculations by New Strategist

Table 1.23 Degree of Religiosity, 2010

"To what extent do you consider yourself a religious person?"

(percent of people aged 18 or older responding by demographic characteristic, 2010)

	very religious	moderately religious	slightly religious	not religious
Total people	**16.8%**	**41.6%**	**23.6%**	**18.1%**
Men	13.8	37.6	26.5	22.1
Women	19.2	44.8	21.2	14.8
Asian	12.5	20.1	46.5	20.9
Black	28.5	39.3	16.8	15.5
Hispanic	11.5	51.8	26.3	10.3
White	14.6	42.5	23.9	19.0
Aged 18 to 44	12.5	38.0	26.9	22.6
Aged 45 to 64	19.8	41.8	22.7	15.6
Aged 65 or older	22.2	51.0	16.1	10.7
Less than a bachelor's degree	17.1	42.7	24.2	15.9
Bachelor's degree or more	15.7	38.4	22.0	23.8

Note: Hispanics may be of any race.
Source: Survey Documentation and Analysis, Computer-assisted Survey Methods Program, University of California, Berkeley, General Social Surveys, 1972–2010 Cumulative Data Files, Internet site http://sda.berkeley.edu/cgi-bin32/hsda?harcsda+gss10; calculations by New Strategist

Table 1.24 Belief in the Bible, 2000 and 2010

"Which of these statements comes closest to describing your feelings about the Bible? 1) The Bible is the actual word of God and is to be taken literally, word for word; 2) The Bible is the inspired word of God but not everything in it should be taken literally, word for word; 3) The Bible is an ancient book of fables, legends, history, and moral precepts recorded by men."

(percent of people aged 18 or older responding, 2000 and 2010; and percent responding by demographic characteristic, 2010)

	word of God	inspired word	book of fables	other
TEN-YEAR TREND				
2010	34.1%	43.6%	20.6%	1.7%
2000	33.8	49.4	15.9	0.9
2010 PROFILE				
Total people	**34.1**	**43.6**	**20.6**	**1.7**
Men	28.4	43.8	26.3	1.5
Women	38.9	43.4	15.8	1.9
Asian	12.5	35.2	49.6	2.7
Black	55.8	29.7	12.8	1.7
Hispanic	41.9	40.6	16.9	0.6
White	29.8	47.6	21.0	1.7
Aged 18 to 44	31.3	44.9	22.3	1.5
Aged 45 to 64	34.9	42.8	20.2	2.1
Aged 65 or older	39.9	42.0	16.5	1.6
Less than a bachelor's degree	41.4	39.7	17.2	1.7
Bachelor's degree or more	14.9	53.9	29.4	1.8

Note: Hispanics may be of any race.
Source: Survey Documentation and Analysis, Computer-assisted Survey Methods Program, University of California, Berkeley, General Social Surveys, 1972–2010 Cumulative Data Files, Internet site http://sda.berkeley.edu/cgi-bin32/hsda?harcsda+gss10; calculations by New Strategist

Table 1.25 Bible in the Public Schools, 2000 and 2010

"The United States Supreme Court has ruled that no state or local government may require the reading of the Lord's Prayer or Bible verses in public schools. What are your views on this? Do you approve or disapprove of the court ruling?"

(percent of people aged 18 or older responding, 2000 and 2010; and percent responding by demographic characteristic, 2010)

	approve	disapprove
TEN-YEAR TREND		
2010	44.1%	55.9%
2000	39.0	61.0
2010 PROFILE		
Total people	**44.1**	**55.9**
Men	47.7	52.3
Women	41.3	58.7
Asian	59.8	40.2
Black	38.3	61.7
Hispanic	43.6	56.4
White	44.9	55.1
Aged 18 to 44	50.2	49.8
Aged 45 to 64	39.5	60.5
Aged 65 or older	37.0	63.0
Less than a bachelor's degree	38.7	61.3
Bachelor's degree or more	58.4	41.6

Note: Hispanics may be of any race.
Source: Survey Documentation and Analysis, Computer-assisted Survey Methods Program, University of California, Berkeley, General Social Surveys, 1972–2010 Cumulative Data Files, Internet site http://sda.berkeley.edu/cgi-bin32/hsda?harcsda+gss10; calculations by New Strategist

Growing Tolerance of Same-Sex Relationships

Most Americans say premarital sex is OK.

The share of Americans who believe premarital sex is not wrong at all grew from 42 percent in 2000 to 53 percent in 2010. Among Americans aged 65 or older, however, only 37 percent think premarital sex is not wrong at all.

When it comes to sexual relations between adults of the same sex, the trend of growing tolerance is there as well, but acceptance is below the 50-percent mark. Overall 43 percent say homosexuality is not wrong at all, up from 29 percent a decade ago. Women are more accepting of same-sex relations than men (47 versus 37 percent), and Asians more so than blacks, Hispanics, or whites (60 versus 25, 30, and 46 percent, respectively). The younger the adult, the more accepting he or she is of same-sex relationships.

On the issue of whether gays and lesbians should have the right to marry, 47 percent of the public agrees. Support is greatest among Asians (71 percent), younger adults (55 percent), and college graduates (56 percent).

■ As younger, more tolerant adults replace older, less tolerant generations, American attitudes toward sexuality will continue to change.

Nearly half the public thinks same-sex couples should have the right to marry

(percent distribution of people aged 18 or older by response to the statement, "Homosexual couples should have the right to marry one another," 2010)

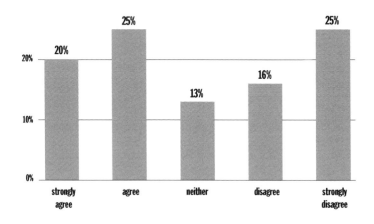

Table 1.26 Premarital Sex, 2000 and 2010

"If a man and woman have sex relations before marriage,
do you think it is always wrong, almost always wrong,
wrong only sometimes, or not wrong at all?"

(percent of people aged 18 or older responding, 2000 and 2010; and percent responding by demographic characteristic, 2010)

	always wrong	almost always wrong	sometimes wrong	not wrong at all
TEN-YEAR TREND				
2010	21.3%	7.8%	17.8%	53.1%
2000	27.7	8.6	21.4	42.2
2010 PROFILE				
Total people	**21.3**	**7.8**	**17.8**	**53.1**
Men	17.8	5.2	19.7	57.2
Women	24.0	9.8	16.2	49.9
Asian	5.5	6.8	21.2	66.4
Black	28.2	11.1	11.3	49.4
Hispanic	23.9	4.6	23.1	48.5
White	20.9	7.3	18.3	53.5
Aged 18 to 44	15.3	6.9	19.4	58.4
Aged 45 to 64	25.0	5.0	16.2	53.8
Aged 65 or older	30.9	15.7	16.5	36.9
Less than a bachelor's degree	24.1	8.3	16.4	51.2
Bachelor's degree or more	13.7	6.5	21.5	58.3

Note: Hispanics may be of any race.
Source: Survey Documentation and Analysis, Computer-assisted Survey Methods Program, University of California, Berkeley, General Social Surveys, 1972–2010 Cumulative Data Files, Internet site http://sda.berkeley.edu/cgi-bin32/hsda?harcsda+gss10; calculations by New Strategist

Table 1.27 Homosexual Relations, 2000 and 2010

"What about sexual relations between two adults of the same sex?"

(percent of people aged 18 or older responding, 2000 and 2010; and percent responding by demographic characteristic, 2010)

	always wrong	almost always wrong	sometimes wrong	not wrong at all
TEN-YEAR TREND				
2010	45.7%	3.7%	7.9%	42.7%
2000	58.7	4.4	8.1	28.8
2010 PROFILE				
Total people	**45.7**	**3.7**	**7.9**	**42.7**
Men	50.4	3.7	8.4	37.5
Women	41.6	3.6	7.4	47.4
Asian	20.1	4.8	15.5	59.6
Black	66.6	3.7	4.3	25.5
Hispanic	59.1	4.3	6.3	30.3
White	42.8	3.7	7.8	45.7
Aged 18 to 44	37.9	3.3	9.4	49.4
Aged 45 to 64	50.1	3.4	6.9	39.6
Aged 65 or older	58.5	5.4	6.0	30.1
Less than a bachelor's degree	52.3	3.5	6.8	37.3
Bachelor's degree or more	29.2	3.9	10.5	56.4

Note: Hispanics may be of any race.
Source: Survey Documentation and Analysis, Computer-assisted Survey Methods Program, University of California, Berkeley, General Social Surveys, 1972–2010 Cumulative Data Files, Internet site http://sda.berkeley.edu/cgi-bin32/ hsda?harcsda+gss10; calculations by New Strategist

Table 1.28 Gay Marriage, 2010

"Do you agree or disagree? Homosexual couples should have the right to marry one another."

(percent of people aged 18 or older responding by demographic characteristic, 2010)

	strongly agree	agree	neither agree nor disagree	disagree	strongly disagree
Total people	**21.1%**	**25.4%**	**12.8%**	**15.6%**	**25.1%**
Men	17.9	24.2	11.6	19.1	27.1
Women	23.8	26.5	13.9	12.5	23.3
Asian	21.1	49.6	3.4	16.9	8.9
Black	13.4	23.2	13.9	22.5	26.9
Hispanic	11.4	23.0	26.6	16.6	22.3
White	23.6	24.4	11.4	14.3	26.4
Aged 18 to 44	26.2	28.7	16.8	11.9	16.4
Aged 45 to 64	17.5	23.5	8.2	17.3	33.5
Aged 65 or older	14.5	19.9	11.8	22.7	31.1
Less than a bachelor's degree	17.8	25.1	14.1	15.7	27.3
Bachelor's degree or more	29.3	26.2	9.6	15.3	19.7

Note: Hispanics may be of any race.
Source: Survey Documentation and Analysis, Computer-assisted Survey Methods Program, University of California, Berkeley, General Social Surveys, 1972–2010 Cumulative Data Files, Internet site http://sda.berkeley.edu/cgi-bin32/hsda?harcsda+gss10; calculations by New Strategist

Television News Is Most Important

The Internet has jumped into the number two position.

Nearly half of Americans get most of their news from television, 22 percent from the Internet, and 18 percent from the newspaper. Together these three news outlets are the main source of news for nearly 90 percent of the public. But there are differences by demographic segment. Men are more likely than women to get news online and less likely to turn to television for news. Asians and whites are much more likely than blacks or Hispanics to get their news from the Internet. Thirty-one percent of adults under age 45 get most of their news from the Internet versus only 2 percent of adults aged 65 or older. Thirty-eight percent of people aged 65 or older rely on the newspaper, compared with only 8 percent of younger adults.

When asked about their political leanings, the largest share of Americans says they are moderates (38 percent). Thirty-four percent say they are slightly to extremely conservative, and 29 percent say they are slightly to extremely liberal. Democrats far outnumber Republicans in political party identification. Forty-six percent of adults say they are at least slight Democrats compared with 33 percent who say they are at least slight Republicans. Among whites, the split is nearly even. Among Asians, blacks, and Hispanics, Democrats vastly outnumber Republicans.

■ The political leanings of Americans have changed surprisingly little over the past 10 years, despite the seeming polarization of the public.

Newspapers have fallen into third place as the source for news

(percent distribution of people aged 18 or older by response to the question, "Where do you get most of your information about current news events?" 2010)

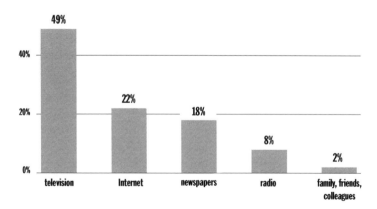

Table 1.29 Main Source of Information about Events in the News, 2010

"We are interested in how people get information about events in the news. Where do you get most of your information about current news events?"

(percent of people aged 18 or older responding by demographic characteristic, 2010)

	television	Internet	newspapers	radio	family, friends, or colleagues	books, other printed	government agencies	magazines
Total people	**49.1%**	**21.6%**	**17.7%**	**7.7%**	**2.2%**	**0.8%**	**0.6%**	**0.3%**
Men	44.3	23.0	19.2	9.0	1.7	1.1	1.1	0.6
Women	55.3	19.7	15.8	6.0	2.9	0.4	0.0	0.0
Asian	60.0	25.0	10.0	5.0	0.0	0.0	0.0	0.0
Black	68.7	6.0	13.4		7.1	0.0	4.8	0.0
Hispanic	71.2	14.8	7.0	0.0	7.0	0.0	0.0	0.0
White	44.0	24.2	19.4	9.7	1.4	0.8	0.0	0.4
Aged 18 to 44	47.8	30.7	7.8	10.5	3.2	0.0	0.0	0.0
Aged 45 to 64	46.9	20.0	19.7	6.5	2.2	2.2	1.7	0.9
Aged 65 or older	56.7	1.8	38.4	3.2	0.0	0.0	0.0	0.0
Less than bachelor's degree	56.6	14.7	16.6	7.1	2.7	1.1	0.8	0.4
Bachelor's degree or more	26.6	42.2	21.0	9.6	0.6	0.0	0.0	0.0

Note: Hispanics may be of any race.
Source: Survey Documentation and Analysis, Computer-assisted Survey Methods Program, University of California, Berkeley, General Social Surveys, 1972–2010 Cumulative Data Files, Internet site http://sda.berkeley.edu/cgi-bin32/hsda?harcsda+gss10; calculations by New Strategist

Table 1.30 Political Leanings, 2000 and 2010

"We hear a lot of talk these days about liberals and conservatives.
On a seven-point scale from extremely liberal (1) to extremely
conservative (7), where would you place yourself?"

(percent of people aged 18 or older responding, 2000 and 2010; and percent responding by demographic characteristic, 2010)

	1 extremely liberal	2 liberal	3 slightly liberal	4 moderate	5 slightly conservative	6 conservative	7 extremely conservative
TEN-YEAR TREND							
2010	3.8%	12.9%	11.9%	37.6%	12.8%	16.6%	4.4%
2000	3.9	11.5	10.8	39.9	14.5	15.9	3.6
2010 PROFILE							
Total people	**3.8**	**12.9**	**11.9**	**37.6**	**12.8**	**16.6**	**4.4**
Men	2.5	12.6	10.8	37.1	13.3	18.0	5.6
Women	4.9	13.1	12.8	38.0	12.4	15.4	3.4
Asian	1.4	22.5	16.5	33.9	14.8	5.9	5.0
Black	7.1	16.7	10.3	38.4	8.3	13.6	5.6
Hispanic	2.8	10.2	18.4	44.4	11.5	9.3	3.3
White	3.2	11.6	11.8	37.3	13.7	18.3	4.0
Aged 18 to 44	3.0	15.4	11.9	39.9	11.6	14.3	4.0
Aged 45 to 64	4.3	10.5	11.7	37.4	13.7	17.4	4.9
Aged 65 or older	4.8	10.8	12.2	31.8	14.4	21.6	4.4
Less than a bachelor's degree	4.0	11.0	10.9	41.5	11.7	15.9	5.1
Bachelor's degree or more	3.4	17.7	14.4	27.9	15.6	18.4	2.5

Note: Hispanics may be of any race.
Source: Survey Documentation and Analysis, Computer-assisted Survey Methods Program, University of California, Berkeley, General Social Surveys, 1972–2010 Cumulative Data Files, Internet site http://sda.berkeley.edu/cgi-bin32/hsda?harcsda+gss10; calculations by New Strategist

Table 1.31 Political Party Affiliation, 2000 and 2010

"Generally speaking, do you usually think of yourself as
a Republican, Democrat, independent, or what?"

(percent of people aged 18 or older responding, 2000 and 2010; and percent responding by demographic characteristic, 2010)

	strong Democrat	not strong Democrat	independent, near Democrat	independent	independent, near Republican	not strong Republican	strong Republican	other party
TEN-YEAR TREND								
2010	16.5%	15.7%	13.5%	18.8%	10.0%	13.4%	9.6%	2.6%
2000	13.8	17.9	11.5	20.4	9.3	14.9	10.6	1.7
2010 PROFILE								
Total people	**16.5**	**15.7**	**13.5**	**18.8**	**10.0**	**13.4**	**9.6**	**2.6**
Men	12.2	13.7	14.8	18.2	12.3	15.1	10.5	3.1
Women	20.0	17.3	12.4	19.2	8.1	11.9	8.9	2.2
Asian	16.3	19.3	17.0	21.9	6.6	10.3	3.2	5.3
Black	40.0	19.1	13.3	14.0	4.2	7.0	1.1	1.3
Hispanic	13.0	22.7	19.9	26.0	6.7	8.0	2.0	1.8
White	12.2	14.9	12.5	18.6	11.8	15.1	12.2	2.7
Aged 18 to 44	12.4	17.4	14.1	21.8	10.2	13.7	7.0	3.3
Aged 45 to 64	17.5	13.1	15.3	17.3	9.9	13.0	11.9	2.1
Aged 65 or older	25.3	16.3	8.0	13.4	9.7	13.2	12.2	1.8
Less than bachelor's degree	15.6	16.1	13.1	22.0	9.3	13.3	8.3	2.2
Bachelor's degree or more	18.7	14.7	14.3	10.1	11.8	13.5	13.0	3.9

Note: Hispanics may be of any race.
Source: Survey Documentation and Analysis, Computer-assisted Survey Methods Program, University of California, Berkeley, General Social Surveys, 1972–2010 Cumulative Data Files, Internet site http://sda.berkeley.edu/cgi-bin32/hsda?harcsda+gss10; calculations by New Strategist

Most Support Right to Die, Gun Permits

More than two-thirds of the public support capital punishment.

Americans have long been in support of the death penalty for convicted murderers. In 2010, 68 percent of the public was in favor of the death penalty, about the same percentage as in 2000. Blacks are the only demographic segment in which the majority opposes the death penalty. The strongest support for the death penalty is found among men (73 percent) and whites (73 percent).

The great majority of Americans favors requiring a permit for gun ownership, but support for gun laws is flagging. In 2010, 74 percent favored requiring a permit before buying a gun, down from 81 percent in 2000. Men are most opposed to gun laws, with 30 percent against requiring a police permit before a gun purchase.

Support for legal abortion under certain circumstances is overwhelming. Eighty-six percent of Americans approve of abortion if a women's health is in serious danger, and about three-quarters do if the pregnancy is the result of rape or there is a chance of serious defect in the baby. Other reasons garner substantially lower approval ratings (42 to 48 percent).

More than two-thirds of Americans support the right of the terminally ill to die with a doctor's assistance. The biggest differences are by race and Hispanic origin. Ninety-two percent of Asians favor the right to die compared with only 54 percent of blacks.

■ Although a growing number of states are outlawing the death penalty, the public continues to overwhelmingly support it.

When abortion should be legal

(percent of people aged 18 or older who responded "yes" to the question, "Should a woman be able to obtain a legal abortion if . . . " 2010)

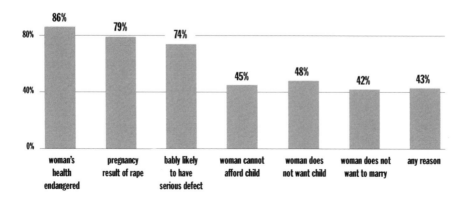

Table 1.32 Favor or Oppose Death Penalty for Murder, 2000 and 2010

"Do you favor or oppose the death penalty for persons convicted of murder?"

(percent of people aged 18 or older responding, 2000 and 2010; and percent responding by demographic characteristic, 2010)

	favor	oppose
TEN-YEAR TREND		
2010	67.8%	32.2%
2000	69.6	30.4
2010 PROFILE		
Total people	**67.8**	**32.2**
Men	72.7	27.3
Women	63.7	36.3
Asian	64.5	35.5
Black	47.8	52.2
Hispanic	53.2	46.8
White	72.9	27.1
Aged 18 to 44	66.1	33.9
Aged 45 to 64	69.0	31.0
Aged 65 or older	70.3	29.7
Less than a bachelor's degree	69.9	30.1
Bachelor's degree or more	62.1	37.9

Note: Hispanics may be of any race.
Source: Survey Documentation and Analysis, Computer-assisted Survey Methods Program, University of California, Berkeley, General Social Surveys, 1972–2010 Cumulative Data Files, Internet site http://sda.berkeley.edu/cgi-bin32/hsda?harcsda+gss10; calculations by New Strategist

Table 1.33 Favor or Oppose Gun Permits, 2000 and 2010

"Would you favor or oppose a law which would require a person
to obtain a police permit before he or she could buy a gun?"

(percent of people aged 18 or older responding, 2000 and 2010; and percent responding by demographic characteristic, 2010)

	favor	oppose
TEN-YEAR TREND		
2010	74.3%	25.7%
2000	81.0	19.0
2010 PROFILE		
Total people	**74.3**	**25.7**
Men	70.3	29.7
Women	77.8	22.2
Asian	93.8	6.2
Black	83.5	16.5
Hispanic	83.1	16.9
White	71.3	28.7
Aged 18 to 44	72.6	27.4
Aged 45 to 64	74.1	25.9
Aged 65 or older	79.4	20.6
Less than a bachelor's degree	72.8	27.2
Bachelor's degree or more	78.2	21.8

Note: Hispanics may be of any race.
Source: Survey Documentation and Analysis, Computer-assisted Survey Methods Program, University of California, Berkeley, General Social Surveys, 1972–2010 Cumulative Data Files, Internet site http://sda.berkeley.edu/cgi-bin32/hsda?harcsda+gss10; calculations by New Strategist

Table 1.34 Support for Legal Abortion by Reason, 2000 and 2010

"Please tell me whether or not you think it should be possible for a pregnant woman to obtain a legal abortion if the woman wants it."

(percent of people aged 18 or older responding "yes," 2000 and 2010; and percent responding by demographic characteristic, 2010)

	her health is seriously endangered	pregnancy is the result of a rape	there is a serious defect in the baby	she cannot afford more children	she is married, but does not want more childen	she is single and does not want to marry the man	for any reason
TEN-YEAR TREND							
2010	86.4%	79.1%	73.9%	44.9%	47.7%	41.9%	42.9%
2000	88.5	79.8	77.9	41.0	39.9	38.0	38.9
2010 PROFILE							
Total people	**86.4**	**79.1**	**73.9**	**44.9**	**47.7**	**41.9**	**42.9**
Men	87.1	82.7	75.4	46.3	50.3	43.5	45.2
Women	85.7	75.9	72.5	43.7	45.3	40.5	40.9
Asian	92.5	85.0	81.2	67.3	73.7	58.7	60.0
Black	83.9	79.9	69.8	48.6	50.7	41.8	43.9
Hispanic	75.4	62.8	63.7	31.1	37.3	24.3	25.8
White	87.2	79.7	75.1	44.2	46.7	42.6	43.3
Aged 18 to 44	85.1	81.3	72.0	45.3	49.8	43.7	46.4
Aged 45 to 64	88.0	76.4	74.4	46.4	49.6	44.0	42.4
Aged 65 or older	86.2	78.6	78.2	39.5	36.7	31.0	33.4
Less than a bachelor's degree	84.7	76.6	71.0	40.1	43.8	36.6	38.0
Bachelor's degree or more	90.6	85.4	81.1	56.8	57.5	55.4	55.2

Note: Hispanics may be of any race.
Source: Survey Documentation and Analysis, Computer-assisted Survey Methods Program, University of California, Berkeley, General Social Surveys, 1972–2010 Cumulative Data Files, Internet site http://sda.berkeley.edu/cgi-bin32/ hsda?harcsda+gss10; calculations by New Strategist

Table 1.35 Allow Patients with Incurable Disease to Die, 2000 and 2010

"When a person has a disease that cannot be cured, do you think
doctors should be allowed by law to end the patient's life by
some painless means if the patient and his family request it?"

(percent of people aged 18 or older responding, 2000 and 2010; and percent responding by demographic characteristic, 2010)

	yes	no
TEN-YEAR TREND		
2010	68.4%	31.6%
2000	68.0	32.0
2010 PROFILE		
Total people	**68.4**	**31.6**
Men	74.1	25.9
Women	64.0	36.0
Asian	92.4	7.6
Black	54.3	45.7
Hispanic	61.2	38.8
White	71.3	28.7
Aged 18 to 44	71.9	28.1
Aged 45 to 64	65.4	34.6
Aged 65 or older	64.9	35.1
Less than a bachelor's degree	66.5	33.5
Bachelor's degree or more	73.7	26.3

Note: Hispanics may be of any race.
Source: Survey Documentation and Analysis, Computer-assisted Survey Methods Program, University of California, Berkeley, General Social Surveys, 1972–2010 Cumulative Data Files, Internet site http://sda.berkeley.edu/cgi-bin32/ hsda?harcsda+gss10; calculations by New Strategist

Education Trends

■ **Middle-aged and younger adults are well educated.**

Most of those under age 65 have college experience, and one-third of those under age 45 have a bachelor's degree.

■ **Asians are much better educated than others.**

The majority of Asians have a bachelor's degree. Among Hispanics, only 14 percent have graduated from college.

■ **Most parents are satisfied with their child's school.**

A substantial 59 percent of parents with children in kindergarten through 12th grade say they are "very satisfied" with their child's school.

■ **College costs and debt have skyrocketed.**

The cost of attending college increased 142 percent between 1977–78 and 2009–10, after adjusting for inflation. Most students take out loans to pay for these costs.

■ **College enrollment is rising.**

But the number of full-time students attending private, four-year schools fell 9 percent between 2005 and 2009.

■ **College campuses are becoming more diverse.**

Non-Hispanic whites account for 62 percent of the nation's college students, down from 68 percent in 2000.

■ **Women earn most degrees.**

Sixty-two percent of associate's degrees went to women in 2008–09, as did 57 percent of bachelor's degrees, 60 percent of master's degrees, and 52 percent of doctorates.

Many Americans Are Well Educated

More than half the adult population has some college experience.

The educational attainment of Americans has increased dramatically over the past few decades. Just 30 years ago, more than half of adults had not even graduated from high school. Today, most adults have at least some college education and 30 percent have at least a bachelor's degree.

Among men, the share with a college degree peaks at 34 percent in the 55-to-64 age group, now filled with the oldest boomers. Boomer men are better educated than younger men because, as young adults during the Vietnam War, many boomers stayed in college to avoid the draft.

Among women aged 65 or older, only 18 percent have a college degree. But among women under age 35, an impressive 37 percent have a bachelor's degree. Women under age 55 are better educated than their male counterparts.

■ Because the educational attainment of younger women is higher than that of younger men, women's incomes should continue to gain on men's.

Among Americans under age 55, women are better educated than men

(percent of people with a bachelor's degree, by age and sex, 2010)

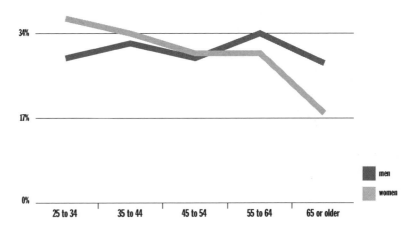

Table 2.1 Educational Attainment by Age, 2010

(number and percent distribution of people aged 25 or older by educational attainment and age, 2010; numbers in thousands)

	total	25 to 34	35 to 44	45 to 54	55 to 64	65 or older
Total people	**199,928**	**41,085**	**40,447**	**44,387**	**35,395**	**38,613**
Not a high school graduate	25,711	4,763	4,715	4,624	3,692	7,917
High school graduate only	62,456	11,186	11,582	14,564	11,068	14,057
Some college, no degree	33,662	7,752	6,593	7,432	6,137	5,748
Associate's degree	18,259	3,903	4,180	4,706	3,269	2,201
Bachelor's degree	38,784	9,840	8,857	8,429	6,593	5,066
Master's degree	15,203	2,773	3,298	3,325	3,405	2,402
Professional degree	3,074	494	649	646	651	635
Doctoral degree	2,779	373	575	662	581	588
High school graduate or more	174,217	36,321	35,734	39,764	31,704	30,697
Some college or more	111,761	25,135	24,152	25,200	20,636	16,640
Associate's degree or more	78,099	17,383	17,559	17,768	14,499	10,892
Bachelor's degree or more	59,840	13,480	13,379	13,062	11,230	8,691
Total people	**100.0%**	**100.0%**	**100.0%**	**100.0%**	**100.0%**	**100.0%**
Not a high school graduate	12.9	11.6	11.7	10.4	10.4	20.5
High school graduate only	31.2	27.2	28.6	32.8	31.3	36.4
Some college, no degree	16.8	18.9	16.3	16.7	17.3	14.9
Associate's degree	9.1	9.5	10.3	10.6	9.2	5.7
Bachelor's degree	19.4	24.0	21.9	19.0	18.6	13.1
Master's degree	7.6	6.7	8.2	7.5	9.6	6.2
Professional degree	1.5	1.2	1.6	1.5	1.8	1.6
Doctoral degree	1.4	0.9	1.4	1.5	1.6	1.5
High school graduate or more	87.1	88.4	88.3	89.6	89.6	79.5
Some college or more	55.9	61.2	59.7	56.8	58.3	43.1
Associate's degree or more	39.1	42.3	43.4	40.0	41.0	28.2
Bachelor's degree or more	29.9	32.8	33.1	29.4	31.7	22.5

Source: Bureau of the Census, 2010 Current Population Survey Annual Social and Economic Supplement, Internet site http://www.census.gov/hhes/www/cpstables/032010/perinc/toc.htm; calculations by New Strategist

Table 2.2 Educational Attainment of Men by Age, 2010

(number and percent distribution of men aged 25 or older by educational attainment and age, 2010; numbers in thousands)

	total	25 to 34	35 to 44	45 to 54	55 to 64	65 or older
Total men	**96,325**	**20,689**	**20,074**	**21,784**	**16,985**	**16,793**
Not a high school graduate	12,916	2,693	2,566	2,475	1,839	3,342
High school graduate only	30,682	6,458	6,269	7,555	5,030	5,370
Some college, no degree	15,908	3,863	3,117	3,537	2,885	2,507
Associate's degree	7,662	1,724	1,729	1,928	1,472	809
Bachelor's degree	18,674	4,457	4,262	3,943	3,414	2,598
Master's degree	6,859	1,069	1,471	1,535	1,532	1,253
Professional degree	1,861	230	311	406	462	452
Doctoral degree	1,763	194	350	405	351	463
High school graduate or more	83,409	17,995	17,509	19,309	15,146	13,452
Some college or more	52,727	11,537	11,240	11,754	10,116	8,082
Associate's degree or more	36,819	7,674	8,123	8,217	7,231	5,575
Bachelor's degree or more	29,157	5,950	6,394	6,289	5,759	4,766
Total men	**100.0%**	**100.0%**	**100.0%**	**100.0%**	**100.0%**	**100.0%**
Not a high school graduate	13.4	13.0	12.8	11.4	10.8	19.9
High school graduate only	31.9	31.2	31.2	34.7	29.6	32.0
Some college, no degree	16.5	18.7	15.5	16.2	17.0	14.9
Associate's degree	8.0	8.3	8.6	8.9	8.7	4.8
Bachelor's degree	19.4	21.5	21.2	18.1	20.1	15.5
Master's degree	7.1	5.2	7.3	7.0	9.0	7.5
Professional degree	1.9	1.1	1.5	1.9	2.7	2.7
Doctoral degree	1.8	0.9	1.7	1.9	2.1	2.8
High school graduate or more	86.6	87.0	87.2	88.6	89.2	80.1
Some college or more	54.7	55.8	56.0	54.0	59.6	48.1
Associate's degree or more	38.2	37.1	40.5	37.7	42.6	33.2
Bachelor's degree or more	30.3	28.8	31.9	28.9	33.9	28.4

Source: Bureau of the Census, 2010 Current Population Survey Annual Social and Economic Supplement, Internet site http:// www.census.gov/hhes/www/cpstables/032010/perinc/toc.htm; calculations by New Strategist

Table 2.3 Educational Attainment of Women by Age, 2010

(number and percent distribution of women aged 25 or older by educational attainment and age, 2010; numbers in thousands)

	total	25 to 34	35 to 44	45 to 54	55 to 64	65 or older
Total women	**103,603**	**20,396**	**20,373**	**22,604**	**18,410**	**21,820**
Not a high school graduate	12,795	2,070	2,149	2,148	1,853	4,576
High school graduate only	31,774	4,728	5,312	7,008	6,038	8,687
Some college, no degree	17,753	3,889	3,476	3,896	3,252	3,241
Associate's degree	10,597	2,179	2,451	2,778	1,797	1,392
Bachelor's degree	20,110	5,383	4,595	4,486	3,179	2,467
Master's degree	8,344	1,704	1,828	1,790	1,873	1,149
Professional degree	1,213	264	338	240	188	183
Doctoral degree	1,015	179	224	257	230	125
High school graduate or more	90,806	18,326	18,224	20,455	16,557	17,244
Some college or more	59,032	13,598	12,912	13,447	10,519	8,557
Associate's degree or more	41,279	9,709	9,436	9,551	7,267	5,316
Bachelor's degree or more	30,682	7,530	6,985	6,773	5,470	3,924
Total women	**100.0%**	**100.0%**	**100.0%**	**100.0%**	**100.0%**	**100.0%**
Not a high school graduate	12.4	10.1	10.5	9.5	10.1	21.0
High school graduate only	30.7	23.2	26.1	31.0	32.8	39.8
Some college, no degree	17.1	19.1	17.1	17.2	17.7	14.9
Associate's degree	10.2	10.7	12.0	12.3	9.8	6.4
Bachelor's degree	19.4	26.4	22.6	19.8	17.3	11.3
Master's degree	8.1	8.4	9.0	7.9	10.2	5.3
Professional degree	1.2	1.3	1.7	1.1	1.0	0.8
Doctoral degree	1.0	0.9	1.1	1.1	1.2	0.6
High school graduate or more	87.6	89.9	89.5	90.5	89.9	79.0
Some college or more	57.0	66.7	63.4	59.5	57.1	39.2
Associate's degree or more	39.8	47.6	46.3	42.3	39.5	24.4
Bachelor's degree or more	29.6	36.9	34.3	30.0	29.7	18.0

Source: Bureau of the Census, 2010 Current Population Survey Annual Social and Economic Supplement, Internet site http:// www.census.gov/hhes/www/cpstables/032010/perinc/toc.htm; calculations by New Strategist

Most Asian Men Have a College Degree

Only 13 percent of Hispanic men are college graduates.

Among both men and women, Asians are far better educated than non-Hispanic whites, blacks, or Hispanics. The 55 percent majority of Asian men have a bachelor's degree versus a much smaller 34 percent of non-Hispanic white men, 18 percent of black men, and just 13 percent of Hispanic men. The story is similar for Asian women. Nearly 50 percent are college graduates versus 32 percent of non-Hispanic white women, 22 percent of black women, and 15 percent of Hispanic women.

Many Hispanics have not graduated from high school. Among Hispanic men, only 61 percent are high school graduates. The figure is a slightly higher 64 percent among Hispanic women. In contrast, 84 to 85 percent of blacks have a high school diploma. The figure ranges from 87 to 92 percent among Asians and non-Hispanic whites.

■ The educational attainment of Hispanics is well below that of the rest of the population because many are immigrants from countries that provide little formal schooling.

Blacks are better educated than Hispanics

(percent of people aged 25 or older with a bachelor's degree, by sex, race, and Hispanic origin, 2010)

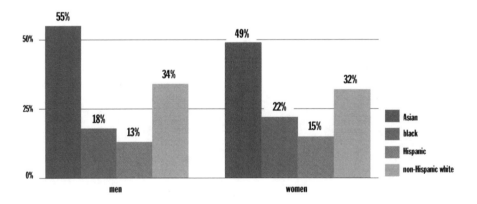

Table 2.4 Educational Attainment by Race and Hispanic Origin, 2010

(number and percent distribution of people aged 25 or older by educational attainment, race, and Hispanic origin, 2010; numbers in thousands)

	total	Asian	black	Hispanic	non-Hispanic white
Total people	**199,928**	**9,882**	**23,702**	**26,375**	**138,482**
Not a high school graduate	25,711	1,077	3,741	9,796	11,007
High school graduate	62,456	2,015	8,279	7,815	43,802
Some college, no degree	33,662	951	4,723	3,392	24,203
Associate's degree	18,259	719	2,243	1,709	13,428
Bachelor's degree	38,784	3,163	3,169	2,652	29,611
Master's degree	15,203	1,321	1,233	733	11,846
Professional degree	3,074	295	187	134	2,444
Doctorate degree	2,779	342	126	146	2,141
High school graduate or more	174,217	8,806	19,960	16,581	127,475
Some college or more	111,761	6,791	11,681	8,766	83,673
Associate's degree or more	78,099	5,840	6,958	5,374	59,470
Bachelor's degree or more	59,840	5,121	4,715	3,665	46,042
Total people	**100.0%**	**100.0%**	**100.0%**	**100.0%**	**100.0%**
Not a high school graduate	12.9	10.9	15.8	37.1	7.9
High school graduate	31.2	20.4	34.9	29.6	31.6
Some college, no degree	16.8	9.6	19.9	12.9	17.5
Associate's degree	9.1	7.3	9.5	6.5	9.7
Bachelor's degree	19.4	32.0	13.4	10.1	21.4
Master's degree	7.6	13.4	5.2	2.8	8.6
Professional degree	1.5	3.0	0.8	0.5	1.8
Doctorate degree	1.4	3.5	0.5	0.6	1.5
High school graduate or more	87.1	89.1	84.2	62.9	92.1
Some college or more	55.9	68.7	49.3	33.2	60.4
Associate's degree or more	39.1	59.1	29.4	20.4	42.9
Bachelor's degree or more	29.9	51.8	19.9	13.9	33.2

*Note: Asians and blacks are those who identify themselves as being of the race alone or in combination with other races. Hispanics may be of any race. Non-Hispanic whites are those who identify themselves as being white alone and not Hispanic.
Source: Bureau of the Census, 2010 Current Population Survey Annual Social and Economic Supplement, Internet site http://www.census.gov/hhes/www/cpstables/032010/perinc/toc.htm; calculations by New Strategist*

Table 2.5 Educational Attainment of Men by Race and Hispanic Origin, 2010

(number and percent distribution of men aged 25 or older by educational attainment, race, and Hispanic origin, 2010; numbers in thousands)

	total	Asian	black	Hispanic	non-Hispanic white
Total men	**96,325**	**4,605**	**10,542**	**13,573**	**66,895**
Not a high school graduate	12,916	404	1,738	5,236	5,499
High school graduate	30,682	886	4,079	4,212	21,246
Some college, no degree	15,908	476	2,020	1,654	11,558
Associate's degree	7,662	318	835	720	5,714
Bachelor's degree	18,674	1,437	1,264	1,245	14,635
Master's degree	6,859	683	468	348	5,330
Professional degree	1,861	165	78	64	1,549
Doctorate degree	1,763	235	60	95	1,364
High school graduate or more	83,409	4,200	8,804	8,338	61,396
Some college or more	52,727	3,314	4,725	4,126	40,150
Associate's degree or more	36,819	2,838	2,705	2,472	28,592
Bachelor's degree or more	29,157	2,520	1,870	1,752	22,878
Total men	**100.0%**	**100.0%**	**100.0%**	**100.0%**	**100.0%**
Not a high school graduate	13.4	8.8	16.5	38.6	8.2
High school graduate	31.9	19.2	38.7	31.0	31.8
Some college, no degree	16.5	10.3	19.2	12.2	17.3
Associate's degree	8.0	6.9	7.9	5.3	8.5
Bachelor's degree	19.4	31.2	12.0	9.2	21.9
Master's degree	7.1	14.8	4.4	2.6	8.0
Professional degree	1.9	3.6	0.7	0.5	2.3
Doctorate degree	1.8	5.1	0.6	0.7	2.0
High school graduate or more	86.6	91.2	83.5	61.4	91.8
Some college or more	54.7	72.0	44.8	30.4	60.0
Associate's degree or more	38.2	61.6	25.7	18.2	42.7
Bachelor's degree or more	30.3	54.7	17.7	12.9	34.2

Note: Asians and blacks are those who identify themselves as being of the race alone or in combination with other races. Hispanics may be of any race. Non-Hispanic whites are those who identify themselves as being white alone and not Hispanic.
Source: Bureau of the Census, 2010 Current Population Survey Annual Social and Economic Supplement, Internet site http://www.census.gov/hhes/www/cpstables/032010/perinc/toc.htm; calculations by New Strategist

Table 2.6 Educational Attainment of Women by Race and Hispanic Origin, 2010

(number and percent distribution of women aged 25 or older by educational attainment, race, and Hispanic origin, 2010; numbers in thousands)

	total	Asian	black	Hispanic	non-Hispanic white
Total women	**103,603**	**5,277**	**13,160**	**12,802**	**71,587**
Not a high school graduate	12,795	672	2,003	4,559	5,509
High school graduate	31,774	1,129	4,200	3,602	22,556
Some college, no degree	17,753	475	2,703	1,738	12,646
Associate's degree	10,597	401	1,408	989	7,714
Bachelor's degree	20,110	1,726	1,905	1,407	14,976
Master's degree	8,344	638	765	385	6,516
Professional degree	1,213	129	109	70	895
Doctorate degree	1,015	107	66	52	776
High school graduate or more	90,806	4,605	11,156	8,243	66,079
Some college or more	59,032	3,476	6,956	4,641	43,523
Associate's degree or more	41,279	3,001	4,253	2,903	30,877
Bachelor's degree or more	30,682	2,600	2,845	1,914	23,163
Total women	**100.0%**	**100.0%**	**100.0%**	**100.0%**	**100.0%**
Not a high school graduate	12.4	12.7	15.2	35.6	7.7
High school graduate	30.7	21.4	31.9	28.1	31.5
Some college, no degree	17.1	9.0	20.5	13.6	17.7
Associate's degree	10.2	7.6	10.7	7.7	10.8
Bachelor's degree	19.4	32.7	14.5	11.0	20.9
Master's degree	8.1	12.1	5.8	3.0	9.1
Professional degree	1.2	2.4	0.8	0.5	1.3
Doctorate degree	1.0	2.0	0.5	0.4	1.1
High school graduate or more	87.6	87.3	84.8	64.4	92.3
Some college or more	57.0	65.9	52.9	36.3	60.8
Associate's degree or more	39.8	56.9	32.3	22.7	43.1
Bachelor's degree or more	29.6	49.3	21.6	15.0	32.4

Note: Asians and blacks are those who identify themselves as being of the race alone or in combination with other races. Hispanics may be of any race. Non-Hispanic whites are those who identify themselves as being white alone and not Hispanic.
Source: Bureau of the Census, 2010 Current Population Survey Annual Social and Economic Supplement, Internet site http://www.census.gov/hhes/www/cpstables/032010/perinc/toc.htm; calculations by New Strategist

Educational Attainment Varies Widely by State

Massachusetts has the largest share of college graduates.

Among regions, the Northeast has the highest level of education. Thirty-two percent of people aged 25 or older in the Northeast have a bachelor's degree. This compares with a low of only 26 percent in the South.

Educational attainment varies more by state than by region. The proportion of state populations that have a high school diploma ranges from less than 80 percent in Texas to a high of 92 percent in Wyoming.

The figures vary for college graduates as well. In West Virginia, only 17 percent of people aged 25 or older have a bachelor's degree, the smallest share among the 50 states. In contrast, at least 35 percent of adults are college graduates in Massachusetts, Colorado, Maryland, Connecticut, and the District of Columbia. Since income rises with education, it is no surprise that the states with the least-educated populations are also some of the poorest.

■ The educational level of the workforce is one factor behind business location decisions. Better-educated populations attract business investment, which increases economic diversity and employment opportunities.

West Virginia's population is least likely to be college educated

(percent of people aged 25 or older with a bachelor's degree in the states with the largest and smallest percentage of college-educated residents, 2009)

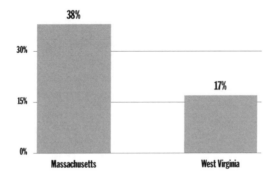

Table 2.7 High School and College Graduates by Region, 2009

(number and percent of people aged 25 or older who are high school or college graduates, by region, 2009; numbers in thousands)

	number	percent
Total with a high school diploma or more	**172,167**	**85.3%**
Northeast	32,648	87.0
Midwest	38,831	88.1
South	61,806	83.4
West	38,882	84.1
Total with a bachelor's degree or more	**56,336**	**27.9**
Northeast	12,041	32.1
Midwest	11,669	26.5
South	19,094	25.8
West	13,532	29.3

Source: Bureau of the Census, 2009 American Community Survey, Internet site http://factfinder.census.gov/servlet/ DatasetMainPageServlet?_program=ACS&_submenuId=&_lang=en&_ts=l; calculations by New Strategist

Table 2.8 Educational Attainment by State, 2009

(percent of people aged 25 or older who have at least a high school diploma or a bachelor's degree, ranked from highest to lowest by state, 2009)

	high school diploma or more		bachelor's degree or more
Total United States	**85.3%**	**Total United States**	**27.9%**
Wyoming	91.8	District of Columbia	48.5
Minnesota	91.5	Massachusetts	38.2
Alaska	91.4	Colorado	35.9
New Hampshire	91.3	Maryland	35.7
Vermont	91.0	Connecticut	35.6
Montana	90.8	New Jersey	34.5
Iowa	90.5	Virginia	34.0
Hawaii	90.4	Vermont	33.1
Utah	90.4	New York	32.4
Maine	90.2	New Hampshire	32.0
North Dakota	90.1	Minnesota	31.5
South Dakota	89.9	Washington	31.0
Nebraska	89.8	Illinois	30.6
Wisconsin	89.8	Rhode Island	30.5
Kansas	89.7	California	29.9
Washington	89.7	Hawaii	29.6
Colorado	89.3	Kansas	29.5
Oregon	89.1	Oregon	29.2
Massachusetts	89.0	Delaware	28.7
Connecticut	88.6	Utah	28.5
Idaho	88.4	Georgia	27.5
Maryland	88.2	Montana	27.4
Michigan	87.9	Nebraska	27.4
Pennsylvania	87.9	Maine	26.9
Ohio	87.6	Alaska	26.6
Delaware	87.4	North Carolina	26.5
New Jersey	87.4	Pennsylvania	26.4
District of Columbia	87.1	North Dakota	25.8
Missouri	86.8	Wisconsin	25.7
Indiana	86.6	Arizona	25.6
Virginia	86.6	Texas	25.5
Illinois	86.4	Florida	25.3
Oklahoma	85.6	New Mexico	25.3
Florida	85.3	Missouri	25.2
New York	84.7	Iowa	25.1
Rhode Island	84.7	South Dakota	25.1
North Carolina	84.3	Michigan	24.6
Arizona	84.2	South Carolina	24.3
Georgia	83.9	Ohio	24.1
Nevada	83.9	Idaho	23.9
South Carolina	83.6	Wyoming	23.8
Tennessee	83.1	Tennessee	23.0
New Mexico	82.8	Oklahoma	22.7
West Virginia	82.8	Indiana	22.5
Arkansas	82.4	Alabama	22.0
Louisiana	82.2	Nevada	21.8
Alabama	82.1	Louisiana	21.4
Kentucky	81.7	Kentucky	21.0
California	80.6	Mississippi	19.6
Mississippi	80.4	Arkansas	18.9
Texas	79.9	West Virginia	17.3

Source: Bureau of the Census, 2009 American Community Survey, Ranking Tables, Internet site http://factfinder.census.gov/ servlet/DatasetMainPageServlet?_program=ACS&_submenuId=&_lang=en&_ts=1; calculations by New Strategist

More than One in Four Americans Are in School

More than 77 million people were enrolled in school in 2009.

Americans start school at a younger age, and many stay in school—or go back to school—well into middle age. In 2009, 27 percent of people aged 3 or older were in school.

Among 3-year-olds, a substantial 41 percent are in school, as are the 65 percent majority of 4-year-olds. Enrollment is above 95 percent for children from ages 6 to 16, and schooling attracts the majority of people through age 20. Even at ages 25 to 29, about one in seven people are still in school.

The nation's elementary schools enrolled 20 million students in 2009, while middle schools enrolled 12 million and high schools 16 million. Only 55 percent of public school students are non-Hispanic white, while a substantial 45 percent are American Indian, Asian, black, or Hispanic. In 11 states and the District of Columbia, minorities account for at least half the student body.

■ The economic downturn is driving more of the nation's young adults into college, but the rising cost of higher education may limit this trend.

The number of people in college now well surpasses the number in high school

(number of people enrolled in school by level, 2009)

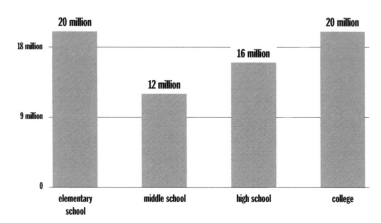

Table 2.9 School Enrollment by Age, 2009

(number of people aged 3 or older, and number and percent enrolled in school by age, fall 2009; numbers in thousands)

	total	enrolled	
		number	percent
Total people	**289,420**	**77,288**	**26.7%**
Aged 3	4,361	1,776	40.7
Aged 4	4,176	2,698	64.6
Aged 5	4,180	3,826	91.5
Aged 6	4,088	3,957	96.8
Aged 7	4,057	3,947	97.3
Aged 8	4,160	4,080	98.1
Aged 9	3,979	3,894	97.9
Aged 10	3,999	3,935	98.4
Aged 11	3,841	3,778	98.4
Aged 12	3,967	3,920	98.8
Aged 13	4,116	4,054	98.5
Aged 14	3,947	3,872	98.1
Aged 15	3,998	3,917	98.0
Aged 16	4,182	4,038	96.6
Aged 17	4,211	3,901	92.6
Aged 18	4,340	3,266	75.3
Aged 19	4,274	2,669	62.4
Aged 20	4,087	2,254	55.2
Aged 21	3,960	1,908	48.2
Aged 22	4,075	1,552	38.1
Aged 23	4,139	1,197	28.9
Aged 24	4,346	1,069	24.6
Aged 25 to 29	20,912	2,819	13.5
Aged 30 to 34	19,516	1,576	8.1
Aged 35 to 39	20,078	1,112	5.5
Aged 40 to 44	20,674	815	3.9
Aged 45 to 49	22,677	640	2.8
Aged 50 to 54	21,779	424	1.9
Aged 55 to 59	19,048	223	1.2
Aged 60 to 64	16,009	94	0.6
Aged 65 or older	38,241	76	0.2

Source: Bureau of the Census, School Enrollment—Social and Economic Characteristics of Students: October 2009, Internet site http://www.census.gov/population/www/socdemo/school/cps2009.html

Table 2.10 School Enrollment by Grade and Year of College, 2009

(number and percent distribution of people attending school by grade and year of college, fall 2009; numbers in thousands)

	number	percent distribution
TOTAL STUDENTS	**77,288**	**100.0%**
Nursery school	**4,708**	**6.1**
Kindergarten	**4,132**	**5.3**
Elementary	**20,363**	**26.3**
First grade	3,976	5.1
Second grade	4,063	5.3
Third grade	4,226	5.5
Fourth grade	4,017	5.2
Fifth grade	4,081	5.3
Middle school	**11,875**	**15.4**
Sixth grade	3,842	5.0
Seventh grade	3,983	5.2
Eighth grade	4,050	5.2
High school	**16,445**	**21.3**
Ninth grade	4,002	5.2
Tenth grade	3,961	5.1
Eleventh grade	4,021	5.2
Twelfth grade	4,461	5.8
College	**19,765**	**25.6**
Undergraduate	16,012	20.7
First year	5,112	6.6
Second year	4,384	5.7
Third year	3,869	5.0
Fourth or higher year	2,647	3.4
Graduate	3,753	4.9
First year	1,467	1.9
Second or higher year	2,286	3.0

Source: Bureau of the Census, School Enrollment—Social and Economic Characteristics of Students: October 2009, Internet site http://www.census.gov/population/www/socdemo/school/cps2009.html

Table 2.11 Enrollment in Public Elementary and Secondary School by State, Race, and Hispanic Origin, 2008

(percent distribution of students enrolled in public elementary and secondary school by state, race, and Hispanic origin, 2008)

	total	minority students					non-Hispanic white
		total	Am. Indian	Asian	black	Hispanic	
Total public school children	**100.0%**	**45.1%**	**1.2%**	**5.0%**	**17.0%**	**21.5%**	**54.9%**
Alabama	100.0	41.2	0.8	1.2	35.3	3.9	58.8
Alaska	100.0	46.7	23.1	7.2	3.5	5.8	53.3
Arizona	100.0	55.6	5.5	3.0	5.8	41.4	44.4
Arkansas	100.0	33.4	0.7	1.6	22.4	8.6	66.6
California	100.0	72.1	0.7	11.7	7.3	49.0	27.9
Colorado	100.0	39.1	1.2	3.6	6.0	28.4	60.9
Connecticut	100.0	35.5	0.4	4.2	13.9	17.1	64.5
Delaware	100.0	47.9	0.4	3.4	33.2	10.9	52.1
District of Columbia	100.0	94.0	0.1	1.6	81.5	10.8	6.0
Florida	100.0	53.0	0.3	2.6	24.0	26.1	47.0
Georgia	100.0	52.8	0.2	3.3	39.0	10.4	47.2
Hawaii	100.0	80.5	0.6	72.9	2.3	4.6	19.5
Idaho	100.0	18.8	1.6	1.7	1.3	14.1	81.2
Illinois	100.0	45.7	0.2	4.2	20.0	21.3	54.3
Indiana	100.0	21.7	0.3	1.5	12.8	7.1	78.3
Iowa	100.0	15.5	0.6	2.2	5.8	7.0	84.5
Kansas	100.0	27.2	1.6	2.8	8.8	14.0	72.8
Kentucky	100.0	15.3	0.1	1.1	11.0	3.0	84.7
Louisiana	100.0	51.2	0.8	1.4	46.1	2.9	48.8
Maine	100.0	6.3	0.8	1.6	2.7	1.2	93.7
Maryland	100.0	53.8	0.4	5.9	38.0	9.5	46.2
Massachusetts	100.0	30.1	0.3	5.2	8.2	14.3	69.9
Michigan	100.0	28.6	0.9	2.7	20.2	4.8	71.4
Minnesota	100.0	24.4	2.2	6.2	9.6	6.4	75.6
Mississippi	100.0	53.7	0.2	0.9	50.5	2.1	46.3
Missouri	100.0	24.0	0.4	1.9	17.8	3.9	76.0
Montana	100.0	16.3	11.4	1.2	1.0	2.6	83.7
Nebraska	100.0	25.4	1.7	2.1	8.1	13.5	74.6
Nevada	100.0	57.7	1.5	8.1	11.2	36.9	42.3
New Hampshire	100.0	8.1	0.3	2.4	2.1	3.3	91.9
New Jersey	100.0	46.0	0.2	8.5	17.1	19.9	54.0
New Mexico	100.0	71.1	11.0	1.4	2.6	56.1	28.9
New York	100.0	48.9	0.5	7.7	19.3	21.4	51.1
North Carolina	100.0	45.7	1.4	2.5	31.2	10.6	54.3
North Dakota	100.0	14.7	9.2	1.1	2.2	2.2	85.3
Ohio	100.0	21.6	0.1	1.7	16.9	2.8	78.4
Oklahoma	100.0	42.7	19.2	2.1	10.9	10.5	57.3
Oregon	100.0	28.3	2.1	5.0	3.1	18.1	71.7
Pennsylvania	100.0	26.4	0.2	2.9	15.8	7.5	73.6
Rhode Island	100.0	31.4	0.7	3.2	9.0	18.5	68.6

| | total | minority students | | | | | non-Hispanic white |
		total	Am. Indian	Asian	black	Hispanic	
South Carolina	100.0%	46.2%	0.4%	1.6%	38.8%	5.5%	53.8%
South Dakota	100.0	18.7	12.2	1.3	2.5	2.7	81.3
Tennessee	100.0	31.7	0.2	1.6	24.6	5.2	68.3
Texas	100.0	66.0	0.4	3.6	14.2	47.9	34.0
Utah	100.0	20.6	1.4	3.3	1.4	14.5	79.4
Vermont	100.0	6.0	0.2	1.5	1.7	1.2	94.0
Virginia	100.0	41.8	0.3	5.9	26.4	9.2	58.2
Washington	100.0	32.9	2.6	8.9	5.7	15.8	67.1
West Virginia	100.0	7.2	0.1	0.7	5.4	0.9	92.8
Wisconsin	100.0	23.7	1.5	3.7	10.5	8.0	76.3
Wyoming	100.0	16.7	3.5	1.1	1.6	10.4	83.3

Note: Minority students by race/Hispanic origin do not sum to total because "other" race is not shown.
*Source: National Center for Education Statistics, Digest of Education Statistics: 2010, Table 43, Internet site http://nces.
ed.gov/programs/digest/d10/*

Table 2.12 Homeschooled Children by Selected Characteristics, 2007

(number and percent of children who are homeschooled, 1999 to 2007; and number and percent distribution of homeschooled children by selected characteristics, 2007; numbers in thousands)

	number	percent of total enrollment
Total homeschooled children		
2007	1,508	2.9%
2003	1,096	2.2
1999	850	1.7

	number	percent distribution
TOTAL HOMESCHOOLED CHILDREN, 2007	**1,508**	**100.0%**
Race and Hispanic origin		
Black	61	4.0
Hispanic	147	9.7
Non-Hispanic white	1,159	76.9
Sex of child		
Male	633	42.0
Female	875	58.0
Number of children in household		
One	187	12.4
Two	412	27.3
Three or more	909	60.3
Number of parents in household		
Two parents	1,348	89.4
One parent	115	7.6
Nonparental guardian	45	3.0
Parents' labor force participation		
Two parents, both in labor force	808	53.6
Two parents, one in labor force	509	33.8
One parent, in labor force	127	8.4
No parent in labor force	64	4.2
Household income		
$25,000 or less	239	15.8
$25,001 to $50,000	364	24.1
$50,001 to $75,000	405	26.9
$75,001 or more	501	33.2
Parents' education		
High school diploma or less	206	13.7
Some college or vocational/technical	549	36.4
Bachelor's degree	444	29.4
Graduate/professional degree	309	20.5

	number	percent distribution
Most important reason for homeschooling		
Desire to provide religious or moral instruction	540	35.8%
Concern about environment of schools	309	20.5
Dissatisfaction with academic instruction at schools	258	17.1
Desire to provide a nontraditional approach to child's education	99	6.6
Child has other special needs	55	3.6
Child has a physical or mental health problem	31	2.1
Other reasons	216	14.3

Note: "Other reasons" include family time, finances, travel, and distance.
Source: National Center for Education Statistics, The Condition of Education, Homeschooled Students, Internet site http://nces
.ed.gov/programs/coe/2009/section1/indicator06.asp

Table 2.13 Children Attending Private School by Selected Characteristics, 1997–98 to 2007–08

(number and percent of children who are attending private elementary or secondary schools, 1997–98 to 2007–08; and percent distribution of enrollment by selected characteristics, 2007–08; numbers in thousands)

	number	percent of total enrollment
Children attending private elementary or secondary schools		
2007–2008	5,910	10.7%
2005–2006	6,073	11.0
2003–2004	6,099	11.2
2001–2002	6,320	11.7
1999–2000	6,018	11.4
1997–1998	5,944	11.4
Attendance by region, 2007–08		
Northeast	1,426	14.9
Midwest	1,352	11.2
South	1,965	9.6
West	1,167	8.9

Enrollment characteristics, 2007–08	percent distribution
TOTAL PRIVATE SCHOOL ENROLLMENT	**100.0%**
Type of school	
Roman Catholic	39.1
Other religious	38.6
Nonsectarian	22.3
School level	
Elementary	54.6
Secondary	14.0
Combined	31.4
Race and Hispanic origin of students	
Asian	5.4
Black	9.8
Hispanic	9.6
Non-Hispanic white	74.5

Source: National Center for Education Statistics, The Condition of Education, Private School Enrollment, Internet site http://nces.ed.gov/programs/coe/2010/section1/indicator03.asp

Parents Are Involved in Their Children's Education

In the past year, most have attended a school meeting, a parent-teacher conference, and a school or class event.

Most parents are actively involved in their children's education. The parents of 89 percent of the nation's elementary and secondary school children say they attended a PTA or general school meeting during the past year, according to a survey by the National Center for Education Statistics. Seventy-eight percent attended a parent-teacher conference, 74 percent attended a class event, and 46 percent volunteered.

Participation in a child's education typically rises with the educational attainment of the parent. The percentage of children whose parents attended a class event, for example, climbs from 48 percent among parents who did not graduate from high school to more than 80 percent among parents with at least a bachelor's degree. Surprisingly, however, the most educated parents are least likely to check their children's homework. Among students with homework, only 81 percent of parents with a graduate degree check to make sure their child has done his homework compared with 94 percent of parents without a high school diploma.

■ Poor parents are more likely than the nonpoor to make sure their children have done their homework.

Educated parents are most likely to attend their children's class events

(percent of children whose parents attended a class event in the past year, by educational attainment of parents, 2006–07)

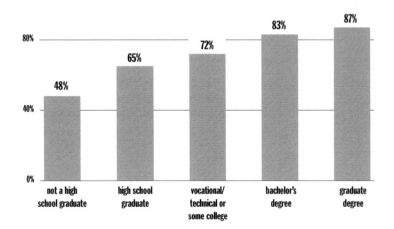

Table 2.14 Parental Involvement in School Activities, 2006–07

(total number and percent of elementary and secondary school children whose parents reported participation in school activities, by selected characteristics of child and parent, 2006–07; numbers in thousands)

	total number	percent	parent attended a PTA or general school meeting	parent attended a parent-teacher conference	parent attended a school or class event	parent volunteered at school	parent participated in school fundraising
TOTAL CHILDREN	51,600	100%	89%	78%	74%	46%	65%
Race and Hispanic origin of child							
Asian, non-Hispanic	1,566	100	90	80	72	46	62
Black, non-Hispanic	7,837	100	87	77	65	35	58
Hispanic	9,767	100	87	80	65	32	51
White, non-Hispanic	29,832	100	91	78	80	54	72
Educational attainment of parent							
Not a high school graduate	3,504	100	75	70	48	20	34
High school graduate	11,070	100	84	74	65	33	55
Vocational/technical or some college	14,844	100	89	77	72	42	67
Bachelor's degree	11,353	100	94	81	83	56	72
Graduate degree	10,829	100	95	82	87	64	77
School type							
Public, assigned	37,168	100	89	76	72	42	63
Public, chosen	7,951	100	88	81	74	45	62
Private, religious	4,560	100	96	96	86	73	85
Private, nonreligious	1,438	100	97	90	86	68	72
Student's grade level							
Kindergarten through 2nd grade	11,516	100	93	90	78	63	72
3rd through 5th grade	11,519	100	94	92	83	57	71
6th through 8th grade	12,058	100	91	76	72	38	63
9th through 12th grade	16,503	100	83	61	68	34	57
Poverty status							
Poor	10,012	100	81	77	56	26	45
Not poor	41,587	100	91	78	79	51	70

Source: National Center for Education Statistics, Parent and Family Involvement in Education, 2006–07 School Year, from the National Household Education Surveys Program of 2007, August 2008, Internet site http://nces.ed.gov/pubsearch/pubsinfo .asp?pubid=2008050; calculations by New Strategist

Table 2.15 Parental Involvement in Child's Homework, 2006–07

(total number and percent of elementary and secondary school children whose parents reported involvement with child's homework, by selected characteristics of child and parent, 2006–07; numbers in thousands)

	total		student does homework outside of school		
	number	percent	total	place in home set aside for homework	adult in household checks that homework is done
TOTAL CHILDREN	**51,600**	**100%**	**94%**	**89%**	**85%**
Race and Hispanic origin of child					
Asian, non-Hispanic	1,566	100	96	93	83
Black, non-Hispanic	7,837	100	94	94	94
Hispanic	9,767	100	94	84	91
White, non-Hispanic	29,832	100	95	89	82
Educational attainment of parent					
Not a high school graduate	3,504	100	90	83	94
High school graduate	11,070	100	93	89	89
Vocational/technical or some college	14,844	100	94	90	86
Bachelor's degree	11,353	100	96	87	83
Graduate degree	10,829	100	96	90	81
School type					
Public, assigned	37,168	100	94	89	86
Public, chosen	7,951	100	95	90	88
Private, religious	4,560	100	97	86	79
Private, nonreligious	1,438	100	90	85	84
Student's grade level					
Kindergarten through 2nd grade	11,516	100	93	84	100
3rd through 5th grade	11,519	100	97	89	97
6th through 8th grade	12,058	100	95	91	88
9th through 12th grade	16,503	100	93	91	65
Poverty status					
Poor	10,012	100	93	87	93
Not poor	41,587	100	95	89	84

Source: National Center for Education Statistics, Parent and Family Involvement in Education, 2006–07 School Year, from the National Household Education Surveys Program of 2007, August 2008, Internet site http://nces.ed.gov/pubsearch/pubsinfo .asp?pubid=2008050; calculations by New Strategist

Most Parents Are Satisfied with Their Child's School

Most are also satisfied with their child's teachers and the amount of homework.

Complaints about the nation's schools are commonplace, but in fact the parents of most children in kindergarten through 12th grade are highly satisfied with various aspects of their child's school. Fifty-nine percent of school children have parents who claim to be "very satisfied" with their child's school. The percentage of parents who are very satisfied with the teachers is an even higher 64 percent. Similar proportions are very satisfied with their school's academic standards and discipline. Seventy-five percent say the amount of homework assigned to their child is about right.

The biggest difference in satisfaction levels is by type of school and grade level. Typically, private school parents are happier than public school parents, and the parents of younger children are happier than the parents of children in middle or high school. Nevertheless, the majority of parents, regardless of type of school or grade level, say they are very satisfied with their child's school.

■ By race and Hispanic origin, non-Hispanic whites are most satisfied with their child's school.

Blacks are least likely to be very satisfied with their child's school

(percent of children in kindergarten through 12th grade whose parents are very satisfied with their child's school, by race and Hispanic origin, 2006–07)

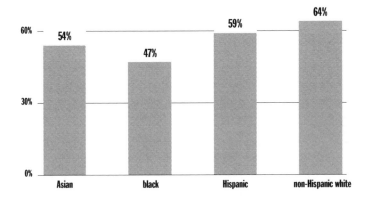

Table 2.16 Parental Satisfaction with School, 2006–07

(total number, percent distribution, and percent of elementary and secondary school children whose parents report satisfaction with school characteristics and amount of homework, by selected characteristics of child and parent, 2006–07; numbers in thousands)

| | total | | parent reports being very satisfied | | | | | |
	number	percent	with the school	with teachers student had this year	with academic standards of the school	with order and discipline at the school	with the way school staff interacts with parents	amount of homework assigned is about right
TOTAL CHILDREN	**51,600**	**100%**	**59%**	**64%**	**63%**	**62%**	**55%**	**75%**
Race and Hispanic origin of child								
Asian, non-Hispanic	1,566	100	54	59	56	57	50	67
Black, non-Hispanic	7,837	100	47	57	55	54	49	66
Hispanic	9,767	100	59	65	60	63	59	78
White, non-Hispanic	29,832	100	64	66	66	65	57	77
Educational attainment of parent								
Not a high school graduate	3,504	100	54	62	56	60	55	79
High school graduate	11,070	100	54	59	56	58	51	74
Vocational/technical or some college	14,844	100	55	61	59	57	53	73
Bachelor's degree	11,353	100	64	67	67	65	57	76
Graduate degree	10,829	100	68	70	71	70	62	76
School type								
Public, assigned	37,168	100	55	61	58	58	51	74
Public, chosen	7,951	100	63	68	67	63	59	72
Private, religious	4,560	100	81	79	84	83	77	80
Private, nonreligious	1,438	100	82	78	84	83	76	88
Student's grade level								
Kindergarten through 2nd grade	11,516	100	69	78	69	72	67	80
3rd through 5th grade	11,519	100	65	69	67	66	63	79
6th through 8th grade	12,058	100	55	58	60	59	51	71
9th through 12th grade	16,503	100	52	54	57	54	46	72
Poverty status								
Poor	10,012	100	56	64	59	57	56	73
Not poor	41,587	100	60	64	63	63	55	75

Source: National Center for Education Statistics, Parent and Family Involvement in Education, 2006–07 School Year, from the National Household Education Surveys Program of 2007, August 2008 Internet site http://nces.ed.gov/pubsearch/pubsinfo .asp?pubid=2008050; calculations by New Strategist

School Enrollment Is Projected to Rise

In the Northeast, however, public school enrollment may decline.

Between 2010 and 2019, enrollment in the nation's elementary and secondary schools is projected to rise by 6 percent, according to projections by the National Center for Education Statistics. Overall, the nation's schools will gain more than 3 million additional students during those years.

High school enrollment is projected to increase by only 3 percent between 2010 and 2019, while enrollment in pre-K through 8th grade is expected to rise 7 percent. Private school enrollment should increase more slowly than public school enrollment overall, and the number of high school students in private school is projected to decline.

Public school enrollment trends should differ dramatically by region and state between 2010 and 2019. In most Northeastern and some Midwestern states, public elementary and secondary school enrollment is projected to fall. In contrast, public school enrollment is projected to increase by 10 percent in the South and West.

■ Public school enrollment growth in Arizona and Nevada may not be as rapid as projected if those states are slow to recover from the Great Recession.

School enrollment is projected to climb the most in the South

(percent change in number of pre-K through 12th grade students in public schools by region, 2010–19)

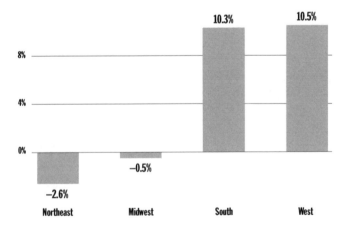

Table 2.17 Projected Enrollment in Prekindergarten through 12th Grade, 2010 and 2019

(projected number of people enrolled in prekindergarten through 12th grade by control of institution, fall 2010 and 2019; percent change, 2010–19; numbers in thousands)

	2010	2019	percent change 2010 to 2019
TOTAL ENROLLED	**55,350**	**58,590**	**5.9%**
Pre-K through grade 8	39,312	42,083	7.0
Grades 9 through 12	16,038	16,507	2.9
Public enrollment	**49,386**	**52,342**	**6.0**
Pre-K through grade 8	34,730	37,156	7.0
Grades 9 through 12	14,657	15,186	3.6
Private enrollment	**5,964**	**6,248**	**4.8**
Pre-K through grade 8	4,582	4,927	7.5
Grades 9 through 12	1,382	1,321	–4.4

Source: National Center for Education Statistics, Projections of Education Statistics to 2019, Internet site http://nces.ed.gov/ programs/projections/projections2019/tables.asp; calculations by New Strategist

Table 2.18 Projected Enrollment in Prekindergarten through 12th Grade in Public Schools by State, 2010 and 2019

(number of people enrolled in prekindergarten through 12th grade in public schools by state, fall 2010 and 2019; percent change, 2010–19; numbers in thousands)

	2010	2019	percent change 2010 to 2019
Total enrolled	**49,386**	**52,342**	**6.0%**
Northeast	7,817	7,611	–2.6
Connecticut	554	538	–3.0
Maine	186	180	–3.2
Massachusetts	930	890	–4.4
New Hampshire	192	195	1.8
New Jersey	1,354	1,339	–1.1
New York	2,620	2,505	–4.4
Pennsylvania	1,755	1,744	–0.7
Rhode Island	138	132	–4.2
Vermont	88	88	–0.1
Midwest	10,525	10,477	–0.5
Illinois	2,084	2,061	–1.1
Indiana	1,040	1,048	0.8
Iowa	476	477	0.3
Kansas	470	492	4.6
Michigan	1,601	1,520	–5.0
Minnesota	826	873	5.7
Missouri	903	926	2.5
Nebraska	290	300	3.5
North Dakota	92	91	–1.1
Ohio	1,768	1,688	–4.5
South Dakota	121	123	1.9
Wisconsin	854	877	2.7
South	18,870	20,806	10.3
Alabama	742	729	–1.7
Arkansas	483	508	5.1
Delaware	124	134	7.6
District of Columbia	79	80	1.9
Florida	2,692	3,051	13.4
Georgia	1,716	1,916	11.7
Kentucky	683	682	–0.1
Louisiana	675	676	0.1
Maryland	814	852	4.7
Mississippi	488	469	–4.0
North Carolina	1,582	1,833	15.9
Oklahoma	650	685	5.4
South Carolina	718	753	4.8
Tennessee	959	1,005	4.8
Texas	4,955	5,838	17.8
Virginia	1,231	1,328	7.9
West Virginia	278	266	–4.5

	2010	2019	percent change 2010 to 2019
West	12,174	13,448	10.5%
Alaska	127	144	12.8
Arizona	1,159	1,447	24.9
California	6,367	6,805	6.9
Colorado	824	909	10.4
Hawaii	177	184	3.8
Idaho	286	329	15.1
Montana	141	147	4.9
Nevada	461	579	25.6
New Mexico	334	363	8.7
Oregon	568	624	9.9
Utah	613	695	13.4
Washington	1,030	1,125	9.3
Wyoming	89	96	7.4

Source: National Center for Education Statistics, Projections of Education Statistics to 2019, Internet site http://nces.ed.gov/ programs/projections/projections2019/tables.asp; calculations by New Strategist

Fewer Students Are Dropping Out of High School

The dropout rate is still high among Hispanics, however.

Among people aged 16 to 24 in 2009, only 8.1 percent were neither high school graduates nor currently enrolled in school, down from 10.9 percent in 2000. Since 2000, dropout rates have fallen for both men and women and for every racial and ethnic group.

Dropout rates remain high for Hispanics. While just 5.2 percent of whites and 9.3 percent of blacks aged 16 to 24 have dropped out of high school, a much larger 17.6 percent of Hispanics are high school dropouts. Among Hispanic men, the dropout rate was 19.0 percent in 2009, down sharply from 31.8 in 2000 but still high. Among Hispanic women aged 16 to 24, a smaller 16.1 percent were high school dropouts in 2009, down from 23.5 percent in 2000.

■ The arrival of millions of poorly educated immigrants to the United States during the past decade explains the high dropout rate among Hispanics. Some did not, in fact, drop out of an American high school, but arrived in the United States without a high school diploma.

Whites have the lowest dropout rate

(percent of people aged 16 to 24 who were neither enrolled in school nor high school graduates, by race and Hispanic origin, 2009)

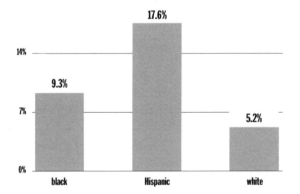

Table 2.19 High School Dropouts by Sex, Race, and Hispanic Origin, 1990 to 2009

(percentage of people aged 16 to 24 who were not enrolled in school and were not high school graduates by sex, race, and Hispanic origin, selected years 1990 to 2009; percentage point change, 1990–2009 and 2000–09)

	2009	2000	1990	percentage point change	
				2000–09	1990–2000
TOTAL PEOPLE	**8.1%**	**10.9%**	**12.1%**	**–2.8**	**–1.2**
Black	9.3	13.1	13.2	–3.8	–0.1
Hispanic	17.6	27.8	32.4	–10.2	–4.6
White	5.2	6.9	9.0	–1.7	–2.1
Total men	**9.1**	**12.0**	**12.3**	**–2.9**	**–0.3**
Black	10.6	15.3	11.9	–4.7	3.4
Hispanic	19.0	31.8	34.3	–12.8	–2.5
White	6.3	7.0	9.3	–0.7	–2.3
Total women	**7.0**	**9.9**	**11.8**	**–2.9**	**–1.9**
Black	8.1	11.1	14.4	–3.0	–3.3
Hispanic	16.1	23.5	30.3	–7.4	–6.8
White	4.1	6.9	8.7	–2.8	–1.8

Note: Whites and blacks include Hispanics.
Source: National Center for Education Statistics, Digest of Education Statistics: 2010, Table 115, Internet site http://nces
.ed.gov/programs/digest/d10/

Stability in High School Graduates

The number of people graduating from high school will decline slightly between 2009–10 and 2019–20.

As the iGeneration (children under age 16 in 2010) enters high school, the number of high school graduates will remain stable at about 3.2 to 3.3 million a year between 2009–10 and 2019–20. The number of public school graduates will barely change during those years, while the number of private school graduates is projected to fall by a substantial 7 percent.

College campuses, which have become accustomed to growing numbers of high school graduates, may have to adjust to a new stability. The changing demographics, coupled with economic uncertainty, suggest that change lies ahead for the nation's institutions of higher education.

■ Nearly 10 percent of the nation's high school graduates attend private school, a figure that is projected to decline to 9 percent by 2019–20.

Little change is forecast in the number of high school graduates

(number of high school graduates, 2009–10 and 2019–20)

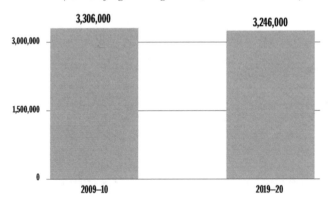

Table 2.20 Projections of High School Graduates, 2009–10 to 2019–20

(number of people graduating from high school by control of institution, 2009–10 to 2019–20; percent change 2009–10 to 2019–20; numbers in thousands)

	total	public	private
2009–10	3,306	2,991	315
2010–11	3,252	2,937	315
2011–12	3,222	2,906	316
2012–13	3,200	2,891	309
2013–14	3,176	2,868	308
2014–15	3,171	2,872	298
2015–16	3,201	2,906	295
2016–17	3,223	2,933	290
2017–18	3,274	2,989	285
2018–19	3,265	2,985	280
2019–20	3,246	2,953	293
Percent change			
2009–10 to 2019–20	–1.8%	–1.3%	–7.0%

Source: National Center for Education Statistics, Projections of Education Statistics to 2019, Internet site http://nces.ed.gov/ programs/projections/projections2019/tables.asp; calculations by New Strategist

Table 2.21 Projections of Public High School Graduates by Race and Hispanic Origin, 2009–10 to 2019–20

(projected number of people graduating from public high schools by race and Hispanic origin, 2009–10 to 2019–20; percent change 2009–10 to 2019–20; numbers in thousands)

	total	Asian	black	Hispanic	white
2009–10	2,991	165	451	495	1,849
2010–11	2,937	168	444	504	1,793
2011–12	2,906	173	432	518	1,754
2012–13	2,891	178	419	536	1,728
2013–14	2,868	184	405	548	1,702
2014–15	2,872	189	406	564	1,685
2015–16	2,906	192	411	585	1,689
2016–17	2,933	197	412	603	1,692
2017–18	2,989	213	418	630	1,697
2018–19	2,985	215	411	650	1,677
2019–20	2,953	215	405	656	1,646

Percent change

	total	Asian	black	Hispanic	white
2009–10 to 2019–20	–1.3%	30.7%	–10.1%	32.5%	–11.0%

Percent distribution by race and Hispanic origin

	total	Asian	black	Hispanic	white
2009–10	100.0%	5.5%	15.1%	16.6%	61.8%
2010–11	100.0	5.7	15.1	17.1	61.0
2011–12	100.0	5.9	14.9	17.8	60.4
2012–13	100.0	6.2	14.5	18.6	59.8
2013–14	100.0	6.4	14.1	19.1	59.4
2014–15	100.0	6.6	14.1	19.6	58.7
2015–16	100.0	6.6	14.1	20.1	58.1
2016–17	100.0	6.7	14.0	20.6	57.7
2017–18	100.0	7.1	14.0	21.1	56.8
2018–19	100.0	7.2	13.8	21.8	56.2
2019–20	100.0	7.3	13.7	22.2	55.8

Note: Race categories exclude Hispanics. Numbers do not add to total because not all races are shown.
Source: National Center for Education Statistics, Projections of Education Statistics to 2019, Internet site http://nces.ed.gov/programs/projections/projections2019/tables.asp; calculations by New Strategist

SAT Scores Vary by Income and Parent's Education

The more educated the parent, the higher the child's score.

It is well known that SAT scores vary by race and Hispanic origin. Asians and whites get higher scores than blacks or Hispanics. It is also no surprise that students with the best grades get the biggest scores. Students with an A+ GPA (97 to 100) averaged a 621 out of 800 on the math section of the SAT in 2009–10, for example. Students with a B GPA (80 to 89) scored a much lower average of 483 on the math section of the test.

SAT scores also vary by family income and parental education. Students with family incomes below $20,000 scored a 460 on average on the math portion of the SAT in 2009–10 compared with an average score of 586 among students with family incomes of $200,000 or more. Parental education also has a big impact on test scores. Among students with a parent who did not graduate from high school, the average SAT math score was 446. Among those whose parent had a graduate degree, the average math score was 575.

■ Affluent, educated parents can afford SAT prep courses for their children, which can boost test scores.

A parent's education influences a child's test score

(average SAT mathematics score by highest level of parental education, 2009–10)

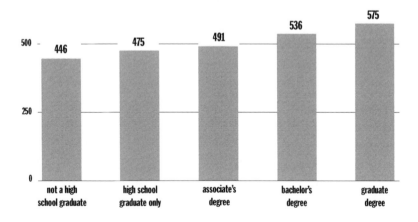

Table 2.22 SAT Scores by Selected Characteristics, 2009–10

(average SAT scores by selected characteristics, 2009–10)

	critical reading	mathematics	writing
TOTAL	**501**	**516**	**492**
Sex			
Men	503	534	486
Women	498	500	498
Race and Hispanic origin			
American Indian, Alaska Native	485	492	467
Asian or Pacific Islander	519	591	526
Black	429	428	420
Mexican American	454	467	448
Puerto Rican	454	452	443
Other Hispanic	454	462	447
White	528	536	516
High school grade point average			
A+ (97 to 100)	599	621	596
A (93 to 96)	563	584	558
A– (90 to 92)	531	550	525
B (80 to 89)	473	483	462
C (70 to 79)	418	424	405
D or F (below 70)	411	422	399
Family income			
Less than $20,000	437	460	432
$20,000 to $39,999	465	479	455
$40,000 o $59,999	490	500	478
$60,000 to $79,999	504	514	492
$80,000 to $99,999	518	529	505
$100,000 to $119,999	528	541	518
$120,000 to $139,999	533	546	523
$140,000 to $159,999	540	554	531
$160,000 to $199,999	547	561	540
$200,000 or more	568	586	567
Highest level of parental education			
Not a high school graduate	422	446	419
High school graduate	464	475	453
Associate's degree	482	491	469
Bachelor's degree	521	536	512
Graduate degree	561	575	554

Source: National Center for Education Statistics, Digest of Education Statistics 2010, Tables 151, 152, and 153, Internet site http://nces.ed.gov/programs/digest/d10/; calculations by New Strategist

College Enrollment Rates Are at a Peak

Among men, however, rates are below their peak.

The rate at which high school graduates enroll in college has never been higher. Among men and women aged 16 to 24 who graduated from high school in 2009, seven out of ten had enrolled in college (either two-year or four-year schools) within 12 months. Women's 2009 enrollment rate of 73.8 percent was 7.6 percentage points higher than their 66.2 percent rate of 2000 and at an all-time high. Men's college enrollment rate grew 6.1 percentage points between 2000 and 2009, but is slightly below the peak rate of 66.5 in 2005.

The 2009 college enrollment rate of blacks (69.5 percent) was the highest ever recorded. Among whites, the 71.3 percent enrollment rate was below the 73.2 percent high reached in 2005. The Hispanic enrollment rate of 62.3 percent was also a record high.

■ The economic downturn is spurring more young adults to go to college in an attempt to boost their credentials for the job market.

Enrollment rates were higher in 2009 than in 2000

(percent of people aged 16 to 24 who graduated from high school in the previous 12 months and were enrolled in college as of October of each year, by sex, 2000 and 2009)

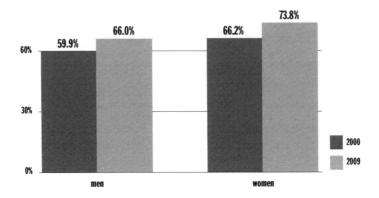

Table 2.23 College Enrollment Rate by Sex, 1990 to 2009

(percentage of people aged 16 to 24 who graduated from high school in the previous 12 months and were enrolled in college as of October, by sex, 1990 to 2009; percentage point change in enrollment rate, for selected years)

	total	men	women
2009	70.1%	66.0%	73.8%
2008	68.6	65.9	71.6
2007	67.2	66.1	68.3
2006	66.0	65.8	66.1
2005	68.6	66.5	70.4
2004	66.7	61.4	71.5
2003	63.9	61.2	66.5
2002	65.2	62.1	68.4
2001	61.8	60.1	63.5
2000	63.3	59.9	66.2
1999	62.9	61.4	64.4
1998	65.6	62.4	69.1
1997	67.0	63.6	70.3
1996	65.0	60.1	69.7
1995	61.9	62.6	61.3
1994	61.9	60.6	63.2
1993	62.6	59.9	65.2
1992	61.9	60.0	63.8
1991	62.5	57.9	67.1
1990	60.1	58.0	62.2

Percentage point change

	total	men	women
2000 to 2009	6.8	6.1	7.6
1990 to 2009	10.0	8.0	11.6

Source: National Center for Education Statistics, Digest of Education Statistics: 2010, Table 208, Internet site http://nces .ed.gov/programs/digest/d10/

Table 2.24 College Enrollment Rate by Race and Hispanic Origin, 1990 to 2009

(percentage of people aged 16 to 24 who graduated from high school in the previous 12 months and were enrolled in college as of October, by race and Hispanic origin, 1990 to 2009; percentage point change in enrollment rate, for selected years)

| | | non-Hispanic | | |
	total	black	white	Hispanic
2009	70.1%	69.5%	71.3%	–
2008	68.6	55.7	71.7	62.3%
2007	67.2	55.7	69.5	62.0
2006	66.0	55.5	68.5	58.5
2005	68.6	55.7	73.2	57.5
2004	66.7	62.5	68.8	57.7
2003	63.9	57.5	66.2	57.7
2002	65.2	59.4	69.1	54.7
2001	61.8	55.0	64.3	52.7
2000	63.3	54.9	65.7	48.6
1999	62.9	58.9	66.3	47.4
1998	65.6	61.9	68.5	51.9
1997	67.0	58.5	68.2	55.3
1996	65.0	56.0	67.4	57.6
1995	61.9	51.2	64.3	51.6
1994	61.9	50.8	64.5	55.0
1993	62.6	55.6	62.9	55.7
1992	61.9	48.2	64.3	58.2
1991	62.5	46.4	65.4	52.6
1990	60.1	46.8	63.0	52.5
Percentage point change				
2000 to 2009	6.8	14.6	5.6	13.7
1990 to 2009	10.0	22.7	8.3	9.8

Note: "–" means data are not available; Hispanic enrollment rate is a three-year moving average. Percentage point change in Hispanic enrollment rate is from 1990 to 2008 and 2000 to 2008 three-year moving averages.
Source: National Center for Education Statistics, Digest of Education Statistics: 2010, Table 209, Internet site http://nces .ed.gov/programs/digest/d10/

College Costs Have More than Doubled in Two Decades

The increasing cost of a college education is making it harder for students to go to school without going into debt.

Between 1977–78 and 2009–10, the average cost of attending a four-year college (including tuition, fees, room, and board) more than doubled, rising by 142 percent. In 1977–78, the cost of one year of college was $8,672. By 2009–10, the price had escalated to $20,986, after adjusting for inflation.

The cost of attending a public college grew 135 percent between 1977–78 to 2009–10 (to $14,870), while private college costs rose by a nearly identical 134 percent (to $32,475). During the past 10 years, however, the cost of public institutions (up 42 percent) increased more than private institutions (up 24 percent). In 1999–00, private institutions cost 2.5 times as much as public institutions. By 2009–10, they cost 2.2 times as much.

Nearly half of first-time full-time undergraduates take out student loans to pay for their education, the proportion climbing from 40 to 49 percent between 2000–01 and 2008–09. At private, for-profit four-year schools, the figure reaches as high as 81 percent. The cumulative amount borrowed for undergraduate education totaled $15,100 per borrower in 2007–08, according to the National Center for Education Statistics.

■ The burden of student loans could hurt the housing industry, preventing young adults from buying a home until their loans are paid off.

The average cost of one year of college exceeds $20,000

(average annual tuition, fees, room, and board for undergraduate programs at four-year institutions, 1977–78 and 2009–10; in 2008–09 dollars)

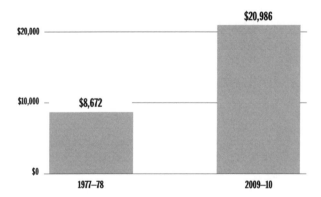

Table 2.25 College Costs, 1977–78 to 2009–10

(average annual tuition, fees, room, and board for undergraduate programs at four-year institutions, by control of school, 1977–78 to 2009–10, percent change in costs for selected years; in 2008–09 dollars)

	total institutions	public institutions	private institutions
2009–10	$20,986	$14,870	$32,475
2008–09	20,385	14,262	32,090
2007–08	19,592	13,616	31,207
2006–07	19,423	13,457	30,409
2005–06	18,820	13,062	29,467
2004–05	18,487	12,795	29,403
2003–04	17,885	12,312	28,918
2002–03	17,020	11,537	28,039
2001–02	16,430	11,078	27,581
2000–01	15,843	10,609	26,795
1999–2000	15,662	10,492	26,255
1998–99	15,509	10,472	25,999
1997–98	14,967	10,184	25,309
1996–97	14,644	9,907	24,912
1995–96	14,352	9,745	24,469
1994–95	13,883	9,519	23,694
1993–94	13,648	9,345	23,348
1992–93	13,190	9,067	22,606
1991–92	12,794	8,843	22,144
1990–91	12,192	8,411	21,218
1989–90	12,185	8,403	20,767
1988–89	11,912	8,286	20,323
1987–88	11,623	8,159	19,752
1986–87	11,509	7,985	19,374
1985–86	10,858	7,611	18,204
1984–85	10,473	7,472	17,151
1983–84	10,012	7,240	16,364
1982–83	9,636	6,990	15,585
1981–82	9,339	6,984	14,532
1980–81	9,142	6,721	14,445
1979–80	9,012	6,548	14,438
1978–79	8,757	6,435	13,861
1977–78	8,672	6,320	13,860
Percent change			
1999–2000 to 2009–10	34.0%	41.7%	23.7%
1977–78 to 2009–10	142.0	135.3	134.3

Source: National Center for Education Statistics, Digest of Education Statistics: 2010, Table 345, Internet site http://nces .ed.gov/programs/digest/d10/

Table 2.26   Student Borrowing, 2000–01 to 2008–09, and Cumulative Amount Borrowed, 2003–04 and 2007–08

(percent of full-time, first-time degree/certificate-seeking undergraduate students enrolled in degree-granting institutions who received student loans and average annual amount of loan, by type and control of institution, 2000–01 to 2008–09; and cumulative amount borrowed for undergraduate education by full-time students who borrowed to finance their education, by type and control of school, 2003–04 and 2007–08)

	all institutions	public four-year	public two-year	private, not-for-profit four-year	private, not-for-profit two-year	private, for-profit four-year	private, for-profit two-year
PERCENT TAKING OUT LOANS							
2008–09	48.6%	46.9%	21.1%	60.6%	58.1%	81.4%	77.5%
2007–08	45.6	45.2	19.4	60.3	54.1	68.7	77.9
2006–07	44.6	44.4	19.0	59.8	55.9	67.2	73.4
2005–06	44.0	44.3	18.2	59.8	55.2	73.6	69.6
2004–05	43.5	43.8	19.6	59.4	53.5	52.0	76.4
2000–01	40.1	40.7	15.3	58.1	49.5	57.7	67.3
AVERAGE ANNUAL AMOUNT BORROWED							
2008–09	$6,974	$5,972	$4,152	$7,638	$6,089	$9,660	$7,734
2007–08	6,009	5,190	3,488	6,435	5,323	8,799	7,195
2006–07	5,014	4,433	2,877	5,558	4,715	6,989	6,007
2005–06	4,831	4,166	2,812	5,264	5,531	7,046	5,951
2004–05	4,463	3,998	2,712	4,991	4,526	5,955	5,274
2000–01	3,764	3,212	2,396	4,000	4,509	5,749	5,387

	all institutions	public four-year doctoral	public all other four-year	public two-year	private, not-for-profit four-year doctoral	private, not-for-profit all other four-year	private, for-profit two-year and above	private, for-profit less than two-year
CUMULULATIVE AMOUNT BORROWED								
2007–08	$15,100	$14,580	$13,280	$8,710	$20,610	$17,920	$17,570	$9,590
2003–04	11,800	11,810	10,790	7,390	15,010	14,040	14,670	7,730

Note: Student loans include only loans made directly to students, not PLUS or other loans to parents.
Source: National Center for Education Statistics, Digest of Education Statistics: 2010, Tables 350 and 353, Internet site http://nces.ed.gov/programs/digest/d10/

More Americans Are Attending College

The number of full-time students attending four-year private schools has fallen since 2005, however.

Between 2000 and 2009, the number of students enrolled in college—from two-year schools through graduate school—climbed 29 percent to nearly 20 million. Enrollment at two-year schools increased more than enrollment at four-year schools during those years (43 versus 23 percent) and full-time enrollment grew much faster than part-time (41 versus 5 percent). But a closer look at the numbers reveals that enrollment in some institutions of higher education is falling. The number of full-time students attending four-year private colleges peaked in 2005 at 2.1 million and has fallen 9 percent since then, to 1.9 million. In contrast, full-time students at four-year public universities reached a record high of more than 6.8 million in 2009.

On the nation's college campuses, women outnumber men by a wide margin. Among students attending two-year schools, women account for 57 percent of students. Among undergraduates at four-year schools, women outnumber men by nearly 1 million and account for 55 percent of the student body. At the graduate school level, women are an even larger 59 percent of the total.

■ The number of full-time students at private four-year colleges had begun to decline even before the economic downturn. Expect to see more declines in the years ahead if college costs continue their relentless rise.

Among undergraduates at four-year schools, women outnumber men by nearly 1 million

(number of undergraduates who attend four-year institutions, by sex, 2009)

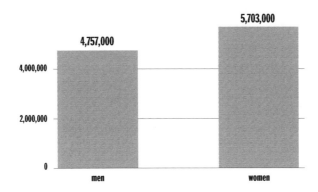

Table 2.27 College Enrollment by Type of College and Attendance Status, 2000 to 2009

(number of students aged 14 or older enrolled in college by type of college and attendance status, 2000 to 2009; percent change in enrollment for selected years; numbers in thousands)

	total	full-time	part-time
TOTAL COLLEGE STUDENTS			
2009	19,765	14,364	5,400
2008	18,631	13,245	5,387
2007	17,956	12,655	5,299
2006	17,232	12,070	5,162
2005	17,473	12,238	5,235
2004	17,382	11,989	5,393
2003	16,638	11,490	5,148
2002	16,498	11,141	5,356
2001	15,873	10,404	5,469
2000	15,314	10,159	5,155
Percent change			
2000–09	29.1%	41.4%	4.8%
Two-year colleges			
2009	5,551	3,633	1,918
2008	5,345	3,397	1,948
2007	4,814	2,988	1,825
2006	4,294	2,699	1,595
2005	4,327	2,632	1,695
2004	4,340	2,602	1,738
2003	4,384	2,563	1,822
2002	4,378	2,464	1,914
2001	4,159	2,310	1,850
2000	3,881	2,193	1,688
Percent change			
2000–09	43.0%	65.7%	13.6%
Four-year colleges			
2009	10,461	8,685	1,775
2008	9,610	7,981	1,629
2007	9,550	7,877	1,673
2006	9,560	7,681	1,879
2005	9,842	8,019	1,823
2004	9,664	7,816	1,848
2003	8,986	7,305	1,680
2002	9,048	7,271	1,776
2001	8,393	6,696	1,696
2000	8,520	6,698	1,822
Percent change			
2000–09	22.8%	29.7%	–2.6%

	total	full-time	part-time
Graduate school			
2009	3,752	2,046	1,707
2008	3,676	1,867	1,810
2007	3,591	1,790	1,801
2006	3,378	1,690	1,688
2005	3,304	1,587	1,717
2004	3,378	1,571	1,807
2003	3,268	1,622	1,646
2002	3,072	1,406	1,666
2001	3,321	1,398	1,923
2000	2,913	1,268	1,645
Percent change			
2000–09	28.8%	61.4%	3.8%

Source: Bureau of the Census, School Enrollment, Historical Tables, Internet site http://www.census.gov/population/www/socdemo/school.html; calculations by New Strategist

Table 2.28 Number of Undergraduates Enrolled Full-Time in Four-Year Colleges by Control of School, 2000 to 2009

(number of students aged 14 or older enrolled full-time in four-year undergraduate institutions of higher education by control of school, 2000 to 2009; percent change in enrollment, 2000–09 and 2005–09; numbers in thousands)

	total	public	private
2009	8,685	6,801	1,884
2008	7,981	6,120	1,861
2007	7,877	6,058	1,819
2006	7,681	5,883	1,798
2005	8,019	5,941	2,077
2004	7,816	5,938	1,878
2003	7,305	5,693	1,612
2002	7,271	5,497	1,774
2001	6,696	5,046	1,650
2000	6,698	4,971	1,726
Percent change			
2005–09	8.3%	14.5%	−9.3%
2000–09	29.7	36.8	9.2

Source: Bureau of the Census, School Enrollment, Historical Tables, Internet site http://www.census.gov/population/www/socdemo/school.html; calculations by New Strategist

Table 2.29 College Students by Age and Sex, 2009

(number, percent, and percent distribution of people aged 15 or older enrolled in institutions of higher education, by type of institution, age, and sex, 2009; numbers in thousands)

	total	men total	men percent of total	women total	women percent of total
TOTAL COLLEGE STUDENTS	**19,765**	**8,642**	**43.7%**	**11,123**	**56.3%**
Aged 15 to 19	4,495	2,016	44.8	2,478	55.1
Aged 20 to 24	7,784	3,712	47.7	4,070	52.3
Aged 25 to 34	4,293	1,843	42.9	2,449	57.0
Aged 35 or older	3,193	1,069	33.5	2,124	66.5
Two-year undergraduates	**5,551**	**2,364**	**42.6**	**3,188**	**57.4**
Aged 15 to 19	1,637	688	42.0	948	57.9
Aged 20 to 24	1,773	885	49.9	889	50.1
Aged 25 to 34	1,222	484	39.6	736	60.2
Aged 35 or older	920	306	33.3	615	66.8
Four-year undergraduates	**10,461**	**4,757**	**45.5**	**5,703**	**54.5**
Aged 15 to 19	2,827	1,316	46.6	1,511	53.4
Aged 20 to 24	5,041	2,403	47.7	2,636	52.3
Aged 25 to 34	1,516	692	45.6	823	54.3
Aged 35 or older	1,078	346	32.1	732	67.9
Graduate students	**3,753**	**1,521**	**40.5**	**2,232**	**59.5**
Aged 15 to 19	32	12	37.5	19	59.4
Aged 20 to 24	969	424	43.8	545	56.2
Aged 25 to 34	1,556	667	42.9	890	57.2
Aged 35 or older	1,194	417	34.9	777	65.1

Source: Bureau of the Census, School Enrollment—Social and Economic Characteristics of Students: October 2009, Internet site http://www.census.gov/population/www/socdemo/school/cps2009.html; calculations by New Strategist

Table 2.30 College Students by Age, Type of School, and Attendance Status, 2009

(number and percent distribution of people aged 15 or older enrolled in institutions of higher education, by age, type of school, and attendance status, 2009; numbers in thousands)

	total	two-year	four-year	graduate school
TOTAL COLLEGE STUDENTS	**19,765**	**5,551**	**10,461**	**3,753**
Aged 15 to 19	4,495	1,637	2,827	32
Aged 20 to 24	7,784	1,773	5,041	969
Aged 25 to 34	4,293	1,222	1,516	1,556
Aged 35 or older	3,193	920	1,078	1,194
Full-time students	**14,364**	**3,633**	**8,685**	**2046**
Aged 15 to 19	4,154	1,410	2,719	26
Aged 20 to 24	6,563	1,228	4,581	752
Aged 25 to 34	2,463	641	907	916
Aged 35 or older	1,184	354	478	351
Part-time students	**5,401**	**1,918**	**1,776**	**1707**
Aged 15 to 19	341	227	108	6
Aged 20 to 24	1,221	545	460	217
Aged 25 to 34	1,830	581	609	640
Aged 35 or older	2,009	566	600	843
Percent distribution by age				
TOTAL COLLEGE STUDENTS	**100.0%**	**100.0%**	**100.0%**	**100.0%**
Aged 15 to 19	22.7	29.5	27.0	0.9
Aged 20 to 24	39.4	31.9	48.2	25.8
Aged 25 to 34	21.7	22.0	14.5	41.5
Aged 35 or older	16.2	16.6	10.3	31.8
Full-time students	**100.0**	**100.0**	**100.0**	**100.0**
Aged 15 to 19	28.9	38.8	31.3	1.3
Aged 20 to 24	45.7	33.8	52.7	36.8
Aged 25 to 34	17.1	17.6	10.4	44.8
Aged 35 or older	8.2	9.7	5.5	17.2
Part-time students	**100.0**	**100.0**	**100.0**	**100.0**
Aged 15 to 19	6.3	11.8	6.1	0.4
Aged 20 to 24	22.6	28.4	25.9	12.7
Aged 25 to 34	33.9	30.3	34.3	37.5
Aged 35 or older	37.2	29.5	33.8	49.4

Source: Bureau of the Census, School Enrollment—Social and Economic Characteristics of Students: October 2009, Internet site http://www.census.gov/population/www/socdemo/school/cps2009.html; calculations by New Strategist

More than One-Third of College Students Are Minorities

Among the nation's 20 million college students, 7 million are black, Hispanic, Asian, or American Indian.

College campuses are becoming more diverse. Non-Hispanic whites accounted for 62 percent of all college students in 2009, down from 68 percent in 2000. Among students at two-years schools, 41 percent are minorities. At four-year schools, the minority share is a smaller 31 percent.

Non-Hispanic whites received 71 percent of bachelor's degrees awarded in 2008–09. Blacks earned 10 percent, Hispanics and Asians 7 to 8 percent. Non-Hispanic whites earn a much smaller proportion of degrees at the doctoral level (59 percent)—not because minorities are better represented, but because foreign students make up a large share of those earning degrees. Twenty-five percent of doctoral degrees awarded in 2008–09 went to nonresident aliens.

■ The educational attainment of blacks and Hispanics is inching upward at a painfully slow rate. The economic downturn has slowed their progress.

Blacks, Hispanics, and Asians account for a significant share of college students

(percent distribution of college students by race and Hispanic origin, 2009)

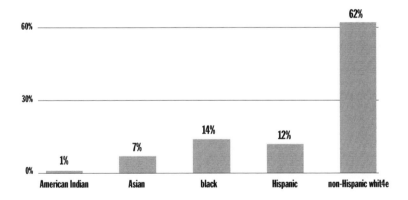

Table 2.31 College Students by Race, Hispanic Origin, and Type of Institution, 2000 and 2009

(number and percent distribution of people enrolled in institutions of higher education by race, Hispanic origin, and type of institution, fall 2000 and fall 2009; percent change in number, 2000–09; numbers in thousands)

| | 2009 | | 2000 | | percent change in number, 2000–09 |
	number	percent distribution	number	percent distribution	
TOTAL ENROLLMENT	**20,428**	**100.0%**	**15,312**	**100.0%**	**33.4%**
White, non-Hispanic	12,731	62.3	10,462	68.3	21.7
Minority	7,012	34.3	4,322	28.2	62.3
American Indian	208	1.0	151	1.0	37.6
Asian	1,338	6.5	978	6.4	36.8
Black, non-Hispanic	2,920	14.3	1,730	11.3	68.8
Hispanic	2,547	12.5	1,462	9.5	74.2
Nonresident alien	685	3.4	529	3.5	29.6
Two-year schools	**7,521**	**100.0**	**5,948**	**100.0**	**26.4**
White, non-Hispanic	4,373	58.1	3,804	64.0	15.0
Minority	3,048	40.5	2,055	34.6	48.3
American Indian	90	1.2	75	1.3	20.5
Asian	496	6.6	402	6.8	23.4
Black, non-Hispanic	1,153	15.3	735	12.4	56.9
Hispanic	1,309	17.4	844	14.2	55.1
Nonresident alien	100	1.3	89	1.5	12.4
Four-year schools	**12,906**	**100.0**	**9,364**	**100.0**	**37.8**
White, non-Hispanic	8,357	64.8	6,658	71.1	25.5
Minority	3,964	30.7	2,266	24.2	74.9
American Indian	118	0.9	76	0.8	55.3
Asian	842	6.5	576	6.2	46.2
Black, non-Hispanic	1,767	13.7	995	10.6	77.6
Hispanic	1,238	9.6	618	6.6	100.3
Nonresident alien	585	4.5	440	4.7	33.0

Source: National Center for Education Statistics, Digest of Education Statistics 2010, Table 236, Internet site http://nces.ed.gov/programs/digest/d10/; calculations by New Strategist

Table 2.32 Degrees Conferred by Student's Race and Hispanic Origin, 2008–09

(number and percent distribution of degrees conferred by institutions of higher education by level of degree, race, and Hispanic origin of degree holder, 2008–09)

	number	percent distribution
TOTAL DEGREES	**3,205,197**	**100.0%**
American Indian	25,806	0.8
Asian	209,425	6.5
Black	339,117	10.6
Hispanic	274,515	8.6
White, non-Hispanic	2,196,872	68.5
Nonresident alien	159,462	5.0
Associate's degrees	**787,325**	**100.0**
American Indian	8,834	1.1
Asian	40,914	5.2
Black	101,487	12.9
Hispanic	97,921	12.4
White, non-Hispanic	522,985	66.4
Nonresident alien	15,184	1.9
Bachelor's degrees	**1,601,368**	**100.0**
American Indian	12,222	0.8
Asian	112,510	7.0
Black	156,615	9.8
Hispanic	129,526	8.1
White, non-Hispanic	1,144,612	71.5
Nonresident alien	45,883	2.9
Master's degrees	**656,784**	**100.0**
American Indian	3,759	0.6
Asian	39,944	6.1
Black	70,010	10.7
Hispanic	39,439	6.0
White, non-Hispanic	424,188	64.6
Nonresident alien	79,444	12.1
Doctoral degrees	**67,716**	**100.0**
American Indian	332	0.5
Asian	3,875	5.7
Black	4,434	6.5
Hispanic	2,540	3.8
White, non-Hispanic	39,648	58.6
Nonresident alien	16,887	24.9
First-professional degrees	**92,004**	**100.0**
American Indian	659	0.7
Asian	12,182	13.2
Black	6,571	7.1
Hispanic	5,089	5.5
White, non-Hispanic	65,439	71.1
Nonresident alien	2,064	2.2

Source: National Center for Education Statistics, Digest of Education Statistics 2010, Tables 293, 296, 299, 302, 305, Internet site http://nces.ed.gov/programs/digest/d10/; calculations by New Strategist

Earning a Bachelor's Degree Often Takes More than Five Years

Earning an associate's degree takes more than four years, on average.

Many students spend more than four years getting their bachelor's degree, according to data from the Census Bureau's Survey of Income and Program Participation. In fact, many students spend more than four years earning an associate's degree. Americans aged 18 or older who have a bachelor's degree report spending an average of 5.6 years working on their degree from start to finish. Those with an associate's degree spent 4.4 years from start to finish.

Among all Americans aged 18 or older with a bachelor's degree, 55 percent finished on time—in four years. A substantial 45 percent spent five or more years working on their degree. Women are more likely than men to graduate in four years (59 versus 51 percent). Non-Hispanic whites are more likely to graduate on time than blacks or Hispanics (56 percent versus 51 and 48 percent, respectively).

■ The high cost of college is one reason it takes many students extra time to finish their degree. Rather than attending school full-time, they take classes part-time while earning money to pay for school.

Nearly half of college graduates spent at least five years earning their bachelor's degree

(percent distribution of bachelor's degree holders by length of time from start to finish of degree, 2004)

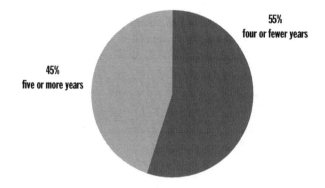

55%
four or fewer years

45%
five or more years

Table 2.33 Average Years to Complete Associate's Degree, 2004

(number and percent distribution of people aged 18 or older whose highest degree is associate, by length of time to start degree and to finish degree, 2004; numbers in thousands)

	total	time from high school to start of degree			time from start to completion of degree			
		same year	within two years	three years or more	under one year	one to three years	four years or more	average years to completion
TOTAL PEOPLE WITH ASSOCIATE'S DEGREE	**16,864**	**8,674**	**3,499**	**4,691**	**415**	**10,661**	**5,788**	**4.4**
Sex								
Men	7,428	3,616	1,637	2,175	157	4,676	2,594	4.4
Women	9,437	5,058	1,863	2,516	258	5,985	3,194	4.3
Race and Hispanic origin								
Black	1,678	699	397	582	63	986	629	4.8
Hispanic	1,376	656	431	289	35	896	445	4.0
Non-Hispanic white	12,847	6,843	2,483	3,521	292	8,167	4,388	4.3
Percent distribution								
TOTAL PEOPLE WITH ASSOCIATE'S DEGREE	**100.0%**	**51.4%**	**20.7%**	**27.8%**	**2.5%**	**63.2%**	**34.3%**	–
Sex								
Men	100.0	48.7	22.0	29.3	2.1	63.0	34.9	–
Women	100.0	53.6	19.7	26.7	2.7	63.4	33.8	–
Race and Hispanic origin								
Black	100.0	41.7	23.7	34.7	3.8	58.8	37.5	–
Hispanic	100.0	47.7	31.3	21.0	2.5	65.1	32.3	–
Non-Hispanic white	100.0	53.3	19.3	27.4	2.3	63.6	34.2	–

Note: "–" means not applicable.
Source: Bureau of the Census, What's It Worth: Field of Training and Economic Status in 2004, Detailed Tables, Internet site http://www.census.gov/population/www/socdemo/education/sipp2004w2.html; calculations by New Strategist

Table 2.34 Average Years to Start and Complete a Bachelor's Degree, 2004

(number and percent distribution of people aged 18 or older whose highest degree is bachelor's, by length of time to start and to finish degree, 2004; numbers in thousands)

| | total | time from high school to start of degree | | | time from start to completion of degree | | continuity of enrollment | | |
		same year	within two years	three years or more	four years or less	five years or more	continuous	not continuous	avg. years to completion
TOTAL PEOPLE WITH BACHELOR'S DEGREE	**33,931**	**25,336**	**4,941**	**3,654**	**18,742**	**15,193**	**26,313**	**7,622**	**5.6**
Sex									
Men	16,401	11,762	2,653	1,986	8,406	7,996	12,425	3,977	5.8
Women	17,530	13,574	2,288	1,668	10,336	7,197	13,888	3,645	5.9
Race and Hispanic origin									
Black	2,444	1,681	446	317	1,242	1,201	1,821	622	6.0
Hispanic	1,635	1,115	325	195	777	857	1,277	357	5.9
Non-Hispanic white	27,137	20,646	3,618	2,873	15,128	12,012	20,980	6,161	5.9
Percent distribution									
TOTAL PEOPLE WITH BACHELOR'S DEGREE	**100.0%**	**74.7%**	**14.6%**	**10.8%**	**55.2%**	**44.8%**	**77.5%**	**22.5%**	–
Sex									
Men	100.0	71.7	16.2	12.1	51.3	48.8	75.8	24.2	–
Women	100.0	77.4	13.1	9.5	59.0	41.1	79.2	20.8	–
Race and Hispanic origin									
Black	100.0	68.8	18.2	13.0	50.8	49.1	74.5	25.5	–
Hispanic	100.0	68.2	19.9	11.9	47.5	52.4	78.1	21.8	–
Non-Hispanic white	100.0	76.1	13.3	10.6	55.7	44.3	77.3	22.7	–

Note: "–" means not applicable.
Source: Bureau of the Census, What's It Worth: Field of Training and Economic Status in 2004, Detailed Tables, Internet site http://www.census.gov/population/www/socdemo/education/sipp2004w2.html; calculations by New Strategist

Women Earn Most Bachelor's Degrees

Women earned more than half of associate's, bachelor's, master's, and doctoral degrees granted in 2008–09.

As women pursue careers, they have been ready customers for credentials that command a higher wage. Women are now the majority presence in most degree programs and fields of study. Sixty-two percent of associate's degrees went to women in 2008–09, as did 57 percent of bachelor's degrees and 60 percent of master's degrees. Women earned only 18 percent of the bachelor's degrees in engineering and computer science in 2008–09. But they accounted for 49 percent of bachelor's degrees awarded in business.

Women earned more than half of all doctorates and slightly less than half of first-professional degrees awarded in 2008–09. They accounted for 49 percent of newly minted physicians, 46 percent of lawyers, 64 percent of pharmacists, and 78 percent of veterinarians.

■ Women's share of the nation's doctors, lawyers, and other professionals will continue to expand in the next few decades as young women now earning degrees replace older men retiring from the professions.

Men earn fewer degrees than women at every level but first-professional

(men's share of degrees awarded, by level of degree, 2008–09)

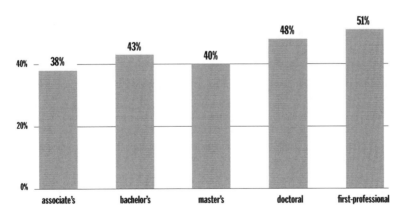

Table 2.35 Associate's Degrees Earned by Field of Study and Sex, 2008–09

(number of associate's degrees conferred by sex, and percent earned by women, by field of study, 2008–09)

	total	men	women number	women percent of total
Total associate's degrees	**787,325**	**298,141**	**489,184**	**62.1%**
Agriculture and natural resources	5,724	3,755	1,969	34.4
Architecture and related services	596	274	322	54.0
Area, ethnic, cultural, and gender studies	173	51	122	70.5
Biological and biomedical sciences	2,364	756	1,608	68.0
Business	127,848	45,735	82,113	64.2
Communications, journalism, and related programs	2,722	1,252	1,470	54.0
Communications technologies	4,803	3,372	1,431	29.8
Computer and information sciences	30,006	22,553	7,453	24.8
Construction trades	4,252	4,035	217	5.1
Education	14,123	2,040	12,083	85.6
Engineering	2,181	1,870	311	14.3
Engineering technologies	30,434	26,143	4,291	14.1
English language and literature/letters	1,525	541	984	64.5
Family and consumer sciences	9,020	356	8,664	96.1
Foreign languages, literatures, and linguistics	1,627	261	1,366	84.0
Health professions and related clinical sciences	165,163	24,270	140,893	85.3
Legal professions and studies	9,062	937	8,125	89.7
Liberal arts and sciences, general studies, and humanities	263,853	102,218	161,635	61.3
Library science	116	15	101	87.1
Mathematics and statistics	930	635	295	31.7
Mechanics and repair technologies	16,066	15,176	890	5.5
Military technologies	721	563	158	21.9
Multi/interdisciplinary studies	15,459	5,955	9,504	61.5
Parks, recreation, leisure, and fitness studies	1,587	946	641	40.4
Philosophy and religious studies	191	136	55	28.8
Physical sciences and science technologies	3,617	2,120	1,497	41.4
Precision production	2,126	1,988	138	6.5
Psychology	3,949	744	3,205	81.2
Public administration and social service professions	4,178	583	3,595	86.0
Security and protective services	33,033	17,230	15,803	47.8
Social sciences and history	9,142	3,253	5,889	64.4
Theology and religious vocations	675	337	338	50.1
Transportation and materials moving	1,430	1,248	182	12.7
Visual and performing arts	18,629	6,793	11,836	63.5

Source: National Center for Education Statistics, Digest of Education Statistics 2010, Table 294, Internet site http://nces.ed.gov/programs/digest/d10/; calculations by New Strategist

Table 2.36 Bachelor's Degrees Earned by Field of Study and Sex, 2008–09

(number of bachelor's degrees conferred by sex, and percent earned by women, by field of study, 2008–09)

	total	men	women number	women percent of total
Total bachelor's degrees	**1,601,368**	**685,382**	**915,986**	**57.2%**
Agriculture and natural resources	24,988	13,101	11,887	47.6
Architecture and related services	10,119	5,797	4,322	42.7
Area, ethnic, cultural, and gender studies	8,772	2,735	6,037	68.8
Biological and biomedical sciences	80,756	32,925	47,831	59.2
Business	347,985	177,862	170,123	48.9
Communications, journalism, and related programs	78,009	27,519	50,490	64.7
Communications technologies	5,100	3,699	1,401	27.5
Computer and information sciences	37,994	31,215	6,779	17.8
Construction trades	168	163	5	3.0
Education	101,708	21,159	80,549	79.2
Engineering	69,133	56,716	12,417	18.0
Engineering technologies	15,112	13,589	1,523	10.1
English language and literature/letters	55,462	17,973	37,489	67.6
Family and consumer sciences	21,905	2,754	19,151	87.4
Foreign languages, literatures, and linguistics	21,158	6,302	14,856	70.2
Health professions and related clinical sciences	120,488	17,792	102,696	85.2
Legal professions and studies	3,822	1,037	2,785	72.9
Liberal arts and sciences, general studies, and humanities	47,096	16,616	30,480	64.7
Library science	78	8	70	89.7
Mathematics and statistics	15,496	8,793	6,703	43.3
Mechanics and repair technologies	223	207	16	7.2
Military technologies	55	54	1	1.8
Multi/interdisciplinary studies	37,444	11,857	25,587	68.3
Parks, recreation, leisure, and fitness studies	31,667	16,666	15,001	47.4
Philosophy and religious studies	12,444	7,761	4,683	37.6
Physical sciences and science technologies	22,466	13,299	9,167	40.8
Precision production	29	19	10	34.5
Psychology	94,271	21,488	72,783	77.2
Public administration and social service professions	23,851	4,374	19,477	81.7
Security and protective services	41,800	21,073	20,727	49.6
Social sciences and history	168,500	85,197	83,303	49.4
Theology and religious vocations	8,940	5,950	2,990	33.4
Transportation and materials moving	5,189	4,631	558	10.8
Visual and performing arts	89,140	35,051	54,089	60.7

Source: National Center for Education Statistics, Digest of Education Statistics 2010, Table 297, Internet site http://nces.ed.gov/ programs/digest/d10/; calculations by New Strategist

Table 2.37 Master's Degrees Earned by Field of Study and Sex, 2008–09

(number of master's degrees conferred by sex, and percent earned by women, by field of study, 2008–09)

	total	men	women number	women percent of total
Total master's degrees	**656,784**	**259,998**	**396,786**	**60.4%**
Agriculture and natural resources	4,877	2,328	2,549	52.3
Architecture and related services	6,587	3,657	2,930	44.5
Area, ethnic, cultural, and gender studies	1,779	607	1,172	65.9
Biological and biomedical sciences	9,898	4,200	5,698	57.6
Business	168,375	91,981	76,394	45.4
Communications, journalism, and related programs	7,092	2,212	4,880	68.8
Communications technologies	475	247	228	48.0
Computer and information sciences	17,907	13,063	4,844	27.1
Education	178,564	40,324	138,240	77.4
Engineering	34,750	26,970	7,780	22.4
Engineering technologies	3,455	2,625	830	24.0
English language and literature/letters	9,261	3,001	6,260	67.6
Family and consumer sciences	2,453	366	2,087	85.1
Foreign languages, literatures, and linguistics	3,592	1,211	2,381	66.3
Health professions and related clinical sciences	62,620	11,869	50,751	81.0
Legal professions and studies	5,150	2,683	2,467	47.9
Liberal arts and sciences, general studies, and humanities	3,728	1,439	2,289	61.4
Library science	7,091	1,344	5,747	81.0
Mathematics and statistics	5,211	3,064	2,147	41.2
Military technologies	3	2	1	33.3
Multi/interdisciplinary studies	5,344	1,946	3,398	63.6
Parks, recreation, leisure, and fitness studies	4,822	2,605	2,217	46.0
Philosophy and religious studies	1,859	1,178	681	36.6
Physical sciences and science technologies	5,658	3,433	2,225	39.3
Precision production	10	5	5	50.0
Psychology	23,415	4,789	18,626	79.5
Public administration and social service professions	33,933	8,346	25,587	75.4
Security and protective services	6,128	2,829	3,299	53.8
Social sciences and history	19,240	9,605	9,635	50.1
Theology and religious vocations	7,541	4,839	2,702	35.8
Transportation and materials moving	1,048	905	143	13.6
Visual and performing arts	14,918	6,325	8,593	57.6

Source: National Center for Education Statistics, Digest of Education Statistics 2010, Table 300, Internet site http://nces.ed.gov/programs/digest/d10/; calculations by New Strategist

Table 2.38 Doctoral Degrees Earned by Field of Study and Sex, 2008–09

(number of doctoral degrees conferred by sex, and percent earned by women, by field of study, 2008–09)

			women	
	total	men	number	percent of total
Total doctoral degrees	**67,716**	**32,279**	**35,437**	**52.3%**
Agriculture and natural resources	1,328	741	587	44.2
Architecture and related services	212	113	99	46.7
Area, ethnic, cultural, and gender studies	239	87	152	63.6
Biological and biomedical sciences	6,957	3,292	3,665	52.7
Business	2,123	1,302	821	38.7
Communications, journalism, and related programs	533	223	310	58.2
Communications technologies	2	2	0	0.0
Computer and information sciences	1,580	1,226	354	22.4
Education	9,028	2,956	6,072	67.3
Engineering	7,931	6,212	1,719	21.7
Engineering technologies	59	47	12	20.3
English language and literature/letters	1,271	464	807	63.5
Family and consumer sciences	333	66	267	80.2
Foreign languages, literatures, and linguistics	1,111	426	685	61.7
Health professions and related clinical sciences	12,112	3,191	8,921	73.7
Legal professions and studies	259	138	121	46.7
Liberal arts and sciences, general studies, and humanities	67	34	33	49.3
Library science	35	14	21	60.0
Mathematics and statistics	1,535	1,059	476	31.0
Multi/interdisciplinary studies	1,273	572	701	55.1
Parks, recreation, leisure, and fitness studies	285	151	134	47.0
Philosophy and religious studies	686	472	214	31.2
Physical sciences and science technologies	5,048	3,416	1,632	32.3
Psychology	5,477	1,478	3,999	73.0
Public administration and social service professions	812	306	506	62.3
Security and protective services	97	46	51	52.6
Social sciences and history	4,234	2,353	1,881	44.4
Theology and religious vocations	1,520	1,166	354	23.3
Visual and performing arts	1,569	726	843	53.7

Source: National Center for Education Statistics, Digest of Education Statistics 2010, Table 303, Internet site http://nces.ed.gov/programs/digest/d10/; calculations by New Strategist

Table 2.39 First-Professional Degrees Earned by Field of Study and Sex, 2008–09

(number of first-professional degrees conferred by sex, and percent earned by women, by field of study, 2008–09)

	total	men	women	
			number	percent of total
Total first-professional degrees	**92,004**	**46,900**	**45,104**	**49.0%**
Dentistry (D.D.S. or D.M.D.)	4,918	2,637	2,281	46.4
Medicine (M.D.)	15,987	8,164	7,823	48.9
Optometry (O.D.)	1,338	466	872	65.2
Osteopathic medicine (D.O.)	3,665	1,798	1,867	50.9
Pharmacy (Pharm.D.)	11,291	4,011	7,280	64.5
Podiatry (Pod.D., D.P., or D.P.M.)	431	250	181	42.0
Veterinary medicine (D.V.M.)	2,377	526	1,851	77.9
Chiropractic (D.C. or D.C.M.)	2,512	1,584	928	36.9
Naturopathic medicine	78	18	60	76.9
Law (LL.B. or J.D.)	44,045	23,860	20,185	45.8
Theology (M.Div., M.H.L., B.D., or Ord.)	5,362	3,586	1,776	33.1

Source: National Center for Education Statistics, Digest of Education Statistics 2010, Table 306, Internet site http://nces.ed.gov/programs/digest/d10/; calculations by New Strategist

3

Health Trends

■ **Most Americans say their health is "excellent" or "very good."**

Only among people aged 65 or older does the share fall below 50 percent.

■ **Weight problems have grown in every age group.**

Sixty-three percent of the nation's adults are overweight, and 28 percent are obese.

■ **The babies being born today promise great diversity tomorrow.**

Of the 4.1 million babies born in 2009, only 54 percent were born to non-Hispanic whites. Fully 24 percent were born to Hispanics and 15 percent to blacks.

■ **Seventeen percent of Americans are without health insurance.**

The number of people without health insurance rose 32 percent between 2000 and 2009, to 51 million.

■ **Many children have asthma.**

Fourteen percent of children under age 18 have been diagnosed with asthma. Eight percent have learning disabilities.

■ **Lower back pain is the most frequently reported health condition.**

More than half of people aged 75 or older have been diagnosed with arthritis. One in four has had a heart attack.

■ **Heart disease and cancer are the biggest killers.**

Alzheimer's is the sixth leading cause of death, and diabetes is the seventh.

Most Americans Feel Very Good or Excellent

Just 14 percent say their health is only fair or poor.

Overall, 56 percent of adults say their health is "very good" or "excellent," ranging from a high of 63 percent among people aged 18 to 24 to a low of just under 40 percent among people aged 65 or older. Among the oldest Americans, those who rate their health as very good or excellent far surpass the 25 percent who say their health is only "fair" or "poor."

The higher their education, the better people feel. Sixty-nine percent of college graduates say their health is very good or excellent compared with just 29 percent of people who did not graduate from high school. One reason for the poorer health of the less educated is that older Americans are disproportionately represented among those with the least education.

■ The proportion of Americans who say their health is very good or excellent rises with household income.

The majority of people under age 65 say their health is very good or excellent

(percent of people aged 18 or older who say their health is "very good" or "excellent," by age, 2009)

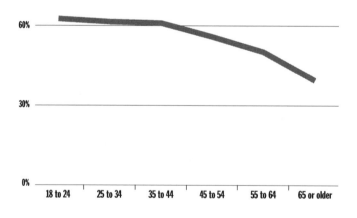

Table 3.1 Health Status, 2009

"How is your general health?"

(percent distribution of people aged 18 or older by health status and selected characteristics, 2009)

| | total | excellent or very good | | | good | fair or poor | | |
		total	excellent	very good		total	fair	poor
Total people	100.0%	56.0%	21.0%	35.0%	29.9%	14.2%	10.5%	3.7%
Sex								
Men	100.0	55.4	20.9	34.5	30.0	13.3	9.9	3.4
Women	100.0	55.2	20.4	34.8	29.6	15.3	11.3	4.0
Age								
Aged 18 to 24	100.0	62.6	26.0	36.6	28.6	8.0	7.1	0.9
Aged 25 to 34	100.0	61.5	25.4	36.1	28.4	9.3	8.0	1.3
Aged 35 to 44	100.0	61.0	23.7	37.3	28.1	10.0	7.6	2.4
Aged 45 to 54	100.0	55.9	20.8	35.1	29.0	14.2	10.3	3.9
Aged 55 to 64	100.0	50.2	17.1	33.1	30.0	18.7	13.4	5.3
Aged 65 or older	100.0	39.5	11.6	27.9	34.7	24.7	17.7	7.0
Race and Hispanic origin								
Black	100.0	42.5	15.9	26.6	35.3	20.2	15.2	5.0
Hispanic	100.0	41.4	17.6	23.8	35.2	18.6	14.7	3.9
White	100.0	58.5	21.9	36.6	28.6	12.5	9.1	3.4
Household income								
Under $15,000	100.0	28.9	10.5	18.4	32.0	37.7	24.0	13.7
$15,000 to $24,999	100.0	36.7	12.4	24.3	36.1	26.4	19.0	7.4
$25,000 to $34,999	100.0	44.1	14.5	29.6	35.6	17.9	13.8	4.1
$35,000 to $49,999	100.0	54.3	18.0	36.3	32.8	12.5	9.8	2.7
$50,000 or more	100.0	69.2	27.3	41.9	24.7	5.9	4.8	1.1
Education								
Not a high school graduate	100.0	29.0	10.5	18.5	34.3	33.5	23.4	10.1
High school graduate	100.0	45.7	15.1	30.6	35.2	18.5	13.7	4.8
Some college	100.0	55.6	18.9	36.7	30.2	13.9	10.6	3.3
College graduate	100.0	69.2	28.2	41.0	23.9	6.6	5.1	1.5

Note: Numbers may not add to total because some people did not report their health status.
Source: Centers for Disease Control and Prevention, Behavioral Risk Factor Surveillance System, Prevalence Data, Internet site http://apps.nccd.cdc.gov/brfss/index.asp; calculations by New Strategist

Weight Problems Are the Norm

Sixty-three percent of adults are overweight.

Americans have a weight problem. A government health survey, which measures the height and weight of a representative sample of Americans, found the average man weighing 195 pounds in 2003–06. The average woman weighed 165 pounds. For both men and women, these figures are substantially larger than they were several decades ago. In 1960–62, the average man weighed 166 pounds and the average woman weighed 140 pounds.

Sixty-three percent of people aged 18 or older are overweight, according to another government survey based on self-reported heights and weights. When Americans self-report their weight, however, they often lowball it, so the 63 percent estimate is conservative. Twenty-eight percent of adults are obese, according to body mass index calculations based on the self-reported heights and weights. Most men and women are overweight, as are the majority in every age, educational, and income group. By race and Hispanic origin, Asians are the only segment in which the overweight are in the minority. Only 42 percent of Asians are overweight.

■ Most overweight Americans lack the willpower to eat less or exercise more—fueling a diet and weight loss industry that never lacks for customers.

The overweight dominate every age group

(percent of people aged 18; or older who are overweight, by age, 2009)

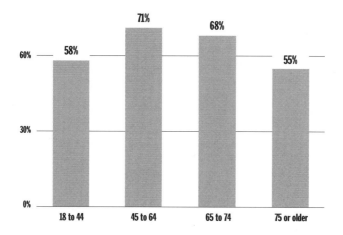

Table 3.2 Average Measured Weight by Age and Sex, 2003–06

(average weight in pounds of people aged 20 or older by age and sex, 2003–06)

	men	women
Total aged 20 or older	**194.7**	**164.7**
Aged 20 to 29	188.3	155.9
Aged 30 to 39	194.1	164.7
Aged 40 to 49	202.3	171.3
Aged 50 to 59	198.8	172.1
Aged 60 to 69	198.3	170.5
Aged 70 to 79	187.4	155.6
Aged 80 or older	168.1	142.2

Note: Data are based on measured weight of a sample of the civilian noninstitutionalized population.
Source: National Center for Health Statistics, Anthropometric Reference Data for Children and Adults: United States, 2003–2006, National Health Statistics Reports, Number 10, 2008, Internet site http://www.cdc.gov/nchs/products/pubs/pubd/ nhsr/nhsr.htm; calculations by New Strategist

Table 3.3 Overweight and Obesity by Selected Characteristics, 2009

(percent distribution of people aged 18 or older by weight status, by selected characteristics, 2009; numbers in thousands)

	total		underweight	healthy weight	overweight	
	number	percent			total	obese
Total people	**227,371**	**100.0%**	**1.7%**	**35.1%**	**63.2%**	**27.6%**
Sex						
Men	109,844	100.0	0.8	29.5	69.6	27.6
Women	117,527	100.0	2.7	41.7	55.7	26.8
Age						
Aged 18 to 44	110,337	100.0	2.0	39.7	58.4	25.6
Aged 45 to 64	79,195	100.0	1.0	28.4	70.6	32.1
Aged 65 to 74	20,597	100.0	1.1	30.9	68.0	29.5
Aged 75 or older	17,242	100.0	3.9	41.1	55.0	17.9
Race and Hispanic origin						
Asian	10,763	100.0	4.2	53.4	42.4	9.0
Black	27,374	100.0	1.3	27.6	71.1	37.6
Hispanic	31,312	100.0	0.8	27.2	72.0	31.7
Non-Hispanic white	155,185	100.0	1.9	37.8	60.3	25.6
Education						
Not a high school graduate	28,439	100.0	1.1	28.2	70.7	33.7
High school graduate	54,242	100.0	1.7	28.1	70.2	33.5
Some college	56,772	100.0	1.2	31.9	66.8	31.1
College graduate	57,660	100.0	1.4	41.7	56.9	20.5
Household income						
Less than $35,000	70,740	100.0	2.0	34.1	63.9	30.7
$35,000 to $49,999	30,679	100.0	1.9	32.4	65.7	29.8
$50,000 to $74,999	40,179	100.0	1.5	34.3	64.2	27.7
$75,000 to $99,999	26,183	100.0	1.6	35.7	62.8	26.3
$100,000 or more	44,827	100.0	1.3	41.7	57.0	21.5

Note: Overweight is defined as a body mass index of 25 or higher. Obesity is defined as a body mass index of 30 or higher. Body mass index is calculated by dividing weight in kilograms by height in meters squared. Data are based on self-reported height and weight of a sample of the civilian noninstitutionalized population. Numbers may not add to total because not all races are shown and Hispanics may be of any race; education is for people aged 25 or older; and some did not report income.
Source: National Center for Health Statistics, Summary Health Statistics for U.S. Adults: National Health Interview Survey, 2009, Vital and Health Statistics, Series 10, No. 249, 2010, Internet site http://www.cdc.gov/nchs/nhis.htm; calculations by New Strategist

Only One-Third of Americans Get Regular Physical Activity

Another one-third do not engage in any physical activity.

Only 35 percent of people aged 18 or older participate in regular physical activity, meaning 30 minutes of light to moderate activity at least five times a week or 20 minutes of vigorous activity at least three times a week. Men are slightly more likely to meet recommended activity levels than women (37 versus 33 percent). The affluent and highly educated are the most active, with 44 percent of respondents with a household income of $100,000 or more getting regular exercise as do 46 percent of those with a college degree.

Exercise walking is the most popular recreational activity, and 93 million people aged 7 or older (35 percent of the population) participated in exercise walking more than once in 2009, according to a survey by the National Sporting Goods Association. The other activities that rank among the top five are exercising with equipment (21 percent), camping (19 percent), swimming (19 percent), and bowling (17 percent).

■ With most Americans not getting enough exercise, it is no surprise that the ranks of the overweight are growing.

Physical activity increases with education

(percent of people aged 18 or older who engage in regular physical activity, by educational attainment, 2009)

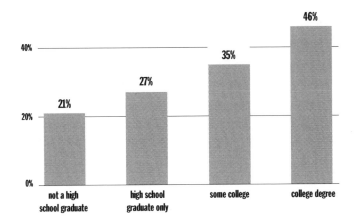

Table 3.4 Participation in Leisure-Time Physical Activity, 2009

(percent distribution of people aged 18 or older by participation in regular leisure-time physical activity, by selected characteristics and level of activity, 2009; numbers in thousands)

| | total | | | | |
	number	percent	inactive	some	regular
Total people	**227,371**	**100.0%**	**32.7%**	**32.6%**	**34.7%**
Sex					
Men	109,844	100.0	30.3	32.3	37.4
Women	117,527	100.0	34.5	32.8	32.7
Age					
Aged 18 to 44	110,337	100.0	27.7	33.0	39.4
Aged 45 to 64	79,195	100.0	33.3	33.8	32.8
Aged 65 to 74	20,597	100.0	38.2	30.4	31.5
Aged 75 or older	17,242	100.0	55.3	27.1	17.6
Race and Hispanic origin					
Asian	10,763	100.0	36.7	35.0	28.3
Black	27,374	100.0	41.1	29.7	29.2
Hispanic	31,312	100.0	44.0	28.2	27.8
Non-Hispanic white	155,185	100.0	28.4	33.5	38.1
Education					
Less than high school	28,439	100.0	53.2	25.4	21.4
High school graduate	54,242	100.0	41.8	31.5	26.8
Some college	56,772	100.0	28.9	35.6	35.4
Bachelor's degree or more	57,660	100.0	18.6	35.4	46.0
Household income					
Less than $35,000	70,740	100.0	43.8	28.0	28.2
$35,000 to $49,999	30,679	100.0	34.8	33.1	32.1
$50,000 to $74,999	40,179	100.0	30.5	33.8	35.7
$75,000 to $99,999	26,183	100.0	26.1	37.1	36.8
$100,000 or more	44,827	100.0	18.9	36.8	44.4

Note: All questions related to leisure-time physical activity were phrased in terms of current behavior and lack a specific reference period. Adults classified as inactive reported no sessions of light to moderate or vigorous leisure-time activity of at least 10 minutes duration. Adults with some leisure-time activity reported at least one session of light to moderate or vigorous physical activity of at least 10 minutes duration but did not meet the definition for regular leisure-time activity. Adults with regular leisure-time activity reported three or more sessions per week of vigorous activity lasting at least 20 minutes or five or more sessions per week of light to moderate activity lasting at least 30 minutes in duration.
Source: National Center for Health Statistics, Summary Health Statistics for U.S. Adults: National Health Interview Survey, 2009, Vital and Health Statistics, Series 10, No. 249, 2010, Internet site http://www.cdc.gov/nchs/nhis.htm; calculations by New Strategist

Table 3.5 Sports Participation of People Aged 7 or Older, 2009

(total number of people aged 7 or older, and number and percent participating in selected sports more than once during past year, 2009; numbers in millions)

	number	percent
Total people	**270.0**	**100.0%**
Exercise walking	93.4	34.6
Exercising with equipment	57.2	21.2
Camping (vacation/overnight)	50.9	18.9
Swimming	50.2	18.6
Bowling	45.0	16.7
Workout at club	38.3	14.2
Bicycle riding	38.1	14.1
Weight lifting	34.5	12.8
Hiking	34.0	12.6
Aerobic exercising	33.1	12.3
Fishing	32.9	12.2
Running/jogging	32.2	11.9
Billiards/pool	28.2	10.4
Basketball	24.4	9.0
Boating (motor)	24.0	8.9
Golf	22.3	8.3
Target shooting (net)	19.8	7.3
Hunting with firearms	18.8	7.0
Yoga	15.7	5.8
Soccer	13.6	5.0
Table tennis	13.3	4.9
Backpacking/wilderness camping	12.3	4.6
Dart throwing	12.2	4.5
Softball	11.8	4.4
Baseball	11.5	4.3
Tennis	10.8	4.0
Volleyball	10.7	4.0
Football (tackle)	8.9	3.3
Skateboarding	8.4	3.1
Mountain biking (off road)	8.4	3.1
Scooter riding	8.1	3.0
Skating (in-line)	7.9	2.9
Archery (target)	7.1	2.6
Skiing (alpine)	7.0	2.6
Paintball	6.3	2.3
Snowboarding	6.2	2.3
Hunting with bow and arrow	6.2	2.3
Water skiing	5.2	1.9
Target shooting (airgun)	5.2	1.9
Kayaking	4.9	1.8
Gymnastics	3.9	1.4
Muzzleloading	3.8	1.4
Hockey (ice)	3.1	1.1
Wrestling	3.0	1.1
Skiing (cross country)	1.7	0.6

Source: National Sporting Goods Association, Internet site http://www.nsga.org

Forty-Six Percent of the Nation's Newborns Are Minorities

The babies being born today promise great diversity tomorrow.

Of the 4.1 million babies born in 2009, fully 24 percent were born to Hispanic mothers and 15 percent to non-Hispanic black mothers. Only 54 percent were born to non-Hispanic whites. As today's children grow up, they will create an increasingly multicultural society with no single racial or ethnic group claiming the majority of the U.S. population.

In the future, many adults will have little experience with married parents. Forty-one percent of births in 2009 were to unwed mothers, up from just 11 percent in 1970. Among non-Hispanic blacks, 73 percent of births are out-of-wedlock compared with just 17 percent among Asians.

Among all women giving birth in 2009, the 40 percent plurality was having a first child, and another 31 percent were having a second child. Only 28 percent of women giving birth in 2009 were having a third or higher-order birth, but among women aged 40 or older who gave birth, about half were having at least their third child.

■ With so many babies born to unmarried mothers, reducing poverty among children is an uphill task.

The nation's newborns are diverse

(percent distribution of births by race and Hispanic origin of mother, 2009)

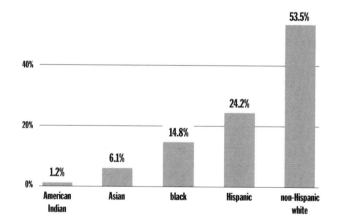

Table 3.6 Births by Age, Race, and Hispanic Origin, 2009

(number and percent distribution of births by age, race, and Hispanic origin, 2009)

	total	American Indian	Asian	non-Hispanic black	Hispanic	non-Hispanic white
Total births	**4,131,019**	**48,660**	**250,935**	**609,552**	**999,632**	**2,211,960**
Under age 15	5,030	108	76	1,704	2,073	1,055
Aged 15 to 19	409,840	8,316	7,041	98,425	136,274	159,526
Aged 20 to 24	1,006,055	16,233	29,395	194,103	274,746	490,555
Aged 25 to 29	1,166,904	12,634	70,496	153,217	270,661	657,466
Aged 30 to 34	955,300	7,394	85,280	98,903	195,746	564,928
Aged 35 to 39	474,143	3,213	48,078	50,006	97,271	273,146
Aged 40 to 44	105,813	722	9,854	12,319	21,640	60,436
Aged 45 to 54	7,934	39	714	875	1,222	4,849
PERCENT DISTRIBUTION BY RACE AND HISPANIC ORIGIN						
Total births	**100.0%**	**1.2%**	**6.1%**	**14.8%**	**24.2%**	**53.5%**
Under age 15	100.0	2.1	1.5	33.9	41.2	21.0
Aged 15 to 19	100.0	2.0	1.7	24.0	33.3	38.9
Aged 20 to 24	100.0	1.6	2.9	19.3	27.3	48.8
Aged 25 to 29	100.0	1.1	6.0	13.1	23.2	56.3
Aged 30 to 34	100.0	0.8	8.9	10.4	20.5	59.1
Aged 35 to 39	100.0	0.7	10.1	10.5	20.5	57.6
Aged 40 to 44	100.0	0.7	9.3	11.6	20.5	57.1
Aged 45 to 54	100.0	0.5	9.0	11.0	15.4	61.1
PERCENT DISTRIBUTION BY AGE						
Total births	**100.0%**	**100.0%**	**100.0%**	**100.0%**	**100.0%**	**100.0%**
Under age 15	0.1	0.2	0.0	0.3	0.2	0.0
Aged 15 to 19	9.9	17.1	2.8	16.1	13.6	7.2
Aged 20 to 24	24.4	33.4	11.7	31.8	27.5	22.2
Aged 25 to 29	28.2	26.0	28.1	25.1	27.1	29.7
Aged 30 to 34	23.1	15.2	34.0	16.2	19.6	25.5
Aged 35 to 39	11.5	6.6	19.2	8.2	9.7	12.3
Aged 40 to 44	2.6	1.5	3.9	2.0	2.2	2.7
Aged 45 to 54	0.2	0.1	0.3	0.1	0.1	0.2

Note: Births by race and Hispanic origin do not add to total because Hispanics may be of any race and not stated is not shown.
Source: National Center for Health Statistics, Births: Preliminary Data for 2009, National Vital Statistics Reports, Vol. 59, No. 3, 2010, Internet site http://www.cdc.gov/nchs/births.htm; calculations by New Strategist

Table 3.7 Births to Unmarried Women by Age, 2009

(total number of births and number and percent of births to unmarried women, by age, 2009)

	total	unmarried women		
		number	percent distribution	percent of total
Total births	**4,131,019**	**1,693,850**	**100.0%**	**41.0%**
Under age 15	5,030	4,980	0.3	99.0
Aged 15 to 19	409,840	357,510	21.1	87.2
Aged 20 to 24	1,006,055	624,354	36.9	62.1
Aged 25 to 29	1,166,904	394,616	23.3	33.8
Aged 30 to 34	955,300	198,183	11.7	20.7
Aged 35 to 39	474,143	89,873	5.3	19.0
Aged 40 to 54	113,747	24,332	1.4	21.4

Source: National Center for Health Statistics, Births: Preliminary Data for 2009, National Vital Statistics Reports, Vol. 59, No. 3, 2010, Internet site http://www.cdc.gov/nchs/births.htm; calculations by New Strategist

Table 3.8 Characteristics of Births by Race and Hispanic Origin, 2009

(total number of births, fertility rate, births in lifetime, and percent of births to unmarried women, by race and Hispanic origin, 2009)

	total	fertility rate	number of births in lifetime	percent of births to unmarried women
Total births	**4,131,019**	**66.7**	**2.01**	**41.0%**
American Indian	48,660	62.8	1.78	65.4
Asian	250,935	68.7	1.96	17.2
Black, non-Hispanic	609,552	68.9	2.03	72.8
Hispanic	999,632	93.3	2.73	53.2
White, non-Hispanic	2,211,960	58.5	1.78	29.0

Note: The fertility rate is the number of births per 1,000 women aged 15 to 44. Births by race and Hispanic origin do not add to total because Hispanics may be of any race and "not stated" is not shown.
Source: National Center for Health Statistics, Births: Preliminary Data for 2009, National Vital Statistics Reports, Vol. 59, No. 3, 2010, Internet site http://www.cdc.gov/nchs/births.htm; calculations by New Strategist

Table 3.9 Births by Age of Mother and Birth Order, 2009

(number and percent distribution of births by age of mother and birth order, 2009)

	total	first child	second child	third child	fourth or later child
Total births	**4,131,019**	**1,660,342**	**1,291,155**	**679,183**	**473,735**
Under age 15	5,030	4,920	70	3	1
Aged 15 to 19	409,840	330,532	65,705	9,739	1,316
Aged 20 to 24	1,006,055	493,880	330,362	127,302	47,821
Aged 25 to 29	1,166,904	426,391	383,698	214,752	134,760
Aged 30 to 34	955,300	272,229	326,916	196,274	153,961
Aged 35 to 39	474,143	106,979	152,566	107,933	103,450
Aged 40 to 44	105,813	23,324	29,803	21,846	30,023
Aged 45 to 54	7,934	2,087	2,035	1,334	2,403

PERCENT DISTRIBUTION BY BIRTH ORDER

Total births	**100.0%**	**40.2%**	**31.3%**	**16.4%**	**11.5%**
Under age 15	100.0	97.8	1.4	0.1	0.0
Aged 15 to 19	100.0	80.6	16.0	2.4	0.3
Aged 20 to 24	100.0	49.1	32.8	12.7	4.8
Aged 25 to 29	100.0	36.5	32.9	18.4	11.5
Aged 30 to 34	100.0	28.5	34.2	20.5	16.1
Aged 35 to 39	100.0	22.6	32.2	22.8	21.8
Aged 40 to 44	100.0	22.0	28.2	20.6	28.4
Aged 45 to 54	100.0	26.3	25.6	16.8	30.3

PERCENT DISTRIBUTION BY AGE

Total births	**100.0%**	**100.0%**	**100.0%**	**100.0%**	**100.0%**
Under age 15	0.1	0.3	0.0	0.0	0.0
Aged 15 to 19	9.9	19.9	5.1	1.4	0.3
Aged 20 to 24	24.4	29.7	25.6	18.7	10.1
Aged 25 to 29	28.2	25.7	29.7	31.6	28.4
Aged 30 to 34	23.1	16.4	25.3	28.9	32.5
Aged 35 to 39	11.5	6.4	11.8	15.9	21.8
Aged 40 to 44	2.6	1.4	2.3	3.2	6.3
Aged 45 to 54	0.2	0.1	0.2	0.2	0.5

Note: Numbers do not add to total by age because "not stated" is not shown.
Source: National Center for Health Statistics, Births: Preliminary Data for 2009, National Vital Statistics Reports, Vol. 59, No. 3, 2010, Internet site http://www.cdc.gov/nchs/births.htm; calculations by New Strategist

More Have Hypertension

Cholesterol is also up among both men and women.

Thirty-two percent of Americans aged 20 or older have high blood pressure or are taking antihypertensive medication. Hypertension increases with age, with the majority of people aged 55 or older having hypertension. The percentage of men and women with hypertension has grown over the past two decades especially among men aged 55 to 64 and women aged 55 to 74.

The percentage of adults with high cholesterol or who take cholesterol-lowering medication increased from 21 to 28 percent between 1988–94 and 2005–08. Double-digit increases occurred among men aged 55 or older and women aged 75 or older. At least half of women aged 55 or older have high cholesterol.

■ Thanks to medications that control blood pressure and cholesterol levels, life expectancy should continue to climb.

Women are slightly more likely than men to have high blood pressure

(percent of people aged 20 or older with elevated blood pressure, by sex, 2005–08)

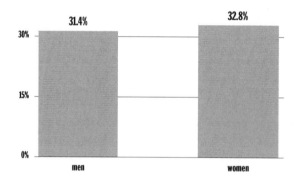

Table 3.10 Hypertension by Sex and Age, 1988–94 and 2005–08

(percent of people aged 20 or older with hypertension or taking anti-hypertensive medication, by sex and age, 1988–94 and 2005–08; percentage point change, 1988-94 to 2005–08)

	2005–08	1988–94	percentage point change
Total people	**32.1%**	**24.1%**	**8.0**
Total men	**31.4**	**23.8**	**7.6**
Aged 20 to 34	9.1	7.1	2.0
Aged 35 to 44	21.1	17.1	0.0
Aged 45 to 54	33.6	29.2	4.4
Aged 55 to 64	51.3	40.6	10.7
Aged 65 to 74	64.0	54.4	9.6
Aged 75 or older	67.2	60.4	6.8
Total women	**32.8**	**24.4**	**8.4**
Aged 20 to 34	3.2	2.9	0.3
Aged 35 to 44	13.8	11.2	2.6
Aged 45 to 54	33.0	23.9	9.1
Aged 55 to 64	52.7	42.6	10.1
Aged 65 to 74	68.4	56.2	12.2
Aged 75 or older	80.4	73.6	6.8

Note: A person is defined as having hypertension if he or she has a systolic pressure of at least 140 mmHg, a diastolic pressure of at least 90 mmHg, or takes antihypertensive medication.
Source: National Center for Health Statistics, Health, United States, 2010, Internet site http://www.cdc.gov/nchs/hus.htm; calculations by New Strategist

Table 3.11 High Cholesterol by Sex and Age, 1988–94 and 2005–08

(percent of people aged 20 or older who have high serum cholesterol or who take cholesterol-lowering medication, by sex and age, 1988–94 and 2005–08; percentage point change, 1988–94 to 2005–08)

	2005–08	1988–94	percentage point change
Total people	**28.4%**	**21.5%**	**6.9**
Total men	**27.7**	**19.6**	**8.1**
Aged 20 to 34	10.1	8.2	1.9
Aged 35 to 44	21.5	21.0	0.5
Aged 45 to 54	33.2	29.6	3.6
Aged 55 to 64	43.4	30.8	12.6
Aged 65 to 74	49.5	27.4	22.1
Aged 75 or older	39.4	24.4	15.0
Total women	**29.1**	**23.2**	**5.9**
Aged 20 to 34	9.5	7.3	2.2
Aged 35 to 44	17.0	13.5	3.5
Aged 45 to 54	29.9	28.2	1.7
Aged 55 to 64	50.0	45.8	4.2
Aged 65 to 74	51.8	46.9	4.9
Aged 75 or older	51.7	41.2	10.5

Note: High cholesterol is defined as 240 mg/dL or more.
Source: National Center for Health Statistics, Health, United States, 2010, Internet site http://www.cdc.gov/nchs/hus.htm; calculations by New Strategist

One in Five Americans Smokes Cigarettes

Drinking is more popular than smoking, with the majority having a drink at least occasionally.

Twenty-one percent of people aged 18 or older smoke cigarettes. Sixteen percent smoke every day. Smoking declines with age, from 23 percent of 18-to-44-year-olds to just 6 percent of those aged 75 or older. Only 9 percent of college graduates smoke versus 30 percent of those who went no further than high school.

Drinking is far more common than smoking, with 52 percent of adults reporting current regular drinking. Those most likely to drink regularly are people aged 18 to 44 (58 percent), non-Hispanic whites (58 percent), college graduates (65 percent), and people with household incomes of $75,000 or more (67 percent).

Fully 47 percent of people aged 12 or older have used an illicit drug at some point in their lives, but only 9 percent have done so in the past month and 15 percent in the past year. Past-month drug use peaks among people aged 18 to 22, with at least one in five using an illicit drug. The majority of Americans ranging in age from 19 to 59 have used an illicit drug at some point in their life.

■ Despite extensive antismoking campaigns, a significant share of the population still adopts the habit.

Men are more likely than women to drink

(percent of people aged 18 or older who are regular drinkers, by sex, 2009)

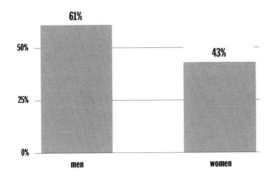

Table 3.12 Percent Distribution of People Aged 18 or Older by Cigarette Smoking Status, 2009

(total number of people aged 18 or older and percent distribution by cigarette smoking status and selected characteristics, 2009; numbers in thousands)

| | total | | all current smokers | | | | |
	number	percent	total	every-day smokers	some-day smokers	former smokers	nonsmokers
Total people	227,371	100.0%	20.6%	16.1%	4.5%	22.0%	57.4%
Sex							
Men	109,844	100.0	23.1	17.6	5.5	25.8	51.1
Women	117,527	100.0	18.1	14.4	3.6	17.8	64.2
Age							
Aged 18 to 44	110,337	100.0	23.4	17.5	6.0	12.5	64.1
Aged 45 to 64	79,195	100.0	21.9	18.2	3.7	26.6	51.5
Aged 65 to 74	20,597	100.0	12.5	9.6	2.9	42.1	45.4
Aged 75 or older	17,242	100.0	6.0	5.1	0.8	38.0	56.1
Race and Hispanic origin							
Asian	10,763	100.0	11.6	8.3	3.3	14.0	74.5
Black	27,374	100.0	20.4	15.1	5.3	15.7	64.0
Hispanic	31,312	100.0	13.6	8.8	4.8	18.8	67.5
Non-Hispanic white	155,185	100.0	22.8	18.3	4.5	23.5	53.6
Education							
Less than high school	28,439	100.0	29.7	24.9	4.7	19.4	50.9
High school graduate	54,242	100.0	29.7	25.0	4.6	21.4	48.9
Some college	56,772	100.0	21.9	16.7	5.2	25.4	52.7
Bachelor's degree or more	57,660	100.0	9.0	5.6	3.4	22.4	68.5
Household income							
Less than $35,000	70,740	100.0	28.3	22.7	5.6	18.4	53.3
$35,000 to $49,999	30,679	100.0	23.7	19.6	4.1	21.5	54.9
$50,000 to $74,999	40,179	100.0	19.8	15.1	4.7	23.1	57.1
$75,000 to $99,999	26,183	100.0	15.7	11.7	4.0	24.5	59.9
$100,000 or more	44,827	100.0	12.1	8.4	3.6	22.8	65.1

Note: Current smokers have smoked at least 100 cigarettes in lifetime and still smoke; every-day smokers are current smokers who smoke every day; some-day smokers are current smokers who smoke on some days; former smokers have smoked at least 100 cigarettes in lifetime but currently do not smoke; nonsmokers have smoked fewer than 100 cigarettes in lifetime. Numbers may not add to total because not all races are shown and Hispanics may be of any race; education is for people aged 25 or older; and some did not report income.
Source: National Center for Health Statistics, Summary Health Statistics for U.S. Adults: National Health Interview Survey, 2009, Vital and Health Statistics, Series 10, No. 249, 2010, Internet site http://www.cdc.gov/nchs/nhis.htm; calculations by New Strategist

Table 3.13 Percent Distribution of People Aged 18 or Older by Alcohol Drinking Status, 2009

(total number of people aged 18 or older and percent distribution by alcohol drinking status and selected characteristics, 2009; numbers in thousands)

	total		current			lifetime
	number	percent	regular	infrequent	former	abstainer
Total people	227,371	100.0%	51.8%	12.9%	15.0%	19.9%
Sex						
Men	109,844	100.0	61.4	9.4	14.8	13.9
Women	117,527	100.0	43.3	16.0	14.5	25.9
Age						
Aged 18 to 44	110,337	100.0	57.9	12.2	8.8	20.8
Aged 45 to 64	79,195	100.0	51.4	14.5	18.2	15.6
Aged 65 to 74	20,597	100.0	40.2	13.2	23.8	22.5
Aged 75 or older	17,242	100.0	29.2	9.8	29.5	31.4
Race and Hispanic origin						
Asian	10,763	100.0	32.8	12.6	11.2	43.1
Black	27,374	100.0	39.4	13.3	17.8	29.3
Hispanic	31,312	100.0	42.0	12.2	15.2	30.3
Non-Hispanic white	155,185	100.0	57.8	12.7	14.1	14.9
Education						
Less than high school	28,439	100.0	37.0	11.5	21.2	29.9
High school graduate	54,242	100.0	46.8	15.2	17.7	19.8
Some college	56,772	100.0	55.1	14.8	15.2	14.6
Bachelor's degree or more	57,660	100.0	65.1	11.5	9.8	13.4
Household income						
Less than $20,000	70,740	100.0	41.7	12.7	18.4	26.9
$20,000 to $34,999	30,679	100.0	47.9	15.1	16.7	20.0
$35,000 to $54,999	40,179	100.0	53.9	13.3	15.1	17.4
$55,000 to $74,999	26,183	100.0	58.9	14.0	11.5	15.4
$75,000 or more	44,827	100.0	66.6	10.4	8.6	14.0

Note: Current drinkers have had 12 or more drinks in lifetime and have had a drink in the past year; regular drinkers have had 12 or more drinks a year; infrequent drinkers have had fewer than 12 drinks a year; former drinkers have had 12 or more drinks in lifetime, but no drinks in past year; lifetime abstainers have had fewer than 12 drinks in lifetime. Numbers by race and Hispanic origin do not sum to total because not all races are shown, Hispanics may be of any race, education is for people aged 25 or older, and some people did not report income.
Source: National Center for Health Statistics, Summary Health Statistics for U.S. Adults: National Health Interview Survey, 2009, Vital and Health Statistics, Series 10, No. 249, 2010, Internet site http://www.cdc.gov/nchs/nhis.htm; calculations by New Strategist

Table 3.14 Illicit Drug Use by People Aged 12 or Older, 2009

(percent of people aged 12 or older who ever used any illicit drug, who used an illicit drug in the past year, and who used an illicit drug in the past month, by age, 2009)

	ever used	used in past year	used in past month
Total people	**47.1%**	**15.1%**	**8.7%**
Aged 12	10.5	6.6	3.6
Aged 13	15.2	9.3	3.6
Aged 14	21.2	14.6	7.0
Aged 15	30.4	22.9	10.9
Aged 16	37.1	28.4	15.1
Aged 17	42.4	32.2	18.3
Aged 18	48.0	37.0	21.3
Aged 19	54.2	39.0	21.6
Aged 20	59.0	38.6	23.9
Aged 21	60.8	39.8	23.5
Aged 22	62.2	37.7	22.4
Aged 23	60.7	33.2	19.1
Aged 24	61.8	32.4	19.9
Aged 25	61.2	29.0	17.4
Aged 26 to 29	60.7	25.5	14.4
Aged 30 to 34	58.1	18.2	10.5
Aged 35 to 39	53.0	13.6	8.0
Aged 40 to 44	57.2	12.6	6.5
Aged 45 to 49	60.9	11.7	6.5
Aged 50 to 54	60.1	10.7	6.9
Aged 55 to 59	51.5	8.4	5.4
Aged 60 to 64	41.5	5.2	3.1
Aged 65 or older	14.9	1.4	0.9

Note: Illicit drugs include marijuana, hashish, cocaine (including crack), heroin, hallucinogens, inhalants, and any prescription-type psychotherapeutic used nonmedically.
Source: SAMHSA, Office of Applied Studies, National Survey on Drug Use and Health, 2009, Internet site http://oas.samhsa .gov/NSDUH/2k9NSDUH/2k9Results.htm

Millions of Americans Do Not Have Health Insurance

The proportion is highest among young adults.

Eighty-three percent of Americans have health insurance, the 56 percent majority being covered by an employer's health plan. Medicare, the federal government's health insurance program for people aged 65 or older, covers 14 percent. Medicaid, the federal health insurance program for the poor, covers a larger 16 percent.

Seventeen percent of Americans do not have health insurance, or 51 million people in 2009. The number of uninsured has grown by 32 percent since 2000. The percentage of people without health insurance is highest among 18-to-24-year-olds, at 30 percent, and Hispanics, at 32 percent. Among all those without health insurance in 2009, the 49 percent plurality say cost is the reason. Twenty-eight percent say they do not have health insurance because they lost or changed jobs. Fourteen percent say their employer did not offer health insurance or the insurance company refused to cover them.

■ The proportion of Americans without health insurance because of job loss has soared during the Great Recession.

One in six Americans does not have health insurance

(percent of people without health insurance coverage, by age, 2009)

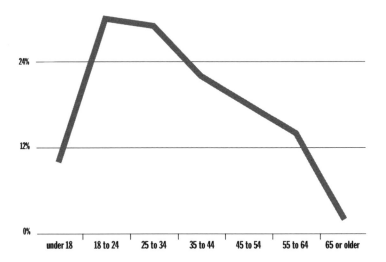

Table 3.15 Health Insurance Coverage by Age, 2009

(number and percent distribution of people by age and health insurance coverage status, 2009; numbers in thousands)

			covered by private or government health insurance								
			private health insurance				government health insurance				
				employment based		direct					not
	total	total	total	total	own	purchase	total	Medicaid	Medicare	military	covered
Total people	**304,280**	**253,606**	**194,545**	**169,689**	**89,696**	**27,219**	**93,167**	**47,758**	**43,440**	**12,412**	**50,674**
Under age 65	265,667	215,669	172,131	156,543	79,491	16,761	56,912	44,109	7,339	9,200	49,998
Under age 18	75,040	67,527	45,288	41,892	192	3,819	27,605	25,331	543	2,365	7,513
Aged 18 to 24	29,313	20,389	16,308	12,802	4,299	1,705	5,366	4,437	199	900	8,923
Aged 25 to 34	41,085	29,122	24,708	22,612	17,362	2,428	5,662	4,236	547	1,209	11,963
Aged 35 to 44	40,447	31,689	27,962	26,125	18,634	2,385	5,043	3,562	934	1,029	8,759
Aged 45 to 54	44,387	36,481	32,147	29,867	21,720	3,134	5,956	3,552	1,796	1,443	7,906
Aged 55 to 64	35,395	30,462	25,718	23,245	17,283	3,290	7,280	2,991	3,318	2,254	4,933
Aged 65 or older	38,613	37,937	22,414	13,146	10,205	10,457	36,255	3,649	36,102	3,213	676

PERCENT DISTRIBUTION BY COVERAGE STATUS

Total people	**100.0%**	**83.3%**	**63.9%**	**55.8%**	**29.5%**	**8.9%**	**30.6%**	**15.7%**	**14.3%**	**4.1%**	**16.7%**
Under age 65	100.0	81.2	64.8	58.9	29.9	6.3	21.4	16.6	2.8	3.5	18.8
Under age 18	100.0	90.0	60.4	55.8	0.3	5.1	36.8	33.8	0.7	3.2	10.0
Aged 18 to 24	100.0	69.6	55.6	43.7	14.7	5.8	18.3	15.1	0.7	3.1	30.4
Aged 25 to 34	100.0	70.9	60.1	55.0	42.3	5.9	13.8	10.3	1.3	2.9	29.1
Aged 35 to 44	100.0	78.3	69.1	64.6	46.1	5.9	12.5	8.8	2.3	2.5	21.7
Aged 45 to 54	100.0	82.2	72.4	67.3	48.9	7.1	13.4	8.0	4.0	3.3	17.8
Aged 55 to 64	100.0	86.1	72.7	65.7	48.8	9.3	20.6	8.5	9.4	6.4	13.9
Aged 65 or older	100.0	98.2	58.0	34.0	26.4	27.1	93.9	9.5	93.5	8.3	1.8

PERCENT DISTRIBUTION BY AGE

Total people	**100.0%**	**100.0%**	**100.0%**	**100.0%**	**100.0%**	**100.0%**	**100.0%**	**100.0%**	**100.0%**	**100.0%**	**100.0%**
Under age 65	87.3	85.0	88.5	92.3	88.6	61.6	61.1	92.4	16.9	74.1	98.7
Under age 18	24.7	26.6	23.3	24.7	0.2	14.0	29.6	53.0	1.3	19.1	14.8
Aged 18 to 24	9.6	8.0	8.4	7.5	4.8	6.3	5.8	9.3	0.5	7.3	17.6
Aged 25 to 34	13.5	11.5	12.7	13.3	19.4	8.9	6.1	8.9	1.3	9.7	23.6
Aged 35 to 44	13.3	12.5	14.4	15.4	20.8	8.8	5.4	7.5	2.2	8.3	17.3
Aged 45 to 54	14.6	14.4	16.5	17.6	24.2	11.5	6.4	7.4	4.1	11.6	15.6
Aged 55 to 64	11.6	12.0	13.2	13.7	19.3	12.1	7.8	6.3	7.6	18.2	9.7
Aged 65 or older	12.7	15.0	11.5	7.7	11.4	38.4	38.9	7.6	83.1	25.9	1.3

Note: Numbers may not add to total because some people have more than one type of health insurance coverage.
Source: Bureau of the Census, Health Insurance, Table HI01, Internet site http://www.census.gov/hhes/www/cpstables/032010/ health/toc.htm; calculations by New Strategist

Table 3.16 People without Health Insurance by Age, 2000 to 2009

(number and percent of people without health insurance coverage by age, 2000 to 2009; percent change in number and percentage point change in share, 2000–09; numbers in thousands)

	2009	2000	percent change
Total without coverage	**50,674**	**38,426**	**31.9%**
Under age 18	7,513	8,385	−10.4
Aged 18 to 24	8,923	7,203	23.9
Aged 25 to 34	11,963	8,318	43.8
Aged 35 to 44	8,759	6,746	29.8
Aged 45 to 54	7,906	4,492	76.0
Aged 55 to 64	4,933	3,031	62.8
Aged 65 or older	676	251	169.3

	2009	2000	percentage point change
Total without coverage	**16.7%**	**13.7%**	**3.0**
Under age 18	10.0	11.6	−1.6
Aged 18 to 24	30.4	26.9	3.5
Aged 25 to 34	29.1	21.4	7.7
Aged 35 to 44	21.7	15.1	6.6
Aged 45 to 54	17.8	11.6	6.2
Aged 55 to 64	13.9	12.3	1.6
Aged 65 or older	1.8	0.7	1.0

Source: Bureau of the Census, Historical Health Insurance Tables, Table HIA-1, Internet site http://www.census.gov/hhes/www/hlthins/historic/index.html; calculations by New Strategist

Table 3.17 People without Health Insurance by Race and Hispanic Origin, 2002 and 2009

(number and percent of people without health insurance coverage by race and Hispanic Origin, 2002 to 2009; percent change in number and percentage point change in share, 2002–09; numbers in thousands)

	2009	2002	percent change
Total without coverage	**50,674**	**42,019**	**20.6%**
Asian	2,503	2,172	15.2
Black	8,414	7,257	15.9
Hispanic	15,820	12,569	25.9
Non-Hispanic white	23,658	19,674	20.3

	2009	2002	percentage point change
Total without coverage	**16.7%**	**14.7%**	**2.0**
Asian	16.4	17.4	−1.0
Black	20.5	19.4	1.1
Hispanic	32.4	31.9	0.5
Non-Hispanic white	12.0	10.1	1.9

Note: Asians and blacks are those who identify themselves as being of the race alone and those who identify themselves as being of the race in combination with other races. Hispanics may be of any race. Non-Hispanic whites are those who identify themselves as being white alone and not Hispanic.
Source: Bureau of the Census, Historical Health Insurance Tables, Table HIA-1, Internet site http://www.census.gov/hhes/www/hlthins/historic/index.html; calculations by New Strategist

Table 3.18 Reason for Lack of Health Insurance Coverage by Selected Characteristics, 2009

(total number and percent distribution of people under age 65 without health insurance by reason for lack of insurance, by selected characteristics, 2009; numbers in thousands)

	total number	total percent	lost job or change in employment	change in marital status or death of parent	ineligible due to age or left school	employer didn't offer or insurance company refused	cost	Medicaid stopped	other reason
Total without health insurance	45,809	100.0%	27.7%	2.7%	9.7%	14.0%	48.6%	10.0%	6.3%
Sex									
Female	20,543	100.0	27.1	3.7	6.7	10.7	46.5	16.1	7.3
Male	25,266	100.0	28.0	1.8	7.8	13.8	49.4	9.0	7.8
Age									
Under age 12	3,535	100.0	23.2	2.5	0.9	5.1	43.0	24.9	13.2
Aged 12 to 17	2,486	100.0	24.8	2.0	1.9	7.6	46.3	16.4	13.0
Aged 18 to 44	28,336	100.0	24.6	2.4	15.1	15.0	47.4	9.8	5.3
Aged 45 to 64	11,451	100.0	37.6	3.6	0.6	15.4	53.9	4.4	5.1
Race and Hispanic origin									
Asian	1,987	100.0	16.3	1.6	5.3	7.2	38.3	6.5	10.4
Black	6,609	100.0	32.1	2.3	8.8	11.2	41.2	15.0	7.6
Hispanic	14,646	100.0	17.8	1.6	3.8	16.5	57.7	13.1	7.3
Non-Hispanic white	21,781	100.0	33.3	3.4	9.4	10.5	42.7	10.7	7.9
Education									
Less than high school	8,454	100.0	21.7	2.0	2.0	21.3	57.9	9.4	6.4
High school graduate	10,329	100.0	35.2	3.9	3.5	14.8	51.9	7.2	4.1
Some college	8,276	100.0	38.5	3.2	4.8	14.3	47.6	8.4	4.0
Bachelor's degree or more	3,482	100.0	36.3	3.0	6.3	14.2	48.7	3.1	7.4
Household income									
Less than $35,000	22,199	100.0	23.5	3.0	6.8	12.1	49.1	16.0	8.2
$35,000 to $49,999	7,859	100.0	30.0	2.2	5.7	14.1	49.0	11.0	7.2
$50,000 to $74,999	6,880	100.0	34.1	2.5	7.4	13.6	45.9	8.0	5.5
$75,000 to $99,999	2,572	100.0	35.9	2.3	10.1	9.1	45.7	6.7	6.2
$100,000 or more	2,628	100.0	33.5	2.6	13.5	12.2	32.9	6.3	–

Note: Figures do not sum to total because more than one reason may have been cited. "Other reason" includes moved, self-employed, never had coverage, does not want or need coverage. "–" means sample is too small to make a reliable estimate.
Source: National Center for Health Statistics, Summary Health Statistics for the U.S. Population: National Health Interview Survey, 2009, Vital and Health Statistics, Series 10, No. 248, 2010, Internet site http://www.cdc.gov/nchs/nhis.htm; calculations by New Strategist

Asthma and Allergies Affect Many Children

Boys are more likely than girls to have learning disabilities.

Asthma is a growing problem among children. Fourteen percent of the nation's 74 million children under age 18 have been diagnosed with asthma. Boys are more likely to have asthma than girls (17 versus 11 percent), and blacks more than other racial or ethnic groups (22 percent versus 11 to 13 percent for Asians, Hispanics, and non-Hispanic whites). Children in single-parent families headed by women are more likely to have asthma than those from two-parent families (20 versus 12 percent).

Five million children (8 percent) have been diagnosed with a learning disability, and 5 million have attention deficit hyperactivity disorder. Boys are far more likely than girls to have these conditions, accounting for 66 percent of those with learning disabilities and 70 percent of those with attention deficit hyperactivity disorder.

Many children use prescription medications. Ten million children have taken prescription medications regularly for at least three months during the past year. That's a substantial 13 percent of the nation's children. Among 12-to-17-year-olds, the figure is an even higher 17 percent.

■ Prescription drug use is becoming common among the nation's children.

Boys are more likely than girls to have attention deficit hyperactivity disorder

(percent of people under age 18 diagnosed with attention deficit hyperactivity disorder, by sex, 2009)

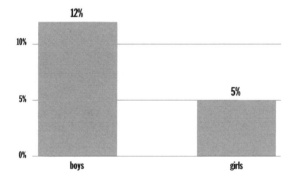

Table 3.19 Health Conditions among Children by Selected Characteristics, 2009

(number of people under age 18 with selected health conditions, by selected characteristics and type of condition, 2009; numbers in thousands)

| | total children | diagnosed with asthma | experienced in past 12 months | | | | | ever told had* | | prescription medication taken regularly at least 3 months |
			still have asthma	hay fever	respiratory allergies	food allergies	skin allergies	learning disability	attention deficit hyperactivity disorder	
Total children	**73,996**	**10,196**	**7,111**	**7,198**	**8,206**	**3,854**	**8,913**	**5,059**	**5,288**	**9,873**
Sex										
Female	36,177	3,986	2,843	3,162	3,455	1,785	4,311	1,738	1,599	3,980
Male	37,818	6,210	4,268	4,036	4,751	2,069	4,602	3,321	3,689	5,892
Age										
Aged 0 to 4	21,134	1,668	1,332	858	1,620	1,185	2,912	245	133	1,383
Aged 5 to 11	27,943	4,246	2,997	3,103	3,664	1,374	3,808	2,120	2,121	4,179
Aged 12 to 17	24,918	4,282	2,781	3,237	2,923	1,295	2,193	2,695	3,035	4,311
Race and Hispanic origin										
Asian	3,023	347	232	236	314	134	410	78	21	163
Black	11,293	2,441	1,893	835	1,242	625	2,005	863	904	1,560
Hispanic	16,522	2,051	1,276	1,063	1,256	652	1,493	940	659	1,339
Non-Hispanic white	40,952	5,056	3,473	4,697	5,143	2,186	4,541	2,963	3,460	6,428
Family structure										
Mother and father	51,421	5,964	4,003	5,073	5,404	2,785	5,683	2,885	3,100	6,324
Mother, no father	18,113	3,546	2,616	1,797	2,296	968	2,897	1,728	1,694	3,000
Father, no mother	2,259	256	170	102	220	41	117	180	178	196
Neither mother nor father	2,203	430	322	226	286	61	215	266	316	352
Parent's education										
Less than high school diploma	9,221	1,172	871	462	618	340	1,051	800	517	953
High school diploma or GED	14,626	2,262	1,555	1,271	1,417	640	1,549	1,124	1,182	1,788
More than high school	47,674	6,306	4,337	5,232	5,881	2,814	6,097	2,857	3,263	6,771
Household income										
Less than $35,000	23,406	3,928	2,906	1,902	2,700	1,169	3,094	2,197	2,030	3,446
$35,000 to $49,999	9,306	1,205	813	770	895	502	948	621	805	1,112
$50,000 to $74,999	12,576	1,341	921	1,293	1,553	593	1,464	896	852	1,519
$75,000 to $99,999	8,946	1,166	785	912	1,028	507	1,113	455	406	1,153
$100,000 or more	16,133	2,225	1,452	1,947	1,776	928	2,055	714	1,027	2,356

* *"Ever told" by a school representative or health professional. Data exclude children under age 3.*
Note: "Mother and father" includes biological, adoptive, step, in-law, or foster relationships. Legal guardians are classified as "neither mother nor father." Parent's education is the education level of the parent with the higher level of education. Race/ Hispanic origin, education, and income categories do not sum to total because not all races are shown and those not reporting education or income are not shown.
Source: National Center for Health Statistics, Summary Health Statistics for U.S. Children: National Health Interview Survey, 2009, Series 10, No. 247, 2010, Internet site http://www.cdc.gov/nchs/nhis.htm

Table 3.20 Distribution of Health Conditions by Selected Characteristics of Children, 2009

(percent distribution of people under age 18 with health condition by selected characteristics, 2009)

	total children	diagnosed with asthma	still have asthma	hay fever	respiratory allergies	food allergies	skin allergies	learning disability	attention deficit hyperactivity disorder	prescription medication taken regularly at least 3 months
			experienced in past 12 months					ever told had*		
Total children	100.0%	100.0%	100.0%	100.0%	100.0%	100.0%	100.0%	100.0%	100.0%	100.0%
Sex										
Female	48.9	39.1	40.0	43.9	42.1	46.3	48.4	34.4	30.2	40.3
Male	51.1	60.9	60.0	56.1	57.9	53.7	51.6	65.6	69.8	59.7
Age										
Aged 0 to 4	28.6	16.4	18.7	11.9	19.7	30.7	32.7	4.8	2.5	14.0
Aged 5 to 11	37.8	41.6	42.1	43.1	44.7	35.7	42.7	41.9	40.1	42.3
Aged 12 to 17	33.7	42.0	39.1	45.0	35.6	33.6	24.6	53.3	57.4	43.7
Race and Hispanic origin										
Asian	4.1	3.4	3.3	3.3	3.8	3.5	4.6	1.5	0.4	1.7
Black	15.3	23.9	26.6	11.6	15.1	16.2	22.5	17.1	17.1	15.8
Hispanic	22.3	20.1	17.9	14.8	15.3	16.9	16.8	18.6	12.5	13.6
Non-Hispanic white	55.3	49.6	48.8	65.3	62.7	56.7	50.9	58.6	65.4	65.1
Family structure										
Mother and father	69.5	58.5	56.3	70.5	65.9	72.3	63.8	57.0	58.6	64.1
Mother, no father	24.5	34.8	36.8	25.0	28.0	25.1	32.5	34.2	32.0	30.4
Father, no mother	3.1	2.5	2.4	1.4	2.7	1.1	1.3	3.6	3.4	2.0
Neither mother nor father	3.0	4.2	4.5	3.1	3.5	1.6	2.4	5.3	6.0	3.6
Parent's education										
Less than high school diploma	12.5	11.5	12.2	6.4	7.5	8.8	11.8	15.8	9.8	9.7
High school diploma or GED	19.8	22.2	21.9	17.7	17.3	16.6	17.4	22.2	22.4	18.1
More than high school	64.4	61.8	61.0	72.7	71.7	73.0	68.4	56.5	61.7	68.6
Household income										
Less than $35,000	31.6	38.5	40.9	26.4	32.9	30.3	34.7	43.4	38.4	34.9
$35,000 to $49,999	12.6	11.8	11.4	10.7	10.9	13.0	10.6	12.3	15.2	11.3
$50,000 to $74,999	17.0	13.2	13.0	18.0	18.9	15.4	16.4	17.7	16.1	15.4
$75,000 to $99,999	12.1	11.4	11.0	12.7	12.5	13.2	12.5	9.0	7.7	11.7
$100,000 or more	21.8	21.8	20.4	27.0	21.6	24.1	23.1	14.1	19.4	23.9

* "Ever told" by a school representative or health professional. Data exclude children under age 3.
Note: "Mother and father" includes biological, adoptive, step, in-law, or foster relationships. Legal guardians are classified as "neither mother nor father." Parent's education is the education level of the parent with the higher level of education. Race/Hispanic origin, education, and income categories do not sum to total because not all races are shown and those not reporting education or income are not shown.
Source: National Center for Health Statistics, Summary Health Statistics for U.S. Children: National Health Interview Survey, 2009, Series 10, No. 247, 2010, Internet site http://www.cdc.gov/nchs/nhis.htm

Table 3.21 Percent of Children with Health Conditions by Selected Characteristics, 2009

(percent of people under age 18 with selected health conditions, by type of condition and selected characteristics, 2009)

| | total children | diagnosed with asthma | experienced in past 12 months | | | | | ever told had* | | prescription medication taken regularly at least 3 months |
			still have asthma	hay fever	respiratory allergies	food allergies	skin allergies	learning disability	attention deficit hyperactivity disorder	
Total children	100.0%	13.8%	9.6%	9.8%	11.1%	5.2%	12.1%	8.2%	8.6%	13.3%
Sex										
Female	100.0	11.1	7.9	8.9	9.7	4.9	12.0	5.8	5.3	11.1
Male	100.0	16.6	11.4	10.8	12.7	5.4	12.2	10.6	11.8	15.8
Age										
Aged 0 to 4	100.0	7.9	6.3	4.1	7.7	5.6	13.8	2.8	1.5	6.5
Aged 5 to 11	100.0	15.2	10.7	11.1	13.1	4.9	13.7	7.6	7.6	15.0
Aged 12 to 17	100.0	17.2	11.2	13.0	11.8	5.2	8.8	10.8	12.2	17.3
Race and Hispanic origin										
Asian	100.0	11.3	7.6	7.6	10.1	4.4	13.4	3.0	0.8	5.3
Black	100.0	21.9	17.0	7.5	11.2	5.5	17.9	9.3	9.8	13.9
Hispanic	100.0	12.9	7.9	6.6	7.7	4.0	9.0	7.3	5.1	8.4
Non-Hispanic white	100.0	12.3	8.4	11.4	12.6	5.3	11.2	8.5	9.9	15.6
Family structure										
Mother and father	100.0	11.9	8.0	10.2	10.7	5.4	11.0	6.9	7.5	12.6
Mother, no father	100.0	19.6	14.5	9.9	12.7	5.3	16.2	11.3	11.0	16.5
Father, no mother	100.0	10.6	7.2	4.2	10.1	1.6	5.2	8.5	8.3	8.3
Neither mother nor father	100.0	20.4	16.1	9.5	12.4	2.7	11.3	12.1	15.0	15.7
Parent's education										
Less than high school diploma	100.0	12.9	9.5	5.1	6.5	3.7	11.3	10.9	7.0	10.4
High school diploma or GED	100.0	15.6	10.7	8.7	9.7	4.4	10.7	9.2	9.7	12.3
More than high school	100.0	13.4	9.2	11.2	12.5	5.9	12.8	7.3	8.4	14.4
Household income										
Less than $35,000	100.0	17.4	12.8	8.5	11.7	5.0	13.3	12.0	11.2	15.3
$35,000 to $49,999	100.0	13.1	8.9	8.3	9.8	5.4	10.4	8.1	10.4	12.1
$50,000 to $74,999	100.0	10.6	7.3	10.2	12.3	4.7	11.7	8.3	8.0	12.1
$75,000 to $99,999	100.0	13.2	8.9	10.4	11.7	5.7	12.4	6.1	5.4	13.0
$100,000 or more	100.0	13.5	8.9	11.8	10.9	5.8	13.1	5.1	7.3	14.3

* "Ever told" by a school representative or health professional. Data exclude children under age 3.
Note: "Mother and father" includes biological, adoptive, step, in-law, or foster relationships. Legal guardians are classified as "neither mother nor father." Parent's education is the education level of the parent with the higher level of education. Race/ Hispanic origin, education, and income categories do not sum to total because not all races are shown and those not reporting education or income are not shown.
Source: National Center for Health Statistics, Summary Health Statistics for U.S. Children: National Health Interview Survey, 2009, Series 10, No. 247, 2010, Internet site http://www.cdc.gov/nchs/nhis.htm

Health Problems Are Common among Older Americans

Lower back pain is the most frequently reported health condition.

Nearly 29 percent of Americans aged 18 or older have experienced lower back pain for at least one full day in the past three months, making it the most frequently reported health problem. Hypertension has been diagnosed in 25 percent of the adult population, and arthritis in 23 percent.

Many ailments are more common among older than younger Americans. Fifty-four percent of people aged 75 or older have been diagnosed with arthritis, for example, compared with only 8 percent of 18-to-44-year-olds. Forty-five percent of the oldest Americans have hearing problems versus 6 percent of the youngest adults. But only 6 percent of people aged 75 or older suffer from migraines or severe headaches compared with a larger 20 percent of people aged 18 to 44.

■ As the baby-boom generation ages into its sixties, the number of people with arthritis and hearing problems will soar.

Most people aged 75 or older have arthritis

(percent of people diagnosed with arthritis, by age, 2009)

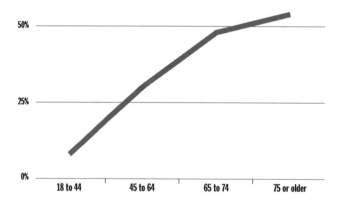

Table 3.22 Number of Adults with Health Conditions by Age, 2009

(number of people aged 18 or older with selected health conditions, by type of condition and age, 2009; numbers in thousands)

	total	18 to 44	45 to 64	aged 65 or older total	65 to 74	75 or older
Total people aged 18 or older	227,371	110,337	79,195	37,839	20,597	17,242
Selected circulatory diseases						
Heart disease, all types	26,845	4,885	10,323	11,637	5,299	6,338
Coronary	14,740	1,258	5,683	7,799	3,445	4,354
Hypertension	56,582	9,558	25,755	21,269	11,081	10,188
Stroke	6,011	627	1,992	3,393	1,317	2,076
Selected respiratory conditions						
Emphysema	4,895	369	2,065	2,462	1,194	1,268
Asthma, ever	29,734	15,743	9,706	4,285	2,466	1,819
Asthma, still	17,456	8,368	6,182	2,906	1,720	1,186
Hay fever	17,738	7,106	7,932	2,701	1,629	1,072
Sinusitis	29,305	11,342	12,792	5,170	3,028	2,142
Chronic bronchitis	9,908	3,093	4,411	2,403	1,329	1,074
Selected types of cancer						
Any cancer	18,648	1,907	7,459	9,282	4,638	4,644
Breast cancer	3,304	166	1,406	1,732	814	918
Cervical cancer	1,289	462	600	227	147	80
Prostate cancer	2,233	–	529	1,704	917	787
Other selected diseases and conditions						
Diabetes	20,490	3,234	9,886	7,370	4,107	3,263
Ulcers	17,665	5,242	7,711	4,711	2,691	2,020
Kidney disease	4,483	1,053	1,551	1,879	761	1,118
Liver disease	3,287	901	1,832	554	337	217
Arthritis	52,107	8,963	23,844	19,300	9,974	9,326
Chronic joint symptoms	64,929	18,476	29,155	17,298	8,883	8,415
Migraines or severe headaches	35,973	21,706	11,893	2,374	1,415	959
Pain in neck	34,954	14,306	15,147	5,501	3,136	2,365
Pain in lower back	64,810	26,973	25,795	12,041	6,198	5,843
Pain in face or jaw	11,501	5,752	4,400	1,349	799	550
Selected sensory problems						
Hearing	34,488	7,059	13,903	13,526	5,840	7,686
Vision	19,441	5,893	8,581	4,966	2,130	2,836
Absence of all natural teeth	17,271	2,408	5,763	9,100	4,276	4,824

Note: The conditions shown are those that have ever been diagnosed by a doctor, except as noted. Hay fever, sinusitis, and chronic bronchitis have been diagnosed in the past 12 months. Kidney and liver diseases have been diagnosed in the past 12 months and exclude kidney stones, bladder infections, and incontinence. Chronic joint symptoms are shown if respondent had pain, aching, or stiffness in or around a joint (excluding back and neck) and the condition began more than three months ago. Migraines and pain in neck, lower back, face, or jaw are shown only if pain lasted a whole day or more. "–" means sample is too small to make a reliable estimate.
Source: National Center for Health Statistics, Summary Health Statistics for U.S. Adults: National Health Interview Survey, 2009, Vital and Health Statistics, Series 10, No. 249, 2010, Internet site http://www.cdc.gov/nchs/nhis.htm; calculations by New Strategist

Table 3.23 Distribution of Health Conditions among Adults by Age, 2009

(percent distribution of people aged 18 or older with selected health conditions, by type of condition and age, 2009)

	total	18 to 44	45 to 64	aged 65 or older total	65 to 74	75 or older
Total people aged 18 or older	**100.0%**	**48.5%**	**34.8%**	**16.6%**	**9.1%**	**7.6%**
Selected circulatory diseases						
Heart disease, all types	100.0	18.2	38.5	43.3	19.7	23.6
Coronary	100.0	8.5	38.6	52.9	23.4	29.5
Hypertension	100.0	16.9	45.5	37.6	19.6	18.0
Stroke	100.0	10.4	33.1	56.4	21.9	34.5
Selected respiratory conditions						
Emphysema	100.0	7.5	42.2	50.3	24.4	25.9
Asthma, ever	100.0	52.9	32.6	14.4	8.3	6.1
Asthma, still	100.0	47.9	35.4	16.6	9.9	6.8
Hay fever	100.0	40.1	44.7	15.2	9.2	6.0
Sinusitis	100.0	38.7	43.7	17.6	10.3	7.3
Chronic bronchitis	100.0	31.2	44.5	24.3	13.4	10.8
Selected types of cancer						
Any cancer	100.0	10.2	40.0	49.8	24.9	24.9
Breast cancer	100.0	5.0	42.6	52.4	24.6	27.8
Cervical cancer	100.0	35.8	46.5	17.6	11.4	6.2
Prostate cancer	100.0	–	23.7	76.3	41.1	35.2
Other selected diseases and conditions						
Diabetes	100.0	15.8	48.2	36.0	20.0	15.9
Ulcers	100.0	29.7	43.7	26.7	15.2	11.4
Kidney disease	100.0	23.5	34.6	41.9	17.0	24.9
Liver disease	100.0	27.4	55.7	16.9	10.3	6.6
Arthritis	100.0	17.2	45.8	37.0	19.1	17.9
Chronic joint symptoms	100.0	28.5	44.9	26.6	13.7	13.0
Migraines or severe headaches	100.0	60.3	33.1	6.6	3.9	2.7
Pain in neck	100.0	40.9	43.3	15.7	9.0	6.8
Pain in lower back	100.0	41.6	39.8	18.6	9.6	9.0
Pain in face or jaw	100.0	50.0	38.3	11.7	6.9	4.8
Selected sensory problems						
Hearing	100.0	20.5	40.3	39.2	16.9	22.3
Vision	100.0	30.3	44.1	25.5	11.0	14.6
Absence of all natural teeth	100.0	13.9	33.4	52.7	24.8	27.9

Note: The conditions shown are those that have ever been diagnosed by a doctor, except as noted. Hay fever, sinusitis, and chronic bronchitis have been diagnosed in the past 12 months. Kidney and liver diseases have been diagnosed in the past 12 months and exclude kidney stones, bladder infections, and incontinence. Chronic joint symptoms are shown if respondent had pain, aching, or stiffness in or around a joint (excluding back and neck) and the condition began more than three months ago. Migraines and pain in neck, lower back, face, or jaw are shown only if pain lasted a whole day or more. "–" means sample is too small to make a reliable estimate.
Source: National Center for Health Statistics, Summary Health Statistics for U.S. Adults: National Health Interview Survey, 2009, Vital and Health Statistics, Series 10, No. 249, 2010, Internet site http://www.cdc.gov/nchs/nhis.htm; calculations by New Strategist

Table 3.24 Percent of Adults with Health Conditions by Age, 2009

(percent of people aged 18 or older with selected health conditions, by type of condition and age, 2009)

	total	18 to 44	45 to 64	65 to 74	75 or older
Total people aged 18 or older	100.0%	100.0%	100.0%	100.0%	100.0%
Selected circulatory diseases					
Heart disease, all types	11.8	4.4	13.1	25.8	36.9
Coronary	6.5	1.1	7.2	16.8	25.4
Hypertension	24.9	8.7	32.6	53.8	59.3
Stroke	2.6	0.6	2.5	6.4	12.1
Selected respiratory conditions					
Emphysema	2.2	0.3	2.6	5.8	7.4
Asthma, ever	13.1	14.3	12.3	12.0	10.6
Asthma, still	7.7	7.6	7.8	8.4	6.9
Hay fever	7.8	6.4	10.0	7.9	6.2
Sinusitis	12.9	10.3	16.2	14.7	12.4
Chronic bronchitis	4.4	2.8	5.6	6.5	6.2
Selected types of cancer					
Any cancer	8.2	1.7	9.4	22.5	26.9
Breast cancer	1.5	0.2	1.8	4.0	5.3
Cervical cancer	1.1	0.8	1.5	1.3	0.8
Prostate cancer	2.0	–	1.4	9.7	11.4
Other selected diseases and conditions					
Diabetes	9.1	3.0	12.7	20.5	19.2
Ulcers	7.8	4.8	9.7	13.1	11.7
Kidney disease	2.0	1.0	2.0	3.7	6.5
Liver disease	1.4	0.8	2.3	1.6	1.3
Arthritis	22.9	8.1	30.2	48.4	54.2
Chronic joint symptoms	28.6	16.8	36.9	43.2	48.9
Migraines or severe headaches	15.8	19.7	15.0	6.9	5.6
Pain in neck	15.4	13.0	19.1	15.2	13.7
Pain in lower back	28.5	24.5	32.6	30.1	33.9
Pain in face or jaw	5.1	5.2	5.6	3.9	3.2
Selected sensory problems					
Hearing	15.2	6.4	17.6	28.4	44.6
Vision	8.6	5.3	10.8	10.3	16.5
Absence of all natural teeth	7.6	2.2	7.3	20.8	28.0

Note: The conditions shown are those that have ever been diagnosed by a doctor, except as noted. Hay fever, sinusitis, and chronic bronchitis have been diagnosed in the past 12 months. Kidney and liver diseases have been diagnosed in the past 12 months and exclude kidney stones, bladder infections, and incontinence. Chronic joint symptoms are shown if respondent had pain, aching, or stiffness in or around a joint (excluding back and neck) and the condition began more than three months ago. Migraines and pain in neck, lower back, face, or jaw are shown only if pain lasted a whole day or more. "–" means sample is too small to make a reliable estimate.
Source: National Center for Health Statistics, Summary Health Statistics for U.S. Adults: National Health Interview Survey, 2009, Vital and Health Statistics, Series 10, No. 249, 2010, Internet site http://www.cdc.gov/nchs/nhis.htm; calculations by New Strategist

Many People Are Disabled

Sixteen percent of Americans have physical difficulties.

Nearly 36 million Americans—or 16 percent of adults— report having physical difficulties performing a variety of tasks, according to the 2009 National Health Interview Survey. Not surprisingly, the percentage of people with physical difficulties rises with age. Among 18-to-44-year-olds, only 6 percent report problems. The figure rises to 48 percent among people aged 75 or older.

Among all adults, two physical difficulties are most common: stooping, bending, and kneeling; and standing for two hours. Nine percent of people aged 18 or older say either activity would be "very difficult" or they "can't do it at all." Among people aged 75 or older, 33 percent say they would have trouble standing for two hours. Twenty-eight percent of people aged 75 or older have problems stooping, bending, or kneeling. Twenty-eight percent also have difficulty walking a quarter of a mile.

■ As the large baby-boom generation ages, the number of Americans with physical difficulties will grow rapidly.

The percentage of people with physical difficulties rises with age

(percent of people with physical difficulties, by age, 2009)

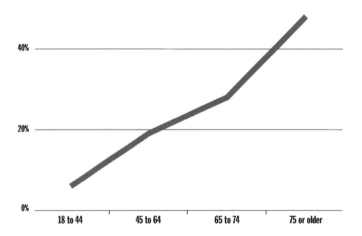

Table 3.25 Difficulties in Physical Functioning among Adults by Age, 2009

(number and percent distribution of people aged 18 or older with difficulties in physical functioning, by type of difficulty and age, 2009; numbers in thousands)

	total	18 to 44	45 to 64	aged 65 or older total	65 to 74	75 or older
Total people aged 18 or older	**227,371**	**110,337**	**79,195**	**37,839**	**20,597**	**17,242**
Total with any physical difficulty	**35,600**	**6,639**	**14,884**	**14,077**	**5,756**	**8,321**
Walk quarter of a mile	15,937	2,215	6,186	7,536	2,704	4,832
Climb 10 steps without resting	11,455	1,459	4,518	5,478	1,883	3,595
Stand for two hours	21,228	3,277	8,945	9,006	3,379	5,627
Sit for two hours	7,898	2,113	4,081	1,704	856	848
Stoop, bend, or kneel	20,651	3,383	9,031	8,237	3,452	4,785
Reach over head	5,415	741	2,480	2,194	780	1,414
Grasp or handle small objects	4,042	608	1,660	1,774	715	1,059
Lift or carry 10 pounds	9,538	1,425	3,879	4,235	1,415	2,820
Push or pull large objects	14,209	2,419	5,987	5,802	2,184	3,618

PERCENT WITH PHYSICAL DIFFICULTY BY AGE

	total	18 to 44	45 to 64	aged 65 or older total	65 to 74	75 or older
Total people aged 18 or older	**100.0%**	**100.0%**	**100.0%**	**100.0%**	**100.0%**	**100.0%**
Total with any physical difficulty	**15.7**	**6.0**	**18.8**	**37.2**	**27.9**	**48.3**
Walk quarter of a mile	7.0	2.0	7.8	19.9	13.1	28.0
Climb 10 steps without resting	5.0	1.3	5.7	14.5	9.1	20.9
Stand for two hours	9.3	3.0	11.3	23.8	16.4	32.6
Sit for two hours	3.5	1.9	5.2	4.5	4.2	4.9
Stoop, bend, or kneel	9.1	3.1	11.4	21.8	16.8	27.8
Reach over head	2.4	0.7	3.1	5.8	3.8	8.2
Grasp or handle small objects	1.8	0.6	2.1	4.7	3.5	6.1
Lift or carry 10 pounds	4.2	1.3	4.9	11.2	6.9	16.4
Push or pull large objects	6.2	2.2	7.6	15.3	10.6	21.0

PERCENT DISTRIBUTION OF THOSE WITH PHYSICAL DIFFICULTIES BY AGE

	total	18 to 44	45 to 64	aged 65 or older total	65 to 74	75 or older
Total people aged 18 or older	**100.0%**	**48.5%**	**34.8%**	**16.6%**	**9.1%**	**7.6%**
Total with any physical difficulty	**100.0**	**18.6**	**41.8**	**39.5**	**16.2**	**23.4**
Walk quarter of a mile	100.0	13.9	38.8	47.3	17.0	30.3
Climb 10 steps without resting	100.0	12.7	39.4	47.8	16.4	31.4
Stand for two hours	100.0	15.4	42.1	42.4	15.9	26.5
Sit for two hours	100.0	26.8	51.7	21.6	10.8	10.7
Stoop, bend, or kneel	100.0	16.4	43.7	39.9	16.7	23.2
Reach over head	100.0	13.7	45.8	40.5	14.4	26.1
Grasp or handle small objects	100.0	15.0	41.1	43.9	17.7	26.2
Lift or carry 10 pounds	100.0	14.9	40.7	44.4	14.8	29.6
Push or pull large objects	100.0	17.0	42.1	40.8	15.4	25.5

Note: Respondents were classified as having difficulties if they responded "very difficult" or "can't do at all."
Source: National Center for Health Statistics, Summary Health Statistics for U.S. Adults: National Health Interview Survey, 2009, Vital and Health Statistics, Series 10, No. 249, 2010, Internet site http://www.cdc.gov/nchs/nhis.htm; calculations by New Strategist

People Aged 45 or Older Account for Most Health Care Visits

Americans visited the doctor more than 900 million times in 2008.

Among the 1.2 billion health care visits in 2008, visits to physician's offices accounted for 80 percent. Another 10 percent of visits were to emergency rooms, and 9 percent were to hospital outpatient facilities. The 53 percent majority of people who visited a doctor in 2008 were aged 45 or older, and 25 percent were aged 65 or older.

Among all adults, 19 percent have not seen a doctor or other health care professional in the past year. The proportion varies considerably by demographic characteristic. Thirty percent of Hispanics have not been to a doctor in the past year compared with only 16 percent of non-Hispanic whites. Nearly half (47 percent) of adults aged 18 to 64 without health insurance did not see a doctor in the past year compared with only 16 percent of those with private health insurance. People aged 75 or older are most likely to see a doctor frequently. Twenty-two percent have been to the doctor at least 10 times in the past year.

■ Among the uninsured under age 65, a substantial 23 percent did not get needed medical care during the past year because of the cost.

Many without health insurance do not go to the doctor

(percent of people aged 18 to 64 who have not visited a doctor or other health care professional in the past year, by health insurance status, 2009)

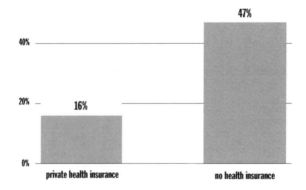

Table 3.26 Health Care Visits by Age, 2008

(number and percent distribution of visits to physician offices, hospital outpatient departments, and hospital emergency departments, and number of visits per 100 persons, by age and place of care, 2008; numbers in thousands)

	total	physician's offices	hospital outpatient departments	hospital emergency rooms
Total visits	**1,189,619**	**955,969**	**109,889**	**123,761**
Under age 18	225,531	171,744	25,907	27,880
Aged 18 to 44	328,438	243,979	34,174	50,285
Aged 45 to 54	169,674	137,776	16,257	15,641
Aged 55 to 64	171,921	146,335	14,893	10,694
Aged 65 or older	294,054	256,135	18,658	19,261
Aged 65 to 74	144,878	127,125	10,273	7,479
Aged 75 or older	149,177	129,010	8,385	11,781
PERCENT DISTRIBUTION BY AGE				
Total visits	**100.0%**	**100.0%**	**100.0%**	**100.0%**
Under age 18	19.0	18.0	23.6	22.5
Aged 18 to 44	27.6	25.5	31.1	40.6
Aged 45 to 54	14.3	14.4	14.8	12.6
Aged 55 to 64	14.5	15.3	13.6	8.6
Aged 65 or older	24.7	26.8	17.0	15.6
Aged 65 to 74	12.2	13.3	9.3	6.0
Aged 75 or older	12.5	13.5	7.6	9.5
PERCENT DISTRIBUTION BY PLACE OF CARE				
Total visits	**100.0%**	**80.4%**	**9.2%**	**10.4%**
Under age 18	100.0	76.2	11.5	12.4
Aged 18 to 44	100.0	74.3	10.4	15.3
Aged 45 to 54	100.0	81.2	9.6	9.2
Aged 55 to 64	100.0	85.1	8.7	6.2
Aged 65 or older	100.0	87.1	6.3	6.6
Aged 65 to 74	100.0	87.7	7.1	5.2
Aged 75 or older	100.0	86.5	5.6	7.9
NUMBER OF VISITS PER 100 PERSONS				
Total visits	**398**	**320**	**37**	**41**
Under age 18	306	233	35	38
Aged 18 to 44	298	221	31	46
Aged 45 to 54	386	313	37	36
Aged 55 to 64	513	437	44	32
Aged 65 or older	790	688	50	52
Aged 65 to 74	729	639	52	38
Aged 75 or older	860	743	48	68

Source: National Center for Health Statistics, Health, United States, 2009, Web Update, Internet site http://www.cdc.gov/nchs/ hus/updatedtables.htm; calculations by New Strategist

Table 3.27 Number of Visits to a Doctor or Other Health Care Professional by Selected Characteristics, 2009

(total number and percent distribution of office visits by people aged 18 or older to a doctor or other health care professional in past 12 months, by selected characteristics, 2009; numbers in thousands)

	total		none	1 or more visits				
	number	percent		total	1	2 to 3	4 to 9	10 or more
Total people	227,371	100.0%	19.0%	81.1%	16.6%	26.2%	24.2%	14.1%
Sex								
Men	109,844	100.0	26.1	73.9	18.6	24.3	20.3	10.7
Women	117,527	100.0	12.7	87.3	14.8	27.7	27.7	17.1
Age								
Aged 18 to 44	110,337	100.0	25.5	74.4	19.4	25.2	18.5	11.3
Aged 45 to 64	79,195	100.0	16.3	83.8	15.8	27.8	25.3	14.9
Aged 65 to 74	20,597	100.0	6.2	93.9	10.2	27.5	36.6	19.6
Aged 75 or older	17,242	100.0	4.3	95.7	9.7	22.9	41.4	21.7
Race and Hispanic origin								
Asian	10,763	100.0	24.7	75.3	21.2	24.3	20.5	9.3
Black	27,374	100.0	19.7	80.3	16.2	25.9	24.3	13.9
Hispanic	31,312	100.0	29.7	70.4	18.2	20.9	20.1	11.2
Non-Hispanic white	155,185	100.0	16.3	83.7	16.2	27.3	25.1	15.1
Education								
Less than high school	28,439	100.0	31.1	68.9	14.3	18.4	21.2	15.0
High school graduate	54,242	100.0	22.9	77.2	16.5	23.6	22.6	14.5
Some college	56,772	100.0	16.8	83.1	16.4	27.8	23.6	15.3
Bachelor's degree or more	57,660	100.0	12.3	87.8	17.3	29.7	27.1	13.7
Household income								
Less than $35,000	70,740	100.0	24.7	75.4	14.9	21.1	23.0	16.4
$35,000 to $49,999	30,679	100.0	21.5	78.4	16.0	24.3	24.1	14.0
$50,000 to $74,999	40,179	100.0	19.1	80.8	17.4	26.9	23.3	13.2
$75,000 to $99,999	26,183	100.0	15.5	84.6	17.4	28.7	25.0	13.5
$100,000 or more	44,827	100.0	12.4	87.6	18.2	30.9	25.9	12.6
Health insurance coverage among people under age 65								
Private	123,528	100.0	15.8	84.2	19.3	30.1	23.1	11.7
Medicaid	17,578	100.0	13.1	86.8	12.1	20.3	26.9	27.5
Other	7,631	100.0	12.1	87.9	11.4	26.1	26.0	24.4
Uninsured	40,141	100.0	47.1	52.9	18.1	16.7	11.3	6.8

Note: Numbers by race and Hispanic origin do not sum to total because not all races are shown, Hispanics may be of any race, education is reported only for persons aged 25 or older, and some did not report income.
Source: National Center for Health Statistics, Summary Health Statistics for U.S. Adults: National Health Interview Survey, 2009, Vital and Health Statistics, Series 10, No. 249, 2010, Internet site http://www.cdc.gov/nchs/nhis.htm; calculations by New Strategist

Table 3.28 Did Not Receive or Delayed Getting Medical Care Due to Cost by Selected Characteristics, 2009

(total number of people and percent who did not receive or delayed getting needed medical care in past year due to cost, by selected characteristics, 2009; numbers in thousands)

	total		did not receive care due to cost	delayed getting care due to cost
	number	percent		
Total people	301,362	100.0%	6.9%	10.1%
Sex				
Female	153,702	100.0	7.3	10.7
Male	147,660	100.0	6.4	9.2
Age				
Under age 12	49,374	100.0	2.2	4.2
Aged 12 to 17	24,621	100.0	3.0	5.8
Aged 18 to 44	110,336	100.0	9.6	13.1
Aged 45 to 64	79,039	100.0	9.5	13.6
Aged 65 or older	37,993	100.0	2.6	4.5
Race and Hispanic origin				
Asian	13,788	100.0	3.7	4.9
Black	38,730	100.0	8.9	10.6
Hispanic	47,833	100.0	8.5	10.9
Non-Hispanic white	196,132	100.0	6.3	9.9
Education				
Less than high school	27,819	100.0	13.1	15.0
High school graduate	55,288	100.0	9.6	13.1
Some college	54,662	100.0	9.5	13.8
Bachelor's degree or more	56,811	100.0	4.4	8.0
Household income				
Less than $35,000	87,673	100.0	13.4	16.9
$35,000 to $49,999	38,725	100.0	8.7	13.0
$50,000 to $74,999	50,336	100.0	6.0	10.0
$75,000 to $99,999	34,250	100.0	3.1	5.8
$100,000 or more	60,451	100.0	1.6	3.4
Health insurance coverage among people under age 65				
Private	165,433	100.0	3.4	6.4
Medicaid	40,568	100.0	7.2	9.1
Other	9,528	100.0	6.5	9.0
Uninsured	45,809	100.0	23.0	29.4

Note: Numbers by race and Hispanic origin do not sum to total because not all races are shown, Hispanics may be of any race, education is reported only for persons aged 25 or older, and some did not report income.
Source: National Center for Health Statistics, Summary Health Statistics for the U.S. Population: National Health Interview Survey, 2009, Vital and Health Statistics, Series 10, No. 248, 2010, Internet site http://www.cdc.gov/nchs/nhis.htm; calculations by New Strategist

Many Americans Turn to Alternative Medicine

Vitamins are the most popular alternative therapy.

Alternative medicine is a big business. In 2007, fully 38 percent of Americans aged 18 or older used a complementary or alternative medicine or therapy, according to a study by the National Center for Health Statistics. Alternative treatments range from popular regimens such as the South Beach diet to chiropractic care, yoga, and acupuncture.

The adults most likely to use alternative medicines are well-educated, middle-aged, and non-Hispanic white. Fifty-five percent of people with a graduate degree used alternative medicine in 2007, as did 43 percent of non-Hispanic whites and 44 percent of people aged 50 to 59. Not surprisingly, adults with multiple health conditions and frequent doctor visits are more likely to have used alternative medicine than those without health problems.

Twelve percent of children used alternative medicine in 2007. Children whose parents use alternative medicine are twice as likely to be users themselves, at 24 percent. Many are taking vitamins.

■ Among all racial and ethnic groups, American Indians are most likely to use alternative medicine, 50 percent doing so in 2007. Many American Indians are visiting traditional healers.

The use of alternative medicine rises with education

(percent of people aged 18 or older who have used alternative medicine in the past 12 months, by education, 2007)

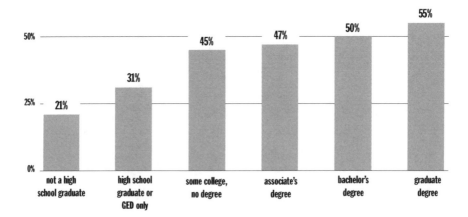

Table 3.29 Use of Alternative and Complementary Medicine by Type, 2007

(number and percent of people who used complementary or alternative medicine in the past 12 months by age, 2007; numbers in thousands)

	children (under age 18)		adults (aged 18 or older)	
	number	percent	number	percent
Any use	**8,720**	**11.8%**	**87,217**	**38.3%**
Alternative medical systems				
Acupuncture	150	0.2	3,141	1.4
Homeopathic treatment	907	1.3	3,909	1.8
Biologically based therapies				
Nonvitamin, nonmineral natural products	2,850	3.9	38,797	17.7
Diet-based therapies	565	0.8	7,893	3.6
Vegetarian diet	367	0.5	3,351	1.5
Atkins diet	88	0.1	2,673	1.2
South Beach diet	128	0.2	2,334	1.1
Manipulative and body-based therapies				
Chiropractic or osteopathic manipulation	2,020	2.8	18,740	8.6
Massage	743	1.0	18,068	8.3
Movement therapies	299	0.4	3,146	1.5
Pilates	245	0.3	3,015	1.4
Mind–body therapies				
Meditation	725	1.0	20,541	9.4
Guided imagery	293	0.4	4,866	2.2
Progressive relaxation	329	0.5	6,454	2.9
Deep breathing exercises	1,558	2.2	27,794	12.7
Yoga	1,505	2.1	13,172	6.1
Tai chi	113	0.2	2,267	1.0
Energy healing therapy/Reiki	161	0.2	1,216	0.5

Note: Only therapies with at least 1 million adult users are shown.
Source: National Center for Health Statistics, Complementary and Alternative Medicine Use Among Adults and Children: United States, 2007, National Health Statistics Report, No. 12, 2008, Internet site http://nccam.nih.gov/news/camstats/2007/index.htm

Table 3.30 Characteristics of Adults Who Use Complementary and Alternative Medicine, 2007

(percent of people aged 18 or older who used complementary or alternative medicine in the past 12 months, by selected characteristics, 2007)

	any	biologically based therapies	mind–body therapies	alternative medical systems	manipulative and body-based therapies
Total adults	**38.3%**	**19.9%**	**19.2%**	**3.4%**	**15.2%**
Sex					
Female	42.8	21.9	23.8	4.2	18.1
Male	33.5	17.8	14.4	2.7	12.2
Age					
Aged 18 to 29	36.3	15.9	21.3	3.2	15.1
Aged 30 to 39	39.6	19.8	19.9	3.6	17.2
Aged 40 to 49	40.1	20.4	19.7	4.6	17.4
Aged 50 to 59	44.1	24.2	22.9	4.9	17.3
Aged 60 to 69	41.0	25.4	17.3	2.8	13.8
Aged 70 to 84	32.1	19.3	11.9	1.8	9.9
Aged 85 or older	24.2	13.7	9.8	1.9	7.0
Race and Hispanic origin					
American Indian	50.3	23.7	23.3	13.2	13.4
Asian	39.9	19.6	23.4	5.4	11.1
Black	25.5	12.3	14.8	1.4	6.5
Hispanic	23.7	11.8	10.6	3.0	6.7
Non-Hispanic white	43.1	22.7	21.4	3.7	18.7
Education					
Not a high school graduate	20.8	9.8	7.6	2.1	6.4
High school graduate or GED	31.0	16.3	12.1	2.0	11.5
Some college, no degree	45.0	24.4	22.0	4.3	18.0
Associate's degree	47.2	24.9	24.3	3.6	18.2
Bachelor's degree	49.6	27.5	25.5	5.4	20.7
Graduate degree	55.4	30.1	34.2	6.1	23.6
Health insurance status of people under age 65					
Private health insurance	42.7	21.3	22.0	3.9	19.0
Public health insurance	30.6	14.9	18.7	2.6	9.6
No health insurance	31.5	17.0	16.2	4.0	9.8
Number of health conditions					
No conditions	21.3	10.0	9.8	1.4	7.5
One to two conditions	33.3	16.5	16.2	2.2	12.5
Three to five conditions	42.3	22.8	19.5	3.9	18.1
Six or more conditions	53.8	28.4	30.6	5.7	22.1

	any	biologically based therapies	mind–body therapies	alternative medical systems	manipulative and body-based therapies
Number of visits to doctor in past 12 months					
No visits	24.5%	13.0%	13.2%	2.0%	6.0%
One visit	32.3	16.8	14.7	2.7	10.7
Two to three visits	39.4	20.9	19.7	3.1	15.0
Four to nine visits	47.2	25.1	23.8	4.2	20.6
10 or more visits	53.4	25.3	28.8	6.7	28.3
Delayed conventional care because of worry about costs					
Yes	48.2	26.3	27.7	5.6	17.6
No	37.0	19.1	18.2	3.2	14.9

Definitions: Biologically based therapies include chelation therapy; nonvitamin, nonmineral, natural products; and diet-based therapies. Mind–body therapies include biofeedback, meditation, guided imagery, progressive relaxation, deep breathing exercises, hypnosis, yoga, tai chi, and qi gong. Alternative medical systems include acupuncture, ayurveda, homeopathic treatment, naturopathy, and traditional healers. Manipulative body-based therapies include chiropractic or osteopathic manipulation, massage, and movement therapies.

Note: Asians and blacks are those who identify themselves as being of the race alone. Non-Hispanic whites are those who identify themselves as being white alone and not Hispanic. American Indians are those who identify themselves as being American Indian or Alaska Native alone.

Source: National Center for Health Statistics, Complementary and Alternative Medicine Use Among Adults and Children: United States, 2007, National Health Statistics Report, No. 12, 2008; Internet site http://nccam.nih.gov/news/camstats/2007/index.htm

Table 3.31 Characteristics of Children Who Use Complementary and Alternative Medicine, 2007

(percent of people under age 18 who used complementary or alternative medicine (CAM) in the past 12 months, by selected characteristics, 2007)

	any	biologically based therapies	mind–body therapies	alternative medical systems	manipulative and body-based therapies
Total children	11.8%	4.7%	4.3%	2.6%	3.7%
Children whose parent uses CAM	23.9	10.3	9.8	4.2	7.5
Sex					
Female	12.6	4.6	4.9	2.8	4.2
Male	11.0	4.8	3.8	2.4	3.2
Age					
Aged 0 to 4	7.6	3.2	1.9	2.9	2.1
Aged 5 to 11	10.7	4.3	3.9	2.5	2.8
Aged 12 to 17	16.4	6.3	6.8	2.5	5.9
Race and Hispanic origin					
Black	5.9	1.7	3.0	1.4	0.8
Hispanic	7.9	2.8	2.8	2.5	1.9
White	12.8	5.2	4.4	2.8	4.4
Family structure					
Mother and father	12.7	5.2	4.3	2.7	4.2
Mother, no father	9.6	3.3	4.8	2.2	2.5
Parent's education					
Not a high school graduate	4.8	1.7	1.9	1.5	1.3
High school graduate or GED	8.0	2.8	2.3	1.7	2.5
More than high school	14.7	6.1	5.6	3.2	4.6
Number of health conditions					
No conditions	4.0	1.3	1.1	1.9	1.4
One to two conditions	8.5	2.9	3.2	1.5	2.3
Three to five conditions	14.1	6.0	4.8	2.9	4.2
Six or more conditions	23.8	8.8	10.2	5.6	5.4
Number of visits to doctor in past 12 months					
No visits	7.7	4.9	2.5	2.6	1.9
One visit	7.8	3.6	2.1	1.6	1.9
Two to three visits	11.1	3.4	4.5	2.6	3.1
Four to nine visits	15.0	6.0	5.0	2.5	5.6
10 or more visits	28.4	12.0	12.9	6.3	10.0
Delayed conventional care because of worry about costs					
Yes	16.9	7.3	6.6	5.0	6.2
No	11.6	4.6	4.2	2.6	3.6

Definitions: Biologically based therapies include chelation therapy; nonvitamin, nonmineral, natural products; and diet-based therapies. Mind–body therapies include biofeedback, meditation, guided imagery, progressive relaxation, deep breathing exercises, hypnosis, yoga, tai chi, and qi gong. Alternative medical systems include acupuncture, ayurveda, homeopathic treatment, naturopathy, and traditional healers. Manipulative body-based therapies include chiropractic or osteopathic manipulation, massage, and movement therapies.

Note: Asians and blacks are those who identify themselves as being of the race alone. Non-Hispanic whites are those who identify themselves as being white alone and not Hispanic. American Indians are those who identify themselves as being American Indian or Alaska Native alone.

Source: National Center for Health Statistics, Complementary and Alternative Medicine Use Among Adults and Children: United States, 2007, National Health Statistics Report, No. 12, 2008; Internet site http://nccam.nih.gov/news/camstats/2007/index.htm

One in 12 Had a Hospital Stay in 2009

Older Americans are most likely to be hospitalized.

As health insurance companies try to cut costs, hospitals have changed their strategy. They are less likely to keep patients overnight and more likely to care for them through outpatient services.

In 2009, only 8 percent of the population was hospitalized overnight. People aged 65 or older are most likely to experience a hospital stay, with 17 percent hospitalized overnight in 2009. The least educated and those with the lowest incomes are also most likely to be hospitalized, in large part because older Americans are disproportionately represented in those groups.

■ While greater outpatient care has cut costs for hospitals and insurers, it has increased the caregiving burden on family members.

Females are more likely than males to be hospitalized

(percent of people who experienced an overnight hospital stay, by sex, 2009)

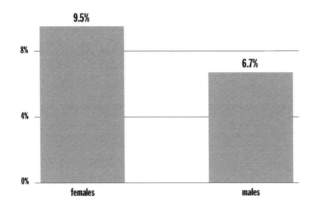

Table 3.32 Number of Overnight Hospital Stays by Selected Characteristics, 2009

(total number of people and percent distribution by experience of an overnight hospital stay in past 12 months, by selected characteristics, 2009; numbers in thousands)

	total		number of stays	
	number	percent	none	one or more
Total people	**301,362**	**100.0%**	**91.8%**	**8.2%**
Sex				
Female	153,702	100.0	90.5	9.5
Male	147,660	100.0	93.3	6.7
Age				
Under age 12	49,374	100.0	92.5	7.5
Aged 12 to 17	24,621	100.0	98.0	2.0
Aged 18 to 44	110,336	100.0	93.4	6.6
Aged 45 to 64	79,039	100.0	91.5	8.5
Aged 65 or older	37,993	100.0	83.0	17.0
Race and Hispanic origin				
Asian	13,788	100.0	94.7	5.3
Black	38,730	100.0	91.0	9.0
Hispanic	47,833	100.0	92.4	7.6
Non-Hispanic white	196,132	100.0	91.8	8.2
Education				
Less than high school	27,819	100.0	88.0	12.0
High school graduate	55,288	100.0	90.7	9.3
Some college	54,662	100.0	90.3	9.7
Bachelor's degree or more	56,811	100.0	92.2	7.8
Household income				
Less than $35,000	87,673	100.0	89.2	10.8
$35,000 to $49,999	38,725	100.0	91.3	8.7
$50,000 to $74,999	50,336	100.0	92.9	7.1
$75,000 to $99,999	34,250	100.0	93.0	7.0
$100,000 or more	60,451	100.0	93.4	6.6
Health insurance coverage among people under age 65				
Private	165,433	100.0	94.2	5.8
Medicaid	40,568	100.0	84.5	15.5
Other	9,528	100.0	88.8	11.2
Uninsured	45,809	100.0	95.4	4.6

Note: Numbers by race and Hispanic origin do not sum to total because not all races are shown, Hispanics may be of any race, education is reported only for persons aged 25 or older, and some did not report income.
Source: National Center for Health Statistics, Summary Health Statistics for the U.S. Population: National Health Interview Survey, 2009, Vital and Health Statistics, Series 10, No. 248, 2010, Internet site http://www.cdc.gov/nchs/nhis.htm; calculations by New Strategist

Over One Million Have Been Diagnosed with AIDS

Nearly eight out of 10 people diagnosed with AIDS are males aged 13 or older.

More than 1 million people had been diagnosed with AIDS through 2008. While new drug therapies have been successful in reducing AIDS mortality, the number of AIDS cases continues to climb.

Males aged 13 or older account for 79 percent of AIDS victims. The 30-to-44 age group accounts for the 58 percent majority of people diagnosed with AIDS over the years. A substantial 42 percent of AIDS cases have occurred among blacks and another 39 percent among non-Hispanic whites. Hispanics account for just 17 percent of AIDS cases.

■ Only 20 percent of people with AIDS are females aged 13 or older. Children under age 13 account for less than 1 percent.

Blacks and non-Hispanic whites account for a nearly equal share of AIDS cases

(percent distribution of people diagnosed with AIDS by race and Hispanic origin, through December 2008)

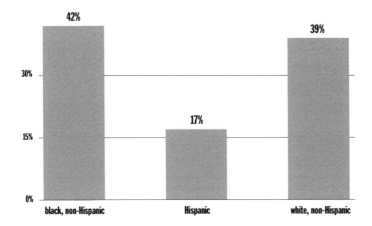

Table 3.33 Cumulative Number of AIDS Cases by Sex and Age, through 2008

(cumulative number and percent distribution of AIDS cases by sex and age at diagnosis, through 2008)

	number	percent distribution
Total cases	**1,073,128**	**100.0%**
Sex		
Males aged 13 or older	851,974	79.4
Females aged 13 or older	211,804	19.7
Age		
Under age 13	9,349	0.9
Aged 13 to 14	1,220	0.1
Aged 15 to 19	6,685	0.6
Aged 20 to 24	40,735	3.8
Aged 25 to 29	125,755	11.7
Aged 30 to 34	209,554	19.5
Aged 35 to 39	229,111	21.3
Aged 40 to 44	187,421	17.5
Aged 45 to 49	121,111	11.3
Aged 50 to 54	68,560	6.4
Aged 55 to 59	36,987	3.4
Aged 60 to 64	19,669	1.8
Aged 65 or older	16,972	1.6

Source: Centers for Disease Control and Prevention, HIV/AIDS, Internet site http://www.cdc.gov/hiv/surveillance/resources/reports/2008report/table2a.htm

Table 3.34 Cumulative Number of AIDS Cases by Race and Hispanic Origin, through 2008

(cumulative number and percent distribution of AIDS cases by race and Hispanic origin, through 2008)

	number	percent distribution
Total cases	**1,073,128**	**100.0%**
American Indian	3,741	0.3
Asian	8,253	0.8
Black	452,916	42.2
Hispanic	180,061	16.8
Non-Hispanic white	419,905	39.1

Note: Numbers do not add to total because not all races are shown and Hispanics may be of any race.
Source: Centers for Disease Control and Prevention, HIV/AIDS, Internet site http://www.cdc.gov/hiv/surveillance/resources/reports/2008report/table2a.htm

Heart Disease and Cancer Are the Biggest Killers

Nearly half of deaths in 2009 were caused by heart disease or cancer.

Heart disease and cancer each kill more than half a million Americans a year. These illnesses are by far the leading causes of death in the United States, accounting for 25 and 23 percent of deaths in 2009, respectively. The third leading cause of death, chronic lower respiratory disease, accounts for only 6 percent of the total.

The number of accidental deaths (in fifth place as a cause of death) has declined over the past few years because of the greater use of seat belts and tougher drunk driving laws. Alzheimer's disease is becoming a more important cause of death as the population ages. In 2009, nearly 79,000 people died of Alzheimer's, putting it in sixth place as a cause of death. Parkinson's disease ranks 14th.

■ Although medical science has made considerable progress in combating the problem, heart disease will remain the number one cause of death for years to come.

Heart disease and cancer are most likely to kill

(percent of deaths caused by the top five causes of death, 2009)

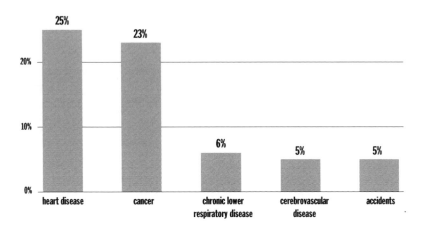

Table 3.35 Leading Causes of Death, 2009

(number and percent distribution of deaths accounted for by the fifteen leading causes of death, 2009)

		number	percent distribution
All causes		**2,436,652**	**100.0%**
1.	Diseases of heart	598,607	24.6
2.	Malignant neoplasms	568,668	23.3
3.	Chronic lower respiratory diseases	137,082	5.6
4.	Cerebrovascular diseases	128,603	5.3
5.	Accidents	117,176	4.8
6.	Alzheimer's disease	78,889	3.2
7.	Diabetes mellitus	68,504	2.8
8.	Influenza and pneumonia	53,582	2.2
9.	Nephritis, nephrotic syndrome, nephrosis	48,714	2.0
10.	Suicide	36,547	1.5
11.	Septicemia	35,587	1.5
12.	Chronic liver disease and cirrhosis	30,444	1.2
13.	Essential (primary) hypertension and hypertensive renal disease	25,651	1.1
14.	Parkinson's disease	20,552	0.8
15.	Assault (homicide)	16,591	0.7
	All other causes	471,455	19.3

Source: National Center for Health Statistics, Deaths: Preliminary Deaths for 2009, National Vital Statistics Report, Vol. 59, No. 4, 2011, Internet site http://www.cdc.gov/nchs/deaths.htm; calculations by New Strategist

Life Expectancy Has Increased

Americans born in 2009 could expect to live 78.2 years.

Since 1950, life expectancy at birth has climbed 10 years, from 68.2 to 78.2 years. Life expectancy at age 65 has grown by almost five years. Someone who turned age 65 in 2009 could expect to live another 18.8 years. Between 2000 and 2009, life expectancy at birth and at age 65 increased by about one year.

Women have longer life expectancies than men at every age. A girl born in 2009 could expect to live to age 80.6. Their male counterparts could expect to live to age 75.7. At age 65, women could expect to live an additional 20.0 years compared with 17.3 years for men. By age 90, however, the difference in life expectancy between men and women is measured in months rather than years.

■ Although life expectancy has increased substantially, the United States ranks well below many other developed nations in expected length of life.

Females live longer than males

(years of life remaining at birth, by sex, 2009)

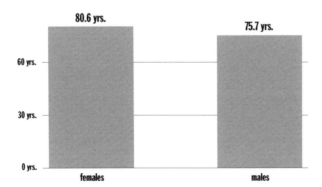

Table 3.36 Life Expectancy by Age, 1950 to 2009

(years of life remaining at birth and age 65, 1950 to 2009; change in years of life remaining for selected years)

	at birth	age 65
2009	78.2	18.8
2000	77.0	17.9
1990	75.4	17.2
1980	73.7	16.4
1970	70.8	15.2
1960	69.7	14.3
1950	68.2	13.9
Change		
2000 to 2009	1.2	0.9
1950 to 2009	10.0	4.9

Source: National Center for Health Statistics, Deaths: Preliminary Deaths for 2009, National Vital Statistics Report, Vol. 59, No. 4, 2011, Internet site http://www.cdc.gov/nchs/deaths.htm; calculations by New Strategist"

Table 3.37 Life Expectancy by Age and Sex, 2009

(years of life remaining at selected ages, by sex, 2009)

	total	females	males
At birth	78.2	80.6	75.7
Aged 1	77.7	80.0	75.3
Aged 5	73.8	76.1	71.4
Aged 10	68.8	71.2	66.4
Aged 15	63.9	66.2	61.5
Aged 20	59.0	61.3	56.7
Aged 25	54.3	56.4	52.0
Aged 30	49.5	51.6	47.3
Aged 35	44.8	46.8	42.7
Aged 40	40.1	42.0	38.0
Aged 45	35.5	37.3	33.5
Aged 50	31.1	32.8	29.1
Aged 55	26.8	28.4	25.0
Aged 60	22.7	24.1	21.1
Aged 65	18.8	20.0	17.3
Aged 70	15.1	16.1	13.8
Aged 75	11.7	12.5	10.7
Aged 80	8.8	9.4	8.0
Aged 85	6.4	6.8	5.8
Aged 90	4.6	4.8	4.1
Aged 95	3.2	3.3	2.9
Aged 100	2.2	2.2	2.0

Source: National Center for Health Statistics, Deaths: Preliminary Deaths for 2009, National Vital Statistics Report, Vol. 59, No. 4, 2011, Internet site http://www.cdc.gov/nchs/deaths.htm; calculations by New Strategist

4

Housing Trends

■ Homeownership rate is falling.

In 2010, 66.9 percent of households owned their home. This was 2.1 percentage points lower than the 69.0 percent peak in 2004, and it was 0.6 percentage points below the 67.5 percent rate of 2000.

■ Non-Hispanic whites are most likely to own a home.

Seventy-four percent of non-Hispanic white households owned their home in 2010. Among blacks the proportion was 45 percent.

■ The Midwest has the highest homeownership rate.

Seventy-one percent of households in the Midwest owned their home in 2010, compared with only 61 percent in the West.

■ American homes have a median of 1,800 square feet of living space.

The average size of houses has fallen slightly because of the housing downturn. Nevertheless, most homes still have three or more bedrooms and two or more bathrooms.

■ Most householders are happy with their home.

When asked how they would rate their housing unit on a scale of 1 (worst) to 10 (best), fully 71 percent of householders rate their home an 8 or higher.

■ Most homeowners do not have public transportation in their area.

Seventy percent of renters have public transportation available to them compared with only 47 percent of owners.

■ The median value of owned homes fell to $170,000 in 2009.

Mortgage loans as a percentage of home values grew from 54 to 63 percent between 2007 and 2009 as housing prices fell.

The Homeownership Rate Is Falling

Rate has decreased in every age group since peaking in 2004.

In 2010, 66.9 percent of households owned their home—2.1 percentage points below the record high of 69.0 percent reached in 2004. Homeownership rates fell in every age group between 2004 and 2010 and in all but the oldest age group between 2000 and 2010. Householders aged 35 to 44 experienced the biggest decline in homeownership since the rate peaked in 2004. Their homeownership rate fell by 4.2 percentage points to 65.0 percent.

The homeownership rate fell for most household types and every race and Hispanic origin group between 2004 and 2010. Eighty-two percent of married couples owned their home in 2010—the highest rate of homeownership among all household types. Seventy-four percent of non-Hispanic whites owned a home in 2010 compared with 45 percent of blacks and 48 percent of Hispanics.

■ Despite the collapse of the housing bubble and the record number of foreclosures, a substantial two-thirds of households are homeowners.

Homeownership rate is highest among older Americans

(percent of householders who own their home, by age, 2010)

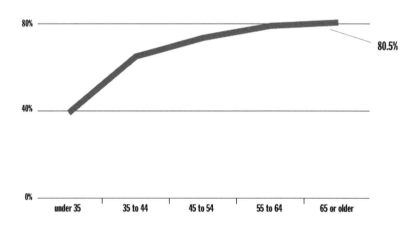

Table 4.1 Homeownership Rates by Age, Household Type, Race, and Hispanic Origin, 2000 to 2010

(percent of households that own their home by age of householder, household type, race, and Hispanic origin of householder, 2000 to 2010; percentage point change for selected years)

	2010	peak year 2004	2000	percentage point change 2000–10	percentage point change 2004–10
Total households	**66.9%**	**69.0%**	**67.5%**	**–0.6**	**–2.1**
Age of householder					
Under age 35	39.1	43.1	40.7	–1.6	–4.0
Aged 35 to 44	65.0	69.2	68.0	–3.0	–4.2
Aged 45 to 54	73.5	77.2	76.8	–3.2	–3.7
Aged 55 to 64	79.0	81.7	80.2	–1.2	–2.7
Aged 65 or older	80.5	81.1	80.5	0.1	–0.6
Type of household					
Married couple	82.1	84.0	82.4	–0.3	–1.9
Female householder, no spouse present	48.6	50.9	48.9	–0.3	–2.3
Male householder, no spouse present	56.9	59.6	58.6	–1.7	–2.7
Women living alone	58.6	59.9	57.9	0.7	–1.3
Men living alone	51.3	50.5	47.8	3.5	0.8
Race and Hispanic origin					
American Indian	52.3	55.6	56.2	–3.9	–3.3
Asian	58.9	59.8	52.8	6.1	–0.9
Black	45.4	49.1	47.2	–1.8	–3.7
Hispanic	47.5	48.1	46.3	1.2	–0.6
Non-Hispanic white	74.4	76.0	73.8	0.6	–1.6

Note: American Indians, Asians, blacks, and whites are those who identified themselves as being of the race alone.
Source: Bureau of the Census, Housing Vacancy Surveys, Internet site http://www.census.gov/hhes/www/housing/hvs/hvs.html; calculations by New Strategist

Table 4.2 Age of Householder by Homeownership Status, 2010

(number and percent distribution of households by age of householder and homeownership status, 2010; numbers in thousands)

	total	owner	renter
Total households	**111,860**	**74,791**	**37,069**
Under age 35	24,578	9,601	14,977
Aged 35 to 44	20,319	13,209	7,110
Aged 45 to 54	23,411	17,212	6,199
Aged 55 to 64	19,781	15,625	4,156
Aged 65 or older	23,772	19,144	4,628
PERCENT DISTRIBUTION BY HOMEOWNERSHIP STATUS			
Total households	**100.0%**	**66.9%**	**33.1%**
Under age 35	100.0	39.1	60.9
Aged 35 to 44	100.0	65.0	35.0
Aged 45 to 54	100.0	73.5	26.5
Aged 55 to 64	100.0	79.0	21.0
Aged 65 or older	100.0	80.5	19.5
PERCENT DISTRIBUTION BY AGE			
Total households	**100.0%**	**100.0%**	**100.0%**
Under age 35	22.0	12.8	40.4
Aged 35 to 44	18.2	17.7	19.2
Aged 45 to 54	20.9	23.0	16.7
Aged 55 to 64	17.7	20.9	11.2
Aged 65 or older	21.3	25.6	12.5

Source: Bureau of the Census, Housing Vacancy Survey, Internet site http://www.census.gov/hhes/www/housing/hvs/hvs.html; calculations by New Strategist

Table 4.3 Type of Household by Homeownership Status, 2010

(number and percent distribution of households by type and homeownership status, 2010; numbers in thousands)

	total	owner	renter
Total households	**111,860**	**74,791**	**37,069**
Married couple	54,898	45,068	9,830
Female householder, no spouse present	14,082	6,846	7,236
Male householder, no spouse present	5,513	3,138	2,375
Women living alone	16,801	9,842	6,959
Men living alone	13,652	7,002	6,650
PERCENT DISTRIBUTION BY HOMEOWNERSHIP STATUS			
Total households	**100.0%**	**66.9%**	**33.1%**
Married couple	100.0	82.1	17.9
Female householder, no spouse present	100.0	48.6	51.4
Male householder, no spouse present	100.0	56.9	43.1
Women living alone	100.0	58.6	41.4
Men living alone	100.0	51.3	48.7
PERCENT DISTRIBUTION BY HOUSEHOLD TYPE			
Total households	**100.0%**	**100.0%**	**100.0%**
Married couple	49.1	60.3	26.5
Female householder, no spouse present	12.6	9.2	19.5
Male householder, no spouse present	4.9	4.2	6.4
Women living alone	15.0	13.2	18.8
Men living alone	12.2	9.4	17.9

Note: Numbers do not sum to total because not all household types are shown.
Source: Bureau of the Census, Housing Vacancy Survey, Internet site http://www.census.gov/hhes/www/housing/hvs/hvs.html; calculations by New Strategist

Table 4.4 Race and Hispanic Origin of Householders by Homeownership Status, 2009

(number and percent distribution of households by race and Hispanic origin of householder and homeownership status, 2009; numbers in thousands)

	total	owner	renter
Total households	**111,806**	**76,428**	**35,378**
American Indian	968	503	466
Asian	4,003	2,516	1,487
Black	13,993	6,547	7,446
Hispanic	12,739	6,439	6,300
Non-Hispanic white	79,333	59,905	19,427
PERCENT DISTRIBUTION BY HOMEOWNERSHIP STATUS			
Total households	**100.0%**	**68.4%**	**31.6%**
American Indian	100.0	51.9	48.1
Asian	100.0	62.9	37.1
Black	100.0	46.8	53.2
Hispanic	100.0	50.5	49.5
Non-Hispanic white	100.0	75.5	24.5
PERCENT DISTRIBUTION BY RACE AND HISPANIC ORIGIN			
Total households	**100.0%**	**100.0%**	**100.0%**
American Indian	0.9	0.7	1.3
Asian	3.6	3.3	4.2
Black	12.5	8.6	21.0
Hispanic	11.4	8.4	17.8
Non-Hispanic white	71.0	78.4	54.9

Note: 2009 data are the latest available on the number of owners and renters by race and Hispanic origin. American Indians, Asians, blacks, and whites are those who identified themselves as being of the race alone.
Source: Bureau of the Census, American Housing Survey for the United States: 2009, Internet site http://www.census.gov/hhes/ www/housing/ahs/ahs09/ahs09.html; calculations by New Strategist

Homeownership Rises with Income

Because educated householders tend to be the most affluent, homeownership also rises with education.

Despite troubles in the housing market and the rise in foreclosures, most Americans are homeowners in all but the lowest-income groups. In 2009, renters outnumbered homeowners only among households with incomes below $15,000. The higher the income, the higher the homeownership rate, with the proportion climbing to 92 percent among households with incomes of $120,000 or more.

Homeownership also rises with education, although not as sharply. Among householders without a high school diploma, 56 percent are homeowners. Among those with a graduate degree the figure is 81 percent.

Native-born Americans are more likely to be homeowners than U.S. residents born in another country. Nevertheless, the 55 percent majority of immigrants are homeowners.

■ Among immigrants who came to the United States before 1995, from 54 to 74 percent are homeowners.

Ninety percent of the most affluent householders own their home

(percent distribution of households with incomes of $100,000 or more by homeownership status, 2009)

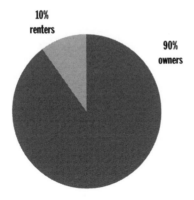

10%
renters

90%
owners

Table 4.5 Household Income by Homeownership Status, 2009

(number and percent distribution of households by household income and homeownership status, 2009; numbers in thousands)

	total	owner	renter
Total households	**111,806**	**76,428**	**35,378**
Less than $5,000	5,849	2,539	3,310
$5,000 to $9,999	4,683	1,884	2,799
$10,000 to $14,999	5,963	2,788	3,175
$15,000 to $19,999	6,062	3,123	2,940
$20,000 to $24,999	5,961	3,110	2,850
$25,000 to $29,999	7,637	4,507	3,131
$30,000 to $34,999	5,966	3,600	2,366
$35,000 to $39,999	5,593	3,482	2,111
$40,000 to $49,999	10,290	6,852	3,438
$50,000 to $59,999	8,654	6,328	2,326
$60,000 to $79,999	13,780	10,535	3,244
$80,000 to $99,999	10,073	8,409	1,663
$100,000 to $119,999	6,840	6,007	833
$120,000 or more	14,456	13,264	1,192
Median income	$47,000	$60,000	$28,400

PERCENT DISTRIBUTION BY HOMEOWNERSHIP STATUS

	total	owner	renter
Total households	**100.0%**	**68.4%**	**31.6%**
Less than $5,000	100.0	43.4	56.6
$5,000 to $9,999	100.0	40.2	59.8
$10,000 to $14,999	100.0	46.8	53.2
$15,000 to $19,999	100.0	51.5	48.5
$20,000 to $24,999	100.0	52.2	47.8
$25,000 to $29,999	100.0	59.0	41.0
$30,000 to $34,999	100.0	60.3	39.7
$35,000 to $39,999	100.0	62.3	37.7
$40,000 to $49,999	100.0	66.6	33.4
$50,000 to $59,999	100.0	73.1	26.9
$60,000 to $79,999	100.0	76.5	23.5
$80,000 to $99,999	100.0	83.5	16.5
$100,000 to $119,999	100.0	87.8	12.2
$120,000 or more	100.0	91.8	8.2

	total	owner	renter
PERCENT DISTRIBUTION BY HOUSEHOLD INCOME			
Total households	**100.0%**	**100.0%**	**100.0%**
Less than $5,000	5.2	3.3	9.4
$5,000 to $9,999	4.2	2.5	7.9
$10,000 to $14,999	5.3	3.6	9.0
$15,000 to $19,999	5.4	4.1	8.3
$20,000 to $24,999	5.3	4.1	8.1
$25,000 to $29,999	6.8	5.9	8.8
$30,000 to $34,999	5.3	4.7	6.7
$35,000 to $39,999	5.0	4.6	6.0
$40,000 to $49,999	9.2	9.0	9.7
$50,000 to $59,999	7.7	8.3	6.6
$60,000 to $79,999	12.3	13.8	9.2
$80,000 to $99,999	9.0	11.0	4.7
$100,000 to $119,999	6.1	7.9	2.4
$120,000 or more	12.9	17.4	3.4

Source: Bureau of the Census, American Housing Survey for the United States: 2009, Internet site http://www.census.gov/hhes/ www/housing/ahs/ahs09/ahs09.html; calculations by New Strategist

Table 4.6 Educational Attainment of Householders by Homeownership Status, 2009

(number and percent distribution of households by educational attainment of householder and homeownership status, 2009; numbers in thousands)

	total	owner	renter
Total households	**111,806**	**76,428**	**35,378**
Not a high school graduate	15,229	8,542	6,687
High school graduate	34,389	22,665	11,724
Some college, no degree	19,583	12,659	6,924
Associate's degree	9,244	6,722	2,522
Bachelor's degree or more	33,361	25,840	7,521
Bachelor's degree	21,077	15,894	5,183
Graduate or professional degree	12,285	9,947	2,338

PERCENT DISTRIBUTION BY HOMEOWNERSHIP STATUS

Total households	**100.0%**	**68.4%**	**31.6%**
Not a high school graduate	100.0	56.1	43.9
High school graduate	100.0	65.9	34.1
Some college, no degree	100.0	64.6	35.4
Associate's degree	100.0	72.7	27.3
Bachelor's degree or more	100.0	77.5	22.5
Bachelor's degree	100.0	75.4	24.6
Graduate or professional degree	100.0	81.0	19.0

PERCENT DISTRIBUTION BY EDUCATIONAL ATTAINMENT

Total households	**100.0%**	**100.0%**	**100.0%**
Not a high school graduate	13.6	11.2	18.9
High school graduate	30.8	29.7	33.1
Some college, no degree	17.5	16.6	19.6
Associate's degree	8.3	8.8	7.1
Bachelor's degree or more	29.8	33.8	21.3
Bachelor's degree	18.9	20.8	14.7
Graduate or professional degree	11.0	13.0	6.6

Source: Bureau of the Census, American Housing Survey for the United States: 2009, Internet site http://www.census.gov/hhes/ www/housing/ahs/ahs09/ahs09.html; calculations by New Strategist

Table 4.7 Nativity of Householder by Homeownership Status, 2009

(number and percent distribution of households headed by native-born and immigrant householders by year of immigration and homeownership status, 2009; numbers in thousands)

	total	owner	renter
Total households	**111,806**	**76,428**	**35,378**
Native-born	97,495	68,602	28,893
Foreign-born	14,310	7,826	6,485
YEAR OF IMMIGRATION			
Total immigrant householders	**14,310**	**7,826**	**6,485**
2005 to 2009	1,129	156	973
2000 to 2004	2,060	659	1,402
1995 to 1999	2,056	998	1,058
1990 to 1994	1,926	1,037	889
1980 to 1989	3,342	2,175	1,167
1979 or earlier	3,797	2,801	996
PERCENT DISTRIBUTION BY HOMEOWNERSHIP STATUS			
Total households	**100.0%**	**68.4%**	**31.6%**
Native-born	100.0	70.4	29.6
Foreign-born	100.0	54.7	45.3
YEAR OF IMMIGRATION			
Total immigrant householders	**100.0%**	**54.7%**	**45.3%**
2005 to 2009	100.0	13.8	86.2
2000 to 2004	100.0	32.0	68.0
1995 to 1999	100.0	48.5	51.5
1990 to 1994	100.0	53.8	46.2
1980 to 1989	100.0	65.1	34.9
1979 or earlier	100.0	73.8	26.2

Source: Bureau of the Census, American Housing Survey for the United States: 2009, Internet site http://www.census.gov/hhes/ www/housing/ahs/ahs09/ahs09.html; calculations by New Strategist

Homeownership Is Highest in the Midwest

Central city households are least likely to own their home.

The Midwest has the highest homeownership rate in the nation—71 percent of households in the region owned their home in 2010. Homeownership rates are lowest in the West, at 61 percent.

Half of homeowners live in the suburbs. Seventy-four percent of suburban householders are homeowners, as are 75 percent of households in nonmetropolitan areas. In the nation's central cities, a much smaller 55 percent of households own their home.

The homeownership rate fell in most states between 2004 (when the overall homeownership rate peaked) and 2010. The biggest decline occurred in Nevada, where the homeownership rate fell 6 percentage points between 2004 and 2010. Homeownership rates increased in seven states during those years. The biggest gain took place in South Dakota—up 2.1 percentage points. In 2010, homeownership was highest in West Virginia (79 percent) and lowest in the District of Columbia (46 percent) and New York (55 percent).

The homeownership rate fell in most of the 75 largest metropolitan areas between 2005 (the earliest year for which data are available) and 2010. The biggest decline came in Toledo, Ohio, an 8.5 percentage point drop. The biggest gain occurred in Albany, New York, a 6.5 percentage point increase. Among the 75 largest metropolitan areas, the homeownership rate is highest in Akron, Ohio (77 percent) and lowest in Fresno, California (49 percent).

■ Despite the downturn in the housing market, homeownership rates are rising in some states and metropolitan areas.

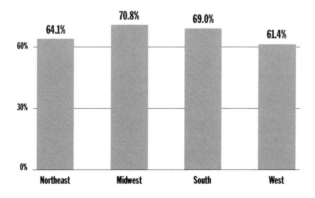

The West has the lowest homeownership rate

(percent of households that own their home, by region, 2010)

Table 4.8 Region of Residence by Homeownership Status, 2010

(number and percent distribution of households by region of residence and homeownership status, 2010; numbers in thousands)

	total	owner	renter
Total housholds	**111,860**	**74,791**	**37,069**
Northeast	20,431	13,102	7,329
Midwest	25,565	18,107	7,458
South	41,476	28,611	12,866
West	24,387	14,971	9,416
PERCENT DISTRIBUTION BY HOMEOWNERSHIP STATUS			
Total housholds	**100.0%**	**66.9%**	**33.1%**
Northeast	100.0	64.1	35.9
Midwest	100.0	70.8	29.2
South	100.0	69.0	31.0
West	100.0	61.4	38.6
PERCENT DISTRIBUTION BY REGION			
Total housholds	**100.0%**	**100.0%**	**100.0%**
Northeast	18.3	17.5	19.8
Midwest	22.9	24.2	20.1
South	37.1	38.3	34.7
West	21.8	20.0	25.4

Source: Bureau of the Census, Housing Vacancy Survey, Internet site http://www.census.gov/hhes/www/housing/hvs/hvs.html; calculations by New Strategist

Table 4.9 Metropolitan Residence by Homeownership Status, 2009

(number and percent distribution of households by metropolitan residence and homeownership status, 2009; numbers in thousands)

	total	owner	renter
Total households	**111,806**	**76,428**	**35,378**
In metropolitan areas	89,949	60,102	29,846
In central cities	32,645	17,809	14,837
In suburbs	57,303	42,294	15,009
Outside metropolitan areas	21,857	16,326	5,532

PERCENT DISTRIBUTION BY HOMEOWNERSHIP STATUS

Total households	**100.0%**	**68.4%**	**31.6%**
In metropolitan areas	100.0	66.8	33.2
In central cities	100.0	54.6	45.4
In suburbs	100.0	73.8	26.2
Outside metropolitan areas	100.0	74.7	25.3

PERCENT DISTRIBUTION BY METROPOLITAN RESIDENCE

Total households	**100.0%**	**100.0%**	**100.0%**
In metropolitan areas	80.5	78.6	84.4
In central cities	29.2	23.3	41.9
In suburbs	51.3	55.3	42.4
Outside metropolitan areas	19.5	21.4	15.6

Source: Bureau of the Census, American Housing Survey for the United States: 2009, Internet site http://www.census.gov/hhes/ www/housing/ahs/ahs09/ahs09.html; calculations by New Strategist

Table 4.10 Homeownership Rate by State, 2000 to 2010

(percent of householders who own their home by state, 2000 to 2010; percentage point change for selected years)

	2010	2004	2000	percentage point change 2000–10	2004–10
Total households	**66.9%**	**69.0%**	**67.4%**	**−0.5**	**−2.1**
Alabama	73.2	78.0	73.2	0.0	−4.8
Alaska	65.7	67.2	66.4	−0.7	−1.5
Arizona	66.6	68.7	68.0	−1.4	−2.1
Arkansas	67.9	69.1	68.9	−1.0	−1.2
California	56.1	59.7	57.1	−1.0	−3.6
Colorado	68.5	71.1	68.3	0.2	−2.6
Connecticut	70.8	71.7	70.0	0.8	−0.9
Delaware	74.7	77.3	72.0	2.7	−2.6
District of Columbia	45.6	45.6	41.9	3.7	0.0
Florida	69.3	72.2	68.4	0.9	−2.9
Georgia	67.1	70.9	69.8	−2.7	−3.8
Hawaii	56.1	60.6	55.2	0.9	−4.5
Idaho	72.4	73.7	70.5	1.9	−1.3
Illinois	68.8	72.7	67.9	0.9	−3.9
Indiana	71.2	75.8	74.9	−3.7	−4.6
Iowa	71.1	73.2	75.2	−4.1	−2.1
Kansas	67.4	69.9	69.3	−1.9	−2.5
Kentucky	70.3	73.3	73.4	−3.1	−3.0
Louisiana	70.4	70.6	68.1	2.3	−0.2
Maine	73.8	74.7	76.5	−2.7	−0.9
Maryland	68.9	72.1	69.9	−1.0	−3.2
Massachusetts	65.3	63.8	59.9	5.4	1.5
Michigan	74.5	77.1	77.2	−2.7	−2.6
Minnesota	72.6	76.4	76.1	−3.5	−3.8
Mississippi	74.8	74.0	75.2	−0.4	0.8
Missouri	71.2	72.4	74.2	−3.0	−1.2
Montana	68.1	72.4	70.2	−2.1	−4.3
Nebraska	70.4	71.2	70.2	0.2	−0.8
Nevada	59.7	65.7	64.0	−4.3	−6.0
New Hampshire	74.9	73.3	69.2	5.7	1.6
New Jersey	66.5	68.8	66.2	0.3	−2.3
New Mexico	68.6	71.5	73.7	−5.1	−2.9
New York	54.5	54.8	53.4	1.1	−0.3
North Carolina	69.5	69.8	71.1	−1.6	−0.3
North Dakota	67.1	70.0	70.7	−3.6	−2.9
Ohio	69.7	73.1	71.3	−1.6	−3.4
Oklahoma	69.2	71.1	72.7	−3.5	−1.9
Oregon	66.3	69.0	65.3	1.0	−2.7
Pennsylvania	72.2	74.9	74.7	−2.5	−2.7
Rhode Island	62.8	61.5	61.5	1.3	1.3

	2010	2004	2000	percentage point change	
				2000–10	2004–10
South Carolina	74.8%	76.2%	76.5%	−1.7	−1.4
South Dakota	70.6	68.5	71.2	−0.6	2.1
Tennessee	71.0	71.6	70.9	0.1	−0.6
Texas	65.3	65.5	63.8	1.5	−0.2
Utah	72.5	74.9	72.7	−0.2	−2.4
Vermont	73.6	72.0	68.7	4.9	1.6
Virginia	68.7	73.4	73.9	−5.2	−4.7
Washington	64.4	66.0	63.6	0.8	−1.6
West Virginia	79.0	80.3	75.9	3.1	−1.3
Wisconsin	71.0	73.3	71.8	−0.8	−2.3
Wyoming	73.4	72.8	71.0	2.4	0.6

Source: Bureau of the Census, Housing Vacancy Surveys, Internet site http://www.census.gov/hhes/www/housing/hvs/hvs.html; calculations by New Strategist

Table 4.11 Homeownership Rate by Metropolitan Area, 2005 and 2010

(percent of householders who own their home in the 75 largest metropolitan areas, 2005 and 2010; percentage point change, 2005–10)

	2010	2005	percentage point change 2005–10
Total inside metropolitan areas	**65.4%**	**67.4%**	**−2.0**
Akron, OH	76.9	78.1	−1.2
Albany–Schenectady–Troy, NY	72.8	66.3	6.5
Alburquerque, NM	65.5	69.2	−3.7
Allentown–Bethlehem–Easton, PA–NJ	71.5	73.5	−2.0
Atlanta–Sandy Springs–Marietta, GA	67.2	66.4	0.8
Austin–Round Rock, TX	65.8	63.9	1.9
Bakersfield, CA	61.7	60.5	1.2
Baltimore–Towson, MD	65.7	70.6	−4.9
Baton Rouge, LA	70.3	71.0	−0.7
Birmingham–Hoover, AL	76.2	75.1	1.1
Boston–Cambridge–Quincy, MA–NH	66.0	63.0	3.0
Bridgeport–Stamford–Norwalk, CT	71.3	68.2	3.1
Buffalo–Cheektowaga–Tonawanda, NY	64.5	66.3	−1.8
Charlotte–Gastonia–Concord, NC–SC	66.1	65.8	0.3
Chicago–Naperville–Joliet, IL	68.2	70.0	−1.8
Cincinnati–Middletown, OH–KY–IN	62.8	68.4	−5.6
Cleveland–Elyria–Mentor, OH	70.7	74.4	−3.7
Columbia, SC	74.1	76.3	−2.2
Columbus, OH	62.2	68.9	−6.7
Dallas–Fort Worth–Arlington, TX	63.8	62.3	1.5
Dayton, OH	67.4	66.1	1.3
Denver–Aurora, CO	65.7	70.7	−5.0
Detroit–Warren–Livonia, MI	73.6	75.1	−1.5
El Paso, TX	70.1	72.6	−2.5
Fresno, CA	49.3	51.8	−2.5
Grand Rapids–Wyoming, MI	76.4	72.6	3.8
Greensboro–High Point, NC	68.8	66.3	2.5
Hartford–West Hartford–East Hartford, CT	71.3	72.2	−0.9
Honolulu, HI	54.9	58.0	−3.1
Houston–Baytown–Sugar Land, TX	61.4	61.7	−0.3
Indianapolis, IN	68.8	77.1	−8.3
Jacksonville, FL	70.0	67.9	2.1
Kansas City, MO–KS	68.8	71.3	−2.5
Las Vegas–Paradise, NV	55.7	61.4	−5.7
Los Angeles–Long Beach–Santa Ana, CA	49.7	54.6	−4.9
Louisville, KY–IN	63.4	62.9	0.5
Memphis, TN–AR–MS	61.9	64.8	−2.9
Miami–Fort Lauderdale–Miami Beach, FL	63.8	69.2	−5.4
Milwaukee–Waukesha–West Allis, WI	62.4	65.7	−3.3
Minneapolis–St. Paul–Bloomington, MN–WI	71.2	74.9	−3.7

	2010	2005	percentage point change 2005–10
Nashville–Davidson–Murfreesboro, TN	70.4%	73.0%	–2.6
New Haven–Milford, CT	65.6	66.9	–1.3
New Orleans–Metairie–Kenner, LA	66.9	71.2	–4.3
New York–Northern New Jersey–Long Island, NY	51.6	54.6	–3.0
Oklahoma City, OK	70.0	72.9	–2.9
Omaha–Council Bluffs, NE–IA	73.2	69.7	3.5
Orlando, FL	70.8	70.5	0.3
Oxnard–Thousand Oaks–Ventura, CA	67.1	73.4	–6.3
Philadelphia–Camden–Wilmington, PA	70.7	73.5	–2.8
Phoenix–Mesa–Scottsdale, AZ	66.5	71.2	–4.7
Pittsburgh, PA	70.4	73.1	–2.7
Portland–Vancouver–Beaverton, OR–WA	63.7	68.3	–4.6
Poughkeepsie–Newburgh–Middletown, NJ	70.8	74.2	–3.4
Providence–New Bedford–Fall River, RI–MA	61.0	63.1	–2.1
Raleigh–Cary, NC	65.9	71.4	–5.5
Richmond, VA	68.1	69.7	–1.6
Riverside–San Bernardino–Ontario, CA	63.9	68.5	–4.6
Rochester, NY	71.4	74.9	–3.5
Sacramento–Arden–Arcade–Roseville, CA	61.1	64.1	–3.0
St. Louis, MO–IL	72.2	74.4	–2.2
Salt Lake City, UT	65.5	68.8	–3.3
San Antonio, TX	70.1	66.0	4.1
San Diego–Carlsbad–San Marcos, CA	54.4	60.5	–6.1
San Francisco–Oakland–Fremont, CA	58.0	57.8	0.2
San Jose–Sunnyvale–Santa Clara, CA	58.9	59.2	–0.3
Seattle–Bellevue–Everett, WA	60.9	64.5	–3.6
Springfield, MA	67.1	64.5	2.6
Syracuse, NY	61.1	59.8	1.3
Tampa–St. Petersburg–Clearwater, FL	68.3	71.7	–3.4
Toledo, OH	63.9	72.4	–8.5
Tucson, AZ	64.3	66.1	–1.8
Tulsa, OK	64.2	71.7	–7.5
Virginia Beach–Norfolk–Newport News, VA	61.4	68.0	–6.6
Washington–Arlington–Alexandria, DC–VA–MD–WV	67.3	68.4	–1.1
Worcester, MA	64.1	65.3	–1.2

Note: 2004 was the peak year for homeownership nationwide, but 2005 is the earliest year for which comparable metropolitan area data are available.
Source: Bureau of the Census, Housing Vacancy Survey, Internet site http://wwwcensusgov/hhes/www/housing/hvs/hvshtml; calculations by New Strategist

Most Americans Live in Single-Family Homes

Thirty-one percent of homes have a room used for business.

Nearly two out of three householders live in a single-family detached home, a reflection of the low population density in the United States compared to many other developed countries. Only 23 percent of householders live in apartments, while 5 percent reside in duplexes and another 6 percent in mobile homes. Not surprisingly, renters are far more likely than homeowners to live in apartments—63 versus just 5 percent.

American homes have a median of 1,800 square feet of living space. Sixty-four percent of housing units have three or more bedrooms and half have two or more bathrooms. Thirty-four percent of homeowners have a room they use for business, as do 23 percent of renters. One in four of the nation's occupied housing units was built in 1990 or later.

Natural gas is the main heating fuel for the 51 percent majority of households. Another 34 percent depend on electricity as their main heating fuel. Renters are far more likely than homeowners to heat with electricity—44 versus 29 percent.

■ The homes of Americans had been growing larger as families demanded more bathrooms, bedrooms, and rooms for business. The slump in the housing market has reversed that trend.

Two bathrooms are a must for most homeowners

(percent distribution of homeowners by number of bathrooms in home, 2009)

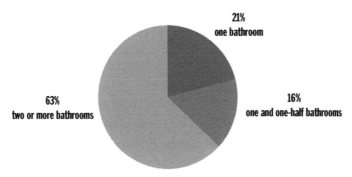

21%
one bathroom

16%
one and one-half bathrooms

63%
two or more bathrooms

Table 4.12 Units in Structure by Homeownership Status, 2009

(number and percent distribution of households by number of units in structure and homeownership status, 2009; numbers in thousands)

	total	owner	renter
Total households	**111,806**	**76,428**	**35,378**
One, detached	73,079	63,324	9,755
One, attached	5,973	3,952	2,021
Two to four	8,350	1,353	6,998
Five to nine	5,269	632	4,637
10 to 19	4,661	483	4,178
20 to 49	3,630	499	3,131
50 or more	4,004	768	3,237
Mobile home	6,839	5,418	1,421
PERCENT DISTRIBUTION BY HOMEOWNERSHIP STATUS			
Total households	**100.0%**	**68.4%**	**31.6%**
One, detached	100.0	86.7	13.3
One, attached	100.0	66.2	33.8
Two to four	100.0	16.2	83.8
Five to nine	100.0	12.0	88.0
10 to 19	100.0	10.4	89.6
20 to 49	100.0	13.7	86.3
50 or more	100.0	19.2	80.8
Mobile home	100.0	79.2	20.8
PERCENT DISTRIBUTION BY NUMBER OF UNITS IN STRUCTURE			
Total households	**100.0%**	**100.0%**	**100.0%**
One, detached	65.4	82.9	27.6
One, attached	5.3	5.2	5.7
Two to four	7.5	1.8	19.8
Five to nine	4.7	0.8	13.1
10 to 19	4.2	0.6	11.8
20 to 49	3.2	0.7	8.9
50 or more	3.6	1.0	9.1
Mobile home	6.1	7.1	4.0

Source: Bureau of the Census, American Housing Survey for the United States: 2009, Internet site http://www.census.gov/hhes/ www/housing/ahs/ahs09/ahs09.html; calculations by New Strategist

Table 4.13 Size of Housing Unit by Homeownership Status, 2009

(number and percent distribution of households by size and characteristics of unit and homeownership status, 2009; numbers in thousands)

	number			percent distribution		
	total	owner	renter	total	owner	renter
Total households	**111,806**	**76,428**	**35,378**	**100.0%**	**100.0%**	**100.0%**
Number of bedrooms						
None	789	45	744	0.7	0.1	2.1
One bedroom	11,434	1,714	9,720	10.2	2.2	27.5
Two bedrooms	27,671	13,471	14,200	24.7	17.6	40.1
Three bedrooms	48,082	39,723	8,359	43.0	52.0	23.6
Four or more bedrooms	23,830	21,475	2,354	21.3	28.1	6.7
Number of bathrooms						
None	403	175	229	0.4	0.2	0.6
One bathroom	38,662	15,767	22,894	34.6	20.6	64.7
One-and-one-half bathrooms	15,656	12,081	3,575	14.0	15.8	10.1
Two or more bathrooms	57,085	48,405	8,680	51.1	63.3	24.5
Room(s) used for business						
Total with room(s) used for business	34,148	26,108	8,040	30.5	34.2	22.7
Business only	15,236	11,479	3,757	13.6	15.0	10.6
Business and other use	18,912	14,629	4,283	16.9	19.1	12.1
Median square footage of unit	1,800	1,800	1,300	–	–	–
Median size of lot (acres)	0.27	0.32	0.22	–	–	–

Note: Square footage of unit and size of lot for single-family detached and mobile homes only; "–" means not applicable.
Source: Bureau of the Census, American Housing Survey for the United States: 2009, Internet site http://www.census.gov/hhes/ www/housing/ahs/ahs09/ahs09.html; calculations by New Strategist

Table 4.14 Year Unit Built by Homeownership Status, 2009

(number and percent distribution of households by year structure was built and homeownership status, 2009; numbers in thousands)

	total	owners	renters
Total households	**111,806**	**76,428**	**35,378**
2005 to 2009	5,884	4,601	1,283
2000 to 2004	8,102	6,371	1,731
1995 to 1999	7,825	6,221	1,603
1990 to 1994	5,995	4,715	1,280
1985 to 1989	7,648	5,159	2,489
1980 to 1984	6,380	4,201	2,179
1975 to 1979	11,835	7,471	4,364
1970 to 1974	9,413	5,696	3,718
1960 to 1969	13,326	8,917	4,409
1950 to 1959	11,771	8,528	3,243
1940 to 1949	6,745	4,423	2,322
1930 to 1939	4,828	2,904	1,924
1920 to 1929	4,331	2,520	1,811
1919 or earlier	7,724	4,703	3,021
Median year built	1974	1975	1971
PERCENT DISTRIBUTION			
Total households	**100.0%**	**100.0%**	**100.0%**
2005 to 2009	5.3	6.0	3.6
2000 to 2004	7.2	8.3	4.9
1995 to 1999	7.0	8.1	4.5
1990 to 1994	5.4	6.2	3.6
1985 to 1989	6.8	6.8	7.0
1980 to 1984	5.7	5.5	6.2
1975 to 1979	10.6	9.8	12.3
1970 to 1974	8.4	7.5	10.5
1960 to 1969	11.9	11.7	12.5
1950 to 1959	10.5	11.2	9.2
1940 to 1949	6.0	5.8	6.6
1930 to 1939	4.3	3.8	5.4
1920 to 1929	3.9	3.3	5.1
1919 or earlier	6.9	6.2	8.5

Source: Bureau of the Census, American Housing Survey for the United States: 2009, Internet site http://www.census.gov/hhes/ www/housing/ahs/ahs09/ahs09.html; calculations by New Strategist

Table 4.15 Fuels Used by Homeownership Status, 2009

(number and percent of households by fuels used and homeownership status, 2009; numbers in thousands)

	total	owner	renter
Total households	**111,806**	**76,428**	**35,378**
Electricity	111,746	76,378	35,368
Piped gas	67,886	46,700	21,186
Bottled gas	9,816	8,391	1,425
Fuel oil	9,208	6,409	2,800
Kerosene or other liquid fuel	616	451	164
Coal or coke	104	97	7
Wood	1,787	1,510	278
Solar energy	147	130	17
Other	405	254	151
All-electric homes	30,166	17,951	12,216

PERCENT USING FUEL

	total	owner	renter
Total households	**100.0%**	**100.0%**	**100.0%**
Electricity	99.9	99.9	100.0
Piped gas	60.7	61.1	59.9
Fuel oil	8.8	11.0	4.0
Wood	8.2	8.4	7.9
Bottled gas	0.6	0.6	0.5
Kerosene or other liquid fuel	0.1	0.1	0.0
Coal or coke	1.6	2.0	0.8
Solar energy	0.1	0.2	0.0
Other	0.4	0.3	0.4
All-electric homes	27.0	23.5	34.5

Note: Figures do not add to total because many householders use more than one fuel.
Source: Bureau of the Census, American Housing Survey for the United States: 2009, Internet site http://www.census.gov/hhes/www/housing/ahs/ahs09/ahs09.html; calculations by New Strategist

Table 4.16 Main Heating Fuel Used by Homeownership Status, 2009

(number and percent distribution of households by main heating fuel used and homeownership status, 2009; numbers in thousands)

	total	owner	renter
Households using heating fuel	**111,420**	**76,222**	**35,198**
Electricity	37,851	22,219	15,632
Piped gas	56,806	41,233	15,573
Bottled gas	5,817	4,889	929
Fuel oil	8,214	5,693	2,521
Kerosene or other liquid fuel	599	444	154
Coal or coke	98	91	7
Wood	1,780	1,503	277
Solar energy	11	8	3
Other	243	142	101

PERCENT DISTRIBUTION BY HOMEOWNERSHIP STATUS

Households using heating fuel	**100.0%**	**68.4%**	**31.6%**
Electricity	100.0	58.7	41.3
Piped gas	100.0	72.6	27.4
Bottled gas	100.0	84.0	16.0
Fuel oil	100.0	69.3	30.7
Kerosene or other liquid fuel	100.0	74.2	25.8
Coal or coke	100.0	92.8	7.2
Wood	100.0	84.4	15.6
Solar energy	100.0	73.7	26.3
Other	100.0	58.4	41.6

PERCENT DISTRIBUTION BY PRIMARY HEATING FUEL

Households using heating fuel	**100.0%**	**100.0%**	**100.0%**
Electricity	34.0	29.2	44.4
Piped gas	51.0	54.1	44.2
Bottled gas	5.2	6.4	2.6
Fuel oil	7.4	7.5	7.2
Kerosene or other liquid fuel	0.5	0.6	0.4
Coal or coke	0.1	0.1	0.0
Wood	1.6	2.0	0.8
Solar energy	0.0	0.0	0.0
Other	0.2	0.2	0.3

Source: Bureau of the Census, American Housing Survey for the United States: 2009, Internet site http://www.census.gov/hhes/ www/housing/ahs/ahs09/ahs09.html; calculations by New Strategist

American Households Are Well Equipped

Most have dishwashers, clothes washers, and clothes dryers.

American households are well equipped with appliances and have a variety of other amenities. Eighty-five percent of households have a porch, deck, balcony, or patio. Sixty-six percent have a garage or carport. Thirty-five percent have a useable fireplace.

Not surprisingly, homeowners are more likely than renters to have various amenities. The 57 percent majority of homeowners have a separate dining room, while the figure is just 28 percent for renters. Seventy-two percent of homeowners have central air conditioning compared with 51 percent of renters. Nearly one in five renters do not have a vehicle compared with just 3 percent of homeowners.

■ Many Americans now think air conditioning is a necessity rather than a luxury.

Most American homes have central air conditioning

(percent of households with central air conditioning, by homeownership status, 2009)

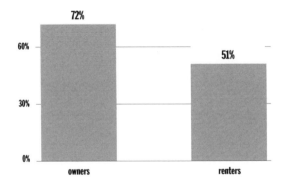

Table 4.17 Kitchen, Laundry, and Safety Equipment by Homeownership Status, 2009

(number and percent of total households by presence of kitchen, laundry, and safety equipment and homeownership status, 2009; numbers in thousands)

	total	owner	renter
Total households	**111,806**	**76,428**	**35,378**
With complete kitchen equipment	110,054	76,050	34,004
Dishwasher	73,584	57,191	16,393
Disposal in kitchen sink	56,531	40,597	15,933
Trash compactor	3,896	3,166	730
Washing machine	93,372	73,826	19,545
Clothes dryer	90,905	72,562	18,343
Working smoke detector	104,362	71,797	32,565
Fire extinguisher	49,902	37,922	11,980
Working carbon monoxide detector	40,698	31,691	9,007
Sprinkler system	5,167	2,086	3,081
PERCENT WITH EQUIPMENT			
Total households	**100.0%**	**100.0%**	**100.0%**
With complete kitchen equipment	98.4	99.5	96.1
Dishwasher	65.8	74.8	46.3
Disposal in kitchen sink	50.6	53.1	45.0
Trash compactor	3.5	4.1	2.1
Washing machine	83.5	96.6	55.2
Clothes dryer	81.3	94.9	51.8
Working smoke detector	93.3	93.9	92.0
Fire extinguisher	44.6	49.6	33.9
Working carbon monoxide detector	36.4	41.5	25.5
Sprinkler system	4.6	2.7	8.7

Note: Complete kitchen equipment includes a sink, refrigerator, and oven or burners.
Source: Bureau of the Census, American Housing Survey for the United States: 2009, Internet site http://www.census.gov/hhes/www/housing/ahs/ahs09/ahs09.html; calculations by New Strategist

Table 4.18 Amenities of Home by Homeownership Status, 2009

(number and percent of households with selected amenities by homeownership status, 2009; numbers in thousands)

	total	owners	renters
Total households	**111,806**	**76,428**	**35,378**
Telephone	109,325	75,129	34,196
Car, truck, or van	103,068	74,359	28,709
Porch, deck, balcony, or patio	95,406	70,421	24,984
Garage or carport	74,236	60,979	13,258
Separate dining room	53,676	43,717	9,959
Usable fireplace	38,998	34,458	4,540
Two or more living or recreation rooms	33,912	30,978	2,934
PERCENT WITH AMENITY			
Total households	**100.0%**	**100.0%**	**100.0%**
Telephone	97.8	98.3	96.7
Car, truck, or van	92.2	97.3	81.1
Porch, deck, balcony, or patio	85.3	92.1	70.6
Garage or carport	66.4	79.8	37.5
Separate dining room	48.0	57.2	28.2
Usable fireplace	34.9	45.1	12.8
Two or more living or recreation rooms	30.3	40.5	8.3

Source: Bureau of the Census, American Housing Survey for the United States: 2009, Internet site http://www.census.gov/hhes/ www/housing/ahs/ahs09/ahs09.html; calculations by New Strategist

Table 4.19 Air Conditioning by Homeownership Status, 2009

(number and percent of households with air conditioning by homeownership status, 2009; numbers in thousands)

	total	owner	renter
Total households	**111,806**	**76,428**	**35,378**
With any air conditioning	97,390	68,355	29,035
With central air conditioning	72,808	54,647	18,161
With room units	24,582	13,707	10,875
One room unit	11,532	5,303	6,229
Two room units	8,132	4,800	3,332
Three or more room units	4,918	3,604	1,314
PERCENT DISTRIBUTION			
Total households	**100.0%**	**100.0%**	**100.0%**
With any air conditioning	87.1	89.4	82.1
With central air conditioning	65.1	71.5	51.3
With room units	22.0	17.9	30.7
One room unit	10.3	6.9	17.6
Two room units	7.3	6.3	9.4
Three or more room units	4.4	4.7	3.7

Source: Bureau of the Census, American Housing Survey for the United States: 2009, Internet site http://www.census.gov/hhes/ www/housing/ahs/ahs09/ahs09.html; calculations by New Strategist

Most Are Satisfied with Home and Neighborhood

Homeowners are happier than renters, but few renters are dissatisfied.

When asked how they would rate their housing unit on a scale of 1 (worst) to 10 (best), 71 percent of householders rate their home an 8 or higher. Homeowners rate their home more highly than renters. While 77 percent of homeowners rate their home an 8 or higher, a smaller 59 percent of renters are that positive. Thirty-one percent of homeowners, but only 20 percent of renters, give their home a 10. Although few rate their home a 5 or less on the 10-point scale, those who do are primarily renters.

The patterns are the same when householders are asked to rate their neighborhood. Sixty-eight percent of householders rate their neighborhood an 8 or higher, including 72 percent of homeowners and 60 percent of renters. Among the few householders who rate their neighborhood at 5 or below, the majority are renters.

■ Householders are likely to rate their homes and neighborhoods highly because most of those who are unhappy find new places to live.

Most householders rate their home and neighborhood highly

(percent of householders who rate their home and neighborhood an 8 or higher on a scale of 1 (worst) to 10 (best), by homeownership status, 2009)

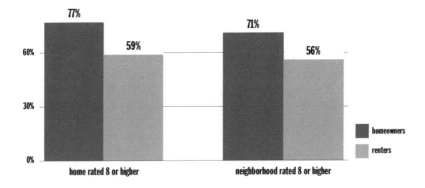

Table 4.20 Opinion of Housing Unit by Homeownership Status, 2009

(number and percent distribution of households by householder's opinion of housing unit and homeownership status, 2009; numbers in thousands)

	total	owner	renter
Total households	**111,806**	**76,428**	**35,378**
1 (worst)	530	203	327
2	331	122	209
3	611	175	436
4	1,153	444	708
5	5,275	2,365	2,910
6	5,208	2,655	2,553
7	15,045	8,899	6,146
8	30,667	21,042	9,625
9	17,844	13,627	4,217
10 (best)	30,909	23,967	6,941

PERCENT DISTRIBUTION BY HOMEOWNERSHIP STATUS

	total	owner	renter
Total households	**100.0%**	**68.4%**	**31.6%**
1 (worst)	100.0	38.4	61.6
2	100.0	37.0	63.0
3	100.0	28.6	71.4
4	100.0	38.6	61.4
5	100.0	44.8	55.2
6	100.0	51.0	49.0
7	100.0	59.1	40.9
8	100.0	68.6	31.4
9	100.0	76.4	23.6
10 (best)	100.0	77.5	22.5

PERCENT DISTRIBUTION BY OPINION OF HOUSING UNIT

	total	owner	renter
Total households	**100.0%**	**100.0%**	**100.0%**
1 (worst)	0.5	0.3	0.9
2	0.3	0.2	0.6
3	0.5	0.2	1.2
4	1.0	0.6	2.0
5	4.7	3.1	8.2
6	4.7	3.5	7.2
7	13.5	11.6	17.4
8	27.4	27.5	27.2
9	16.0	17.8	11.9
10 (best)	27.6	31.4	19.6

Note: Numbers do not add to total because "not reported" is not shown.
Source: Bureau of the Census, American Housing Survey for the United States: 2009, Internet site http://www.census.gov/hhes/www/housing/ahs/ahs09/ahs09.html; calculations by New Strategist

Table 4.21 Opinion of Neighborhood by Homeownership Status, 2009

(number and percent distribution of households by householder's opinion of neighborhood and homeownership status, 2009; numbers in thousands)

	total	owner	renter
Total households	**111,806**	**76,428**	**35,378**
1 (worst)	837	338	499
2	637	289	348
3	1,002	459	543
4	1,633	766	867
5	6,332	3,356	2,976
6	5,919	3,454	2,465
7	14,767	9,603	5,164
8	29,794	20,808	8,986
9	18,017	13,454	4,563
10 (best)	28,465	20,891	7,575

PERCENT DISTRIBUTION BY HOMEOWNERSHIP STATUS

	total	owner	renter
Total households	**100.0%**	**68.4%**	**31.6%**
1 (worst)	100.0	40.4	59.6
2	100.0	45.4	54.6
3	100.0	45.8	54.2
4	100.0	46.9	53.1
5	100.0	53.0	47.0
6	100.0	58.3	41.7
7	100.0	65.0	35.0
8	100.0	69.8	30.2
9	100.0	74.7	25.3
10 (best)	100.0	73.4	26.6

PERCENT DISTRIBUTION BY OPINION OF NEIGHBORHOOD

	total	owner	renter
Total households	**100.0%**	**100.0%**	**100.0%**
1 (worst)	0.7	0.4	1.4
2	0.6	0.4	1.0
3	0.9	0.6	1.5
4	1.5	1.0	2.5
5	5.7	4.4	8.4
6	5.3	4.5	7.0
7	13.2	12.6	14.6
8	26.6	27.2	25.4
9	16.1	17.6	12.9
10 (best)	25.5	27.3	21.4

Note: Numbers do not add to total because "not reported" and "no neighborhood" are not shown.
Source: Bureau of the Census, American Housing Survey for the United States: 2009, Internet site http://www.census.gov/hhes/ www/housing/ahs/ahs09/ahs09.html; calculations by New Strategist

Many People Live Near Open Space, Woodlands

Street noise and crime bother renters more than homeowners.

Of the 112 million households in the United States, 86 percent report having single-family detached houses within 300 feet of their home—90 percent of homeowners and 76 percent of renters. Forty-three percent of homeowners and 36 percent of renters report having open space, park, woods, farm, or ranchland close by.

A minority of households report bothersome neighborhood problems. The most common problem is street noise or traffic, reported by 20 percent of homeowners and 29 percent of renters. Crime ranks second and is considered a serious neighborhood problem by 15 percent of homeowners and 22 percent of renters.

Some public services are more readily available to renters than homeowners. Public transportation is available to only 47 percent of homeowners, for example, but to a much larger 70 percent of renters. Both owners and renters are about equally satisfied with police protection in their area. Most parents of children under age 14 are also satisfied with the local elementary school.

■ The lack of public transportation in many parts of the United States makes owning a car a necessity.

Most homeowners do not have public transportation available to them

(percent of households with public transportation available in the area, by homeownership status, 2009)

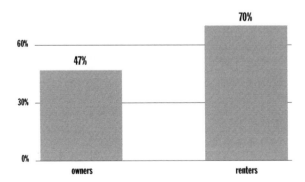

Table 4.22 Characteristics of Neighborhood by Homeownership Status, 2009

(number and percent of households by description of area within 300 feet and homeownership status, 2009; numbers in thousands)

	total	owner	renter
Total households	**111,806**	**76,428**	**35,378**
Single-family detached houses	95,916	68,909	27,007
Single-family attached	21,832	10,973	10,860
Multiunit residential buildings	33,635	11,514	22,121
One-to-three-story multiunit is tallest	25,143	9,014	16,130
Four-to-six-story multiunit is tallest	4,937	1,464	3,473
Seven-or-more-story multiunit is tallest	3,172	929	2,243
Mobile homes	13,388	10,276	3,112
Commercial or institutional establishments	35,649	16,992	18,657
Industrial sites or factories	5,376	2,520	2,856
Open space, park, woods, farm, or ranch	45,816	33,110	12,706
Four-or-more-lane highway, railroad, or airport	19,612	10,380	9,232
Water in area	18,656	13,824	4,832
Waterfront property	3,331	2,653	678
PERCENT WITH NEIGHBORHOOD CHARACTERISTIC			
Total households	**100.0%**	**100.0%**	**100.0%**
Single-family detached houses	85.8	90.2	76.3
Single-family attached	19.5	14.4	30.7
Multiunit residential buildings	30.1	15.1	62.5
One-to-three-story multiunit is tallest	22.5	11.8	45.6
Four-to-six-story multiunit is tallest	4.4	1.9	9.8
Seven-or-more-story multiunit is tallest	2.8	1.2	6.3
Mobile homes	12.0	13.4	8.8
Commerical or institutional establishments	31.9	22.2	52.7
Industrial sites or factories	4.8	3.3	8.1
Open space, park, woods, farm, or ranch	41.0	43.3	35.9
Four-or-more-lane highway, railroad, or airport	17.5	13.6	26.1
Water in area	16.7	18.1	13.7
Waterfront property	3.0	3.5	1.9

Note: Numbers may not add to total because of nonresponse.
Source: Bureau of the Census, American Housing Survey for the United States: 2009, Internet site http://www.census.gov/hhes/www/housing/ahs/ahs09/ahs09.html; calculations by New Strategist

Table 4.23 Neighborhood Problems by Homeownership Status, 2009

(number and percent of households with neighborhood problems, by homeownership status, 2009; numbers in thousands)

	total	owner	renter
Total households	**111,806**	**76,428**	**35,378**
Bothersome street noise or heavy traffic	25,381	15,223	10,158
Serious crime in past 12 months	19,299	11,649	7,650
Bothersome smoke, gas, or bad smells	5,434	3,278	2,156
Noise problem	2,950	1,733	1,217
Litter or housing deterioration	1,691	1,101	590
Poor city or county services	694	440	254
Undesirable commercial, institutional, industrial establishments	415	247	168
People problem	4,521	2,706	1,815
PERCENT PROBLEM			
Total households	**100.0%**	**100.0%**	**100.0%**
Bothersome street noise or heavy traffic	22.7	19.9	28.7
Serious crime in past 12 months	17.3	15.2	21.6
Bothersome smoke, gas, or bad smells	4.9	4.3	6.1
Noise problem	2.6	2.3	3.4
Litter or housing deterioration	1.5	1.4	1.7
Poor city or county services	0.6	0.6	0.7
Undesirable commercial, institutional, industrial establishments	0.4	0.3	0.5
People problem	4.0	3.5	5.1

Source: Bureau of the Census, American Housing Survey for the United States: 2009, Internet site http://www.census.gov/hhes/ www/housing/ahs/ahs09/ahs09.html; calculations by New Strategist

Table 4.24 Public Services in Neighborhood by Homeownership Status, 2009

(number and percent of households by public services in neighborhood and homeownership status, 2009; numbers in thousands)

	total	owner	renter
Total households	**111,806**	**76,428**	**35,378**
With public transportation in area	60,257	35,616	24,641
Household uses public transportation regularly	10,212	3,817	6,395
Grocery or drug stores within 15 minutes of home	106,737	72,548	34,189
Satisfactory police protection in area	101,373	69,633	31,740
PERCENT WITH SERVICES			
Total households	**100.0%**	**100.0%**	**100.0%**
With public transportation	53.9	46.6	69.6
Household uses public transportation regularly	9.1	5.0	18.1
Grocery or drug stores within 15 minutes of home	95.5	94.9	96.6
Satisfactory police protection	90.7	91.1	89.7

Source: Bureau of the Census, American Housing Survey for the United States: 2009, Internet site http://www.census.gov/hhes/ www/housing/ahs/ahs09/ahs09.html; calculations by New Strategist

Table 4.25 Public School in Neighborhood by Homeownership Status, 2009

(number and percent distribution of households with children by type of school attended, opinion of public school in area, and homeownership status, 2009; numbers in thousands)

	number			percent distribution		
	total	owner	renter	total	owner	renter
SCHOOL ATTENDANCE						
Households with children aged 5 to 15	**26,636**	**18,509**	**8,127**	**100.0%**	**100.0%**	**100.0%**
Attend public school (K–12)	22,140	14,932	7,208	83.1	80.7	88.7
Attend private school (K–12)	2,583	2,203	380	9.7	11.9	4.7
Attend ungraded school, preschool	438	327	111	1.6	1.8	1.4
Home schooled	382	294	88	1.4	1.6	1.1
Not in school	497	317	180	1.9	1.7	2.2
OPINION OF SCHOOL						
Households with children aged 0 to 13	**30,976**	**20,490**	**10,486**	**100.0**	**100.0**	**100.0**
Satisfactory public elementary school	25,297	16,966	8,331	81.7	82.8	79.5
Unsatisfactory public elementary school	2,146	1,422	724	6.9	6.9	6.9
DISTANCE TO SCHOOL						
Households with children aged 0 to 13	**30,976**	**20,490**	**10,486**	**100.0**	**100.0**	**100.0**
Public elementary school less than one mile from home	18,667	11,571	7,096	60.3	56.5	67.7
Public elementary school one mile or more from home	10,526	7,785	2,741	34.0	38.0	26.1

Note: Numbers may not add to total because "not reported" is not shown.
Source: Bureau of the Census, American Housing Survey for the United States: 2009, Internet site http://www.census.gov/hhes/www/housing/ahs/ahs09/ahs09.html; calculations by New Strategist

Few Americans Live in Gated Communities

Among those who do, most are renters.

Overall, 15 percent of the nation's renters and 7 percent of homeowners live in gated communities. About half of those living in gated communities have a special system in place that allows them entry into their community. The rest depend on walls or fences alone to keep intruders out.

Among the 46 million households with people aged 55 or older, only 7 percent are in communities with age restrictions. Again, renters are more likely than homeowners to live in age-restricted communities, many of them in senior-citizen apartment complexes.

Many households are in communities that offer a variety of services and amenities. Twenty-two percent have a community center or clubhouse available to them, 19 percent have trails, 14 percent have a daycare center, and 19 percent have a private park, beach, or shoreline.

■ To attract buyers during the housing boom, home builders added amenities to their developments, which are evident in these statistics.

Renters are more likely than homeowners to live in a gated community

(percent of households living in a community where access is secured by walls or fences, by homeownership status, 2009)

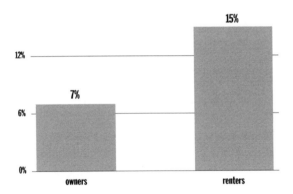

Table 4.26 Characteristics of Community by Homeownership Status, 2009

(number and percent distribution of households by community characteristics and homeownership status, 2009; numbers in thousands)

	number			percent distribution		
	total	owner	renter	total	owner	renter
SECURED COMMUNITIES						
Total households	**111,806**	**76,428**	**35,378**	**100.0%**	**100.0%**	**100.0%**
Community access secured with walls or fences	10,759	5,337	5,422	9.6	7.0	15.3
Special entry system present	6,091	2,682	3,410	5.4	3.5	9.6
Special entry system not present	4,653	2,648	2,005	4.2	3.5	5.7
Community access not secured	100,124	70,410	29,714	89.6	92.1	84.0
SENIOR CITIZEN COMMUNITIES						
Households with persons aged 55 or older	**45,684**	**36,591**	**9,093**	**100.0**	**100.0**	**100.0**
Community age restricted	3,080	1,457	1,624	6.7	4.0	17.9
No age restriction	42,603	35,134	7,469	93.3	96.0	82.1
Community age specific	10,302	8,867	1,435	22.6	24.2	15.8
Community not age specific	29,683	24,100	5,583	65.0	65.9	61.4
COMMUNITY AMENITIES						
Total households	**111,806**	**76,428**	**35,378**	**100.0**	**100.0**	**100.0**
Community center or clubhouse	24,410	14,707	9,703	21.8	19.2	27.4
Golf in community	16,709	12,762	3,947	14.9	16.7	11.2
Trails in community	21,609	15,300	6,309	19.3	20.0	17.8
Shuttle bus available	9,933	5,718	4,215	8.9	7.5	11.9
Daycare center	15,883	10,633	5,249	14.2	13.9	14.8
Private or restricted beach, park, or shoreline	21,432	15,124	6,308	19.2	19.8	17.8

Note: Numbers may not add to total because "not reported" is not shown.
Source: Bureau of the Census, American Housing Survey for the United States: 2009, Internet site http://www.census.gov/hhes/ www/housing/ahs/ahs09/ahs09.html; calculations by New Strategist

Monthly Housing Costs Are Higher for Homeowners

But renters devote a much larger share of their income to housing.

Homeowners had median monthly housing costs of $1,000 in 2009, while the median for renters was a smaller $808. Because homeowners have higher incomes than renters, however, housing costs absorb only 21 percent of the monthly income of owners versus a larger 34 percent of renters' income.

Homeowners pay more than renters for utilities, in large part because their homes are bigger. Homeowners pay a median of $117 per month for electricity, for example, versus the $84 paid by renters. The 95 percent of homeowners who have property insurance pay a median of $55 a month for coverage. Just 27 percent of renters have property insurance, which costs them a median of $16 per month.

■ Homeowners who have paid off their mortgages have much lower monthly housing costs than those with mortgages.

One in four homeowners pays less than $500 per month for housing

(percent distribution of homeowners by total monthly housing costs, 2009)

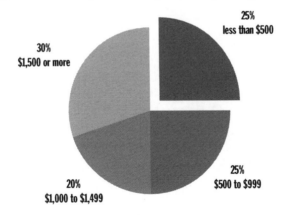

25%
less than $500

30%
$1,500 or more

25%
$500 to $999

20%
$1,000 to $1,499

Table 4.27 Monthly Housing Costs by Homeownership Status, 2009

(number and percent distribution of households by monthly housing costs and housing costs as a percent of current income, by homeownership status, 2009; households in thousands)

	number			percent distribution		
	total	owner	renter	total	owner	renter
MONTHLY HOUSING COSTS						
Total households	**111,806**	**76,428**	**35,378**	**100.0%**	**100.0%**	**100.0%**
Less than $300	10,344	7,987	2,357	9.3	10.5	6.7
$300 to $499	14,782	11,329	3,453	13.2	14.8	9.8
$500 to $799	22,240	11,738	10,502	19.9	15.4	29.7
$800 to $999	13,200	7,139	6,060	11.8	9.3	17.1
$1,000 to $1,249	12,933	8,156	4,777	11.6	10.7	13.5
$1,250 to $1,499	9,459	6,828	2,631	8.5	8.9	7.4
$1,500 to $1,999	11,692	9,445	2,247	10.5	12.4	6.4
$2,000 to $2,499	6,140	5,422	718	5.5	7.1	2.0
$2,500 or more	8,980	8,383	596	8.0	11.0	1.7
No cash rent	2,037	–	2,037	1.8	–	5.8
Median monthly costs	$909	$1,000	$808	–	–	–

	number			percent distribution		
	total	owner	renter	total	owner	renter
MONTHLY HOUSING COSTS AS A PERCENT OF CURRENT INCOME						
Total households	**111,806**	**76,428**	**35,378**	**100.0%**	**100.0%**	**100.0%**
Less than 5 percent	3,065	2,903	162	2.7	3.8	0.5
5 to 9 percent	10,334	9,614	721	9.2	12.6	2.0
10 to 14 percent	13,111	11,147	1,964	11.7	14.6	5.6
15 to 19 percent	14,210	10,986	3,224	12.7	14.4	9.1
20 to 24 percent	13,271	9,589	3,682	11.9	12.5	10.4
25 to 29 percent	10,775	7,167	3,608	9.6	9.4	10.2
30 to 34 percent	8,116	5,160	2,956	7.3	6.8	8.4
35 to 39 percent	6,071	3,753	2,317	5.4	4.9	6.6
40 to 49 percent	7,851	4,529	3,322	7.0	5.9	9.4
50 to 59 percent	4,859	2,649	2,210	4.3	3.5	6.2
60 to 69 percent	3,099	1,676	1,423	2.8	2.2	4.0
70 to 99 percent	4,795	2,380	2,415	4.3	3.1	6.8
100 percent or more	8,091	4,016	4,076	7.2	5.3	11.5
Median percent of current income	24%	21%	34%	–	–	–

Note: Housing costs include mortgages, rent, utilities, real estate taxes, property insurance, and regime fees; monthly cost as a percent of income excludes "no cash rent" and zero income; "–" means not applicable.
Source: Bureau of the Census, American Housing Survey for the United States: 2009, Internet site http://www.census.gov/hhes/www/housing/ahs/ahs09/ahs09.html; calculations by New Strategist

Table 4.28 Monthly Utility and Property Insurance Costs by Homeownership Status, 2009

(total number of households, number and percent with utility or insurance expense, and median monthly cost of utility or insurance for households with expense, by homeownership status, 2009; numbers in thousands)

	total	owner	renter
Total households	**111,806**	**76,428**	**35,378**
Electricity			
Number with electricity	111,746	76,378	35,368
Percent with electricity	99.9%	99.9%	100.0%
Median monthly cost of electricity	$107	$117	$84
Piped gas			
Number with piped gas	67,886	46,700	21,186
Percent with piped gas	60.7%	61.1%	59.9%
Median monthly cost of piped gas	$73	$80	$55
Fuel oil			
Number with fuel oil	9,208	6,409	2,800
Percent with fuel oil	8.2%	8.4%	7.9%
Median monthly cost of fuel oil	$133	$133	$100
Water			
Number paying for water separately	62,789	53,552	9,237
Percent paying for water separately	56.2%	70.1%	26.1%
Median monthly cost for water	$35	$38	$29
Trash			
Number paying for trash separately	52,525	44,974	7,551
Percent paying for trash separately	47.0%	58.8%	21.3%
Median monthly cost for trash removal	$21	$21	$20
Property insurance			
Number paying for property insurance	81,711	72,313	9,397
Percent paying for property insurance	73.1%	94.6%	26.6%
Median monthly cost for property insurance	$50	$55	$16

Source: Bureau of the Census, American Housing Survey for the United States: 2009, Internet site http://www.census.gov/hhes/www/housing/ahs/ahs09/ahs09.html; calculations by New Strategist

The Median Value of Owned Homes Fell Sharply

Most homeowners with mortgages owe less than their home is worth.

The median value of the homes owned by Americans stood at $170,000 in 2009, down from $191,471 in 2007—an 11 percent decline. Ten percent of homeowners report that their home is worth more than $500,000. With home values slipping, some of these homeowners may be overestimating the value of their home.

Homeowners paid a median of $107,500 for their home. Only 12 percent say they paid $300,000 or more.

Among the nation's 76 million homeowners, 63 percent have a mortgage on their home. Those with a mortgage have a median of 23 years left to pay it off. Median outstanding principal is $106,909. Homeowners with a mortgage in 2009 owed a median of 63 percent of the value of their home, up sharply from the 54 percent of 2007.

■ Although homeowners have seen their home's value decline, most still have considerable equity in their home.

Homeowners have less equity in their homes

(median current mortgage as a percent of home value, 2007 and 2009)

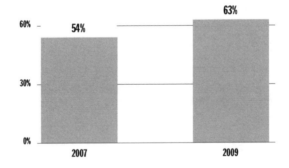

Table 4.29 Homeowners by Housing Value and Purchase Price, 2007 and 2009

(number and percent distribution of homeowners by value of home, purchase price, first-home status, and major source of down payment, 2007 and 2009; households in thousands)

	2009 number	2009 percent distribution	2007 number	2007 percent distribution
VALUE OF HOME				
Total homeowners	**76,428**	**100.0%**	**75,647**	**100.0%**
Under $100,000	19,685	25.8	18,779	24.8
$100,000 to $119,999	4,980	6.5	4,313	5.7
$120,000 to $149,999	7,629	10.0	6,735	8.9
$150,000 to $199,999	11,141	14.6	9,643	12.7
$200,000 to $299,999	13,494	17.7	13,132	17.4
$300,000 to $399,999	7,924	10.4	8,060	10.7
$400,000 to $499,999	4,200	5.5	4,740	6.3
$500,000 to $749,999	4,577	6.0	6,234	8.2
$750,000 or more	2,798	3.7	4,013	5.3
Median value	$170,000	–	$191,471	–
PURCHASE PRICE				
Total homes purchased or built	**71,877**	**100.0**	**70,334**	**100.0**
Under $50,000	17,168	23.9	17,976	25.6
$50,000 to $99,999	14,832	20.6	14,816	21.1
$100,000 to $119,999	4,288	6.0	4,216	6.0
$120,000 to $149,999	6,691	9.3	6,320	9.0
$150,000 to $199,999	8,055	11.2	7,581	10.8
$200,000 to $249,999	5,029	7.0	4,522	6.4
$250,000 to $299,999	3,024	4.2	2,820	4.0
$300,000 or more	8,594	12.0	7,483	10.6
Median purchase price	$107,500	–	$100,539	–
FIRST-HOME STATUS				
Total homeowners (reporting status)	**74,909**	**100.0**	**73,090**	**100.0**
First home	31,676	42.3	30,267	41.4
Not first home	43,233	57.7	42,823	58.6
MAJOR SOURCE OF DOWN PAYMENT				
Total homes purchased or built	**71,877**	**100.0**	**70,334**	**100.0**
Savings or cash on hand	31,437	43.7	31,005	44.1
Sale of previous home	21,946	30.5	22,897	32.6
Borrowing, other than mortgage on property	2,409	3.4	2,444	3.5
Inheritance or gift	1,358	1.9	1,375	2.0
Sale of other investment	750	1.0	737	1.0
Land where building built used for financing	639	0.9	584	0.8
Other	3,125	4.3	3,060	4.4
No down payment	8,346	11.6	6,616	9.4

	2009		2007	
	number	percent distribution	number	percent distribution
DOWN PAYMENT AS PERCENT OF PURCHASE PRICE				
Total homes purchased or built	**71,877**	**100.0%**	**70,334**	**100.0%**
No down payment	8,346	11.6	6,616	9.4
Less than three percent	5,034	7.0	4,700	6.7
Three to five percent	7,289	10.1	5,933	8.4
Six to 10 percent	9,895	13.8	8,545	12.1
11 to 15 percent	3,946	5.5	3,355	4.8
16 to 20 percent	8,200	11.4	6,881	9.8
21 to 40 percent	7,999	11.1	6,841	9.7
41 to 99 percent	4,478	6.2	3,904	5.6
Bought outright	6,377	8.9	5,668	8.1

Note: Numbers may not add to total because "not reported" is not shown; "–" means not applicable.
Source: Bureau of the Census, American Housing Survey for the United States: 2007 and 2009, Internet site http://www.census
.gov/hhes/www/housing/ahs/nationaldata.html; calculations by New Strategist

Table 4.30 Homeowners by Mortgage Characteristics, 2007 and 2009

(number and percent distribution of homeowners with mortgages by mortgage characteristics, 2007 and 2009; numbers in thousands)

	2009		2007	
	number	percent	number	percent
Total homeowners	**76,428**	**100.0%**	**75,647**	**100.0%**
Homeowners with mortgages	47,945	62.7	46,461	61.4
REMAINING YEARS MORTGAGED				
Homeowners with mortgages	**47,945**	**100.0**	**46,461**	**100.0**
Less than 8 years	6,160	12.8	5,981	12.9
8 to 12 years	5,188	10.8	5,549	11.9
13 to 17 years	5,077	10.6	4,602	9.9
18 to 22 years	6,568	13.7	4,879	10.5
23 to 27 years	14,948	31.2	12,263	26.4
28 to 32 years	9,569	20.0	12,791	27.5
33 years or more	164	0.3	241	0.5
Variable	271	0.6	156	0.3
Median years remaining	23	–	24	–
TOTAL OUTSTANDING PRINCIPAL				
Homeowners with mortgages	**47,945**	**100.0**	**46,461**	**100.0**
Under $10,000	2,797	5.8	3,122	6.7
$10,000 to $19,999	1,972	4.1	2,011	4.3
$20,000 to $29,999	1,877	3.9	2,038	4.4
$30,000 to $39,999	1,978	4.1	2,188	4.7
$40,000 to $49,999	2,338	4.9	2,220	4.8
$50,000 to $59,999	2,328	4.9	2,246	4.8
$60,000 to $69,999	2,504	5.2	2,373	5.1
$70,000 to $79,999	2,484	5.2	2,414	5.2
$80,000 to $99,999	4,420	9.2	4,447	9.6
$100,000 to $119,999	3,751	7.8	3,790	8.2
$120,000 to $149,999	5,029	10.5	4,751	10.2
$150,000 to $199,999	5,926	12.4	5,511	11.9
$200,000 to $249,999	3,575	7.5	3,081	6.6
$250,000 to $299,999	2,267	4.7	2,008	4.3
$300,000 or more	4,700	9.8	4,261	9.2
Median outstanding principal	$106,909	–	$100,904	–

	2009		2007	
	number	percent	number	percent
CURRENT TOTAL LOAN AS PERCENT OF VALUE				
Homeowners with mortgages	**47,945**	**100.0%**	**46,461**	**100.0%**
Less than 20 percent	6,174	12.9	7,204	15.5
20 to 39 percent	7,478	15.6	9,102	19.6
40 to 59 percent	8,524	17.8	9,626	20.7
60 to 79 percent	9,924	20.7	10,365	22.3
80 to 89 percent	5,128	10.7	4,489	9.7
90 to 99 percent	4,928	10.3	3,220	6.9
100 percent or more	5,789	12.1	2,456	5.3
Median percent of value	63.0%	–	54.4%	–

Note: "–" means not applicable.
Source: Bureau of the Census, American Housing Survey for the United States: 2007 and 2009, Internet site http://www.census
.gov/hhes/www/housing/ahs/nationaldata.html; calculations by New Strategist

5

Income Trends

■ Median household income fell between 2000 and 2009.

Householders aged 35 to 54 had a lower median income in 2009 than they did in 1990, after adjusting for inflation.

■ Four percent of households had an income of $200,000 or more in 2009.

With more than one in five households having an income of $100,000 or more, the Census Bureau has expanded the upper income brackets for which it publishes income data.

■ Among married couples, blacks have higher incomes than Hispanics.

The $61,553 median income of black couples is 24 percent above the all-household median. The $48,471 median income of Hispanic couples is 3 percent below average.

■ College-educated householders had a median income of $82,722 in 2009.

The median income of households headed by college graduates has fallen by 8 percent since 2000, after adjusting for inflation.

■ Women have been catching up to men.

Among full-time workers in 2009, women's earnings were 77 percent as high as men's, up from 72 percent in 1990.

■ Most of the nation's poor are Asian, black, or Hispanic.

Among non-Hispanic whites, 9.4 percent are poor. The figure exceeds 25 percent among blacks and Hispanics.

Few Households Have Incomes of $200,000 or More

The percentage of households with incomes of $100,000 or more peaked in 2007.

The proportion of households with incomes of $100,000 or more reached a peak of 21.4 percent in 2007, after adjusting for inflation. The figure fell slightly, to 20.1 percent in 2009. Because this high-income bracket had grown to encompass more than one in five households, the Census Bureau expanded the upper range to $200,000-plus beginning with the 2010 Current Population Survey (which collected income data for 2009). In 2009, 8 percent of households had an income of $150,000 or more, and 4 percent had an income of $200,000 or more. The percentage of households in the high-income brackets has grown since 1990 because of the aging of the baby-boom generation into the peak-earning years.

The share of households with incomes below $35,000 stood at 36 percent in 2009, little changed from 1990. The proportion of households with incomes in the middle of the distribution (from $35,000 to $75,000) fell from 36 to 32 percent during those years.

■ The proportion of households with incomes of $100,000 or more is likely to decline in the years ahead as boomers retire.

More than 20 percent of households have incomes of $100,000 or more

(percent of households with incomes of $100,000 or more, 1990 to 2009; in 2009 dollars)

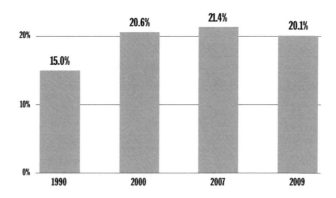

Table 5.1 Distribution of Households by Income, 1990 to 2009

(number of households and percent distribution by income, 1990 to 2009, in 2009 dollars; households in thousands as of the following year)

	total households		under $15,000	$15,000– $24,999	$25,000– $34,999	$35,000– $49,999	$50,000– $74,999	$75,000– $99,999	$100,000– $149,999	$150,000– $199,999	$200,000 or more
	number	percent									
2009	117,538	100.0%	13.0%	11.9%	11.1%	14.1%	18.1%	11.5%	11.9%	4.4%	3.8%
2008	117,181	100.0	13.4	12.0	11.0	14.1	17.6	11.9	11.9	4.3	3.7
2007	116,783	100.0	12.9	11.3	10.5	14.0	18.0	12.0	12.7	4.7	4.0
2006	116,011	100.0	12.6	11.2	11.1	14.1	18.2	11.6	12.5	4.7	4.0
2005	114,384	100.0	13.0	11.5	10.8	14.2	18.1	12.1	12.0	4.3	4.0
2004	113,343	100.0	13.3	11.6	11.0	14.1	18.1	12.0	11.9	4.4	3.6
2003	112,000	100.0	13.2	11.6	10.9	14.0	17.7	12.2	12.3	4.4	3.7
2002	111,278	100.0	12.9	11.4	10.6	14.5	18.0	12.5	12.3	4.2	3.7
2001	109,297	100.0	12.4	11.4	10.5	14.8	17.9	12.6	12.2	4.3	3.9
2000	108,209	100.0	12.1	11.1	10.5	14.5	18.4	12.7	12.3	4.5	3.8
1999	106,434	100.0	11.8	11.3	10.9	14.0	18.4	12.8	12.5	4.3	4.0
1998	103,874	100.0	12.7	11.4	10.7	14.5	18.7	12.6	12.0	4.0	3.4
1997	102,528	100.0	13.2	11.8	11.3	14.4	18.8	12.2	11.4	3.7	3.1
1996	101,018	100.0	13.7	12.3	11.2	14.7	18.8	12.3	10.7	3.5	2.8
1995	99,627	100.0	13.7	12.2	11.4	15.0	19.2	12.1	10.6	3.1	2.6
1994	98,990	100.0	14.6	12.6	11.5	14.8	19.0	11.6	10.3	3.2	2.6
1993	97,107	100.0	15.1	12.6	11.0	15.8	18.5	11.7	10.0	3.0	2.3
1992	96,426	100.0	15.0	12.5	11.1	15.5	19.3	12.1	9.7	2.7	2.1
1991	95,669	100.0	14.5	12.3	11.3	15.9	19.3	12.0	9.9	2.9	1.9
1990	94,312	100.0	14.0	11.8	11.2	15.7	20.0	12.2	9.9	3.0	2.1

Source: Bureau of the Census, Income, Poverty, and Health Insurance Coverage in the United States: 2009, Current Population Reports, P60-238, Internet site http://www.census.gov/hhes/www/income/data/incpovhlth/2009/index.html; calculations by New Strategist

Income Inequality Has Grown

The richest 20 percent of households control more than half of household income.

If you add up all the money going to American households, including earnings, interest, dividends, Social Security benefits, and so on, the result is called aggregate household income. Year-to-year changes in how this aggregate is divided among the nation's households can reveal trends in income inequality. The numbers on the next page show how much aggregate income is received by each fifth of households, from poorest to richest. It also shows how much accrues to the 5 percent of households with the highest incomes.

For years, a growing share of income had been accruing to the most affluent households. The percentage of aggregate income received by the richest 20 percent of households (with an income of $100,000 or more in 2009) rose from 46.6 percent in 1990 to 50.3 percent in 2009. During those years, the percentage of aggregate income received by the bottom four-fifths of households fell from 53.4 to 49.7 percent. Despite the recession, the richest 20 percent of households have maintained their hold on the majority of aggregate household income.

■ A rise or fall in the amount of income accruing to each fifth of households reveals trends in the distribution of income among households, not the economic wellbeing of individual households.

The wealthiest households control more than half of the nation's riches

(percent of aggregate household income accruing to the richest 20 percent of households, 1990 to 2009)

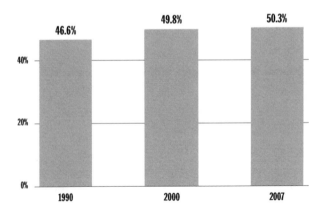

Table 5.2 Distribution of Aggregate Household Income, 1990 to 2009

(total number of households and percent of aggregate household income received by each fifth and top 5 percent of households, 1990 to 2009; households in thousands as of the following year)

	total households		lowest fifth	second fifth	middle fifth	fourth fifth	highest fifth	top 5 percent
	number	percent						
2009	117,538	100.0%	3.4%	8.6%	14.6%	23.2%	50.3%	21.7%
2008	117,181	100.0	3.4	8.6	14.7	23.3	50.0	21.5
2007	116,783	100.0	3.4	8.7	14.8	23.4	49.7	21.2
2006	116,011	100.0	3.4	8.6	14.5	22.9	50.5	22.3
2005	114,384	100.0	3.4	8.6	14.6	23.0	50.4	22.2
2004	113,343	100.0	3.4	8.7	14.7	23.2	50.1	21.8
2003	112,000	100.0	3.4	8.7	14.8	23.4	49.8	21.4
2002	111,278	100.0	3.5	8.8	14.8	23.3	49.7	21.7
2001	109,297	100.0	3.5	8.7	14.6	23.0	50.1	22.4
2000	108,209	100.0	3.6	8.9	14.8	23.0	49.8	22.1
1999	106,434	100.0	3.6	8.9	14.9	23.2	49.4	21.5
1998	103,874	100.0	3.6	9.0	15.0	23.2	49.2	21.4
1997	102,528	100.0	3.6	8.9	15.0	23.2	49.4	21.7
1996	101,018	100.0	3.6	9.0	15.1	23.3	49.0	21.4
1995	99,627	100.0	3.7	9.1	15.2	23.3	48.7	21.0
1994	98,990	100.0	3.6	8.9	15.0	23.4	49.1	21.2
1993	97,107	100.0	3.6	9.0	15.1	23.5	48.9	21.0
1992	96,426	100.0	3.8	9.4	15.8	24.2	46.9	18.6
1991	95,669	100.0	3.8	9.6	15.9	24.2	46.5	18.1
1990	94,312	100.0	3.8	9.6	15.9	24.0	46.6	18.5

Source: Bureau of the Census, Current Population Survey, Historical Tables, Internet site http://www.census.gov/hhes/www/ income/data/historical/index.html; calculations by New Strategist

Rich and Poor Have Unique Characteristics

High-income households have more earners than low-income households.

One common way to examine income differences among households is to divide the total number of households into five equally sized groups (called quintiles) based on income and compare household characteristics. The numbers on the next two pages show the distribution of households by income quintile and the characteristics of households within income quintile.

The demographics of the poorest and the richest households are strikingly different and account in large part for their income differences. Among households with two or more earners, for example, only 3 percent are in the lowest income quintile (with incomes below $20,450) and 37 percent are in the highest income quintile (with incomes of $100,000 or more). To look at the numbers another way, among households in the highest income quintile, more than three out of four have two or more earners. Among households in the lowest income quintile, only 5.5 percent have two or more earners. The 58 percent majority of households in the lowest income quintile has no earners.

■ Households in the highest income quintile are disproportionately headed by 35-to-54-year-olds, married couples, Asians, and non-Hispanic whites. The elderly, people living alone, blacks, and Hispanics head a disproportionate share of households in the lowest income quintile.

Married couples are typically found in the higher income quintiles because their households are likely to include two or more earners

(percent distribution of married couples by income quintile, 2009)

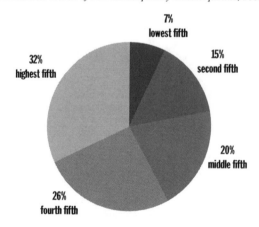

7%
lowest fifth

15%
second fifth

20%
middle fifth

26%
fourth fifth

32%
highest fifth

Table 5.3 Distribution of Households by Income Quintile, 2009

(total number of households by income quintile and top 5 percent, lower income limit of quintile and top 5 percent, and percent distribution of households by income quintile and selected characteristics, 2009; households in thousands as of 2010)

	total	lowest fifth	second fifth	middle fifth	fourth fifth	highest fifth	top 5 percent
Number of households	117,538	23,508	23,508	23,508	23,508	23,508	5,879
Lower income limit	–	–	$20,450	$38,530	$61,800	$100,000	$180,000
AGE OF HOUSEHOLDER							
Aged 15 to 24	100.0%	34.8%	25.5%	21.3%	11.8%	6.5%	1.0%
Aged 25 to 34	100.0	17.4	20.9	23.0	22.8	16.0	2.8
Aged 35 to 44	100.0	13.7	16.4	20.9	23.6	25.5	6.3
Aged 45 to 54	100.0	14.8	14.7	18.9	23.5	28.2	7.6
Aged 55 to 64	100.0	17.3	17.4	19.1	20.7	25.4	7.1
Aged 65 or older	100.0	31.0	28.4	18.5	12.9	9.3	2.3
RACE AND HISPANIC ORIGIN OF HOUSEHOLDER							
Asian	100.0	16.5	14.8	16.8	20.3	31.6	10.0
Black	100.0	32.7	23.9	18.8	15.4	9.2	1.6
Hispanic	100.0	25.7	24.8	20.9	16.9	11.6	2.2
Non-Hispanic white	100.0	16.9	18.9	20.3	21.3	22.7	5.8
TYPE OF HOUSEHOLD							
Married couples	100.0	7.2	14.9	20.0	26.2	31.7	8.4
Female householder, no spouse present	100.0	17.1	23.1	24.4	21.3	14.1	2.8
Male householder, no spouse present	100.0	31.4	26.3	20.7	14.4	7.1	1.1
Women living alone	100.0	46.5	26.1	16.0	7.6	3.8	0.6
Men living alone	100.0	33.0	26.5	20.9	12.2	7.4	1.6
NUMBER OF EARNERS							
No earners	100.0	52.5	27.2	12.6	5.4	2.4	0.4
One earner	100.0	19.4	27.2	25.0	16.4	12.0	2.9
Two or more earners	100.0	2.7	9.5	19.5	31.3	37.1	9.4

Note: Asians and blacks are those who identify themselves as being of the race alone and those who identify themselves as being of the race in combination with other races. Non-Hispanic whites are those who identify themselves as being white alone and not Hispanic. Hispanics may be of any race. "–" means not applicable.
Source: Bureau of the Census, 2010 Current Population Survey, Internet site http://www.census.gov/hhes/www/cpstables/032010/hhinc/toc.htm; calculations by New Strategist

Table 5.4 Characteristics of Households within Income Quintiles, 2009

(total number of households by income quintile and top 5 percent, lower income limit of quintile and top 5 percent, and percent distribution of households within income quintiles by selected characteristics, 2009; households in thousands as of 2010)

	total	lowest fifth	second fifth	middle fifth	fourth fifth	highest fifth	top 5 percent
Number of households	117,538	23,508	23,508	23,508	23,508	23,508	5,879
Lower income limit	–	–	$20,450	$38,530	$61,800	$100,000	$180,000
AGE OF HOUSEHOLDER							
Total households	100.0%	100.0%	100.0%	100.0%	100.0%	100.0%	100.0%
Aged 15 to 24	5.3	9.2	6.8	5.7	3.1	1.7	1.1
Aged 25 to 34	16.4	14.2	17.1	18.8	18.7	13.1	9.2
Aged 35 to 44	18.3	12.5	15.0	19.1	21.6	23.3	23.0
Aged 45 to 54	21.2	15.6	15.5	19.9	24.8	29.9	32.0
Aged 55 to 64	17.3	15.0	15.1	16.6	18.0	22.1	24.7
Aged 65 or older	21.5	33.3	30.5	19.9	13.8	9.9	10.0
RACE AND HISPANIC ORIGIN OF HOUSEHOLDER							
Total households	100.0	100.0	100.0	100.0	100.0	100.0	100.0
Asian	4.2	3.5	3.1	3.5	4.3	6.6	8.4
Black	12.9	21.2	15.5	12.2	9.9	5.9	4.2
Hispanic	11.3	14.6	14.0	11.8	9.6	6.6	5.0
Non-Hispanic white	70.7	59.7	66.7	71.7	75.4	80.3	81.8
TYPE OF HOUSEHOLD							
Total households	100.0	100.0	100.0	100.0	100.0	100.0	100.0
Married couples	49.7	17.9	37.1	49.7	65.0	78.8	83.6
Female householder, no spouse present	12.6	19.8	16.6	13.1	9.1	4.5	2.8
Male householder, no spouse present	4.7	4.1	5.5	5.8	5.1	3.4	2.6
Women living alone	14.8	34.5	19.3	11.9	5.6	2.8	1.8
Men living alone	11.9	19.6	15.7	12.4	7.3	4.4	3.9
NUMBER OF EARNERS							
Total households	100.0	100.0	100.0	100.0	100.0	100.0	100.0
No earners	22.3	58.4	30.3	14.0	6.0	2.6	1.8
One earner	37.2	36.1	50.6	46.5	30.5	22.2	21.8
Two earners or more	40.5	5.5	19.2	39.5	63.5	75.1	76.4

Note: Asians and blacks are those who identify themselves as being of the race alone and those who identify themselves as being of the race in combination with other races. Non-Hispanic whites are those who identify themselves as being white alone and not Hispanic. Hispanics may be of any race. "–" means not applicable.
Source: Bureau of the Census, 2010 Current Population Survey, Internet site http://www.census.gov/hhes/www/cpstables/032010/hhinc/toc.htm; calculations by New Strategist

Median Household Income Fell between 2000 and 2009

Householders aged 35 to 54 have been hit harder than others.

Household income growth has varied significantly by age over the past 20 years. Between 1990 and 2009, median household income climbed from $47,637 to $49,777 after adjusting for inflation—a 4 percent increase. Householders aged 55 or older experienced the largest boost, a median income gain of 11 to 17 percent. In contrast, householders aged 35 to 54 saw their median household income fall over the past two decades.

Between 2000 and 2009, median household income fell sharply among householders under age 55. The decline in median income ranged from 9 to 11 percent, after adjusting for inflation. Householders aged 55 to 64 saw their median income rise 2 percent during those years, and the median income of those aged 65 or older grew by an even larger 9 percent. Behind these increases is the growing labor force participation of older Americans.

■ The median income of households headed by people aged 65 or older reached a record high in 2009.

Householders under age 55 saw their median income fall sharply between 2000 and 2009

(percent change in median household income by age of householder, 2000 to 2009)

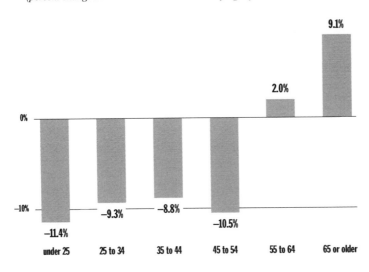

Table 5.5 Median Household Income by Age of Householder, 1990 to 2009

(median household income by age of householder, 1990 to 2009; percent change for selected years; in 2009 dollars)

	total households	under 25	25 to 34	35 to 44	45 to 54	55 to 64	65 or older
2009	$49,777	$30,733	$50,199	$61,083	$64,235	$56,973	$31,354
2008	50,112	32,148	51,205	62,715	64,105	57,048	29,631
2007	51,965	32,886	52,775	64,266	67,734	59,365	29,281
2006	51,278	32,912	52,302	64,261	69,015	58,077	29,572
2005	50,899	31,610	52,056	63,817	68,586	57,419	28,606
2004	50,343	31,313	51,628	64,365	69,299	57,222	27,839
2003	50,519	31,550	52,223	64,194	70,256	57,396	27,741
2002	50,563	33,179	54,046	63,812	70,369	56,279	27,604
2001	51,161	34,161	54,616	64,599	70,324	55,566	28,008
2000	52,301	34,685	55,320	66,963	71,796	55,867	28,751
1999	52,388	32,373	54,182	65,406	73,248	57,496	29,346
1998	51,100	30,966	52,656	63,672	71,158	56,728	28,555
1997	49,309	30,092	50,866	61,773	69,123	55,106	27,664
1996	48,315	29,183	48,854	60,468	68,706	54,199	26,474
1995	47,622	29,318	48,495	60,743	67,162	53,213	26,687
1994	46,175	27,679	47,445	59,632	67,638	50,423	25,897
1993	45,665	28,259	45,724	59,729	67,542	48,930	25,947
1992	45,888	26,457	46,792	59,694	66,559	50,917	25,666
1991	46,269	28,126	47,368	60,434	67,194	51,149	26,071
1990	47,637	28,640	48,298	61,347	66,694	51,490	26,815

Percent change

2000 to 2009	−4.8%	−11.4%	−9.3%	−8.8%	−10.5%	2.0%	9.1%
1990 to 2009	4.5	7.3	3.9	−0.4	−3.7	10.6	16.9

Source: Bureau of the Census, Current Population Survey, Historical Tables, Internet site http://www.census.gov/hhes/www/income/data/historical/index.html; calculations by New Strategist

Most Household Types Lost Ground between 2000 and 2009

Incomes were higher in 2009 than in 1990 for most households, however.

Few households have escaped unscathed from the Great Recession. Only one type of household saw its median income grow between 2000 and 2009—women who live alone (most of them aged 55 or older) enjoyed a record-high median income in 2009. Between 2000 and 2009, their median income climbed by 0.5 percent. Although a small gain, it stands in sharp contrast to the substantial declines in income experienced by every other type of household. Married couples saw their median income fall by 3 percent between 2000 and 2009, female-headed families experienced a 7 percent decline, and male-headed families were hit with an even larger 8 percent decline.

Most household types had a higher median income in 2009 than in 1990, after adjusting for inflation. The only losers were male-headed families (down 4 percent) and men who live alone (down 0.5 percent).

■ The incomes of married couples peaked in 2007 at just over $75,000, then fell by nearly 5 percent to the $71,830 of 2009.

Only women who live alone have seen their household income grow since 2000

(percent change in median household income by household type, 2000 to 2009; in 2009 dollars)

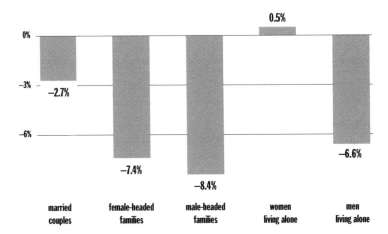

Table 5.6 Median Household Income by Type of Household, 1990 to 2009

(median household income by type of household, 1990 to 2009; percent change for selected years; income in 2009 dollars)

| | total households | family households | | | | nonfamily households | | | | |
		total	married couples	female hh, no spouse present	male hh, no spouse present	total	female householder total	female householder living alone	male householder total	male householder living alone
2009	$49,777	$61,265	$71,830	$32,597	$48,084	$30,444	$25,269	$22,324	$36,611	$31,595
2008	50,112	62,383	72,733	32,947	48,999	29,964	24,919	21,934	35,869	30,609
2007	51,965	64,509	75,295	34,521	51,558	31,217	25,132	22,289	38,035	32,696
2006	51,278	63,717	74,166	33,849	50,083	30,939	25,400	22,709	37,887	33,264
2005	50,899	62,932	72,588	33,675	51,371	30,023	24,928	22,157	37,409	32,983
2004	50,343	62,829	72,461	33,869	51,122	29,809	24,826	22,158	36,351	31,129
2003	50,519	62,966	72,779	34,179	48,934	30,020	24,856	21,781	37,236	31,999
2002	50,563	62,838	73,032	34,577	49,731	30,291	24,934	21,327	37,442	31,963
2001	51,161	63,333	73,263	34,095	49,328	31,053	24,551	21,648	39,147	34,266
2000	52,301	64,410	73,826	35,204	52,506	31,520	25,509	22,204	39,209	33,819
1999	52,388	64,129	72,929	33,719	53,770	31,392	25,452	22,246	39,466	34,466
1998	51,100	62,381	71,326	32,056	51,796	30,805	24,463	21,560	39,968	34,195
1997	49,309	60,424	68,864	30,701	48,814	28,922	23,469	20,694	36,766	31,808
1996	48,315	58,647	67,871	29,355	48,540	28,550	22,322	19,910	37,117	32,739
1995	47,622	57,611	65,864	29,834	46,864	27,851	22,209	20,028	36,368	31,564
1994	46,175	56,374	64,461	28,440	43,611	27,116	21,393	19,222	35,197	30,364
1993	45,665	54,791	63,042	27,108	43,631	27,597	21,755	18,995	36,145	31,240
1992	45,888	55,407	62,859	27,510	45,400	26,557	21,626	19,372	34,617	29,926
1991	46,269	55,909	63,084	27,591	47,626	27,304	22,004	19,711	35,358	31,115
1990	47,637	56,807	63,630	28,746	50,196	28,143	22,430	19,963	35,778	31,761
Percent change										
2000 to 2009	−4.8%	−4.9%	−2.7%	−7.4%	−8.4%	−3.4%	−0.9%	0.5%	−6.6%	−6.6%
1990 to 2009	4.5	7.8	12.9	13.4	−4.2	8.2	12.7	11.8	2.3	−0.5

Source: Bureau of the Census, Current Population Survey, Historical Tables, Internet site http://www.census.gov/hhes/www/income/data/historical/index.html; calculations by New Strategist

Every Racial and Ethnic Group Has Lost Ground

Black households experienced the biggest decline in income between 2000 and 2009.

Overall, median household income fell 5 percent between 2000 and 2009, after adjusting for inflation. Black households experienced the biggest loss, with an 11 percent decline in median household income during those years. The median was down 6 percent for Asians, 8 percent for Hispanics, and 4 percent for non-Hispanic whites.

Despite these declines, median household income was higher in 2009 than in 1990 for every racial and ethnic group. The median income of black households climbed 10 percent during those years, more than double the 4.5 percent rise in the overall median. The median income of black households was only 62 percent as high as the national median in 1990. By 2009, it reached 66 percent of the national median. Despite the gain, blacks continue to have lower household incomes than any other racial or ethnic group, with a median of just $32,750 in 2009. Asians have the highest median household income, at $65,073—well above the $54,461 median income of households headed by non-Hispanic whites. Hispanic households had a median income of $38,039.

■ Black households have low incomes because many are female-headed families—one of the poorest household types.

The median income of non-Hispanic whites fell 4 percent between 2000 and 2009

(percent change in median household income by race and Hispanic origin, 2000 to 2009; in 2009 dollars)

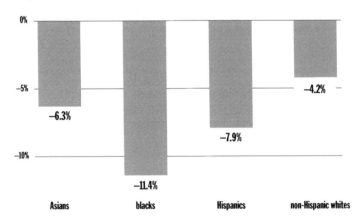

Table 5.7 Median Household Income by Race and Hispanic Origin of Householder, 1990 to 2009

(median household income by race and Hispanic origin of householder, 1990 to 2009; percent change in median for selected years; in 2009 dollars)

	total households	Asian	black	Hispanic	non-Hispanic white
2009	$49,777	$65,073	$32,750	$38,039	$54,461
2008	50,112	65,318	34,215	37,769	55,319
2007	51,965	68,148	35,267	40,013	56,814
2006	51,278	67,979	34,183	40,193	55,769
2005	50,899	67,074	34,009	39,517	55,797
2004	50,343	65,236	34,333	38,916	55,539
2003	50,519	64,448	34,624	38,482	55,719
2002	50,563	62,338	34,787	39,468	55,918
2001	51,161	64,981	35,704	40,665	56,100
2000	52,301	69,448	36,952	41,312	56,826
1999	52,388	65,600	35,928	39,579	56,843
1998	51,100	61,288	33,315	37,230	55,771
1997	49,309	60,294	33,379	35,481	54,068
1996	48,315	58,911	31,966	33,904	52,800
1995	47,622	56,759	31,295	31,947	51,957
1994	46,175	57,937	30,093	33,519	50,271
1993	45,665	56,052	28,552	33,453	49,951
1992	45,888	56,621	28,092	33,847	49,864
1991	46,269	55,980	28,884	34,850	49,643
1990	47,637	61,170	29,712	35,525	50,822
Percent change					
2000 to 2009	−4.8%	−6.3%	−11.4%	−7.9%	−4.2%
1990 to 2009	4.5	6.4	10.2	7.1	7.2

Note: Asians and blacks in 2002 through 2009 are those who identify themselves as being of the race alone and those who identify themselves as being of the race in combination with other races. Non-Hispanic whites in 2002 through 2009 are those who identify themselves as being white alone and not Hispanic. Hispanics may be of any race.
Source: Bureau of the Census, Current Population Survey, Historical Tables, Internet site http://www.census.gov/hhes/www/income/data/historical/index.html; calculations by New Strategist

College Graduates Are Not Immune from Recession

Households headed by college graduates have experienced sharp income declines since 2000.

Among households headed by people aged 25 or older, median income fell 5 percent between 2000 and 2009, after adjusting for inflation. Income declines have been steep for nearly every educational group. Households headed by high school graduates saw their median income fall 13 percent during those years, as did households headed by people with only some college. Households headed by people with a bachelor's degree experienced a 9 percent decline in median income.

Between 1991 (the earliest year with comparable data) and 2009, median income increased slightly for people with at least a bachelor's degree (up 3 percent). It dropped 9 percent for high school graduates and 10 percent for people with some college.

■ The least educated householders saw their incomes grow between 1991 and 2009 because many are older Americans who receive Social Security benefits, which are indexed to inflation.

The median income of college graduates fell between 2000 and 2009

(median income of households headed by people aged 25 or older with a bachelor's degree or more education, 2000 to 2009; in 2009 dollars)

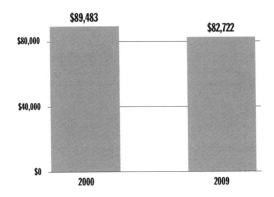

Table 5.8 Median Household Income by Education of Householder, 1991 to 2009

(median income of households headed by people aged 25 or older by educational attainment of householder, 1991 to 2009; percent change for selected years; in 2009 dollars)

	total	less than 9th grade	9th to 12th grade, no diploma	high school graduate	some college, no degree	assoc. degree	bachelor's degree or more total	bachelor's degree	master's degree	prof. degree	doctoral degree
2009	$50,971	$21,635	$25,604	$39,647	$48,413	$56,789	$82,722	$75,518	$91,660	$123,784	$120,873
2008	51,193	21,161	25,225	39,810	50,132	58,938	84,804	77,993	92,290	99,620	99,620
2007	53,200	21,522	25,337	41,851	52,158	62,206	87,422	80,281	93,786	103,448	103,448
2006	53,196	22,235	27,566	41,943	52,863	59,593	86,939	80,703	94,066	106,383	106,383
2005	52,426	22,220	27,111	41,961	53,050	60,109	84,797	79,573	89,021	109,871	109,871
2004	52,182	22,150	25,537	42,390	53,768	61,217	84,374	77,691	90,993	113,554	113,554
2003	52,499	21,910	26,495	42,958	53,477	60,609	85,655	80,153	91,597	116,623	112,927
2002	52,507	21,914	27,741	42,500	54,050	60,875	87,752	82,453	91,174	119,228	117,597
2001	52,813	21,953	28,169	43,682	55,501	61,985	87,575	81,373	95,593	121,154	112,438
2000	53,907	21,803	28,239	45,495	55,580	62,902	89,483	82,974	97,564	124,555	118,425
1999	53,921	22,167	27,963	45,857	56,664	63,304	89,749	82,712	95,742	128,729	125,037
1998	52,955	21,229	27,234	45,171	54,745	63,873	87,356	81,724	93,417	125,250	110,519
1997	50,888	20,708	26,451	45,010	53,319	60,306	84,336	78,681	90,762	122,893	116,236
1996	49,708	20,931	26,752	43,963	52,270	60,589	81,647	75,057	86,968	122,983	110,480
1995	49,241	21,023	25,572	43,848	51,926	58,861	81,129	73,868	90,783	114,610	111,808
1994	47,924	20,430	25,107	43,037	51,349	57,616	82,206	74,950	87,366	111,634	111,856
1993	47,018	20,347	26,261	41,951	51,482	57,859	82,026	75,249	88,201	128,143	109,268
1992	47,331	20,101	25,946	43,320	52,779	57,332	80,766	73,966	86,497	126,893	104,877
1991	47,660	20,305	26,931	43,751	53,985	60,973	80,278	74,803	84,737	119,717	107,994

Percent change

	total	less than 9th grade	9th to 12th grade, no diploma	high school graduate	some college, no degree	assoc. degree	bachelor's degree or more total	bachelor's degree	master's degree	prof. degree	doctoral degree
2000 to 2009	−5.4%	−0.8%	−9.3%	−12.9%	−12.9%	−9.7%	−7.6%	−9.0%	−6.1%	−0.6%	2.1%
1991 to 2009	6.9	6.5	−4.9	−9.4	−10.3	−6.9	3.0	1.0	8.2	3.4	11.9

Source: Bureau of the Census, Current Population Survey, Historical Tables, Internet site http://www.census.gov/hhes/www/income/data/historical/index.html; calculations by New Strategist

The Median Income of Middle-Aged Married Couples Tops $88,000

The median income of couples aged 45 to 54 is 77 percent above average.

The median income of the average household stood at $49,777 in 2009. Incomes vary considerably by age and household type. The most affluent households are married couples with a householder in the 45-to-54 age group. Their median income stood at $88,011 in 2009. Not only are 45-to-54-year-olds in their peak earning years, but most couples are dual earners, boosting incomes well above average.

Women who live alone have the lowest incomes. Households headed by women under age 25 who live by themselves had a median income of $18,147 in 2009—just 36 percent of the national median. Many of these women are in college and are likely to make more money in the future. Women aged 65 or older who live by themselves had a median income of just $18,280.

■ Married couples spanning the ages from 25 to 64 have well above average median incomes.

Incomes vary sharply by age and living arrangement

(median income of the richest and poorest households, by household type and age of householder, 2009)

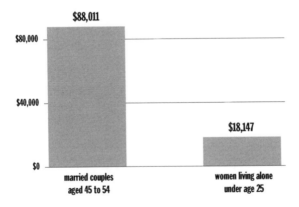

Table 5.9 Median Household Income by Household Type and Age of Householder, 2009

(median household income by type of household and age of householder; and index of age median to national median by household type, 2009)

	total	under 25	25 to 34	35 to 44	45 to 54	55 to 64	65 or older
Total households	$49,777	$30,733	$50,199	$61,083	$64,235	$56,973	$31,354
Family households	61,265	33,996	53,026	66,986	76,738	72,324	43,913
Married couples	71,830	39,830	65,307	81,232	88,011	78,627	46,086
Female householder, no spouse present	32,597	24,109	24,553	32,314	40,995	41,693	34,018
Male householder, no spouse present	48,084	40,879	48,325	47,170	53,834	51,870	43,112
Nonfamily households	30,444	26,980	45,221	42,800	36,016	31,702	20,054
Female householder	25,269	24,974	42,839	40,710	32,081	29,560	18,630
Living alone	22,324	18,147	33,370	35,272	28,534	27,278	18,280
Male householder	36,611	29,364	46,074	45,527	38,324	34,161	25,387
Living alone	31,595	21,121	37,575	40,102	35,208	31,787	24,172
INDEX							
Total households	**100**	**62**	**101**	**123**	**129**	**114**	**63**
Family households	123	68	107	135	154	145	88
Married couples	144	80	131	163	177	158	93
Female householder, no spouse present	65	48	49	65	82	84	68
Male householder, no spouse present	97	82	97	95	108	104	87
Nonfamily households	61	54	91	86	72	64	40
Female householder	51	50	86	82	64	59	37
Living alone	45	36	67	71	57	55	37
Male householder	74	59	93	91	77	69	51
Living alone	63	42	75	81	71	64	49

Note: The index is calculated by dividing the median income of each age/household type group by the national median and multiplying by 100.
Source: Bureau of the Census, Current Population Survey, Historical Tables, Internet site http://www.census.gov/hhes/www/income/data/historical/index.html; calculations by New Strategist

The Median Income of Black Married Couples Tops $60,000

The median income of black couples is well above the national household median.

The $32,750 median income of the average black household is 34 percent below the national household median of $49,777 (with an index of 66). But the median income of black married couples is 24 percent above the all-household median (with an index of 124). In 2009, black couples had a median household income of $61,553. Asian couples had the highest median income, at $83,453 in 2009.

Interestingly, while the median income of the average Hispanic household is higher than that of the average black household ($38,039 versus $32,750), the median income of Hispanic couples is well below that of their black counterparts ($48,471 versus $61,553). Behind this pattern are differences in the living arrangements of Hispanics and blacks. The average Hispanic household has a higher income than the average black household because Hispanic households are more likely to be headed by married couples. But black couples have higher incomes than Hispanic couples because black couples are better educated and more likely to be dual-earners.

■ Hispanic incomes are low regardless of household type because many Hispanics are recent immigrants with little education or earning power.

The incomes of married couples are lowest among Hispanics

(median income of households headed by married couples, by race and Hispanic origin, 2009)

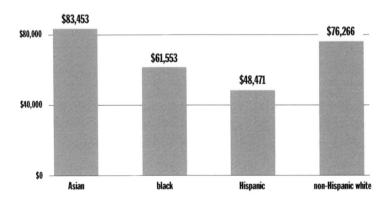

Table 5.10 Median Household Income by Household Type and Race and Hispanic Origin of Householder, 2009

(median household income by type of household and race and Hispanic origin of householder; and index of race/ Hispanic origin median to national median by household type, 2009)

	total	Asian	black	Hispanic	non-Hispanic white
Total households	**$49,777**	**$65,073**	**$32,750**	**$38,039**	**$54,461**
Family households	61,265	76,089	40,695	41,653	68,758
Married couples	71,830	83,453	61,553	48,471	76,266
Female householder, no spouse present	32,597	53,353	26,479	27,882	38,490
Male householder, no spouse present	48,084	57,340	40,441	43,545	51,575
Nonfamily households	30,444	35,259	22,726	26,561	32,158
Female householder	25,269	28,480	20,693	20,145	26,413
Living alone	22,324	24,645	18,923	16,140	23,473
Male householder	36,611	40,633	25,692	31,249	39,971
Living alone	31,595	36,058	22,953	25,898	34,305
INDEX					
Total households	**100**	**131**	**66**	**76**	**109**
Family households	123	153	82	84	138
Married couples	144	168	124	97	153
Female householder, no spouse present	65	107	53	56	77
Male householder, no spouse present	97	115	81	87	104
Nonfamily households	61	71	46	53	65
Female householder	51	57	42	40	53
Living alone	45	50	38	32	47
Male householder	74	82	52	63	80
Living alone	63	72	46	52	69

Note: The index is calculated by dividing the median income of each race/Hispanic origin/household type group by the national median and multiplying by 100. Asians and blacks are those who identify themselves as being of the race alone and those who identify themselves as being of the race in combination with other races. Non-Hispanic whites are those who identify themselves as being white alone and not Hispanic. Hispanics may be of any race.
Source: Bureau of the Census, 2010 Current Population Survey, Internet site http://www.census.gov/hhes/www/cpstables/ 032010/hhinc/toc.htm; calculations by New Strategist

Householders Aged 45 to 54 Have the Highest Incomes

Median household income peaks at $64,235 in the 45-to-54 age group.

A hefty 28 percent of householders aged 45 to 54 had an income of $100,000 or more in 2009—so many, in fact, that the Census Bureau expanded, beginning with the 2010 Current Population Survey, the income brackets to show detailed demographic data for households with incomes up to $200,000 or more. More than 4 million households (3.8 percent) had an income of $200,000 or more in 2009. Among householders aged 45 to 54, the figure was 6 percent. One-third of households with incomes of $200,000 or more are headed by 45-to-54-year-olds.

Households headed by people aged 75 or older have the lowest incomes, a median of just $25,693. Householders aged 65 to 74 have a higher median income ($38,895) than those under age 25 ($30,733).

■ With boomers entering their sixties, the household incomes of 55-to-64-year-olds should rise as early retirement becomes less common.

Household income peaks in middle age

(median income of households by age of householder, 2009)

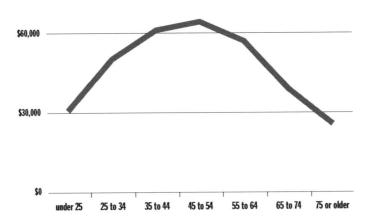

Table 5.11 Household Income by Age of Householder, 2009: Total Households

(number and percent distribution of households by household income and age of householder, 2009; households in thousands as of 2010)

	total	under 25	25 to 34	35 to 44	45 to 54	55 to 64	aged 65 or older total	65 to 74	75 or older
Total households	117,538	6,233	19,257	21,519	24,871	20,387	25,270	13,164	12,106
Under $25,000	29,352	2,567	4,276	3,671	4,513	4,351	9,973	4,091	5,881
$25,000 to $49,999	29,610	1,936	5,306	4,946	5,024	4,689	7,709	3,957	3,752
$50,000 to $74,999	21,280	956	4,115	4,239	4,733	3,649	3,586	2,253	1,334
$75,000 to $99,999	13,549	351	2,432	3,133	3,516	2,482	1,632	1,107	525
$100,000 to $124,999	8,967	230	1,389	2,093	2,569	1,768	918	636	283
$125,000 to $149,999	5,067	79	718	1,189	1,462	1,111	509	377	134
$150,000 to $174,999	3,354	39	409	787	1,029	770	321	250	72
$175,000 to $199,999	1,855	32	209	439	548	440	183	139	45
$200,000 or more	4,506	42	405	1,018	1,475	1,126	440	356	85
Median income	$49,777	$30,733	$50,199	$61,083	$64,235	$56,973	$31,354	$38,895	$25,693
Total households	100.0%	100.0%	100.0%	100.0%	100.0%	100.0%	100.0%	100.0%	100.0%
Under $25,000	25.0	41.2	22.2	17.1	18.1	21.3	39.5	31.1	48.6
$25,000 to $49,999	25.2	31.1	27.6	23.0	20.2	23.0	30.5	30.1	31.0
$50,000 to $74,999	18.1	15.3	21.4	19.7	19.0	17.9	14.2	17.1	11.0
$75,000 to $99,999	11.5	5.6	12.6	14.6	14.1	12.2	6.5	8.4	4.3
$100,000 to $124,999	7.6	3.7	7.2	9.7	10.3	8.7	3.6	4.8	2.3
$125,000 to $149,999	4.3	1.3	3.7	5.5	5.9	5.4	2.0	2.9	1.1
$150,000 to $174,999	2.9	0.6	2.1	3.7	4.1	3.8	1.3	1.9	0.6
$175,000 to $199,999	1.6	0.5	1.1	2.0	2.2	2.2	0.7	1.1	0.4
$200,000 or more	3.8	0.7	2.1	4.7	5.9	5.5	1.7	2.7	0.7

Source: Bureau of the Census, 2010 Current Population Survey, Internet site http://www.census.gov/hhes/www/cpstables/032010/hhinc/toc.htm; calculations by New Strategist

Income Peaks in Middle Age for Asians, Blacks, Hispanics, and Non-Hispanic Whites

Median household income peaks at ages 45 to 54 for every racial and ethnic group except Asians.

Among non-Hispanic whites, the median income of householders aged 45 to 54 stood at $71,559 in 2009. Among blacks and Hispanics, incomes peak in the same age group but at a much lower level—$41,727 for blacks and $46,772 for Hispanics. Among Asian households, the income peak occurs at a younger age. Asian householders aged 35 to 44 have the highest incomes of all, a median of $82,005 in 2009. Eleven percent of Asian households headed by someone aged 35 to 44 had an income of $200,000 or more.

Householders aged 65 or older have the lowest incomes among Asians ($31,926), Hispanics ($24,051), and non-Hispanic whites ($32,825). Among blacks, householders under age 25 have the lowest incomes ($20,708).

■ The incomes of black households are far below those of non-Hispanic whites because black households are much less likely to be headed by married couples—the most affluent household type. Hispanic household incomes are low because many are immigrants with little earning power.

Nearly one-third of Asian households have an income of $100,000 or more

(percent of households with incomes of $100,000 or more, by race and Hispanic origin, 2009)

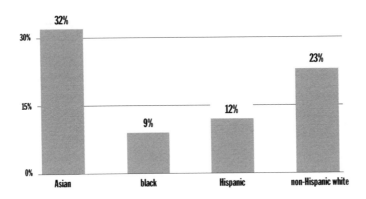

Table 5.12 Household Income by Age of Householder, 2009: Asian Households

(number and percent distribution of Asian households by household income and age of householder, 2009; households in thousands as of 2010)

	total	under 25	25 to 34	35 to 44	45 to 54	55 to 64	65 or older
Total Asian households	**4,940**	**292**	**1,057**	**1,180**	**1,020**	**709**	**682**
Under $25,000	972	105	196	139	142	113	278
$25,000 to $49,999	968	81	207	188	203	136	155
$50,000 to $74,999	822	50	208	203	166	113	82
$75,000 to $99,999	588	18	153	151	118	91	58
$100,000 to $124,999	507	20	108	151	110	79	40
$125,000 to $149,999	318	4	60	103	83	47	24
$150,000 to $174,999	238	4	51	60	59	50	16
$175,000 to $199,999	145	4	28	53	42	11	7
$200,000 or more	381	7	46	132	103	70	23
Median income	$65,073	$36,521	$63,066	$82,005	$75,335	$72,367	$31,926
Total Asian households	**100.0%**	**100.0%**	**100.0%**	**100.0%**	**100.0%**	**100.0%**	**100.0%**
Under $25,000	19.7	36.0	18.5	11.8	13.9	15.9	40.8
$25,000 to $49,999	19.6	27.7	19.6	15.9	19.9	19.2	22.7
$50,000 to $74,999	16.6	17.1	19.7	17.2	16.3	15.9	12.0
$75,000 to $99,999	11.9	6.2	14.5	12.8	11.6	12.8	8.5
$100,000 to $124,999	10.3	6.8	10.2	12.8	10.8	11.1	5.9
$125,000 to $149,999	6.4	1.4	5.7	8.7	8.1	6.6	3.5
$150,000 to $174,999	4.8	1.4	4.8	5.1	5.8	7.1	2.3
$175,000 to $199,999	2.9	1.4	2.6	4.5	4.1	1.6	1.0
$200,000 or more	7.7	2.4	4.4	11.2	10.1	9.9	3.4

Note: Asians are those who identify themselves as being of the race alone and those who identify themselves as being of the race in combination with other races.
Source: Bureau of the Census, 2010 Current Population Survey, Internet site http://www.census.gov/hhes/www/cpstables/032010/hhinc/toc.htm; calculations by New Strategist

Table 5.13 Household Income by Age of Householder, 2009: Black Households

(number and percent distribution of black households by household income and age of householder, 2009; households in thousands as of 2010)

	total	under 25	25 to 34	35 to 44	45 to 54	55 to 64	65 or older
Total black households	**15,212**	**1,074**	**2,937**	**3,134**	**3,284**	**2,413**	**2,370**
Under $25,000	5,900	630	1,155	929	1,048	900	1,241
$25,000 to $49,999	4,253	302	920	963	815	638	615
$50,000 to $74,999	2,308	87	396	576	630	362	259
$75,000 to $99,999	1,322	25	256	309	353	243	137
$100,000 to $124,999	641	15	101	166	201	109	50
$125,000 to $149,999	316	5	59	76	88	66	23
$150,000 to $174,999	203	2	26	59	65	33	19
$175,000 to $199,999	76	2	1	27	24	16	7
$200,000 or more	189	5	22	30	61	50	21
Median income	$32,750	$20,708	$31,181	$40,291	$41,727	$34,978	$23,549
Total black households	**100.0%**	**100.0%**	**100.0%**	**100.0%**	**100.0%**	**100.0%**	**100.0%**
Under $25,000	38.8	58.7	39.3	29.6	31.9	37.3	52.4
$25,000 to $49,999	28.0	28.1	31.3	30.7	24.8	26.4	25.9
$50,000 to $74,999	15.2	8.1	13.5	18.4	19.2	15.0	10.9
$75,000 to $99,999	8.7	2.3	8.7	9.9	10.7	10.1	5.8
$100,000 to $124,999	4.2	1.4	3.4	5.3	6.1	4.5	2.1
$125,000 to $149,999	2.1	0.5	2.0	2.4	2.7	2.7	1.0
$150,000 to $174,999	1.3	0.2	0.9	1.9	2.0	1.4	0.8
$175,000 to $199,999	0.5	0.2	0.0	0.9	0.7	0.7	0.3
$200,000 or more	1.2	0.5	0.7	1.0	1.9	2.1	0.9

Note: Blacks are those who identify themselves as being of the race alone and those who identify themselves as being of the race in combination with other races.
Source: Bureau of the Census, 2010 Current Population Survey, Internet site http://www.census.gov/hhes/www/cpstables/032010/hhinc/toc.htm; calculations by New Strategist

Table 5.14 Household Income by Age of Householder, 2009: Hispanic Households

(number and percent distribution of Hispanic households by household income and age of householder, 2009; households in thousands as of 2010)

	total	under 25	25 to 34	35 to 44	45 to 54	55 to 64	65 or older
Total Hispanic households	**13,298**	**1,152**	**3,147**	**3,320**	**2,618**	**1,570**	**1,490**
Under $25,000	4,221	484	973	869	655	472	771
$25,000 to $49,999	3,960	374	1,024	1,058	715	400	391
$50,000 to $74,999	2,342	170	590	580	498	329	174
$75,000 to $99,999	1,215	54	285	382	300	133	58
$100,000 to $124,999	688	39	139	185	187	94	44
$125,000 to $149,999	354	19	73	93	88	57	20
$150,000 to $174,999	192	2	27	64	60	33	8
$175,000 to $199,999	97	7	9	36	27	15	3
$200,000 or more	230	6	28	51	87	39	20
Median income	$38,039	$29,612	$36,662	$41,722	$46,772	$44,608	$24,051
Total Hispanic households	**100.0%**	**100.0%**	**100.0%**	**100.0%**	**100.0%**	**100.0%**	**100.0%**
Under $25,000	31.7	42.0	30.9	26.2	25.0	30.1	51.7
$25,000 to $49,999	29.8	32.5	32.5	31.9	27.3	25.5	26.2
$50,000 to $74,999	17.6	14.8	18.7	17.5	19.0	21.0	11.7
$75,000 to $99,999	9.1	4.7	9.1	11.5	11.5	8.5	3.9
$100,000 to $124,999	5.2	3.4	4.4	5.6	7.1	6.0	3.0
$125,000 to $149,999	2.7	1.6	2.3	2.8	3.4	3.6	1.3
$150,000 to $174,999	1.4	0.2	0.9	1.9	2.3	2.1	0.5
$175,000 to $199,999	0.7	0.6	0.3	1.1	1.0	1.0	0.2
$200,000 or more	1.7	0.5	0.9	1.5	3.3	2.5	1.3

Source: Bureau of the Census, 2010 Current Population Survey, Internet site http://www.census.gov/hhes/www/cpstables/ 032010/hhinc/toc.htm; calculations by New Strategist

Table 5.15 Household Income by Age of Householder, 2009: Non-Hispanic White Households

(number and percent distribution of non-Hispanic white households by household income and age of householder, 2009; households in thousands as of 2010)

	total	under 25	25 to 34	35 to 44	45 to 54	55 to 64	65 or older
Total non-Hispanic white households	**83,158**	**3,693**	**12,030**	**13,746**	**17,713**	**15,456**	**20,520**
Under $25,000	17,969	1,335	1,930	1,711	2,596	2,810	7,589
$25,000 to $49,999	20,217	1,182	3,131	2,705	3,263	3,445	6,492
$50,000 to $74,999	15,639	647	2,899	2,857	3,389	2,814	3,035
$75,000 to $99,999	10,310	247	1,721	2,265	2,717	1,991	1,368
$100,000 to $124,999	7,076	159	1,037	1,586	2,050	1,466	778
$125,000 to $149,999	4,038	49	524	907	1,193	928	437
$150,000 to $174,999	2,710	30	310	598	841	651	278
$175,000 to $199,999	1,523	21	171	319	452	396	165
$200,000 or more	3,679	22	309	800	1,213	956	380
Median income	$54,461	$35,179	$57,406	$71,172	$71,559	$61,829	$32,825
Total non-Hispanic white households	**100.0%**	**100.0%**	**100.0%**	**100.0%**	**100.0%**	**100.0%**	**100.0%**
Under $25,000	21.6	36.1	16.0	12.4	14.7	18.2	37.0
$25,000 to $49,999	24.3	32.0	26.0	19.7	18.4	22.3	31.6
$50,000 to $74,999	18.8	17.5	24.1	20.8	19.1	18.2	14.8
$75,000 to $99,999	12.4	6.7	14.3	16.5	15.3	12.9	6.7
$100,000 to $124,999	8.5	4.3	8.6	11.5	11.6	9.5	3.8
$125,000 to $149,999	4.9	1.3	4.4	6.6	6.7	6.0	2.1
$150,000 to $174,999	3.3	0.8	2.6	4.4	4.7	4.2	1.4
$175,000 to $199,999	1.8	0.6	1.4	2.3	2.6	2.6	0.8
$200,000 or more	4.4	0.6	2.6	5.8	6.8	6.2	1.9

Note: Non-Hispanic whites are those who identify themselves as being white alone and not Hispanic.
Source: Bureau of the Census, 2010 Current Population Survey, Internet site http://www.census.gov/hhes/www/cpstables/032010/hhinc/toc.htm; calculations by New Strategist

Nearly Four Million Couples Have Incomes of $200,000 or More

Married couples are by far the most affluent household type.

Most married couples are dual earners, which accounts for their higher incomes. Nearly one-third of couples had an income of $100,000 or more in 2009. Six percent had an income of $200,000 or more, accounting for 84 percent of all households with incomes that high.

Married couples are the only household type whose median income is significantly above the all-household average of $49,777. Female-headed families had a median income of just $32,597, while male-headed families had a median income only slightly below the national median, at $48,084. Fourteen percent of male-headed families had an income of $100,000 or more in 2009 compared with only 7 percent of female-headed families.

Women who live alone have the lowest incomes, a median of $22,324 in 2009. Most women who live alone are older widows, which accounts for their low incomes. Men who live alone have much higher incomes than their female counterparts—a median of $31,595—because most are under age 55 and in the labor force.

■ The incomes of women who live alone are likely to rise in the decades ahead as baby-boom women with their own retirement income become widows.

Women who live alone have the lowest incomes

(median income of people who live alone, by sex, 2009)

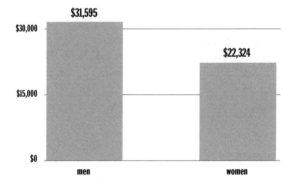

Table 5.16 Household Income by Household Type, 2009: Total Households

(number and percent distribution of households by household income and type of householder, 2009; households in thousands as of 2010)

		family households				nonfamily households				
							female householders		male householders	
	total	total	married couples	female hh, no spouse present	male hh, no spouse present	total	total	living alone	total	living alone
Total households	**117,538**	**78,833**	**58,410**	**14,843**	**5,580**	**38,705**	**20,442**	**17,428**	**18,263**	**13,971**
Under $25,000	29,352	12,999	6,056	5,707	1,235	16,352	10,123	9,528	6,228	5,547
$25,000 to $49,999	29,610	18,676	12,458	4,552	1,664	10,934	5,490	4,696	5,442	4,335
$50,000 to $74,999	21,280	15,633	12,011	2,376	1,246	5,646	2,594	1,929	3,053	2,126
$75,000 to $99,999	13,549	10,983	9,204	1,143	634	2,567	1,033	607	1,535	902
$100,000 to $124,999	8,967	7,534	6,718	488	330	1,433	555	335	877	474
$125,000 to $149,999	5,067	4,423	3,985	248	189	646	229	134	416	210
$150,000 to $174,999	3,354	2,924	2,663	150	110	429	176	92	253	132
$175,000 to $199,999	1,855	1,625	1,537	44	42	230	67	24	162	74
$200,000 or more	4,506	4,038	3,777	133	128	468	174	86	294	172
Median income	$49,777	$61,265	$71,830	$32,597	$48,084	$30,444	$25,269	$22,324	$36,611	$31,595
Total households	**100.0%**	**100.0%**	**100.0%**	**100.0%**	**100.0%**	**100.0%**	**100.0%**	**100.0%**	**100.0%**	**100.0%**
Under $25,000	25.0	16.5	10.4	38.4	22.1	42.2	49.5	54.7	34.1	39.7
$25,000 to $49,999	25.2	23.7	21.3	30.7	29.8	28.2	26.9	26.9	29.8	31.0
$50,000 to $74,999	18.1	19.8	20.6	16.0	22.3	14.6	12.7	11.1	16.7	15.2
$75,000 to $99,999	11.5	13.9	15.8	7.7	11.4	6.6	5.1	3.5	8.4	6.5
$100,000 to $124,999	7.6	9.6	11.5	3.3	5.9	3.7	2.7	1.9	4.8	3.4
$125,000 to $149,999	4.3	5.6	6.8	1.7	3.4	1.7	1.1	0.8	2.3	1.5
$150,000 to $174,999	2.9	3.7	4.6	1.0	2.0	1.1	0.9	0.5	1.4	0.9
$175,000 to $199,999	1.6	2.1	2.6	0.3	0.8	0.6	0.3	0.1	0.9	0.5
$200,000 or more	3.8	5.1	6.5	0.9	2.3	1.2	0.9	0.5	1.6	1.2

Source: Bureau of the Census, 2010 Current Population Survey, Internet site http://www.census.gov/hhes/www/cpstables/ 032010/hhinc/toc.htm; calculations by New Strategist

From Young to Old, Incomes Vary by Household Type

In all but the youngest age group, married couples have the highest incomes.

Married couples are the most affluent household type, while the middle aged are the most affluent age group. Combine those characteristics and you have the most affluent households in the country. Married couples in the 45-to-54 age group had a median income of $88,011 in 2009, 42 percent having an income of $100,000 or more and 9 percent having an income of $200,000 or more. Among couples aged 35 to 44 and 55 to 64, a substantial 37 percent have an income of $100,000 or more.

Only 18 percent of households headed by people under age 25 are married couples, which is one reason for the low incomes of the age group. Among householders under age 25, male-headed families have the highest incomes, a median of $40,879 versus $39,830 for married couples.

■ The number of earners in a household is the major determinant of income. Because most married couples are dual-earners, their incomes typically are far higher than the incomes of other household types.

Many married couples have incomes of $100,000 or more

(percent of married couples with household incomes of $100,000 or more, by age of householder, 2009)

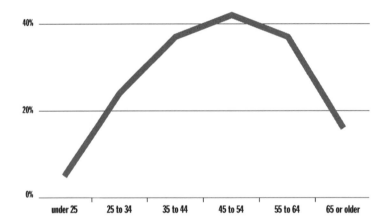

Table 5.17 Household Income by Household Type, 2009: Householders under Age 25

(number and percent distribution of households headed by people under age 25 by household income and type of householder, 2009; households in thousands as of 2010)

		family households				nonfamily households				
				female hh, no spouse present	male hh, no spouse present		female householders		male householders	
	total	total	married couples			total	total	living alone	total	living alone
Householders under 25	6,233	3,399	1,125	1,435	838	2,835	1,299	643	1,535	724
Under $25,000	2,567	1,270	309	734	225	1,297	649	447	647	425
$25,000 to $49,999	1,936	1,051	407	364	281	883	393	168	492	211
$50,000 to $74,999	956	592	262	183	147	365	141	20	225	58
$75,000 to $99,999	351	226	84	89	53	125	40	1	85	22
$100,000 to $124,999	230	126	37	32	58	106	60	7	45	4
$125,000 to $149,999	79	57	12	15	29	22	8	0	15	0
$150,000 to $174,999	39	26	2	6	18	12	0	0	12	1
$175,000 to $199,999	32	16	0	5	11	16	8	0	8	0
$200,000 or more	42	34	10	8	16	8	0	0	8	4
Median income	$30,733	$33,996	$39,830	$24,109	$40,879	$26,980	$24,974	$18,147	$29,364	$21,121
Householders under 25	100.0%	100.0%	100.0%	100.0%	100.0%	100.0%	100.0%	100.0%	100.0%	100.0%
Under $25,000	41.2	37.4	27.5	51.1	26.8	45.7	50.0	69.5	42.1	58.7
$25,000 to $49,999	31.1	30.9	36.2	25.4	33.5	31.1	30.3	26.1	32.1	29.1
$50,000 to $74,999	15.3	17.4	23.3	12.8	17.5	12.9	10.9	3.1	14.7	8.0
$75,000 to $99,999	5.6	6.6	7.5	6.2	6.3	4.4	3.1	0.2	5.5	3.0
$100,000 to $124,999	3.7	3.7	3.3	2.2	6.9	3.7	4.6	1.1	2.9	0.6
$125,000 to $149,999	1.3	1.7	1.1	1.0	3.5	0.8	0.6	0.0	1.0	0.0
$150,000 to $174,999	0.6	0.8	0.2	0.4	2.1	0.4	0.0	0.0	0.8	0.1
$175,000 to $199,999	0.5	0.5	0.0	0.3	1.3	0.6	0.6	0.0	0.5	0.0
$200,000 or more	0.7	1.0	0.9	0.6	1.9	0.3	0.0	0.0	0.5	0.6

Source: Bureau of the Census, 2010 Current Population Survey, Internet site http://www.census.gov/hhes/www/cpstables/032010/hhinc/toc.htm; calculations by New Strategist

Table 5.18 Household Income by Household Type, 2009: Householders Aged 25 to 34

(number and percent distribution of households headed by people aged 25 to 34 by household income and type of householder, 2009; households in thousands as of 2010)

| | | family households | | | | nonfamily households | | | | |
| | | | | female hh, | male hh, | | female householders | | male householders | |
	total	total	married couples	no spouse present	no spouse present	total	total	living alone	total	living alone
Householders 25 to 34	**19,257**	**13,093**	**8,634**	**3,199**	**1,260**	**6,164**	**2,436**	**1,623**	**3,728**	**2,294**
Under $25,000	4,276	2,837	950	1,627	261	1,438	643	573	795	657
$25,000 to $49,999	5,306	3,297	2,009	896	392	2,008	793	612	1,215	874
$50,000 to $74,999	4,115	2,803	2,147	377	279	1,309	510	282	800	465
$75,000 to $99,999	2,432	1,772	1,474	152	147	662	249	81	413	169
$100,000 to $124,999	1,389	1,041	901	82	60	349	88	32	259	80
$125,000 to $149,999	718	574	492	30	52	142	54	18	90	9
$150,000 to $174,999	409	291	246	18	29	117	39	9	77	29
$175,000 to $199,999	209	158	149	2	7	52	18	7	33	3
$200,000 or more	405	318	267	13	38	87	43	10	44	7
Median income	$50,199	$53,026	$65,307	$24,553	$48,325	$45,221	$42,839	$33,370	$46,074	$37,575
Householders 25 to 34	**100.0%**	**100.0%**	**100.0%**	**100.0%**	**100.0%**	**100.0%**	**100.0%**	**100.0%**	**100.0%**	**100.0%**
Under $25,000	22.2	21.7	11.0	50.9	20.7	23.3	26.4	35.3	21.3	28.6
$25,000 to $49,999	27.6	25.2	23.3	28.0	31.1	32.6	32.6	37.7	32.6	38.1
$50,000 to $74,999	21.4	21.4	24.9	11.8	22.1	21.2	20.9	17.4	21.5	20.3
$75,000 to $99,999	12.6	13.5	17.1	4.8	11.7	10.7	10.2	5.0	11.1	7.4
$100,000 to $124,999	7.2	8.0	10.4	2.6	4.8	5.7	3.6	2.0	6.9	3.5
$125,000 to $149,999	3.7	4.4	5.7	0.9	4.1	2.3	2.2	1.1	2.4	0.4
$150,000 to $174,999	2.1	2.2	2.8	0.6	2.3	1.9	1.6	0.6	2.1	1.3
$175,000 to $199,999	1.1	1.2	1.7	0.1	0.6	0.8	0.7	0.4	0.9	0.1
$200,000 or more	2.1	2.4	3.1	0.4	3.0	1.4	1.8	0.6	1.2	0.3

Source: Bureau of the Census, 2010 Current Population Survey, Internet site http://www.census.gov/hhes/www/cpstables/ 032010/hhinc/toc.htm; calculations by New Strategist

Table 5.19 Household Income by Household Type, 2009: Householders Aged 35 to 44

(number and percent distribution of households headed by people aged 35 to 44 by household income and type of householder, 2009; households in thousands as of 2010)

		family households				nonfamily households				
				female hh, no spouse	male hh, no spouse		female householders		male householders	
	total	total	married couples	present	present	total	total	living alone	total	living alone
Householders 35 to 44	**21,519**	**17,062**	**12,465**	**3,473**	**1,124**	**4,457**	**1,622**	**1,280**	**2,834**	**2,173**
Under $25,000	3,671	2,442	926	1,277	241	1,229	501	440	727	661
$25,000 to $49,999	4,946	3,636	2,076	1,207	354	1,310	491	417	821	676
$50,000 to $74,999	4,239	3,369	2,548	542	280	870	335	252	534	400
$75,000 to $99,999	3,133	2,649	2,269	243	137	484	131	68	353	221
$100,000 to $124,999	2,093	1,859	1,707	89	60	235	80	54	155	82
$125,000 to $149,999	1,189	1,075	1,006	50	20	115	26	15	90	46
$150,000 to $174,999	787	716	662	37	18	71	20	9	52	28
$175,000 to $199,999	439	401	388	8	6	39	9	5	29	8
$200,000 or more	1,018	916	882	20	13	102	31	19	71	50
Median income	$61,083	$66,986	$81,232	$32,314	$47,170	$42,800	$40,710	$35,272	$45,527	$40,102
Householders 35 to 44	**100.0%**	**100.0%**	**100.0%**	**100.0%**	**100.0%**	**100.0%**	**100.0%**	**100.0%**	**100.0%**	**100.0%**
Under $25,000	17.1	14.3	7.4	36.8	21.4	27.6	30.9	34.4	25.7	30.4
$25,000 to $49,999	23.0	21.3	16.7	34.8	31.5	29.4	30.3	32.6	29.0	31.1
$50,000 to $74,999	19.7	19.7	20.4	15.6	24.9	19.5	20.7	19.7	18.8	18.4
$75,000 to $99,999	14.6	15.5	18.2	7.0	12.2	10.9	8.1	5.3	12.5	10.2
$100,000 to $124,999	9.7	10.9	13.7	2.6	5.3	5.3	4.9	4.2	5.5	3.8
$125,000 to $149,999	5.5	6.3	8.1	1.4	1.8	2.6	1.6	1.2	3.2	2.1
$150,000 to $174,999	3.7	4.2	5.3	1.1	1.6	1.6	1.2	0.7	1.8	1.3
$175,000 to $199,999	2.0	2.4	3.1	0.2	0.5	0.9	0.6	0.4	1.0	0.4
$200,000 or more	4.7	5.4	7.1	0.6	1.2	2.3	1.9	1.5	2.5	2.3

Source: Bureau of the Census, 2010 Current Population Survey, Internet site http://www.census.gov/hhes/www/cpstables/ 032010/hhinc/toc.htm; calculations by New Strategist

Table 5.20 Household Income by Household Type, 2009: Householders Aged 45 to 54

(number and percent distribution of households headed by people aged 45 to 54 by household income and type of householder, 2009; households in thousands as of 2010)

| | | family households | | | | nonfamily households | | | | |
| | | total | married couples | female hh, no spouse present | male hh, no spouse present | total | female householders | | male householders | |
	total						total	living alone	total	living alone
Householders 45 to 54	**24,871**	**18,176**	**13,896**	**3,048**	**1,233**	**6,695**	**3,005**	**2,476**	**3,690**	**3,005**
Under $25,000	4,513	2,077	912	906	259	2,436	1,213	1,100	1,224	1,108
$25,000 to $49,999	5,024	3,146	1,950	901	296	1,879	857	748	1,022	887
$50,000 to $74,999	4,733	3,619	2,682	629	310	1,114	471	357	644	492
$75,000 to $99,999	3,516	2,954	2,453	328	174	562	218	139	345	239
$100,000 to $124,999	2,569	2,266	2,049	131	87	302	113	67	189	121
$125,000 to $149,999	1,462	1,318	1,204	72	42	144	44	26	100	61
$150,000 to $174,999	1,029	940	880	37	26	87	31	22	56	34
$175,000 to $199,999	548	508	488	11	6	41	13	0	29	13
$200,000 or more	1,475	1,347	1,279	34	33	128	46	19	82	53
Median income	$64,235	$76,738	$88,011	$40,995	$53,834	$36,016	$32,081	$28,534	$38,324	$35,208
Householders 45 to 54	**100.0%**	**100.0%**	**100.0%**	**100.0%**	**100.0%**	**100.0%**	**100.0%**	**100.0%**	**100.0%**	**100.0%**
Under $25,000	18.1	11.4	6.6	29.7	21.0	36.4	40.4	44.4	33.2	36.9
$25,000 to $49,999	20.2	17.3	14.0	29.6	24.0	28.1	28.5	30.2	27.7	29.5
$50,000 to $74,999	19.0	19.9	19.3	20.6	25.1	16.6	15.7	14.4	17.5	16.4
$75,000 to $99,999	14.1	16.3	17.7	10.8	14.1	8.4	7.3	5.6	9.3	8.0
$100,000 to $124,999	10.3	12.5	14.7	4.3	7.1	4.5	3.8	2.7	5.1	4.0
$125,000 to $149,999	5.9	7.3	8.7	2.4	3.4	2.2	1.5	1.1	2.7	2.0
$150,000 to $174,999	4.1	5.2	6.3	1.2	2.1	1.3	1.0	0.9	1.5	1.1
$175,000 to $199,999	2.2	2.8	3.5	0.4	0.5	0.6	0.4	0.0	0.8	0.4
$200,000 or more	5.9	7.4	9.2	1.1	2.7	1.9	1.5	0.8	2.2	1.8

Source: Bureau of the Census, 2010 Current Population Survey, Internet site http://www.census.gov/hhes/www/cpstables/032010/hhinc/toc.htm; calculations by New Strategist

Table 5.21 Household Income by Household Type, 2009: Householders Aged 55 to 64

(number and percent distribution of households headed by people aged 55 to 64 by household income and type of householder, 2009; households in thousands as of 2010)

| | | family households | | | | nonfamily households | | | | |
| | | | | female hh, no spouse present | male hh, no spouse present | | female householders | | male householders | |
	total	total	married couples	female hh, no spouse present	male hh, no spouse present	total	total	living alone	total	living alone
Householders 55 to 64	**20,387**	**13,706**	**11,405**	**1,672**	**629**	**6,681**	**3,676**	**3,286**	**3,005**	**2,578**
Under $25,000	4,351	1,629	1,024	460	145	2,724	1,599	1,510	1,125	1,038
$25,000 to $49,999	4,689	2,775	2,114	502	159	1,913	1,037	950	877	771
$50,000 to $74,999	3,649	2,700	2,249	326	126	949	517	449	432	352
$75,000 to $99,999	2,482	2,027	1,763	173	91	456	237	185	219	160
$100,000 to $124,999	1,768	1,511	1,393	82	36	253	124	98	129	107
$125,000 to $149,999	1,111	946	879	44	24	165	70	52	94	67
$150,000 to $174,999	770	681	629	37	15	88	45	14	44	31
$175,000 to $199,999	440	396	376	12	9	45	10	4	35	25
$200,000 or more	1,126	1,038	978	36	24	88	36	24	52	29
Median income	$56,973	$72,324	$78,627	$41,693	$51,870	$31,702	$29,560	$27,278	$34,161	$31,787
Householders 55 to 64	**100.0%**	**100.0%**	**100.0%**	**100.0%**	**100.0%**	**100.0%**	**100.0%**	**100.0%**	**100.0%**	**100.0%**
Under $25,000	21.3	11.9	9.0	27.5	23.1	40.8	43.5	46.0	37.4	40.3
$25,000 to $49,999	23.0	20.2	18.5	30.0	25.3	28.6	28.2	28.9	29.2	29.9
$50,000 to $74,999	17.9	19.7	19.7	19.5	20.0	14.2	14.1	13.7	14.4	13.7
$75,000 to $99,999	12.2	14.8	15.5	10.3	14.5	6.8	6.4	5.6	7.3	6.2
$100,000 to $124,999	8.7	11.0	12.2	4.9	5.7	3.8	3.4	3.0	4.3	4.2
$125,000 to $149,999	5.4	6.9	7.7	2.6	3.8	2.5	1.9	1.6	3.1	2.6
$150,000 to $174,999	3.8	5.0	5.5	2.2	2.4	1.3	1.2	0.4	1.5	1.2
$175,000 to $199,999	2.2	2.9	3.3	0.7	1.4	0.7	0.3	0.1	1.2	1.0
$200,000 or more	5.5	7.6	8.6	2.2	3.8	1.3	1.0	0.7	1.7	1.1

Source: Bureau of the Census, 2010 Current Population Survey, Internet site http://www.census.gov/hhes/www/cpstables/032010/hhinc/toc.htm; calculations by New Strategist

Table 5.22 Household Income by Household Type, 2009: Householders Aged 65 or Older

(number and percent distribution of households headed by people aged 65 or older by household income and type of householder, 2009; households in thousands as of 2010)

| | | family households | | | | nonfamily households | | | | |
| | total | total | married couples | female hh, no spouse present | male hh, no spouse present | total | female householders | | male householders | |
							total	living alone	total	living alone
Householders 65+	**25,270**	**13,397**	**10,885**	**2,016**	**496**	**11,874**	**8,403**	**8,120**	**3,470**	**3,197**
Under $25,000	9,973	2,743	1,934	706	103	7,230	5,518	5,455	1,710	1,659
$25,000 to $49,999	7,709	4,771	3,901	685	185	2,938	1,922	1,802	1,015	917
$50,000 to $74,999	3,586	2,547	2,122	319	106	1,039	620	568	419	360
$75,000 to $99,999	1,632	1,354	1,163	155	36	279	159	134	120	93
$100,000 to $124,999	918	731	631	69	30	188	87	75	99	80
$125,000 to $149,999	509	454	392	38	23	56	28	25	28	26
$150,000 to $174,999	321	268	243	18	6	53	43	40	12	9
$175,000 to $199,999	183	145	137	6	2	36	8	8	28	25
$200,000 or more	440	385	360	21	4	55	18	14	37	30
Median income	$31,354	$43,913	$46,086	$34,018	$43,112	$20,054	$18,630	$18,280	$25,387	$24,172
Householders 65+	**100.0%**	**100.0%**	**100.0%**	**100.0%**	**100.0%**	**100.0%**	**100.0%**	**100.0%**	**100.0%**	**100.0%**
Under $25,000	39.5	20.5	17.8	35.0	20.8	60.9	65.7	67.2	49.3	51.9
$25,000 to $49,999	30.5	35.6	35.8	34.0	37.3	24.7	22.9	22.2	29.3	28.7
$50,000 to $74,999	14.2	19.0	19.5	15.8	21.4	8.8	7.4	7.0	12.1	11.3
$75,000 to $99,999	6.5	10.1	10.7	7.7	7.3	2.3	1.9	1.7	3.5	2.9
$100,000 to $124,999	3.6	5.5	5.8	3.4	6.0	1.6	1.0	0.9	2.9	2.5
$125,000 to $149,999	2.0	3.4	3.6	1.9	4.6	0.5	0.3	0.3	0.8	0.8
$150,000 to $174,999	1.3	2.0	2.2	0.9	1.2	0.4	0.5	0.5	0.3	0.3
$175,000 to $199,999	0.7	1.1	1.3	0.3	0.4	0.3	0.1	0.1	0.8	0.8
$200,000 or more	1.7	2.9	3.3	1.0	0.8	0.5	0.2	0.2	1.1	0.9

Source: Bureau of the Census, 2010 Current Population Survey, Internet site http://www.census.gov/hhes/www/cpstables/032010/hhinc/toc.htm; calculations by New Strategist

Asian Married Couples Have the Highest Incomes

Hispanic women who live alone have the lowest.

Married couples are the most affluent household type, and Asians are the most affluent racial or ethnic group. Combine those characteristics and you have the most affluent households in the country. Asian married couples had a median income of $83,453 in 2009, 42 percent having an income of $100,000 or more. Eleven percent of Asian couples have an income of $200,000 or more. Black couples have much higher incomes than Hispanic couples—a median of $61,553 compared with $48,471 for Hispanics. Twenty-two percent of black couples have an income of $100,000 or more compared with only 16 percent of Hispanic couples.

Hispanic women who live alone have the lowest incomes, a median of just $16,140 in 2009. Women who live alone account for only 7 percent of Hispanic households. In contrast, a much larger 16 percent of non-Hispanic white households are headed by women who live alone. Their median income is $23,473.

■ Black couples have much higher incomes than Hispanic couples because they are better educated and more likely to be managers or professionals.

Asian married couples are most likely to have incomes of $100,000 or more

(percent of married couples with household incomes of $100,000 or more, by race and Hispanic origin of householder, 2009)

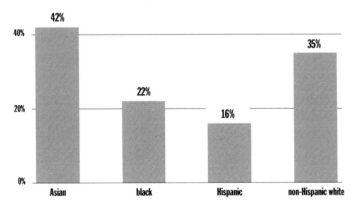

Table 5.23 Household Income by Household Type, 2009: Asian Households

(number and percent distribution of Asian households by household income and type of householder, 2009; households in thousands as of 2010)

| | | family households | | | | nonfamily households | | | | |
| | | | | female hh, no spouse present | male hh, no spouse present | | female householders | | male householders | |
	total	total	married couples			total	total	living alone	total	living alone
Asian households	**4,940**	**3,742**	**2,987**	**481**	**273**	**1,198**	**581**	**465**	**617**	**450**
Under $25,000	972	505	338	118	49	467	266	235	200	161
$25,000 to $49,999	968	686	512	107	69	281	124	104	157	121
$50,000 to $74,999	822	650	492	98	61	171	81	66	88	59
$75,000 to $99,999	588	474	379	68	28	115	38	25	77	57
$100,000 to $124,999	507	435	378	36	21	72	36	27	35	23
$125,000 to $149,999	318	293	257	20	16	26	7	4	19	12
$150,000 to $174,999	238	210	188	13	9	28	10	2	18	12
$175,000 to $199,999	145	133	122	9	1	12	4	2	8	1
$200,000 or more	381	354	320	13	22	26	14	2	12	5
Median income	$65,073	$76,089	$83,453	$53,353	$57,340	$35,259	$28,480	$24,645	$40,633	$36,058
Asian households	**100.0%**	**100.0%**	**100.0%**	**100.0%**	**100.0%**	**100.0%**	**100.0%**	**100.0%**	**100.0%**	**100.0%**
Under $25,000	19.7	13.5	11.3	24.5	17.9	39.0	45.8	50.5	32.4	35.8
$25,000 to $49,999	19.6	18.3	17.1	22.2	25.3	23.5	21.3	22.4	25.4	26.9
$50,000 to $74,999	16.6	17.4	16.5	20.4	22.3	14.3	13.9	14.2	14.3	13.1
$75,000 to $99,999	11.9	12.7	12.7	14.1	10.3	9.6	6.5	5.4	12.5	12.7
$100,000 to $124,999	10.3	11.6	12.7	7.5	7.7	6.0	6.2	5.8	5.7	5.1
$125,000 to $149,999	6.4	7.8	8.6	4.2	5.9	2.2	1.2	0.9	3.1	2.7
$150,000 to $174,999	4.8	5.6	6.3	2.7	3.3	2.3	1.7	0.4	2.9	2.7
$175,000 to $199,999	2.9	3.6	4.1	1.9	0.4	1.0	0.7	0.4	1.3	0.2
$200,000 or more	7.7	9.5	10.7	2.7	8.1	2.2	2.4	0.4	1.9	1.1

Note: Asians are those who identify themselves as being of the race alone and those who identify themselves as being of the race in combination with other races.
Source: Bureau of the Census, 2010 Current Population Survey, Internet site http://www.census.gov/hhes/www/cpstables/032010/hhinc/toc.htm; calculations by New Strategist

Table 5.24 Household Income by Household Type, 2009: Black Households

(number and percent distribution of black households by household income and type of householder, 2009; households in thousands as of 2010)

| | | family households | | | | nonfamily households | | | | |
| | | total | married couples | female hh, no spouse present | male hh, no spouse present | total | female householders | | male householders | |
	total						total	living alone	total	living alone
Black households	**15,212**	**9,652**	**4,427**	**4,257**	**968**	**5,560**	**3,103**	**2,779**	**2,457**	**2,060**
Under $25,000	5,900	2,930	636	2,011	284	2,971	1,769	1,671	1,201	1,094
$25,000 to $49,999	4,253	2,745	1,117	1,310	318	1,510	796	703	715	583
$50,000 to $74,999	2,308	1,691	930	542	221	617	325	266	292	235
$75,000 to $99,999	1,322	1,068	768	227	73	254	124	77	131	80
$100,000 to $124,999	641	535	411	89	36	105	46	32	58	36
$125,000 to $149,999	316	264	212	32	18	53	29	25	23	15
$150,000 to $174,999	203	179	141	32	6	24	9	3	16	5
$175,000 to $199,999	76	73	63	7	4	3	1	0	2	2
$200,000 or more	189	167	148	10	9	22	3	2	19	9
Median income	$32,750	$40,695	$61,553	$26,479	$40,441	$22,726	$20,693	$18,923	$25,692	$22,953
Black households	**100.0%**	**100.0%**	**100.0%**	**100.0%**	**100.0%**	**100.0%**	**100.0%**	**100.0%**	**100.0%**	**100.0%**
Under $25,000	38.8	30.4	14.4	47.2	29.3	53.4	57.0	60.1	48.9	53.1
$25,000 to $49,999	28.0	28.4	25.2	30.8	32.9	27.2	25.7	25.3	29.1	28.3
$50,000 to $74,999	15.2	17.5	21.0	12.7	22.8	11.1	10.5	9.6	11.9	11.4
$75,000 to $99,999	8.7	11.1	17.3	5.3	7.5	4.6	4.0	2.8	5.3	3.9
$100,000 to $124,999	4.2	5.5	9.3	2.1	3.7	1.9	1.5	1.2	2.4	1.7
$125,000 to $149,999	2.1	2.7	4.8	0.8	1.9	1.0	0.9	0.9	0.9	0.7
$150,000 to $174,999	1.3	1.9	3.2	0.8	0.6	0.4	0.3	0.1	0.7	0.2
$175,000 to $199,999	0.5	0.8	1.4	0.2	0.4	0.1	0.0	0.0	0.1	0.1
$200,000 or more	1.2	1.7	3.3	0.2	0.9	0.4	0.1	0.1	0.8	0.4

Note: Blacks are those who identify themselves as being of the race alone and those who identify themselves as being of the race in combination with other races.
Source: Bureau of the Census, 2010 Current Population Survey, Internet site http://www.census.gov/hhes/www/cpstables/032010/hhinc/toc.htm; calculations by New Strategist

Table 5.25 Household Income by Household Type, 2009: Hispanic Households

(number and percent distribution of Hispanic households by household income and type of householder, 2009; households in thousands as of 2010)

| | | family households | | | | nonfamily households | | | | |
| | | | | | | | female householders | | male householders | |
	total	total	married couples	female hh, no spouse present	male hh, no spouse present	total	total	living alone	total	living alone
Hispanic households	**13,298**	**10,412**	**6,589**	**2,745**	**1,079**	**2,885**	**1,260**	**976**	**1,625**	**1,078**
Under $25,000	4,221	2,857	1,364	1,232	260	1,364	727	648	637	521
$25,000 to $49,999	3,960	3,174	2,011	814	349	787	289	210	497	332
$50,000 to $74,999	2,342	1,957	1,343	390	224	384	123	73	259	133
$75,000 to $99,999	1,215	1,068	801	153	114	148	57	21	91	42
$100,000 to $124,999	688	589	448	87	56	97	31	11	66	24
$125,000 to $149,999	354	318	241	37	40	35	10	6	25	9
$150,000 to $174,999	192	161	139	10	12	32	11	3	20	6
$175,000 to $199,999	97	85	74	4	7	12	3	0	8	2
$200,000 or more	230	202	170	15	16	29	10	5	19	8
Median income	$38,039	$41,653	$48,471	$27,882	$43,545	$26,561	$20,145	$16,140	$31,249	$25,898
Hispanic households	**100.0%**	**100.0%**	**100.0%**	**100.0%**	**100.0%**	**100.0%**	**100.0%**	**100.0%**	**100.0%**	**100.0%**
Under $25,000	31.7	27.4	20.7	44.9	24.1	47.3	57.7	66.4	39.2	48.3
$25,000 to $49,999	29.8	30.5	30.5	29.7	32.3	27.3	22.9	21.5	30.6	30.8
$50,000 to $74,999	17.6	18.8	20.4	14.2	20.8	13.3	9.8	7.5	15.9	12.3
$75,000 to $99,999	9.1	10.3	12.2	5.6	10.6	5.1	4.5	2.2	5.6	3.9
$100,000 to $124,999	5.2	5.7	6.8	3.2	5.2	3.4	2.5	1.1	4.1	2.2
$125,000 to $149,999	2.7	3.1	3.7	1.3	3.7	1.2	0.8	0.6	1.5	0.8
$150,000 to $174,999	1.4	1.5	2.1	0.4	1.1	1.1	0.9	0.3	1.2	0.6
$175,000 to $199,999	0.7	0.8	1.1	0.1	0.6	0.4	0.2	0.0	0.5	0.2
$200,000 or more	1.7	1.9	2.6	0.5	1.5	1.0	0.8	0.5	1.2	0.7

Source: Bureau of the Census, 2010 Current Population Survey, Internet site http://www.census.gov/hhes/www/cpstables/ 032010/hhinc/toc.htm; calculations by New Strategist

Table 5.26 Household Income by Household Type, 2009: Non-Hispanic White Households

(number and percent distribution of non-Hispanic white households by household income and type of householder, 2009; households in thousands as of 2010)

| | | family households | | | | nonfamily households | | | | |
| | | | | female hh, no spouse present | male hh, no spouse present | | female householders | | male householders | |
	total	total	married couples			total	total	living alone	total	living alone
Non-Hispanic white households	**83,158**	**54,445**	**43,954**	**7,291**	**3,200**	**28,712**	**15,317**	**13,051**	**13,396**	**10,249**
Under $25,000	17,969	6,592	3,674	2,307	612	11,376	7,268	6,888	4,107	3,698
$25,000 to $49,999	20,217	11,957	8,733	2,312	913	8,260	4,233	3,634	4,026	3,263
$50,000 to $74,999	15,639	11,207	9,124	1,342	741	4,429	2,035	1,508	2,396	1,689
$75,000 to $99,999	10,310	8,271	7,172	688	410	2,040	812	482	1,228	714
$100,000 to $124,999	7,076	5,928	5,438	275	216	1,148	439	264	710	386
$125,000 to $149,999	4,038	3,517	3,244	161	114	520	180	97	343	172
$150,000 to $174,999	2,710	2,363	2,187	94	84	346	145	83	201	110
$175,000 to $199,999	1,523	1,320	1,265	23	31	203	58	22	144	68
$200,000 or more	3,679	3,290	3,117	93	79	390	147	75	243	149
Median income	$54,461	$68,758	$76,266	$38,490	$51,575	$32,158	$26,413	$23,473	$39,971	$34,305
Non-Hispanic white households	**100.0%**	**100.0%**	**100.0%**	**100.0%**	**100.0%**	**100.0%**	**100.0%**	**100.0%**	**100.0%**	**100.0%**
Under $25,000	21.6	12.1	8.4	31.6	19.1	39.6	47.5	52.8	30.7	36.1
$25,000 to $49,999	24.3	22.0	19.9	31.7	28.5	28.8	27.6	27.8	30.1	31.8
$50,000 to $74,999	18.8	20.6	20.8	18.4	23.2	15.4	13.3	11.6	17.9	16.5
$75,000 to $99,999	12.4	15.2	16.3	9.4	12.8	7.1	5.3	3.7	9.2	7.0
$100,000 to $124,999	8.5	10.9	12.4	3.8	6.8	4.0	2.9	2.0	5.3	3.8
$125,000 to $149,999	4.9	6.5	7.4	2.2	3.6	1.8	1.2	0.7	2.6	1.7
$150,000 to $174,999	3.3	4.3	5.0	1.3	2.6	1.2	0.9	0.6	1.5	1.1
$175,000 to $199,999	1.8	2.4	2.9	0.3	1.0	0.7	0.4	0.2	1.1	0.7
$200,000 or more	4.4	6.0	7.1	1.3	2.5	1.4	1.0	0.6	1.8	1.5

Note: Non-Hispanic whites are those who identify themselves as being white alone and not Hispanic.
Source: Bureau of the Census, 2010 Current Population Survey, Internet site http://www.census.gov/hhes/www/cpstables/032010/hhinc/toc.htm; calculations by New Strategist

Dual-Earner Couples Have the Highest Incomes

Most have incomes of $100,000 or more, and many have incomes of $200,000 or more.

The median income of all married-couple families stood at $71,627 in 2009. Among dual-income couples, median income was a much higher $103,527. Eleven percent of dual-income couples have an income of $200,000 or more. Twenty-eight percent of the nation's couples are dual earners in which both husband and wife work full-time.

Among all married couples, those with children under age 18 at home have higher incomes than those without children—$76,649 versus $67,376. Those with children at home have higher incomes because they are more likely to be in the labor force, and many are in their peak-earning years. Couples without children at home have lower incomes because many are older and retired.

Among couples in which both husband and wife work full-time, however, those without children at home—many of them empty-nesters—have the highest incomes—a median of $105,554 in 2009. Dual-income couples with children under age 18 have a lower median income of $101,968.

■ The incomes of married couples without children at home may continue to grow in the years ahead as aging boomers postpone retirement.

Dual-earner married couples without children at home have the highest incomes

(median income of married couples by work status and presence of children under age 18 at home, 2009)

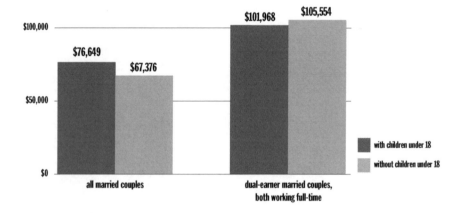

Table 5.27 Income of Married Couples by Presence of Children, 2009

(number and percent distribution of married-couple families by income and presence and age of related children under age 18 at home, 2009; couples in thousands as of 2010)

	total	no children	with one or more children			
			total	all under 6	some under 6, some 6 to 17	all 6 to 17
Total couples	**58,428**	**32,309**	**26,119**	**6,505**	**5,653**	**13,961**
Under $25,000	6,100	3,722	2,378	697	727	953
$25,000 to $49,999	12,510	7,573	4,940	1,376	1,257	2,306
$50,000 to $74,999	12,018	6,657	5,362	1,276	1,218	2,867
$75,000 to $99,999	9,182	4,855	4,327	1,076	843	2,409
$100,000 to $124,999	6,711	3,421	3,292	785	594	1,912
$125,000 to $149,999	3,964	2,027	1,936	466	332	1,138
$150,000 to $174,999	2,655	1,355	1,300	280	242	778
$175,000 to $199,999	1,539	832	709	150	134	422
$200,000 or more	3,748	1,870	1,877	400	305	1,173
Median income	$71,627	$67,376	$76,649	$72,584	$66,250	$82,308
Total couples	**100.0%**	**100.0%**	**100.0%**	**100.0%**	**100.0%**	**100.0%**
Under $25,000	10.4	11.5	9.1	10.7	12.9	6.8
$25,000 to $49,999	21.4	23.4	18.9	21.2	22.2	16.5
$50,000 to $74,999	20.6	20.6	20.5	19.6	21.5	20.5
$75,000 to $99,999	15.7	15.0	16.6	16.5	14.9	17.3
$100,000 to $124,999	11.5	10.6	12.6	12.1	10.5	13.7
$125,000 to $149,999	6.8	6.3	7.4	7.2	5.9	8.2
$150,000 to $174,999	4.5	4.2	5.0	4.3	4.3	5.6
$175,000 to $199,999	2.6	2.6	2.7	2.3	2.4	3.0
$200,000 or more	6.4	5.8	7.2	6.1	5.4	8.4

Note: The median income of married couples in this table is slightly different from the figure shown in the household income tables because this figure includes the incomes of only the family members and not any unrelated members of the household. Source: Bureau of the Census, 2010 Current Population Survey, Internet site http://www.census.gov/hhes/www/cpstables/032010/faminc/toc.htm; calculations by New Strategist

Table 5.28 Income of Dual-Earner Married Couples by Presence of Children, 2009

(number and percent distribution of married couples in which both husband and wife work full-time, year-round, by income and presence and age of related children under age 18 at home, 2009; couples in thousands as of 2010)

	total	no children	with one or more children			
			total	all under 6	some under 6 some 6 to 17	all 6 to 17
Total dual-earner couples	**16,538**	**8,156**	**8,383**	**1,927**	**1,478**	**4,977**
Under $25,000	105	48	57	9	14	34
$25,000 to $49,999	1,007	458	550	107	135	305
$50,000 to $74,999	3,038	1,493	1,545	356	321	869
$75,000 to $99,999	3,572	1,711	1,861	440	312	1,110
$100,000 to $124,999	2,988	1,465	1,522	336	240	944
$125,000 to $149,999	1,922	925	998	248	173	578
$150,000 to $174,999	1,311	710	599	138	98	365
$175,000 to $199,999	840	456	383	100	61	220
$200,000 or more	1,757	888	869	191	125	553
Median income	$103,527	$105,554	$101,968	$102,204	$95,453	$103,344
Total dual-earner couples	**100.0%**	**100.0%**	**100.0%**	**100.0%**	**100.0%**	**100.0%**
Under $25,000	0.6	0.6	0.7	0.5	0.9	0.7
$25,000 to $49,999	6.1	5.6	6.6	5.6	9.1	6.1
$50,000 to $74,999	18.4	18.3	18.4	18.5	21.7	17.5
$75,000 to $99,999	21.6	21.0	22.2	22.8	21.1	22.3
$100,000 to $124,999	18.1	18.0	18.2	17.4	16.2	19.0
$125,000 to $149,999	11.6	11.3	11.9	12.9	11.7	11.6
$150,000 to $174,999	7.9	8.7	7.1	7.2	6.6	7.3
$175,000 to $199,999	5.1	5.6	4.6	5.2	4.1	4.4
$200,000 or more	10.6	10.9	10.4	9.9	8.5	11.1

Source: Bureau of the Census, 2010 Current Population Survey, Internet site http://www.census.gov/hhes/www/cpstables/ 032010/faminc/toc.htm; calculations by New Strategist

Single Parents Have Low Incomes

But many male- and female-headed families have incomes close to the average.

Single-parent families are families with children under age 18 headed by a man or woman without a spouse. Single parents account for 66 percent of female-headed families and 51 percent of families headed by men. The incomes of single-parent families are lower than those of other male- and female-headed families. Female-headed single-parent families had a median income of $25,172 in 2009, while their male counterparts had a median income of $36,085.

Male- and female-headed families without children under age 18 at home have substantially higher incomes. Many of these householders live with other adults such as parents, brothers, or sisters—which adds earners to the household. The median income of male-headed families without children under age 18 at home stood at $48,947, close to the national median. A substantial 15 percent had incomes of $100,000 or more. Their female counterparts had a median income of $39,375.

■ Both male- and female-headed families have seen their incomes fall because of the recession.

Female-headed families with children have lower incomes

(median income of female- and male-headed families by presence of children under age 18 at home, 2009)

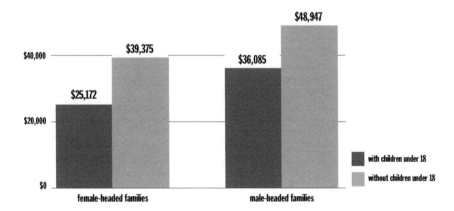

Table 5.29 Income of Female- and Male-Headed Families by Presence of Children, 2009

(number and percent distribution of female- and male-headed families with no spouse present, by family income and presence of children under age 18 at home, 2009; families in thousands as of 2010)

	female-headed families			male-headed families		
	total	no children	one or more children	total	no children	one or more children
Total families	**14,857**	**4,985**	**9,872**	**5,582**	**2,753**	**2,829**
Under $25,000	6,368	1,460	4,907	1,551	574	977
$25,000 to $49,999	4,537	1,667	2,871	1,713	827	885
$50,000 to $74,999	2,149	919	1,231	1,095	613	480
$75,000 to $99,999	931	480	452	555	325	229
$100,000 to $124,999	419	214	205	277	163	113
$125,000 to $149,999	192	116	77	157	90	69
$150,000 to $174,999	120	52	68	88	63	25
$175,000 to $199,999	39	26	13	25	19	6
$200,000 or more	100	49	51	121	78	44
Median income	$29,770	$39,375	$25,172	$41,501	$48,947	$36,085
Total families	**100.0%**	**100.0%**	**100.0%**	**100.0%**	**100.0%**	**100.0%**
Under $25,000	42.9	29.3	49.7	27.8	20.8	34.5
$25,000 to $49,999	30.5	33.4	29.1	30.7	30.0	31.3
$50,000 to $74,999	14.5	18.4	12.5	19.6	22.3	17.0
$75,000 to $99,999	6.3	9.6	4.6	9.9	11.8	8.1
$100,000 to $124,999	2.8	4.3	2.1	5.0	5.9	4.0
$125,000 to $149,999	1.3	2.3	0.8	2.8	3.3	2.4
$150,000 to $174,999	0.8	1.0	0.7	1.6	2.3	0.9
$175,000 to $199,999	0.3	0.5	0.1	0.4	0.7	0.2
$200,000 or more	0.7	1.0	0.5	2.2	2.8	1.6

Note: Median incomes in this table are slightly different from the figures shown in the household income tables because these figures include the incomes of only the family members and not any unrelated members of the household.
Source: Bureau of the Census, 2010 Current Population Survey, Internet site http://www.census.gov/hhes/www/cpstables/ 032010/faminc/toc.htm; calculations by New Strategist

Most Women Who Live Alone Have Low Incomes

The youngest and oldest women who live alone have median incomes of less than $19,000.

Among the nation's 31 million single-person households, women head the 56 percent majority. The median income of all women who live alone was just $22,324 in 2009. The median income of all men who live alone was a higher $31,595. The gap in median incomes can be explained largely by the age differences between men and women who live alone. The 65 percent majority of women who live alone are aged 55 or older, many of them elderly widows dependent on Social Security. Fifty-nine percent of men who live alone are under age 55, many in their peak earning years.

For both men and women who live alone, income is lowest in the youngest age group. Women under age 25 who live alone had a median income of just $18,147. Men under age 25 who live alone had a median income of $21,121. For people who live alone, income peaks in the 35-to-44 age group. The median income of women in the age group who live alone was $35,272 in 2009. For their male counterparts, it was a larger $40,102.

■ The only household type that experienced a gain in median income between 2000 and 2009, after adjusting for inflation, was women who live alone.

Among women who live alone, those aged 35 to 44 have the highest median income

(median income of women who live alone, by age, 2009)

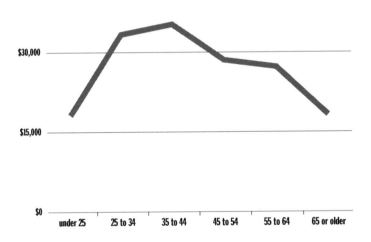

Table 5.30 Household Income of Men Who Live Alone, 2009

(number and percent distribution of male-headed single-person households by household income and age of householder, 2009; households in thousands as of 2010)

	total	15 to 24	25 to 34	35 to 44	45 to 54	55 to 64	65 or older
Total men living alone	**13,971**	**724**	**2,294**	**2,173**	**3,005**	**2,578**	**3,197**
Under $25,000	5,547	425	657	661	1,108	1,038	1,659
$25,000 to $49,999	4,335	211	874	676	887	771	917
$50,000 to $74,999	2,126	58	465	400	492	352	360
$75,000 to $99,999	902	22	169	221	239	160	93
$100,000 to $124,999	474	4	80	82	121	107	80
$125,000 to $149,999	210	0	9	46	61	67	26
$150,000 to $174,999	132	1	29	28	34	31	9
$175,000 to $199,999	74	0	3	8	13	25	25
$200,000 or more	172	4	7	50	53	29	30
Median income	$31,595	$21,121	$37,575	$40,102	$35,208	$31,787	$24,172
Total men living alone	**100.0%**	**100.0%**	**100.0%**	**100.0%**	**100.0%**	**100.0%**	**100.0%**
Under $25,000	39.7	58.7	28.6	30.4	36.9	40.3	51.9
$25,000 to $49,999	31.0	29.1	38.1	31.1	29.5	29.9	28.7
$50,000 to $74,999	15.2	8.0	20.3	18.4	16.4	13.7	11.3
$75,000 to $99,999	6.5	3.0	7.4	10.2	8.0	6.2	2.9
$100,000 to $124,999	3.4	0.6	3.5	3.8	4.0	4.2	2.5
$125,000 to $149,999	1.5	0.0	0.4	2.1	2.0	2.6	0.8
$150,000 to $174,999	0.9	0.1	1.3	1.3	1.1	1.2	0.3
$175,000 to $199,999	0.5	0.0	0.1	0.4	0.4	1.0	0.8
$200,000 or more	1.2	0.6	0.3	2.3	1.8	1.1	0.9

Source: Bureau of the Census, 2010 Current Population Survey, Internet site http://www.census.gov/hhes/www/cpstables/032010/hhinc/toc.htm; calculations by New Strategist

Table 5.31 Household Income of Women Who Live Alone, 2009

(number and percent distribution of female-headed single-person households by household income and age of householder, 2009; households in thousands as of 2010)

	total	15 to 24	25 to 34	35 to 44	45 to 54	55 to 64	65 or older
Total women living alone	**17,428**	**643**	**1,623**	**1,280**	**2,476**	**3,286**	**8,120**
Under $25,000	9,528	447	573	440	1,100	1,510	5,455
$25,000 to $49,999	4,696	168	612	417	748	950	1,802
$50,000 to $74,999	1,929	20	282	252	357	449	568
$75,000 to $99,999	607	1	81	68	139	185	134
$100,000 to $124,999	335	7	32	54	67	98	75
$125,000 to $149,999	134	0	18	15	26	52	25
$150,000 to $174,999	92	0	9	9	22	14	40
$175,000 to $199,999	24	0	7	5	0	4	8
$200,000 or more	86	0	10	19	19	24	14
Median income	$22,324	$18,147	$33,370	$35,272	$28,534	$27,278	$18,280
Total women living alone	**100.0%**	**100.0%**	**100.0%**	**100.0%**	**100.0%**	**100.0%**	**100.0%**
Under $25,000	54.7	69.5	35.3	34.4	44.4	46.0	67.2
$25,000 to $49,999	26.9	26.1	37.7	32.6	30.2	28.9	22.2
$50,000 to $74,999	11.1	3.1	17.4	19.7	14.4	13.7	7.0
$75,000 to $99,999	3.5	0.2	5.0	5.3	5.6	5.6	1.7
$100,000 to $124,999	1.9	1.1	2.0	4.2	2.7	3.0	0.9
$125,000 to $149,999	0.8	0.0	1.1	1.2	1.1	1.6	0.3
$150,000 to $174,999	0.5	0.0	0.6	0.7	0.9	0.4	0.5
$175,000 to $199,999	0.1	0.0	0.4	0.4	0.0	0.1	0.1
$200,000 or more	0.5	0.0	0.6	1.5	0.8	0.7	0.2

Source: Bureau of the Census, 2010 Current Population Survey, Internet site http://www.census.gov/hhes/www/cpstables/032010/hhinc/toc.htm; calculations by New Strategist

College-Educated Householders Have the Highest Incomes

The median income of households headed by college graduates is 62 percent higher than the national average.

The higher the educational degree, the greater the household income. At the top are householders with professional degrees, such as doctors or lawyers. Their median household income was $123,784 in 2009, with 28 percent having household incomes of $200,000 or more.

Thirty-one percent of householders aged 25 or older have at least a bachelor's degree. Their median income stood at $82,722 in 2009. In contrast, householders who went no further than high school had a median income that was far below average at just $39,647. Those who did not graduate from high school had a median household income of less than $26,000.

■ Households headed by college graduates account for 76 percent of all households with incomes of $200,000 or more.

Incomes rise with education

(median income of householders aged 25 or older by educational attainment, 2009)

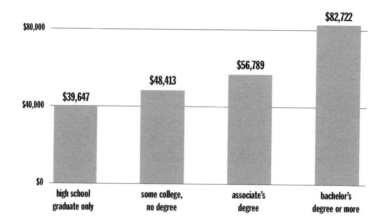

Table 5.32 Household Income by Education of Householder, 2009

(number and percent distribution of householders aged 25 or older by household income and educational attainment of householder, 2009; households in thousands as of 2010)

	total	less than 9th grade	9th to 12th grade, no diploma	high school graduate	some college, no degree	assoc. degree	bachelor's degree or more				
							total	bachelor's degree	master's degree	prof. degree	doctoral degree
Total households	**111,305**	**5,091**	**8,356**	**32,770**	**19,938**	**10,531**	**34,618**	**22,134**	**9,000**	**1,746**	**1,738**
Under $25,000	26,784	2,884	4,086	9,880	4,667	1,902	3,364	2,484	685	116	79
$25,000 to $49,999	27,675	1,332	2,458	9,970	5,550	2,634	5,731	4,164	1,205	201	160
$50,000 to $74,999	20,322	520	1,046	6,151	4,041	2,262	6,304	4,321	1,573	207	201
$75,000 to $99,999	13,197	190	455	3,290	2,471	1,606	5,184	3,345	1,446	172	221
$100,000 to $124,999	8,737	96	159	1,763	1,402	960	4,357	2,700	1,245	181	231
$125,000 to $149,999	4,989	22	75	810	804	501	2,778	1,587	890	124	180
$150,000 to $174,999	3,314	18	26	394	374	269	2,235	1,290	608	158	179
$175,000 to $199,999	1,822	17	10	188	209	135	1,262	672	367	99	124
$200,000 or more	4,465	11	43	327	421	260	3,402	1,568	984	489	362
Median income	$50,971	$21,635	$25,604	$39,647	$48,413	$56,789	$82,722	$75,518	$91,660	$123,784	$120,873
Total households	**100.0%**	**100.0%**	**100.0%**	**100.0%**	**100.0%**	**100.0%**	**100.0%**	**100.0%**	**100.0%**	**100.0%**	**100.0%**
Under $25,000	24.1	56.6	48.9	30.1	23.4	18.1	9.7	11.2	7.6	6.6	4.5
$25,000 to $49,999	24.9	26.2	29.4	30.4	27.8	25.0	16.6	18.8	13.4	11.5	9.2
$50,000 to $74,999	18.3	10.2	12.5	18.8	20.3	21.5	18.2	19.5	17.5	11.9	11.6
$75,000 to $99,999	11.9	3.7	5.4	10.0	12.4	15.3	15.0	15.1	16.1	9.9	12.7
$100,000 to $124,999	7.8	1.9	1.9	5.4	7.0	9.1	12.6	12.2	13.8	10.4	13.3
$125,000 to $149,999	4.5	0.4	0.9	2.5	4.0	4.8	8.0	7.2	9.9	7.1	10.4
$150,000 to $174,999	3.0	0.4	0.3	1.2	1.9	2.6	6.5	5.8	6.8	9.0	10.3
$175,000 to $199,999	1.6	0.3	0.1	0.6	1.0	1.3	3.6	3.0	4.1	5.7	7.1
$200,000 or more	4.0	0.2	0.5	1.0	2.1	2.5	9.8	7.1	10.9	28.0	20.8

Source: Bureau of the Census, 2010 Current Population Survey, Internet site http://www.census.gov/hhes/www/cpstables/032010/hhinc/toc.htm; calculations by New Strategist

Incomes Have Plummeted among Men under Age 65

Most young and middle-aged women have also lost ground.

Between 2000 and 2009, older men and women experienced substantial gains in income, after adjusting for inflation. Among men aged 65 or older, median income climbed 7 percent during those years. Among women aged 55 or older, median income rose 11 to 19 percent. Most younger men and women lost ground between 2000 and 2009. Men under age 55 experienced double-digit declines in median income during those years.

Women's median income stood at $20,957 in 2009, well below the $32,184 median income of men. Men's incomes are higher than women's in part because men are more likely to work full-time. Incomes peak among men aged 45 to 54 at $44,731. Women's income peak is also in the 45-to-54 age group at $28,617—including both full- and part-time workers.

■ Behind the income gains for older men and women is increased labor force participation.

The median income of men aged 45 to 54 fell 12 percent between 2000 and 2009

(median income of men aged 25 or older by age, 2000 and 2009; in 2009 dollars)

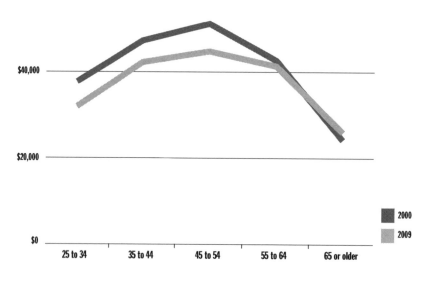

Table 5.33 Median Income of Men by Age, 1990 to 2009

(median income of men aged 15 or older with income by age, 1990 to 2009; percent change in income, 2000–09 and 1990–2009; in 2009 dollars)

	total men	under 25	25 to 34	35 to 44	45 to 54	55 to 64	65 or older
2009	$32,184	$10,036	$31,914	$42,224	$44,731	$41,296	$25,877
2008	33,035	10,737	33,288	44,021	45,367	41,599	25,406
2007	34,341	11,596	34,009	46,570	47,430	43,582	25,162
2006	34,324	11,664	34,182	45,359	48,610	44,124	25,000
2005	34,362	11,502	34,237	45,008	47,933	44,667	23,934
2004	34,652	11,449	35,193	46,028	47,540	44,613	23,995
2003	34,907	11,617	35,642	45,711	49,074	45,384	23,748
2002	34,860	11,496	36,576	45,178	48,846	43,252	23,173
2001	35,257	11,269	36,964	46,450	49,799	43,176	23,853
2000	35,303	11,890	37,683	47,234	51,116	42,584	24,177
1999	35,134	10,749	37,817	46,854	52,527	43,105	24,845
1998	34,814	10,763	36,950	46,228	51,149	43,072	23,873
1997	33,595	9,951	34,639	43,774	50,134	41,516	23,676
1996	32,445	9,475	34,276	43,788	49,322	40,193	22,712
1995	31,531	9,661	32,994	43,910	49,732	40,500	23,037
1994	31,085	10,087	32,353	43,947	49,995	38,749	21,825
1993	30,845	9,397	32,051	44,351	48,462	36,746	21,901
1992	30,639	9,432	32,200	44,173	48,203	38,368	21,864
1991	31,437	9,647	33,166	45,002	48,807	39,102	22,050
1990	32,284	10,053	34,034	47,366	49,329	39,461	22,564
Percent change							
2000 to 2009	−8.8%	−15.6%	−15.3%	−10.6%	−12.5%	−3.0%	7.0%
1990 to 2009	−0.3	−0.2	−6.2	−10.9	−9.3	4.7	14.7

Source: Bureau of the Census, Current Population Surveys, Internet site http://www.census.gov/hhes/www/income/data/historical/people/index.html; calculations by New Strategist

Table 5.34 Median Income of Women by Age, 1990 to 2009

(median income of women aged 15 or older with income by age, 1990 to 2009; percent change in income, 2000–09 and 1990–2009; in 2009 dollars)

	total women	under 25	25 to 34	35 to 44	45 to 54	55 to 64	65 or older
2009	$20,957	$8,950	$25,236	$27,894	$28,617	$25,112	$15,282
2008	20,788	8,867	25,456	27,267	28,129	25,418	14,504
2007	21,643	9,268	26,777	28,657	30,469	26,133	14,504
2006	21,291	9,205	25,722	28,051	29,621	25,730	14,471
2005	20,410	9,031	25,067	27,946	29,089	24,306	13,728
2004	20,062	8,747	25,058	27,710	29,788	23,622	13,719
2003	20,128	8,671	25,648	27,374	30,166	23,754	13,814
2002	20,045	9,040	25,812	26,614	30,004	22,850	13,599
2001	20,129	9,047	26,015	27,224	29,240	21,593	13,706
2000	20,007	9,167	26,218	27,498	29,559	21,075	13,730
1999	19,701	8,597	24,855	26,595	29,052	20,522	14,106
1998	18,963	8,587	23,992	26,657	28,370	19,285	13,804
1997	18,259	8,451	23,514	24,926	27,361	19,156	13,407
1996	17,445	8,006	22,303	25,112	25,927	18,127	13,104
1995	16,952	7,421	21,741	24,313	24,768	17,303	13,074
1994	16,410	7,883	21,301	23,169	24,403	15,552	12,809
1993	16,146	7,822	20,446	23,159	23,861	15,829	12,423
1992	16,048	7,744	20,417	23,093	23,744	15,178	12,257
1991	16,089	7,982	19,911	23,230	22,614	15,208	12,577
1990	16,020	7,799	20,028	23,075	22,639	14,955	12,797
Percent change							
2000 to 2009	4.7%	–2.4%	–3.7%	1.4%	–3.2%	19.2%	11.3%
1990 to 2009	30.8	14.8	26.0	20.9	26.4	67.9	19.4

Source: Bureau of the Census, Current Population Surveys, Internet site http://www.census.gov/hhes/www/income/data/ historical/people/index.html; calculations by New Strategist

Between 2000 and 2009, Men in Every Racial or Ethnic Group Lost Ground

Most women saw their incomes grow, but black women fell behind.

The median income of black men fell 11 percent between 2000 and 2009, after adjusting for inflation. The income of Hispanic men fell 8 percent, non-Hispanic white men's income was down 6 percent, and Asians lost 4 percent. In contrast, Asian, Hispanic, and non-Hispanic white women experienced an increase in their median income between 2000 and 2009. Asian women experienced the biggest gain, with their median income rising by 12 percent. Black women's median income fell 2 percent during those years.

Among both men and women, Hispanics have the lowest median income—just $16,210 for women and $22,256 for men in 2009. Asians and non-Hispanic whites have the highest incomes among men, a median of just under $37,000. Among women, Asians have the highest median income—$24,170 in 2009.

■ Until recently, the incomes of black men and women had been growing faster than the incomes of other racial or ethnic groups.

The median income of black men and women fell between 2000 and 2009

(percent change in median income of people aged 15 or older, by sex, race, and Hispanic origin, 2000 to 2009; in 2009 dollars)

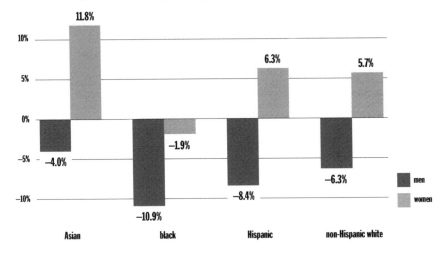

Table 5.35 Median Income of Men by Race and Hispanic Origin, 1990 to 2009

(median income of men aged 15 or older with income by race and Hispanic origin, 1990 to 2009; percent change in income, 2000–09 and 1990–2009; in 2009 dollars)

	total men	Asian	black	Hispanic	non-Hispanic white
2009	$32,184	$36,886	$23,674	$22,256	$36,785
2008	33,035	36,067	25,023	23,912	37,267
2007	34,341	37,996	26,681	25,294	38,662
2006	34,324	39,473	26,676	24,949	38,898
2005	34,362	36,297	24,841	24,269	38,834
2004	34,652	36,867	25,792	24,478	38,243
2003	34,907	37,013	25,581	24,553	37,706
2002	34,860	36,769	25,645	24,683	38,193
2001	35,257	37,674	26,007	24,460	38,516
2000	35,303	38,404	26,584	24,286	39,245
1999	35,134	35,887	26,314	23,000	39,737
1998	34,814	33,017	25,391	22,678	39,243
1997	33,595	33,373	24,113	21,608	36,722
1996	32,445	31,819	22,449	21,014	35,788
1995	31,531	30,972	22,369	20,739	35,610
1994	31,085	32,759	21,442	20,752	34,523
1993	30,845	31,633	21,348	20,009	33,869
1992	30,639	29,792	19,568	20,083	33,551
1991	31,437	30,145	19,908	21,222	34,056
1990	32,284	30,854	20,472	21,430	34,933

Percent change

	total men	Asian	black	Hispanic	non-Hispanic white
2000 to 2009	–8.8%	–4.0%	–10.9%	–8.4%	–6.3%
1990 to 2009	–0.3	19.5	15.6	3.9	5.3

Note: Asians and blacks in 2002 through 2009 are those who identify themselves as being of the race alone and those who identify themselves as being of the race in combination with other races. Non-Hispanic whites in 2002 through 2009 are those who identify themselves as being white alone and not Hispanic. Hispanics may be of any race.
Source: Bureau of the Census, Current Population Surveys, Internet site http://www.census.gov/hhes/www/income/data/historical/people/index.html; calculations by New Strategist

Table 5.36 Median Income of Women by Race and Hispanic Origin, 1990 to 2009

(median income of women aged 15 or older with income by race and Hispanic origin, 1990 to 2009; percent change in income, 2000–09 and 1990–2009; in 2009 dollars)

	total women	Asian	black	Hispanic	non-Hispanic white
2009	$20,957	$24,170	$19,413	$16,210	$21,939
2008	20,788	22,928	20,126	16,355	21,666
2007	21,643	24,926	20,392	17,326	22,435
2006	21,291	23,491	20,282	16,764	22,050
2005	20,410	23,757	19,332	16,520	21,371
2004	20,062	23,410	19,698	16,411	20,934
2003	20,128	20,851	19,290	15,910	21,343
2002	20,045	21,339	19,876	15,934	20,733
2001	20,129	22,444	19,726	15,245	20,874
2000	20,007	21,618	19,781	15,256	20,757
1999	19,701	21,623	19,021	14,644	20,482
1998	18,963	20,012	17,264	14,274	19,997
1997	18,259	19,071	17,386	13,671	19,173
1996	17,445	19,921	16,025	12,910	18,396
1995	16,952	17,975	15,318	12,477	17,898
1994	16,410	17,692	15,090	12,327	17,095
1993	16,146	18,074	13,898	11,840	16,954
1992	16,048	17,781	13,311	12,444	16,854
1991	16,089	16,934	13,540	12,307	16,894
1990	16,020	17,637	13,249	11,983	16,833
Percent change					
2000 to 2009	4.7%	11.8%	–1.9%	6.3%	5.7%
1990 to 2009	30.8	37.0	46.5	35.3	30.3

Note: Asians and blacks in 2002 through 2009 are those who identify themselves as being of the race alone and those who identify themselves as being of the race in combination with other races. Non-Hispanic whites in 2002 through 2009 are those who identify themselves as being white alone and not Hispanic. Hispanics may be of any race.
Source: Bureau of the Census, Current Population Surveys, Internet site http://www.census.gov/hhes/www/income/data/ historical/people/index.html; calculations by New Strategist

The Incomes of Men and Women Peak in the 45-to-54 Age Group

Men's income peak is much higher than women's.

Men aged 45 to 54 had a median income of $44,731 in 2009. Their female counterparts had a median income of $28,617—just 64 percent as high as men's. The income gap between men and women is somewhat smaller when comparing only full-time workers. Among full-time workers aged 45 to 54, women's income was 74 percent as high as men's ($40,392 versus $54,333).

A substantial 14 percent of men aged 45 to 64 had an income of $100,000 or more in 2009, as did 12 percent of 35-to-44-year-olds. Incomes are lowest for men under age 25, a median of just $10,036, because many are college students working part-time. Among young men who work full-time, median income was a higher $25,404 in 2009.

Women are much less likely than men to have high incomes. Only 4 to 5 percent of women ranging in age from 35 to 64 had an income of $100,000 or more. But more than one in five women aged 45 to 54 had an income of $50,000 or more in 2009. Older women have much lower incomes than their male counterparts because fewer are covered by pensions. Women aged 65 or older had a median income of just $15,282 versus $25,877 for men.

■ The percentage of men who work full-time peaks at 70 percent in the 35-to-44 age group. Among women, the peak is 52 percent in the 45-to-54 age group.

Even among full-time workers, men's incomes are much higher

(median income of people aged 45 to 54, by work status and sex, 2009)

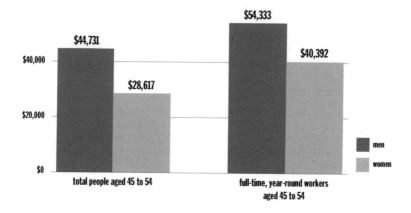

Table 5.37 Income of Men by Age, 2009

(number and percent distribution of men aged 15 or older with income, median income of those with income and of those working full-time year-round, and percent working full-time year-round, by income and age, 2009; men in thousands as of 2010)

	total	15 to 24	25 to 34	35 to 44	45 to 54	55 to 64	65 or older
Total men	**117,728**	**21,403**	**20,689**	**20,074**	**21,784**	**16,985**	**16,793**
Without income	12,703	8,123	1,408	987	1,065	733	387
With income	105,025	13,280	19,281	19,087	20,719	16,252	16,406
Under $10,000	14,950	6,624	2,181	1,383	1,763	1,469	1,532
$10,000 to $19,999	17,803	3,029	3,183	2,251	2,421	2,337	4,583
$20,000 to $29,999	15,585	1,767	3,407	2,527	2,443	2,139	3,299
$30,000 to $39,999	12,835	915	2,893	2,542	2,504	1,886	2,096
$40,000 to $49,999	10,240	427	2,336	2,291	2,313	1,591	1,283
$50,000 to $59,999	8,249	227	1,741	1,789	2,014	1,432	1,042
$60,000 to $69,999	5,806	128	1,008	1,372	1,541	1,129	630
$70,000 to $79,999	4,464	53	835	1,133	1,167	867	410
$80,000 to $89,999	3,007	37	474	740	914	561	279
$90,000 to $99,999	2,244	24	257	630	621	501	212
$100,000 or more	9,842	46	966	2,429	3,016	2,342	1,044
Median income of men with income	$32,184	$10,036	$31,914	$42,224	$44,731	$41,296	$25,877
Median income of full-time workers	49,164	25,404	41,240	51,208	54,333	57,041	61,308
Percent working full-time	47.6%	16.9%	61.0%	69.9%	67.1%	53.7%	12.3%
Total men	**100.0%**	**100.0%**	**100.0%**	**100.0%**	**100.0%**	**100.0%**	**100.0%**
Without income	10.8	38.0	6.8	4.9	4.9	4.3	2.3
With income	89.2	62.0	93.2	95.1	95.1	95.7	97.7
Under $10,000	12.7	30.9	10.5	6.9	8.1	8.6	9.1
$10,000 to $19,999	15.1	14.2	15.4	11.2	11.1	13.8	27.3
$20,000 to $29,999	13.2	8.3	16.5	12.6	11.2	12.6	19.6
$30,000 to $39,999	10.9	4.3	14.0	12.7	11.5	11.1	12.5
$40,000 to $49,999	8.7	2.0	11.3	11.4	10.6	9.4	7.6
$50,000 to $59,999	7.0	1.1	8.4	8.9	9.2	8.4	6.2
$60,000 to $69,999	4.9	0.6	4.9	6.8	7.1	6.6	3.8
$70,000 to $79,999	3.8	0.2	4.0	5.6	5.4	5.1	2.4
$80,000 to $89,999	2.6	0.2	2.3	3.7	4.2	3.3	1.7
$90,000 to $99,999	1.9	0.1	1.2	3.1	2.9	2.9	1.3
$100,000 or more	8.4	0.2	4.7	12.1	13.8	13.8	6.2

Source: Bureau of the Census, 2010 Current Population Survey, Internet site http://www.census.gov/hhes/www/cpstables/ 032010/ perinc/toc.htm; calculations by New Strategist

Table 5.38 Income of Women by Age, 2009

(number and percent distribution of women aged 15 or older with income, median income of those with income and of those working full-time year-round, and percent working full-time year-round, by income and age, 2009; women in thousands as of 2010)

	total	15 to 24	25 to 34	35 to 44	45 to 54	55 to 64	65 or older
Total women	**124,440**	**20,837**	**20,396**	**20,373**	**22,604**	**18,410**	**21,820**
Without income	18,211	8,033	2,898	2,460	2,186	1,716	919
With income	106,229	12,804	17,498	17,913	20,418	16,694	20,901
Under $10,000	26,970	6,862	3,496	3,496	3,695	3,599	5,819
$10,000 to $19,999	23,958	3,211	3,382	3,052	3,460	3,305	7,551
$20,000 to $29,999	16,924	1,634	3,317	2,813	3,374	2,620	3,167
$30,000 to $39,999	12,326	699	2,603	2,631	2,809	2,029	1,554
$40,000 to $49,999	8,151	186	1,783	1,832	2,051	1,427	873
$50,000 to $59,999	5,748	103	1,130	1,194	1,481	1,083	756
$60,000 to $69,999	3,635	51	604	866	1,025	726	363
$70,000 to $79,999	2,500	16	435	589	718	507	232
$80,000 to $89,999	1,534	5	213	327	473	366	148
$90,000 to $99,999	1,057	4	170	249	299	228	106
$100,000 or more	3,426	33	362	862	1,034	806	328
Median income of women with income	$20,957	$8,950	$25,236	$27,894	$28,617	$25,112	$15,282
Median income of full-time workers	37,234	22,616	35,608	39,642	40,392	40,850	47,229
Percent working full-time	34.8%	13.6%	47.4%	49.7%	52.4%	40.3%	6.2%
Total women	**100.0%**	**100.0%**	**100.0%**	**100.0%**	**100.0%**	**100.0%**	**100.0%**
Without income	14.6	38.6	14.2	12.1	9.7	9.3	4.2
With income	85.4	61.4	85.8	87.9	90.3	90.7	95.8
Under $10,000	21.7	32.9	17.1	17.2	16.3	19.5	26.7
$10,000 to $19,999	19.3	15.4	16.6	15.0	15.3	18.0	34.6
$20,000 to $29,999	13.6	7.8	16.3	13.8	14.9	14.2	14.5
$30,000 to $39,999	9.9	3.4	12.8	12.9	12.4	11.0	7.1
$40,000 to $49,999	6.6	0.9	8.7	9.0	9.1	7.8	4.0
$50,000 to $59,999	4.6	0.5	5.5	5.9	6.6	5.9	3.5
$60,000 to $69,999	2.9	0.2	3.0	4.3	4.5	3.9	1.7
$70,000 to $79,999	2.0	0.1	2.1	2.9	3.2	2.8	1.1
$80,000 to $89,999	1.2	0.0	1.0	1.6	2.1	2.0	0.7
$90,000 to $99,999	0.8	0.0	0.8	1.2	1.3	1.2	0.5
$100,000 or more	2.8	0.2	1.8	4.2	4.6	4.4	1.5

Source: Bureau of the Census, 2010 Current Population Survey, Internet site http://www.census.gov/hhes/www/cpstables/032010/perinc/toc.htm; calculations by New Strategist

Among both Men and Women, Asians Have the Highest Incomes

Asian men are most likely to work full-time.

Among full-time workers, Asian men had the highest incomes, a median of $52,849 in 2009. Non-Hispanic white men were only a few hundred dollars behind them, with a median income of $52,469. Black men who worked full-time had a lower median income, at $39,280, and Hispanic men had the lowest—just $31,638. Asian men are most likely to work full-time (54 percent), black men the least (39 percent).

Among women who work full-time, Asians again have the highest incomes, a median of $45,020. Non-Hispanic white women are next, with a median of $40,265. Black women who work full-time have a median income of $32,723, while Hispanic women have the lowest incomes—a median of just $27,883. Asian and black women are most likely to work full-time (36 percent), Hispanic women the least (31 percent).

■ More than one in ten Asian and non-Hispanic white men had an income of $100,000 or more in 2009.

Black men and women have higher incomes than their Hispanic counterparts

(median income of people aged 15 or older who work full-time, year-round, by sex, race, and Hispanic origin, 2009)

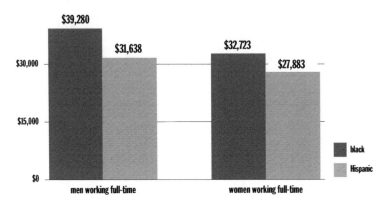

Table 5.39 Income of Men by Race and Hispanic Origin, 2009

(number and percent distribution of men aged 15 or older with income, median income of those with income and of those working full-time year-round, and percent working full-time year-round, by income, race, and Hispanic origin, 2009; men in thousands as of 2010)

	total men	Asian	black	Hispanic	non-Hispanic white
Total men	**117,728**	**5,614**	**13,830**	**17,679**	**79,763**
Without income	12,703	786	2,766	2,760	6,278
With income	105,025	4,828	11,064	14,919	73,485
Under $10,000	14,950	719	2,458	2,728	8,959
$10,000 to $19,999	17,803	672	2,335	3,749	10,911
$20,000 to $29,999	15,585	592	1,754	2,887	10,237
$30,000 to $39,999	12,835	562	1,338	1,948	8,891
$40,000 to $49,999	10,240	410	975	1,184	7,601
$50,000 to $59,999	8,249	350	721	796	6,318
$60,000 to $69,999	5,806	255	471	468	4,574
$70,000 to $79,999	4,464	245	306	364	3,513
$80,000 to $89,999	3,007	160	186	172	2,467
$90,000 to $99,999	2,244	159	122	134	1,811
$100,000 or more	9,842	701	399	489	8,203
Median income of men with income	$32,184	$36,886	$23,674	$22,256	$36,785
Median income of full-time workers	49,164	52,849	39,280	31,638	52,469
Percent working full-time	47.6%	54.3%	38.8%	46.2%	49.1%
Total men	**100.0%**	**100.0%**	**100.0%**	**100.0%**	**100.0%**
Without income	10.8	14.0	20.0	15.6	7.9
With income	89.2	86.0	80.0	84.4	92.1
Under $10,000	12.7	12.8	17.8	15.4	11.2
$10,000 to $19,999	15.1	12.0	16.9	21.2	13.7
$20,000 to $29,999	13.2	10.5	12.7	16.3	12.8
$30,000 to $39,999	10.9	10.0	9.7	11.0	11.1
$40,000 to $49,999	8.7	7.3	7.0	6.7	9.5
$50,000 to $59,999	7.0	6.2	5.2	4.5	7.9
$60,000 to $69,999	4.9	4.5	3.4	2.6	5.7
$70,000 to $79,999	3.8	4.4	2.2	2.1	4.4
$80,000 to $89,999	2.6	2.9	1.3	1.0	3.1
$90,000 to $99,999	1.9	2.8	0.9	0.8	2.3
$100,000 or more	8.4	12.5	2.9	2.8	10.3

Note: Asians and blacks are those who identify themselves as being of the race alone and those who identify themselves as being of the race in combination with other races. Non-Hispanic whites are those who identify themselves as being white alone and not Hispanic. Hispanics may be of any race.
Source: Bureau of the Census, 2010 Current Population Survey, Internet site http://www.census.gov/hhes/www/cpstables/032010/perinc/toc.htm; calculations by New Strategist

Table 5.40 Income of Women by Race and Hispanic Origin, 2009

(number and percent distribution of women aged 15 or older with income, median income of those with income and of those working full-time year-round, and percent working full-time year-round, by income, race, and Hispanic origin, 2009; women in thousands as of 2010)

	total women	Asian	black	Hispanic	non-Hispanic white
Total women	**124,440**	**6,260**	**16,638**	**16,609**	**84,049**
Without income	18,211	1,337	2,845	4,574	9,356
With income	106,229	4,923	13,793	12,035	74,693
Under $10,000	26,970	1,315	3,581	3,765	18,083
$10,000 to $19,999	23,958	831	3,460	3,318	16,173
$20,000 to $29,999	16,924	703	2,315	2,013	11,757
$30,000 to $39,999	12,326	495	1,674	1,206	8,864
$40,000 to $49,999	8,151	376	989	620	6,083
$50,000 to $59,999	5,748	286	635	377	4,446
$60,000 to $69,999	3,635	209	389	235	2,779
$70,000 to $79,999	2,500	174	252	159	1,898
$80,000 to $89,999	1,534	113	150	86	1,173
$90,000 to $99,999	1,057	103	90	50	812
$100,000 or more	3,426	316	257	207	2,622
Median income of women with income	$20,957	$24,170	$19,413	$16,210	$21,939
Median income of full-time workers	37,234	45,020	32,723	27,883	40,265
Percent working full-time	34.8%	36.9%	36.4%	31.2%	35.0%
Total women	**100.0%**	**100.0%**	**100.0%**	**100.0%**	**100.0%**
Without income	14.6	21.4	17.1	27.5	11.1
With income	85.4	78.6	82.9	72.5	88.9
Under $10,000	21.7	21.0	21.5	22.7	21.5
$10,000 to $19,999	19.3	13.3	20.8	20.0	19.2
$20,000 to $29,999	13.6	11.2	13.9	12.1	14.0
$30,000 to $39,999	9.9	7.9	10.1	7.3	10.5
$40,000 to $49,999	6.6	6.0	5.9	3.7	7.2
$50,000 to $59,999	4.6	4.6	3.8	2.3	5.3
$60,000 to $69,999	2.9	3.3	2.3	1.4	3.3
$70,000 to $79,999	2.0	2.8	1.5	1.0	2.3
$80,000 to $89,999	1.2	1.8	0.9	0.5	1.4
$90,000 to $99,999	0.8	1.6	0.5	0.3	1.0
$100,000 or more	2.8	5.0	1.5	1.2	3.1

Note: Asians and blacks are those who identify themselves as being of the race alone and those who identify themselves as being of the race in combination with other races. Non-Hispanic whites are those who identify themselves as being white alone and not Hispanic. Hispanics may be of any race.
Source: Bureau of the Census, 2010 Current Population Survey, Internet site http://www.census.gov/hhes/www/cpstables/032010/perinc/toc.htm; calculations by New Strategist

Women Have Gained on Men

Among full-time workers, women have been closing the gap.

Among men working full-time, year-round in 2009, median earnings stood at $47,127. Among their female counterparts, median earnings were a smaller $36,278—or 77 percent as high as men's. Women are closing the gap with men. Their earnings have grown from 72 percent of men's in 1990 to 77 percent today.

Women have been closing the gap with men because their earnings are growing faster. Among full-time workers, women's median earnings grew 15 percent between 1990 and 2009, after adjusting for inflation. Men's median earnings grew only 7 percent during those years. Women continued to gain on men in the 2000 to 2009 time period. Between 2000 and 2009, the median earnings of women who work full-time grew 6 percent compared with a gain of 2 percent for men.

■ Despite the Great Recession, workers who have managed to keep their full-time jobs are seeing their earnings grow.

Income gap narrows between the sexes

(women's median earnings as a percent of men's median earnings among full-time, year-round workers, 1990 to 2009)

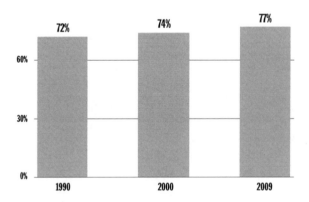

Table 5.41 Median Earnings of Full-Time Workers by Sex, 1990 to 2009

(median earnings of people aged 15 or older who work full-time, year-round, by sex, and index of men's earnings to women's, 1990 to 2009; percent change in earnings for selected years; in 2009 dollars)

	men	women	index of women's earnings to men's
2009	$47,127	$36,278	77
2008	46,191	35,609	77
2007	46,669	36,312	78
2006	44,959	34,590	77
2005	45,471	35,003	77
2004	46,326	35,474	77
2003	47,428	35,831	76
2002	47,010	36,010	77
2001	46,372	35,395	76
2000	46,399	34,205	74
1999	46,846	33,876	72
1998	46,448	33,986	73
1997	44,870	33,276	74
1996	43,757	32,276	74
1995	44,016	31,440	71
1994	44,157	31,779	72
1993	44,446	31,788	72
1992	45,231	32,017	71
1991	45,186	31,566	70
1990	44,033	31,535	72
Percent change			
2000 to 2009	1.6%	6.1%	–
1990 to 2009	7.0	15.0	–

Note: The index is calculated by dividing the median earnings of women by the median earnings of men and multiplying by 100. "–" means not applicable.
Source: Bureau of the Census, Current Population Surveys, Internet site http://www.census.gov/hhes/www/income/data/historical/people/index.html; calculations by New Strategist

Education Boosts Earnings

Although college costs are soaring, the payback has been worth the investment.

Among full-time workers, men with at least a bachelor's degree earned a median of $71,466 in 2009. Those who went no further than high school earned just $39,478. Women with at least a bachelor's degree earned a median of $51,878 versus the $29,150 earned by those who went no further than high school. Women's earnings are much lower than men's in part because the average working woman is younger than the average working man, and job experience increases earnings.

The highest-paid men are those with professional degrees, such as doctors and lawyers. Their median personal earnings stood at $123,243 in 2009. The highest-paid women are also those with professional degrees, with median earnings of $83,905.

■ The enormous increase in the cost of getting a college degree is reducing the economic return of a college education.

Earnings are much higher for college graduates

(median earnings of full-time, year-round workers, by educational attainment and sex, 2009)

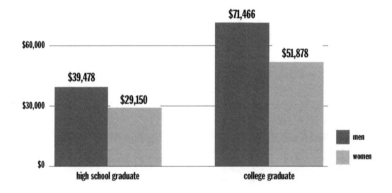

Table 5.42 Earnings of Men Who Work Full-Time by Education, 2009

(number and percent distribution of men aged 25 or older working full-time, year-round by earnings and educational attainment, and median earnings of those with earnings, 2009; men in thousands as of 2010)

| | total | less than 9th grade | 9th to 12th grade, no degree | high school graduate, incl. GED | some college, no degree | associate's degree | bachelor's degree or more | | | | |
							total	bachelor's degree	master's degree	prof. degree	doctoral degree
Total men with earnings	**52,445**	**1,561**	**2,795**	**15,258**	**8,609**	**4,828**	**19,395**	**12,290**	**4,575**	**1,319**	**1,212**
Under $10,000	796	71	85	247	116	75	199	124	52	6	16
$10,000 to $19,999	3,658	460	657	1,432	473	208	429	308	92	8	20
$20,000 to $29,999	6,779	497	762	2,908	1,168	521	925	760	119	26	18
$30,000 to $39,999	7,703	265	564	3,138	1,442	704	1,587	1,283	235	32	36
$40,000 to $49,999	7,288	121	288	2,591	1,368	855	2,066	1,522	389	68	88
$50,000 to $59,999	6,288	69	170	1,883	1,221	780	2,165	1,515	519	58	76
$60,000 to $69,999	4,534	38	99	1,080	949	519	1,849	1,294	414	69	70
$70,000 to $79,999	3,532	16	71	745	613	378	1,709	1,073	473	58	104
$80,000 to $89,999	2,380	11	41	406	348	258	1,318	839	345	64	70
$90,000 to $99,999	1,690	4	9	282	199	159	1,035	646	261	48	82
$100,000 or more	7,797	7	51	546	710	370	6,112	2,923	1,673	882	634
Median earnings	$49,994	$23,945	$28,023	$39,478	$47,097	$50,303	$71,466	$62,444	$79,342	$123,243	$100,740
Total men with earnings	**100.0%**	**100.0%**	**100.0%**	**100.0%**	**100.0%**	**100.0%**	**100.0%**	**100.0%**	**100.0%**	**100.0%**	**100.0%**
Under $10,000	1.5	4.5	3.0	1.6	1.3	1.6	1.0	1.0	1.1	0.5	1.3
$10,000 to $19,999	7.0	29.5	23.5	9.4	5.5	4.3	2.2	2.5	2.0	0.6	1.7
$20,000 to $29,999	12.9	31.8	27.3	19.1	13.6	10.8	4.8	6.2	2.6	2.0	1.5
$30,000 to $39,999	14.7	17.0	20.2	20.6	16.7	14.6	8.2	10.4	5.1	2.4	3.0
$40,000 to $49,999	13.9	7.8	10.3	17.0	15.9	17.7	10.7	12.4	8.5	5.2	7.3
$50,000 to $59,999	12.0	4.4	6.1	12.3	14.2	16.2	11.2	12.3	11.3	4.4	6.3
$60,000 to $69,999	8.6	2.4	3.5	7.1	11.0	10.7	9.5	10.5	9.0	5.2	5.8
$70,000 to $79,999	6.7	1.0	2.5	4.9	7.1	7.8	8.8	8.7	10.3	4.4	8.6
$80,000 to $89,999	4.5	0.7	1.5	2.7	4.0	5.3	6.8	6.8	7.5	4.9	5.8
$90,000 to $99,999	3.2	0.3	0.3	1.8	2.3	3.3	5.3	5.3	5.7	3.6	6.8
$100,000 or more	14.9	0.4	1.8	3.6	8.2	7.7	31.5	23.8	36.6	66.9	52.3

Source: Bureau of the Census, 2010 Current Population Survey, Internet site http://www.census.gov/hhes/www/cpstables/032010/perinc/toc.htm; calculations by New Strategist

Table 5.43 Earnings of Women Who Work Full-Time by Education, 2009

(number and percent distribution of women aged 25 or older working full-time, year-round by earnings and educational attainment, and median earnings of those with earnings, 2009; women in thousands as of 2010)

| | total | less than 9th grade | 9th to 12th grade, no degree | high school graduate, incl. GED | some college, no degree | associate's degree | bachelor's degree or more | | | | |
							total	bachelor's degree	master's degree	prof. degree	doctoral degree
Total women with earnings	**40,376**	**776**	**1,519**	**10,467**	**7,164**	**4,924**	**15,526**	**10,066**	**4,261**	**606**	**592**
Under $10,000	812	74	74	241	194	79	149	114	20	6	8
$10,000 to $19,999	4,525	366	598	1,855	742	447	516	406	93	10	7
$20,000 to $29,999	8,148	223	487	3,314	1,772	1,017	1,336	1,145	159	18	16
$30,000 to $39,999	8,083	80	186	2,487	1,793	1,141	2,398	1,945	410	17	25
$40,000 to $49,999	5,943	17	96	1,242	1,171	826	2,590	1,847	633	65	44
$50,000 to $59,999	3,993	13	41	605	631	557	2,146	1,332	687	57	70
$60,000 to $69,999	2,769	1	21	278	329	351	1,787	1,038	616	60	74
$70,000 to $79,999	1,877	0	8	184	238	202	1,246	691	431	52	72
$80,000 to $89,999	1,097	0	5	78	95	106	812	410	324	34	45
$90,000 to $99,999	778	0	1	32	48	62	636	307	256	38	36
$100,000 or more	2,352	1	5	151	154	134	1,907	830	633	248	196
Median earnings	$37,264	$18,480	$21,226	$29,150	$34,087	$37,267	$51,878	$46,832	$61,068	$83,905	$76,581
Total women with earnings	**100.0%**	**100.0%**	**100.0%**	**100.0%**	**100.0%**	**100.0%**	**100.0%**	**100.0%**	**100.0%**	**100.0%**	**100.0%**
Under $10,000	2.0	9.5	4.9	2.3	2.7	1.6	1.0	1.1	0.5	1.0	1.4
$10,000 to $19,999	11.2	47.2	39.4	17.7	10.4	9.1	3.3	4.0	2.2	1.7	1.2
$20,000 to $29,999	20.2	28.7	32.1	31.7	24.7	20.7	8.6	11.4	3.7	3.0	2.7
$30,000 to $39,999	20.0	10.3	12.2	23.8	25.0	23.2	15.4	19.3	9.6	2.8	4.2
$40,000 to $49,999	14.7	2.2	6.3	11.9	16.3	16.8	16.7	18.3	14.9	10.7	7.4
$50,000 to $59,999	9.9	1.7	2.7	5.8	8.8	11.3	13.8	13.2	16.1	9.4	11.8
$60,000 to $69,999	6.9	0.1	1.4	2.7	4.6	7.1	11.5	10.3	14.5	9.9	12.5
$70,000 to $79,999	4.6	0.0	0.5	1.8	3.3	4.1	8.0	6.9	10.1	8.6	12.2
$80,000 to $89,999	2.7	0.0	0.3	0.7	1.3	2.2	5.2	4.1	7.6	5.6	7.6
$90,000 to $99,999	1.9	0.0	0.1	0.3	0.7	1.3	4.1	3.0	6.0	6.3	6.1
$100,000 or more	5.8	0.1	0.3	1.4	2.1	2.7	12.3	8.2	14.9	40.9	33.1

Source: Bureau of the Census, 2010 Current Population Survey, Internet site http://www.census.gov/hhes/www/cpstables/ 032010/perinc/toc.htm; calculations by New Strategist

Among Wage and Salary Workers, Women Earn 80 Percent as Much as Men

The gap varies greatly by occupation, however.

Men who work full-time as wage or salary workers earned a median of $819 a week in 2009. Women earned a median of $657—or 80 percent of what men earn. Although a substantial gap exists between men's and women's earnings, women have been closing the gap. In many occupations, women now make almost as much or even more than men.

Women in management occupations earn only 72 percent as much as their male counterparts. For women in professional occupations, the figure is 74 percent. But in many individual occupations, the gap is smaller. Among computer software engineers, women earn 85 percent as much as men. Among social workers, the figure is 90 percent.

A big earnings gap exists in some occupations. Among physicians and surgeons, women earn only 64 percent as much as men—largely because the average male doctor is much older and more experienced than the average female doctor. Among human resource managers, women earn only 69 percent as much as their male counterparts. But in a handful of occupations, women earned more than men in 2009. These include teacher assistants, cafeteria attendants, and bakers.

■ One reason for the earnings gap is that the average male worker has been on the job longer than the average female worker. As women gain job experience, the earnings gap should continue to shrink.

In most occupations, women earn less than men

(women's median weekly earnings as a percent of men's among full-time wage and salary workers, by occupation, 2009)

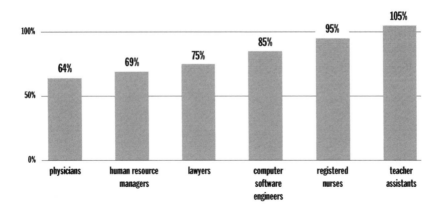

Table 5.44 Median Weekly Earnings of Full-Time Workers by Occupation and Sex, 2009

(median weekly earnings of full-time wage and salary workers aged 16 or older by selected occupation and sex, and index of women's to men's earnings, 2009)

	men	women	index of women's earnings to men's
TOTAL FULL-TIME WORKERS AGED 16 OR OLDER	**$819**	**$657**	**80**
Management, professional, and related occupations	**1,248**	**907**	**73**
Management, business, and financial operations occupations	1,334	955	72
Management occupations	1,384	1,002	72
Chief executives	2,084	1,553	75
General and operations managers	1,372	1,110	81
Marketing and sales managers	1,536	1,052	68
Administrative services managers	1,148	–	–
Computer and information systems managers	1,788	1,411	79
Financial managers	1,443	961	67
Human resources managers	1,548	1,072	69
Industrial production managers	1,332	–	–
Purchasing managers	1,383	1,029	74
Transportation, storage, and distribution managers	899	–	–
Farm, ranch, and other agricultural managers	812	–	–
Construction managers	1,236	–	–
Education administrators	1,432	1,093	76
Engineering managers	1,855	–	–
Food service managers	754	602	80
Lodging managers	864	731	85
Medical and health services managers	1,448	1,143	79
Property, real estate, and community association managers	982	791	81
Social and community service managers	1,147	898	78
Managers, all other	1,292	1,037	80
Business and financial operations occupations	1,171	894	76
Wholesale and retail buyers, except farm products	958	770	80
Purchasing agents, except wholesale, retail, and farm products	999	783	78
Claims adjusters, appraisers, examiners, and investigators	1,128	845	75
Compliance officers, except agriculture, construction, health and safety, and transportation	1,162	970	83
Cost estimators	1,050	–	–
Human resources, training, and labor relations specialists	1,103	845	77
Management analysts	1,371	1,177	86
Other business operations specialists	1,207	808	67
Accountants and auditors	1,190	902	76
Personal financial advisors	1,450	1,088	75
Insurance underwriters	–	987	–
Loan counselors and officers	1,118	754	67
Tax examiners, collectors, and revenue agents	–	912	–
Professional and related occupations	1,191	880	74
Computer and mathematical occupations	1,304	1,149	88
Computer scientists and systems analysts	1,268	1,167	92
Computer programmers	1,267	1,182	93
Computer software engineers	1,550	1,311	85
Computer support specialists	930	857	92
Database administrators	1,391	–	–
Network and computer systems administrators	1,109	–	–
Network systems and data communications analysts	1,187	1,032	87
Operations research analysts	1,380	–	–

	men	women	index of women's earnings to men's
Architecture and engineering occupations	$1,318	$1,061	81
Architects, except naval	1,197	–	–
Aerospace engineers	1,505	–	–
Civil engineers	1,336	–	–
Electrical and electronics engineers	1,521	–	–
Industrial engineers, including health and safety	1,358	–	–
Mechanical engineers	1,350	–	–
Engineers, all other	1,495	–	–
Drafters	936	–	–
Engineering technicians, except drafters	959	799	83
Surveying and mapping technicians	769	–	–
Life, physical, and social science occupations	1,190	940	79
Biological scientists	1,158	–	–
Medical scientists	1,388	975	70
Chemists and materials scientists	1,303	–	–
Environmental scientists and geoscientists	1,238	–	–
Physical scientists, all other	1,587	–	–
Psychologists	–	1,091	–
Other life, physical, and social science technicians	723	740	102
Community and social services occupations	897	741	83
Counselors	797	750	94
Social workers	864	774	90
Miscellaneous community and social service specialists	826	680	82
Clergy	976	–	–
Legal occupations	1,741	985	57
Lawyers	1,934	1,449	75
Paralegals and legal assistants	–	845	–
Miscellaneous legal support workers	–	791	–
Education, training, and library occupations	1,068	836	78
Postsecondary teachers	1,342	1,030	77
Preschool and kindergarten teachers	–	614	–
Elementary and middle school teachers	1,040	891	86
Secondary school teachers	1,028	940	91
Special education teachers	990	967	98
Other teachers and instructors	959	723	75
Librarians	–	875	–
Teacher assistants	453	474	105
Arts, design, entertainment, sports, and media occupations	960	775	81
Designers	956	730	76
Producers and directors	1,131	–	–
Athletes, coaches, umpires, and related workers	856	–	–
Public relations specialists	1,044	922	88
Editors	992	923	93
Broadcast and sound engineering technicians and radio operators	954	–	–
Health care practitioners and technical occupations	1,184	924	78
Dietitians and nutritionists	–	770	–
Pharmacists	1,954	1,475	75
Physicians and surgeons	1,914	1,228	64
Registered nurses	1,090	1,035	95
Occupational therapists	–	1,155	–
Physical therapists	–	1,104	–
Respiratory therapists	–	935	–
Speech-language pathologists	–	1,148	–
Therapists, all other	–	786	–
Clinical laboratory technologists and technicians	925	791	86

	men	women	index of women's earnings to men's
Diagnostic related technologists and technicians	$1,018	$893	88
Emergency medical technicians and paramedics	717	–	–
Health diagnosing and treating practitioner support technicians	733	560	76
Licensed practical and licensed vocational nurses	–	702	–
Medical records and health information technicians	–	607	–
Opticians, dispensing	–	–	–
Miscellaneous health technologists and technicians	–	645	–
Service occupations	**524**	**418**	**80**
Health care support occupations	544	464	85
Nursing, psychiatric, and home health aides	519	430	83
Dental assistants	–	532	–
Medical assistants and other health care support occupations	579	504	87
Protective service occupations	798	599	75
First-line supervisors/managers of police and detectives	1,169	–	–
Supervisors, protective service workers, all other	828	–	–
Fire fighters	982	–	–
Bailiffs, correctional officers, and jailers	726	623	86
Detectives and criminal investigators	1,073	–	–
Police and sheriff's patrol officers	971	805	83
Security guards and gaming surveillance officers	520	462	89
Food preparation and serving related occupations	416	378	91
Chefs and head cooks	565	–	–
First-line supervisors/managers of food preparation and serving workers	495	435	88
Cooks	400	371	93
Food preparation workers	385	367	95
Bartenders	560	418	75
Combined food preparation and serving workers, including fast food	357	347	97
Waiters and waitresses	419	363	87
Dining room and cafeteria attendants and bartender helpers	360	400	111
Dishwashers	339	–	–
Building and grounds cleaning and maintenance occupations	488	388	80
First-line supervisors/managers of housekeeping and janitorial workers	645	453	70
First-line supervisors/managers of landscaping, lawn service, and groundskeeping workers	740	–	–
Janitors and building cleaners	494	401	81
Maids and housekeeping cleaners	444	371	84
Grounds maintenance workers	435	–	–
Personal care and service occupations	546	415	76
Hairdressers, hair stylists, and cosmetologists	–	413	–
Miscellaneous personal appearance workers	–	434	–
Transportation attendants	–	606	–
Child care workers	–	364	–
Personal and home care aides	424	406	96
Recreation and fitness workers	677	487	72
Sales and office occupations	**737**	**590**	**80**
Sales and related occupations	793	525	66
First-line supervisors/managers of retail sales workers	770	597	78
First-line supervisors/managers of nonretail sales workers	1,059	780	74
Cashiers	422	361	86
Counter and rental clerks	557	–	–
Parts salespersons	589	–	–
Retail salespersons	624	443	71
Advertising sales agents	1,201	847	71
Insurance sales agents	860	692	80

	men	women	index of women's earnings to men's
Securities, commodities, and financial services sales agents	$1,237	$798	65
Sales representatives, services, all other	936	747	80
Sales representatives, wholesale and manufacturing	986	736	75
Real estate brokers and sales agents	939	745	79
Sales and related workers, all other	828	726	88
Office and administrative support occupations	657	602	92
First-line supervisors/managers of office and administrative support workers	837	705	84
Bill and account collectors	590	563	95
Billing and posting clerks and machine operators	–	579	–
Bookkeeping, accounting, and auditing clerks	671	627	93
Payroll and timekeeping clerks	–	648	–
Tellers	–	477	–
Court, municipal, and license clerks	–	705	–
Customer service representatives	617	587	95
Eligibility interviewers, government programs	–	757	–
File clerks	–	581	–
Hotel, motel, and resort desk clerks	–	408	–
Interviewers, except eligibility and loan	–	608	–
Loan interviewers and clerks	–	625	–
Order clerks	–	595	–
Receptionists and information clerks	537	516	96
Information and record clerks, all other	–	681	–
Couriers and messengers	719	–	–
Dispatchers	747	614	82
Postal service clerks	905	904	100
Postal service mail carriers	944	908	96
Production, planning, and expediting clerks	928	644	69
Shipping, receiving, and traffic clerks	538	525	98
Stock clerks and order fillers	485	479	99
Secretaries and administrative assistants	666	619	93
Computer operators	740	–	–
Data entry keyers	689	568	82
Word processors and typists	–	604	–
Insurance claims and policy processing clerks	–	620	–
Office clerks, general	647	594	92
Office and administrative support workers, all other	822	617	75
Natural resources, construction, and maintenance occupations	**727**	**542**	**75**
Farming, fishing, and forestry occupations	428	372	87
Miscellaneous agricultural workers	405	346	85
Construction and extraction occupations	719	673	94
First-line supervisors/managers of construction trades and extraction workers	963	–	–
Brickmasons, blockmasons, and stonemasons	701	–	–
Carpenters	665	–	–
Carpet, floor, and tile installers and finishers	590	–	–
Cement masons, concrete finishers, and terrazzo workers	631	–	–
Construction laborers	595	–	–
Operating engineers and other construction equipment operators	750	–	–
Drywall installers, ceiling tile installers, and tapers	592	–	–
Electricians	858	–	–
Painters, construction and maintenance	524	–	–
Pipelayers, plumbers, pipefitters, and steamfitters	795	–	–
Roofers	600	–	–
Sheet metal workers	765	–	–
Structural iron and steel workers	779	–	–

	men	women	index of women's earnings to men's
Helpers, construction trades	$520	–	–
Construction and building inspectors	926	–	–
Highway maintenance workers	766	–	–
Mining machine operators	1,017	–	–
Installation, maintenance, and repair occupations	787	$644	82
First-line supervisors/managers of mechanics, installers, and repairers	988	–	–
Computer, automated teller, and office machine repairers	808	–	–
Radio and telecommunications equipment installers and repairers	911	–	–
Electronic home entertainment equipment installers and repairers	671	–	–
Security and fire alarm systems installers	722	–	–
Aircraft mechanics and service technicians	946	–	–
Automotive body and related repairers	663	–	–
Automotive service technicians and mechanics	669	–	–
Bus and truck mechanics and diesel engine specialists	804	–	–
Heavy vehicle and mobile equipment service technicians and mechanics	848	–	–
Miscellaneous vehicle and mobile equipment mechanics, installers, and repairers	445	–	–
Heating, air conditioning, and refrigeration mechanics and installers	764	–	–
Industrial and refractory machinery mechanics	805	–	–
Maintenance and repair workers, general	731	–	–
Electrical power-line installers and repairers	1,026	–	–
Telecommunications line installers and repairers	799	–	–
Other installation, maintenance, and repair workers	621	–	–
Production, transportation, and material-moving occupations	**648**	**472**	**73**
Production occupations	678	472	70
First-line supervisors/managers of production and operating workers	895	680	76
Electrical, electronics, and electromechanical assemblers	611	486	80
Miscellaneous assemblers and fabricators	592	488	82
Bakers	448	466	104
Butchers and other meat, poultry, and fish processing workers	510	418	82
Computer control programmers and operators	745	–	–
Cutting, punching, and press machine setters, operators, and tenders, metal and plastic	603	–	–
Machinists	722	–	–
Welding, soldering, and brazing workers	682	–	–
Metalworkers and plastic workers, all other	623	–	–
Printing machine operators	672	–	–
Laundry and dry-cleaning workers	493	362	73
Sewing machine operators	–	383	–
Stationary engineers and boiler operators	925	–	–
Water and liquid waste treatment plant and system operators	787	–	–
Crushing, grinding, polishing, mixing, and blending workers	606	–	–
Cutting workers	541	–	–
Inspectors, testers, sorters, samplers, and weighers	754	513	68
Packaging and filling machine operators and tenders	497	415	84
Painting workers	606	–	–
Production workers, all other	635	481	76
Transportation and material-moving occupations	618	472	76
Supervisors, transportation and material-moving workers	799	–	–
Aircraft pilots and flight engineers	1,652	–	–
Bus drivers	605	527	87
Driver/sales workers and truck drivers	690	512	74
Taxi drivers and chauffeurs	519	–	–
Locomotive engineers and operators	1,140	–	–
Parking lot attendants	415	–	–

	men	women	index of women's earnings to men's
Crane and tower operators	$778	–	–
Industrial truck and tractor operators	532	–	–
Cleaners of vehicles and equipment	423	–	–
Laborers and freight, stock, and material movers, hand	511	$421	82
Packers and packagers, hand	453	389	86
Refuse and recyclable material collectors	473	–	–

Note: The index is calculated by dividing the median earnings of women by the median earnings of men and multiplying by 100.
"–" means sample is too small to make a reliable estimate because fewer than 50,000 are employed in occupation.
Source: Bureau of Labor Statistics, Labor Force Statistics from the Current Population Survey, Internet site ftp://ftp.bls.gov/ pub/special.requests/lf/aat39.txt; calculations by New Strategist

Incomes Are Highest in the Suburbs

Households in nonmetropolitan areas have the lowest incomes.

Households in the suburbs of the nation's metropolitan areas (outside principal cities) have the highest incomes, a median of $56,582 in 2009—14 percent higher than the national median. Many suburban householders are middle-aged married couples in their peak-earning years. Nonmetropolitan households have the lowest incomes, a median of $40,135 in 2009, or just 81 percent of the national average. The elderly head a larger share of households in nonmetro areas.

Households in the Northeast and West have above-average incomes, while those in the Midwest have average incomes and those in the South have incomes well below average. Among the 50 states, New Hampshire has the highest household income, with a 2007–09 median of $66,654, 32 percent above average. Mississippi has the lowest median household income, just $36,650 in 2007–09—28 percent below average. Arkansas is also close to the bottom, with a median income of less than $40,000. The gap in the median household income of New Hampshire and Mississippi was fully $30,000 in 2007–09.

■ The Great Recession has not reduced the income gap between the richest and poorest states.

Households in the South have the lowest incomes

(median household income by region, 2009)

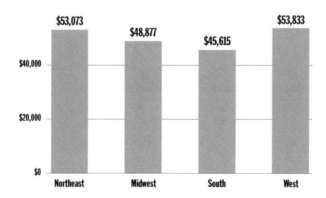

Table 5.45 Median Household Income by Metropolitan Status and Region of Residence, 2009

(number of households, median household income, and index of category median to national median, by metropolitan status, and region and division of residence, 2009; households in thousands as of 2010)

	number of households	median income	index
Total households	**117,538**	**$49,777**	**100**
Metropolitan status			
Inside metropolitan areas	98,379	51,522	104
Inside principal cities	38,850	44,852	90
Outside principal cities	59,529	56,582	114
Outside metropolitan areas	19,159	40,135	81
Region			
Northeast	21,479	53,073	107
New England	5,756	58,709	118
Middle Atlantic	15,723	51,583	104
Midwest	26,390	48,877	98
East North Central	18,215	48,137	97
West North Central	8,175	50,408	101
South	43,611	45,615	92
South Atlantic	23,281	47,408	95
East South Central	7,180	39,958	80
West South Central	13,150	45,905	92
West	26,058	53,833	108
Mountain	8,305	50,419	101
Pacific	17,753	56,232	113

Note: The index is calculated by dividing the median for each metropolitan status and region by the national median and multiplying by 100.
Source: Bureau of the Census, 2010 Current Population Survey, Internet site http://www.census.gov/hhes/www/cpstables/032010/hhinc/toc.htm; calculations by New Strategist

Table 5.46 Median Household Income by State, 2007–09

(median income of households by state, and index of state to national median, three-year average, 2007–09; ranked by median income)

	median income	index		median income	index
United States	**$50,618**	**100**	Pennsylvania	$49,829	98
New Hampshire	66,654	132	North Dakota	49,450	98
Connecticut	65,213	129	Michigan	48,888	97
Maryland	65,183	129	South Dakota	48,416	96
New Jersey	64,143	127	Idaho	48,299	95
Alaska	63,505	125	Maine	48,032	95
Virginia	61,151	121	Ohio	47,809	94
Hawaii	61,055	121	Kansas	47,527	94
Massachusetts	59,981	118	Missouri	47,408	94
Colorado	59,964	118	Texas	47,143	93
Washington	58,964	116	Arizona	47,106	93
Utah	58,722	116	Indiana	46,579	92
Minnesota	56,956	113	Georgia	46,570	92
California	56,862	112	Florida	45,897	91
Nevada	53,964	107	Oklahoma	45,507	90
D.C.	53,685	106	New Mexico	43,790	87
Rhode Island	53,584	106	North Carolina	43,229	85
Illinois	53,413	106	South Carolina	42,945	85
Delaware	53,032	105	Montana	42,778	85
Wyoming	52,010	103	Alabama	42,652	84
Wisconsin	51,763	102	Louisiana	42,528	84
Oregon	50,866	100	Kentucky	41,489	82
Vermont	50,619	100	Tennessee	40,895	81
Iowa	50,422	100	West Virginia	40,627	80
New York	50,372	100	Arkansas	39,392	78
Nebraska	50,333	99	Mississippi	36,650	72

Note: The index is calculated by dividing the median income of each state by the national median and multiplying by 100.
Source: Bureau of the Census, Current Population Surveys, Internet site http://www.census.gov/hhes/www/income/data/ historical/household/index.htmll; calculations by New Strategist

Wages and Salaries Rank Number One

Wages and salaries are the most important source of income for the largest share of Americans.

Among the 211 million Americans aged 15 or older with income in 2009, just over 73 percent received income from earnings—such as wages and salaries (69 percent), nonfarm self-employment income (6 percent), or farm self-employment income (less than 1 percent). Among those with income from earnings, the median amount received was $30,899. Twenty-one percent of Americans received Social Security income, averaging $12,384 per person.

Forty-five percent of the population received property income in 2009, such as interest, dividends, rent, or royalties. More than 88 million people received interest income in 2009, getting a median of $1,455 from this source. Fourteen percent of the population received dividend income (a median of $1,625). Ten percent received retirement income, and 8 percent received pensions. Six percent of people aged 15 or older received unemployment compensation in 2009, a median of $5,740. Only 1 percent received public assistance, and those who did received an average of $2,398.

■ While most people of working age are dependent primarily on wages and salaries, older Americans depend on a wider variety of income sources—from Social Security and pensions to interest and dividends.

Social Security is the third most common source of income

(percent of people aged 15 or older receiving income by source, for the six most common souces of income, 2009)

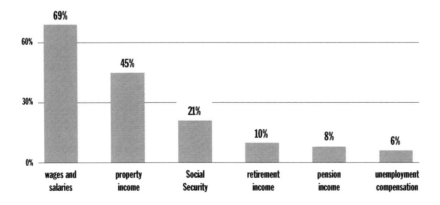

Table 5.47 Sources of Income, 2009

(number and percent of people aged 15 or older with income by source and median income for those with income, 2009; people in thousands as of 2010; ranked by number receiving income)

	number with income	percent with income	median amount received by those with income
Total	**211,254**	**100.0%**	**$26,134**
Earnings	154,906	73.3	30,899
Wages and salary	145,725	69.0	31,219
Nonfarm self-employment	11,887	5.6	14,783
Farm self-employment	1,920	0.9	2,316
Property income	94,485	44.7	1,611
Interest	88,449	41.9	1,455
Dividends	29,778	14.1	1,625
Rents, royalties, estates, or trusts	10,802	5.1	2,158
Social Security	43,630	20.7	12,384
Retirement income	20,235	9.6	12,162
Company or union retirement	11,307	5.4	8,606
State or local government retirement	4,496	2.1	18,790
Federal government retirement	1,768	0.8	20,672
Military retirement	1,210	0.6	18,691
Annuities	525	0.2	7,371
IRA, Keogh, or 401(k)	503	0.2	9,292
Railroad retirement	318	0.2	20,307
Pension income	16,637	7.9	12,866
Company or union retirement	9,777	4.6	8,905
State or local government retirement	3,948	1.9	20,153
Federal government retirement	1,375	0.7	23,904
Military Retirement	976	0.5	20,204
Annuities	251	0.1	7,238
Railroad retirement	234	0.1	21,992
Unemployment compensation	12,960	6.1	5,740
Educational assistance	8,634	4.1	4,067
SSI (Supplemental Security Income)	5,460	2.6	7,624
Child support	4,826	2.3	3,627
Survivor benefits	2,918	1.4	8,073
Veteran's benefits	2,771	1.3	8,516
Financial assistance from other household	2,305	1.1	4,356
Public assistance	2,028	1.0	2,398
Disability benefits	1,546	0.7	8,754
Worker's compensation	1,517	0.7	3,875
Alimony	349	0.2	7,146
Other income	1,105	0.5	1,729

Source: Bureau of the Census, 2010 Current Population Survey, Internet site http://www.census.gov/hhes/www/ cpstables/032010/perinc/toc.htm; calculations by New Strategist

Minorities Account for Most of the Poor

Among the nation's 44 million poor, the 57 percent majority are Asian, black, or Hispanic.

Poverty rates have grown sharply during the Great Recession. In 2009, 14.3 percent of Americans were poor, up from a low of 11.3 percent in 2000. The poverty rate of 2009 was higher than the 13.5 percent of 1990.

Some segments of society are poorer than others. Only 9.4 percent of non-Hispanic whites are poor versus 26 percent of blacks and 25 percent of Hispanics. Overall, 21 percent of the nation's children are poor. The figure is 35 percent among black children and 33 percent among Hispanic children.

The poverty rate varies sharply by family type. Regardless of race or Hispanic origin, poverty rates are low among married couples. Overall, only 5.8 percent of married couples are poor compared with 29.9 percent of female-headed families. Among female-headed families with children, the poverty rate is an even higher 38.5 percent.

■ Childhood poverty will remain a chronic problem until single parents become a smaller share of all families.

Poverty rates are low for married couples

(percent of families in poverty by race, Hispanic origin, and family type, 2009)

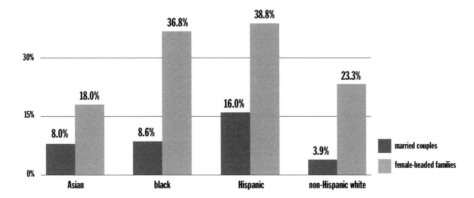

Table 5.48 People in Poverty, 1990 to 2009

(number and percent of people below poverty level, 1990 to 2009; percent and percentage point change for selected years; people in thousands as of the following year)

	number	percent
2009	43,569	14.3%
2008	39,829	13.2
2007	37,276	12.5
2006	36,460	12.3
2005	36,950	12.6
2004	37,040	12.7
2003	35,861	12.5
2002	34,570	12.1
2001	32,907	11.7
2000	31,581	11.3
1999	32,791	11.9
1998	34,476	12.7
1997	35,574	13.3
1996	36,529	13.7
1995	36,425	13.8
1994	38,059	14.5
1993	39,265	15.1
1992	38,014	14.8
1991	35,708	14.2
1990	33,585	13.5

	percent change	percentage point change
2000 to 2009	38.0%	3.0
1990 to 2009	29.7	0.8

Source: Bureau of the Census, Current Population Surveys, Internet site http://www.census.gov/hhes/www/poverty/data/ historical/index.html; calculations by New Strategist

Table 5.49 People in Poverty by Age, Race, and Hispanic Origin, 2009

(number and percent of people in poverty and percent distribution of poor, by age, race, and Hispanic origin, 2009; people in thousands as of 2010)

	total	Asian	black	Hispanic	non-Hispanic white
NUMBER OF POOR					
Total people in poverty	43,569	1,901	10,575	12,350	18,530
Under age 18	15,451	531	4,480	5,610	4,850
Aged 18 to 24	6,071	332	1,392	1,440	2,903
Aged 25 to 34	6,123	281	1,382	1,864	2,544
Aged 35 to 44	4,756	222	994	1,495	1,996
Aged 45 to 54	4,421	180	984	914	2,283
Aged 55 to 59	1,792	60	385	284	1,030
Aged 60 to 64	1,520	79	304	227	902
Aged 65 or older	3,433	216	655	516	2,022
PERCENT IN POVERTY					
Total people	14.3%	12.4%	25.9%	25.3%	9.4%
Under age 18	20.7	13.3	35.4	33.1	11.9
Aged 18 to 24	20.7	23.8	30.8	26.3	16.3
Aged 25 to 34	14.9	11.2	23.8	23.0	10.4
Aged 35 to 44	11.8	9.0	18.9	21.2	7.9
Aged 45 to 54	10.0	8.8	18.0	17.3	7.3
Aged 55 to 59	9.3	7.1	18.7	15.6	7.2
Aged 60 to 64	9.4	12.0	17.6	17.6	7.3
Aged 65 or older	8.9	15.7	19.2	18.3	6.6
PERCENT DISTRIBUTION OF POOR BY RACE AND HISPANIC ORIGIN					
Total people in poverty	100.0%	4.4%	24.3%	28.3%	42.5%
Under age 18	100.0	3.4	29.0	36.3	31.4
Aged 18 to 24	100.0	5.5	22.9	23.7	47.8
Aged 25 to 34	100.0	4.6	22.6	30.4	41.5
Aged 35 to 44	100.0	4.7	20.9	31.4	42.0
Aged 45 to 54	100.0	4.1	22.3	20.7	51.6
Aged 55 to 59	100.0	3.3	21.5	15.8	57.5
Aged 60 to 64	100.0	5.2	20.0	14.9	59.3
Aged 65 or older	100.0	6.3	19.1	15.0	58.9

Note: Numbers do not add to total because Asians and blacks are those who identify themselves as being of the race alone and those who identify themselves as being of the race in combination with other races. Non-Hispanic whites are those who identify themselves as being white alone and not Hispanic. Hispanics may be of any race.
Source: Bureau of the Census, 2010 Current Population Survey, Internet site http://www.census.gov/hhes/www/cpstables/032010/pov/toc.htm; calculations by New Strategist

Table 5.50 Families in Poverty by Family Type, Race, and Hispanic Origin, 2009

(number and percent of families in poverty, and percent distribution of families in poverty, by type of family and race and Hispanic origin of householder, 2009; families in thousands as of 2010)

	total	Asian	black	Hispanic	non-Hispanic white
NUMBER IN POVERTY					
Total families in poverty	**8,792**	**359**	**2,193**	**2,369**	**3,797**
Married couples	3,409	239	383	1,054	1,697
Female householders, no spouse present	4,441	87	1,569	1,066	1,701
Male householders, no spouse present	942	34	241	249	399
PERCENT IN POVERTY					
Total families	**11.1%**	**9.6%**	**22.7%**	**22.7%**	**7.0%**
Married couples	5.8	8.0	8.6	16.0	3.9
Female householders, no spouse present	29.9	18.0	36.8	38.8	23.3
Male householders, no spouse present	16.9	12.3	24.9	23.0	12.5
PERCENT DISTRIBUTION OF FAMILIES IN POVERTY BY RACE AND HISPANIC ORIGIN					
Total families in poverty	**100.0%**	**4.1%**	**24.9%**	**26.9%**	**43.2%**
Married couples	100.0	7.0	11.2	30.9	49.8
Female householders, no spouse present	100.0	2.0	35.3	24.0	38.3
Male householders, no spouse present	100.0	3.6	25.6	26.4	42.4
PERCENT DISTRIBUTION OF FAMILIES IN POVERTY BY FAMILY TYPE					
Total families in poverty	**100.0%**	**100.0%**	**100.0%**	**100.0%**	**100.0%**
Married couples	38.8	66.6	17.5	44.5	44.7
Female householders, no spouse present	50.5	24.2	71.5	45.0	44.8
Male householders, no spouse present	10.7	9.5	11.0	10.5	10.5

Note: Numbers do not add to total because Asians and blacks are those who identify themselves as being of the race alone and those who identify themselves as being of the race in combination with other races. Non-Hispanic whites are those who identify themselves as being white alone and not Hispanic. Hispanics may be of any race.
Source: Bureau of the Census, 2010 Current Population Survey, Internet site http://www.census.gov/hhes/www/cpstables/032010/pov/toc.htm; calculations by New Strategist

Table 5.51 Families with Children in Poverty by Family Type, Race, and Hispanic Origin, 2009

(number and percent of families with children under age 18 in poverty, and percent distribution of families with children in poverty, by type of family and race and Hispanic origin of householder, 2009; families in thousands as of 2010)

	total	Asian	black	Hispanic	non-Hispanic white
NUMBER IN POVERTY					
Total families with children in poverty	**6,630**	**238**	**1,787**	**2,004**	**2,553**
Married couples	2,161	153	259	876	854
Female householders, no spouse present	3,800	64	1,365	945	1,412
Male householders, no spouse present	670	21	163	183	286
PERCENT IN POVERTY					
Total families with children	**17.1%**	**11.5%**	**30.4%**	**28.4%**	**10.8%**
Married couples	8.3	9.0	11.4	19.9	4.9
Female householders, no spouse present	38.5	23.4	44.3	46.0	31.7
Male householders, no spouse present	23.7	20.7	30.5	30.2	18.5
PERCENT DISTRIBUTION OF FAMILIES IN POVERTY BY RACE AND HISPANIC ORIGIN					
Total families with children in poverty	**100.0%**	**3.6%**	**27.0%**	**30.2%**	**38.5%**
Married couples	100.0	7.1	12.0	40.5	39.5
Female householders, no spouse present	100.0	1.7	35.9	24.9	37.2
Male householders, no spouse present	100.0	3.1	24.3	27.3	42.7
PERCENT DISTRIBUTION OF FAMILIES IN POVERTY BY FAMILY TYPE					
Total families with children in poverty	**100.0%**	**100.0%**	**100.0%**	**100.0%**	**100.0%**
Married couples	32.6	64.3	14.5	43.7	33.5
Female householders, no spouse present	57.3	26.9	76.4	47.2	55.3
Male householders, no spouse present	10.1	8.8	9.1	9.1	11.2

Note: Numbers do not add to total because Asians and blacks are those who identify themselves as being of the race alone and those who identify themselves as being of the race in combination with other races. Non-Hispanic whites are those who identify themselves as being white alone and not Hispanic. Hispanics may be of any race.
Source: Bureau of the Census, 2010 Current Population Survey, Internet site http://www.census.gov/hhes/www/ cpstables/ 032010/pov/toc.htm; calculations by New Strategist

6

Labor Force Trends

■ **Older Americans are increasingly likely to work.**

Twenty-two percent of men aged 65 or older are in the labor force, up from 16 percent in 1990.

■ **Unemployment has surged.**

Nearly 15 million Americans were unemployed in 2010, 9.6 percent of the labor force.

■ **Many workers have part-time jobs.**

Twenty-six million Americans work part-time, including 20 percent of men and 33 percent of women. Many part-time workers want full-time jobs.

■ **Long-term employment is less common among middle-aged workers.**

The proportion of workers who have been with their employer for 10 or more years has fallen sharply among men aged 35 to 49.

■ **Service workers are less likely to have benefits.**

Only 50 percent of service workers have access to medical care benefits through their employer. Among management and professional workers, the figure is 88 percent.

■ **Big gains for older workers.**

The labor force as a whole will grow 8 percent between 2008 and 2018, but the number of men aged 65 or older in the labor force is projected to expand by 72 percent.

Labor Force Participation Has Dropped

Older men and women are more likely to work, however.

Men's and women's labor force participation rates fell between 2000 and 2010, with the decline greater for men than for women. One factor behind the decline was the economic downturn, although participation rates include people who are looking for a job. Many Americans are too discouraged by the troubled economy to even look for work, pushing labor force participation rates down.

Labor force participation rates fell for men and women under age 55, the steepest decline occurring among teenagers. Among the reasons for the drop in the labor force participation rate of teenagers are the increase in extracurricular activities among high school students and the rise in college enrollment rates among recent high school graduates.

The labor force participation rate of older men and women increased significantly between 2000 and 2010. Among men and women aged 65 or older, labor force participation climbed 4.4 percentage points. In 2010, a substantial 22.1 percent of men aged 65 or older were in the labor force. The labor force participation rate of men aged 65 or older has not been that high since 1974.

■ As older Americans postpone retirement, it is harder for young and middle-aged adults to find jobs.

More older men are working

(percent of men aged 65 or older in the civilian labor force, by age, 2000 and 2010)

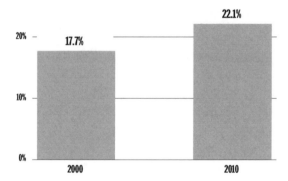

Table 6.1 Labor Force Participation by Sex and Age, 1990 to 2010

(civilian labor force participation rate of people aged 16 or older by sex and age, selected years, 1990 to 2010; percentage point change, 1990–2010 and 2000–10)

	2010	2000	1990	percentage point change 2000–10	percentage point change 1990–2010
Total men	**71.2%**	**74.8%**	**76.1%**	**–3.6**	**–4.9**
Aged 16 to 19	34.9	52.8	55.7	–17.9	–20.8
Aged 20 to 24	74.5	82.6	84.3	–8.1	–9.8
Aged 25 to 34	89.7	93.4	94.2	–3.7	–4.5
Aged 35 to 44	91.5	92.7	94.4	–1.2	–2.9
Aged 45 to 54	86.8	88.6	90.7	–1.8	–3.9
Aged 55 to 64	70.0	67.3	67.7	2.7	2.3
Aged 65 or older	22.1	17.7	16.4	4.4	5.7
Total women	**58.6**	**59.9**	**57.5**	**–1.3**	**1.1**
Aged 16 to 19	35.0	51.2	51.8	–16.2	–16.8
Aged 20 to 24	68.3	73.1	71.6	–4.8	–3.3
Aged 25 to 34	74.7	76.1	73.6	–1.4	1.1
Aged 35 to 44	75.2	77.2	76.5	–2.0	–1.3
Aged 45 to 54	75.7	76.8	71.2	–1.1	4.5
Aged 55 to 64	60.2	51.9	45.3	8.3	14.9
Aged 65 or older	13.8	9.4	8.7	4.4	5.1

Source: Bureau of Labor Statistics, Employment and Earnings, January 1991, and Current Population Survey data for 2000 and 2010, Internet site http://www.bls.gov/cps/tables.htm#empstat; calculations by New Strategist

Sixty-Five Percent of Americans Are in the Labor Force

Among them, nearly 15 million were unemployed in 2010.

Of the nation's 238 million people aged 16 or older, 154 million were in the civilian labor force in 2010. Labor force statistics include both the employed and the unemployed. In 2010, a substantial 14.8 million people were unemployed—9.6 percent of the labor force.

Men's and women's labor force participation rates are similar for 16-to-19-year-olds, 35 percent of whom are in the labor force. Men's participation rises to a peak of 91 percent in the 35-to-44 age group. Women's participation rate peaks at 76 percent in the 45-to-54 age group. Both men's and women's participation falls in the 55-to-64 age group as some workers retire, although most in the age group remain in the labor force. A significant 22 percent of men and 14 percent of women aged 65 or older are still in the labor force, however.

Unemployment is highest among the youngest workers. The unemployment rate among 16-to-19-year-olds was nearly 29 percent among men and 23 percent among women in 2010.

■ The economic downturn is forcing some aging boomers to postpone retirement and driving others to retire earlier than they had planned because they cannot find jobs.

Unemployment is highest among young men

(percent of men who are unemployed, by age, 2010)

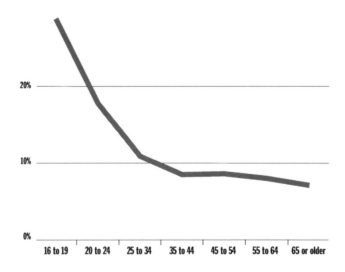

Table 6.2 Employment Status by Sex and Age, 2010

(number and percent of people aged 16 or older in the civilian labor force by sex, age, and employment status, 2010; numbers in thousands)

	civilian noninstitutional population	civilian labor force			unemployed	
		total	percent of population	employed	number	percent of labor force
Total people	**237,830**	**153,889**	**64.7%**	**139,064**	**14,825**	**9.6%**
Aged 16 to 19	16,901	5,906	34.9	4,378	1,528	25.9
Aged 20 to 24	21,047	15,028	71.4	12,699	2,329	15.5
Aged 25 to 34	40,903	33,614	82.2	30,229	3,386	10.1
Aged 35 to 44	40,090	33,366	83.2	30,663	2,703	8.1
Aged 45 to 54	44,297	35,960	81.2	33,191	2,769	7.7
Aged 55 to 64	35,885	23,297	64.9	21,636	1660	7.1
Aged 65 or older	38,706	6,718	17.4	6,268	449	6.7
Total men	**115,174**	**81,985**	**71.2**	**73,359**	**8,626**	**10.5**
Aged 16 to 19	8,578	2,991	34.9	2,129	863	28.8
Aged 20 to 24	10,550	7,864	74.5	6,466	1398	17.8
Aged 25 to 34	20,465	18,352	89.7	16,358	1,993	10.9
Aged 35 to 44	19,807	18,119	91.5	16,585	1534	8.5
Aged 45 to 54	21,713	18,856	86.8	17,242	1614	8.6
Aged 55 to 64	17,291	12,103	70.0	11,140	962	8.0
Aged 65 or older	16,769	3,701	22.1	3,439	262	7.1
Total women	**122,656**	**71,904**	**58.6**	**65,705**	**6,199**	**8.6**
Aged 16 to 19	8,323	2,914	35.0	2,249	665	22.8
Aged 20 to 24	10,497	7,164	68.3	6,233	931	13.0
Aged 25 to 34	20,438	15,263	74.7	13,870	1392	9.1
Aged 35 to 44	20,283	15,247	75.2	14,078	1169	7.7
Aged 45 to 54	22,584	17,104	75.7	15,949	1156	6.8
Aged 55 to 64	18,594	11,194	60.2	10,496	698	6.2
Aged 65 or older	21,937	3,017	13.8	2,830	187	6.2

Note: The civilian labor force equals the number of the employed plus the number of the unemployed. The civilian population equals the number in the labor force plus the number not in the labor force.
Source: Bureau of Labor Statistics, Current Population Survey, Internet site http://www.bls.gov/cps/tables.htm#empstat

Labor Force Participation Varies by Race and Hispanic Origin

Unemployment rates have surged in every racial and ethnic group.

The labor force participation rate of men ranges from a high of 78 percent among Hispanics to a low of 65 percent among blacks (the labor force includes both the employed and the unemployed). Among women, the labor force participation rate ranges from a high of 60 percent among blacks to a low of 56 percent among Hispanics.

Unemployment has surged in every racial and ethnic group over the past few years. In 2010, the unemployment rate ranged from a high of 16.0 percent among blacks to a low of 7.5 percent among Asians. Young black men have the highest unemployment rate of all. Among black men aged 16 to 19 who are in the labor force, 45 percent are unemployed.

■ In every racial and ethnic group, the unemployment rate is higher for men than for women.

Blacks have the highest unemployment rate

(percent of the civilian labor force aged 16 or older who are unemployed, by race and Hispanic origin, 2010)

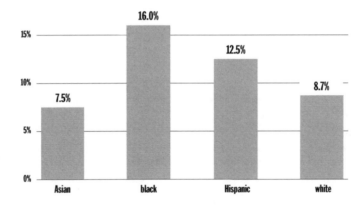

Table 6.3 Employment Status of Asians by Sex and Age, 2010

(number and percent of Asians aged 16 or older in the civilian labor force by sex, age, and employment status, 2010; numbers in thousands)

	civilian noninstitutional population	civilian labor force			unemployed	
		total	percent of population	employed	number	percent of labor force
Total Asians	**11,199**	**7,248**	**64.7%**	**6,705**	**543**	**7.5%**
Aged 16 to 19	649	143	22.0	108	35	24.8
Aged 20 to 24	940	504	53.6	442	62	12.3
Aged 25 to 34	2,314	1,740	75.2	1,620	120	6.9
Aged 35 to 44	2,430	1,987	81.8	1,869	118	6.0
Aged 45 to 54	1,975	1,642	83.2	1,530	112	6.8
Aged 55 to 64	1,472	990	67.2	916	74	7.5
Aged 65 or older	1,419	243	17.1	221	22	8.9
Total Asian men	**5,315**	**3,893**	**73.2**	**3,588**	**305**	**7.8**
Aged 16 to 19	331	73	22.1	54	19	25.8
Aged 20 to 24	472	265	56.3	228	38	14.2
Aged 25 to 34	1,108	946	85.3	887	58	6.2
Aged 35 to 44	1,174	1,074	91.4	1,005	69	6.5
Aged 45 to 54	940	858	91.3	794	64	7.5
Aged 55 to 64	676	529	78.2	487	42	7.9
Aged 65 or older	614	149	24.3	133	15	7.5
Total Asian women	**5,884**	**3,355**	**57.0**	**3,117**	**238**	**7.1**
Aged 16 to 19	318	70	22.0	53	17	23.7
Aged 20 to 24	468	238	50.9	214	24	10.2
Aged 25 to 34	1,206	794	65.8	732	62	7.8
Aged 35 to 44	1,255	913	72.7	864	49	5.4
Aged 45 to 54	1,035	784	75.8	737	48	6.1
Aged 55 to 64	796	461	57.9	429	33	7.1
Aged 65 or older	806	94	11.7	88	6	6.4

Note: The civilian labor force equals the number of the employed plus the number of the unemployed. The civilian population equals the number in the labor force plus the number not in the labor force.
Source: Bureau of Labor Statistics, Current Population Survey, Internet site http://www.bls.gov/cps/tables.htm#empstat

Table 6.4 Employment Status of Blacks by Sex and Age, 2010

(number and percent of blacks aged 16 or older in the civilian labor force by sex, age, and employment status, 2010; numbers in thousands)

| | civilian noninstitutional population | civilian labor force | | | | |
| | | total | percent of population | employed | unemployed | |
					number	percent of labor force
Total blacks	**28,708**	**17,862**	**62.2%**	**15,010**	**2,852**	**16.0%**
Aged 16 to 19	2,657	677	25.5	386	291	43.0
Aged 20 to 24	3,097	2,072	66.9	1,532	539	26.0
Aged 25 to 34	5,491	4,418	80.5	3,641	776	17.6
Aged 35 to 44	5,031	4,095	81.4	3,561	534	13.0
Aged 45 to 54	5,322	3,991	75.0	3,531	461	11.5
Aged 55 to 64	3,773	2,104	55.7	1,899	204	9.7
Aged 65 or older	3,337	506	15.2	460	47	9.2
Total black men	**12,939**	**8,415**	**65.0**	**6,865**	**1,550**	**18.4**
Aged 16 to 19	1,313	339	25.8	185	154	45.4
Aged 20 to 24	1,474	986	66.9	692	294	29.8
Aged 25 to 34	2,540	2,118	83.4	1,710	408	19.3
Aged 35 to 44	2,234	1,924	86.1	1,638	286	14.9
Aged 45 to 54	2,406	1,862	77.4	1,594	268	14.4
Aged 55 to 64	1,673	950	56.8	834	116	12.2
Aged 65 or older	1,299	236	18.1	211	24	10.4
Total black women	**15,769**	**9,447**	**59.9**	**8,145**	**1,302**	**13.8**
Aged 16 to 19	1,344	337	25.1	201	137	40.5
Aged 20 to 24	1,623	1,086	66.9	841	245	22.6
Aged 25 to 34	2,951	2,299	77.9	1,931	369	16.0
Aged 35 to 44	2,796	2,171	77.7	1,923	248	11.4
Aged 45 to 54	2,916	2,129	73.0	1,936	193	9.1
Aged 55 to 64	2,101	1,153	54.9	1,065	88	7.6
Aged 65 or older	2,038	270	13.3	248	22	8.2

Note: The civilian labor force equals the number of the employed plus the number of the unemployed. The civilian population equals the number in the labor force plus the number not in the labor force.
Source: Bureau of Labor Statistics, Current Population Survey, Internet site http://www.bls.gov/cps/tables.htm#empstat

Table 6.5 Employment Status of Hispanics by Sex and Age, 2010

(number and percent of Hispanics aged 16 or older in the civilian labor force by sex, age, and employment status, 2010; numbers in thousands)

	civilian noninstitutional population	civilian labor force			unemployed	
		total	percent of population	employed	number	percent of labor force
Total Hispanics	**33,713**	**22,748**	**67.5%**	**19,906**	**2,843**	**12.5%**
Aged 16 to 19	3,243	1,002	30.9	680	322	32.2
Aged 20 to 24	3,880	2,760	71.1	2,281	479	17.4
Aged 25 to 34	8,084	6,517	80.6	5,781	736	11.3
Aged 35 to 44	7,123	5,783	81.2	5,185	598	10.3
Aged 45 to 54	5,351	4,238	79.2	3,779	459	10.8
Aged 55 to 64	3,167	1,936	61.1	1,737	199	10.3
Aged 65 or older	2,864	513	17.9	464	49	9.5
Total Hispanic men	**17,359**	**13,511**	**77.8**	**11,800**	**1,711**	**12.7**
Aged 16 to 19	1,666	553	33.2	361	191	34.6
Aged 20 to 24	2,016	1,612	80.0	1,319	294	18.2
Aged 25 to 34	4,381	4,061	92.7	3,591	470	11.6
Aged 35 to 44	3,783	3,515	92.9	3,169	346	9.8
Aged 45 to 54	2,741	2,407	87.8	2,137	269	11.2
Aged 55 to 64	1,538	1,061	69.0	949	112	10.6
Aged 65 or older	1,234	302	24.5	273	28	9.4
Total Hispanic women	**16,354**	**9,238**	**56.5**	**8,106**	**1,132**	**12.3**
Aged 16 to 19	1,578	449	28.5	318	131	29.1
Aged 20 to 24	1,864	1,147	61.6	962	186	16.2
Aged 25 to 34	3,703	2,456	66.3	2,189	267	10.9
Aged 35 to 44	3,340	2,268	67.9	2,016	252	11.1
Aged 45 to 54	2,610	1,831	70.2	1,642	190	10.4
Aged 55 to 64	1,628	875	53.7	788	87	9.9
Aged 65 or older	1,630	211	13.0	191	20	9.6

Note: The civilian labor force equals the number of the employed plus the number of the unemployed. The civilian population equals the number in the labor force plus the number not in the labor force.
Source: Bureau of Labor Statistics, Current Population Survey, Internet site http://www.bls.gov/cps/tables.htm#empstat

Table 6.6 Employment Status of Whites by Sex and Age, 2010

(number and percent of whites aged 16 or older in the civilian labor force by sex, age, and employment status, 2010; numbers in thousands)

| | civilian noninstitutional population | civilian labor force | | | unemployed | |
		total	percent of population	employed	number	percent of labor force
Total whites	**192,075**	**125,084**	**65.1%**	**114,168**	**10,916**	**8.7%**
Aged 16 to 19	12,891	4,861	37.7	3,733	1,128	23.2
Aged 20 to 24	16,280	11,948	73.4	10,334	1,614	13.5
Aged 25 to 34	31,813	26,455	83.2	24,097	2,358	8.9
Aged 35 to 44	31,647	26,510	83.8	24,540	1,969	7.4
Aged 45 to 54	36,064	29,632	82.2	27,502	2,130	7.2
Aged 55 to 64	29,983	19,808	66.1	18,464	1,344	6.8
Aged 65 or older	33,396	5,869	17.6	5,496	373	6.4
Total white men	**94,082**	**67,728**	**72.0**	**61,252**	**6,476**	**9.6**
Aged 16 to 19	6,580	2,463	37.4	1,815	648	26.3
Aged 20 to 24	8,240	6,342	77.0	5,347	995	15.7
Aged 25 to 34	16,174	14,734	91.1	13,282	1,452	9.9
Aged 35 to 44	15,920	14,713	92.4	13,583	1,131	7.7
Aged 45 to 54	17,919	15,791	88.1	14,542	1,249	7.9
Aged 55 to 64	14,634	10,422	71.2	9,637	785	7.5
Aged 65 or older	14,615	3,263	22.3	3,047	216	6.6
Total white women	**97,993**	**57,356**	**58.5**	**52,916**	**4,440**	**7.7**
Aged 16 to 19	6,311	2,398	38.0	1,918	480	20.0
Aged 20 to 24	8,040	5,607	69.7	4,988	619	11.0
Aged 25 to 34	15,640	11,721	74.9	10,815	906	7.7
Aged 35 to 44	15,727	11,796	75.0	10,958	839	7.1
Aged 45 to 54	18,146	13,841	76.3	12,960	881	6.4
Aged 55 to 64	15,349	9,386	61.1	8,827	559	6.0
Aged 65 or older	18,781	2,607	13.9	2,450	157	6.0

Note: The civilian labor force equals the number of the employed plus the number of the unemployed. The civilian population equals the number in the labor force plus the number not in the labor force.
Source: Bureau of Labor Statistics, Current Population Survey, Internet site http://www.bls.gov/cps/tables.htm#empstat

Working Mothers Are the Norm

Most working mothers have full-time jobs.

Working mothers are the norm—even among women with infants. Fifty-seven percent of mothers with children under age 1 were in the labor force in 2010. Among the employed, most had full-time jobs.

Labor force participation is higher for mothers with school-aged children than for those with preschoolers. Seventy-six percent of women with children aged 6 to 17 were in the labor force in 2010. This compares with 64 percent of women with children under age 6. Among the workers in both groups, the majority has a full-time job.

Fifty-nine percent of the nation's married couples with children under age 18 are dual-earners, with both mother and father employed. In just 30 percent of couples, only the father is employed. Even among couples with preschoolers, the 53 percent majority are dual-earners.

■ As unemployment rises, many two-earner families have been forced to make ends meet on only one income.

Most mothers are in the labor force

(percent of women in the labor force by age of children at home, 2010)

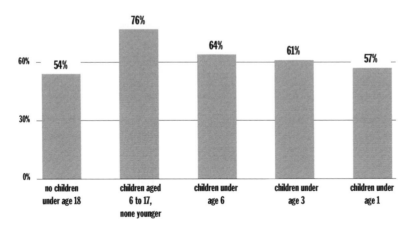

Table 6.7 Labor Force Status of Women by Presence of Children, 2010

(number and percent distribution of women aged 16 or older by labor force status and presence and age of own children under age 18 at home, 2010; numbers in thousands)

			civilian labor force				
				employed			
		civilian population	total	total	full-time	part-time	not in labor force
Total women	**122,656**	**71,904**	**65,705**	**48,214**	**17,491**	**6,199**	**50,752**
No children under age 18	86,631	46,405	42,495	31,108	11,387	3,910	40,226
With children under age 18	36,025	25,499	23,210	17,106	6,104	2,289	10,526
Children aged 6 to 17, none younger	19,763	15,110	13,939	10,514	3,425	1,172	4,653
Children under age 6	16,262	10,388	9,271	6,592	2,679	1,117	5,874
Children under age 3	9,503	5,770	5,114	3,570	1,543	656	3,733
Children under age 1	3,184	1,800	1,590	1,128	462	210	1,384
Total women	**100.0%**	**58.6%**	**53.6%**	**39.3%**	**14.3%**	**5.1%**	**41.4%**
No children under age 18	100.0	53.6	49.1	35.9	13.1	4.5	46.4
With children under age 18	100.0	70.8	64.4	47.5	16.9	6.4	29.2
Children aged 6 to 17, none younger	100.0	76.5	70.5	53.2	17.3	5.9	23.5
Children under age 6	100.0	63.9	57.0	40.5	16.5	6.9	36.1
Children under age 3	100.0	60.7	53.8	37.6	16.2	6.9	39.3
Children under age 1	100.0	56.5	49.9	35.4	14.5	6.6	43.5

Source: Bureau of Labor Statistics, Employment Characteristics of Families, Internet sites http://www.bls.gov/news.release/famee.t05.htm and http://www.bls.gov/news.release/famee.t06.htm

Table 6.8 Labor Force Status of Families with Children under Age 18, 2010

(number and percent distribution of families by employment status of parent and age of youngest own child under age 18 at home, by family type, 2010; numbers in thousands)

	total	youngest child 6 to 17	youngest child under 6
NUMBER			
Married couples with children under age 18	**23,804**	**13,203**	**10,601**
One or both parents employed	22,776	12,650	10,125
Mother employed	15,577	9,333	6,244
Both parents employed	13,822	8,256	5,566
Mother employed not father	1,755	1,076	678
Father employed, not mother	7,199	3,318	3,881
Neither parent employed	1,028	553	475
Female-headed families with children under age 18	**8,401**	**4,987**	**3,414**
Mother employed	5,627	3,594	2,033
Mother not employed	2,774	1,393	1,381
Male-headed families with chlidren under age 18	**2,308**	**1,290**	**1,018**
Father employed	1,750	979	771
Father not employed	557	311	247
PERCENT DISTRIBUTION			
Married couples with children under age 18	**100.0%**	**100.0%**	**100.0%**
One or both parents employed	95.7	95.8	95.5
Mother employed	65.4	70.7	58.9
Both parents employed	58.1	62.5	52.5
Mother employed not father	7.4	8.1	6.4
Father employed, not mother	30.2	25.1	36.6
Neither parent employed	4.3	4.2	4.5
Female-headed families with children under age 18	**100.0**	**100.0**	**100.0**
Mother employed	67.0	72.1	59.5
Mother not employed	33.0	27.9	40.5
Male-headed families with chlidren under age 18	**100.0**	**100.0**	**100.0**
Father employed	75.8	75.9	75.7
Father not employed	24.1	24.1	24.3

Source: Bureau of Labor Statistics, Employment Characteristics of Families, Internet site http://www.bls.gov/news.release/famee.t04.htm

More than Half of Couples Are Dual Earners

In just 22 percent of married couples is only the husband in the labor force.

Dual incomes are by far the norm among married couples. Both husband and wife are in the labor force in 54 percent of married couples. In another 22 percent, the husband is the only worker. Not far behind are the 17 percent of couples in which neither spouse is in the labor force. The wife is the sole worker among 7 percent of couples.

At least two-thirds of couples aged 30 to 54 are dual earners. This lifestyle accounts for half of couples aged 55 to 64. The wife is the only spouse employed in a substantial 13.5 percent of couples aged 55 to 64. In these homes, typically, the older husband is retired while the younger wife is still at work. For 67 percent of couples aged 65 or older, neither husband nor wife is working.

■ As boomers retire, the number of couples in which neither spouse is in the labor force may surpass the number in which only the husband is employed.

Dual earners outnumber single earners

(percent distribution of married couples by labor force status of husband and wife, 2010)

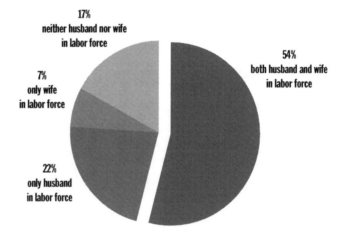

17%
neither husband nor wife
in labor force

7%
only wife
in labor force

22%
only husband
in labor force

54%
both husband and wife
in labor force

Table 6.9 Labor Force Status of Married-Couple Family Groups, 2010

(number and percent distribution of married-couple family groups aged 20 or older by age of householder and labor force status of husband and wife, 2010; numbers in thousands)

	total	husband and wife	husband only	wife only	neither husband nor wife in labor force
Married couples	**60,384**	**32,731**	**13,074**	**4,526**	**10,053**
Under age 25	1,359	730	505	60	61
Aged 25 to 29	3,796	2,460	1,137	150	49
Aged 30 to 34	5,246	3,470	1,525	143	109
Aged 35 to 39	6,343	4,421	1,636	195	91
Aged 40 to 44	6,496	4,481	1,616	280	119
Aged 45 to 54	14,336	10,140	2,848	878	470
Aged 55 to 64	11,699	5,861	2,518	1,580	1,739
Aged 65 or older	11,109	1,166	1,291	1,238	7,415
Aged 65 to 74	6,953	1,023	1,008	1,001	3,922
Aged 75 or older	4,156	143	283	237	3,493
Married couples	**100.0%**	**54.2%**	**21.7%**	**7.5%**	**16.6%**
Aged 20 to 24	100.0	53.7	37.2	4.4	4.5
Aged 25 to 29	100.0	64.8	30.0	4.0	1.3
Aged 30 to 34	100.0	66.1	29.1	2.7	2.1
Aged 35 to 39	100.0	69.7	25.8	3.1	1.4
Aged 40 to 44	100.0	69.0	24.9	4.3	1.8
Aged 45 to 54	100.0	70.7	19.9	6.1	3.3
Aged 55 to 64	100.0	50.1	21.5	13.5	14.9
Aged 65 or older	100.0	10.5	11.6	11.1	66.7
Aged 65 to 74	100.0	14.7	14.5	14.4	56.4
Aged 75 or older	100.0	3.4	6.8	5.7	84.0

Source: Bureau of the Census, America's Families and Living Arrangements: 2010, Internet site http://www.census.gov/population/www/socdemo/hh-fam/cps2010.html; calculations by New Strategist

Most Preschoolers Are in Day Care

The children of working mothers are most likely to attend day care centers.

Among the nation's preschoolers, only 39 percent are cared for only by their parents. The 61 percent majority are in nonparental care some of the time. More than one in three are in center-based programs, such as a day care center, prekindergarten, nursery school, or Head Start. The children of mothers with a college degree are most likely to use nonparental care (69.5 percent) and be in a center-based program (45.8 percent).

Among children in kindergarten through 3rd grade, 53 percent are cared for by their parents before and after school and 47 percent are in nonparental care. Among children in 4th through 8th grade, a larger 53 percent are in nonparental care before and after school, but that's because 22 percent take care of themselves. Most 4th through 8th graders participate in after-school activities, religious activities and sports being most popular. Non-Hispanic white children are far more likely than black or Hispanic children to take part in after-school activities (63 percent versus 40 and 35 percent, respectively).

■ The differences in participation in after-school activities by race and Hispanic origin have long-term effects on school performance and college admissions.

Non-Hispanic white children are much more likely than others to participate in after-school activities

(percent of children in 4th–8th grade participating in after-school activities, by race and Hispanic origin, 2005)

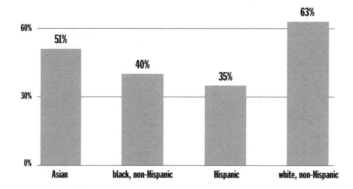

Table 6.10 Day Care Arrangements of Preschoolers, 2005

(percent distribution of children aged 0 to 6 not yet in kindergarten, by type of care, child and family character-istics, 2005)

| | | | nonparental care | | | |
| | | | | care in a home | | |
	total	parental care only	total	by a relative	by a nonrelative	center-based program
Total children	100.0%	39.2%	60.8%	22.3%	13.9%	36.1%
Age						
Aged 0 to 2	100.0	49.3	50.7	22.0	15.6	19.6
Aged 3 to 6	100.0	23.6	73.7	22.7	11.7	57.1
Race and Hispanic origin						
Asian	100.0	43.5	56.5	21.3	9.0	37.0
Black, non-Hispanic	100.0	30.1	69.9	27.7	10.2	43.9
Hispanic	100.0	50.5	49.5	21.2	10.4	25.2
White, non-Hispanic	100.0	37.2	62.8	21.0	17.0	37.8
Poverty status						
Below poverty level	100.0	49.2	50.8	23.3	8.0	28.3
100 to 199 percent above poverty level	100.0	47.2	52.8	23.5	9.3	29.4
200 percent or more above poverty level	100.0	31.6	68.4	21.4	18.3	42.2
Family type						
Two parents	100.0	42.9	57.1	18.8	14.1	34.4
Two parents, married	100.0	41.8	58.2	18.6	14.2	35.8
Two parents, unmarried	100.0	53.0	47.0	20.4	13.0	21.7
One parent	100.0	24.9	75.1	36.0	13.4	42.3
No parents	100.0	33.1	66.9	28.3	10.0	43.6
Mother's educational attainment						
Less than high school	100.0	63.7	36.3	16.1	5.5	18.9
High school graduate/GED	100.0	44.4	55.6	24.1	9.9	30.7
Vocational/technical/some college	100.0	36.5	63.5	25.8	14.5	35.2
College graduate	100.0	30.5	69.5	19.1	19.2	45.8
Mother's employment status						
Employed 35 or more hours/week	100.0	14.7	85.3	31.8	23.3	47.6
Employed fewer than 35 hours/week	100.0	30.3	69.7	30.5	18.0	37.8
Looking for work	100.0	53.3	46.7	20.7	7.5	23.3
Not in labor force	100.0	66.1	33.9	7.8	3.6	25.8
Region						
Northeast	100.0	38.3	61.7	21.0	15.1	37.9
Midwest	100.0	38.0	62.0	22.3	11.1	38.8
South	100.0	36.7	63.3	23.8	18.8	33.5
West	100.0	43.9	56.1	21.8	12.6	33.1

Note: Numbers may not sum to total because there may be more than one type of nonparental care arrangement. Center-based care includes day care centers, prekindergartens, nursery schools, Head Start programs, and other early childhood education programs.
Source: Federal Interagency Forum on Child and Family Statistics, America's Children in Brief: Key National Indicators of Well-Being, 2010, Internet site http://childstats.gov/americaschildren/tables.asp

Table 6.11 Before- and After-School Activities of Children, 2005

(percent distribution of children in kindergarten through eighth grade, by type of before- and after-school care, poverty status, race, and Hispanic origin, 2005)

| | total | poverty status | | | race and Hispanic origin | | | |
		below poverty	100%–199% above poverty level	200% or more above poverty level	Asian	black non-Hispanic	Hispanic	white non-Hispanic
KINDERGARTEN TO THIRD GRADE								
Total children	100.0%	100.0%	100.0%	100.0%	100.0%	100.0%	100.0%	100.0%
Care arrangements								
Parent care only	53.1	52.0	54.5	53.0	49.9	34.6	55.3	58.3
Nonparental care	46.9	48.0	45.5	47.0	50.1	65.4	44.7	41.7
Home-based care	23.6	25.2	24.5	22.6	26.5	32.2	20.4	22.0
Center-based care	24.4	25.0	21.6	25.2	21.4	39.8	23.4	20.5
Activities used for supervision	5.2	3.1	5.3	6.0	13.4	5.8	3.2	4.8
Self-care	2.6	5.1	3.6	1.3	3.6	4.1	4.2	1.6
ACTIVITIES*								
Any activity	**46.2**	**24.3**	**34.0**	**59.5**	**45.8**	**30.4**	**30.4**	**56.2**
Sports	31.8	12.1	19.5	44.3	29.3	16.8	20.8	40.2
Religious activities	19.4	13.5	14.8	23.4	11.5	14.6	11.9	24.0
Arts	17.2	6.0	10.8	24.1	27.1	8.3	8.2	21.8
Scouts	12.9	5.3	8.0	17.8	11.1	4.9	3.8	18.2
Academic activities	4.7	3.8	3.8	5.3	7.4	4.4	3.5	5.1
Community services	4.2	1.9	3.0	5.5	2.6	3.3	1.7	5.3
Clubs	3.2	1.3	2.4	4.3	4.2	1.1	1.8	4.3
FOURTH TO EIGHTH GRADE								
Total children	100.0	100.0	100.0	100.0	100.0	100.0	100.0	100.0
Care arrangements								
Parent care only	46.9	46.7	45.2	47.6	44.2	34.5	45.0	51.2
Nonparental care	53.1	53.3	54.8	52.4	55.8	65.5	55.0	48.8
Home-based care	18.1	15.0	20.0	18.4	17.5	24.1	18.6	16.4
Center-based care	19.0	21.3	21.3	17.4	21.9	28.9	25.4	14.2
Activities used for supervision	9.0	7.8	6.9	10.2	11.9	10.5	7.5	8.9
Self-care	22.2	23.5	23.8	21.2	21.0	27.1	19.6	21.1
ACTIVITIES*								
Any activity	**53.7**	**30.4**	**40.5**	**65.9**	**51.2**	**39.7**	**35.4**	**63.3**
Sports	39.3	18.6	26.1	50.8	37.2	24.2	26.7	47.8
Religious activities	24.9	12.5	20.0	30.7	18.3	20.9	14.8	29.7
Arts	21.5	9.7	12.5	28.5	25.5	13.3	13.2	25.8
Community services	12.7	5.0	10.6	15.9	13.1	8.2	7.1	15.6
Scouts	10.1	4.8	6.4	13.2	7.7	5.6	5.4	13.3
Academic activities	9.7	6.6	7.1	11.6	13.0	12.0	5.9	10.0
Clubs	8.7	3.7	4.6	11.8	8.9	4.9	4.1	11.0

* *"Activities" are organized programs outside of school hours that are not part of a before- or after-school program.*
Note: Numbers may not sum to total because there may be more than one type of arrangement or activity.
Source: Federal Interagency Forum on Child and Family Statistics, America's Children in Brief: Key National Indicators of Well-Being, 2010, Internet site http://childstats.gov/americaschildren/tables.asp

More than One in Four Workers Are Part-Timers

Among women workers, one-third work part-time.

Most of the nation's nonagricultural workers have full-time jobs. Part-timers outnumber those with full-time jobs only in the 16-to-19 age group. Seventy-eight percent of workers aged 16 to 19 work part-time. Among 20-to-24-year-olds, a smaller 42 percent work part-time. The figure drops to 21 percent among 25-to-54-year-olds, then rises again to 29 percent among those aged 55 or older.

Many part-time workers would rather have full-time jobs. Among the 35 million part-time workers, 32 percent of men and 20 percent of women are working part-time for economic reasons—meaning either their hours have been reduced or they cannot find a full-time job. The proportion of part-timers who would rather work full-time peaks at 41 percent among men aged 25 to 54.

■ The economic downturn has forced many Americans into part-time employment to make ends meet.

Part-time work is most common among teens and young adults

(percent of people aged 16 or older in nonagricultural industries who work part-time, by age, 2010)

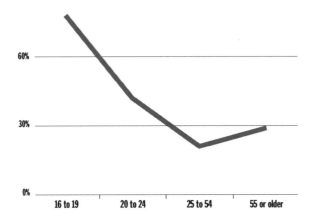

Table 6.12 Full-Time and Part-Time Workers by Age and Sex, 2010

(number and percent distribution of people aged 16 or older at work in nonagricultural industries by age, employment status, and sex, 2010; numbers in thousands)

	total			men			women		
	total	full-time	part-time	total	full-time	part-time	total	full-time	part-time
Total at work	**131,891**	**97,386**	**34,505**	**69,556**	**55,591**	**13,964**	**62,335**	**41,795**	**20,540**
Aged 16 to 19	4,124	920	3,204	1,981	528	1,453	2,143	391	1,751
Aged 20 to 24	12,185	7,023	5,161	6,190	3,849	2,340	5,995	3,174	2,821
Aged 25 to 54	89,751	71,227	18,524	47,976	40,966	7,010	41,776	30,262	11,514
Aged 55 or older	25,831	18,216	7,615	13,409	10,248	3,161	12,422	7,968	4,454

PERCENT DISTRIBUTION BY EMPLOYMENT STATUS

	total			men			women		
Total at work	**100.0%**	**73.8%**	**26.2%**	**100.0%**	**79.9%**	**20.1%**	**100.0%**	**67.0%**	**33.0%**
Aged 16 to 19	100.0	22.3	77.7	100.0	26.7	73.3	100.0	18.2	81.7
Aged 20 to 24	100.0	57.6	42.4	100.0	62.2	37.8	100.0	52.9	47.1
Aged 25 to 54	100.0	79.4	20.6	100.0	85.4	14.6	100.0	72.4	27.6
Aged 55 or older	100.0	70.5	29.5	100.0	76.4	23.6	100.0	64.1	35.9

PERCENT DISTRIBUTION BY AGE

	total			men			women		
Total at work	**100.0%**	**100.0%**	**100.0%**	**100.0%**	**100.0%**	**100.0%**	**100.0%**	**100.0%**	**100.0%**
Aged 16 to 19	3.1	0.9	9.3	2.8	0.9	10.4	3.4	0.9	8.5
Aged 20 to 24	9.2	7.2	15.0	8.9	6.9	16.8	9.6	7.6	13.7
Aged 25 to 54	68.0	73.1	53.7	69.0	73.7	50.2	67.0	72.4	56.1
Aged 55 or older	19.6	18.7	22.1	19.3	18.4	22.6	19.9	19.1	21.7

Note: Part-time work is less than 35 hours per week. Part-time workers exclude those who worked less than 35 hours in the previous week because of vacation, holidays, child care problems, weather issues, and other temporary, noneconomic reasons. Source: Bureau of Labor Statistics, Current Population Survey, Internet site http://www.bls.gov/cps/tables.htm#empstat; calculations by New Strategist

Table 6.13 Part-Time Workers by Age, Sex, and Reason, 2010

(total number of people aged 16 or older who work in nonagricultural industries part-time, and number and percent working part-time for economic reasons, by sex and age, 2010; numbers in thousands)

	total	working part-time for economic reasons	
		number	share of total
Men working part-time	**13,964**	**4,536**	**32.5%**
Aged 16 to 19	1,453	236	16.2
Aged 20 to 24	2,340	780	33.3
Aged 25 to 54	7,010	2,863	40.8
Aged 55 or older	3,161	657	20.8
Women working part-time	**20,540**	**4,208**	**20.5**
Aged 16 to 19	1,751	212	12.1
Aged 20 to 24	2,821	703	24.9
Aged 25 to 54	11,514	2,643	23.0
Aged 55 or older	4,454	650	14.6

Note: Part-time work is less than 35 hours per week. Part-time workers exclude those who worked less than 35 hours in the previous week because of vacation, holidays, child care problems, weather issues, and other temporary, noneconomic reasons. "Economic reasons" means a worker's hours have been reduced or workers cannot find full-time employment.
Source: Bureau of Labor Statistics, Current Population Survey, Internet site http://www.bls.gov/cps/tables.htm#empstat; calculations by New Strategist

Occupations Differ by Sex

Occupational differences are also considerable by race and Hispanic origin.

Women are more likely than men to work in education or health care occupations. Men are more likely than women to work in computer, construction, and production occupations. Occupational differences are even greater by race and Hispanic origin. While 47 percent of Asians work in management or professional occupations, the proportion is just 19 percent among Hispanics. Ten percent of Hispanics work in construction versus fewer than 2 percent of Asians.

Women account for the majority of workers in many occupations, including public relations managers, education administrators, registered nurses, librarians, and secretaries. Asians are well represented in many professional occupations. Although they account for fewer than 5 percent of all workers, Asians are 28 percent of computer software engineers. Blacks are 11 percent of all workers, but a larger 23 percent of social workers, 24 percent of licensed practical nurses, and 15 percent of dietitians. Hispanics are 14 percent of all workers but fully 41 percent of maids and housekeepers, 43 percent of construction laborers, and 44 percent of grounds maintenance workers.

■ Women account for 32 percent of doctors and lawyers, but only 10 percent of civil engineers.

Nearly half of Asians work in management or professional jobs

(percent of workers in management or professional occupations, by race and Hispanic origin, 2010)

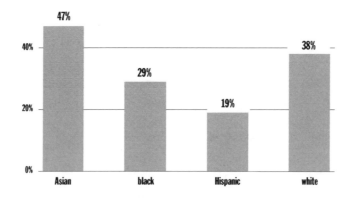

Table 6.14 Workers by Occupation and Sex, 2010

(number of employed people aged 16 or older in the civilian labor force, by occupation and sex, 2010; numbers in thousands)

	total	men	women
TOTAL EMPLOYED	**139,064**	**73,359**	**65,705**
Management, professional and related occupations	**51,743**	**25,070**	**26,673**
Management, business, and financial operations	20,938	11,945	8,993
Management	15,001	9,266	5,735
Business and financial operations	5,937	2,679	3,258
Professional and related occupations	30,805	13,125	17,680
Computer and mathematical	3,531	2,620	911
Architecture and engineering	2,619	2,282	337
Life, physical, and social science	1,409	755	655
Community and social services	2,337	836	1,500
Legal	1,716	878	838
Education, training, and library	8,628	2,261	6,367
Art, design, entertainment, sports, and media	2,759	1,484	1,276
Health care practitioner and technical	7,805	2,009	5,796
Service occupations	**24,634**	**10,652**	**13,982**
Health care support	3,332	370	2,962
Protective service	3,289	2,587	703
Food preparation and serving related	7,660	3,439	4,221
Building and grounds cleaning and maintenance	5,328	3,164	2,164
Personal care and service	5,024	1,092	3,932
Sales and office occupations	**33,433**	**12,419**	**21,015**
Sales and related	15,386	7,703	7,683
Office and administrative support	18,047	4,716	13,331
Natural resources, construction, and maintenance occupations	**13,073**	**12,467**	**606**
Farming, fishing, and forestry	987	755	231
Construction and extraction	7,175	6,990	185
Installation, maintenance, and repair	4,911	4,721	190
Production, transportation, and material-moving occupations	**16,180**	**12,751**	**3,429**
Production	7,998	5,792	2,206
Transportation and material moving	8,182	6,959	1,224

Source: Bureau of Labor Statistics, Current Population Survey, Internet site http://www.bls.gov/cps/tables.htm#empstat; calculations by New Strategist

Table 6.15 Occupational Distribution of Workers by Sex, 2010

(occupational distribution of employed people aged 16 or older in the civilian labor force, by sex, 2010)

	total	men	women
TOTAL EMPLOYED	100.0%	100.0%	100.0%
Management, professional and related occupations	37.2	34.2	40.6
Management, business, and financial operations	15.1	16.3	13.7
Management	10.8	12.6	8.7
Business and financial operations	4.3	3.7	5.0
Professional and related occupations	22.2	17.9	26.9
Computer and mathematical	2.5	3.6	1.4
Architecture and engineering	1.9	3.1	0.5
Life, physical, and social science	1.0	1.0	1.0
Community and social services	1.7	1.1	2.3
Legal	1.2	1.2	1.3
Education, training, and library	6.2	3.1	9.7
Art, design, entertainment, sports, and media	2.0	2.0	1.9
Health care practitioner and technical	5.6	2.7	8.8
Service occupations	17.7	14.5	21.3
Health care support	2.4	0.5	4.5
Protective service	2.4	3.5	1.1
Food preparation and serving related	5.5	4.7	6.4
Building and grounds cleaning and maintenance	3.8	4.3	3.3
Personal care and service	3.6	1.5	6.0
Sales and office occupations	24.0	16.9	32.0
Sales and related	11.1	10.5	11.7
Office and administrative support	13.0	6.4	20.3
Natural resources, construction, maintenance occupations	9.4	17.0	0.9
Farming, fishing, and forestry	0.7	1.0	0.4
Construction and extraction	5.2	9.5	0.3
Installation, maintenance, and repair	3.5	6.4	0.3
Production, transportation, material-moving occupations	11.6	17.4	5.2
Production	5.8	7.9	3.4
Transportation and material moving	5.9	9.5	1.9

Source: Bureau of Labor Statistics, Current Population Survey, Internet site http://www.bls.gov/cps/tables.htm#empstat; calculations by New Strategist

Table 6.16 Distribution of Men and Women by Occupation, 2010

(percent distribution of employed people aged 16 or older in occupations by sex, 2010)

	total	men	women
TOTAL EMPLOYED	**100.0%**	**52.8%**	**47.2%**
Management, professional and related occupations	**100.0**	**48.5**	**51.5**
Management, business, and financial operations	100.0	57.0	43.0
Management	100.0	61.8	38.2
Business and financial operations	100.0	45.1	54.9
Professional and related occupations	100.0	42.6	57.4
Computer and mathematical	100.0	74.2	25.8
Architecture and engineering	100.0	87.1	12.9
Life, physical, and social science	100.0	53.6	46.5
Community and social services	100.0	35.8	64.2
Legal	100.0	51.2	48.8
Education, training, and library	100.0	26.2	73.8
Art, design, entertainment, sports, and media	100.0	53.8	46.2
Health care practitioner and technical	100.0	25.7	74.3
Service occupations	**100.0**	**43.2**	**56.8**
Health care support	100.0	11.1	88.9
Protective service	100.0	78.7	21.4
Food preparation and serving related	100.0	44.9	55.1
Building and grounds cleaning and maintenance	100.0	59.4	40.6
Personal care and service	100.0	21.7	78.3
Sales and office occupations	**100.0**	**37.1**	**62.9**
Sales and related	100.0	50.1	49.9
Office and administrative support	100.0	26.1	73.9
Natural resources, construction, maintenance occupations	**100.0**	**95.4**	**4.6**
Farming, fishing, and forestry	100.0	76.5	23.4
Construction and extraction	100.0	97.4	2.6
Installation, maintenance, and repair	100.0	96.1	3.9
Production, transportation, material-moving occupations	**100.0**	**78.8**	**21.2**
Production	100.0	72.4	27.6
Transportation and material moving	100.0	85.1	15.0

Source: Bureau of Labor Statistics, Current Population Survey, Internet site http://www.bls.gov/cps/tables.htm#empstat; calculations by New Strategist

Table 6.17 Workers by Occupation, Race, and Hispanic Origin, 2010

(number of employed people aged 16 or older in the civilian labor force, by occupation, race, and Hispanic origin, 2010; numbers in thousands)

	total	Asian	black	Hispanic	white
TOTAL EMPLOYED	**139,064**	**6,705**	**15,010**	**19,906**	**114,168**
Management, professional and related occupations	**51,743**	**3,149**	**4,363**	**3,755**	**43,268**
Management, business, and financial operations	20,938	999	1,537	1,562	18,043
Management	15,001	662	954	1,142	13,137
Business and financial operations	5,937	336	583	420	4,906
Professional and related occupations	30,805	2,150	2,826	2,194	25,225
Computer and mathematical	3,531	568	237	194	2,663
Architecture and engineering	2,619	236	135	177	2,205
Life, physical, and social science	1,409	152	88	85	1,139
Community and social services	2,337	77	451	229	1,750
Legal	1,716	58	111	94	1,510
Education, training, and library	8,628	330	810	686	7,325
Art, design, entertainment, sports, and media	2,759	117	152	244	2,430
Health care practitioner and technical	7,805	612	842	484	6,204
Service occupations	**24,634**	**1,205**	**3,763**	**5,257**	**18,938**
Health care support	3,332	137	849	506	2,252
Protective service	3,289	79	585	437	2,530
Food preparation and serving related	7,660	431	866	1,703	6,110
Building and grounds cleaning and maintenance	5,328	166	722	1,877	4,290
Personal care and service	5,024	392	741	734	3,756
Sales and office occupations	**33,433**	**1,416**	**3,762**	**4,228**	**27,470**
Sales and related	15,386	766	1,503	1,814	12,785
Office and administrative support	18,047	649	2,259	2,413	14,685
Natural resources, construction, maintenance occupations	**13,073**	**261**	**876**	**3,272**	**11,619**
Farming, fishing, and forestry	987	19	51	412	889
Construction and extraction	7,175	102	441	2,090	6,449
Installation, maintenance, and repair	4,911	140	384	769	4,281
Production, transportation, material-moving occupations	**16,180**	**674**	**2,247**	**3,395**	**12,873**
Production	7,998	441	908	1,755	6,468
Transportation and material moving	8,182	232	1,339	1,640	6,405

Source: Bureau of Labor Statistics, Current Population Survey, Internet site http://www.bls.gov/cps/tables.htm#empstat; calculations by New Strategist

Table 6.18 Occupational Distribution of Workers by Race and Hispanic Origin, 2010

(occupational distribution of employed people aged 16 or older in the civilian labor force by race and Hispanic origin, 2010)

	total	Asian	black	Hispanic	white
TOTAL EMPLOYED	100.0%	100.0%	100.0%	100.0%	100.0%
Management, professional and related occupations	**37.2**	**47.0**	**29.1**	**18.9**	**37.9**
Management, business, and financial operations	15.1	14.9	10.2	7.8	15.8
Management	10.8	9.9	6.4	5.7	11.5
Business and financial operations	4.3	5.0	3.9	2.1	4.3
Professional and related occupations	22.2	32.1	18.8	11.0	22.1
Computer and mathematical	2.5	8.5	1.6	1.0	2.3
Architecture and engineering	1.9	3.5	0.9	0.9	1.9
Life, physical, and social science	1.0	2.3	0.6	0.4	1.0
Community and social services	1.7	1.1	3.0	1.2	1.5
Legal	1.2	0.9	0.7	0.5	1.3
Education, training, and library	6.2	4.9	5.4	3.4	6.4
Art, design, entertainment, sports, and media	2.0	1.7	1.0	1.2	2.1
Health care practitioner and technical	5.6	9.1	5.6	2.4	5.4
Service occupations	**17.7**	**18.0**	**25.1**	**26.4**	**16.6**
Health care support	2.4	2.0	5.7	2.5	2.0
Protective service	2.4	1.2	3.9	2.2	2.2
Food preparation and serving related	5.5	6.4	5.8	8.6	5.4
Building and grounds cleaning and maintenance	3.8	2.5	4.8	9.4	3.8
Personal care and service	3.6	5.8	4.9	3.7	3.3
Sales and office occupations	**24.0**	**21.1**	**25.1**	**21.2**	**24.1**
Sales and related	11.1	11.4	10.0	9.1	11.2
Office and administrative support	13.0	9.7	15.0	12.1	12.9
Natural resources, construction, maintenance occupations	**9.4**	**3.9**	**5.8**	**16.4**	**10.2**
Farming, fishing, and forestry	0.7	0.3	0.3	2.1	0.8
Construction and extraction	5.2	1.5	2.9	10.5	5.6
Installation, maintenance, and repair	3.5	2.1	2.6	3.9	3.7
Production, transportation, material-moving occupations	**11.6**	**10.1**	**15.0**	**17.1**	**11.3**
Production	5.8	6.6	6.0	8.8	5.7
Transportation and material moving	5.9	3.5	8.9	8.2	5.6

Source: Bureau of Labor Statistics, Current Population Survey, Internet site http://www.bls.gov/cps/tables.htm#empstat; calculations by New Strategist

Table 6.19 Race and Hispanic Origin Distributions of Occupations, 2010

(percent distribution of employed people aged 16 or older in occupations by race and Hispanic origin, 2010)

	total	Asian	black	Hispanic	white
TOTAL EMPLOYED	**100.0%**	**4.8%**	**10.8%**	**14.3%**	**82.1%**
Management, professional and related occupations	**100.0**	**6.1**	**8.4**	**7.3**	**83.6**
Management, business, and financial operations	100.0	4.8	7.3	7.5	86.2
Management	100.0	4.4	6.4	7.6	87.6
Business and financial operations	100.0	5.7	9.8	7.1	82.6
Professional and related occupations	100.0	7.0	9.2	7.1	81.9
Computer and mathematical	100.0	16.1	6.7	5.5	75.4
Architecture and engineering	100.0	9.0	5.2	6.8	84.2
Life, physical, and social science	100.0	10.8	6.2	6.0	80.8
Community and social services	100.0	3.3	19.3	9.8	74.9
Legal	100.0	3.4	6.5	5.5	88.0
Education, training, and library	100.0	3.8	9.4	8.0	84.9
Art, design, entertainment, sports, and media	100.0	4.2	5.5	8.8	88.1
Health care practitioner and technical	100.0	7.8	10.8	6.2	79.5
Service occupations	**100.0**	**4.9**	**15.3**	**21.3**	**76.9**
Health care support	100.0	4.1	25.5	15.2	67.6
Protective service	100.0	2.4	17.8	13.3	76.9
Food preparation and serving related	100.0	5.6	11.3	22.2	79.8
Building and grounds cleaning and maintenance	100.0	3.1	13.6	35.2	80.5
Personal care and service	100.0	7.8	14.7	14.6	74.8
Sales and office occupations	**100.0**	**4.2**	**11.3**	**12.6**	**82.2**
Sales and related	100.0	5.0	9.8	11.8	83.1
Office and administrative support	100.0	3.6	12.5	13.4	81.4
Natural resources, construction, maintenance occupations	**100.0**	**2.0**	**6.7**	**25.0**	**88.9**
Farming, fishing, and forestry	100.0	1.9	5.2	41.7	90.1
Construction and extraction	100.0	1.4	6.1	29.1	89.9
Installation, maintenance, and repair	100.0	2.9	7.8	15.7	87.2
Production, transportation, material-moving occupations	**100.0**	**4.2**	**13.9**	**21.0**	**79.6**
Production	100.0	5.5	11.4	21.9	80.9
Transportation and material moving	100.0	2.8	16.4	20.0	78.3

Source: Bureau of Labor Statistics, Current Population Survey, Internet site http://www.bls.gov/cps/tables.htm#empstat; calculations by New Strategist

Table 6.20 Workers by Detailed Occupation, Sex, Race, and Hispanic Origin, 2010

(percentage of employed civilians aged 16 or older who are women, Asians, blacks, or Hispanics, by selected detailed occupation, 2010)

	women	Asians	blacks	Hispanics
TOTAL EMPLOYED	**47.2%**	**4.8%**	**10.8%**	**14.3%**
Management, professional, and related occupations	**51.5**	**6.1**	**8.4**	**7.3**
Management, business, and financial operations occupations	43.0	4.8	7.3	7.5
Management occupations	38.2	4.4	6.4	7.6
Chief executives	25.5	3.2	2.8	4.8
General and operations managers	29.9	3.3	5.8	5.9
Advertising and promotions managers	61.1	2.3	0.8	9.6
Marketing and sales managers	45.2	5.0	5.9	5.1
Public relations managers	60.0	4.8	4.4	5.2
Administrative services managers	34.4	5.5	9.0	9.5
Computer and information systems managers	29.9	9.0	6.8	7.2
Financial managers	53.2	6.9	6.7	8.1
Human resources managers	69.3	3.0	9.1	7.9
Industrial production managers	17.9	4.4	3.0	9.4
Purchasing managers	46.1	2.8	7.6	7.8
Transportation, storage, and distribution managers	17.4	2.8	9.5	11.7
Farm, ranch, and other agricultural managers	18.1	0.8	0.6	9.8
Farmers and ranchers	24.6	0.7	0.6	1.5
Construction managers	6.8	2.0	3.5	8.5
Education administrators	63.0	2.0	11.1	6.4
Engineering managers	7.7	13.3	5.4	3.5
Food service managers	47.4	10.8	8.5	14.6
Lodging managers	48.4	11.3	5.1	5.8
Medical and health services managers	72.5	3.2	12.4	7.2
Property, real estate, and community association managers	49.2	2.6	7.7	11.4
Social and community service managers	70.2	1.6	13.1	7.0
Managers, all other	35.0	4.8	6.8	8.5
Business and financial operations occupations	54.9	5.7	9.8	7.1
Wholesale and retail buyers, except farm products	52.1	2.2	4.4	9.7
Purchasing agents, except wholesale, retail, and farm products	54.9	3.2	8.0	5.7
Claims adjusters, appraisers, examiners, and investigators	57.4	3.3	13.8	7.4
Compliance officers, except agriculture, construction, health and safety, and transportation	47.0	2.2	11.5	7.8
Cost estimators	11.6	0.6	1.5	7.5
Human resources, training, and labor relations specialists	70.3	2.6	14.0	10.2
Logisticians	42.8	8.7	10.6	7.9
Management analysts	43.7	7.6	7.2	6.7
Meeting and convention planners	78.8	3.0	9.4	6.8
Other business operations specialists	63.0	4.4	10.3	7.1
Accountants and auditors	60.1	9.1	8.6	5.8
Appraisers and assessors of real estate	34.0	1.8	3.0	2.5
Financial analysts	35.7	6.9	11.6	3.0
Personal financial advisors	30.8	4.9	5.2	3.5
Insurance underwriters	59.3	4.2	13.2	4.7
Loan counselors and officers	51.8	4.6	9.9	10.6
Tax examiners, collectors, and revenue agents	66.1	3.5	25.6	7.1
Tax preparers	71.1	6.1	13.0	11.1
Financial specialists, all other	64.1	5.3	13.7	12.1

	women	Asians	blacks	Hispanics
Professional and related occupations	57.4%	7.0%	9.2%	7.1%
Computer and mathematical occupations	25.8	16.1	6.7	5.5
Computer scientists and systems analysts	30.5	14.9	7.3	5.1
Computer programmers	22.0	12.4	5.1	6.5
Computer software engineers	20.9	28.0	5.1	3.9
Computer support specialists	27.6	7.9	11.3	6.9
Database administrators	36.4	11.8	9.0	8.6
Network and computer systems administrators	16.5	9.4	5.6	6.0
Network systems and data communications analysts	26.2	7.4	6.6	6.7
Operations research analysts	46.2	5.8	10.7	8.4
Architecture and engineering occupations	12.9	9.0	5.2	6.8
Architects, except naval	24.4	1.9	2.1	7.8
Aerospace engineers	10.8	3.7	6.7	3.8
Chemical engineers	17.4	11.5	3.1	1.0
Civil engineers	9.7	8.9	4.9	6.9
Computer hardware engineers	10.3	26.7	3.1	7.3
Electrical and electronics engineers	7.2	16.7	5.3	7.0
Industrial engineers, including health and safety	20.0	10.2	5.0	7.8
Mechanical engineers	6.7	11.0	3.2	3.7
Engineers, all other	12.9	12.5	7.1	5.2
Drafters	21.4	4.1	3.6	11.3
Engineering technicians, except drafters	13.2	4.6	8.2	8.9
Surveying and mapping technicians	10.9	0.3	1.6	10.9
Life, physical, and social science occupations	46.5	10.8	6.3	6.0
Biological scientists	45.8	9.8	8.0	6.2
Medical scientists	53.7	28.4	7.0	7.5
Chemists and materials scientists	33.5	18.2	9.9	4.3
Environmental scientists and geoscientists	26.2	3.0	5.4	2.9
Physical scientists, all other	39.5	21.1	4.0	3.2
Market and survey researchers	55.7	7.7	5.1	2.8
Psychologists	66.7	3.3	3.9	7.3
Chemical technicians	32.4	8.4	12.8	13.8
Other life, physical, and social science technicians	54.6	6.9	7.4	8.4
Community and social services occupations	64.2	3.3	19.3	9.8
Counselors	71.2	3.8	21.4	9.5
Social workers	80.8	3.3	22.8	11.3
Miscellaneous community and social service specialists	68.0	1.7	21.6	13.0
Clergy	17.5	2.9	12.6	6.3
Directors, religious activities and education	79.2	4.3	2.0	4.0
Religious workers, all other	69.3	6.2	6.0	9.0
Legal occupations	48.8	3.4	6.5	5.5
Lawyers	31.5	3.4	4.3	3.4
Judges, magistrates, and other judicial workers	36.4	3.9	12.5	7.8
Paralegals and legal assistants	85.8	2.4	8.8	9.6
Miscellaneous legal support workers	72.6	4.4	10.4	7.7
Education, training, and library occupations	73.8	3.8	9.4	8.0
Postsecondary teachers	45.9	11.0	6.3	5.0
Preschool and kindergarten teachers	97.0	2.7	13.4	9.6
Elementary and middle school teachers	81.8	2.4	9.3	7.3
Secondary school teachers	57.0	1.6	8.0	6.7
Special education teachers	85.1	2.0	6.8	6.2
Other teachers and instructors	66.5	4.8	9.6	8.0
Archivists, curators, and museum technicians	56.4	0.6	3.3	2.5
Librarians	82.8	1.7	9.2	5.2
Teacher assistants	92.4	2.9	12.7	15.1
Other education, training, and library workers	75.9	1.7	16.1	11.2

	women	Asians	blacks	Hispanics
Arts, design, entertainment, sports, and media occupations	46.2%	4.3%	5.5%	8.8%
Artists and related workers	47.1	3.6	2.7	6.6
Designers	53.7	5.2	3.3	9.0
Producers and directors	37.7	5.5	9.1	10.9
Athletes, coaches, umpires, and related workers	34.6	4.1	7.3	10.6
Musicians, singers, and related workers	31.9	2.1	13.9	8.7
Announcers	18.0	2.0	12.9	18.0
News analysts, reporters, and correspondents	46.9	6.0	3.0	7.2
Public relations specialists	58.8	2.6	2.8	8.7
Editors	53.2	5.0	4.9	3.9
Technical writers	54.3	3.8	5.4	2.0
Writers and authors	63.5	2.3	3.8	1.5
Miscellaneous media and communication workers	67.9	10.6	6.6	32.5
Broadcast and sound engineering technicians and radio operators	9.9	4.1	5.7	10.8
Photographers	39.4	3.3	6.5	8.1
Television, video, and motion picture camera operators and editors	7.2	4.0	5.5	7.1
Health care practitioner and technical occupations	74.3	7.8	10.8	6.2
Chiropractors	20.2	5.3	–	2.0
Dentists	25.5	13.7	0.3	5.7
Dietitians and nutritionists	92.3	9.1	14.9	5.2
Pharmacists	53.0	15.1	5.2	4.3
Physicians and surgeons	32.3	15.7	5.8	6.8
Physician assistants	68.7	5.8	5.0	9.2
Registered nurses	91.1	7.5	12.0	4.9
Occupational therapists	87.8	2.6	2.5	6.1
Physical therapists	68.5	7.6	5.8	5.4
Respiratory therapists	63.6	4.8	11.9	6.6
Speech-language pathologists	96.3	0.7	2.9	6.1
Therapists, all other	76.9	4.0	6.6	10.4
Veterinarians	56.0	1.8	2.6	3.9
Clinical laboratory technologists and technicians	76.8	10.3	15.1	7.4
Dental hygienists	95.1	5.9	4.3	3.0
Diagnostic related technologists and technicians	73.3	4.8	7.2	7.7
Emergency medical technicians and paramedics	34.1	0.9	4.4	3.7
Health diagnosing and treating practitioner support technicians	75.9	6.8	13.6	10.8
Licensed practical and licensed vocational nurses	91.7	3.8	24.4	6.2
Medical records and health information technicians	87.6	6.5	19.9	12.7
Opticians, dispensing	66.5	4.5	15.3	8.1
Miscellaneous health technologists and technicians	71.1	6.5	17.6	8.5
Other health care practitioners and technical occupations	43.1	3.0	8.7	9.6
Service occupations	**56.8**	**4.9**	**15.3**	**21.3**
Health care support occupations	88.9	4.1	25.5	15.2
Nursing, psychiatric, and home health aides	88.2	4.0	34.6	14.7
Physical therapist assistants and aides	71.5	6.6	6.2	14.5
Massage therapists	87.1	4.9	5.3	6.0
Dental assistants	97.5	5.6	5.7	20.0
Medical assistants and other health care support occupations	89.7	3.5	17.8	16.4
Protective service occupations	21.4	2.4	17.8	13.3
First-line supervisors/managers of police and detectives	15.4	2.5	8.7	7.4
Supervisors, protective service workers, all other	30.7	2.3	19.9	8.2
Fire fighters	3.6	0.5	6.4	9.6
Bailiffs, correctional officers, and jailers	26.1	1.2	22.0	13.3
Detectives and criminal investigators	22.8	3.7	10.6	13.3
Police and sheriff's patrol officers	13.0	2.7	12.1	15.2

	women	Asians	blacks	Hispanics
Private detectives and investigators	37.6%	3.2%	5.7%	12.1%
Security guards and gaming surveillance officers	20.8	3.4	28.8	15.9
Crossing guards	66.4	1.8	26.4	9.4
Lifeguards and other protective service workers	54.4	2.2	4.2	6.7
Food preparation and serving related occupations	55.1	5.6	11.3	22.2
Chefs and head cooks	19.0	16.5	12.0	17.9
First-line supervisors/managers of food preparation and serving workers	56.6	3.0	15.4	14.9
Cooks	40.5	5.0	15.0	32.5
Food preparation workers	59.2	5.3	13.4	23.7
Bartenders	55.2	2.1	3.8	10.7
Combined food preparation and serving workers, including fast food	61.3	4.6	12.8	16.6
Counter attendants, cafeteria, food concession, and coffee shop	65.7	5.7	11.3	18.5
Waiters and waitresses	71.1	6.1	7.1	16.6
Food servers, nonrestaurant	64.9	6.5	18.6	16.3
Dining room and cafeteria attendants and bartender helpers	47.9	7.0	10.7	29.0
Dishwashers	21.1	4.2	10.5	38.5
Hosts and hostesses, restaurant, lounge, and coffee shop	84.7	4.0	8.1	14.3
Building and grounds cleaning and maintenance occupations	40.6	3.1	13.6	35.2
First-line supervisors/managers of housekeeping and janitorial workers	41.7	2.8	13.3	19.8
First-line supervisors/managers of landscaping, lawn service, and grounds keeping workers	7.3	1.1	3.8	20.5
Janitors and building cleaners	33.2	3.2	17.1	30.9
Maids and housekeeping cleaners	89.0	5.0	16.3	40.8
Pest control workers	3.3	1.7	5.3	15.9
Grounds maintenance workers	5.8	1.3	6.3	43.8
Personal care and service occupations	78.3	7.8	14.8	14.6
First-line supervisors/managers of gaming workers	52.2	8.3	5.4	8.9
First-line supervisors/managers of personal service workers	71.6	14.5	7.7	9.0
Nonfarm animal caretakers	71.7	2.0	2.7	12.7
Gaming services workers	38.1	29.6	5.0	10.5
Ushers, lobby attendants, and ticket takers	42.7	7.9	24.0	16.4
Miscellaneous entertainment attendants and related workers	42.8	3.1	12.8	14.4
Barbers	17.9	1.2	37.2	12.1
Hairdressers, hairstylists, and cosmetologists	91.9	4.7	10.6	12.7
Miscellaneous personal appearance workers	86.6	51.4	7.5	10.9
Baggage porters, bellhops, and concierges	17.9	6.9	29.8	25.8
Transportation attendants	71.6	4.9	12.2	16.6
Child care workers	94.7	3.4	16.0	19.1
Personal and home care aides	86.1	6.4	23.8	17.6
Recreation and fitness workers	67.2	1.8	11.3	6.9
Residential advisors	64.1	2.0	25.4	5.1
Personal care and service workers, all other	48.9	3.6	5.9	9.5
Sales and office occupations	**62.9**	**4.2**	**11.3**	**12.6**
Sales and related occupations	49.9	5.0	9.8	11.8
First-line supervisors/managers of retail sales workers	43.9	5.4	7.9	10.3
First-line supervisors/managers of nonretail sales workers	28.0	5.6	5.9	9.6
Cashiers	73.7	6.8	16.1	16.3
Counter and rental clerks	49.0	6.9	7.9	12.7
Parts salespersons	12.5	0.5	3.7	12.9
Retail salespersons	51.9	4.1	11.3	13.7
Advertising sales agents	47.6	2.7	6.3	4.9
Insurance sales agents	49.4	3.2	6.6	10.1
Securities, commodities, and financial services sales agents	30.8	8.0	6.4	4.8
Travel agents	84.0	6.5	9.9	8.7

	women	Asians	blacks	Hispanics
Sales representatives, services, all other	34.4%	4.9%	9.6%	9.9%
Sales representatives, wholesale and manufacturing	25.0	3.3	4.0	9.3
Models, demonstrators, and product promoters	87.7	2.7	8.0	9.5
Real estate brokers and sales agents	54.0	3.8	5.3	7.1
Telemarketers	68.3	1.2	25.0	11.9
Door-to-door sales workers, news and street vendors, related workers	64.3	3.6	12.9	15.7
Sales and related workers, all other	59.4	4.1	7.0	8.1
Office and administrative support occupations	73.9	3.6	12.5	13.4
First-line supervisors/managers of office and administrative support workers	68.7	3.8	9.7	11.1
Bill and account collectors	65.4	2.9	17.5	18.9
Billing and posting clerks and machine operators	92.2	4.1	13.7	14.0
Bookkeeping, accounting, and auditing clerks	90.9	3.4	6.5	8.8
Payroll and timekeeping clerks	90.8	1.9	10.4	10.7
Tellers	88.0	5.2	11.3	14.0
Court, municipal, and license clerks	75.9	3.1	17.9	12.1
Customer service representatives	66.6	3.9	17.5	15.2
Eligibility interviewers, government programs	83.8	6.2	20.2	23.0
File clerks	82.0	3.9	16.0	14.3
Hotel, motel, and resort desk clerks	69.1	4.4	15.3	11.6
Interviewers, except eligibility and loan	76.0	5.8	17.3	12.0
Library assistants, clerical	77.1	3.2	5.9	12.3
Loan interviewers and clerks	78.3	4.7	11.5	11.0
Order clerks	68.0	6.4	8.0	16.2
Receptionists and information clerks	92.7	3.3	9.8	16.8
Reservation and transportation ticket agents and travel clerks	58.2	3.9	24.0	14.9
Information and record clerks, all other	86.8	2.8	16.7	10.0
Couriers and messengers	15.4	2.4	16.4	15.6
Dispatchers	60.9	1.6	13.5	14.4
Postal service clerks	45.3	8.3	29.5	11.1
Postal service mail carriers	37.7	6.6	11.7	11.1
Postal service mail sorters, processors, processing machine operators	48.8	16.2	30.5	7.5
Production, planning, and expediting clerks	54.9	3.4	9.5	7.2
Shipping, receiving, and traffic clerks	27.5	3.6	12.5	21.9
Stock clerks and order fillers	36.0	3.4	16.7	19.3
Weighers, measurers, checkers, and samplers, recordkeeping	38.3	3.1	10.8	22.3
Secretaries and administrative assistants	96.1	1.9	8.6	9.4
Computer operators	48.5	9.1	10.8	11.8
Data entry keyers	80.5	4.2	13.2	11.4
Word processors and typists	92.5	2.5	12.3	13.9
Insurance claims and policy processing clerks	82.6	2.3	16.5	11.5
Mail clerks and mail machine operators, except postal service	51.3	3.5	21.4	18.1
Office clerks, general	84.2	5.2	13.0	15.6
Office and administrative support workers, all other	79.0	3.2	12.7	12.6
Natural resources, construction, and maintenance occupations	**4.6**	**2.0**	**6.7**	**25.0**
Farming, fishing, and forestry occupations	23.5	1.9	5.2	41.8
Graders and sorters, agricultural products	67.8	7.3	9.2	50.3
Miscellaneous agricultural workers	18.8	1.3	3.9	47.9
Logging workers	1.1	0.7	13.6	6.2
Construction and extraction occupations	2.6	1.4	6.1	29.1
First-line supervisors/managers of construction trades, extraction workers	3.9	1.0	4.9	16.5
Brickmasons, blockmasons, and stonemasons	0.1	0.8	6.7	35.5
Carpenters	1.4	1.4	4.0	25.7
Carpet, floor, and tile installers and finishers	0.5	3.3	3.8	39.5

	women	Asians	blacks	Hispanics
Cement masons, concrete finishers, and terrazzo workers	0.3%	–	12.0%	51.5%
Construction laborers	2.7	2.2%	9.0	43.1
Operating engineers and other construction equipment operators	1.5	1.1	4.7	13.7
Drywall installers, ceiling tile installers, and tapers	2.5	0.3	2.5	58.6
Electricians	1.5	1.6	7.0	14.0
Painters, construction and maintenance	7.2	1.3	4.8	41.0
Pipelayers, plumbers, pipefitters, and steamfitters	1.5	1.3	7.2	20.8
Roofers	1.0	1.3	4.0	46.4
Sheet metal workers	4.0	0.4	5.8	18.8
Structural iron and steel workers	0.6	–	0.6	11.5
Helpers, construction trades	3.3	0.2	4.5	41.6
Construction and building inspectors	8.7	2.3	8.3	9.0
Highway maintenance workers	2.5	2.6	14.2	11.0
Mining machine operators	3.0	–	2.4	20.8
Other extraction workers	1.4	–	10.0	24.6
Installation, maintenance, and repair occupations	3.9	2.9	7.8	15.7
First-line supervisors/managers of mechanics, installers, repairers	6.3	1.9	7.5	9.9
Computer, automated teller, and office machine repairers	11.0	8.0	10.0	10.1
Radio and telecommunications equipment installers and repairers	9.1	6.2	9.3	10.4
Electronic home entertainment equipment installers and repairers	6.0	6.0	12.1	11.3
Security and fire alarm systems installers	4.4	1.9	6.0	16.7
Aircraft mechanics and service technicians	2.3	7.1	7.1	15.3
Automotive body and related repairers	1.2	0.8	6.3	22.6
Automotive service technicians and mechanics	1.6	3.5	6.8	20.3
Bus and truck mechanics and diesel engine specialists	0.7	1.6	7.6	13.2
Heavy vehicle and mobile equipment service technicians and mechanics	1.2	1.1	4.6	14.1
Small-engine mechanics	2.0	2.7	6.4	14.0
Miscellaneous vehicle and mobile equipment mechanics, installers, and repairers	0.8	0.7	7.3	25.7
Heating, air conditioning, and refrigeration mechanics and installers	0.6	2.2	8.0	17.2
Home appliance repairers	8.1	6.1	7.7	17.5
Industrial and refractory machinery mechanics	3.5	2.2	8.1	14.4
Maintenance and repair workers, general	3.8	2.7	11.1	18.0
Electrical power-line installers and repairers	0.4	0.7	8.2	10.3
Telecommunications line installers and repairers	7.5	1.6	9.4	17.5
Precision instrument and equipment repairers	13.8	0.5	10.8	12.4
Other installation, maintenance, and repair workers	6.3	1.4	5.4	18.5
Production, transportation, and material-moving occupations	**21.2**	**4.2**	**13.9**	**21.0**
Production occupations	27.6	5.5	11.4	21.9
First-line supervisors/managers of production and operating workers	18.1	5.5	7.3	15.7
Electrical, electronics, and electromechanical assemblers	54.9	22.6	15.1	17.1
Miscellaneous assemblers and fabricators	36.5	6.1	15.3	20.5
Bakers	57.0	5.8	9.8	30.6
Butchers and other meat, poultry, and fish processing workers	21.2	10.4	14.0	36.2
Food batchmakers	55.5	2.6	9.7	27.6
Computer control programmers and operators	3.9	2.1	6.9	18.3
Cutting, punching, and press machine setters, operators, and tenders, metal and plastic	21.1	2.6	11.1	15.2
Grinding, lapping, polishing, and buffing machine tool setters, operators, and tenders, metal and plastic	9.0	1.5	11.3	16.7
Machinists	3.9	5.5	4.3	15.1
Molders and molding machine setters, operators, and tenders, metal and plastic	17.6	1.9	10.7	19.0
Tool and die makers	0.9	1.0	1.8	7.4

	women	Asians	blacks	Hispanics
Welding, soldering, and brazing workers	5.4%	3.6%	7.0%	22.7%
Metalworkers and plastic workers, all other	18.1	7.2	11.2	24.2
Job printers	17.3	4.4	13.5	11.7
Printing machine operators	21.5	1.8	13.7	19.6
Laundry and dry-cleaning workers	55.8	9.3	15.9	30.1
Pressers, textile, garment, and related materials	66.4	9.2	19.3	36.6
Sewing machine operators	78.5	10.8	13.3	40.2
Tailors, dressmakers, and sewers	70.0	20.9	4.9	19.6
Cabinetmakers and bench carpenters	2.8	2.8	4.0	20.8
Stationary engineers and boiler operators	1.7	5.3	9.8	14.5
Water and liquid waste treatment plant and system operators	5.9	3.4	6.8	10.1
Chemical processing machine setters, operators, and tenders	17.7	2.7	17.6	17.0
Crushing, grinding, polishing, mixing, and blending workers	15.7	2.2	16.0	23.2
Cutting workers	23.2	3.0	10.1	27.6
Inspectors, testers, sorters, samplers, and weighers	34.3	5.3	11.1	16.9
Medical, dental, and ophthalmic laboratory technicians	49.0	7.8	5.5	12.5
Packaging and filling machine operators and tenders	47.6	4.1	16.4	42.3
Painting workers	7.9	0.5	9.3	26.4
Production workers, all other	28.8	4.2	14.9	22.8
Transportation and material-moving occupations	15.0	2.8	16.4	20.0
Supervisors, transportation and material-moving workers	23.4	3.0	18.3	15.1
Aircraft pilots and flight engineers	5.2	1.0	1.0	6.3
Bus drivers	47.0	2.2	25.1	12.3
Driver/sales workers and truck drivers	4.6	1.5	13.6	17.5
Taxi drivers and chauffeurs	14.4	13.0	26.6	15.7
Motor vehicle operators, all other	15.8	2.7	7.8	22.0
Locomotive engineers and operators	2.6	2.4	5.7	4.7
Railroad conductors and yardmasters	6.5	1.2	19.9	8.4
Parking lot attendants	6.3	12.8	25.7	18.0
Service station attendants	13.5	4.0	8.6	17.1
Crane and tower operators	–	0.4	6.9	12.2
Dredge, excavating, and loading machine operators	3.2	0.1	3.3	9.6
Industrial truck and tractor operators	6.2	1.2	22.0	32.0
Cleaners of vehicles and equipment	15.0	3.7	14.8	35.6
Laborers and freight, stock, and material movers, hand	17.4	3.0	16.9	21.3
Packers and packagers, hand	56.5	4.2	17.3	41.3
Refuse and recyclable material collectors	7.9	0.2	23.9	21.2
Material-moving workers, all other	8.7	2.7	13.2	17.8

Note: "–" means sample is too small to make a reliable estimate.
Source: Bureau of Labor Statistics, Current Population Survey, Internet site http://www.bls.gov/cps/tables.htm#empstat

Job Tenure Has Crept Up

But long-term employment has diminished sharply among middle-aged men.

The economic downturn has boosted job tenure as workers cling to their jobs. Between 2000 and 2010, the median job tenure of workers aged 25 or older increased from 4.7 to 5.2 years—an increase of half a year.

Median job tenure among men aged 25 or older climbed by 0.4 years, while women's job tenure climbed 0.7 years. But among men aged 45 to 54, job tenure fell by one full year as layoffs took their toll on the middle aged. Among women in the same age group, job tenure fell 0.2 years.

Job tenure has diminished among the middle aged because long-term employment has become less common. The proportion of men and women who have been with their current employer for 10 or more years fell in most age groups between 2000 and 2010. Among men aged 45 to 49, the percentage with long-term jobs fell by more than 5 percentage points. Among men aged 60 or older and women aged 65 or older, long-term employment increased as more postponed retirement.

■ Long-term employment will continue to erode until the economy recovers.

About one-third of workers have been with their current employer for 10 or more years

(percent of workers aged 25 or older who have worked for their current employer for 10 or more years, by sex, 2010)

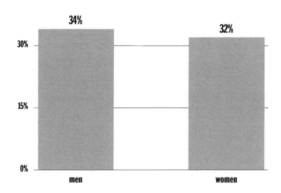

Table 6.21 Job Tenure by Sex and Age, 2000 and 2010

(median number of years workers aged 25 or older have been with their current employer by sex and age, and change in years, 2000 and 2010)

	2010	2000	change in years 2000–10
Total aged 25 or older	**5.2**	**4.7**	**0.5**
Aged 25 to 34	3.1	2.6	0.5
Aged 35 to 44	5.1	4.8	0.3
Aged 45 to 54	7.8	8.2	–0.4
Aged 55 to 64	10.0	10.0	0.0
Aged 65 or older	9.9	9.4	0.5
Men aged 25 or older	**5.3**	**4.9**	**0.4**
Aged 25 to 34	3.2	2.7	0.5
Aged 35 to 44	5.3	5.3	0.0
Aged 45 to 54	8.5	9.5	–1.0
Aged 55 to 64	10.4	10.2	0.2
Aged 65 or older	9.7	9.0	0.7
Women aged 25 or older	**5.1**	**4.4**	**0.7**
Aged 25 to 34	3.0	2.5	0.5
Aged 35 to 44	4.9	4.3	0.6
Aged 45 to 54	7.1	7.3	–0.2
Aged 55 to 64	9.7	9.9	–0.2
Aged 65 or older	10.1	9.7	0.4

Source: Bureau of Labor Statistics, Employee Tenure, Internet site http://www.bls.gov/news.release/tenure.toc.htm; calculations by New Strategist

Table 6.22 Long-Term Employment by Sex and Age, 2000 and 2010

(percent of employed wage and salary workers aged 25 or older who have been with their current employer for 10 or more years, by sex and age, 2000 and 2010; percentage point change in share, 2000–10)

	2010	2000	percentage point change 2000–10
Total aged 25 or older	**33.1%**	**31.5%**	**1.6**
Men aged 25 or older	**34.3**	**33.4**	**0.9**
Aged 25 to 29	3.1	3.0	0.1
Aged 30 to 34	14.3	15.1	−0.8
Aged 35 to 39	27.2	29.4	−2.2
Aged 40 to 44	37.5	40.2	−2.7
Aged 45 to 49	43.7	49.0	−5.3
Aged 50 to 54	51.3	51.6	−0.3
Aged 55 to 59	53.6	53.7	−0.1
Aged 60 to 64	56.8	52.4	4.4
Aged 65 or older	51.9	48.6	3.3
Women aged 25 or older	**31.9**	**29.5**	**2.4**
Aged 25 to 29	1.6	1.9	−0.3
Aged 30 to 34	11.1	12.5	−1.4
Aged 35 to 39	24.0	22.3	1.7
Aged 40 to 44	32.9	31.2	1.7
Aged 45 to 49	38.0	41.4	−3.4
Aged 50 to 54	46.5	45.8	0.7
Aged 55 to 59	51.2	52.5	−1.3
Aged 60 to 64	52.2	53.6	−1.4
Aged 65 or older	54.3	51.0	3.3

Source: Bureau of Labor Statistics, Employee Tenure, Internet site http://www.bls.gov/news.release/tenure.toc.htm; calculations by New Strategist

Self-Employment Rises with Age

Older workers are more than twice as likely as the average worker to be self-employed.

Among the 139 million employed wage and salary workers in 2010, only about 10 million were self-employed—or just 7 percent of workers. The figure undoubtedly underestimates the number of people who work for themselves because it excludes those who have a business on the side if it is not their primary source of income. It also excludes sole proprietorships that are incorporated.

Self-employment rises with age, peaking at 17 percent among workers aged 65 or older. Older workers are most likely to be self-employed because Medicare, which begins at age 65, frees them from the need to find a job with health insurance coverage.

■ Many more Americans would be self-employed if health insurance was more affordable.

Older workers are most likely to choose self-employment

(percent of workers who are self-employed, by age, 2010)

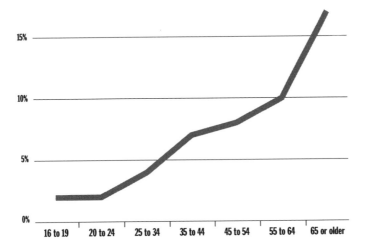

Table 6.23 Self-Employed Workers by Age, 2010

(number of employed workers aged 16 or older, number and percent who are self-employed, and percent distribution of self-employed by age, 2010; numbers in thousands)

	total employed	self-employed		
		number	percent of total	percent distribution
Total aged 16 or older	139,064	9,681	7.0%	100.0%
Aged 16 to 19	4,379	74	1.7	0.8
Aged 20 to 24	12,699	266	2.1	2.7
Aged 25 to 34	30,228	1,339	4.4	13.8
Aged 35 to 44	30,663	2,081	6.8	21.5
Aged 45 to 54	33,191	2,667	8.0	27.5
Aged 55 to 64	21,636	2,167	10.0	22.4
Aged 65 or older	6,268	1,088	17.4	11.2

Source: Bureau of Labor Statistics, Current Population Survey, Internet site http://www.bls.gov/cps/tables.htm#empstat; calculations by New Strategist

Few Workers Are Represented by Unions

The differences are greatest by occupation.

Union representation has fallen sharply over the past few decades. In 1970, 30 percent of nonagricultural workers were represented by labor unions. In 2010, the figure was just 13 percent.

Unions represent 14 percent of male workers and 12 percent of female workers. Men are more likely than women to be represented by unions because they are more likely to work in jobs that are traditional union strongholds. In fact, the decline of labor unions is partly the result of the shift in jobs from manufacturing to services.

Union representation is higher for blacks than for Asians, Hispanics, or whites. Full-time workers are more likely to be represented than part-time workers. The biggest differences are by occupation. Forty-one percent of workers in education, training, and library occupations are represented by unions, as are 37 percent of protective service workers. In contrast, unions represent only 4 percent of food preparation workers and farm workers.

■ Union representation has declined in part because the global economy makes it increasingly risky for American workers to make demands on their employers.

Union representation is much greater in some occupations

(percent of employed wage and salary workers aged 16 or older who are represented by unions, by occupation, 2010)

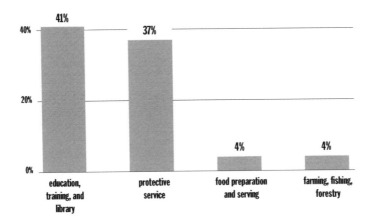

Table 6.24 Workers Represented by Unions by Sex, Race, and Hispanic Origin, 2010

(number of employed wage and salary workers aged 16 or older, and number and percent who are represented by unions, by sex, race, and Hispanic origin, 2010; numbers in thousands)

	total	represented by unions	
		number	percent
Total employed	**124,073**	**16,290**	**13.1%**
Men	63,531	8,761	13.8
Women	60,542	7,528	12.4
Asians	5,900	713	12.1
Blacks	14,195	2,115	14.9
Hispanics	18,263	2,021	11.1
Whites	101,042	13,111	13.0
Full-time workers	99,531	14,498	14.6
Part-time workers	24,351	1,760	7.2

Source: Bureau of Labor Statistics, Current Population Survey, Internet site http://www.bls.gov/cps/tables.htm#empstat

Table 6.25 Workers Represented by Unions by Occupation, 2010

(number of employed wage and salary workers aged 16 or older, and number and percent represented by unions, by occupation, 2010; numbers in thousands)

	total	represented by unions	
		number	percent
TOTAL EMPLOYED	**124,073**	**16,290**	**13.1%**
Management, professional and related occupations	**44,871**	**6,674**	**14.9**
Management, business, and financial operations	16,684	973	5.8
Management	11,386	599	5.3
Business and financial operations	5,299	373	7.0
Professional and related occupations	28,187	5,701	20.2
Computer and mathematical	3,350	180	5.4
Architecture and engineering	2,468	244	9.9
Life, physical, and social science	1,256	145	11.5
Community and social services	2,260	390	17.3
Legal	1,352	87	6.4
Education, training, and library	8,415	3,441	40.9
Art, design, entertainment, sports, and media	1,899	139	7.3
Health care practitioner and technical occupations	7,188	1,076	15.0
Service occupations	**22,463**	**2,683**	**11.9**
Health care support	3,214	296	9.2
Protective service	3,287	1,202	36.6
Food preparation and serving related	7,555	328	4.3
Building and grounds cleaning and maintenance	4,549	518	11.4
Personal care and service	3,858	338	8.8
Sales and office occupations	**30,673**	**2,388**	**7.8**
Sales and related	13,033	496	3.8
Office and administrative support	17,641	1,892	10.7
Natural resources, construction, maintenance occupations	**10,879**	**1,912**	**17.6**
Farming, fishing, and forestry	869	36	4.1
Construction and extraction	5,579	1,100	19.7
Installation, maintenance, and repair	4,431	776	17.5
Production, transportation, material-moving occupations	**15,186**	**2,633**	**17.3**
Production	7,540	1,210	16.0
Transportation and material moving	7,647	1,423	18.6

Source: Bureau of Labor Statistics, Current Population Survey, Internet site http://www.bls.gov/cps/tables.htm#empstat; calculations by New Strategist

More than Four Million Earn Minimum Wage or Less

Many who earn minimum wage are food service workers.

Among the nation's 73 million workers who are paid hourly rates, just over 4 million (6.0 percent) earn the minimum wage or less, according to the Bureau of Labor Statistics. Of minimum-wage workers, nearly half are under age 25.

Women are more likely than men to earn minimum wage or less, and they account for 63 percent of the nation's minimum-wage workers. Part-time workers also dominate the minimum-wage labor force, accounting for the 62 percent majority. By occupation, 39 percent of minimum-wage workers are in food service occupations. Twenty-six percent of those with food-service jobs are paid minimum wage or less.

■ As the minimum wage increased over the past few years, the percentage of workers earning minimum wage also rose.

Young adults account for nearly half of minimum wage workers

(percent distribution of workers who make minimum wage or less, by age, 2010)

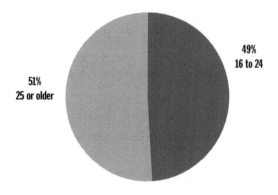

49%
16 to 24

51%
25 or older

Table 6.26 Workers Earning Minimum Wage by Selected Characteristics, 2010

(number and percent distribution of employed wage and salary workers paid hourly rates at or below minimum wage, by selected characteristics, 2010; numbers in thousands)

	total paid hourly rates	paid at or below minimum wage		
		number	percent of total	percent distribution
Total aged 16 or older	**72,902**	**4,360**	**6.0%**	**100.0%**
Aged 16 to 24	14,061	2,135	15.2	49.0
Aged 25 or older	58,842	2,225	3.8	51.0
Sex				
Men	35,498	1,612	4.5	37.0
Women	37,404	2,748	7.3	63.0
Race and Hispanic origin				
Asian	2,920	140	4.8	3.2
Black	9,436	650	6.9	14.9
Hispanic	12,977	822	6.3	18.9
White	58,529	3,429	5.9	78.6
Work status				
Full-time workers	52,803	1,634	3.1	37.5
Part-time workers	19,994	2,716	13.6	62.3
Occupation				
Management, business, financial occupations	4,013	52	1.3	1.2
Professional and related occupations	11,195	171	1.5	3.9
Service occupations	17,732	2,511	14.2	57.6
Health care support	2,727	135	5.0	3.1
Protective service	2,093	76	3.6	1.7
Food preparation and serving related	6,604	1,695	25.7	38.9
Building and grounds cleaning and maintenance	3,606	281	7.8	6.4
Personal care and service	2,703	325	12.0	7.5
Sales and related occupations	7,670	733	9.6	16.8
Office and administrative support occupations	12,103	326	2.7	7.5
Farming, fishing, and forestry occupations	621	34	5.4	0.8
Construction and extraction occupations	4,355	39	0.9	0.9
Installation, maintenance, and repair occupations	3,224	31	1.0	0.7
Production occupations	6,356	171	2.7	3.9
Transportation and material-moving occupations	5,633	292	5.2	6.7

Source: Bureau of Labor Statistics, Characteristics of Minimum Wage Workers, 2010, Internet site http://www.bls.gov/cps/minwage2010tbls.htm; calculations by New Strategist

Millions Work at Home

College graduates are most likely to report working at home.

The Bureau of Labor Statistics' American Time Use Survey reveals just how many Americans work at home. Among the 101 million people who worked on the survey's diary day, 24 percent reported working at least part of their day at home. Those working at home logged an average of 2.98 work hours at home.

Interestingly, there is not much variation in the percentage of workers who work at home by full- or part-time status or by sex. Twenty-three percent of full-time workers say they worked at home on diary day, as did 24 percent of part-time workers. Twenty-three to 24 percent of men and women reported working at home. There are substantial differences by education, however. Fully 40 percent of college graduates worked at home on diary day versus only 13 percent of those who went no further than high school. Not surprisingly, the self-employed are far more likely to work at home (60 percent) than wage and salary workers (20 percent).

■ The percentage of people who work at home may rise as employers attempt to cut overhead by eliminating office space.

More than 40 percent of college graduates work at home on the average day

(percent of workers aged 25 or older who reported working at home on diary day, by educational attainment, 2009)

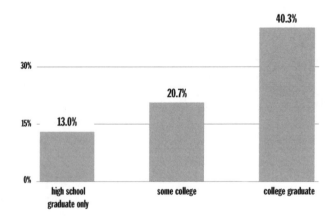

Table 6.27 People Who Work at Home, 2009

(total number of employed workers aged 15 or older, number and percent who worked on diary day and average hours of work, number and percent who worked at home on diary day and average number of hours worked at home, by selected characteristics, 2009)

		total who worked on average day			total who worked at home on average day		
	total employed	number	percent of employed	hours of work	number	percent of those who worked	hours of work
Total workers	**148,720**	**101,379**	**68.2%**	**7.48**	**23,925**	**23.6%**	**2.98**
Full-time	114,618	82,511	72.0	7.97	19,353	23.5	3.13
Part-time	34,102	18,868	55.3	5.34	4,572	24.2	2.35
Sex of worker							
Men	78,264	55,676	71.1	7.90	13,033	23.4	3.12
Women	70,456	45,703	64.9	6.97	10,892	23.8	2.81
Educational attainment, aged 25+							
Not a high school graduate	9,087	5,968	65.7	7.75	609	10.2	–
High school graduate only	36,852	24,251	65.8	8.03	3,154	13.0	4.97
Some college or associate's degree	33,136	23,045	69.5	7.76	4,759	20.7	3.02
Bachelor's degree or more	47,722	34,855	73.0	7.20	14,049	40.3	2.64
Class of worker							
Wage and salary	137,890	92,192	66.9	7.48	18,022	19.5	2.62
Self-employed	10,753	7,198	66.9	6.46	4,324	60.1	4.66

Note: Time spent working excludes travel time related to work. Working at home includes any time the respondent reported doing activities that were identified as part of one's job, and is not restricted to persons whose usual workplace is their home. "–" means sample too small to make a reliable estimate.
Source: Bureau of Labor Statistics, American Time Use Survey, Internet site http://www.bls.gov/news.release/atus.toc.htm; calculations by New Strategist

Most Workers Drive to Work Alone

Public transportation is most popular in the Northeast.

Despite the efforts of many to encourage carpooling and the use of public transportation during the commute to work, the great majority of workers drive to work alone. In 2009, fully 76 percent of workers aged 16 or older drove alone. Only 10 percent carpooled, while just 5 percent used mass transit. Three percent of workers walked to work, and 4 percent worked at home.

Workers in the Northeast are least likely to drive to work alone, with 68 percent doing so. Fourteen percent of workers in the Northeast take public transportation to work. In the Midwest and South, 80 percent of workers drive to work alone. Only 2 percent of workers in the South use public transportation for their commute, largely because public transportation is unavailable in many areas of the South.

■ Although higher gasoline prices might encourage more workers to use mass transit, cars will continue to dominate the commute to work because many Americans do not have access to public transportation.

Driving to work alone is most common in the Midwest and South

(percent of workers who drive alone to work, by region, 2009)

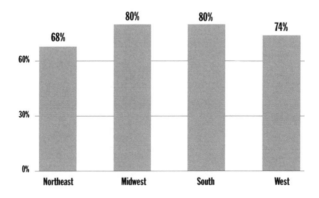

Table 6.28 Journey to Work by Region, 2009

(number and percent distribution of workers aged 16 or older by principal means of transportation to work, by region, 2009; numbers in thousands)

	total	Northeast	Midwest	South	West
Total workers	**138,592**	**25,827**	**30,894**	**50,004**	**31,867**
Drove car, truck, or van alone	105,476	17,517	24,635	39,839	23,485
Carpooled in car, truck, or van	13,917	2,136	2,828	5,326	3,627
Public transportation (including taxis)	6,922	3,517	914	1,128	1,364
Walked	3,966	1,220	855	944	947
Other means	2,393	404	416	807	765
Worked at home	5,918	1,034	1,245	1,960	1,679
Average travel time to work (minutes)	25.1	28.2	23.1	25.0	24.9

PERCENT DISTRIBUTION

	total	Northeast	Midwest	South	West
Total workers	**100.0%**	**100.0%**	**100.0%**	**100.0%**	**100.0%**
Drove car, truck, or van alone	76.1	67.8	79.7	79.7	73.7
Carpooled in car, truck, or van	10.0	8.3	9.2	10.7	11.4
Public transportation (including taxis)	5.0	13.6	3.0	2.3	4.3
Walked	2.9	4.7	2.8	1.9	3.0
Other means	1.7	1.6	1.3	1.6	2.4
Worked at home	4.3	4.0	4.0	3.9	5.3

Source: Bureau of the Census, 2009 American Community Survey, Internet site http://factfinder.census.gov/servlet/ DatasetMainPageServlet?_program=ACS&_submenuId=&_lang=en&_ts=; calculations by New Strategist

Many Workers Lack Benefits

Service workers are less likely than managers or professionals to have access to most employee benefits.

Some workers are far more likely than others to have access to important health insurance and retirement benefits. Among management and professional workers, fully 88 percent have access to medical care benefits at work compared with only 50 percent of service workers, according to the Bureau of Labor Statistics' Employee Benefits Survey. Among workers with access to medical benefits, most must contribute towards coverage. The average contribution for employees with family coverage is $377 per month.

The 69 percent majority of workers had access to a retirement plan at work in 2010, but the proportion is 83 percent among management and professional workers and just 49 percent among service workers. Less than one-third of workers have access to a defined benefit retirement plan—which guarantees a certain level of income in retirement.

The percentage of workers with access to a broad array of other benefits is much greater among management and professional workers than among service workers. Only 28 percent of service workers can take paid personal leave, for example, compared with 58 percent of management and professional workers.

■ The lack of access to health insurance at work is one of the barriers to universal health insurance coverage.

Most management and professional workers have access to health insurance coverage through their employer

(percent of civilian workers with access to health insurance coverage through their employer, by occupation, 2010

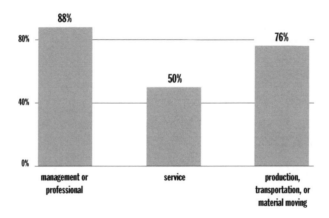

Table 6.29 Employee Benefits by Occupation, 2010

(employed civilian workers with access to selected employee benefits, by selected occupation, 2010; in percent unless otherwise noted)

	total workers	management or profesional	service	production, transportion, and material-moving
Access to retirement benefits	69%	83%	49%	67%
Defined benefit	31	43	18	28
Defined contribution	54	61	36	54
Access to medical care benefits	73	88	50	76
Access to dental care benefits	47	59	31	49
Access to vision care benefits	28	36	19	30
Access to prescription drug coverage	72	86	49	75
Employee required to contribute for single-coverage medical plan	77	76	77	76
Average flat monthly employee contribution for participants	$96.56	$94.74	$94.99	$94.62
Employee required to contribute for family coverage medical plan	88%	90%	90%	84%
Average flat monthly employee contribution for participants	$376.96	$375.65	$393.83	$336.76
Access to paid holidays	76%	79%	58%	84%
Access to paid sick leave	67	87	48	55
Access to paid vacation days	74	74	61	82
Access to paid personal leave	41	58	28	33
Access to paid jury duty leave	72	87	56	70
Access to paid family leave	11	17	8	6
Access to unpaid family leave	86	91	81	85
Access to life insurance	62	79	40	65
Access to short-term disability benefits	37	42	23	46
Access to long-term disability benefits	33	52	15	28
Access to long-term care insurance	17	20	9	11
Retiree health care benefits, under age 65	26	41	15	19
Retiree health care benefits, aged 65 or older	23	37	13	15
Access to health savings account	15	20	8	11
Access to pretax benefits				
Flexible benefits	21	32	12	16
Dependent care reimbursement account	37	56	23	27
Health care reimbursement account	39	59	25	28
Employer provides assistance for child care	10	17	9	5
Employer provides a flexible work schedule	5	10	1	1
Access to subsidized commuting	6	11	3	3
Access to wellness programs	34	49	22	27
Access to employee assistance programs	50	66	35	42
Access to any nonproduction bonus	42	45	31	44

Source: Bureau of Labor Statistics, Employee Benefits Survey, Internet site http://www.bls.gov/ncs/ebs/benefits/2010/ownership_civilian.htm

The Number of Older Workers Will Expand Rapidly

Early retirement will become less common.

As the baby-boom generation enters its late sixties during the next decade, the number of workers aged 65 or older will surge. While the labor force as a whole is projected to increase 8 percent between 2008 and 2018, the number of working men aged 65 or older will grow by 78 percent. The number of working women in the age group will expand by an even larger 84 percent. In contrast, the number of workers aged 35 to 54 will decline.

The Bureau of Labor Statistics projects an increase in the labor force participation rate of men aged 65 or older, the rate rising by 5 percentage points to 26.7 percent. The bureau foresees declines in labor force participation among men under age 55.

Women's labor force participation should also climb in the older age groups between 2008 and 2018. Among women aged 65 or older, labor force participation is projected to rise by nearly 6 percentage points.

■ If unemployed older boomers give up looking for a job and retire sooner than they had planned, then labor force participation rates among Americans aged 65 or older may rise less than projected.

Rapid growth is projected for workers aged 65 or older

(percent change in number of total workers and workers aged 65 or older, by sex, 2008–18)

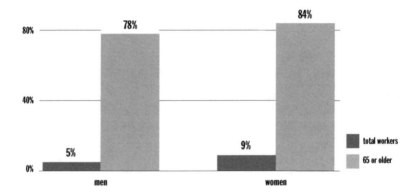

Table 6.30 Labor Force Projections by Sex and Age, 2008 and 2018

(number and percent of people aged 16 or older in the civilian labor force by sex and age, 2008 and 2018; percent change in number and percentage point change in rate 2008–18; numbers in thousands)

	number			participation rate		
	2008	2018	percent change 2008–18	2008	2018	percentage point change 2008–18
Total labor force	**154,287**	**166,911**	**8.2%**	**66.0%**	**64.5%**	**−1.5**
Aged 16 to 19	6,858	5,868	−14.4	40.2	33.8	−6.4
Aged 20 to 24	15,174	15,263	0.6	74.4	71.3	−3.1
Aged 25 to 34	33,332	36,814	10.4	83.3	82.4	−0.9
Aged 35 to 44	35,061	34,787	−0.8	84.1	83.2	−0.9
Aged 45 to 54	36,003	34,343	−4.6	81.9	81.7	−0.2
Aged 55 to 64	21,615	28,754	33.0	64.5	68.1	3.6
Aged 65 or older	6,243	11,082	77.5	16.8	22.4	5.6
Aged 65 to 74	4,985	9,045	81.4	25.1	30.5	5.4
Aged 75 or older	1,258	2,037	61.9	7.3	10.3	3.0
Men in labor force	**82,520**	**86,682**	**5.0**	**73.0**	**70.6**	**−2.4**
Aged 16 to 19	3,472	2,923	−15.8	40.1	33.2	−6.9
Aged 20 to 24	8,065	8,064	0.0	78.7	75.2	−3.5
Aged 25 to 34	18,302	20,173	10.2	91.5	90.6	−0.9
Aged 35 to 44	18,972	19,109	0.7	92.2	92.0	−0.2
Aged 45 to 54	18,928	18,027	−4.8	88.0	87.1	−0.9
Aged 55 to 64	11,345	14,479	27.6	70.4	71.2	0.8
Aged 65 or older	3,435	5,907	72.0	21.5	26.7	5.2
Aged 65 to 74	2,724	4,753	74.5	29.7	34.4	4.7
Aged 75 or older	711	1,154	62.3	10.4	13.9	3.5
Women in labor force	**71,767**	**78,229**	**9.0**	**59.5**	**58.7**	**−0.8**
Aged 16 to 19	3,385	2,946	−13.0	40.2	34.4	−5.8
Aged 20 to 24	7,109	7,198	1.3	70.0	67.3	−2.7
Aged 25 to 34	15,030	16,641	10.7	75.2	74.2	−1.0
Aged 35 to 44	16,089	15,678	−2.6	76.1	74.6	−1.5
Aged 45 to 54	17,075	16,316	−4.4	76.1	76.6	0.5
Aged 55 to 64	10,270	14,275	39.0	59.1	65.3	6.2
Aged 65 or older	2,808	5,174	84.3	13.3	18.9	5.6
Aged 65 to 74	2,261	4,291	89.8	21.1	27.1	6.0
Aged 75 or older	547	883	61.4	5.2	7.7	2.5

Source: Bureau of Labor Statistics, Labor Force Projections to 2018: Older Workers Staying More Active, Monthly Labor Review, November 2009, Internet site http://www.bls.gov/opub/mlr/2009/11/home.htm; calculations by New Strategist

Number of Asian and Hispanic Workers Will Grow the Fastest

Non-Hispanic whites will decline as a share of workers.

Between 2008 and 2018, the labor force will grow by 8 percent—to 167 million, according to projections by the Bureau of Labor Statistics. The number of minority workers will grow much faster than the number of non-Hispanic whites. The pool of Asian and Hispanic workers will expand by 30 and 33 percent, respectively, during those years. The black labor force will grow by 14 percent. The non-Hispanic white labor force is projected to increase by less than 2 percent.

The non-Hispanic white share of the labor force will fall from 68 to 64 percent between 2008 and 2018. In contrast, the Hispanic share will climb from 14 to 18 percent during those years, and the Asian share will increase from 5 to 6 percent.

■ The ability to manage a diverse workforce will become increasingly important as the minority share of American workers grows.

The labor force is becoming increasingly diverse

(percent distribution of the labor force by race and Hispanic origin, 2008 and 2018)

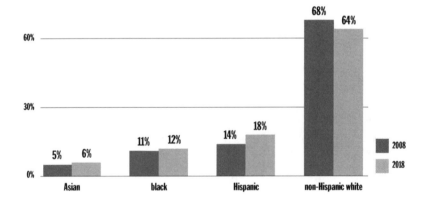

Table 6.31 Labor Force Projections by Race and Hispanic Origin, 2008 and 2018

(number and percent of people aged 16 or older in the civilian labor force by sex, race, and Hispanic origin, 2008 and 2018; percent change in number and percentage point change in rate 2008–18; numbers in thousands)

	number			participation rate		
	2008	2018	percent change 2008–18	2008	2018	percentage point change 2008–18
Total in labor force	**154,287**	**166,911**	**8.2%**	**66.0%**	**64.5%**	**–1.5**
Asian	7,202	9,345	29.8	67.0	65.0	–2.0
Black	17,740	20,244	14.1	63.7	63.3	–0.4
Hispanic	22,024	29,304	33.1	68.5	67.3	–1.2
Non-Hispanic white	105,210	106,834	1.5	65.9	64.7	–1.2
Men in labor force	**82,520**	**88,682**	**7.5**	**73.0**	**70.6**	**–2.4**
Asian	3,852	4,895	27.1	75.3	73.8	–1.5
Black	8,347	9,579	14.8	66.7	65.7	–1.0
Hispanic	13,255	17,051	28.6	80.2	78.2	–2.0
Non-Hispanic white	55,971	57,075	2.0	72.4	70.7	–1.7
Women in labor force	**71,767**	**78,229**	**9.0**	**59.5**	**58.7**	**–0.8**
Asian	3,350	4,450	32.8	59.4	57.4	–2.0
Black	9,393	10,665	13.5	61.3	61.2	–0.1
Hispanic	8,769	12,253	39.7	56.2	56.4	0.2
Non-Hispanic white	49,238	49,759	1.1	59.8	59.0	–0.8

Source: Bureau of Labor Statistics, Labor Force Projections to 2018: Older Workers Staying More Active, Monthly Labor Review, November 2009, Internet site http://www.bls.gov/opub/mlr/2009/11/home.htm; calculations by New Strategist

Table 6.32 Distribution of the Labor Force by Race and Hispanic Origin, 2008 and 2018

(number and percent distribution of people aged 16 or older in the civilian labor force by sex, race, and Hispanic origin, 2008 and 2018; numbers in thousands)

	2008 number	2008 percent distribution	2018 number	2018 percent distribution
Total in labor force	**154,287**	**100.0%**	**166,911**	**100.0%**
Asian	7,202	4.7	9,345	5.6
Black	17,740	11.5	20,244	12.1
Hispanic	22,024	14.3	29,304	17.6
Non-Hispanic white	105,210	68.2	106,834	64.0
Men in labor force	**82,520**	**100.0**	**88,682**	**100.0**
Asian	3,852	4.7	4,895	5.5
Black	8,347	10.1	9,579	10.8
Hispanic	13,255	16.1	17,051	19.2
Non-Hispanic white	55,971	67.8	57,075	64.4
Women in labor force	**71,767**	**100.0**	**78,229**	**100.0**
Asian	3,350	4.7	4,450	5.7
Black	9,393	13.1	10,665	13.6
Hispanic	8,769	12.2	12,253	15.7
Non-Hispanic white	49,238	68.6	49,759	63.6

Source: Bureau of Labor Statistics, Labor Force Projections to 2018: Older Workers Staying More Active, Monthly Labor Review, November 2009, Internet site http://www.bls.gov/opub/mlr/2009/11/home.htm; calculations by New Strategist

The Biggest Job Gains Are Forecast for Registered Nurses

Many health care positions are projected to be among the fastest-growing jobs.

Overall employment in the United States is projected to grow by 10 percent between 2008 and 2018 according to the Bureau of Labor Statistics. The bureau projects a hefty 17 percent growth in professional occupations between 2008 and 2018. This is much greater than the 5 percent increase forecast for management occupations and contrasts with the decline projected for production jobs. The bureau forecasts a 13 percent gain in construction jobs by 2018 as that sector recovers from the Great Recession.

Health care jobs appear repeatedly in the list of occupations projected to grow the most and the fastest between 2008 and 2018. This trend is likely to continue despite the ailing economy. Registered nurses top the list of the biggest gainers, followed by home health aides. Among the occupations projected to grow the fastest are skin care specialists and computer software engineers.

■ Many occupations involved in processing paper—such as file clerks, shipping clerks, and records clerks—are projected to be among the biggest losers.

Health care and computer jobs are projected to grow the fastest

(percent change in employment in the five occupations projected to grow the fastest, 2008 to 2018)

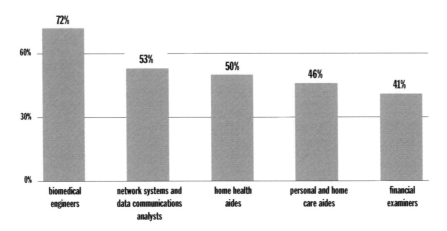

Table 6.33 Employment by Major Occupational Group, 2008 and 2018

(number and percent distribution of people aged 16 or older employed by major occupational group, 2008 and 2018; percent change, 2008–18; numbers in thousands)

	2008 number	2008 percent distribution	2018 number	2018 percent distribution	percent change 2008–18
Total employed	**150,932**	**100.0%**	**166,206**	**100.0%**	**10.1%**
Management occupations	8,912	5.9	9,367	5.6	5.1
Business and financial operations occupations	6,834	4.5	8,044	4.8	17.7
Professional and related occupations	31,054	20.6	36,280	21.8	16.8
Computer and mathematical	3,540	2.3	4,326	2.6	22.2
Architecture and engineering	2,636	1.7	2,907	1.7	10.3
Life, physical, and social science	1,461	1.0	1,738	1.0	19.0
Community and social services	2,724	1.8	3,172	1.9	16.5
Legal	1,251	0.8	1,439	0.9	15.1
Education, training, and library	9,210	6.1	10,534	6.3	14.4
Art, design, entertainment, sports, and media	2,741	1.8	3,073	1.8	12.1
Health care practitioner and technical occupations	7,491	5.0	9,091	5.5	21.4
Service occupations	29,576	19.6	33,645	20.2	13.8
Health care support	3,982	2.6	5,130	3.1	28.8
Protective service	3,270	2.2	3,670	2.2	12.2
Food preparation and serving related	11,552	7.7	12,560	7.6	8.7
Building and grounds cleaning and maintenance	5,727	3.8	6,211	3.7	8.5
Personal care and service	5,044	3.3	6,074	3.7	20.4
Sales and related occupations	15,903	10.5	16,883	10.2	6.2
Office and administrative support occupations	24,101	16.0	25,943	15.6	7.6
Farming, fishing, and forestry occupations	1,035	0.7	1,026	0.6	-0.9
Construction and extraction occupations	7,810	5.2	8,828	5.3	13.0
Installation, maintenance, and repair occupations	5,798	3.8	6,238	3.8	7.6
Production occupations	10,083	6.7	9,734	5.9	-3.5
Transportation and material-moving occupations	9,826	6.5	10,217	6.1	4.0

Source: Bureau of Labor Statistics, Economic and Employment Projections, Internet site http://www.bls.gov/news.release/ecopro.toc.htm; calculations by New Strategist

Table 6.34 Fastest-Growing Occupations, 2008 to 2018

(number of people aged 16 or older employed in the 30 fastest-growing occupations, 2008 to 2018; numerical and percent change, 2008–18; numbers in thousands)

	2008	2018	change, 2008–18 number	change, 2008–18 percent
Biomedical engineers	16	28	12	72.0%
Network systems and data communications analysts	292	448	156	53.4
Home health aides	922	1383	461	50.0
Personal and home care aides	817	1193	376	46.0
Financial examiners	27	38	11	41.2
Medical scientists, except epidemiologists	109	154	44	40.4
Physician assistants	75	104	29	39.0
Skin care specialists	39	54	15	37.9
Biochemists and biophysicists	23	32	9	37.4
Athletic trainers	16	22	6	37.0
Physical therapist aides	46	63	17	36.3
Dental hygienists	174	237	63	36.1
Veterinary technologists and technicians	80	108	29	35.8
Dental assistants	295	401	106	35.8
Computer software engineers, applications	515	690	175	34.0
Medical assistants	484	648	164	33.9
Physical therapist assistants	64	85	21	33.3
Veterinarians	60	79	20	33.0
Self-enrichment education teachers	254	335	81	32.1
Compliance officers, except agriculture, construction, health and safety, and transportation	260	341	81	31.1
Occupational therapist aides	8	10	2	30.7
Environmental engineers	54	71	17	30.6
Pharmacy technicians	326	426	100	30.6
Computer software engineers, systems software	395	515	120	30.4
Survey researchers	23	31	7	30.4
Physical therapists	186	242	56	30.3
Personal financial advisors	208	271	63	30.1
Environmental engineering technicians	21	28	6	30.1
Occupational therapist assistants	27	35	8	29.8
Fitness trainers and aerobics instructors	261	338	77	29.4

Note: Changes are based on unrounded figures.
Source: Bureau of Labor Statistics, Economic and Employment Projections, Internet site http://www.bls.gov/news.release/ecopro.toc.htm; calculations by New Strategist

Table 6.35 Occupations with the Largest Job Growth, 2008 to 2018

(number of people aged 16 or older employed in the 30 occupations with the largest projected job growth, 2008 to 2018; numerical and percent change, 2008–18; numbers in thousands)

	2008	2018	change, 2008–18 number	change, 2008–18 percent
Registered nurses	2,619	3,200	582	22.2%
Home health aides	922	1,383	461	50.0
Customer service representatives	2,252	2,652	400	17.7
Food preparation and serving workers, including fast food	2,702	3,096	394	14.6
Personal and home care aides	817	1,193	376	46.0
Retail salespersons	4,489	4,864	375	8.4
Office clerks, general	3,024	3,383	359	11.9
Accountants and auditors	1,291	1,570	279	21.7
Nursing aides, orderlies, and attendants	1,470	1,746	276	18.8
Postsecondary teachers	1,699	1,956	257	15.1
Construction laborers	1,249	1,505	256	20.5
Elementary school teachers, except special education	1,550	1,794	244	15.8
Truck drivers, heavy and tractor-trailer	1,798	2,031	233	13.0
Landscaping and groundskeeping workers	1,206	1,423	217	18.0
Bookkeeping, accounting, and auditing clerks	2,064	2,276	212	10.3
Executive secretaries and administrative assistants	1,594	1,799	204	12.8
Management analysts	747	925	178	23.9
Computer software engineers, applications	515	690	175	34.0
Receptionists and information clerks	1,139	1,312	173	15.2
Carpenters	1,285	1,450	165	12.9
Medical assistants	484	648	164	33.9
First-line supervisors of office and administrative support workers	1,457	1,618	160	11.0
Network systems and data communications analysts	292	448	156	53.4
Licensed practical nurses	754	909	156	20.7
Security guards	1,077	1,229	153	14.2
Waiters and waitresses	2,382	2,533	152	6.4
Maintenance and repair workers, general	1,361	1,509	148	10.9
Physicians and surgeons	661	806	144	21.8
Child care workers	1,302	1,444	142	10.9
Teacher assistants	1,313	1,448	135	10.3

Note: Changes are based on unrounded figures.
Source: Bureau of Labor Statistics, Economic and Employment Projections, Internet site http://www.bls.gov/news.release/ecopro.toc.htm; calculations by New Strategist

Table 6.36 Occupations with the Largest Job Decline, 2008 to 2018

(number of people aged 16 or older employed in the 30 occupations with the largest projected employment decline, 2008 to 2018; numerical and percent change, 2008–18; numbers in thousands)

	2008	2018	change, 2008–18	
			number	percent
Farmers and ranchers	986	907	–79	–8.0%
Sewing machine operators	212	141	–72	–33.7
Order clerks	246	182	–64	–26.1
Postal service mail sorters, processors, and processing machine operators	180	125	–55	–30.3
File clerks	212	163	–50	–23.4
Shipping, receiving, and traffic clerks	751	701	–49	–6.6
Telemarketers	342	304	–38	–11.1
First-line supervisors of production and operating workers	681	646	–36	–5.2
Office and administrative support workers, all other	307	271	–36	–11.6
Packers and packagers, hand	759	725	–34	–4.5
Cutting, punching, and press machine workers, metal and plastic	237	204	–33	–14.1
Electrical and electronic equipment assemblers	213	182	–31	–14.7
Machine feeders and offbearers	141	110	–31	–22.2
Door-to-door sales workers, news and street vendors, and related workers	182	155	–27	–14.8
Information and record clerks, all other	227	200	–27	–11.8
Paper goods machine setters, operators, and tenders	103	81	–22	–21.5
Computer operators	110	90	–21	–18.6
Machinists	422	402	–19	–4.6
Laborers and freight, stock, and material movers, hand	2,317	2,299	–19	–0.8
Miscellaneous agricultural workers	807	789	–18	–2.3
Data entry keyers	284	267	–17	–6.1
Inspectors, testers, sorters, samplers, and weighers	465	448	–17	–3.6
Switchboard operators, including answering service	155	138	–17	–10.9
Mail clerks and mail machine operators, except postal	141	125	–17	–11.8
Lathe and turning machine tool setters, operators, and tenders, metal and plastic	56	41	–15	–26.7
Grinding, lapping, polishing, and buffing machine tool setters, operators, and tenders, metal and plastic	93	78	–15	–15.9
Textile winding, twisting, and drawing out machine setters, operators, and tenders	35	21	–14	–40.7
Postal service clerks	76	62	–14	–18.0
Multiple machine tool setters, operators, and tenders, metal and plastic	86	73	–13	–14.7
Photographic processing machine operators	51	39	–13	–24.3

Note: Changes are based on unrounded figures.
Source: Bureau of Labor Statistics, Economic and Employment Projections, Internet site http://www.bls.gov/news.release/ecopro.toc.htm; calculations by New Strategist

Management, Scientific, and Technical Consulting Services Will Grow the Fastest

Among industries, offices of physicians ranks second in projected growth.

The number of jobs in the management, scientific, and technical consulting services industry will expand by 83 percent between 2008 and 2018, according to Bureau of Labor Statistics projections published in 2009. Offices of physicians ranks second, and computer systems design is third.

Overall, jobs in goods-producing industries are projected to increase by just 0.1 percent between 2008 and 2018. This miniscule growth includes a decline in manufacturing and mining employment and an increase in construction jobs. Employment in service-producing industries is projected to increase by 13 percent between 2008 and 2018. Among the service-providing industries, education, health care, and professional and business services are expected to grow the most.

■ The Bureau of Labor Statistics projects a 19 percent increase in construction industry employment as the economy recovers from the Great Recession.

Goods-producing industries will see little employment growth

(percent change in employment by industry group, 2008–18)

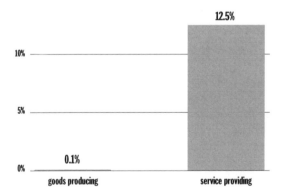

Table 6.37 Employment by Major Industry, 2008 and 2018

(number and percent distribution of people aged 16 or older employed by major industry, 2008 and 2018; percent change in number, 2008–18; numbers in thousands)

	2008		2018		
	number	percent distribution	number	percent distribution	percent change 2008–18
Total employed	**150,932**	**100.0%**	**166,206**	**100.0%**	**10.1%**
Nonagriculture wage and salary	137,815	91.3	152,443	91.7	10.6
Goods producing	21,363	14.2	21,390	12.9	0.1
Mining	717	0.5	613	0.4	−14.5
Construction	7,215	4.8	8,552	5.1	18.5
Manufacturing	13,431	8.9	12,225	7.4	−9.0
Service providing	116,452	77.2	131,053	78.8	12.5
Utilities	560	0.4	500	0.3	−10.7
Wholesale trade	5,964	4.0	6,220	3.7	4.3
Retail trade	15,356	10.2	16,010	9.6	4.3
Transportation and warehousing	4,505	3.0	4,950	3.0	9.9
Information	2,997	2.0	3,115	1.9	3.9
Financial activities	8,146	5.4	8,703	5.2	6.8
Professional and business services	17,778	11.8	21,968	13.2	23.6
Education	3,037	2.0	3,842	2.3	26.5
Health care and social assistance	15,819	10.5	19,816	11.9	25.3
Leisure and hospitality	13,459	8.9	14,601	8.8	8.5
Other services	6,333	4.2	7,142	4.3	12.8
Federal government	2,764	1.8	2,859	1.7	3.4
State and local government	19,735	13.1	21,327	12.8	8.1
Agriculture, forestry, fishing, and hunting	2,098	1.4	2,020	1.2	−3.7
Agriculture, wage and salary	1,210	0.8	1,206	0.7	−0.3
Agriculture, self-employed and unpaid family workers	889	0.6	814	0.5	−8.4
Nonagricultural self-employed and unpaid family workers	9,313	6.2	9,943	6.0	6.8
Secondary wage, salary jobs in agriculture, forestry, fishing, or private households	182	0.1	192	0.1	5.5
Secondary jobs as self-employed or unpaid family workers	1,524	1.0	1,607	1.0	5.4

Source: Bureau of Labor Statistics, Economic and Employment Projections, Internet site http://www.bls.gov/news.release/ecopro.toc.htm; calculations by New Strategist

Table 6.38 Industries with the Largest Wage and Salary Employment Growth, 2008 to 2018

(number of people aged 16 or older employed in industries with the largest wage and salary employment growth, 2008–2018; numerical and percent change in employment, 2008–18; ranked by numberical change; numbers in thousands)

	2008	2018	change, 2008–2018	
			number	percent
Management, scientific, technical consulting services	1,009	1,844	835	82.8%
Offices of physicians	2,266	3,038	772	34.1
Computer systems design and related services	1,450	2,107	656	45.3
Other general merchandise stores	1,490	2,097	607	40.7
Employment services	3,144	3,744	600	19.1
Local government, excluding education and hospitals	5,819	6,306	487	8.4
Home health care services	958	1,399	441	46.1
Service for the elderly and persons with disabilities	585	1,016	431	73.8
Nursing care facilities	1,614	2,007	394	24.4
Full-service restaurants	4,598	4,942	343	7.5

Note: Changes are based on unrounded figures.
Source: Bureau of Labor Statistics, Economic and Employment Projections, Internet site http://www.bls.gov/news.release/ ecopro.toc.htm; calculations by New Strategist

7

Living Arrangement Trends

■ **Married couples are slipping as a share of households.**

Married couples account for only 50 percent of households, and couples with children under age 18 are just 22 percent of the total.

■ **The number of households headed by older adults is growing rapidly.**

Between 2000 and 2010, the number of households headed by 55-to-64-year-olds grew by 50 percent. In contrast, the number of households headed by 35-to-44-year-olds fell 10 percent.

■ **The number of single-person households fell between 2008 and 2010.**

The Great Recession is taking its toll on single-person households as fewer people can afford to live alone.

■ **Only 59 percent of children live with their married, biological parents.**

The figure ranges from a low of 30 percent among black children to a high of 78 percent among Asian children.

■ **Most husbands and wives are close in age and education.**

Seven percent of couples are of mixed race or Hispanic origin.

■ **Men and women in their fifties are most likely to have experienced divorce.**

Divorce is more likely for those marrying young.

■ **More than half a million households are headed by same-sex couples.**

For the first time, demographers have estimated the number of same-sex couples.

Married Couples Account for Less than Half of Households

Their dominance is eroding as other household types grow faster.

Between 2000 and 2010, the number of married couples increased only 6 percent, less than the 12 percent gain for all households. Consequently, the married couple share of households slipped from 52.8 to 49.7 percent. The number of married couples with children under age 18 actually declined by 0.7 percent during those years. Married couples with children account for only 22 percent of the nation's households, well below the 27 percent share held by people who live alone.

Male-headed families are growing the fastest, up 39 percent in number between 2000 and 2010. The 5.6 million male-headed families account for a tiny 5 percent of the total, however. They are greatly outnumbered by the 14.8 million female-headed families.

The number of nonfamily households grew 18 percent between 2000 and 2010, with male-headed nonfamily households growing faster than their female counterparts. This pattern should reverse as the baby-boom generation enters the older age groups and an increasing number of women become widowed and live alone.

■ The Great Recession has slowed the growth in single-person households as fewer people can afford to live by themselves.

Married couples are the most common type of household

(percent distribution of households, by type, 2010)

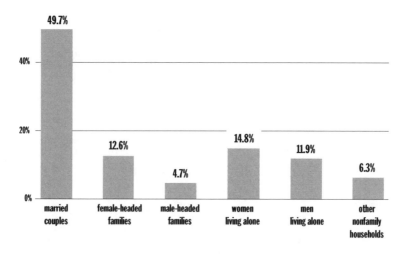

Table 7.1 Households by Type, 2000 and 2010

(number and percent distribution of households by household type, 2000 and 2010; percent change in number, 2000–10; numbers in thousands)

	2010		2000		percent change in number 2000–10
	number	percent distribution	number	percent distribution	
TOTAL HOUSEHOLDS	**117,538**	**100.0%**	**104,705**	**100.0%**	**12.3%**
Family households	**78,833**	**67.1**	**72,025**	**68.8**	**9.5**
Married couples	58,410	49.7	55,311	52.8	5.6
With children under age 18	26,171	22.3	26,359	25.2	–0.7
Female householders, no spouse present	14,843	12.6	12,687	12.1	17.0
With children under age 18	9,867	8.4	8,727	8.3	13.1
Male householders, no spouse present	5,580	4.7	4,028	3.8	38.5
With children under age 18	2,851	2.4	2,164	2.1	31.7
Nonfamily households	**38,705**	**32.9**	**32,680**	**31.2**	**18.4**
Female householders	20,442	17.4	18,039	17.2	13.3
Living alone	17,428	14.8	15,543	14.8	12.1
Male householders	18,263	15.5	14,641	14.0	24.7
Living alone	13,971	11.9	11,181	10.7	25.0

Source: Bureau of the Census, Current Population Survey Annual Social and Economic Supplement, Internet site http://www .census.gov/hhes/www/income/dinctabs.html; calculations by New Strategist

Number of Households Headed by 55-to-64-Year-Olds Is Growing Rapidly

The number of households headed by 35-to-44-year-olds fell between 2000 and 2010.

Between 2000 and 2010, the number of households headed by 55-to-64-year-olds grew 50 percent, more than four times as much as the 12 percent gain for all households during those years. Behind the rapid growth was the aging of the baby-boom generation.

The 35-to-44 age group was the only one to see its household numbers decline between 2000 and 2010. As the small generation X entered its late thirties and early forties, the number of householders aged 35 to 44 fell 10 percent. In contrast, the number of householders under age 25 rose by 6 percent as the large millennial generation entered its twenties.

■ The number of households headed by people aged 65 or older is now growing rapidly because boomers began to enter the age group in 2011.

The number of households headed by the oldest Americans is about to expand rapidly

(percent change in number of households, by age of householder, 2000–10)

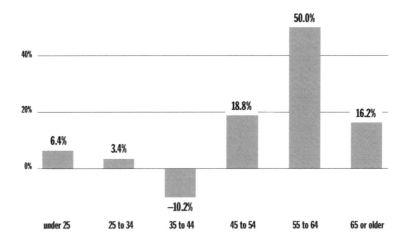

Table 7.2 Households by Age of Householder, 2000 and 2010

(number and percent distribution of households by age of householder, 2000 and 2010; percent change in number, 2000–10; numbers in thousands)

	2010		2000		percent change in number 2000–10
	number	percent distribution	number	percent distribution	
Total households	**117,538**	**100.0%**	**104,705**	**100.0%**	**12.3%**
Under age 25	6,233	5.3	5,860	5.6	6.4
Aged 25 to 34	19,257	16.4	18,627	17.8	3.4
Aged 35 to 44	21,519	18.3	23,955	22.9	–10.2
Aged 45 to 54	24,871	21.2	20,927	20.0	18.8
Aged 55 to 64	20,387	17.3	13,592	13.0	50.0
Aged 65 or older	25,270	21.5	21,745	20.8	16.2

Source: Bureau of the Census, Current Population Survey Annual Social and Economic Supplement, Internet site http://www .census.gov/hhes/www/income/dinctabs.html; calculations by New Strategist

Lifestyles Change with Age

The households of young adults are different from those of middle-aged and older Americans.

Married couples are far less common among the youngest and oldest householders than they are among the middle aged. Only 18 percent of households headed by people under age 25 are comprised of married couples. Among the elderly, married couples head a 43 percent minority of households. In contrast, couples account for the 56 to 58 percent majority of households headed by people aged 35 to 64.

Female-headed families are most commonly found among the youngest householders, at 23 percent. They account for just 8 percent of households headed by people aged 55 or older. Women who live alone are most common among the oldest householders, at 32 percent of households. They are least common among 35-to-44-year-olds, at 6 percent. Men who live alone account for 10 to 13 percent of households regardless of age.

■ With the baby-boom generation now in middle age, household composition has been stable. Change is coming, however, as boomers age.

Married couples head most households in the 35-to-64 age groups

(percent of households headed by married couples, by age of householder, 2010)

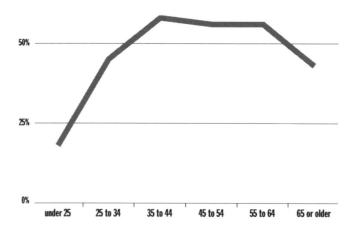

Table 7.3 Households by Household Type and Age of Householder, 2010

(number and percent distribution of households by household type and age of householder, 2010; numbers in thousands)

	total	under 25	25 to 34	35 to 44	45 to 54	55 to 64	65 or older
Total households	**117,538**	**6,233**	**19,257**	**21,519**	**24,871**	**20,387**	**25,270**
Married couples	58,410	1,125	8,634	12,465	13,896	11,405	10,885
Female family householders	14,843	1,435	3,199	3,473	3,048	1,672	2,016
Male family householders	5,580	838	1,260	1,124	1,233	629	496
Women living alone	17,428	643	1,623	1,280	2,476	3,286	8,120
Men living alone	13,971	724	2,294	2,173	3,005	2,578	3,197
Other nonfamily households	7,306	1,468	2,247	1,004	1,213	817	556

PERCENT DISTRIBUTION BY HOUSEHOLD TYPE

	total	under 25	25 to 34	35 to 44	45 to 54	55 to 64	65 or older
Total households	**100.0%**	**100.0%**	**100.0%**	**100.0%**	**100.0%**	**100.0%**	**100.0%**
Married couples	49.7	18.0	44.8	57.9	55.9	55.9	43.1
Female family householders	12.6	23.0	16.6	16.1	12.3	8.2	8.0
Male family householders	4.7	13.4	6.5	5.2	5.0	3.1	2.0
Women living alone	14.8	10.3	8.4	5.9	10.0	16.1	32.1
Men living alone	11.9	11.6	11.9	10.1	12.1	12.6	12.7
Other nonfamily households	6.2	23.6	11.7	4.7	4.9	4.0	2.2

PERCENT DISTRIBUTION BY AGE

	total	under 25	25 to 34	35 to 44	45 to 54	55 to 64	65 or older
Total households	**100.0%**	**5.3%**	**16.4%**	**18.3%**	**21.2%**	**17.3%**	**21.5%**
Married couples	100.0	1.9	14.8	21.3	23.8	19.5	18.6
Female family householders	100.0	9.7	21.6	23.4	20.5	11.3	13.6
Male family householders	100.0	15.0	22.6	20.1	22.1	11.3	8.9
Women living alone	100.0	3.7	9.3	7.3	14.2	18.9	46.6
Men living alone	100.0	5.2	16.4	15.6	21.5	18.5	22.9
Other nonfamily households	100.0	20.1	30.8	13.7	16.6	11.2	7.6

Source: Bureau of the Census, 2010 Current Population Survey Annual Social and Economic Supplement, Internet site http://www.census.gov/hhes/www/cpstables/032010/hhinc/new02_000.htm; calculations by New Strategist

Big Differences in Household Type by Race and Hispanic Origin

Married couples head 60 percent of Asian households, but only 29 percent of black households.

Although the Hispanic population is now larger than the black population, black households still far outnumber Hispanic ones—15 million versus 13 million in 2010. But Hispanic married couples greatly outnumber black married couples—6.6 million to 4.4 million. There are nearly 3 million Asian married couples.

Among blacks, married couples outnumber female-headed families by only 170,000, with married couples accounting for 29 percent of black households and female-headed families for 28 percent. Among Hispanics, married couples account for 50 percent of households and female-headed families for a much smaller 21 percent. Female-headed families account for only 10 percent of Asian and 9 percent of non-Hispanic white households.

Hispanic women are much less likely to live alone than are women from other racial and ethnic groups. Only 7 percent of Hispanic households are headed by women who live alone compared with 18 percent of black, 16 percent of non-Hispanic white, and 9 percent of Asian households.

■ Blacks have lower incomes than Asians and non-Hispanic whites in part because a much smaller proportion of their households are headed by married couples.

Married couples head most Asian, Hispanic, and non-Hispanic white households

(percent of households headed by married couples, by race and Hispanic origin, 2010)

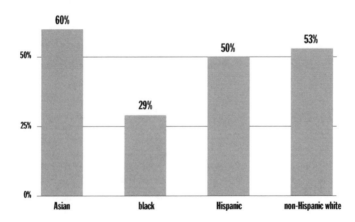

Table 7.4 Households by Household Type, Race, and Hispanic Origin of Householder, 2010

(number and percent distribution of households by household type, race, and Hispanic origin of householder, 2010; numbers in thousands)

	total	Asian	black	Hispanic	non-Hispanic white
TOTAL HOUSEHOLDS	**117,538**	**4,940**	**15,212**	**13,298**	**83,158**
Family households	**78,833**	**3,742**	**9,652**	**10,412**	**54,445**
Married couples	58,410	2,987	4,427	6,589	43,954
With children under age 18	26,171	1,698	2,276	4,416	17,605
Female householders, no spouse present	14,843	481	4,257	2,745	7,291
With children under age 18	9,867	277	3,077	2,047	4,445
Male householders, no spouse present	5,580	273	968	1,079	3,200
With children under age 18	2,851	99	538	611	1,561
Nonfamily households	**38,705**	**1,198**	**5,560**	**2,885**	**28,712**
Female householders	20,442	581	3,103	1,260	15,317
Living alone	17,428	465	2,779	976	13,051
Male householders	18,263	617	2,457	1,625	13,396
Living alone	13,971	450	2,060	1,078	10,249
Percent distribution by household type					
TOTAL HOUSEHOLDS	**100.0%**	**100.0%**	**100.0%**	**100.0%**	**100.0%**
Family households	**67.1**	**75.7**	**63.4**	**78.3**	**65.5**
Married couples	49.7	60.5	29.1	49.5	52.9
With children under age 18	22.3	34.4	15.0	33.2	21.2
Female householders, no spouse present	12.6	9.7	28.0	20.6	8.8
With children under age 18	8.4	5.6	20.2	15.4	5.3
Male householders, no spouse present	4.7	5.5	6.4	8.1	3.8
With children under age 18	2.4	2.0	3.5	4.6	1.9
Nonfamily households	**32.9**	**24.3**	**36.6**	**21.7**	**34.5**
Female householders	17.4	11.8	20.4	9.5	18.4
Living alone	14.8	9.4	18.3	7.3	15.7
Male householders	15.5	12.5	16.2	12.2	16.1
Living alone	11.9	9.1	13.5	8.1	12.3
Percent distribution by race and Hispanic origin					
TOTAL HOUSEHOLDS	**100.0%**	**4.2%**	**12.9%**	**11.3%**	**70.7%**
Family households	**100.0**	**4.7**	**12.2**	**13.2**	**69.1**
Married couples	100.0	5.1	7.6	11.3	75.3
With children under age 18	100.0	6.5	8.7	16.9	67.3
Female householders, no spouse present	100.0	3.2	28.7	18.5	49.1
With children under age 18	100.0	2.8	31.2	20.7	45.0
Male householders, no spouse present	100.0	4.9	17.3	19.3	57.3
With children under age 18	100.0	3.5	18.9	21.4	54.8
Nonfamily households	**100.0**	**3.1**	**14.4**	**7.5**	**74.2**
Female householders	100.0	2.8	15.2	6.2	74.9
Living alone	100.0	2.7	15.9	5.6	74.9
Male householders	100.0	3.4	13.5	8.9	73.4
Living alone	100.0	3.2	14.7	7.7	73.4

Note: Numbers do not add to total because Hispanics may be of any race, not all races are shown, and some householders may be of more than one race. Asians and blacks are those who identify themselves as being of the race alone and those who identify themselves as being of the race in combination with other races. Non-Hispanic whites are those who identify themselves as being white alone and not Hispanic.
Source: Bureau of the Census, 2010 Current Population Survey Annual Social and Economic Supplement, Internet site http://www.census.gov/hhes/www/cpstables/032010/hhinc/new01_000.htm; calculations by New Strategist

Most Households Are Small

The number of single-person households is declining because of the Great Recession.

Sixty percent of the nation's households are home to only one or two people. The number of single-person households climbed 17 percent between 2000 and 2010, significantly faster than the 12 percent growth in households overall. But the growth in single-person households occurred before the Great Recession. Between 2008 and 2010, the number of single-person households fell 2 percent as fewer Americans could afford to live by themselves.

Two-person households are most common, accounting for 34 percent of the 118 million households in the nation. Single-person households constitute 27 percent of the total. Only 10 percent of households have five or more people. Overall, the average household in the United States was home to 2.59 people in 2010, down from 2.62 in 2000 but up from 2.56 in 2008.

■ Household size is growing in part because many unemployed young adults are moving back in with their parents.

Two-person households are most common

(percent distribution of households by size, 2010)

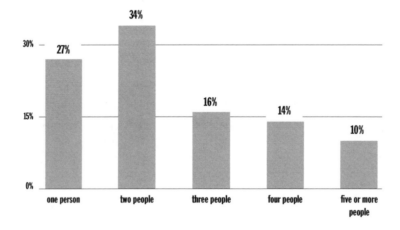

Table 7.5 Households by Size, 2000 to 2010

(number and percent distribution of households by size, 2000 to 2010; percent change in number, 2000–10 and 2008–10; number of households in thousands)

	2010		2008		2000		percent change in number	
	number	percent distribution	number	percent distribution	number	percent distribution	2000–10	2008–10
Total households	**117,538**	**100.0%**	**116,783**	**100.0%**	**104,705**	**100.0%**	**12.3%**	**0.6%**
One person	31,399	26.7	32,167	27.5	26,724	25.5	17.5	–2.4
Two people	39,487	33.6	38,737	33.2	34,666	33.1	13.9	1.9
Three people	18,638	15.9	18,522	15.9	17,152	16.4	8.7	0.6
Four people	16,122	13.7	15,865	13.6	15,309	14.6	5.3	1.6
Five people	7,367	6.3	7,332	6.3	6,981	6.7	5.5	0.5
Six people	2,784	2.4	2,694	2.3	2,445	2.3	13.9	3.3
Seven or more people	1,740	1.5	1,467	1.3	1,428	1.4	21.8	18.6
Average number of persons per household	2.59	–	2.56	–	2.62	–	–	–

Note: "–" means not applicable.
Source: Bureau of the Census, Current Population Survey Annual Social and Economic Supplement, Internet site http://www .census.gov/hhes/www/income/dinctabs.html; calculations by New Strategist

More than Eight Million Elderly Women Live Alone

Nearly half of the women who live alone are aged 65 or older.

Among the nation's 31 million single-person households, women head the 56 percent majority. People aged 55 or older head 55 percent of single-person households.

There are sharp differences in the ages of men and women who live alone. Most men who live alone are under age 55, while most women who live alone are aged 55 or older. Among men, those aged 75 or older are most likely to live alone, but the proportion is only 23 percent. In contrast, 47 percent of their female counterparts live by themselves. Most men live alone before marriage or after divorce. Most women live alone following the death of a spouse.

■ The number of single-person households has declined since 2008 because fewer Americans can afford to live by themselves.

Women are increasingly likely to live alone after middle age

(percent of women who live alone, by age, 2010)

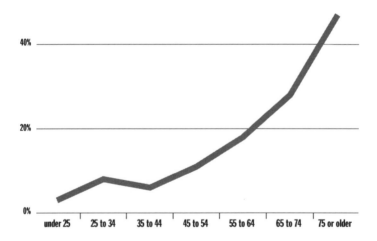

Table 7.6 People Living Alone by Sex and Age, 2010

(total number of people aged 15 or older, number and percent living alone, and percent distribution of people who live alone, by sex and age, 2010; numbers in thousands)

| | | living alone | | |
	total	number	percent of total	percent distribution
Total people	**242,168**	**31,399**	**13.0%**	**100.0%**
Under age 25	42,240	1,367	3.2	4.4
Aged 25 to 34	41,085	3,917	9.5	12.5
Aged 35 to 44	40,447	3,453	8.5	11.0
Aged 45 to 54	44,387	5,481	12.3	17.5
Aged 55 to 64	35,395	5,864	16.6	18.7
Aged 65 to 74	20,956	4,710	22.5	15.0
Aged 75 or older	17,657	6,609	37.4	21.0
Total men	**117,728**	**13,971**	**11.9**	**100.0**
Under age 25	21,403	724	3.4	5.2
Aged 25 to 34	20,689	2,294	11.1	16.4
Aged 35 to 44	20,074	2,173	10.8	15.6
Aged 45 to 54	21,784	3,005	13.8	21.5
Aged 55 to 64	16,985	2,578	15.2	18.5
Aged 65 to 74	9,735	1,600	16.4	11.5
Aged 75 or older	7,058	1,598	22.6	11.4
Total women	**124,440**	**17,428**	**14.0**	**100.0**
Under age 25	20,837	643	3.1	3.7
Aged 25 to 34	20,396	1,623	8.0	9.3
Aged 35 to 44	20,373	1,280	6.3	7.3
Aged 45 to 54	22,604	2,476	11.0	14.2
Aged 55 to 64	18,410	3,286	17.8	18.9
Aged 65 to 74	11,221	3,110	27.7	17.8
Aged 75 or older	10,599	5,011	47.3	28.8

Source: Bureau of the Census, 2010 Current Population Survey Annual Social and Economic Supplement, Internet site http://www.census.gov/hhes/www/income/data/incpovhlth/2009/dtables.html; calculations by New Strategist

Number of Households Is Declining in the West

The South is home to the majority of black households.

Household growth has slowed dramatically because of the Great Recession. Between 2000 and 2010, the number of households in the United States grew by 12 percent, but during the last two years of that time period households increased by only 0.6 percent. The number of households in the West actually fell by 0.2 percent. Even during the recession, the number of households in the South continued to grow faster than average, up 1 percent.

The nation's minority populations are heavily concentrated in some regions. The 55 percent majority of black households are in the South. Forty-six percent of Asian households are in the West. The West is also home to 39 percent of Hispanic households, while the South claims another 38 percent. Blacks are the largest minority in the South, heading 19 percent of households. Hispanics are the largest minority in the West, accounting for 20 percent of households in that region. The Asian presence is also greatest in the West, where Asians head 9 percent of households.

■ The nation's markets and politics will be shaped increasingly by the concentration of Asians, blacks, and Hispanics in certain regions and states.

Only 41 percent of households are in the Northeast and Midwest

(percent distribution of households by region, 2010)

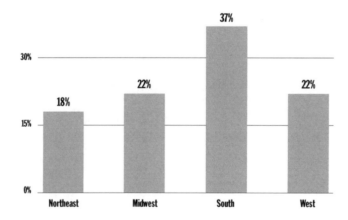

Table 7.7 Households by Region, 2000 to 2010

(number and percent distribution of households by region, 2000 to 2010; percent change in number, 2000–10 and 2008–10; numbers in thousands)

	2010 number	2010 percent distribution	2008 number	2008 percent distribution	2000 number	2000 percent distribution	percent change in number 2000–10	percent change in number 2008–10
Total households	**117,538**	**100.0%**	**116,783**	**100.0%**	**104,705**	**100.0%**	**12.3%**	**0.6%**
Northeast	21,479	18.3	21,351	18.3	20,087	19.2	6.9	0.6
Midwest	26,390	22.5	26,266	22.5	24,508	23.4	7.7	0.5
South	43,611	37.1	43,062	36.9	37,303	35.6	16.9	1.3
West	26,058	22.2	26,105	22.4	22,808	21.8	14.2	−0.2

Source: Bureau of the Census, Current Population Survey Annual Social and Economic Supplement, Internet site http://www .census.gov/hhes/www/income/dinctabs.html; calculations by New Strategist

Table 7.8 Households by Region, Race, and Hispanic Origin, 2010

(number and percent distribution of households by region, race, and Hispanic origin of householder, 2010; numbers in thousands)

	total	Asian	black	Hispanic	non-Hispanic white
Total households	**117,538**	**4,940**	**15,212**	**13,298**	**83,158**
Northeast	21,479	1,076	2,602	2,004	15,902
Midwest	26,390	558	2,761	1,041	21,825
South	43,611	1,059	8,419	5,062	28,721
West	26,058	2,248	1,430	5,191	16,709
PERCENT DISTRIBUTION BY REGION					
Total households	**100.0%**	**100.0%**	**100.0%**	**100.0%**	**100.0%**
Northeast	18.3	21.8	17.1	15.1	19.1
Midwest	22.5	11.3	18.2	7.8	26.2
South	37.1	21.4	55.3	38.1	34.5
West	22.2	45.5	9.4	39.0	20.1
PERCENT DISTRIBUTION BY RACE AND HISPANIC ORIGIN					
Total households	**100.0%**	**4.2%**	**12.9%**	**11.3%**	**70.7%**
Northeast	100.0	5.0	12.1	9.3	74.0
Midwest	100.0	2.1	10.5	3.9	82.7
South	100.0	2.4	19.3	11.6	65.9
West	100.0	8.6	5.5	19.9	64.1

Note: Numbers do not add to total because Hispanics may be of any race, not all races are shown, and some householders may be of more than one race. Asians and blacks are those who identify themselves as being of the race alone and those who identify themselves as being of the race in combination with other races. Non-Hispanic whites are only those who identify themselves as being white alone and not Hispanic.
Source: Bureau of the Census, 2010 Current Population Survey Annual Social and Economic Supplement, Internet site http:// www.census.gov/hhes/www/cpstables/032010/hhinc/new01_000.htm; calculations by New Strategist

More than 80 Percent of Households Are in Metropolitan Areas

Non-Hispanic whites are more likely to live in nonmetropolitan areas than Asians, blacks, or Hispanics.

Of the nation's 118 million households, 84 percent are in metropolitan areas, defined as counties with a city of 50,000 or more population plus any adjacent counties with economic ties to the core county. Only 16 percent of households are in nonmetropolitan areas. Asians are more likely than blacks, Hispanics, or non-Hispanic whites to be metropolitan residents.

About half the nation's Asian, black, and Hispanic households are in the principal (central) cities of metropolitan areas. The figure is a much smaller 26 percent among non-Hispanic whites. Conversely, the 54 percent majority of non-Hispanic white households are in the suburbs of metropolitan areas (outside principal cities) compared with 39 to 47 percent of Asian, black, and Hispanic households. Nineteen percent of non-Hispanic white households are in nonmetropolitan areas versus only 3 percent of Asian households.

■ The nation's central cities are much more diverse than the suburbs or nonmetropolitan areas.

Few non-Hispanic white households are in the principal cities of metro areas

(percent of households in the principal cities of metropolitan areas, by race and Hispanic origin, 2010)

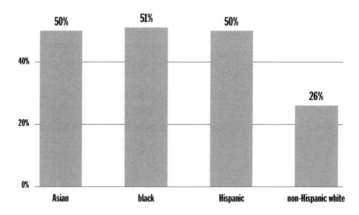

Table 7.9 Households by Metropolitan Status, Race, and Hispanic Origin, 2010

(number and percent distribution of households by metropolitan status, race, and Hispanic origin, 2010; numbers in thousands)

	total	Asian	black	Hispanic	non-Hispanic white
Total households	**117,538**	**4,940**	**15,212**	**13,298**	**83,158**
Inside metropolitan areas	98,379	4,789	13,706	12,368	67,090
Inside principal cities	38,850	2,486	7,827	6,602	21,870
Outside principal cities	59,529	2,302	5,878	5,766	45,220
Outside metropolitan areas	19,159	151	1,506	930	16,068
PERCENT DISTRIBUTION BY METROPOLITAN STATUS					
Total households	**100.0%**	**100.0%**	**100.0%**	**100.0%**	**100.0%**
Inside metropolitan areas	83.7	96.9	90.1	93.0	80.7
Inside principal cities	33.1	50.3	51.5	49.6	26.3
Outside principal cities	50.6	46.6	38.6	43.4	54.4
Outside metropolitan areas	16.3	3.1	9.9	7.0	19.3
PERCENT DISTRIBUTION BY RACE AND HISPANIC ORIGIN					
Total households	**100.0%**	**4.2%**	**12.9%**	**11.3%**	**70.7%**
Inside metropolitan areas	100.0	4.9	13.9	12.6	68.2
Inside principal cities	100.0	6.4	20.1	17.0	56.3
Outside principal cities	100.0	3.9	9.9	9.7	76.0
Outside metropolitan areas	100.0	0.8	7.9	4.9	83.9

Note: Numbers do not add to total because Hispanics may be of any race, not all races are shown, and some householders may be of more than one race. Asians and blacks are those who identify themselves as being of the race alone and those who identify themselves as being of the race in combination with other races. Non-Hispanic whites are those who identify themselves as being white alone and not Hispanic.
Source: Bureau of the Census, 2010 Current Population Survey Annual Social and Economic Supplement, Internet site http://www.census.gov/hhes/www/cpstables/032010/hhinc/new01_000.htm; calculations by New Strategist

Nearly One in Four Children Lives with Mother Only

Fewer than 4 percent live with their father only.

Among the nation's 75 million children under age 18, only 69 percent lived with two parents in 2010—down from 85 percent in 1970. The proportion of children who live with two parents (married or unmarried) ranges from a low of 41 percent among black children to a high of 85 percent among Asian children. A smaller share of children lives with two married biological parents, ranging from 30 percent of blacks to 78 percent of Asians.

The proportion of children who live with their mother only ranges from a low of 11 percent among Asians to a high of 48 percent among blacks. Only 3 percent of children live with their father only, and another 4 percent live with neither parent.

■ The poverty rate among children is unlikely to decline significantly until fewer children live in single-parent families.

Children's living arrangements vary greatly by race and Hispanic origin

(percent of children living with two married, biological parents, by race and Hispanic origin, 2010)

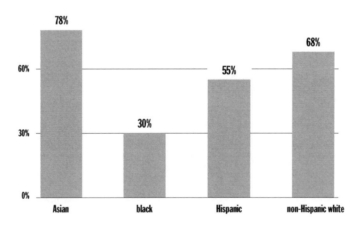

Table 7.10 Living Arrangements of Children, 1970 to 2010

(number and percent distribution of children under age 18 by living arrangement, 1970 to 2010; numbers in thousands)

| | total | | children living with | | | |
	number	percent	two parents	mother only	father only	neither parent
Total children						
2010	74,718	100.0%	69.4%	23.1%	3.4%	4.1%
2009	74,230	100.0	69.8	22.8	3.4	4.0
2008	74,104	100.0	69.9	22.8	3.5	3.8
2007*	73,746	100.0	70.7	22.6	3.2	3.5
2007*	73,746	100.0	67.8	24.2	4.5	3.5
2006	73,664	100.0	67.4	23.3	4.7	4.6
2005	73,523	100.0	67.4	23.4	4.7	4.5
2000	72,012	100.0	69.1	22.4	4.2	4.2
1995	70,254	100.0	68.7	23.5	3.5	4.3
1990	64,137	100.0	72.5	21.6	3.1	2.8
1985	62,475	100.0	73.9	20.9	2.5	2.7
1980	63,427	100.0	76.7	18.0	1.7	3.7
1975	66,087	100.0	80.3	15.5	1.5	2.7
1970	69,162	100.0	85.2	10.8	1.1	2.9

* Before 2007, the Current Population Survey classified children as living with two parents only if the parents were married. Beginning in 2007, children were counted as living with two parents if there were two parents in the home regardless of marital status. Results for both the original and new methodology in 2007 are shown here for comparative purposes.
Source: Bureau of the Census, Families and Living Arrangements, Historical Time Series, Internet site http://www.census .gov/population/www/socdemo/hh-fam.html; calculations by New Strategist

Table 7.11 Living Arrangements of Children, 2010: Total Children

(number and percent distribution of total children under age 18 by living arrangement, 2010; numbers in thousands)

	number	percent distribution
Total children	**74,718**	**100.0%**
Living with two parents	51,823	69.4
Married parents	49,106	65.7
Unmarried parents	2,717	3.6
Biological mother and father	46,438	62.2
Married parents	44,099	59.0
Biological mother and stepfather	3,252	4.4
Biological father and stepmother	955	1.3
Biological mother and adoptive father	167	0.2
Biological father and adoptive mother	33	0.0
Adoptive mother and father	768	1.0
Other	210	0.3
Living with one parent	19,857	26.6
Mother only	17,285	23.1
Father only	2,572	3.4
Living with no parents	3,038	4.1
Grandparents	1,655	2.2
Other	1,383	1.9
At least one biological parent	70,236	94.0
At least one stepparent	4,615	6.2
At least one adoptive parent	1,258	1.7

Source: Bureau of the Census, Current Population Survey Annual Social and Economic Supplement, America's Families and Living Arrangements: 2010, detailed tables, Internet site http://www.census.gov/population/www/socdemo/hh-fam/cps2010 .html; calculations by New Strategist

Table 7.12 Living Arrangements of Children, 2010: Asian Children

(number and percent distribution of Asian children under age 18 by living arrangement, 2010; numbers in thousands)

	number	percent distribution
Asian children	**3,984**	**100.0%**
Living with two parents	3,372	84.6
Married parents	3,314	83.2
Unmarried parents	58	1.5
Biological mother and father	3,171	79.6
Married parents	3,123	78.4
Biological mother and stepfather	68	1.7
Biological father and stepmother	29	0.7
Biological mother and adoptive father	3	0.1
Biological father and adoptive mother	–	–
Adoptive mother and father	93	2.3
Other	7	0.2
Living with one parent	535	13.4
Mother only	441	11.1
Father only	94	2.4
Living with no parents	77	1.9
Grandparents	24	0.6
Other	53	1.3
At least one biological parent	3,776	94.8
At least one stepparent	113	2.8
At least one adoptive parent	120	3.0

Note: Asians are those who identify themselves as being of the race alone and those who identify themselves as being of the race in combination with other races. "–" means sample is too small to make a reliable estimate.
Source: Bureau of the Census, Current Population Survey Annual Social and Economic Supplement, America's Families and Living Arrangements: 2010, detailed tables, Internet site http://www.census.gov/population/www/socdemo/hh-fam/cps2010 .html; calculations by New Strategist

Table 7.13 Living Arrangements of Children, 2010: Black Children

(number and percent distribution of black children under age 18 by living arrangement, 2010; numbers in thousands)

	number	percent distribution
Black children	**12,653**	**100.0%**
Living with two parents	5,163	40.8
Married parents	4,541	35.9
Unmarried parents	622	4.9
Biological mother and father	4,324	34.2
Married parents	3,765	29.8
Biological mother and stepfather	533	4.2
Biological father and stepmother	115	0.9
Biological mother and adoptive father	12	0.1
Biological father and adoptive mother	4	0.0
Adoptive mother and father	144	1.1
Other	31	0.2
Living with one parent	6,573	51.9
Mother only	6,135	48.5
Father only	439	3.5
Living with no parents	917	7.2
Grandparents	563	4.4
Other	354	2.8
At least one biological parent	11,436	90.4
At least one stepparent	719	5.7
At least one adoptive parent	253	2.0

Note: Blacks are those who identify themselves as being of the race alone and those who identify themselves as being of the race in combination with other races.
Source: Bureau of the Census, Current Population Survey Annual Social and Economic Supplement, America's Families and Living Arrangements: 2010, detailed tables, Internet site http://www.census.gov/population/www/socdemo/hh-fam/cps2010 .html; calculations by New Strategist

Table 7.14 Living Arrangements of Children, 2010: Hispanic Children

(number and percent distribution of Hispanic children under age 18 by living arrangement, 2010; numbers in thousands)

	number	percent distribution
Hispanic children	**16,941**	**100.0%**
Living with two parents	11,345	67.0
Married parents	10,325	60.9
Unmarried parents	1,020	6.0
Biological mother and father	10,298	60.8
Married parents	9,387	55.4
Biological mother and stepfather	681	4.0
Biological father and stepmother	150	0.9
Biological mother and adoptive father	25	0.1
Biological father and adoptive mother	11	0.1
Adoptive mother and father	131	0.8
Other	50	0.3
Living with one parent	4,919	29.0
Mother only	4,456	26.3
Father only	463	2.7
Living with no parents	677	4.0
Grandparents	330	1.9
Other	347	2.0
At least one biological parent	16,008	94.5
At least one stepparent	933	5.5
At least one adoptive parent	193	1.1

Source: Bureau of the Census, Current Population Survey Annual Social and Economic Supplement, America's Families and Living Arrangements: 2010, detailed tables, Internet site http://www.census.gov/population/www/socdemo/hh-fam/cps2010 .html; calculations by New Strategist

Table 7.15 Living Arrangements of Children, 2010: Non-Hispanic White Children

(number and percent distribution of non-Hispanic white children under age 18 by living arrangement, 2010; numbers in thousands)

	number	percent distribution
Non-Hispanic white children	**41,089**	**100.0%**
Living with two parents	31,859	77.5
Married parents	30,835	75.0
Unmarried parents	1,024	2.5
Biological mother and father	28,581	69.6
Married parents	27,749	67.5
Biological mother and stepfather	1,948	4.7
Biological father and stepmother	651	1.6
Biological mother and adoptive father	124	0.3
Biological father and adoptive mother	18	0.0
Adoptive mother and father	414	1.0
Other	123	0.3
Living with one parent	7,938	19.3
Mother only	6,382	15.5
Father only	1,555	3.8
Living with no parents	1,292	3.1
Grandparents	692	1.7
Other	600	1.5
At least one biological parent	39,033	95.0
At least one stepparent	2,818	6.9
At least one adoptive parent	701	1.7

Note: Non-Hispanic whites are those who identify themselves as being white alone and not Hispanic.
Source: Bureau of the Census, Current Population Survey Annual Social and Economic Supplement, America's Families and Living Arrangements: 2010, detailed tables, Internet site http://www.census.gov/population/www/socdemo/hh-fam/cps2010 .html; calculations by New Strategist

Most Married Couples Have Children at Home

Most do not have children under age 18 at home, however.

Among the nation's 118 million households, only 30 percent include children under age 18. When children aged 18 or older are also considered, a larger 40 percent of households include children of the householder. Among married couples, only 42 percent have children under age 18 at home and a larger 54 percent have children of any age living with them. Female-headed families are more likely to have children at home—57 percent include children under age 18 and 85 percent include children of any age. A much smaller 40 percent of male-headed families include children under age 18.

Among married couples with children under age 18 in their home, 39 percent have only one and another 39 percent have two. Female-headed families are more likely to have only one child under age 18 at home (50 percent), and male-headed families are most likely to have only one (62 percent).

■ The traditional nuclear family—husband, wife, and children under age 18—accounts for a shrinking share of households as a growing proportion of baby boomers become empty-nesters.

Only 19 percent of married couples have preschoolers

(percent of married-couple households with own children of selected ages in the home, 2010)

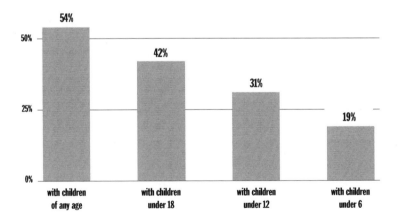

Table 7.16 Households by Presence and Age of Children, 2010

(number and percent distribution of households by presence and age of own children under age 18 and type of household, 2010; numbers in thousands)

	total	married couples	female householder, no spouse present	male householder, no spouse present
Total households	**117,538**	**58,410**	**14,843**	**5,580**
With children of any age	47,463	31,514	12,624	3,325
With children under age 18	35,218	24,575	8,419	2,224
With children under age 12	25,867	18,304	5,986	1,577
With children under age 6	15,506	11,170	3,382	954
PERCENT DISTRIBUTION BY PRESENCE AND AGE OF CHILDREN				
Total households	**100.0%**	**100.0%**	**100.0%**	**100.0%**
With children of any age	40.4	54.0	85.1	59.6
With children under age 18	30.0	42.1	56.7	39.9
With children under age 12	22.0	31.3	40.3	28.3
With children under age 6	13.2	19.1	22.8	17.1
PERCENT DISTRIBUTION BY FAMILY TYPE				
Total households	**100.0%**	**49.7%**	**12.6%**	**4.7%**
With children of any age	100.0	66.4	26.6	7.0
With children under age 18	100.0	69.8	23.9	6.3
With children under age 12	100.0	70.8	23.1	6.1
With children under age 6	100.0	72.0	21.8	6.2

Source: Bureau of the Census, America's Families and Living Arrangements: 2010, Current Population Survey Annual Social and Economic Supplement, Internet site http://www.census.gov/population/www/socdemo/hh-fam/cps2010.html; calculations by New Strategist

Table 7.17 Families by Number of Children under Age 18, 2010

(number and percent distribution of family households with own children under age 18 by number of children and type of family, 2010; numbers in thousands)

	total	married couples	female householders, no spouse present	male householders, no spouse present
Total families with children under age 18	**35,218**	**24,575**	**8,419**	**2,224**
One child	15,149	9,567	4,207	1,375
Two children	12,947	9,658	2,714	576
Three children	5,062	3,842	1,034	187
Four or more children	2,060	1,509	465	86

PERCENT DISTRIBUTION BY NUMBER OF CHILDREN

Total families with children under age 18	**100.0%**	**100.0%**	**100.0%**	**100.0%**
One child	43.0	38.9	50.0	61.8
Two children	36.8	39.3	32.2	25.9
Three children	14.4	15.6	12.3	8.4
Four or more children	5.8	6.1	5.5	3.9

PERCENT DISTRIBUTION BY FAMILY TYPE

Total families with children under age 18	**100.0%**	**69.8%**	**23.9%**	**6.3%**
One child	100.0	63.2	27.8	9.1
Two children	100.0	74.6	21.0	4.4
Three children	100.0	75.9	20.4	3.7
Four or more children	100.0	73.3	22.6	4.2

Source: Bureau of the Census, America's Families and Living Arrangements: 2010, Current Population Survey Annual Social and Economic Supplement, Internet site http://www.census.gov/population/www/socdemo/hh-fam/cps2010.html; calculations by New Strategist

Most Moms Are in the Labor Force

Stay-at-home mothers are not the norm, even among couples with preschoolers.

Among married couples with children under age 15, the 70 percent majority has a mother in the labor force. Only 26 percent have a mom who stays home to care for her family. Stay-at-home dads are even less common. Only 1 percent of married couples with children under age 15 have a father who is not in the labor force because he is caring for the family.

Couples with preschoolers are only slightly more likely than average to have a stay-at-home mother, at 31 percent. They are about equally as likely to have a stay-at-home father, at 1 percent.

■ Perhaps no characteristic distinguishes today's children from those in the past more than working parents. With both mother and father in the labor force, family life has become much more complicated.

Thirty-one percent of couples with preschoolers have a stay-at-home mom

(percent distribution of married-couple family groups with children under age 6, by labor force status of mother during past year, 2010)

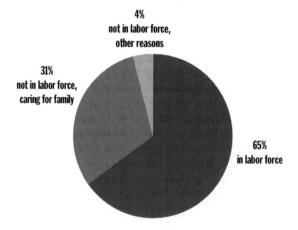

4%
not in labor force,
other reasons

31%
not in labor force,
caring for family

65%
in labor force

Table 7.18 Stay-at-Home Parents among Married Couples, 2010

(number and percent distribution of married-couple family groups with children under age 15 by stay-at-home status of mother and father and age of child, 2010; numbers in thousands)

	with children under age 15		with children under age 6	
	number	percent distribution	number	percent distribution
Total married couple family groups	**22,138**	**100.0%**	**11,599**	**100.0%**
Mother's labor force status in past year				
In labor force one or more weeks	15,454	69.8	7,559	65.2
Not in labor force, caring for family	5,701	25.8	3,561	30.7
Not in labor force, other reason	984	4.4	479	4.1
Father's labor force status in past year				
In labor force one or more weeks	20,728	93.6	10,954	94.4
Not in labor force, caring for family	238	1.1	140	1.2
Not in labor force, other reason	1,172	5.3	505	4.4

Note: Married-couple family groups include married-couple householders and married couples living in households headed by others.
Source: Bureau of the Census, America's Families and Living Arrangements: 2010, Current Population Survey Annual Social and Economic Supplement, Internet site http://www.census.gov/population/www/socdemo/hh-fam/cps2010.html; calculations by New Strategist

Most Americans Live in Family Households

Women aged 65 or older are more likely to live in a nonfamily household.

The 78 percent majority of the nation's 242 million people aged 15 or older live in a family household. Nearly half are married-couple householders or their spouses. Another 15 percent are children of the householder. Twenty-two percent of Americans aged 15 or older live in nonfamily households—meaning they live alone or with nonrelatives.

Women aged 65 or older are much more likely to live in a nonfamily household than is the average American, with a large proportion of older women living by themselves. Only 60 percent of women aged 65 or older live in a family household, and 40 percent live in a nonfamily household. Thirty-seven percent of women aged 65 or older live alone.

■ As the baby-boom generation ages, the proportion of people who live alone should rise.

The lifestyles of men and women diverge in old age

(percent distribution of people aged 65 or older by living arrangement and sex, 2010)

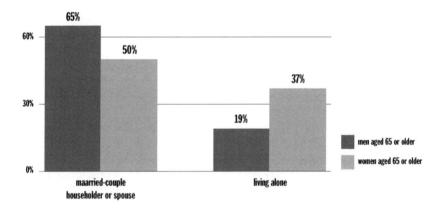

Table 7.19 Living Arrangements by Sex, 2010

(number and percent distribution of noninstitutionalized people aged 15 or older by living arrangement and sex, 2010; numbers in thousands)

	total		female		male	
	number	percent distribution	number	percent distribution	number	percent distribution
Total people	**242,047**	**100.0%**	**124,361**	**100.0%**	**117,686**	**100.0%**
Living in family household	188,315	77.8	97,058	78.0	91,257	77.5
Living in nonfamily household	53,732	22.2	27,302	22.0	26,430	22.5
Householder	**117,538**	**48.6**	**57,858**	**46.5**	**59,680**	**50.7**
Family householder	78,833	32.6	37,416	30.1	41,417	35.2
Married-couple householder	58,410	24.1	22,573	18.2	35,837	30.5
Other family householder	20,423	8.4	14,843	11.9	5,580	4.7
Nonfamily householder	38,705	16.0	20,442	16.4	18,263	15.5
Living alone	31,399	13.0	17,428	14.0	13,971	11.9
Living with nonrelatives	7,306	3.0	3,014	2.4	4,291	3.6
Not a householder	**124,509**	**51.4**	**66,502**	**53.5**	**58,007**	**49.3**
In family household	109,482	45.2	59,642	48.0	49,840	42.3
Spouse of householder	58,410	24.1	35,837	28.8	22,573	19.2
Child of householder	36,596	15.1	16,430	13.2	20,166	17.1
Other relative of householder	14,476	6.0	7,375	5.9	7,101	6.0
In nonfamily household	15,027	6.2	6,860	5.5	8,167	6.9

Source: Bureau of the Census, America's Families and Living Arrangements: 2010, Current Population Survey Annual Social and Economic Supplement, Internet site http://www.census.gov/population/www/socdemo/hh-fam/cps2010.html; calculations by New Strategist

Table 7.20 Living Arrangements of People Aged 65 or Older by Sex, 2010

(number and percent distribution of noninstitutionalized people aged 65 or older by living arrangement and sex, 2010; numbers in thousands)

	total aged 65 or older		female		male	
	number	percent distribution	number	percent distribution	number	percent distribution
Total people aged 65 or older	**38,569**	**100.0%**	**21,784**	**100.0%**	**16,787**	**100.0%**
Living in family household	26,139	67.8	13,125	60.3	13,014	77.5
Living in nonfamily household	12,430	32.2	8,658	39.7	3,771	22.5
Householder	**25,270**	**65.5**	**13,551**	**62.2**	**11,718**	**69.8**
Family householder	13,396	34.7	5,148	23.6	8,248	49.1
Married-couple householder	10,885	28.2	3,133	14.4	7,753	46.2
Other family householder	2,511	6.5	2,015	9.2	495	2.9
Nonfamily householder	11,874	30.8	8,403	38.6	3,470	20.7
Living alone	11,317	29.3	8,121	37.3	3,198	19.1
Living with nonrelatives	556	1.4	284	1.3	273	1.6
Not a householder	**13,299**	**34.5**	**8,232**	**37.8**	**5,067**	**30.2**
In family household	12,743	33.0	7,977	36.6	4,766	28.4
Spouse of householder	10,885	28.2	7,753	35.6	3,133	18.7
Child of householder	59	0.2	36	0.2	23	0.1
Other relative of householder	1,799	4.7	188	0.9	1,610	9.6
In nonfamily household	556	1.4	255	1.2	301	1.8

Source: Bureau of the Census, America's Families and Living Arrangements: 2010, Current Population Survey Annual Social and Economic Supplement, Internet site http://www.census.gov/population/www/socdemo/hh-fam/cps2010.html; calculations by New Strategist

More than Three Out of Four Women Aged 20 to 24 Are Single

Many young adults live with a romantic partner before marrying.

Men and women are remaining single longer than they once did as more attend college and try to establish themselves in a career before tying the knot. Among women aged 20 to 24, fully 79 percent have not yet married. The figure is 89 percent for their male counterparts. The proportion of women who are still single falls below 50 percent in the 25-to-29 age group. Among men, it falls below the 50 percent threshold in the 30-to-34 age group.

Just because young adults are unmarried does not mean they are living the single life. Many live together outside of marriage—called cohabiting. Among women aged 15 to 44 in 2002 (the latest data available), half have lived with a romantic partner outside of marriage. The figures for men are about the same, with 49 percent having cohabited at some point.

■ The percentage of adults under age 45 who have ever cohabited exceeds 60 percent in some age groups.

Most women have married by their late twenties

(percent of women who have never married, by age, 2010)

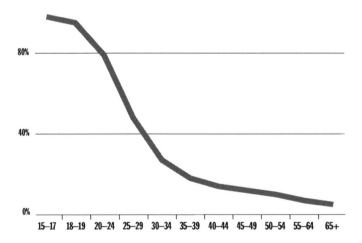

Table 7.21 Never-Married People by Age and Sex, 2010

(percent of people aged 15 or older who have never married, by age and sex, 2010)

	total	men	women
Total never-married	**30.7%**	**34.2%**	**27.4%**
Aged 15 to 17	98.3	98.4	98.2
Aged 18 to 19	96.4	97.4	95.3
Aged 20 to 24	84.0	88.7	79.3
Aged 25 to 29	55.1	62.2	47.8
Aged 30 to 34	31.8	36.5	27.2
Aged 35 to 39	20.6	23.5	17.7
Aged 40 to 44	17.1	20.4	13.8
Aged 45 to 49	14.2	16.5	12.0
Aged 50 to 54	11.6	13.3	10.0
Aged 55 to 64	8.1	9.1	7.1
Aged 65 or older	4.3	4.1	4.5

Source: Bureau of the Census, America's Families and Living Arrangements: 2010, Current Population Survey Annual Social and Economic Supplement, Internet site http://www.census.gov/population/www/socdemo/hh-fam/cps2010.html; calculations by New Strategist

Table 7.22 Cohabitation Experience of Women, 2002

(total number of women aged 15 to 44, and percent who have ever cohabited or are currently cohabiting, by selected characteristics, 2002; numbers in thousands)

	total number	percent	ever cohabited	currently cohabiting
Total women aged 15 to 44	**61,561**	**100.0%**	**50.0%**	**9.1%**
Aged 15 to 19	9,834	100.0	11.7	5.6
Aged 20 to 24	9,840	100.0	43.1	15.7
Aged 25 to 29	9,249	100.0	60.9	12.9
Aged 30 to 34	10,272	100.0	63.2	7.9
Aged 35 to 39	10,853	100.0	61.3	6.7
Aged 40 to 44	11,512	100.0	57.4	6.6
Number of children ever borne				
None	25,622	100.0	31.8	8.9
One	11,193	100.0	63.1	10.7
Two	13,402	100.0	61.4	6.1
Three or more	11,343	100.0	64.9	11.2
Race and Hispanic origin				
Black, non-Hispanic	8,250	100.0	51.1	9.6
Hispanic	9,107	100.0	48.8	13.4
White, non-Hispanic	39,498	100.0	50.5	7.9
Education				
Not a high school graduate	5,627	100.0	69.4	17.2
High school graduate or GED	14,264	100.0	68.5	11.3
Some college, no degree	14,279	100.0	58.3	7.6
Bachelor's degree or more	13,551	100.0	46.3	5.4
Family structure at age 14				
Living with both parents	43,921	100.0	45.5	7.4
Other	17,640	100.0	61.3	13.2

Note: Education categories include only people aged 22 to 44.
Source: National Center for Health Statistics, Fertility, Family Planning, and Reproductive Health of U.S. Women: Data from the 2002 National Survey of Family Growth, Vital and Health Statistics, Series 23, No. 25, 2005, Internet site http://www.cdc.gov/nchs/nsfg.htm

Table 7.23 Cohabitation Experience of Men, 2002

(total number of men aged 15 to 44, and percent who have ever cohabited or are currently cohabiting, by selected characteristics, 2002; numbers in thousands)

	total number	percent	ever cohabited	currently cohabiting
Total men aged 15 to 44	**61,147**	**100.0%**	**48.8%**	**9.2%**
Aged 15 to 19	10,208	100.0	5.5	1.9
Aged 20 to 24	9,883	100.0	33.9	13.4
Aged 25 to 29	9,226	100.0	58.5	17.8
Aged 30 to 34	10,138	100.0	62.3	9.6
Aged 35 to 39	10,557	100.0	64.7	8.2
Aged 40 to 44	11,135	100.0	66.5	6.0
Number of biological children				
None	32,593	100.0	32.6	7.9
One	10,457	100.0	68.4	13.7
Two	9,829	100.0	63.0	7.9
Three or more	8,269	100.0	71.2	10.7
Race and Hispanic origin				
Black, non-Hispanic	6,940	100.0	52.6	10.0
Hispanic	10,188	100.0	47.3	14.0
White, non-Hispanic	38,738	100.0	49.4	7.9
Education				
Not a high school graduate	6,355	100.0	67.2	16.6
High school graduate or GED	15,659	100.0	66.6	12.3
Some college, no degree	13,104	100.0	55.0	9.8
Bachelor's degree or more	11,901	100.0	54.0	7.0
Family structure at age 14				
Living with both parents	45,166	100.0	46.5	8.4
Other	15,981	100.0	55.5	11.7

Note: Education categories include only people aged 22 to 44.
Source: National Center for Health Statistics, Fertility, Contraception, and Fatherhood: Data on Men and Women from Cycle 6 of the 2002 National Survey of Family Growth, Vital and Health Statistics, Series 23, No. 26, 2006, Internet site http://www.cdc .gov/nchs/nsfg.htm

Most Men and Women Are Currently Married

Some of the married have gone to the altar more than once, however.

Over the past few decades, Americans have increasingly postponed marriage to pursue a college degree and start a career. The median age at first marriage stood at 28.2 years for men and 26.1 years for women in 2010—more than five years later than the median age of marriage in 1950. Overall, 50 percent of Americans aged 15 or older are currently married and living with their spouse, 10 percent are currently divorced, and 6 percent are widowed.

Many men and women have been married more than once. Among 15-to-44-year-olds in 2002 (the latest data available), 8.5 percent of women and 7.2 percent of men are now in their second or higher marriage. Among women aged 40 to 44, nearly half—46 percent—are currently in their first marriage and 21 percent are in a second or higher marriage. The figures are similar for men in the age group, with 43 percent in their first marriage and 20 percent in their second or higher marriage.

■ Divorce and multiple marriages are much more common among baby boomers and younger adults than among older generations of Americans.

Only 10 percent of Americans are currently divorced

(percent distribution of people aged 15 or older by current marital status, 2010)

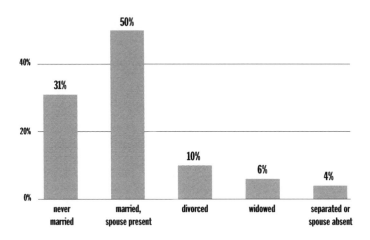

Table 7.24 Median Age at First Marriage by Sex, 1890 to 2010

(median age at first marriage by sex, selected years 1890 to 2010; change in years, 1890–1950 and 1950–2010)

	men	women
2010	28.2	26.1
2000	26.8	25.1
1990	26.1	23.9
1980	24.7	22.0
1970	23.2	20.8
1960	22.8	20.3
1950	22.8	20.3
1940	24.3	21.5
1930	24.3	21.3
1920	24.6	21.2
1910	25.1	21.6
1900	25.9	21.9
1890	26.1	22.0
Change in years		
1950 to 2010	5.4	5.8
1890 to 1950	–3.3	–1.7

Source: Bureau of the Census, Families and Living Arrangements, Historical Time Series, Internet site, http://www.census
.gov/population/www/socdemo/hh-fam.html; calculations by New Strategist

Table 7.25 Marital Status by Sex, 2010

(number and percent distribution of people aged 15 or older by marital status and sex, 2010; numbers in thousands)

	total	men	women
Total people	**242,047**	**117,686**	**124,361**
Never married	74,243	40,206	34,037
Married, spouse present	120,768	60,384	60,384
Married, spouse absent	3,415	1,789	1,626
Separated	5,539	2,352	3,187
Divorced	23,742	9,981	13,760
Widowed	14,341	2,974	11,368
PERCENT DISTRIBUTION BY MARITAL STATUS			
Total people	**100.0%**	**100.0%**	**100.0%**
Never married	30.7	34.2	27.4
Married, spouse present	49.9	51.3	48.6
Married, spouse absent	1.4	1.5	1.3
Separated	2.3	2.0	2.6
Divorced	9.8	8.5	11.1
Widowed	5.9	2.5	9.1
PERCENT DISTRIBUTION BY SEX			
Total people	**100.0%**	**48.6%**	**51.4%**
Never married	100.0	54.2	45.8
Married, spouse present	100.0	50.0	50.0
Married, spouse absent	100.0	52.4	47.6
Separated	100.0	42.5	57.5
Divorced	100.0	42.0	58.0
Widowed	100.0	20.7	79.3

Source: Bureau of the Census, America's Families and Living Arrangements: 2010, Current Population Survey Annual Social and Economic Supplement, Internet site http://www.census.gov/population/www/socdemo/hh-fam/cps2010.html; calculations by New Strategist

Table 7.26 Current Marital Status of Women, 2002

(total number of women aged 15 to 44, and percent distribution by current marital status, by selected characteristics, 2002; numbers in thousands)

	total number	total percent	never married	currently married total	currently married first marriage	currently married second or higher marriage	formerly married separated	formerly married divorced	formerly married widowed
Total women aged 15 to 44	**61,561**	**100.0%**	**41.8%**	**46.0%**	**37.5%**	**8.5%**	**3.0%**	**8.7%**	**0.4%**
Aged 15 to 19	9,834	100.0	97.6	2.0	2.0	0.0	0.3	0.1	0.0
Aged 20 to 24	9,840	100.0	72.7	23.1	22.6	0.5	2.1	2.0	0.1
Aged 25 to 29	9,249	100.0	39.8	51.6	47.7	4.0	3.0	5.3	0.3
Aged 30 to 34	10,272	100.0	22.4	61.8	54.1	7.8	5.6	9.9	0.2
Aged 35 to 39	10,853	100.0	16.7	64.4	49.5	14.9	3.3	14.7	0.9
Aged 40 to 44	11,512	100.0	10.1	67.2	46.3	20.9	3.6	18.0	1.0
Number of children ever borne									
None	25,622	100.0	75.2	20.1	18.1	2.0	0.9	3.7	0.1
One	11,193	100.0	28.9	56.8	47.9	9.0	3.2	10.4	0.6
Two	13,402	100.0	11.9	70.2	57.4	12.8	4.8	12.5	0.7
Three or more	11,343	100.0	14.2	65.4	47.6	17.8	5.7	14.0	0.7
Race and Hispanic origin									
Black, non-Hispanic	8,250	100.0	60.7	25.8	22.0	3.8	4.6	8.5	0.4
Hispanic	9,107	100.0	42.1	45.4	39.5	5.9	5.5	6.1	0.8
White, non-Hispanic	39,498	100.0	37.2	50.8	40.3	10.5	2.1	9.6	0.3
Education									
Not a high school graduate	5,627	100.0	32.2	49.1	39.0	10.2	8.1	9.4	1.2
High school graduate or GED	14,264	100.0	25.1	56.7	39.8	17.0	3.8	13.6	0.8
Some college, no degree	14,279	100.0	24.9	57.4	47.2	10.2	3.8	13.4	0.5
Bachelor's degree or more	13,551	100.0	28.2	62.9	57.0	5.9	1.7	7.0	0.2
Family structure at age 14									
Living with both parents	43,921	100.0	39.0	49.3	41.2	8.1	2.9	8.5	0.5
Other	17,640	100.0	48.9	38.0	28.3	9.7	3.3	9.4	0.3

Note: Education categories include only people aged 22 to 44.
Source: National Center for Health Statistics, Fertility, Family Planning, and Reproductive Health of U.S. Women: Data from the 2002 National Survey of Family Growth, Vital and Health Statistics, Series 23, No. 25, 2005, Internet site http://www.cdc .gov/nchs/nsfg.htm

Table 7.27 Current Marital Status of Men, 2002

(total number of men aged 15 to 44, and percent distribution by current marital status, by selected characteristics, 2002; numbers in thousands)

	total		never married	currently married			formerly married		
	number	percent		total	first marriage	second or higher marriage	separated	divorced	widowed
Total men aged 15 to 44	**61,147**	**100.0%**	**49.4%**	**42.2%**	**35.0%**	**7.2%**	**1.7%**	**6.6%**	**0.1%**
Aged 15 to 19	10,208	100.0	99.3	0.4	0.4	0.0	–	0.0	0.0
Aged 20 to 24	9,883	100.0	83.2	15.4	15.4	0.0	1.2	–	0.0
Aged 25 to 29	9,226	100.0	50.3	45.3	44.4	0.9	1.3	3.2	0.0
Aged 30 to 34	10,138	100.0	29.9	60.6	52.0	8.6	2.4	6.9	–
Aged 35 to 39	10,557	100.0	21.8	65.5	53.8	11.7	2.2	10.3	–
Aged 40 to 44	11,135	100.0	16.6	62.9	43.1	19.8	2.8	17.7	–
Number of biological children									
None	32,593	100.0	79.7	16.8	15.0	1.8	0.6	2.8	–
One	10,457	100.0	23.7	61.5	50.5	11.0	3.4	11.4	–
Two	9,829	100.0	9.4	76.3	67.6	8.7	3.2	11.0	–
Three or more	8,269	100.0	9.7	77.3	55.5	21.8	2.4	10.5	–
Race and Hispanic origin									
Black, non-Hispanic	6,940	100.0	58.3	31.5	24.9	6.6	2.8	7.1	–
Hispanic	10,188	100.0	50.3	42.7	38.6	4.1	2.5	4.5	0.0
White, non-Hispanic	38,738	100.0	46.8	44.4	36.2	8.2	1.5	7.3	–
Education									
Not a high school graduate	6,355	100.0	36.5	53.2	41.6	11.6	3.6	6.7	–
High school graduate or GED	15,659	100.0	31.1	53.9	41.1	12.8	2.8	12.0	–
Some college, no degree	13,104	100.0	41.3	48.7	40.7	8.0	1.6	8.3	–
Bachelor's degree or more	11,901	100.0	31.7	61.7	56.6	5.1	1.0	5.6	–
Family structure at age 14									
Living with both parents	45,166	100.0	48.5	43.8	36.5	7.3	1.7	6.0	0.1
Other	15,981	100.0	51.8	37.8	30.9	6.9	1.9	8.4	–

Note: Education categories include only people aged 22 to 44. "–" means sample is too small to make a reliable estimate.
Source: National Center for Health Statistics, Fertility, Contraception, and Fatherhood: Data on Men and Women from Cycle 6 of the 2002 National Survey of Family Growth, Vital and Health Statistics, Series 23, No. 26, 2006, Internet site http://www .cdc.gov/nchs/nsfg.htm

Husbands and Wives Are Alike in Many Ways

Most couples are close in age and education.

Women usually marry slightly older men, but most husbands and wives are close in age. Thirty-two percent are within one year of each other in age, and in another 21 percent the husband is only two to three years older than the wife. In only 1 percent of couples is the husband 20 or more years older than the wife.

In the 56 percent majority of married couples, neither spouse has a bachelor's degree. In another 21 percent, both husband and wife have a bachelor's degree. Only 23 percent of couples are educationally dissimilar, with one spouse having a bachelor's degree and the other having less education.

There are bigger differences between spouses by earnings. Only 25 percent of couples are within $4,999 of one another's earnings. For 54 percent of couples, the husband earns at least $5,000 more than his wife. In another 21 percent of couples, the wife earn at least $5,000 more than her husband.

Changing racial and ethnic categories make the analysis of interracial marriage a complex task. The Census Bureau estimates that 7 percent of married couples are of mixed race or Hispanic origin, numbering 4.5 million. No single type of mixed marriage accounts for more than 2 percent of all marriages.

■ The similarities between husbands and wives mean that well-educated high earners tend to marry one another, boosting incomes.

Most husbands and wives share the same educational level

(percent distribution of married couples by education of husband and wife, 2010)

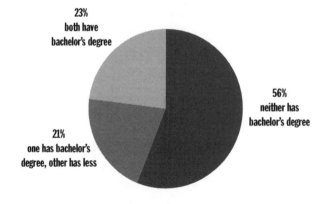

23%
both have
bachelor's degree

56%
neither has
bachelor's degree

21%
one has bachelor's
degree, other has less

Table 7.28 Age Difference between Husbands and Wives, 2010

(number and percent distribution of married-couple family groups by age difference between husband and wife, 2010; numbers in thousands)

	number	percent distribution
AGE DIFFERENCE		
Total married couples	**60,384**	**100.0%**
Husband 20 or more years older than wife	588	1.0
Husband 15 to 19 years older than wife	890	1.5
Husband 10 to 14 years older than wife	3,105	5.1
Husband 6 to 9 years older than wife	7,103	11.8
Husband 4 to 5 years older than wife	7,674	12.7
Husband 2 to 3 years older than wife	12,953	21.5
Husband and wife within 1 year	19,574	32.4
Wife 2 to 3 years older than husband	3,972	6.6
Wife 4 to 5 years older than husband	1,957	3.2
Wife 6 to 9 years older than husband	1,593	2.6
Wife 10 to 14 years older than husband	651	1.1
Wife 15 to 19 years older than husband	154	0.3
Wife 20 or more years older than husband	170	0.3

Note: Married-couple family groups include married-couple householders and married couples living in households headed by others.
Source: Bureau of the Census, America's Families and Living Arrangements: 2010, Current Population Survey Annual Social and Economic Supplement, Internet site http://www.census.gov/population/www/socdemo/hh-fam/cps2010.html; calculations by New Strategist

Table 7.29 Educational Difference between Husbands and Wives, 2010

(number and percent distribution of married-couple family groups by educational difference between husband and wife, 2010; numbers in thousands)

	number	percent distribution
EDUCATIONAL DIFFERENCE		
Total married couples	**60,384**	**100.0%**
Neither has bachelor's degree	33,843	56.0
One has bachelor's degree, other has less	12,841	21.3
Both have bachelor's degree	13,701	22.7

Note: Married-couple family groups include married-couple householders and married couples living in households headed by others.
Source: Bureau of the Census, America's Families and Living Arrangements: 2010, Current Population Survey Annual Social and Economic Supplement, Internet site http://www.census.gov/population/www/socdemo/hh-fam/cps2010.html; calculations by New Strategist

Table 7.30 Earnings Difference between Husbands and Wives, 2010

(number and percent distribution of married-couple family groups by earnings difference between husbands and wives, 2010; numbers in thousands)

	number	percent distribution
Total married couples	**60,384**	**100.0%**
Husband earns at least $50,000 more than wife	12,171	20.2
Husband earns $30,000 to $49,999 more than wife	7,556	12.5
Husband earns $10,000 to $29,999 more than wife	10,356	17.2
Husband earns $5,000 to $9,999 more than wife	2,714	4.5
Husband earns within $4,999 of wife	15,087	25.0
Wife earns $5,000 to $9,999 more than husband	2,062	3.4
Wife earns $10,000 to $29,999 more than husband	5,554	9.2
Wife earns $30,000 to $49,999 more than husband	2,649	4.4
Wife earns at least $50,000 more than husband	2,235	3.7

Note: Married-couple family groups include married-couple householders and married couples living in households headed by others.
Source: Bureau of the Census, America's Families and Living Arrangements: 2010, Current Population Survey Annual Social and Economic Supplement, Internet site http://www.census.gov/population/www/socdemo/hh-fam/cps2010.html; calculations by New Strategist

Table 7.31 Race and Hispanic Origin Differences between Husband and Wife, 2010

(number and percent distribution of married-couple family groups by race and Hispanic origin differences between husband and wife, 2010; numbers in thousands)

	number	percent distribution
Total married-couple family groups	**60,384**	**100.0%**
Both non-Hispanic white	42,611	70.6
Both Hispanic	6,166	10.2
Both non-Hispanic black	3,869	6.4
Both non-Hispanic other	3,231	5.4
Mixed race/Hispanic origin couples	4,507	7.5
Husband non-Hispanic white, wife non-Hispanic black	147	0.2
Husband non-Hispanic white, wife Hispanic	1,043	1.7
Husband non-Hispanic white, wife non-Hispanic other	940	1.6
Husband non-Hispanic black, wife non-Hispanic white	357	0.6
Husband non-Hispanic black, wife Hispanic	92	0.2
Husband non-Hispanic black, wife non-Hispanic other	103	0.2
Husband Hispanic, wife non-Hispanic white	962	1.6
Husband Hispanic, wife non-Hispanic black	37	0.1
Husband Hispanic, wife non-Hispanic other	88	0.1
Husband non-Hispanic other, wife non-Hispanic white	644	1.1
Husband non-Hispanic other, wife non-Hispanic black	25	0.0
Husband non-Hispanic other, wife Hispanic	69	0.1

Note: "Other" race category includes Asians and American Indians. Hispanics may be of any race. Married-couple family groups include married-couple householders and married couples living in households headed by others.
Source: Bureau of the Census, America's Families and Living Arrangements: 2010, Current Population Survey Annual Social and Economic Supplement, Internet site http://www.census.gov/population/www/socdemo/hh-fam/cps2010.html; calculations by New Strategist

Divorce Is Highest among Men and Women in Their Fifties and Sixties

The oldest boomers are most likely to have gone through a divorce.

The experience of divorce is most common among men and women aged 50 to 69. From 35 to 37 percent of men and women in the age group had ever divorced, according to a Census Bureau study of marriage and divorce. Among all Americans aged 15 or older, 41 percent of women and 43 percent of men had married once and were still married. The figure topped 50 percent for men aged 35 or older and for women aged 30 to 49.

Among ever-married women aged 15 to 44 in 2002 (the latest data available), a substantial 35 percent have seen their first marriage dissolve, according to a survey by the National Center for Health Statistics. For men, the figure is 31 percent. Marital problems are much more likely for those marrying at a young age. Among women who married for the first time before age 18, the 63 percent majority has seen the marriage dissolve. For men who married for the first time before age 20, fully 59 percent have seen the marriage end.

■ Government studies have suggested that the Vietnam War and women's changing roles are factors in the higher divorce rates of boomers.

One in five adults has experienced divorce

(percent of people aged 15 or older, by selected marital history and sex, 2009)

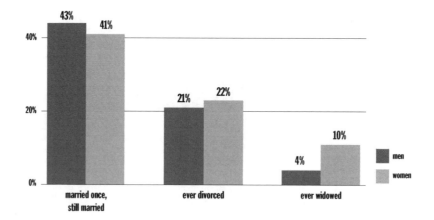

Table 7.32 Marital History of Women by Age, 2009

(number of women aged 15 or older and percent distribution by marital history and age, 2009; numbers in thousands)

	total	15–19	20–24	25–29	30–34	35–39	40–49	50–59	60–69	70+
Total women, number	123,272	10,478	10,158	10,408	9,645	10,267	22,119	20,702	14,288	15,207
Total women, percent	100.0%	100.0%	100.0%	100.0%	100.0%	100.0%	100.0%	100.0%	100.0%	100.0%
Never married	27.2	97.5	77.3	46.8	26.7	17.3	13.0	9.1	6.0	4.3
Ever married	72.8	2.5	22.7	53.2	73.3	82.7	87.0	90.9	94.0	95.7
Married once	57.5	2.5	22.4	50.8	64.5	69.3	67.4	65.5	67.7	76.1
Still married	40.6	1.9	19.7	43.2	54.5	55.8	51.6	47.5	45.7	30.1
Married twice	12.1	0.1	0.3	2.3	8.0	11.6	15.8	19.5	20.1	15.2
Still married	7.9	0.6	0.2	2.0	6.9	9.1	11.3	13.4	13.2	5.2
Married three or more times	3.2	0.0	0.0	0.0	0.8	1.9	3.8	5.9	6.2	4.4
Still married	1.9	0.0	0.0	0.0	0.7	1.4	2.5	4.1	3.6	1.4
Ever divorced	22.4	0.2	1.8	7.3	15.6	22.7	31.0	37.3	34.5	21.4
Currently divorced	11.3	0.1	1.5	5.3	8.1	11.8	16.4	18.6	16.0	9.9
Ever widowed	10.0	0.3	0.1	0.2	0.6	1.4	2.6	6.5	17.0	51.2
Currently widowed	8.9	0.3	0.1	0.1	0.4	0.8	1.8	4.9	13.9	48.3

Source: Bureau of the Census, Number, Timing, and Duration of Marriages and Divorces: 2009, Current Population Reports P70-125, 2011, Internet site http://www.census.gov/hhes/socdemo/marriage/data/sipp/index.html; calculations by New Strategist

Table 7.33 Marital History of Men by Age, 2009

(number of men aged 15 or older and percent distribution by marital history and age, 2009; numbers in thousands)

	total	15–19	20–24	25–29	30–34	35–39	40–49	50–59	60–69	70+
Total men, number	115,797	10,870	10,152	10,567	9,518	9,995	21,504	19,568	12,774	10,849
Total men, percent	100.0%	100.0%	100.0%	100.0%	100.0%	100.0%	100.0%	100.0%	100.0%	100.0%
Never married	33.0	98.0	87.5	59.7	35.6	23.5	16.4	10.8	4.6	3.4
Ever married	67.0	2.0	12.5	40.3	64.4	76.5	83.6	89.2	95.4	96.6
Married once	52.3	1.9	12.5	38.8	59.4	66.9	65.8	63.4	64.8	72.3
Still married	42.5	1.3	11.2	34.2	52.2	56.1	52.2	50.4	53.5	54.0
Married twice	11.6	0.1	0.0	1.5	4.8	8.7	14.8	20.0	22.1	18.9
Still married	9.0	0.1	0.0	1.3	4.0	7.4	11.3	15.5	17.5	13.2
Married three or more times	3.1	0.0	0.0	0.1	0.2	1.0	3.0	5.8	8.5	5.4
Still married	2.3	0.0	0.0	0.1	0.2	0.8	2.2	4.3	6.5	3.8
Ever divorced	20.5	0.3	0.8	5.0	10.5	17.9	28.5	35.7	36.5	23.4
Currently divorced	9.1	0.2	0.7	3.7	6.2	9.5	14.2	15.5	12.4	7.2
Ever widowed	3.6	0.4	0.1	0.3	0.2	0.5	1.3	2.5	6.4	22.6
Currently widowed	2.6	0.3	0.1	0.3	0.1	0.3	0.9	1.6	3.9	17.4

Source: Bureau of the Census, Number, Timing, and Duration of Marriages and Divorces: 2009, Current Population Reports P70-125, 2011, Internet site http://www.census.gov/hhes/socdemo/marriage/data/sipp/index.html; calculations by New Strategist

Table 7.34 Cumulative Percentage of Women Whose First Marriage Has Dissolved, 2002

(number of ever-married women aged 15 to 44 and cumulative percentage of women whose first marriage dissolved through separation, annulment, or divorce, by selected characteristics and years since first marriage, 2002; numbers in thousands)

	total		years since first marriage			
	number	percent	one year	five years	ten years	all marital durations
Total ever-married women aged 15 to 44	**35,849**	**100.0%**	**5.5%**	**19.9%**	**29.1%**	**34.7%**
Age at first marriage						
Under age 18	2,983	100.0	6.7	34.2	48.1	62.6
Aged 18 to 19	6,155	100.0	10.4	28.3	39.1	50.1
Aged 20 to 22	10,094	100.0	5.6	21.5	31.9	37.8
Aged 23 or older	16,617	100.0	3.5	13.3	20.2	22.0
First cohabitation relative to first marriage						
Did not cohabit before first marriage	18,572	100.0	5.0	18.4	28.6	35.3
Cohabited with first husband	13,385	100.0	6.1	22.2	30.9	35.9
Cohabited with someone else	3,892	100.0	6.3	19.2	25.2	27.1
Race and Hispanic origin						
Black, non-Hispanic	3,242	100.0	7.7	23.9	37.1	42.8
Hispanic	5,269	100.0	4.7	17.4	25.6	30.0
White, non-Hispanic	24,817	100.0	5.1	19.6	28.9	35.1
Education						
Not a high school graduate	3,816	100.0	7.6	23.5	31.7	40.6
High school graduate or GED	10,691	100.0	7.0	25.0	38.2	45.4
Some college, no degree	10,728	100.0	5.5	21.3	31.3	36.4
Bachelor's degree or more	9,728	100.0	2.9	11.8	17.0	20.3
Family structure at age 14						
Living with both parents	26,839	100.0	5.1	18.0	25.8	31.6
Other	9,009	100.0	6.9	25.6	38.8	43.8

Note: Education categories include only people aged 22 to 44.
Source: National Center for Health Statistics, Fertility, Family Planning, and Reproductive Health of U.S. Women: Data from the 2002 National Survey of Family Growth, Vital and Health Statistics, Series 23, No. 25, 2005, Internet site http://www.cdc.gov/nchs/nsfg.htm

Table 7.35 Cumulative Percentage of Men Whose First Marriage Has Dissolved, 2002

(number of ever-married men aged 15 to 44 and cumulative percentage of men whose first marriage dissolved through separation, annulment, or divorce, by selected characteristics and years since first marriage, 2002; numbers in thousands)

	total		years since first marriage			
	number	percent	one year	five years	ten years	all marital durations
Total ever-married men aged 15 to 44	**30,972**	**100.0%**	**5.8%**	**19.3%**	**26.7%**	**30.6%**
Age at first marriage						
Under age 20	3,854	100.0	15.8	42.6	50.2	58.6
Aged 20 to 22	7,249	100.0	6.3	20.8	30.1	35.5
Aged 23 to 25	8,101	100.0	5.0	19.3	27.2	29.8
Aged 25 or older	11,767	100.0	2.7	10.8	16.7	18.9
First cohabitation relative to first marriage						
Did not cohabit before first marriage	13,649	100.0	5.9	18.8	25.5	29.8
Cohabited with first wife	12,734	100.0	5.4	20.7	28.0	31.8
Cohabited with someone else	4,566	100.0	5.8	16.8	26.5	29.2
Race and Hispanic origin						
Black, non-Hispanic	2,894	100.0	5.6	22.8	34.8	39.2
Hispanic	5,064	100.0	5.2	15.3	19.7	22.3
White, non-Hispanic	20,611	100.0	5.5	19.8	27.7	31.8
Education						
Not a high school graduate	4,037	100.0	9.7	26.2	32.0	34.4
High school graduate or GED	10,793	100.0	6.1	23.0	33.9	39.9
Some college, no degree	7,695	100.0	5.6	19.7	27.6	30.5
Bachelor's degree or more	8,131	100.0	3.3	10.8	14.2	17.0
Family structure at age 14						
Living with both parents	23,270	100.0	5.5	17.9	24.5	29.0
Other	7,702	100.0	6.5	23.7	33.5	35.5

Note: Education categories include only people aged 22 to 44.
Source: National Center for Health Statistics, Fertility, Contraception, and Fatherhood: Data on Men and Women from Cycle 6 of the 2002 National Survey of Family Growth, Vital and Health Statistics, Series 23, No. 26, 2006, Internet site http://www.cdc .gov/nchs/nsfg.htm

Same-Sex Couples Estimated by Demographers

A study of Census Bureau data finds more than half a million households headed by same-sex couples in the United States.

An analysis of American Community Survey data by demographers finds 581,300 same-sex couples in the United States as of 2009. This figure includes 280,410 male couples and 300,890 female couples.

On average, same-sex couples are a bit younger than married couples, but significantly older than unmarried opposite-sex couples. They are better educated than opposite-sex couples. Fewer than one in five same-sex couples has children under age 18 living in the household compared with a larger 42 percent of opposite-sex couples. Female same-sex couples are about as affluent as opposite-sex married couples (average income of $92,213 and $93,351, respectively). Male same-sex couples are far more affluent than opposite-sex married couples, with an average income of $116,749.

■ Same-sex couples are found in every state, with the largest number in the most populous states such as California, Florida, New York, and Texas.

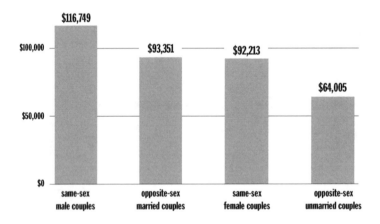

Same-sex couples are relatively affluent

(average income of couples, by type, 2009)

Table 7.36 Characteristics of Opposite-Sex and Same-Sex Couple Households, 2009

(number of households with opposite and same-sex spouses or partners and percent distribution by selected characteristics, 2009)

| | opposite-sex couples | | same-sex couples | | |
	married	unmarried	total	male	female
Total couples	**55,811,477**	**5,920,821**	**581,300**	**280,410**	**300,890**
Age of householder					
Under age 25	1.7%	15.2%	4.3%	3.7%	4.8%
Aged 25 to 34	14.2	35.5	16.8	16.5	17.1
Aged 35 to 44	21.5	20.8	25.1	26.9	23.3
Aged 45 to 54	24.0	16.1	27.7	28.1	27.4
Aged 55 to 64	19.8	8.1	15.2	15.3	15.1
Aged 65 or older	18.8	4.3	10.9	9.4	12.3
Average age of householder (years)	50.5	37.6	46.6	46.1	47.0
Average age of spouse/partner (years)	49.5	36.8	44.7	44.1	45.3
Race and Hispanic origin					
Asian	4.7%	2.0%	2.3%	2.7%	1.9%
Black	6.8	11.7	6.4	5.3	7.5
Hispanic	11.3	17.0	9.5	10.0	9.0
Non-Hispanic white	75.7	66.7	80.1	80.7	79.5
Educational attainment					
Householder has at least a bachelor's degree	34.8	20.6	47.6	49.9	45.5
Both partners have at least a bachelor's degree	21.4	10.3	30.1	29.8	30.3
Employment status					
Householder employed	68.7	76.2	75.8	77.3	74.3
Both partners employed	48.6	56.1	60.1	61.4	58.9
Children in the household	**42.0**	**42.1**	**18.1**	**11.8**	**23.9**
Household income					
Under $35,000	17.1	31.8	15.6	13.2	17.9
$35,000 to $49,999	13.1	17.2	10.7	9.8	11.5
$50,000 to $74,999	21.2	22.1	19.3	17.9	20.6
$75,000 to $99,999	16.8	13.2	15.5	15.0	16.0
$100,000 or more	31.7	15.7	38.9	44.1	34.0
Average household income	**$93,351**	**$64,005**	**$104,048**	**$116,749**	**$92,213**
Housing tenure					
Owner	81.9%	44.0%	70.5%	69.6%	71.2%
Renter	18.1	56.0	29.5	30.4	28.8

Source: Census Bureau, 2009 American Community Survey, Internet site http://www.census.gov/population/www/socdemo/hh-fam.html

Table 7.37 Same-Sex Couple Households by State, 2009

(number and percent distribution of households headed by same-sex couples by state, 2009)

	number	percent distribution		number	percent distribution
United States total	**581,300**	**100.0%**	Missouri	9,691	1.7%
Alabama	4,527	0.8	Montana	1,184	0.2
Alaska	1,136	0.2	Nebraska	2,052	0.4
Arizona	14,375	2.5	Nevada	5,504	0.9
Arkansas	3,769	0.6	New Hampshire	2,966	0.5
California	81,954	14.1	New Jersey	14,838	2.6
Colorado	12,558	2.2	New Mexico	4,172	0.7
Connecticut	6,698	1.2	New York	42,618	7.3
Delaware	2,677	0.5	North Carolina	17,042	2.9
District of Columbia	4,479	0.8	North Dakota	875	0.2
Florida	41,847	7.2	Ohio	21,416	3.7
Georgia	18,263	3.1	Oklahoma	5,438	0.9
Hawaii	3,507	0.6	Oregon	12,258	2.1
Idaho	2,065	0.4	Pennsylvania	22,086	3.8
Illinois	23,397	4.0	Rhode Island	2,097	0.4
Indiana	10,948	1.9	South Carolina	7,363	1.3
Iowa	4,299	0.7	South Dakota	802	0.1
Kansas	4,063	0.7	Tennessee	10,377	1.8
Kentucky	6,934	1.2	Texas	39,289	6.8
Louisiana	5,083	0.9	Utah	3,478	0.6
Maine	4,369	0.8	Vermont	2,013	0.3
Maryland	10,058	1.7	Virginia	12,795	2.2
Massachusetts	20,056	3.5	Washington	15,290	2.6
Michigan	13,512	2.3	West Virginia	2,259	0.4
Minnesota	10,464	1.8	Wisconsin	9,773	1.7
Mississippi	2,028	0.3	Wyoming	558	0.1

Source: Census Bureau, 2009 American Community Survey, Internet site http://www.census.gov/population/www/socdemo/ hh-fam.html

8

Population Trends

■ **The number of people in their sixties is growing rapidly.**

The 60-to-64 age group grew the fastest between 2000 and 2010—up 56 percent as the oldest boomers entered their sixties.

■ **The non-Hispanic white population is growing slowly.**

Between 2000 and 2010, the non-Hispanic white population grew by only 1.2 percent. Sixty-four percent of Americans are non-Hispanic white, down from 69 percent in 2000.

■ **In four states, minorities are the majority.**

In California, the nation's most populous state, only 40 percent of residents are non-Hispanic white, according to the 2010 census. In the nation's second most-populous state, Texas, non-Hispanic whites accounted for only 45 percent of the population.

■ **In 2010, 51 metropolitan areas had more than 1 million residents.**

New York is by far the largest metropolitan area, and minorities account for more than half of its population.

■ **The mobility rate is close to a record low.**

Among homeowners, the mobility rate has never been lower. Only 5.2 percent of homeowners moved between 2009 and 2010.

■ **Most immigrants settle in only five states.**

California, New York, Florida, Texas, and New Jersey receive most of the nation's immigrants.

More Women than Men

Females outnumber males by more than 5 million.

Although there are more females than males in the population, females do not begin to outnumber males until the 35-to-39 age group. Among people aged 85 or older, there are only 48 men for every 100 women. Males slightly outnumber females at younger ages because boys outnumber girls at birth. Women outnumber men at older ages because, throughout life, males have higher death rates than females. Research has shown that higher male death rates are due primarily to biological factors rather than lifestyle differences.

Between 2000 and 2010, the U.S. population grew by 10 percent, to more than 308 million. The most populous five-year age group is 45 to 49, numbering nearly 23 million in 2010. This age group is larger than any other because it is filled with the youngest members of the baby-boom generation. The 60-to-64 age group grew the fastest between 2000 and 2010—up 56 percent as the oldest boomers aged into their sixties. Another relatively large generation is now entering adulthood. Millennials, spanning the ages from 16 to 33 in 2010, are behind the 9 to 14 percent increase in the number of 20-to-29-year-olds since 2000.

■ Because death rates are higher for males than for females, women will always greatly outnumber men in old age.

Women increasingly outnumber men with age

(number of males per 100 females at selected ages, 2010)

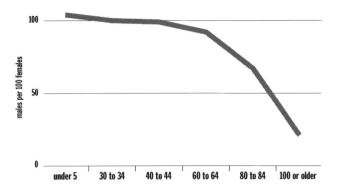

Table 8.1 Population by Age and Sex, 2010

(number of people by age and sex, and sex ratio by age, 2010)

	total	female	male	sex ratio
Total people	**308,745,538**	**156,964,212**	**151,781,326**	**97**
Under age 5	20,201,362	9,881,935	10,319,427	104
Aged 5 to 9	20,348,657	9,959,019	10,389,638	104
Aged 10 to 14	20,677,194	10,097,332	10,579,862	105
Aged 15 to 19	22,040,343	10,736,677	11,303,666	105
Aged 20 to 24	21,585,999	10,571,823	11,014,176	104
Aged 25 to 29	21,101,849	10,466,258	10,635,591	102
Aged 30 to 34	19,962,099	9,965,599	9,996,500	100
Aged 35 to 39	20,179,642	10,137,620	10,042,022	99
Aged 40 to 44	20,890,964	10,496,987	10,393,977	99
Aged 45 to 49	22,708,591	11,499,506	11,209,085	97
Aged 50 to 54	22,298,125	11,364,851	10,933,274	96
Aged 55 to 59	19,664,805	10,141,157	9,523,648	94
Aged 60 to 64	16,817,924	8,740,424	8,077,500	92
Aged 65 or older	40,267,984	22,905,024	17,362,960	76
Aged 65 to 69	12,435,263	6,582,716	5,852,547	89
Aged 70 to 74	9,278,166	5,034,194	4,243,972	84
Aged 75 to 79	7,317,795	4,135,407	3,182,388	77
Aged 80 to 84	5,743,327	3,448,953	2,294,374	67
Aged 85 or older	5,493,433	3,703,754	1,789,679	48
Aged 85 to 89	3,620,459	2,346,592	1,273,867	54
Aged 90 to 94	1,448,366	1,023,979	424,387	41
Aged 95 to 99	371,244	288,981	82,263	28
Aged 100 or older	53,364	44,202	9,162	21
Median age (years)	37.2	38.5	35.8	–

Note: The sex ratio is the number of men per 100 women; "–" means not applicable.
Source: Bureau of the Census, Age and Sex Composition: 2010, 2010 Census Briefs, Internet site http://2010.census.gov/2010census/data/; calculations by New Strategist

Table 8.2 Population by Age, 2000 and 2010

(number of people by age, 2000 and 2010, and percent change, 2000–10)

	2010	2000	percent change
Total people	**308,745,538**	**281,421,906**	**9.7%**
Under age 5	20,201,362	19,175,798	5.3
Aged 5 to 9	20,348,657	20,549,505	−1.0
Aged 10 to 14	20,677,194	20,528,072	0.7
Aged 15 to 19	22,040,343	20,219,890	9.0
Aged 20 to 24	21,585,999	18,964,001	13.8
Aged 25 to 29	21,101,849	19,381,336	8.9
Aged 30 to 34	19,962,099	20,510,388	−2.7
Aged 35 to 39	20,179,642	22,706,664	−11.1
Aged 40 to 44	20,890,964	22,441,863	−6.9
Aged 45 to 49	22,708,591	20,092,404	13.0
Aged 50 to 54	22,298,125	17,585,548	26.8
Aged 55 to 59	19,664,805	13,469,237	46.0
Aged 60 to 64	16,817,924	10,805,447	55.6
Aged 65 to 69	12,435,263	9,533,545	30.4
Aged 70 to 74	9,278,166	8,857,441	4.7
Aged 75 to 79	7,317,795	7,415,813	−1.3
Aged 80 to 84	5,743,327	4,945,367	16.1
Aged 85 to 89	3,620,459	2,789,818	29.8
Aged 90 to 94	1,448,366	1,112,531	30.2
Aged 95 to 99	371,244	286,784	29.5
Aged 100 or older	53,364	50,454	5.8
Aged 18 to 24	30,672,088	27,143,454	13.0
Aged 18 or older	234,564,071	209,128,094	12.2
Aged 65 or older	40,267,984	34,991,753	15.1
Median age (years)	37.2	35.3	−

Note: Numbers are for April 1 of each year; "−" means not applicable.
Source: Bureau of the Census, Age and Sex Composition: 2010, 2010 Census Briefs, Internet site http://2010.census.gov/2010census/data/; calculations by New Strategist

The Non-Hispanic White Population Is Growing Slowly

Minorities account for nearly half of children and young adults.

The United States is a nation of diversity, according to 2010 census results. Only 64 percent of Americans are non-Hispanic white, down from 69 percent in 2000. The majority non-Hispanic white population grew by only 1.2 percent between 2000 and 2010. This compares with a 43 percent increase in the Asian (alone) population and an identical 43 percent increase in the Hispanic population. The black (alone) population increased by 12 percent. The mixed-race population—people who identify themselves as being of two or more races—grew by 32 percent.

Hispanic origin is an ethnic identity, not a race. In fact, Hispanics may be of any race. Because many Hispanics see things differently, however, a substantial 37 percent of Hispanics identified themselves as "other race" when they did not see "Hispanic" as a racial option on the 2010 census questionnaire. Most "other race" Hispanics are white.

According to the Census Bureau's estimates of the population by age, race, and Hispanic origin for 2009 (age data from the 2010 census were not available at the time of publication), the non-Hispanic white share of the population varies greatly by age. It ranges from a low of 52 percent among children under age 5 to a high of 80 percent among people aged 65 or older.

■ Among the mixed-race population, those who identify themselves as black *and* white are the largest and fastest-growing group.

The non-Hispanic white population barely grew between 2000 and 2010

(percent change in population by race and Hispanic origin, 2000–10)

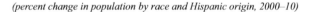

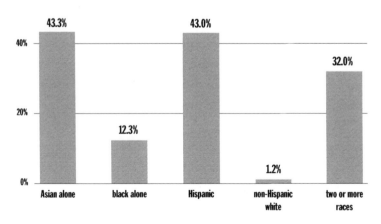

Table 8.3 Population by Race and Hispanic Origin, 2000 and 2010

(number of people by race and Hispanic origin, 2000 and 2010; numerical and percent change, 2000–10)

	2010		2000		change	
	number	percent distribution	number	percent distribution	numerical	percent
Total population	**308,745,538**	**100.0%**	**281,421,906**	**100.0%**	**27,323,632**	**9.7%**
Race alone						
American Indian	2,932,248	0.9	2,475,956	0.9	456,292	18.4
Asian	14,674,252	4.8	10,242,998	3.6	4,431,254	43.3
Black	38,929,319	12.6	34,658,190	12.3	4,271,129	12.3
Native Hawaiian	540,013	0.2	398,835	0.1	141,178	35.4
White	223,553,265	72.4	211,460,626	75.1	12,092,639	5.7
Other race	19,107,368	6.2	15,359,073	5.5	3,748,295	24.4
Two or more races	**9,009,073**	**2.9**	**6,826,228**	**2.4**	**2,182,845**	**32.0**
Race alone or in combination						
American Indian	5,220,579	1.7	4,225,058	1.5	995,521	23.6
Asian	17,320,856	5.6	12,006,894	4.3	5,313,962	44.3
Black	42,020,743	13.6	37,104,248	13.2	4,916,495	13.3
Native Hawaiian	1,225,195	0.4	906,785	0.3	318,410	35.1
White	231,040,398	74.8	231,434,388	82.2	–393,990	–0.2
Hispanic	**50,477,594**	**16.3**	**35,305,818**	**12.5**	**15,171,776**	**43.0**
Non-Hispanic white	**196,817,552**	**63.7**	**194,552,774**	**69.1**	**2,264,778**	**1.2**

Note: Numbers by race in combination do not add to total because they include those who identify themselves as being of the race alone and those who identify themselves as being of the race in combination with other races. Hispanics may be of any race. Non-Hispanic whites are those who identify themselves as being white alone and not Hispanic. Numbers are for April 1 of each year.
Source: Bureau of the Census, An Overview: Race and Hispanic Origin and the 2010 Census, 2010 Census Briefs, Internet site http://2010.census.gov/2010census/data/; calculations by New Strategist

Table 8.4 Two-or-More-Races Population, 2010

(number and percent of people who identify themselves as being of two or more races, by racial identification, 2010)

	number	percent distribution
TOTAL POPULATION	**308,745,538**	**100.0%**
One race	**299,736,465**	**97.1**
White	223,553,265	72.4
Black	38,929,319	12.6
American Indian	2,932,248	0.9
Asian	14,674,252	4.8
Native Hawaiian	540,013	0.2
Other race	19,107,368	6.2
Two races	**8,265,318**	**2.7**
White and black	1,834,212	0.6
White and American Indian	1,432,309	0.5
White and Asian	1,623,234	0.5
White and Native Hawaiian	169,991	0.1
White and some other race	1,740,924	0.6
Black and American Indian	269,421	0.1
Black and Asian	185,595	0.1
Black and Native Hawaiian	50,308	0.0
Black and other race	314,571	0.1
American Indian and Asian	58,829	0.0
American Indian and Native Hawaiian	11,039	0.0
American Indian and other race	115,752	0.0
Asian and Native Hawaiian	165,690	0.1
Asian and other race	234,462	0.1
Native Hawaiian and other race	58,981	0.0
Three races	**676,469**	**0.2**
White, black, and American Indian	230,848	0.1
White, black, and Asian	61,511	0.0
White, black, and Native Hawaiian	9,245	0.0
White, black, and other race	46,641	0.0
White, American Indian, and Asian	45,960	0.0
White, American Indian, and Native Hawaiian	8,656	0.0
White, American Indian, and other race	30,941	0.0
White, Asian, and Native Hawaiian	143,126	0.0
White, Asian, and other race	35,786	0.0
White, Native Hawaiian, and other race	9,181	100.0%
Black, American Indian, and Asian	9,460	0.0
Black, American Indian, and Native Hawaiian	2,142	0.0
Black, American Indian, and other race	8,236	0.0
Black, Asian, and Native Hawaiian	7,295	0.0
Black, Asian, and other race	8,122	0.0

	number	percent distribution
Black, Native Hawaiian, and other race	4,233	0.0%
American Indian, Asian, and Native Hawaiian	3,827	0.0
American Indian, Asian, and other race	3,785	0.0
American Indian, Native Hawaiian, and other race	2,000	0.0
Asian, Native Hawaiian, and other race	5,474	0.0
Four races	**57,875**	**0.0**
White, black, American Indian, and Asian	19,018	0.0
White, black, American Indian, and Native Hawaiian	2,673	0.0
White, black, American Indian, and other race	8,757	0.0
White, black, Asian, and Native Hawaiian	4,852	0.0
White, black, Asian, and other race	2,420	0.0
White, black, Native Hawaiian, and other race	560	0.0
White, American Indian, Asian, and Native Hawaiian	11,500	0.0
White, American Indian, Asian, and other race	1,535	0.0
White, American Indian, Native Hawaiian, and other race	454	0.0
White, Asian, Native Hawaiian, and other race	3,486	0.0
Black, American Indian, Asian, and Native Hawaiian	1,011	0.0
Black, American Indian, Asian, and other race	539	0.0
Black, American Indian, Native Hawaiian, and other race	212	0.0
Black, Asian, Native Hawaiian, and other race	574	0.0
American Indian, Asian, Native Hawaiian, and other race	284	0.0
Five races	**8,619**	**0.0**
White, black, American Indian, Asian, and Native Hawaiian	6,605	0.0
White, black, American Indian, Asian, and other race	1,023	0.0
White, black, American Indian, Native Hawaiian, and other race	182	0.0
White, black, Asian, Native Hawaiian, and other race	268	0.0
White, American Indian, Asian, Native Hawaiian, and other race	443	0.0
Black, American Indian, Asian, Native Hawaiian, and other race	98	0.0
Six races	**792**	**0.0**
White, black, American Indian, Asian, Native Hawaiian, and other race	792	0.0

Note: Most who identify themselves as "other race" are Hispanics who consider Hispanic a race rather than an ethnicity. Census racial categories are shown in the order provided by the Census Bureau. For readability, the names of some census racial categories have been shortened. Blacks include those who identify themselves as African American; American Indians include Alaska Natives; Native Hawaiians include other Pacific Islanders.
Source: Bureau of the Census, An Overview: Race and Hispanic Origin and the 2010 Census, 2010 Census Briefs, Internet site http://2010.census.gov/2010census/data/

Table 8.5 Hispanics and Non-Hispanics by Race, 2010

(number and percent distribution of Hispanics and non-Hispanics by race, 2010; numbers in thousands)

	Hispanics		non-Hispanics	
	number	percent distribution	number	percent of distribution
Total population	**50,477,594**	**100.0%**	**258,267,944**	**100.0%**
Race alone				
American Indian	685,150	1.4	2,247,098	0.9
Asian	209,128	0.4	14,465,124	5.6
Black	1,243,471	2.5	37,685,848	14.6
Native Hawaiian	58,437	0.1	481,576	0.2
White	26,735,713	53.0	196,817,552	76.2
Other race	18,503,103	36.7	604,265	0.2
Two or more races	**3,042,592**	**6.0**	**5,966,481**	**2.3**

Note: Hispanics may be of any race.
Source: Bureau of the Census, An Overview: Race and Hispanic Origin and the 2010 Census, 2010 Census Briefs, Internet site http://2010.census.gov/2010census/data/; calculations by New Strategist

Table 8.6 Population by Age, Race, and Hispanic Origin, 2009

(number and percent distribution of people by age, race, and Hispanic origin, 2009)

	total	Asian	black	Hispanic	non-Hispanic white
Total people	307,006,550	15,989,876	41,804,073	48,419,324	199,851,240
Under age 5	21,299,656	1,324,610	3,665,743	5,484,770	11,015,942
Aged 5 to 9	20,609,634	1,224,385	3,360,097	4,792,409	11,275,215
Aged 10 to 14	19,973,564	1,064,448	3,336,589	4,059,590	11,516,062
Aged 15 to 19	21,537,837	1,046,803	3,693,533	4,031,986	12,707,408
Aged 20 to 24	21,539,559	1,082,709	3,424,321	3,883,925	13,046,112
Aged 25 to 29	21,677,719	1,277,866	3,233,759	4,149,692	12,927,386
Aged 30 to 34	19,888,603	1,352,729	2,817,172	4,029,775	11,646,269
Aged 35 to 39	20,538,351	1,387,280	2,806,264	3,757,576	12,535,066
Aged 40 to 44	20,991,605	1,208,863	2,782,519	3,306,453	13,615,945
Aged 45 to 49	22,831,092	1,118,181	2,895,949	2,893,985	15,794,375
Aged 50 to 54	21,761,391	992,591	2,625,762	2,273,831	15,727,167
Aged 55 to 59	18,975,026	841,936	2,135,788	1,720,174	14,144,970
Aged 60 to 64	15,811,923	652,282	1,572,724	1,274,195	12,197,748
Aged 65 or older	39,570,590	1,415,193	3,453,853	2,760,963	31,701,575

PERCENT DISTRIBUTION BY RACE AND HISPANIC ORIGIN

Total people	**100.0%**	**5.2%**	**13.6%**	**15.8%**	**65.1%**
Under age 5	100.0	6.2	17.2	25.8	51.7
Aged 5 to 9	100.0	5.9	16.3	23.3	54.7
Aged 10 to 14	100.0	5.3	16.7	20.3	57.7
Aged 15 to 19	100.0	4.9	17.1	18.7	59.0
Aged 20 to 24	100.0	5.0	15.9	18.0	60.6
Aged 25 to 29	100.0	5.9	14.9	19.1	59.6
Aged 30 to 34	100.0	6.8	14.2	20.3	58.6
Aged 35 to 39	100.0	6.8	13.7	18.3	61.0
Aged 40 to 44	100.0	5.8	13.3	15.8	64.9
Aged 45 to 49	100.0	4.9	12.7	12.7	69.2
Aged 50 to 54	100.0	4.6	12.1	10.4	72.3
Aged 55 to 59	100.0	4.4	11.3	9.1	74.5
Aged 60 to 64	100.0	4.1	9.9	8.1	77.1
Aged 65 or older	100.0	3.6	8.7	7.0	80.1

	total	Asian	black	Hispanic	non-Hispanic white
PERCENT DISTRIBUTION BY AGE					
Total people	**100.0%**	**100.0%**	**100.0%**	**100.0%**	**100.0%**
Under age 5	6.9	8.3	8.8	11.3	5.5
Aged 5 to 9	6.7	7.7	8.0	9.9	5.6
Aged 10 to 14	6.5	6.7	8.0	8.4	5.8
Aged 15 to 19	7.0	6.5	8.8	8.3	6.4
Aged 20 to 24	7.0	6.8	8.2	8.0	6.5
Aged 25 to 29	7.1	8.0	7.7	8.6	6.5
Aged 30 to 34	6.5	8.5	6.7	8.3	5.8
Aged 35 to 39	6.7	8.7	6.7	7.8	6.3
Aged 40 to 44	6.8	7.6	6.7	6.8	6.8
Aged 45 to 49	7.4	7.0	6.9	6.0	7.9
Aged 50 to 54	7.1	6.2	6.3	4.7	7.9
Aged 55 to 59	6.2	5.3	5.1	3.6	7.1
Aged 60 to 64	5.2	4.1	3.8	2.6	6.1
Aged 65 or older	12.9	8.9	8.3	5.7	15.9

Note: Numbers by race and Hispanic origin do not add to total because Asians and blacks are those who identify themselves as being of the race alone and those who identify themselves as being of the race in combination with other races. Hispanics may be of any race. Non-Hispanic whites are those who identify themselves as being white alone and not Hispanic.
Source: Bureau of the Census, National Population Estimates, Internet site http://www.census.gov/popest/national/asrh/; calculations by New Strategist

The South Is the Most Populous Region

The West is the most diverse.

The South is by far the most populous region. Slightly more than 37 percent of Americans live in the South, according to the 2010 census. The Northeast is the least populous region, home to 18 percent of the total population. Between 2000 and 2010, the population of the South grew by 14.3 percent, slightly faster than the 13.8 percent growth in the West. The Midwest population grew by only 3.9 percent and the Northeast by an even slower 3.2 percent.

The West is the most diverse region, with minorities accounting for 47 percent of its population. The Midwest is the least diverse region, with minorities accounting for only 22 percent of the population.

The South is home to the 55 percent majority of the nation's blacks. Within the region, blacks account for one-fifth of the population. Forty-one percent of Hispanics live in the West, where they account for 29 percent of the population. Forty-six percent of Asians live in the West, and they account for more than one in ten Western residents.

■ Asians, blacks, and Hispanics together will soon account for the majority of the population in the Western states.

The Midwest is the least diverse region

(minority share of population, by region, 2010)

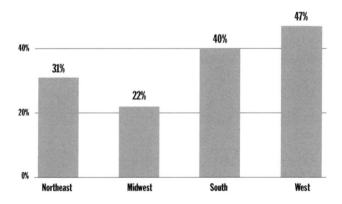

Table 8.7 Population by Region, 2000 and 2010

(number and percent distribution of population by region, 2000 and 2010; percent change in number 2000–10)

	2010		2000		
	number	percent distribution	number	percent distribution	percent change 2000–10
Total population	**308,745,538**	**100.0%**	**281,421,906**	**100.0%**	**9.7%**
Northeast	55,317,240	17.9	53,594,378	19.0	3.2
Midwest	66,927,001	21.7	64,392,776	22.9	3.9
South	114,555,744	37.1	100,236,820	35.6	14.3
West	71,945,553	23.3	63,197,932	22.5	13.8

Note: Numbers in 2000 and 2010 are from the April 1 censuses.
Source: Bureau of the Census, State Population Distribution and Change: 2000 to 2010, 2010 Census Briefs, Internet site hhttp://2010.census.gov/2010census/data/; calculations by New Strategist

Table 8.8 Minority Population by Region, 2010

(number and percent distribution of people by region, race, and Hispanic origin, 2010)

	total	non-Hispanic white	minority
Total population	**308,745,538**	**196,817,552**	**111,927,986**
Northeast	55,317,240	38,008,094	17,309,146
Midwest	66,927,001	52,096,633	14,830,368
South	114,555,744	68,706,462	45,849,282
West	71,945,553	38,006,363	33,939,190
PERCENT DISTRIBUTION BY RACE AND HISPANIC ORIGIN			
Total population	**100.0%**	**63.7%**	**36.3%**
Northeast	100.0	68.7	31.3
Midwest	100.0	77.8	22.2
South	100.0	60.0	40.0
West	100.0	52.8	47.2
PERCENT DISTRIBUTION BY REGION			
Total population	**100.0%**	**100.0%**	**100.0%**
Northeast	17.9	19.3	15.5
Midwest	21.7	26.5	13.2
South	37.1	34.9	41.0
West	23.3	19.3	30.3

Note: "Minority" is defined as not non-Hispanic white alone.
Source: Bureau of the Census, An Overview: Race and Hispanic Origin and the 2010 Census, 2010 Census Briefs, Internet site http://2010.census.gov/2010census/data/; calculations by New Strategist

Table 8.9 Population by Region, Race, and Hispanic Origin, 2010

(number and percent distribution of people by region, race, and Hispanic origin, 2010)

	total	Asian	black	Hispanic	non-Hispanic white
Total population	308,745,538	17,320,856	42,020,743	50,477,594	196,817,552
Northeast	55,317,240	3,428,624	7,187,488	6,991,969	38,008,094
Midwest	66,927,001	2,053,971	7,594,486	4,661,678	52,096,633
South	114,555,744	3,835,242	23,105,082	18,227,508	68,706,462
West	71,945,553	8,003,019	4,133,687	20,596,439	38,006,363

PERCENT DISTRIBUTION BY RACE AND HISPANIC ORIGIN

Total population	**100.0%**	**5.6%**	**13.6%**	**16.3%**	**63.7%**
Northeast	100.0	6.2	13.0	12.6	68.7
Midwest	100.0	3.1	11.3	7.0	77.8
South	100.0	3.3	20.2	15.9	60.0
West	100.0	11.1	5.7	28.6	52.8

PERCENT DISTRIBUTION BY REGION

Total population	**100.0%**	**100.0%**	**100.0%**	**100.0%**	**100.0%**
Northeast	17.9	19.8	17.1	13.9	19.3
Midwest	21.7	11.9	18.1	9.2	26.5
South	37.1	22.1	55.0	36.1	34.9
West	23.3	46.2	9.8	40.8	19.3

Note: Asians and blacks are those who identify themselves as being of the race alone and those who identify themselves as being of the race in combination with other races. Hispanics may be of any race.
Source: Bureau of the Census, An Overview: Race and Hispanic Origin and the 2010 Census, 2010 Census Briefs, Internet site http://2010.census.gov/2010census/data/; calculations by New Strategist

Nevada Grew the Fastest

Arizona was second in growth.

Nevada had the fastest-growing population between 2000 and 2010, with a 35 percent gain according to the 2010 census. Arizona ranked second in growth with a 25 percent population increase. Three other state populations grew by more than 20 percent during the decade: Idaho (21.1 percent), Texas (20.6 percent), and Utah (23.8 percent). Texas gained the most people, its population increasing by more than 4 million.

Michigan was the only state to lose population between 2000 and 2010, down by nearly 55,000 people. Three states grew by less than 2 percent during the decade: Rhode Island (0.4 percent), Louisiana (1.4 percent), and Ohio (1.6 percent).

■ Although Nevada and Arizona grew rapidly between 2000 and 2010, it is likely that growth in both states slowed or even stopped late in the decade because of the Great Recession.

Michigan was the only state to lose population

(percent change in population in the three fastest- and slowest-growing states, 2000 to 2010)

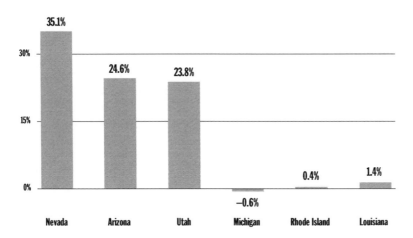

Table 8.10 Population by State, 2000 and 2010

(number of people by state, 2000 and 2010; numerical and percent change, 2000–10)

	2010	2000	change, 2000–10 numerical	change, 2000–10 percent
United States	**308,745,538**	**281,421,906**	**27,323,632**	**9.7%**
Alabama	4,779,736	4,447,100	332,636	7.5
Alaska	710,231	626,932	83,299	13.3
Arizona	6,392,017	5,130,632	1,261,385	24.6
Arkansas	2,915,918	2,673,400	242,518	9.1
California	37,253,956	33,871,648	3,382,308	10.0
Colorado	5,029,196	4,301,261	727,935	16.9
Connecticut	3,574,097	3,405,565	168,532	4.9
Delaware	897,934	783,600	114,334	14.6
District of Columbia	601,723	572,059	29,664	5.2
Florida	18,801,310	15,982,378	2,818,932	17.6
Georgia	9,687,653	8,186,453	1,501,200	18.3
Hawaii	1,360,301	1,211,537	148,764	12.3
Idaho	1,567,582	1,293,953	273,629	21.1
Illinois	12,830,632	12,419,293	411,339	3.3
Indiana	6,483,802	6,080,485	403,317	6.6
Iowa	3,046,355	2,926,324	120,031	4.1
Kansas	2,853,118	2,688,418	164,700	6.1
Kentucky	4,339,367	4,041,769	297,598	7.4
Louisiana	4,533,372	4,468,976	64,396	1.4
Maine	1,328,361	1,274,923	53,438	4.2
Maryland	5,773,552	5,296,486	477,066	9.0
Massachusetts	6,547,629	6,349,097	198,532	3.1
Michigan	9,883,640	9,938,444	−54,804	−0.6
Minnesota	5,303,925	4,919,479	384,446	7.8
Mississippi	2,967,297	2,844,658	122,639	4.3
Missouri	5,988,927	5,595,211	393,716	7.0
Montana	989,415	902,195	87,220	9.7
Nebraska	1,826,341	1,711,263	115,078	6.7
Nevada	2,700,551	1,998,257	702,294	35.1
New Hampshire	1,316,470	1,235,786	80,684	6.5
New Jersey	8,791,894	8,414,350	377,544	4.5
New Mexico	2,059,179	1,819,046	240,133	13.2
New York	19,378,102	18,976,457	401,645	2.1
North Carolina	9,535,483	8,049,313	1,486,170	18.5
North Dakota	672,591	642,200	30,391	4.7
Ohio	11,536,504	11,353,140	183,364	1.6
Oklahoma	3,751,351	3,450,654	300,697	8.7
Oregon	3,831,074	3,421,399	409,675	12.0
Pennsylvania	12,702,379	12,281,054	421,325	3.4
Rhode Island	1,052,567	1,048,319	4,248	0.4
South Carolina	4,625,364	4,012,012	613,352	15.3

	2010	2000	change, 2000–10	
			numerical	percent
South Dakota	814,180	754,844	59,336	7.9%
Tennessee	6,346,105	5,689,283	656,822	11.5
Texas	25,145,561	20,851,820	4,293,741	20.6
Utah	2,763,885	2,233,169	530,716	23.8
Vermont	625,741	608,827	16,914	2.8
Virginia	8,001,024	7,078,515	922,509	13.0
Washington	6,724,540	5,894,121	830,419	14.1
West Virginia	1,852,994	1,808,344	44,650	2.5
Wisconsin	5,686,986	5,363,675	323,311	6.0
Wyoming	563,626	493,782	69,844	14.1

Note: Numbers in 2000 and 2010 are from the April 1 censuses.
Source: Bureau of the Census, State Population Distribution and Change: 2000 to 2010, 2010 Census Briefs, Internet site http://2010.census.gov/2010census/data/; calculations by New Strategist

Four States Have Minority Majorities

Maine, New Hampshire, and Vermont are more than 90 percent non-Hispanic white.

Among the 50 states, Hawaii has the smallest share of non-Hispanic whites—only 23 percent of its population is non-Hispanic white, while 57 percent is Asian. In New Mexico, non-Hispanic whites account for 40 percent of the population and Hispanics for a larger 46 percent. In California, the nation's most populous state, 38 percent of residents are Hispanic, 15 percent are Asian, and 40 percent are non-Hispanic white. In the nation's second most-populous state, Texas, non-Hispanic whites account for 45 percent of the population. Thirty-eight percent of Texas residents are Hispanic and 13 percent are black.

At the other extreme, non-Hispanic whites account for more than 90 percent of the populations of Maine, New Hampshire, and Vermont. In 15 additional states, minorities account for less than 20 percent of the population.

■ Although Hispanics and Asians are growing in number, their political power is muted by low voter participation rates.

California is one of the nation's most diverse states

(percent distribution of population in California, by race and Hispanic origin, 2010)

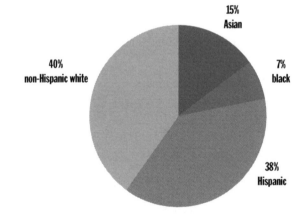

Table 8.11 Minority Population by State, 2010

(number of total people, non-Hispanic whites, and minorities by state; percent distribution of minority population by state, and minority share of total, 2010)

	total	non-Hispanic white	minority number	minority percent distribution	minority percent of total
United States	**308,745,538**	**196,817,552**	**111,927,986**	**100.0%**	**36.3%**
Alabama	4,779,736	3,204,402	1,575,334	1.4	33.0
Alaska	710,231	455,320	254,911	0.2	35.9
Arizona	6,392,017	3,695,647	2,696,370	2.4	42.2
Arkansas	2,915,918	2,173,469	742,449	0.7	25.5
California	37,253,956	14,956,253	22,297,703	19.9	59.9
Colorado	5,029,196	3,520,793	1,508,403	1.3	30.0
Connecticut	3,574,097	2,546,262	1,027,835	0.9	28.8
Delaware	897,934	586,752	311,182	0.3	34.7
District of Columbia	601,723	209,464	392,259	0.4	65.2
Florida	18,801,310	10,884,722	7,916,588	7.1	42.1
Georgia	9,687,653	5,413,920	4,273,733	3.8	44.1
Hawaii	1,360,301	309,343	1,050,958	0.9	77.3
Idaho	1,567,582	1,316,243	251,339	0.2	16.0
Illinois	12,830,632	8,167,753	4,662,879	4.2	36.3
Indiana	6,483,802	5,286,453	1,197,349	1.1	18.5
Iowa	3,046,355	2,701,123	345,232	0.3	11.3
Kansas	2,853,118	2,230,539	622,579	0.6	21.8
Kentucky	4,339,367	3,745,655	593,712	0.5	13.7
Louisiana	4,533,372	2,734,884	1,798,488	1.6	39.7
Maine	1,328,361	1,254,297	74,064	0.1	5.6
Maryland	5,773,552	3,157,958	2,615,594	2.3	45.3
Massachusetts	6,547,629	4,984,800	1,562,829	1.4	23.9
Michigan	9,883,640	7,569,939	2,313,701	2.1	23.4
Minnesota	5,303,925	4,405,142	898,783	0.8	16.9
Mississippi	2,967,297	1,722,287	1,245,010	1.1	42.0
Missouri	5,988,927	4,850,748	1,138,179	1.0	19.0
Montana	989,415	868,628	120,787	0.1	12.2
Nebraska	1,826,341	1,499,753	326,588	0.3	17.9
Nevada	2,700,551	1,462,081	1,238,470	1.1	45.9
New Hampshire	1,316,470	1,215,050	101,420	0.1	7.7
New Jersey	8,791,894	5,214,878	3,577,016	3.2	40.7
New Mexico	2,059,179	833,810	1,225,369	1.1	59.5
New York	19,378,102	11,304,247	8,073,855	7.2	41.7
North Carolina	9,535,483	6,223,995	3,311,488	3.0	34.7
North Dakota	672,591	598,007	74,584	0.1	11.1
Ohio	11,536,504	9,359,263	2,177,241	1.9	18.9
Oklahoma	3,751,351	2,575,381	1,175,970	1.1	31.3
Oregon	3,831,074	3,005,848	825,226	0.7	21.5
Pennsylvania	12,702,379	10,094,652	2,607,727	2.3	20.5

	total	non-Hispanic white	minority		
			number	percent distribution	percent of total
Rhode Island	1,052,567	803,685	248,882	0.2%	23.6%
South Carolina	4,625,364	2,962,740	1,662,624	1.5	35.9
South Dakota	814,180	689,502	124,678	0.1	15.3
Tennessee	6,346,105	4,800,782	1,545,323	1.4	24.4
Texas	25,145,561	11,397,345	13,748,216	12.3	54.7
Utah	2,763,885	2,221,719	542,166	0.5	19.6
Vermont	625,741	590,223	35,518	0.0	5.7
Virginia	8,001,024	5,186,450	2,814,574	2.5	35.2
Washington	6,724,540	4,876,804	1,847,736	1.7	27.5
West Virginia	1,852,994	1,726,256	126,738	0.1	6.8
Wisconsin	5,686,986	4,738,411	948,575	0.8	16.7
Wyoming	563,626	483,874	79,752	0.1	14.1

Note: "Minority" is defined as not non-Hispanic white alone.
Source: Bureau of the Census, An Overview: Race and Hispanic Origin and the 2010 Census, 2010 Census Briefs, Internet site http://2010.census.gov/2010census/data/; calculations by New Strategist

Table 8.12 Population by State, Race, and Hispanic Origin, 2010

(number of people by state, race, and Hispanic origin, 2010)

	total	Asian	black	Hispanic	non-Hispanic white
United States	**308,745,538**	**17,320,856**	**42,020,743**	**50,477,594**	**196,817,552**
Alabama	4,779,736	67,036	1,281,118	185,602	3,204,402
Alaska	710,231	50,402	33,150	39,249	455,320
Arizona	6,392,017	230,907	318,665	1,895,149	3,695,647
Arkansas	2,915,918	44,943	468,710	186,050	2,173,469
California	37,253,956	5,556,592	2,683,914	14,013,719	14,956,253
Colorado	5,029,196	185,589	249,812	1,038,687	3,520,793
Connecticut	3,574,097	157,088	405,600	479,087	2,546,262
Delaware	897,934	33,701	205,923	73,221	586,752
District of Columbia	601,723	26,857	314,352	54,749	209,464
Florida	18,801,310	573,083	3,200,663	4,223,806	10,884,722
Georgia	9,687,653	365,497	3,054,098	853,689	5,413,920
Hawaii	1,360,301	780,968	38,820	120,842	309,343
Idaho	1,567,582	29,698	15,940	175,901	1,316,243
Illinois	12,830,632	668,694	1,974,113	2,027,578	8,167,753
Indiana	6,483,802	126,750	654,415	389,707	5,286,453
Iowa	3,046,355	64,512	113,225	151,544	2,701,123
Kansas	2,853,118	83,930	202,149	300,042	2,230,539
Kentucky	4,339,367	62,029	376,213	132,836	3,745,655
Louisiana	4,533,372	84,335	1,486,885	192,560	2,734,884
Maine	1,328,361	18,333	21,764	16,935	1,254,297
Maryland	5,773,552	370,044	1,783,899	470,632	3,157,958
Massachusetts	6,547,629	394,211	508,413	627,654	4,984,800
Michigan	9,883,640	289,607	1,505,514	436,358	7,569,939
Minnesota	5,303,925	247,132	327,548	250,258	4,405,142
Mississippi	2,967,297	32,560	1,115,801	81,481	1,722,287
Missouri	5,988,927	123,571	747,474	212,470	4,850,748
Montana	989,415	10,482	7,917	28,565	868,628
Nebraska	1,826,341	40,561	98,959	167,405	1,499,753
Nevada	2,700,551	242,916	254,452	716,501	1,462,081
New Hampshire	1,316,470	34,522	21,736	36,704	1,215,050
New Jersey	8,791,894	795,163	1,300,363	1,555,144	5,214,878
New Mexico	2,059,179	40,456	57,040	953,403	833,810
New York	19,378,102	1,579,494	3,334,550	3,416,922	11,304,247
North Carolina	9,535,483	252,585	2,151,456	800,120	6,223,995
North Dakota	672,591	9,193	11,086	13,467	598,007
Ohio	11,536,504	238,292	1,541,771	354,674	9,359,263
Oklahoma	3,751,351	84,170	327,621	332,007	2,575,381
Oregon	3,831,074	186,281	98,479	450,062	3,005,848
Pennsylvania	12,702,379	402,587	1,507,965	719,660	10,094,652
Rhode Island	1,052,567	36,763	77,754	130,655	803,685
South Carolina	4,625,364	75,674	1,332,188	235,682	2,962,740

	total	Asian	black	Hispanic	non-Hispanic white
South Dakota	814,180	10,216	14,705	22,119	689,502
Tennessee	6,346,105	113,398	1,107,178	290,059	4,800,782
Texas	25,145,561	1,110,666	3,168,469	9,460,921	11,397,345
Utah	2,763,885	77,748	43,209	358,340	2,221,719
Vermont	625,741	10,463	9,343	9,208	590,223
Virginia	8,001,024	522,199	1,653,563	631,825	5,186,450
Washington	6,724,540	604,251	325,004	755,790	4,876,804
West Virginia	1,852,994	16,465	76,945	22,268	1,726,256
Wisconsin	5,686,986	151,513	403,527	336,056	4,738,411
Wyoming	563,626	6,729	7,285	50,231	483,874

Note: Asians and blacks are those who identify themselves as being of the race alone and those who identify themselves as being of the race in combination with other races. Hispanics may be of any race.
Source: Bureau of the Census, 2010 Census, American Factfinder, Internet site http://factfinder2.census.gov/faces/nav/jsf/pages/index.xhtml; calculations by New Strategist

Table 8.13 Population Distribution by State, Race, and Hispanic Origin, 2010

(percent distribution of people by state, race, and Hispanic origin, 2010)

	total	Asian	black	Hispanic	non-Hispanic white
United States	**100.0%**	**5.6%**	**13.6%**	**16.3%**	**63.7%**
Alabama	100.0	1.4	26.8	3.9	67.0
Alaska	100.0	7.1	4.7	5.5	64.1
Arizona	100.0	3.6	5.0	29.6	57.8
Arkansas	100.0	1.5	16.1	6.4	74.5
California	100.0	14.9	7.2	37.6	40.1
Colorado	100.0	3.7	5.0	20.7	70.0
Connecticut	100.0	4.4	11.3	13.4	71.2
Delaware	100.0	3.8	22.9	8.2	65.3
District of Columbia	100.0	4.5	52.2	9.1	34.8
Florida	100.0	3.0	17.0	22.5	57.9
Georgia	100.0	3.8	31.5	8.8	55.9
Hawaii	100.0	57.4	2.9	8.9	22.7
Idaho	100.0	1.9	1.0	11.2	84.0
Illinois	100.0	5.2	15.4	15.8	63.7
Indiana	100.0	2.0	10.1	6.0	81.5
Iowa	100.0	2.1	3.7	5.0	88.7
Kansas	100.0	2.9	7.1	10.5	78.2
Kentucky	100.0	1.4	8.7	3.1	86.3
Louisiana	100.0	1.9	32.8	4.2	60.3
Maine	100.0	1.4	1.6	1.3	94.4
Maryland	100.0	6.4	30.9	8.2	54.7
Massachusetts	100.0	6.0	7.8	9.6	76.1
Michigan	100.0	2.9	15.2	4.4	76.6
Minnesota	100.0	4.7	6.2	4.7	83.1
Mississippi	100.0	1.1	37.6	2.7	58.0
Missouri	100.0	2.1	12.5	3.5	81.0
Montana	100.0	1.1	0.8	2.9	87.8
Nebraska	100.0	2.2	5.4	9.2	82.1
Nevada	100.0	9.0	9.4	26.5	54.1
New Hampshire	100.0	2.6	1.7	2.8	92.3
New Jersey	100.0	9.0	14.8	17.7	59.3
New Mexico	100.0	2.0	2.8	46.3	40.5
New York	100.0	8.2	17.2	17.6	58.3
North Carolina	100.0	2.6	22.6	8.4	65.3
North Dakota	100.0	1.4	1.6	2.0	88.9
Ohio	100.0	2.1	13.4	3.1	81.1
Oklahoma	100.0	2.2	8.7	8.9	68.7
Oregon	100.0	4.9	2.6	11.7	78.5
Pennsylvania	100.0	3.2	11.9	5.7	79.5
Rhode Island	100.0	3.5	7.4	12.4	76.4
South Carolina	100.0	1.6	28.8	5.1	64.1

	total	Asian	black	Hispanic	non-Hispanic white
South Dakota	100.0%	1.3%	1.8%	2.7%	84.7%
Tennessee	100.0	1.8	17.4	4.6	75.6
Texas	100.0	4.4	12.6	37.6	45.3
Utah	100.0	2.8	1.6	13.0	80.4
Vermont	100.0	1.7	1.5	1.5	94.3
Virginia	100.0	6.5	20.7	7.9	64.8
Washington	100.0	9.0	4.8	11.2	72.5
West Virginia	100.0	0.9	4.2	1.2	93.2
Wisconsin	100.0	2.7	7.1	5.9	83.3
Wyoming	100.0	1.2	1.3	8.9	85.9

Note: Asians and blacks are those who identify themselves as being of the race alone and those who identify themselves as being of the race in combination with other races. Hispanics may be of any race.
Source: Bureau of the Census, 2010 Census, American Factfinder, Internet site http://factfinder2.census.gov/faces/nav/jsf/pages/index.xhtml; calculations by New Strategist

Most People Live in Metropolitan Areas

New York–Northern New Jersey–Long Island is the largest.

Eighty-three percent of Americans live in a metropolitan area, according to the 2010 census. In 1950, only 56 percent of Americans were metropolitan residents.

Among the nation's largest metropolitan areas, New York is by far the most populous, with nearly 19 million people. Overall, 51 metropolitan areas are home to at least 1 million people.

The minority share of the nation's metropolitan areas varies greatly, from 4 percent in Parkersburg–Marietta–Vienna, West Virginia–Ohio, to 97 percent in Laredo, Texas. In a substantial 46 metropolitan areas, minorities are the majority. These include Houston, Los Angeles, Miami, New York, San Francisco, and Washington, D.C.

■ The New York metropolitan area is growing more slowly than many others, but it will remain the largest for decades to come.

Minorities are the majority in New York and Los Angeles

(minority share of the population in the five most populous metropolitan areas, 2010)

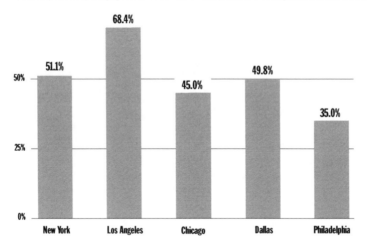

Table 8.14 Population by Metropolitan Status, 1950 to 2010

(number and percent distribution of people by metropolitan status, selected years, 1950 to 2010; numbers in thousands; metropolitan areas as defined at the respective time periods)

	number			percent distribution		
	total	metropolitan	nonmetropolitan	total	metropolitan	nonmetropolitan
2010	308,746	258,318	50,428	100.0%	82.8%	17.2%
2000	281,422	225,968	55,454	100.0	80.3	19.7
1990	249,464	198,249	51,215	100.0	77.5	22.5
1980	227,225	177,361	49,864	100.0	74.8	25.2
1970	203,212	139,480	63,732	100.0	69.0	31.0
1960	179,323	112,885	66,438	100.0	63.3	36.7
1950	150,697	84,501	66,196	100.0	56.1	43.9

Source: Bureau of the Census, Population Distributon and Change: 2000 to 2010, 2010 Census Briefs; 2000 Census, Table DP-1: Profile of General Demographic Characteristics: 2000; and Metropolitan Areas and Cities, 1990 Census Profile, No. 3, 1991; and Historical Statistics of the United States, Colonial Times to 1970, Part 1, 1975; calculations by New Strategist

Table 8.15 Population of Large Metropolitan Areas, 2010

(number of people in metropolitan areas with at least 1 million residents, 2010)

New York–Northern New Jersey–Long Island, NY–NJ–PA	18,897,109
Los Angeles–Long Beach–Santa Ana, CA	12,828,837
Chicago–Joliet–Naperville, IL–IN–WI	9,461,105
Dallas–Fort Worth–Arlington, TX	6,371,773
Philadelphia–Camden–Wilmington, PA–NJ–DE–MD	5,965,343
Houston–Sugar Land–Baytown, TX	5,946,800
Washington–Arlington–Alexandria, DC–VA–MD–WV	5,582,170
Miami–Fort Lauderdale–Pompano Beach, FL	5,564,635
Atlanta–Sandy Springs–Marietta, GA	5,268,860
Boston–Cambridge–Quincy, MA–NH	4,552,402
San Francisco–Oakland–Fremont, CA	4,335,391
Detroit–Warren–Livonia, MI	4,296,250
Riverside–San Bernardino–Ontario, CA	4,224,851
Phoenix–Mesa–Glendale, AZ	4,192,887
Seattle–Tacoma–Bellevue, WA	3,439,809
Minneapolis–St. Paul–Bloomington, MN–WI	3,279,833
San Diego–Carlsbad–San Marcos, CA	3,095,313
St. Louis, MO–IL	2,812,896
Tampa–St. Petersburg–Clearwater, FL	2,783,243
Baltimore–Towson, MD	2,710,489
Denver–Aurora–Broomfield, CO	2,543,482
Pittsburgh, PA	2,356,285
Portland–Vancouver–Hillsboro, OR–WA	2,226,009
Sacramento–Arden-Arcade–Roseville, CA	2,149,127
San Antonio–New Braunfels, TX	2,142,508
Orlando–Kissimmee–Sanford, FL	2,134,411
Cincinnati–Middletown, OH–KY–IN	2,130,151
Cleveland–Elyria–Mentor, OH	2,077,240
Kansas City, MO–KS	2,035,334
Las Vegas–Paradise, NV	1,951,269
San Jose–Sunnyvale–Santa Clara, CA	1,836,911
Columbus, OH	1,836,536
Charlotte–Gastonia–Rock Hill, NC–SC	1,758,038
Indianapolis–Carmel, IN	1,756,241
Austin–Round Rock–San Marcos, TX	1,716,289
Virginia Beach–Norfolk–Newport News, VA–NC	1,671,683
Providence–New Bedford–Fall River, RI–MA	1,600,852
Nashville–Davidson–Murfreesboro–Franklin, TN	1,589,934
Milwaukee–Waukesha–West Allis, WI	1,555,908
Jacksonville, FL	1,345,596
Memphis, TN–MS–AR	1,316,100
Louisville/Jefferson County, KY–IN	1,283,566
Richmond, VA	1,258,251

Oklahoma City, OK	1,252,987
Hartford–West Hartford–East Hartford, CT	1,212,381
New Orleans–Metairie–Kenner, LA	1,167,764
Buffalo–Niagara Falls, NY	1,135,509
Raleigh–Cary, NC	1,130,490
Birmingham–Hoover, AL	1,128,047
Salt Lake City, UT	1,124,197
Rochester, NY	1,054,323

Source: Bureau of the Census, 2010 census, Internet site http://factfinder2.census.gov/faces/nav/jsf/pages/index.xhtml

Table 8.16 Minority Population of Metropolitan Areas, 2010

(number of total people, non-Hispanic whites, and minorities by metropolitan area, and minority share of total, 2010)

	total	non-Hispanic white	minorities number	percent of total
Abilene, TX	165,252	112,735	52,517	31.8%
Akron, OH	703,200	579,151	124,049	17.6
Albany–Schenectady–Troy, NY	870,716	721,505	149,211	17.1
Albany, GA	157,308	68,820	88,488	56.3
Albuquerque, NM	887,077	374,214	512,863	57.8
Alexandria, LA	153,922	98,984	54,938	35.7
Allentown–Bethlehem–Easton, PA–NJ	821,173	645,741	175,432	21.4
Altoona, PA	127,089	121,495	5,594	4.4
Amarillo, TX	249,881	160,881	89,000	35.6
Ames, IA	89,542	77,812	11,730	13.1
Anchorage, AK	380,821	256,490	124,331	32.6
Anderson, IN	131,636	113,577	18,059	13.7
Anderson, SC	187,126	147,362	39,764	21.2
Ann Arbor, MI	344,791	248,675	96,116	27.9
Anniston–Oxford, AL	118,572	87,285	31,287	26.4
Appleton, WI	225,666	203,691	21,975	9.7
Asheville, NC	424,858	366,448	58,410	13.7
Athens–Clarke County, GA	192,541	130,515	62,026	32.2
Atlanta–Sandy Springs–Marietta, GA	5,268,860	2,671,757	2,597,103	49.3
Atlantic City–Hammonton, NJ	274,549	160,871	113,678	41.4
Auburn–Opelika, AL	140,247	97,900	42,347	30.2
Augusta–Richmond County, GA–SC	556,877	314,669	242,208	43.5
Austin–Round Rock–San Marcos, TX	1,716,289	938,474	777,815	45.3
Bakersfield–Delano, CA	839,631	323,794	515,837	61.4
Baltimore–Towson, MD	2,710,489	1,626,199	1,084,290	40.0
Bangor, ME	153,923	145,700	8,223	5.3
Barnstable Town, MA	215,888	197,327	18,561	8.6
Baton Rouge, LA	802,484	465,308	337,176	42.0
Battle Creek, MI	136,146	108,664	27,482	20.2
Bay City, MI	107,771	98,241	9,530	8.8
Beaumont–Port Arthur, TX	388,745	228,486	160,259	41.2
Bellingham, WA	201,140	164,675	36,465	18.1
Bend, OR	157,733	139,470	18,263	11.6
Billings, MT	158,050	140,131	17,919	11.3
Binghamton, NY	251,725	222,179	29,546	11.7
Birmingham–Hoover, AL	1,128,047	733,656	394,391	35.0
Bismarck, ND	108,779	100,591	8,188	7.5
Blacksburg–Christiansburg–Radford, VA	162,958	143,718	19,240	11.8
Bloomington–Normal, IL	169,572	138,835	30,737	18.1
Bloomington, IN	192,714	172,163	20,551	10.7
Boise City–Nampa, ID	616,561	505,202	111,359	18.1
Boston–Cambridge–Quincy, MA–NH	4,552,402	3,408,585	1,143,817	25.1
Boulder, CO	294,567	233,741	60,826	20.6
Bowling Green, KY	125,953	104,540	21,413	17.0
Bremerton–Silverdale, WA	251,133	198,745	52,388	20.9

	total	non-Hispanic white	minorities number	percent of total
Bridgeport–Stamford–Norwalk, CT	916,829	606,716	310,113	33.8%
Brownsville–Harlingen, TX	406,220	43,427	362,793	89.3
Brunswick, GA	112,370	77,516	34,854	31.0
Buffalo–Niagara Falls, NY	1,135,509	903,063	232,446	20.5
Burlington–South Burlington, VT	211,261	194,738	16,523	7.8
Burlington, NC	151,131	101,718	49,413	32.7
Canton–Massillon, OH	404,422	357,541	46,881	11.6
Cape Coral–Fort Myers, FL	618,754	439,048	179,706	29.0
Cape Girardeau–Jackson, MO–IL	96,275	83,552	12,723	13.2
Carson City, NV	55,274	39,083	16,191	29.3
Casper, WY	75,450	67,191	8,259	10.9
Cedar Rapids, IA	257,940	233,695	24,245	9.4
Champaign–Urbana, IL	231,891	172,266	59,625	25.7
Charleston–North Charleston–Summerville, SC	664,607	420,240	244,367	36.8
Charleston, WV	304,284	279,242	25,042	8.2
Charlotte–Gastonia–Rock Hill, NC–SC	1,758,038	1,076,021	682,017	38.8
Charlottesville, VA	201,559	154,343	47,216	23.4
Chattanooga, TN–GA	528,143	420,172	107,971	20.4
Cheyenne, WY	91,738	74,120	17,618	19.2
Chicago–Joliet–Naperville, IL–IN–WI	9,461,105	5,204,489	4,256,616	45.0
Chico, CA	220,000	165,416	54,584	24.8
Cincinnati–Middletown, OH–KY–IN	2,130,151	1,738,775	391,376	18.4
Clarksville, TN–KY	273,949	191,406	82,543	30.1
Cleveland–Elyria–Mentor, OH	2,077,240	1,490,074	587,166	28.3
Cleveland, TN	115,788	103,851	11,937	10.3
Coeur d'Alene, ID	138,494	127,454	11,040	8.0
College Station–Bryan, TX	228,660	136,769	91,891	40.2
Colorado Springs, CO	645,613	469,095	176,518	27.3
Columbia, MO	172,786	140,917	31,869	18.4
Columbia, SC	767,598	447,927	319,671	41.6
Columbus, GA–AL	294,865	147,518	147,347	50.0
Columbus, IN	76,794	66,817	9,977	13.0
Columbus, OH	1,836,536	1,394,399	442,137	24.1
Corpus Christi, TX	428,185	155,550	272,635	63.7
Corvallis, OR	85,579	71,552	14,027	16.4
Crestview–Fort Walton Beach–Destin, FL	180,822	139,500	41,322	22.9
Cumberland, MD–WV	103,299	92,937	10,362	10.0
Dallas–Fort Worth–Arlington, TX	6,371,773	3,201,677	3,170,096	49.8
Dalton, GA	142,227	97,484	44,743	31.5
Danville, IL	81,625	65,590	16,035	19.6
Danville, VA	106,561	67,357	39,204	36.8
Davenport–Moline–Rock Island, IA–IL	379,690	311,053	68,637	18.1
Dayton, OH	841,502	663,353	178,149	21.2
Decatur, AL	153,829	119,005	34,824	22.6
Decatur, IL	110,768	86,822	23,946	21.6
Deltona–Daytona Beach–Ormond Beach, FL	494,593	372,982	121,611	24.6
Denver–Aurora–Broomfield, CO	2,543,482	1,673,709	869,773	34.2
Des Moines–West Des Moines, IA	569,633	476,434	93,199	16.4
Detroit–Warren–Livonia, MI	4,296,250	2,916,144	1,380,106	32.1
Dothan, AL	145,639	104,154	41,485	28.5

	total	non-Hispanic white	minorities	
			number	percent of total
Dover, DE	162,310	105,891	56,419	34.8%
Dubuque, IA	93,653	86,981	6,672	7.1
Duluth, MN–WI	279,771	257,081	22,690	8.1
Durham–Chapel Hill, NC	504,357	278,907	225,450	44.7
Eau Claire, WI	161,151	149,946	11,205	7.0
El Centro, CA	174,528	23,927	150,601	86.3
El Paso, TX	800,647	105,246	695,401	86.9
Elizabethtown, KY	119,736	95,235	24,501	20.5
Elkhart–Goshen, IN	197,559	152,555	45,004	22.8
Elmira, NY	88,830	77,643	11,187	12.6
Erie, PA	280,566	242,787	37,779	13.5
Eugene–Springfield, OR	351,715	297,808	53,907	15.3
Evansville, IN–KY	358,676	318,979	39,697	11.1
Fairbanks, AK	97,581	72,259	25,322	25.9
Fargo, ND–MN	208,777	188,964	19,813	9.5
Farmington, NM	130,044	55,254	74,790	57.5
Fayetteville–Springdale–Rogers, AR–MO	463,204	353,302	109,902	23.7
Fayetteville, NC	366,383	169,891	196,492	53.6
Flagstaff, AZ	134,421	74,231	60,190	44.8
Flint, MI	425,790	309,683	116,107	27.3
Florence–Muscle Shoals, AL	147,137	122,562	24,575	16.7
Florence, SC	205,566	112,098	93,468	45.5
Fond du Lac, WI	101,633	93,398	8,235	8.1
Fort Collins–Loveland, CO	299,630	253,047	46,583	15.5
Fort Smith, AR–OK	298,592	226,828	71,764	24.0
Fort Wayne, IN	416,257	330,540	85,717	20.6
Fresno, CA	930,450	304,522	625,928	67.3
Gadsden, AL	104,430	82,789	21,641	20.7
Gainesville, FL	264,275	172,348	91,927	34.8
Gainesville, GA	179,684	114,300	65,384	36.4
Glens Falls, NY	128,923	121,581	7,342	5.7
Goldsboro, NC	122,623	68,216	54,407	44.4
Grand Forks, ND–MN	98,461	87,768	10,693	10.9
Grand Junction, CO	146,723	121,944	24,779	16.9
Grand Rapids–Wyoming, MI	774,160	615,337	158,823	20.5
Great Falls, MT	81,327	71,100	10,227	12.6
Greeley, CO	252,825	170,827	81,998	32.4
Green Bay, WI	306,241	263,593	42,648	13.9
Greensboro–High Point, NC	723,801	449,177	274,624	37.9
Greenville–Mauldin–Easley, SC	636,986	467,055	169,931	26.7
Greenville, NC	189,510	106,076	83,434	44.0
Gulfport–Biloxi, MS	248,820	177,475	71,345	28.7
Hagerstown–Martinsburg, MD–WV	269,140	229,076	40,064	14.9
Hanford–Corcoran, CA	152,982	53,879	99,103	64.8
Harrisburg–Carlisle, PA	549,475	442,343	107,132	19.5
Harrisonburg, VA	125,228	105,031	20,197	16.1
Hartford–West Hartford–East Hartford, CT	1,212,381	868,016	344,365	28.4
Hattiesburg, MS	142,842	95,576	47,266	33.1
Hickory–Lenoir–Morganton, NC	365,497	302,096	63,401	17.3
Hinesville–Fort Stewart, GA	77,917	35,576	42,341	54.3

	total	non-Hispanic white	minorities number	percent of total
Holland–Grand Haven, MI	263,801	226,156	37,645	14.3%
Honolulu, HI	953,207	181,684	771,523	80.9
Hot Springs, AR	96,024	80,621	15,403	16.0
Houma–Bayou Cane–Thibodaux, LA	208,178	151,869	56,309	27.0
Houston–Sugar Land–Baytown, TX	5,946,800	2,360,472	3,586,328	60.3
Huntington–Ashland, WV–KY–OH	287,702	270,988	16,714	5.8
Huntsville, AL	417,593	286,557	131,036	31.4
Idaho Falls, ID	130,374	111,798	18,576	14.2
Indianapolis–Carmel, IN	1,756,241	1,310,092	446,149	25.4
Iowa City, IA	152,586	128,881	23,705	15.5
Ithaca, NY	101,564	81,490	20,074	19.8
Jackson, MI	160,248	137,588	22,660	14.1
Jackson, MS	539,057	260,512	278,545	51.7
Jackson, TN	115,425	71,897	43,528	37.7
Jacksonville, FL	1,345,596	885,040	460,556	34.2
Jacksonville, NC	177,772	122,558	55,214	31.1
Janesville, WI	160,331	135,526	24,805	15.5
Jefferson City, MO	149,807	131,411	18,396	12.3
Johnson City, TN	198,716	183,099	15,617	7.9
Johnstown, PA	143,679	134,073	9,606	6.7
Jonesboro, AR	121,026	98,641	22,385	18.5
Joplin, MO	175,518	151,986	23,532	13.4
Kalamazoo–Portage, MI	326,589	263,075	63,514	19.4
Kankakee–Bradley, IL	113,449	83,218	30,231	26.6
Kansas City, MO–KS	2,035,334	1,514,888	520,446	25.6
Kennewick–Pasco–Richland, WA	253,340	164,241	89,099	35.2
Killeen–Temple–Fort Hood, TX	405,300	218,901	186,399	46.0
Kingsport–Bristol–Bristol, TN–VA	309,544	293,968	15,576	5.0
Kingston, NY	182,493	149,099	33,394	18.3
Knoxville, TN	698,030	606,269	91,761	13.1
Kokomo, IN	98,688	87,446	11,242	11.4
La Crosse, WI–MN	133,665	122,899	10,766	8.1
Lafayette, IN	201,789	166,341	35,448	17.6
Lafayette, LA	273,738	182,803	90,935	33.2
Lake Charles, LA	199,607	140,168	59,439	29.8
Lake Havasu City–Kingman, AZ	200,186	159,378	40,808	20.4
Lakeland–Winter Haven, FL	602,095	388,769	213,326	35.4
Lancaster, PA	519,445	440,969	78,476	15.1
Lansing–East Lansing, MI	464,036	363,242	100,794	21.7
Laredo, TX	250,304	8,345	241,959	96.7
Las Cruces, NM	209,233	62,992	146,241	69.9
Las Vegas–Paradise, NV	1,951,269	935,955	1,015,314	52.0
Lawrence, KS	110,826	90,532	20,294	18.3
Lawton, OK	124,098	73,122	50,976	41.1
Lebanon, PA	133,568	116,010	17,558	13.1
Lewiston–Auburn, ME	107,702	98,931	8,771	8.1
Lewiston, ID–WA	60,888	54,861	6,027	9.9
Lexington–Fayette, KY	472,099	372,839	99,260	21.0
Lima, OH	106,331	87,708	18,623	17.5
Lincoln, NE	302,157	256,854	45,303	15.0

	total	non-Hispanic white	minorities number	percent of total
Little Rock–North Little Rock–Conway, AR	699,757	487,009	212,748	30.4%
Logan, UT–ID	125,442	108,026	17,416	13.9
Longview, TX	214,369	141,499	72,870	34.0
Longview, WA	102,410	87,825	14,585	14.2
Los Angeles–Long Beach–Santa Ana, CA	12,828,837	4,056,820	8,772,017	68.4
Louisville/Jefferson County, KY–IN	1,283,566	1,012,081	271,485	21.2
Lubbock, TX	284,890	162,440	122,450	43.0
Lynchburg, VA	252,634	194,849	57,785	22.9
Macon, GA	232,293	119,766	112,527	48.4
Madera–Chowchilla, CA	150,865	57,380	93,485	62.0
Madison, WI	568,593	476,020	92,573	16.3
Manchester–Nashua, NH	400,721	351,224	49,497	12.4
Manhattan, KS	127,081	96,848	30,233	23.8
Mankato–North Mankato, MN	96,740	88,338	8,402	8.7
Mansfield, OH	124,475	107,726	16,749	13.5
McAllen–Edinburg–Mission, TX	774,769	60,553	714,216	92.2
Medford, OR	203,206	170,023	33,183	16.3
Memphis, TN–MS–AR	1,316,100	608,449	707,651	53.8
Merced, CA	255,793	81,599	174,194	68.1
Miami–Fort Lauderdale–Pompano Beach, FL	5,564,635	1,937,939	3,626,696	65.2
Michigan City–La Porte, IN	111,467	90,695	20,772	18.6
Midland, TX	136,872	72,822	64,050	46.8
Milwaukee–Waukesha–West Allis, WI	1,555,908	1,073,109	482,799	31.0
Minneapolis–St. Paul–Bloomington, MN–WI	3,279,833	2,578,117	701,716	21.4
Missoula, MT	109,299	99,489	9,810	9.0
Mobile, AL	412,992	243,904	169,088	40.9
Modesto, CA	514,453	240,423	274,030	53.3
Monroe, LA	176,441	106,971	69,470	39.4
Monroe, MI	152,021	140,609	11,412	7.5
Montgomery, AL	374,536	192,543	181,993	48.6
Morgantown, WV	129,709	118,855	10,854	8.4
Morristown, TN	136,608	121,337	15,271	11.2
Mount Vernon–Anacortes, WA	116,901	89,694	27,207	23.3
Muncie, IN	117,671	103,721	13,950	11.9
Muskegon–Norton Shores, MI	172,188	133,132	39,056	22.7
Myrtle Beach–North Myrtle Beach–Conway, SC	269,291	208,096	61,195	22.7
Napa, CA	136,484	76,967	59,517	43.6
Naples–Marco Island, FL	321,520	211,156	110,364	34.3
Nashville–Davidson–Murfreesboro–Franklin, TN	1,589,934	1,176,069	413,865	26.0
New Haven–Milford, CT	862,477	582,384	280,093	32.5
New Orleans–Metairie–Kenner, LA	1,167,764	628,878	538,886	46.1
New York–Northern New Jersey–Long Island, NY–NJ–PA	18,897,109	9,233,812	9,663,297	51.1
Niles–Benton Harbor, MI	156,813	119,389	37,424	23.9
North Port–Bradenton–Sarasota, FL	702,281	558,928	143,353	20.4
Norwich–New London, CT	274,055	214,605	59,450	21.7
Ocala, FL	331,298	245,136	86,162	26.0
Ocean City, NJ	97,265	84,522	12,743	13.1
Odessa, TX	137,130	56,306	80,824	58.9

	total	non-Hispanic white	minorities	
			number	percent of total
Ogden–Clearfield, UT	547,184	452,785	94,399	17.3%
Oklahoma City, OK	1,252,987	845,104	407,883	32.6
Olympia, WA	252,264	199,019	53,245	21.1
Omaha–Council Bluffs, NE–IA	865,350	681,172	184,178	21.3
Orlando–Kissimmee–Sanford, FL	2,134,411	1,136,863	997,548	46.7
Oshkosh–Neenah, WI	166,994	151,509	15,485	9.3
Owensboro, KY	114,752	104,565	10,187	8.9
Oxnard–Thousand Oaks–Ventura, CA	823,318	400,868	422,450	51.3
Palm Bay–Melbourne–Titusville, FL	543,376	421,466	121,910	22.4
Palm Coast, FL	95,696	72,860	22,836	23.9
Panama City–Lynn Haven–Panama City Beach, FL	168,852	133,790	35,062	20.8
Parkersburg–Marietta–Vienna, WV–OH	162,056	155,597	6,459	4.0
Pascagoula, MS	162,246	117,679	44,567	27.5
Pensacola–Ferry Pass–Brent, FL	448,991	325,627	123,364	27.5
Peoria, IL	379,186	319,493	59,693	15.7
Philadelphia–Camden–Wilmington, PA–NJ–DE–MD	5,965,343	3,875,845	2,089,498	35.0
Phoenix–Mesa–Glendale, AZ	4,192,887	2,460,541	1,732,346	41.3
Pine Bluff, AR	100,258	48,740	51,518	51.4
Pittsburgh, PA	2,356,285	2,051,163	305,122	12.9
Pittsfield, MA	131,219	118,926	12,293	9.4
Pocatello, ID	90,656	76,730	13,926	15.4
Port St. Lucie, FL	424,107	287,564	136,543	32.2
Portland–South Portland–Biddeford, ME	514,098	480,553	33,545	6.5
Portland–Vancouver–Hillsboro, OR–WA	2,226,009	1,698,126	527,883	23.7
Poughkeepsie–Newburgh–Middletown, NY	670,301	476,071	194,230	29.0
Prescott, AZ	211,033	172,968	38,065	18.0
Providence–New Bedford–Fall River, RI–MA	1,600,852	1,273,029	327,823	20.5
Provo–Orem, UT	526,810	444,339	82,471	15.7
Pueblo, CO	159,063	86,054	73,009	45.9
Punta Gorda, FL	159,978	137,628	22,350	14.0
Racine, WI	195,408	145,414	49,994	25.6
Raleigh–Cary, NC	1,130,490	716,883	413,607	36.6
Rapid City, SD	126,382	105,389	20,993	16.6
Reading, PA	411,442	316,406	95,036	23.1
Redding, CA	177,223	146,044	31,179	17.6
Reno–Sparks, NV	425,417	281,745	143,672	33.8
Richmond, VA	1,258,251	754,328	503,923	40.0
Riverside–San Bernardino–Ontario, CA	4,224,851	1,546,666	2,678,185	63.4
Roanoke, VA	308,707	248,968	59,739	19.4
Rochester, MN	186,011	159,840	26,171	14.1
Rochester, NY	1,054,323	824,425	229,898	21.8
Rockford, IL	349,431	254,953	94,478	27.0
Rocky Mount, NC	152,392	73,130	79,262	52.0
Rome, GA	96,317	70,959	25,358	26.3
Sacramento–Arden-Arcade–Roseville, CA	2,149,127	1,197,389	951,738	44.3
Saginaw–Saginaw Township North, MI	200,169	141,187	58,982	29.5
Salem, OR	390,738	277,460	113,278	29.0
Salinas, CA	415,057	136,435	278,622	67.1

	total	non-Hispanic white	minorities number	percent of total
Salisbury, MD	125,203	79,563	45,640	36.5%
Salt Lake City, UT	1,124,197	842,071	282,126	25.1
San Angelo, TX	111,823	64,952	46,871	41.9
San Antonio–New Braunfels, TX	2,142,508	773,807	1,368,701	63.9
San Diego–Carlsbad–San Marcos, CA	3,095,313	1,500,047	1,595,266	51.5
San Francisco–Oakland–Fremont, CA	4,335,391	1,840,372	2,495,019	57.6
San Jose–Sunnyvale–Santa Clara, CA	1,836,911	648,063	1,188,848	64.7
San Luis Obispo–Paso Robles, CA	269,637	191,696	77,941	28.9
Sandusky, OH	77,079	65,463	11,616	15.1
Santa Barbara–Santa Maria–Goleta, CA	423,895	203,122	220,773	52.1
Santa Cruz–Watsonville, CA	262,382	156,397	105,985	40.4
Santa Fe, NM	144,170	63,291	80,879	56.1
Santa Rosa–Petaluma, CA	483,878	320,027	163,851	33.9
Savannah, GA	347,611	199,249	148,362	42.7
Scranton–Wilkes-Barre, PA	563,631	502,578	61,053	10.8
Seattle–Tacoma–Bellevue, WA	3,439,809	2,340,274	1,099,535	32.0
Sebastian–Vero Beach, FL	138,028	106,780	31,248	22.6
Sheboygan, WI	115,507	100,520	14,987	13.0
Sherman–Denison, TX	120,877	95,103	25,774	21.3
Shreveport–Bossier City, LA	398,604	218,052	180,552	45.3
Sioux City, IA–NE–SD	143,577	109,779	33,798	23.5
Sioux Falls, SD	228,261	202,388	25,873	11.3
South Bend–Mishawaka, IN–MI	319,224	247,405	71,819	22.5
Spartanburg, SC	284,307	199,184	85,123	29.9
Spokane, WA	471,221	408,629	62,592	13.3
Springfield, IL	210,170	175,307	34,863	16.6
Springfield, MA	692,942	516,073	176,869	25.5
Springfield, MO	436,712	399,431	37,281	8.5
Springfield, OH	138,333	117,976	20,357	14.7
St. Cloud, MN	189,093	172,353	16,740	8.9
St. George, UT	138,115	118,282	19,833	14.4
St. Joseph, MO–KS	127,329	111,905	15,424	12.1
St. Louis, MO–IL	2,812,896	2,112,954	699,942	24.9
State College, PA	153,990	135,427	18,563	12.1
Steubenville–Weirton, OH–WV	124,454	115,903	8,551	6.9
Stockton, CA	685,306	245,919	439,387	64.1
Sumter, SC	107,456	50,423	57,033	53.1
Syracuse, NY	662,577	555,047	107,530	16.2
Tallahassee, FL	367,413	211,958	155,455	42.3
Tampa–St. Petersburg–Clearwater, FL	2,783,243	1,879,437	903,806	32.5
Terre Haute, IN	172,425	155,488	16,937	9.8
Texarkana, TX–Texarkana, AR	136,027	92,034	43,993	32.3
Toledo, OH	651,429	503,966	147,463	22.6
Topeka, KS	233,870	186,502	47,368	20.3
Trenton–Ewing, NJ	366,513	199,909	166,604	45.5
Tucson, AZ	980,263	541,700	438,563	44.7
Tulsa, OK	937,478	635,628	301,850	32.2
Tuscaloosa, AL	219,461	134,386	85,075	38.8
Tyler, TX	209,714	130,246	79,468	37.9
Utica–Rome, NY	299,397	260,944	38,453	12.8

	total	non-Hispanic white	minorities number	percent of total
Valdosta, GA	139,588	80,113	59,475	42.6%
Vallejo–Fairfield, CA	413,344	168,628	244,716	59.2
Victoria, TX	115,384	55,695	59,689	51.7
Vineland–Millville–Bridgeton, NJ	156,898	78,931	77,967	49.7
Virginia Beach–Norfolk–Newport News, VA–NC	1,671,683	955,896	715,787	42.8
Visalia–Porterville, CA	442,179	143,935	298,244	67.4
Waco, TX	234,906	138,295	96,611	41.1
Warner Robins, GA	139,900	84,703	55,197	39.5
Washington–Arlington–Alexandria, DC–VA–MD–WV	5,582,170	2,711,258	2,870,912	51.4
Waterloo–Cedar Falls, IA	167,819	145,617	22,202	13.2
Wausau, WI	134,063	121,007	13,056	9.7
Wenatchee–East Wenatchee, WA	110,884	77,272	33,612	30.3
Wheeling, WV–OH	147,950	139,308	8,642	5.8
Wichita Falls, TX	151,306	108,124	43,182	28.5
Wichita, KS	623,061	459,730	163,331	26.2
Williamsport, PA	116,111	106,710	9,401	8.1
Wilmington, NC	362,315	281,017	81,298	22.4
Winchester, VA–WV	128,472	108,821	19,651	15.3
Winston–Salem, NC	477,717	317,660	160,057	33.5
Worcester, MA	798,552	644,299	154,253	19.3
Yakima, WA	243,231	116,024	127,207	52.3
York–Hanover, PA	434,972	374,779	60,193	13.8
Youngstown–Warren–Boardman, OH–PA	565,773	476,794	88,979	15.7
Yuba City, CA	166,892	90,198	76,694	46.0
Yuma, AZ	195,751	69,022	126,729	64.7

Note: "Minority" is defined as not non-Hispanic white alone.
Source: Bureau of the Census, 2010 census, Internet site, http://factfinder2.census.gov/faces/nav/jsf/pages/index.xhtml; calculations by New Strategist

Americans Are Moving Less

The mobility rate of homeowners is the lowest ever recorded.

Only 12.5 percent of Americans moved between March 2009 and March 2010, down from 14.2 percent in 2000–01 and 21.2 percent in 1950–51. The 2009–10 rate was the same as in 2008–09, during the depths of the recession, and only slightly higher than the all-time low of 11.9 percent in 2007–08. Among homeowners, the 2009–10 mobility rate of 5.2 percent was the same as in the previous year and still the lowest ever recorded because the collapse of the housing market has made it difficult to buy and sell houses. Mobility among renters was a much higher 29.0 percent, not much different from the 30.3 percent of 2000–01.

Most moves are local, motivated by housing needs rather than job relocations. Among movers between 2009 and 2010, the 69 percent majority remained in the same county. Only 12 percent moved to a different state. In 2000–01, a smaller 56 percent of movers stayed in the same county and a larger 20 percent moved to a different state.

Young adults are most likely to move, many of them graduating from college and looking for work. From 26 to 27 percent of 20-to-29-year-olds moved between 2009 and 2010. Mobility rates fall with age to less than 10 percent among people aged 45 or older and to less than 5 percent among people aged 62 or older.

Although mobility rates are lower than they once were, they add up to big changes over the years. Only 59 percent of Americans were born in their state of residence, according to the Census Bureau's 2009 American Community Survey.

■ With so many Americans unable to sell their homes, millions are stuck until the housing market stabilizes.

Mobility has decreased

(percent of people aged 1 or older who moved in a 12-month period, selected years, 1950–51 to 2009–10)

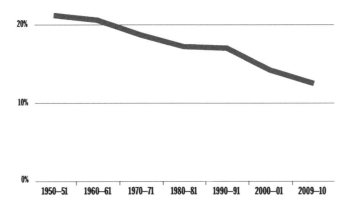

Table 8.17 Geographical Mobility, 1950 to 2010

(number and percent distribution of people aged 1 or older by mobility status, selected years, 1950–51 to 2009–10; numbers in thousands)

| | total people aged 1+ | same house (nonmovers) | total movers | different house in United States | | different county | | | movers from abroad |
				total	same county	total	same state	different state	
2009–10	300,074	262,534	37,540	36,594	26,017	10,578	6,252	4,326	946
2008–09	297,182	260,077	37,105	36,017	24,984	11,034	6,374	4,660	1,087
2007–08	294,851	259,685	35,166	34,022	23,013	11,009	6,282	4,727	1,145
2000–01	275,611	236,605	39,006	37,251	21,918	15,333	7,550	7,783	1,756
1990–91	244,884	203,345	41,539	40,154	25,151	15,003	7,881	7,122	1,385
1980–81	221,641	183,442	38,199	36,887	23,097	13,789	7,614	6,175	1,313
1970–71	201,506	163,800	37,706	36,161	23,018	13,143	6,197	6,946	1,544
1960–61	177,354	140,821	36,533	35,535	24,289	11,246	5,493	5,753	998
1950–51	148,400	116,936	31,464	31,158	20,694	10,464	5,276	5,188	306

PERCENT DISTRIBUTION OF POPULATION BY MOBILITY STATUS

2009–10	100.0%	87.5%	12.5%	12.2%	8.7%	3.5%	2.1%	1.4%	0.3%
2008–09	100.0	87.5	12.5	12.1	8.4	3.7	2.1	1.6	0.4
2007–08	100.0	88.1	11.9	11.5	7.8	3.7	2.1	1.6	0.4
2000–01	100.0	85.8	14.2	13.5	8.0	5.6	2.7	2.8	0.6
1990–91	100.0	83.0	17.0	16.4	10.3	6.1	3.2	2.9	0.6
1980–81	100.0	82.8	17.2	16.6	10.4	6.2	3.4	2.8	0.6
1970–71	100.0	81.3	18.7	17.9	11.4	6.5	3.1	3.4	0.8
1960–61	100.0	79.4	20.6	20.0	13.7	6.3	3.1	3.2	0.6
1950–51	100.0	78.8	21.2	21.0	13.9	7.1	3.6	3.5	0.2

PERCENT DISTRIBUTION OF MOVERS BY TYPE OF MOVE

2009–10	–	–	100.0%	97.5%	69.3%	28.2%	16.7%	11.5%	2.5%
2008–09	–	–	100.0	97.1	67.3	29.7	17.2	12.6	2.9
2007–08	–	–	100.0	96.7	65.4	31.3	17.9	13.4	3.3
2000–01	–	–	100.0	95.5	56.2	39.3	19.4	20.0	4.5
1990–91	–	–	100.0	96.7	60.5	36.1	19.0	17.1	3.3
1980–81	–	–	100.0	96.6	60.5	36.1	19.9	16.2	3.4
1970–71	–	–	100.0	95.9	61.0	34.9	16.4	18.4	4.1
1960–61	–	–	100.0	97.3	66.5	30.8	15.0	15.7	2.7
1950–51	–	–	100.0	99.0	65.8	33.3	16.8	16.5	1.0

Note: "–" means not applicable.
Source: Bureau of the Census, Geographical Mobility/Migration, Internet site http://www.census.gov/population/www/socdemo/migrate.html; calculations by New Strategist

Table 8.18 Geographical Mobility of Homeowners, 2000 to 2010

(number and percent distribution of people aged 1 or older living in owner-occupied homes by mobility status, 2000–01 to 2009–10; numbers in thousands)

	total aged 1+ in owner-occupied housing	same house (nonmovers)	total movers	total	different house in United States		different county			movers from abroad
					same county	total	same state	different state	
2009–2010	206,274	195,504	10,770	10,477	7,010	3,467	2,050	1,417	293
2008–2009	206,924	196,146	10,778	10,445	6,873	3,572	2,013	1,559	333
2007–2008	208,212	197,055	11,157	10,875	6,850	4,025	2,306	1,719	283
2006–2007	207,774	194,014	13,760	13,378	8,467	4,911	2,881	2,030	381
2005–2006	206,136	191,579	14,558	14,214	8,708	5,506	3,414	2,092	344
2004–2005	206,955	191,509	15,446	15,018	8,494	6,524	3,477	3,048	427
2003–2004	203,302	188,461	14,841	14,525	8,303	6,222	3,398	2,824	316
2002–2003	200,627	185,686	14,942	14,641	8,549	6,092	3,195	2,897	301
2001–2002	196,488	180,518	15,971	15,692	9,142	6,550	3,563	2,987	279
2000–2001	194,329	179,990	14,339	13,920	7,737	6,183	3,284	2,899	420

PERCENT DISTRIBUTION OF POPULATION BY MOBILITY STATUS

2009–2010	100.0%	94.8%	5.2%	5.1%	3.4%	1.7%	1.0%	0.7%	0.1%
2008–2009	100.0	94.8	5.2	5.0	3.3	1.7	1.0	0.8	0.2
2007–2008	100.0	94.6	5.4	5.2	3.3	1.9	1.1	0.8	0.1
2006–2007	100.0	93.4	6.6	6.4	4.1	2.4	1.4	1.0	0.2
2005–2006	100.0	92.9	7.1	6.9	4.2	2.7	1.7	1.0	0.2
2004–2005	100.0	92.5	7.5	7.3	4.1	3.2	1.7	1.5	0.2
2003–2004	100.0	92.7	7.3	7.1	4.1	3.1	1.7	1.4	0.2
2002–2003	100.0	92.6	7.4	7.3	4.3	3.0	1.6	1.4	0.2
2001–2002	100.0	91.9	8.1	8.0	4.7	3.3	1.8	1.5	0.1
2000–2001	100.0	92.6	7.4	7.2	4.0	3.2	1.7	1.5	0.2

PERCENT DISTRIBUTION OF MOVERS BY TYPE OF MOVE

2009–2010	–	–	100.0%	97.3%	65.1%	32.2%	19.0%	13.2%	2.7%
2008–2009	–	–	100.0	96.9	63.8	33.1	18.7	14.5	3.1
2007–2008	–	–	100.0	97.5	61.4	36.1	20.7	15.4	2.5
2006–2007	–	–	100.0	97.2	61.5	35.7	20.9	14.8	2.8
2005–2006	–	–	100.0	97.6	59.8	37.8	23.5	14.4	2.4
2004–2005	–	–	100.0	97.2	55.0	42.2	22.5	19.7	2.8
2003–2004	–	–	100.0	97.9	55.9	41.9	22.9	19.0	2.1
2002–2003	–	–	100.0	98.0	57.2	40.8	21.4	19.4	2.0
2001–2002	–	–	100.0	98.3	57.2	41.0	22.3	18.7	1.7
2000–2001	–	–	100.0	97.1	54.0	43.1	22.9	20.2	2.9

Note: "–" means not applicable.
Source: Bureau of the Census, Geographical Mobility/Migration, Internet site http://www.census.gov/population/www/socdemo/migrate.html; calculations by New Strategist

Table 8.19 Geographical Mobility of Renters, 2000 to 2010

(number and percent distribution of people aged 1 or older living in renter-occupied homes by mobility status, 2000–01 to 2009–10; numbers in thousands)

	total aged 1+ in renter-occupied housing	same house (nonmovers)	total movers	total	same county	total	same state	different state	movers from abroad
						different county			
				different house in United States					
2009–2010	89,982	63,903	26,079	25,445	18,614	6,832	4,020	2,812	634
2008–2009	90,257	63,931	26,326	25,572	18,111	7,461	4,361	3,101	754
2007–2008	86,639	62,630	24,010	23,147	16,163	6,984	3,976	3,009	862
2006–2007	84,975	60,053	24,922	24,111	16,725	7,386	4,555	2,831	809
2005–2006	83,646	58,366	25,280	24,327	16,143	8,184	4,596	3,588	953
2004–2005	80,193	55,752	24,442	23,004	14,242	8,763	4,370	4,393	1,437
2003–2004	81,065	56,911	24,153	23,196	14,248	8,948	4,443	4,505	957
2002–2003	81,929	56,777	25,151	24,183	14,919	9,264	4,533	4,731	968
2001–2002	81,673	56,532	25,142	23,857	14,570	9,287	4,504	4,783	1,285
2000–2001	81,282	56,615	24,667	23,329	14,181	9,148	4,265	4,883	1,337

PERCENT DISTRIBUTION OF POPULATION BY MOBILITY STATUS

2009–2010	100.0%	71.0%	29.0%	28.3%	20.7%	7.6%	4.5%	3.1%	0.7%
2008–2009	100.0	70.8	29.2	28.3	20.1	8.3	4.8	3.4	0.8
2007–2008	100.0	72.3	27.7	26.7	18.7	8.1	4.6	3.5	1.0
2006–2007	100.0	70.7	29.3	28.4	19.7	8.7	5.4	3.3	1.0
2005–2006	100.0	69.8	30.2	29.1	19.3	9.8	5.5	4.3	1.1
2004–2005	100.0	69.5	30.5	28.7	17.8	10.9	5.4	5.5	1.8
2003–2004	100.0	70.2	29.8	28.6	17.6	11.0	5.5	5.6	1.2
2002–2003	100.0	69.3	30.7	29.5	18.2	11.3	5.5	5.8	1.2
2001–2002	100.0	69.2	30.8	29.2	17.8	11.4	5.5	5.9	1.6
2000–2001	100.0	69.7	30.3	28.7	17.4	11.3	5.2	6.0	1.6

PERCENT DISTRIBUTION OF MOVERS BY TYPE OF MOVE

2009–2010	–	–	100.0%	97.6%	71.4%	26.2%	15.4%	10.8%	2.4%
2008–2009	–	–	100.0	97.1	68.8	28.3	16.6	11.8	2.9
2007–2008	–	–	100.0	96.4	67.3	29.1	16.6	12.5	3.6
2006–2007	–	–	100.0	96.7	67.1	29.6	18.3	11.4	3.2
2005–2006	–	–	100.0	96.2	63.9	32.4	18.2	14.2	3.8
2004–2005	–	–	100.0	94.1	58.3	35.9	17.9	18.0	5.9
2003–2004	–	–	100.0	96.0	59.0	37.0	18.4	18.7	4.0
2002–2003	–	–	100.0	96.2	59.3	36.8	18.0	18.8	3.8
2001–2002	–	–	100.0	94.9	58.0	36.9	17.9	19.0	5.1
2000–2001	–	–	100.0	94.6	57.5	37.1	17.3	19.8	5.4

Note: "–" means not applicable.
Source: Bureau of the Census, Geographical Mobility/Migration, Internet site http://www.census.gov/population/www/socdemo/migrate.html; calculations by New Strategist

Table 8.20 Geographic Mobility by Age of Mover and Type of Move, 2009–10

(total number of people aged 1 or older, and number and percent who moved between March 2009 and March 2010, by age of mover and type of move; numbers in thousands)

	total	same house (nonmovers)	total movers	same county	different county, same state	different state total	different state same region	different state different region	movers from abroad
Total, aged 1 or older	300,074	262,534	37,540	26,017	6,252	4,326	2,137	2,189	946
Aged 1 to 4	17,228	13,844	3,384	2,451	508	364	180	184	61
Aged 5 to 9	20,785	17,800	2,985	2,208	416	321	153	168	40
Aged 10 to 14	19,893	17,650	2,243	1,653	335	226	101	125	29
Aged 15 to 17	12,928	11,617	1,311	946	201	120	66	54	44
Aged 18 to 19	8,159	6,987	1,172	772	245	120	59	61	35
Aged 20 to 24	21,154	15,499	5,655	3,812	1,025	641	331	310	177
Aged 25 to 29	21,453	15,890	5,563	3,806	901	692	361	331	166
Aged 30 to 34	19,632	15,951	3,681	2,494	603	450	216	234	134
Aged 35 to 39	19,888	17,235	2,653	1,890	405	295	145	150	62
Aged 40 to 44	20,559	18,466	2,093	1,485	341	221	103	118	46
Aged 45 to 49	22,527	20,676	1,851	1,308	313	194	90	104	37
Aged 50 to 54	21,860	20,218	1,642	1,136	258	197	100	97	51
Aged 55 to 59	19,172	18,106	1,066	673	230	145	65	80	18
Aged 60 to 61	7,023	6,657	366	229	67	64	28	36	7
Aged 62 to 64	9,200	8,748	452	280	107	54	27	27	11
Aged 65 to 69	12,020	11,435	585	334	130	110	58	52	12
Aged 70 to 74	8,936	8,646	290	186	61	40	22	18	4
Aged 75 to 79	7,181	6,969	212	136	52	20	11	9	4
Aged 80 to 84	5,783	5,618	165	110	28	23	13	10	5
Aged 85 or older	4,693	4,523	170	107	28	31	10	21	3

PERCENT DISTRIBUTION BY MOBILITY STATUS

Total, aged 1 or older	100.0%	87.5%	12.5%	8.7%	2.1%	1.4%	0.7%	0.7%	0.3%
Aged 1 to 4	100.0	80.4	19.6	14.2	2.9	2.1	1.0	1.1	0.4
Aged 5 to 9	100.0	85.6	14.4	10.6	2.0	1.5	0.7	0.8	0.2
Aged 10 to 14	100.0	88.7	11.3	8.3	1.7	1.1	0.5	0.6	0.1
Aged 15 to 17	100.0	89.9	10.1	7.3	1.6	0.9	0.5	0.4	0.3
Aged 18 to 19	100.0	85.6	14.4	9.5	3.0	1.5	0.7	0.7	0.4
Aged 20 to 24	100.0	73.3	26.7	18.0	4.8	3.0	1.6	1.5	0.8
Aged 25 to 29	100.0	74.1	25.9	17.7	4.2	3.2	1.7	1.5	0.8
Aged 30 to 34	100.0	81.3	18.8	12.7	3.1	2.3	1.1	1.2	0.7
Aged 35 to 39	100.0	86.7	13.3	9.5	2.0	1.5	0.7	0.8	0.3
Aged 40 to 44	100.0	89.8	10.2	7.2	1.7	1.1	0.5	0.6	0.2
Aged 45 to 49	100.0	91.8	8.2	5.8	1.4	0.9	0.4	0.5	0.2
Aged 50 to 54	100.0	92.5	7.5	5.2	1.2	0.9	0.5	0.4	0.2
Aged 55 to 59	100.0	94.4	5.6	3.5	1.2	0.8	0.3	0.4	0.1
Aged 60 to 61	100.0	94.8	5.2	3.3	1.0	0.9	0.4	0.5	0.1
Aged 62 to 64	100.0	95.1	4.9	3.0	1.2	0.6	0.3	0.3	0.1
Aged 65 to 69	100.0	95.1	4.9	2.8	1.1	0.9	0.5	0.4	0.1
Aged 70 to 74	100.0	96.8	3.2	2.1	0.7	0.4	0.2	0.2	0.0
Aged 75 to 79	100.0	97.0	3.0	1.9	0.7	0.3	0.2	0.1	0.1
Aged 80 to 84	100.0	97.1	2.9	1.9	0.5	0.4	0.2	0.2	0.1
Aged 85 or older	100.0	96.4	3.6	2.3	0.6	0.7	0.2	0.4	0.1

Note: "–" means not applicable.
Source: Bureau of the Census, Geographic Mobility: 2009 to 2010, Detailed Tables, Internet site http://www.census.gov/hhes/migration/data/cps/cps2010.html; calculations by New Strategist

Table 8.21 Movers by Age and Type of Move, 2009–10

(number and percent distribution of people aged 1 or older who moved between March 2009 and March 2010, by age of mover and type of move; numbers in thousands)

	total movers	same county	different county, same state	different state total	different state same region	different state different region	movers from abroad
Total, aged 1 or older	37,540	26,017	6,252	4,326	2,137	2,189	946
Aged 1 to 4	3,384	2,451	508	364	180	184	61
Aged 5 to 9	2,985	2,208	416	321	153	168	40
Aged 10 to 14	2,243	1,653	335	226	101	125	29
Aged 15 to 17	1,311	946	201	120	66	54	44
Aged 18 to 19	1,172	772	245	120	59	61	35
Aged 20 to 24	5,655	3,812	1,025	641	331	310	177
Aged 25 to 29	5,563	3,806	901	692	361	331	166
Aged 30 to 34	3,681	2,494	603	450	216	234	134
Aged 35 to 39	2,653	1,890	405	295	145	150	62
Aged 40 to 44	2,093	1,485	341	221	103	118	46
Aged 45 to 49	1,851	1,308	313	194	90	104	37
Aged 50 to 54	1,642	1,136	258	197	100	97	51
Aged 55 to 59	1,066	673	230	145	65	80	18
Aged 60 to 61	366	229	67	64	28	36	7
Aged 62 to 64	452	280	107	54	27	27	11
Aged 65 to 69	585	334	130	110	58	52	12
Aged 70 to 74	290	186	61	40	22	18	4
Aged 75 to 79	212	136	52	20	11	9	4
Aged 80 to 84	165	110	28	23	13	10	5
Aged 85 or older	170	107	28	31	10	21	3

PERCENT DISTRIBUTION BY TYPE OF MOVE

Total, aged 1 or older	100.0%	69.3%	16.7%	11.5%	5.7%	5.8%	2.5%
Aged 1 to 4	100.0	72.4	15.0	10.8	5.3	5.4	1.8
Aged 5 to 9	100.0	74.0	13.9	10.8	5.1	5.6	1.3
Aged 10 to 14	100.0	73.7	14.9	10.1	4.5	5.6	1.3
Aged 15 to 17	100.0	72.2	15.3	9.2	5.0	4.1	3.4
Aged 18 to 19	100.0	65.9	20.9	10.2	5.0	5.2	3.0
Aged 20 to 24	100.0	67.4	18.1	11.3	5.9	5.5	3.1
Aged 25 to 29	100.0	68.4	16.2	12.4	6.5	6.0	3.0
Aged 30 to 34	100.0	67.8	16.4	12.2	5.9	6.4	3.6
Aged 35 to 39	100.0	71.2	15.3	11.1	5.5	5.7	2.3
Aged 40 to 44	100.0	71.0	16.3	10.6	4.9	5.6	2.2
Aged 45 to 49	100.0	70.7	16.9	10.5	4.9	5.6	2.0
Aged 50 to 54	100.0	69.2	15.7	12.0	6.1	5.9	3.1
Aged 55 to 59	100.0	63.1	21.6	13.6	6.1	7.5	1.7
Aged 60 to 61	100.0	62.6	18.3	17.5	7.7	9.8	1.9
Aged 62 to 64	100.0	61.9	23.7	11.9	6.0	6.0	2.4
Aged 65 to 69	100.0	57.1	22.2	18.8	9.9	8.9	2.1
Aged 70 to 74	100.0	64.1	21.0	13.8	7.6	6.2	1.4
Aged 75 to 79	100.0	64.2	24.5	9.4	5.2	4.2	1.9
Aged 80 to 84	100.0	66.7	17.0	13.9	7.9	6.1	3.0
Aged 85 or older	100.0	62.9	16.5	18.2	5.9	12.4	1.8

Source: Bureau of the Census, Geographic Mobility: 2009 to 2010, Detailed Tables, Internet site http://www.census.gov/hhes/migration/data/cps/cps2010.html; calculations by New Strategist

Table 8.22 Place of Birth, 2009

(number and percent distribution of people by place of birth, 2009; numbers in thousands)

	number	percent
TOTAL POPULATION	**307,007**	**100.0%**
Native born	**268,489**	**87.5**
Born in United States	264,367	86.1
Born in state of residence	181,118	59.0
Born in other state in the U.S.	83,249	27.1
Born outside United States	4,122	1.3
Puerto Rico	1,508	0.5
Other*	2,614	0.9
Foreign born	**38,517**	**12.5**

* U.S. Island areas or born abroad to American parents.
Source: Bureau of the Census, 2009 American Community Survey, Internet site http://www.census.gov/acs/www/; calculations by New Strategist

Legal Immigration Adds Millions to the Population

Illegal immigration adds even more, especially in California.

Between 2001 and 2009, more than 10 million immigrants were granted permanent legal residence in the United States, more than in any other decade in U.S. history. In 2010, another 1 million legal immigrants came to the United States despite the ongoing employment problems caused by the Great Recession. As of 2010, there were also an estimated 10.8 million unauthorized immigrants (illegals) living in the United States—28 percent more than in 2000.

The impact of immigration varies dramatically by state. The 58 percent majority of legal immigrants who came to the United States in 2010 planned to live in one of just five states: California, New York, Florida, Texas, and New Jersey. California is the number-one state for immigrants, both legal and illegal. Twenty percent of legal immigrants coming to the United States in 2010 said they planned to live in California. Twenty-four percent of unauthorized immigrants in the United States in 2010 lived in California.

Mexico sends the largest number of legal immigrants to the United States, accounting for 13 percent of the total in 2010. Mexico has also sent the largest number of illegals to the United States. Unauthorized immigrants from Mexico accounted for 62 percent of all illegals in the U.S. in 2010.

■ Although unauthorized immigration to the United States has slowed because of the Great Recession, legal immigration remains high.

Mexico sends the largest number of legal and illegal immigrants to the United States

(Mexico's share of total legal immigrants coming to the United States in 2010 and share of unauthorized immigrants living in the United States as of 2010)

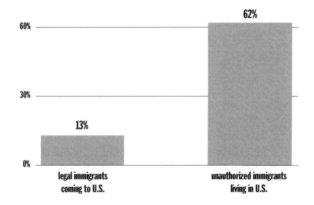

Table 8.23 Legal Immigration to the United States, 1900 to 2010

(number of legal immigrants granted permanent residence in the United States by single year, 2000 to 2010, and by decade, 1900 to 2010)

Single year	immigrants
2010	1,042,625
2009	1,130,818
2008	1,107,126
2007	1,052,415
2006	1,266,129
2005	1,122,257
2004	957,883
2003	703,542
2002	1,059,356
2001	1,058,902
2000	841,002
Decade	
2000–09	10,299,430
1990–99	9,775,398
1980–89	6,244,379
1970–79	4,248,203
1960–69	3,213,749
1950–59	2,499,268
1940–49	856,608
1930–39	699,375
1920–29	4,295,510
1910–19	6,347,380
1900–09	8,202,388

Note: "Immigrants" are those granted legal permanent residence in the United States. They either arrive in the United States with immigrant visas issued abroad or adjust their status in the United States from temporary to permanent residence.
Source: Department of Homeland Security, 2010 Yearbook of Immigration Statistics, Internet site http://www.uscis.gov/ graphics/shared/statistics/yearbook/index.htm

Table 8.24 Legal Immigrants by Country of Birth and State of Intended Residence, 2010

(number and percent distribution of legal immigrants admitted to the United States from the 10 leading countries of birth and percent distribution by intended state of residence, 2010; for the five states receiving the largest total number of legal immigrants in 2010)

	total	total in top five states	California	New York	Florida	Texas	New Jersey
Total legal immigrants	**1,042,625**	**608,391**	**208,446**	**147,999**	**107,276**	**87,750**	**56,920**
Total from top 10 countries	522,608	337,719	129,336	65,327	61,942	52,116	28,998
Mexico	139,120	89,954	50,645	2,437	3,113	32,811	948
China, People's Republic	70,863	44,692	18,680	18,859	1,620	3,280	2,253
India	69,162	36,134	15,099	5,116	2,019	5,777	8,123
Philippines	58,173	33,629	24,082	2,361	2,320	2,545	2,321
Dominican Republic	53,870	39,040	172	26,249	3,900	275	8,444
Cuba	33,573	29,842	450	416	27,301	1,023	652
Vietnam	30,632	17,237	11,501	473	1,164	3,700	399
Haiti	22,582	17,978	81	4,240	11,865	73	1,719
Colombia	22,406	16,342	1,159	3,089	8,277	1,352	2,465
Korea, South	22,227	12,871	7,467	2,087	363	1,280	1,674

PERCENT DISTRIBUTION BY STATE OF INTENDED RESIDENCE

	total	total in top five states	California	New York	Florida	Texas	New Jersey
Total legal immigrants	**100.0%**	**58.4%**	**20.0%**	**14.2%**	**10.3%**	**8.4%**	**5.5%**
Total from top 10 countries	100.0	64.6	24.7	12.5	11.9	10.0	5.5
Mexico	100.0	64.7	36.4	1.8	2.2	23.6	0.7
China, People's Republic	100.0	63.1	26.4	26.6	2.3	4.6	3.2
India	100.0	52.2	21.8	7.4	2.9	8.4	11.7
Philippines	100.0	57.8	41.4	4.1	4.0	4.4	4.0
Dominican Republic	100.0	72.5	0.3	48.7	7.2	0.5	15.7
Cuba	100.0	88.9	1.3	1.2	81.3	3.0	1.9
Vietnam	100.0	56.3	37.5	1.5	3.8	12.1	1.3
Haiti	100.0	79.6	0.4	18.8	52.5	0.3	7.6
Colombia	100.0	72.9	5.2	13.8	36.9	6.0	11.0
Korea, South	100.0	57.9	33.6	9.4	1.6	5.8	7.5

PERCENT DISTRIBUTION BY COUNTRY OF BIRTH

	total	total in top five states	California	New York	Florida	Texas	New Jersey
Total legal immigrants	**100.0%**	**100.0%**	**100.0%**	**100.0%**	**100.0%**	**100.0%**	**100.0%**
Total from top 10 countries	50.1	55.5	62.0	44.1	57.7	59.4	50.9
Mexico	13.3	14.8	24.3	1.6	2.9	37.4	1.7
China, People's Republic	6.8	7.3	9.0	12.7	1.5	3.7	4.0
India	6.6	5.9	7.2	3.5	1.9	6.6	14.3
Philippines	5.6	5.5	11.6	1.6	2.2	2.9	4.1
Dominican Republic	5.2	6.4	0.1	17.7	3.6	0.3	14.8
Cuba	3.2	4.9	0.2	0.3	25.4	1.2	1.1
Vietnam	2.9	2.8	5.5	0.3	1.1	4.2	0.7
Haiti	2.2	3.0	0.0	2.9	11.1	0.1	3.0
Colombia	2.1	2.7	0.6	2.1	7.7	1.5	4.3
Korea, South	2.1	2.1	3.6	1.4	0.3	1.5	2.9

Note: Total includes immigrants from other countries not shown separately. Immigrants are people granted legal permanent residence in the United States. They either arrive in the United States with immigrant visas issued abroad or adjust their status in the United States from temporary to permanent residence.
Source: Department of Homeland Security, 2010 Yearbook of Immigration Statistics, Internet site http://www.dhs.gov/files/statistics/publications/LPR10.shtm; calculations by New Strategist

Table 8.25 Unauthorized Immigrant Population, 2000 to 2010

(number and percent distribution of unauthorized immigrants in the United States by country of birth and state of residence, selected years, 2000 to 2010; percent change in number, 2007–10 and 2000–10; numbers in thousands)

	2010		2007		2000		percent change	
	number	percent distribution	number	percent distribution	number	percent distribution	2007–10	2000–10
COUNTRY OF BIRTH								
Total unauthorized immigrants	**10,790**	**100.0%**	**11,780**	**100.0%**	**8,460**	**100.0%**	**–8.4%**	**27.5%**
Mexico	6,640	61.5	6,980	59.3	4,680	55.3	–4.9	41.9
El Salvador	620	5.7	540	4.6	430	5.1	14.8	44.2
Guatemala	520	4.8	500	4.2	290	3.4	4.0	79.3
Honduras	330	3.1	280	2.4	160	1.9	17.9	106.3
Philippines	280	2.6	290	2.5	200	2.4	–3.4	40.0
India	200	1.9	220	1.9	120	1.4	–9.1	66.7
Ecuador	180	1.7	160	1.4	180	2.1	12.5	0.0
Brazil	180	1.7	190	1.6	110	1.3	–5.3	63.6
Korea	170	1.6	230	2.0	100	1.2	–26.1	70.0
China	130	1.2	290	2.5	190	2.2	–55.2	–31.6
Other countries	1,550	14.4	2,100	17.8	2,000	23.6	–26.2	–22.5
STATE OF RESIDENCE								
Total unauthorized immigrants	**10,790**	**100.0**	**11,780**	**100.0**	**8,460**	**100.0**	**–8.4**	**27.5**
California	2,570	23.8	2,840	24.1	2,510	29.7	–9.5	2.4
Texas	1,770	16.4	1,710	14.5	1,090	12.9	3.5	62.4
Florida	760	7.0	960	8.1	800	9.5	–20.8	–5.0
Illinois	490	4.5	560	4.8	540	6.4	–12.5	–9.3
Arizona	470	4.4	530	4.5	440	5.2	–11.3	6.8
Georgia	460	4.3	490	4.2	220	2.6	–6.1	109.1
New York	460	4.3	640	5.4	330	3.9	–28.1	39.4
North Carolina	390	3.6	380	3.2	260	3.1	2.6	50.0
New Jersey	370	3.4	470	4.0	350	4.1	–21.3	5.7
Nevada	260	2.4	260	2.2	170	2.0	0.0	52.9
Other states	2,790	25.9	2,950	25.0	1,760	20.8	–5.4	58.5

Note: Percent change calculations are based on unrounded figures.
Source: Department of Homeland Security, Estimates of the Unauthorized Immigrant Population Residing in the United States: January 2010, Internet site http://www.uscis.gov/graphics/shared/statistics/yearbook/index.htm

Many U.S. Residents Are Foreign-Born

One in eight was born in another country.

More than 38 million U.S. residents were born in a foreign country, according to the Census Bureau's 2009 American Community Survey, accounting for 12.5 percent of the population. Nearly one-third of the foreign-born came to the United States since 2000. The 53 percent majority of the foreign-born hail from Latin America. Twenty-eight percent are from Asia, and only 13 percent from Europe.

The foreign-born share of the population varies by age, peaking at 20 percent among people aged 25 to 44. Only 5 percent of school-aged children were born in another country. Among people aged 65 or older, the figure is 12 percent.

Thanks to immigration, the population of the United States is a diverse mixture of ancestries. German is the single-most-common ancestry, reported by 17 percent of Americans or 51 million people. The second-most-common ancestry is Irish, specified by 12 percent. Nineteen million people say their ancestry is American.

■ The number of foreign-born in the United States will continue to expand as long as immigration remains high, creating a dynamic multicultural market.

More than 40 percent of the foreign-born are naturalized citizens

(percent distribution of foreign-born by citizenship status, 2009)

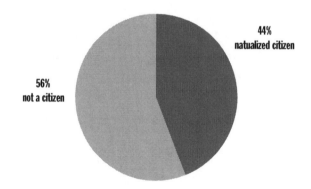

44%
natualized citizen

56%
not a citizen

Table 8.26   Foreign-Born by Year of Entry, World Region of Birth, and Citizenship Status, 2009

(number and percent distribution of foreign-born by year of entry, world region of birth, and citizenship status, 2009; numbers in thousands)

	total	naturalized citizen	not a citizen
Total foreign-born	**38,517**	**16,832**	**21,685**
YEAR OF ENTRY			
Total foreign-born	**38,517**	**16,832**	**21,685**
Entered U.S. 2000 or later	12,163	1,435	10,728
Entered U.S. before 2000	26,354	15,422	10,933
WORLD REGION OF BIRTH			
Total foreign-born	**38,517**	**16,832**	**21,685**
Asia	10,652	6,193	4,459
Europe	4,887	3,000	1,887
Latin America	20,456	6,556	13,899
Mexico	11,478	2,609	8,869
Other Latin America	8,978	3,947	5,030
Other areas	2,522	1,097	1,425
Percent distribution by characteristics			
Total foreign-born	**100.0%**	**100.0%**	**100.0%**
YEAR OF ENTRY			
Total foreign-born	**100.0**	**100.0**	**100.0**
Entered U.S. 2000 or later	31.6	8.5	49.5
Entered U.S. before 2000	68.4	91.6	50.4
WORLD REGION OF BIRTH			
Total foreign-born	**100.0**	**100.0**	**100.0**
Asia	27.7	36.8	20.6
Europe	12.7	17.8	8.7
Latin America	53.1	38.9	64.1
Mexico	29.8	15.5	40.9
Other Latin America	23.3	23.4	23.2
Other areas	6.5	6.5	6.6
Percent distribution by citizenship status			
Total foreign-born	**100.0%**	**43.7%**	**56.3%**
YEAR OF ENTRY			
Total foreign-born	**100.0**	**43.7**	**56.3**
Entered U.S. 2000 or later	100.0	11.8	88.2
Entered U.S. before 2000	100.0	58.5	41.5
WORLD REGION OF BIRTH			
Total foreign-born	100.0	43.7	56.3
Asia	100.0	58.1	41.9
Europe	100.0	61.4	38.6
Latin America	100.0	32.0	67.9
Mexico	100.0	22.7	77.3
Other Latin America	100.0	44.0	56.0
Other areas	100.0	43.5	56.5

Source: Bureau of the Census, 2009 American Community Survey, Internet site http://www.census.gov/acs/www/; calculations by New Strategist

Table 8.27 Foreign-Born Population by Age, 2009

(total number of people, and number and percent who are foreign born, by age, 2009; numbers in thousands)

	total	foreign-born	
		number	percent
Total people	**307,007**	**38,517**	**12.5%**
Under age 5	21,209	270	1.3
Aged 5 to 17	53,288	2,504	4.7
Aged 18 to 24	30,558	3,235	10.6
Aged 25 to 44	83,048	16,370	19.7
Aged 45 to 54	44,597	6,856	15.4
Aged 55 to 64	34,800	4,545	13.1
Aged 65 to 74	20,826	2,696	12.9
Aged 75 to 84	13,169	1,502	11.4
Aged 85 or older	5,512	539	9.8

Source: Bureau of the Census, 2009 American Community Survey, Internet site http://www.census.gov/acs/www/; calculations by New Strategist

Table 8.28 Ancestry of the U.S. Population, 2009

(number and percent distribution of U.S. residents by selected ancestry group, 2009; numbers in thousands)

	number	percent
Total people	**307,007**	**100.0%**
German	50,709	16.5
Irish	36,915	12.0
English	27,659	9.0
American	18,699	6.1
Italian	18,087	5.9
Polish	10,091	3.3
French (except Basque)	9,412	3.1
Scottish	5,847	1.9
Dutch	5,024	1.6
Norwegian	4,643	1.5
Swedish	4,348	1.4
Scotch-Irish	3,570	1.2
European	3,197	1.0
Russian	3,163	1.0
Subsaharan African	2,866	0.9
West Indian (excluding Hispanic-origin groups)	2,572	0.8
French Canadian	2,151	0.7
Welsh	1,987	0.6
Arab	1,707	0.6
Czech	1,616	0.5
Hungarian	1,547	0.5
Danish	1,487	0.5
Portuguese	1,478	0.5
Greek	1,390	0.5
British	1,172	0.4
Swiss	1,018	0.3
Ukrainian	976	0.3
Slovak	801	0.3
Lithuanian	727	0.2

Note: Ancestries sum to more than the total population because more than one ancestry could be reported.
Source: Bureau of the Census, 2009 American Community Survey, Internet site http://www.census.gov/acs/www/; calculations by New Strategist

Millions of U.S. Residents Speak Spanish at Home

Most Spanish speakers also speak English.

More than 57 million U.S. residents speak a language other than English at home, or 20 percent of the population aged 5 or older according to the Census Bureau's 2009 American Community Survey. Spanish is by far the most common non-English language spoken at home, with 35 million speaking Spanish—or 62 percent of all those who speak a language other than English at home.

Among people who speak Spanish at home, 46 percent say they do not speak English very well. Among people who speak a Chinese language at home, a larger 55 percent say they do not speak English very well.

■ The number of Spanish speakers in the United States will continue to grow rapidly because of immigration from Mexico and other Latin American countries.

Spanish is much more likely to be spoken than other non-English languages

(number of people aged 5 or older who speak a language other than English at home, by language group, 2009; numbers in millions)

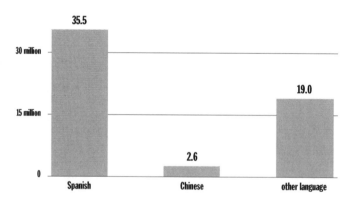

Table 8.29 Language Spoken at Home, 2009

(number and percent distribution of people aged 5 or older who speak Spanish or Chinese at home, and percent who speak English less than very well, 2009; numbers in thousands)

	number	percent distribution
Total population aged 5 or older	**285,797**	**100.0%**
Speak only English at home	228,700	80.0
Speak a language other than English at home	57,097	20.0
Total who speak a language other than English at home	**57,097**	**100.0**
Speak Spanish	35,469	62.1
Speak Chinese	2,600	4.6
Speak other language	19,028	33.3
Total who speak Spanish at home	**35,469**	**100.0**
Speak English less than very well	16,223	45.7
Total who speak Chinese at home	**2,600**	**100.0**
Speak English less than very well	1,429	55.0

Source: Bureau of the Census, 2009 American Community Survey, Internet site http://www.census.gov/acs/www/; calculations by New Strategist

9

Spending Trends

■ **Average household spending fell 5 percent between 2006 and 2009, after adjusting for inflation.**

Spending had increased 9 percent between 2000 and 2006 (the peak spending year), then fell with the onset of the Great Recession.

■ **Households headed by people aged 45 to 54 spend the most—$58,708 in 2009.**

The youngest householders, under age 25, spend the least—only $28,119.

■ **Households with incomes of $100,000 or more spend about twice as much as the average household.**

While the affluent represent only 18 percent of households, they control 36 percent of spending.

■ **Married couples with children spend much more than average.**

In 2009, couples with kids spent an average of $68,481 versus the $49,067 spent by the average household.

■ **Asians spend more than non-Hispanic whites, blacks, or Hispanics.**

Hispanics and blacks spend more than average on children's clothes and rent.

■ **Spending is higher in the Northeast than in the other regions.**

Households in the Northeast spent $53,868 in 2009, or 10 percent more than average.

■ **College graduates earn more and spend more than the average household.**

In 2009, households headed by college graduates spent $69,389—41 percent more than average.

Average Household Spending Fell between 2006 and 2009

Household spending has declined because of the Great Recession. In 2009, the average household spent $49,067—more than in 2000, but less than in 2006, after adjusting for inflation. According to data collected annually by the Bureau of Labor Statistics' Consumer Expenditure Survey, average household spending reached an all-time high in 2006 of $51,504. Spending peaked not only because of the easy money of the housing bubble, but also because the cost of necessities (housing, health, college, etc.) was climbing. Then the recession took hold. Between 2006 and 2009, spending by the average household fell 5 percent—down $2,437—as the hard times hit.

Although overall household spending was rising between 2000 and 2006, an examination of spending trends during those years reveals two opposing forces at work. On the one hand, the numbers show that some households were awash in the easy money that resulted from surging housing prices and the abuse of home equity loans. On the other hand, the cost of necessities was rising, forcing many households to trim their spending on discretionary items well before the official start of the recession.

Average household spending on housing increased 13 percent between 2000 and 2006, after adjusting inflation. That figure includes a 24 percent rise in property taxes as well as a 21 percent rise in spending on mortgage interest as the rate of homeownership reached a record high and some families bought larger homes than they could afford. Spending on audio and visual equipment and services grew 24 percent as many bought big-screen televisions and other electronics.

Households spent more, then cut back, on many items

(percent change in spending by the average household on selected products and services, 2000–06 and 2006–09; in 2009 dollars)

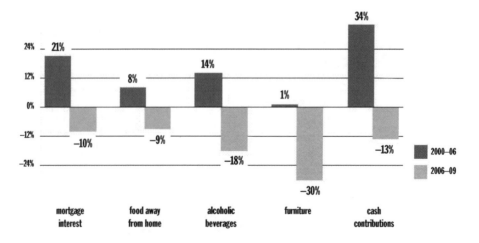

Ominously, however, the cost of necessities was climbing sharply. The average household spent 47 percent more on gasoline in 2006 than in 2000, after adjusting for inflation. Spending on utilities and heating fuels rose 17 percent during those years. Health insurance spending climbed 27 percent, and education spending increased 20 percent. The middle class was being squeezed, and consumers were cutting back. Spending on used vehicles plummeted 24 percent between 2000 and 2006, while spending on new vehicles fell 4 percent. Spending on women's clothes declined 11 percent, and spending on footwear dropped 24 percent. Despite the record-high homeownership rate, spending on household furnishings and equipment fell 6 percent between 2000 and 2006.

Those who track the government's Consumer Expenditure Survey could not have been surprised by these declines or the even deeper cuts that followed. For years, spending trends have suggested that American households were struggling. Between 2006 and 2009, spending on mortgage interest fell 10 percent. Cash contributions declined 13 percent. Spending on clothing and vehicles continued to plummet. Households also cut their spending on alcoholic beverages, food away from home, and furniture. American consumers have become cautious spenders, with enormous consequences for our economy.

Table 9.1 Household Spending Trends, 2000 to 2009

(average annual spending of consumer units, 2000 to 2009; percent change, 2000–06, 2006–09, and 2000–09; in 2009 dollars)

	2009	2006	2000	percent change 2000–06	2006–09	2000–09
Number of consumer units (in 000s)	120,847	118,843	109,367	8.7%	1.7%	10.5%
Average annual spending of consumer units	$49,067	$51,504	$47,399	8.7	–4.7	3.5
FOOD	6,372	6,503	6,426	1.2	–2.0	–0.8
Food at home	3,753	3,636	3,764	–3.4	3.2	–0.3
Cereals and bakery products	506	475	564	–15.9	6.6	–10.3
Cereals and cereal products	173	152	194	–21.7	13.7	–11.0
Bakery products	334	324	370	–12.6	3.2	–9.7
Meats, poultry, fish, and eggs	841	848	990	–14.4	–0.8	–15.1
Beef	226	251	297	–15.3	–10.0	–23.8
Pork	168	167	208	–19.7	0.6	–19.3
Other meats	114	112	126	–11.2	2.0	–9.4
Poultry	154	150	181	–16.9	2.6	–14.8
Fish and seafood	135	130	137	–5.3	4.0	–1.5
Eggs	44	39	42	–7.0	11.7	3.9
Dairy products	406	392	405	–3.3	3.7	0.3
Fresh milk and cream	144	149	163	–8.7	–3.3	–11.8
Other dairy products	262	243	240	0.9	8.0	9.0
Fruits and vegetables	656	630	649	–2.9	4.1	1.1
Fresh fruits	220	208	203	2.2	6.0	8.3
Fresh vegetables	209	205	198	3.7	1.8	5.5
Processed fruits	118	116	143	–19.0	1.7	–17.6
Processed vegetables	110	101	105	–3.4	8.8	5.1
Other food at home	1,343	1,290	1,155	11.7	4.1	16.3
Sugar and other sweets	141	133	146	–8.7	6.0	–3.3
Fats and oils	102	92	103	–11.5	11.5	–1.4
Miscellaneous foods	715	667	544	22.6	7.2	31.3
Nonalcoholic beverages	337	353	311	13.4	–4.6	8.2
Food prepared by consumer unit on trips	49	46	50	–8.2	7.1	–1.7
Food away from home	2,619	2,867	2,662	7.7	–8.6	–1.6
ALCOHOLIC BEVERAGES	435	529	463	14.1	–17.8	–6.1
HOUSING	16,895	17,416	15,348	13.5	–3.0	10.1
Shelter	10,075	10,294	8,863	16.1	–2.1	13.7
Owned dwellings	6,543	6,934	5,733	20.9	–5.6	14.1
Mortgage interest and charges	3,594	3,994	3,288	21.5	–10.0	9.3
Property taxes	1,811	1,755	1,419	23.7	3.2	27.6
Maintenance, repair, insurance, other expenses	1,138	1,187	1,028	15.4	–4.1	10.7
Rented dwellings	2,860	2,756	2,534	8.8	3.8	12.9
Other lodging	672	603	596	1.3	11.4	12.8
Utilities, fuels, and public services	3,645	3,615	3,101	16.6	0.8	17.5
Natural gas	483	542	382	41.6	–10.8	26.3
Electricity	1,377	1,347	1,135	18.7	2.2	21.3
Fuel oil and other fuels	141	147	121	21.5	–4.0	16.7
Telephone services	1,162	1,157	1,093	5.9	0.5	6.3
Water and other public services	481	422	369	14.6	13.9	30.4

	2009	2006	2000	percent change		
				2000–06	2006–09	2000–09
Household services	**$1,011**	**$1,009**	**$852**	**18.4%**	**0.2%**	**18.6%**
Personal services	389	418	406	3.0	−7.0	−4.2
Other household services	622	591	446	32.4	5.3	39.5
Housekeeping supplies	**659**	**681**	**601**	**13.4**	**−3.2**	**9.7**
Laundry and cleaning supplies	156	161	163	−1.5	−2.9	−4.4
Other household products	360	351	282	24.7	2.5	27.9
Postage and stationery	143	169	157	7.8	−15.5	−8.9
Household furnishings and equipment	**1,506**	**1,818**	**1,930**	**−5.8**	**−17.1**	**−22.0**
Household textiles	124	164	132	24.1	−24.3	−6.1
Furniture	343	493	487	1.1	−30.4	−29.6
Floor coverings	30	51	55	−6.8	−41.3	−45.3
Major appliances	194	256	235	8.9	−24.4	−17.6
Small appliances and miscellaneous housewares	93	116	108	7.0	−19.8	−14.2
Miscellaneous household equipment	721	737	911	−19.0	−2.2	−20.8
APPAREL AND RELATED SERVICES	**1,725**	**1,994**	**2,312**	**−13.8**	**−13.5**	**−25.4**
Men and boys	**383**	**472**	**548**	**−13.8**	**−18.9**	**−30.1**
Men, aged 16 or older	304	376	429	−12.3	−19.1	−29.1
Boys, aged 2 to 15	79	97	120	−19.0	−18.4	−33.9
Women and girls	**678**	**799**	**903**	**−11.5**	**−15.2**	**−24.9**
Women, aged 16 or older	561	669	756	−11.5	−16.2	−25.8
Girls, aged 2 to 15	118	130	147	−11.7	−9.1	−19.7
Children under age 2	**91**	**102**	**102**	**0.0**	**−10.9**	**−10.9**
Footwear	**323**	**324**	**427**	**−24.3**	**−0.2**	**−24.4**
Other apparel products and services	**249**	**298**	**331**	**−10.1**	**−16.4**	**−24.9**
TRANSPORTATION	**7,658**	**9,054**	**9,241**	**−2.0**	**−15.4**	**−17.1**
Vehicle purchases	**2,657**	**3,641**	**4,258**	**−14.5**	**−27.0**	**−37.6**
Cars and trucks, new	1,297	1,913	2,000	−4.3	−32.2	−35.1
Cars and trucks, used	1,304	1,669	2,205	−24.3	−21.9	−40.9
Other vehicles	55	57	54	7.3	−4.3	2.7
Gasoline and motor oil	**1,986**	**2,370**	**1,608**	**47.3**	**−16.2**	**23.5**
Other vehicle expenses	**2,536**	**2,506**	**2,842**	**−11.8**	**1.2**	**−10.8**
Vehicle finance charges	281	317	409	−22.4	−11.4	−31.2
Maintenance and repairs	733	732	777	−5.8	0.1	−5.7
Vehicle insurance	1,075	943	969	−2.7	14.0	10.9
Vehicle rentals, leases, licenses, other charges	447	513	686	−25.3	−12.9	−34.9
Public transportation	**479**	**537**	**532**	**1.0**	**−10.9**	**−10.0**
HEALTH CARE	**3,126**	**2,943**	**2,574**	**14.4**	**6.2**	**21.4**
Health insurance	1,785	1,559	1,225	27.3	14.5	45.8
Medical services	736	713	708	0.8	3.2	4.0
Drugs	486	547	518	5.5	−11.1	−6.2
Medical supplies	119	125	123	0.9	−4.4	−3.5
ENTERTAINMENT	**2,693**	**2,528**	**2,321**	**8.9**	**6.5**	**16.0**
Fees and admissions	628	645	642	0.5	−2.6	−2.1
Audio and visual equipment and services	975	964	775	24.4	1.1	25.8
Pets, toys, and playground equipment	690	438	416	5.4	57.4	65.8
Other entertainment products and services	400	480	490	−2.0	−16.7	−18.3
PERSONAL CARE PRODUCTS AND SERVICES	**596**	**623**	**703**	**−11.4**	**−4.3**	**−15.2**
READING	**110**	**125**	**182**	**−31.5**	**−11.7**	**−39.5**
EDUCATION	**1,068**	**945**	**787**	**20.0**	**13.0**	**35.6**

	2009	2006	2000	percent change		
				2000–06	2006–09	2000–09
TOBACCO PRODUCTS AND SMOKING SUPPLIES	**$380**	**$348**	**$397**	**–12.4%**	**9.2%**	**–4.4%**
MISCELLANEOUS	**816**	**900**	**967**	**–6.9**	**–9.4**	**–15.6**
CASH CONTRIBUTIONS	**1,723**	**1,989**	**1,485**	**33.9**	**–13.4**	**16.0**
PERSONAL INSURANCE, PENSIONS	**5,471**	**5,608**	**4,192**	**33.8**	**–2.4**	**30.5**
Life and other personal insurance	309	343	497	–31.1	–9.8	–37.8
Pensions and Social Security	5,162	5,266	3,695	–	–2.0	–
PERSONAL TAXES	**2,104**	**2,588**	**3,883**	**–33.4**	**–18.7**	**–45.8**
Federal income taxes	1,404	1,821	3,001	–39.3	–22.9	–53.2
State and local income taxes	177	215	182	18.2	–17.7	–2.7
Other taxes	1,067	1,228	1,349	–9.0	–13.1	–20.9
GIFTS FOR PEOPLE IN OTHER HOUSEHOLDS	**1,209**	**1,232**	**1,354**	**–9.0**	**–1.9**	**–10.7**

Note: Spending by category does not add to total spending because gift spending is also included in the preceding product and service categories and personal taxes are not included in the total. "–" means calculation is meaningless because of a change in methodology.
Source: Bureau of Labor Statistics, 2000, 2006, and 2009 Consumer Expenditure Surveys, Internet site http://www.bls.gov/cex/; calculations by New Strategist

Householders Aged 35 to 54 Spend the Most

The youngest householders spend the least.

Households headed by people aged 45 to 54 spent an average of $58,708 in 2009—20 percent more than the average household. Close behind are householders aged 35 to 44, who spent an average of $57,301, according to the Bureau of Labor Statistics' Consumer Expenditure Survey. Middle-aged householders spend more than younger and older householders not only because they have higher incomes, but also because their households typically are larger than average because they include children.

Households headed by people under age 25 spend less than any other age group, just $28,119 in 2009. This figure is well below the spending of householders aged 75 or older, which stood at $31,676 in 2009.

The Indexed Spending table shows spending by age of householder in comparison with average household spending. An index of 100 means households in the age group spend an average amount on the item. An index above 100 indicates that households in the age group spend more than average on the item, while an index below 100 reveals below-average spending.

A look at Table 9.3 shows that spending is below average on most items for households headed by the youngest and the oldest householders—those under age 25 and those aged 75 or older. Spending is much closer to the average on most items for households headed by 25-to-34-year-olds and

Spending peaks in middle age

(average annual spending of consumer units by age of consumer unit reference person, 2009)

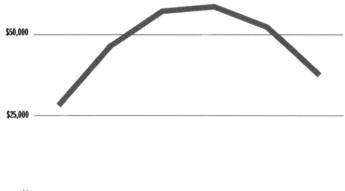

65-to-74-year-olds. Spending is above average in most categories for householders spanning the ages from 35 to 64. There are some exceptions, however. Householders under age 25 spend 71 percent more than average on rent (with an index of 171). They spend 68 percent more than average on baby clothes and 79 percent more than average on education because many are in college. The oldest householders spend 22 percent more than the average household on reading material, 38 percent more on cash contributions, and 16 percent more on postage and stationery.

The Market Share table shows how much of total spending by category is accounted for by the various age groups. Householders aged 35 to 54 accounted for 47 percent of total household spending in 2009, down from their 51 percent share a few years ago as boomers exit the age group. Nevertheless, the 35-to-54 age group still accounts for more than half of spending on many products and services such as boys' clothes (58 percent), girls' clothes (60 percent), mortgage interest (57 percent), fees and admissions to entertainment events (54 percent), and education (57 percent). Householders under age 35 control only 19 percent of spending, while a larger 34 percent is accounted for by householders aged 55 or older.

■ The share of spending controlled by householders aged 55 to 64 is growing as boomers fill the age group and early retirement becomes less common.

Table 9.2 Average Spending by Age of Householder, 2009

(average annual spending of consumer units (CUs) by product and service category and age of consumer unit reference person, 2009)

	total consumer units	under 25	25 to 34	35 to 44	45 to 54	55 to 64	aged 65 or older total	65 to 74	75 or older
Number of CUs (in 000s)	120,847	7,875	20,044	22,199	25,440	20,731	24,557	12,848	11,709
Average number of persons per CU	2.5	2.0	2.8	3.3	2.8	2.1	1.7	1.9	1.6
Average annual spending	**$49,067**	**$28,119**	**$46,494**	**$57,301**	**$58,708**	**$52,463**	**$37,562**	**$42,957**	**$31,676**
FOOD	**6,372**	**4,179**	**6,169**	**7,760**	**7,445**	**6,303**	**4,901**	**5,561**	**4,189**
Food at home	**3,753**	**2,449**	**3,478**	**4,446**	**4,343**	**3,678**	**3,222**	**3,567**	**2,851**
Cereals and bakery products	506	307	473	629	586	465	439	463	414
Cereals and cereal products	173	124	177	223	188	152	138	151	124
Bakery products	334	183	296	406	397	313	301	312	290
Meats, poultry, fish, and eggs	841	571	757	983	978	849	720	849	581
Beef	226	146	196	263	263	242	192	246	133
Pork	168	130	147	198	196	166	145	168	120
Other meats	114	68	102	139	129	110	101	114	87
Poultry	154	120	160	188	177	147	111	121	100
Fish and seafood	135	75	111	145	166	142	129	153	104
Eggs	44	33	40	50	47	43	42	48	37
Dairy products	406	281	376	495	465	386	346	381	308
Fresh milk and cream	144	110	144	179	155	127	125	136	113
Other dairy products	262	171	232	315	310	259	221	244	195
Fruits and vegetables	656	398	593	739	750	663	618	684	546
Fresh fruits	220	116	189	249	249	227	215	244	185
Fresh vegetables	209	130	184	229	247	219	192	220	161
Processed fruits	118	86	114	135	136	105	109	107	110
Processed vegetables	110	67	106	126	118	111	102	113	91
Other food at home	1,343	891	1,280	1,600	1,564	1,314	1,100	1,190	1,002
Sugar and other sweets	141	88	112	162	170	147	127	138	115
Fats and oils	102	63	94	116	117	106	91	104	77
Miscellaneous foods	715	495	729	869	810	664	576	584	568
Nonalcoholic beverages	337	232	315	401	405	329	264	309	216
Food prepared by consumer unit on trips	49	13	31	51	62	68	42	56	27
Food away from home	**2,619**	**1,731**	**2,691**	**3,314**	**3,102**	**2,626**	**1,679**	**1,994**	**1,338**
ALCOHOLIC BEVERAGES	**435**	**344**	**481**	**498**	**502**	**440**	**292**	**389**	**188**
HOUSING	**16,895**	**9,735**	**17,258**	**20,705**	**19,004**	**16,991**	**13,196**	**14,462**	**11,811**
Shelter	**10,075**	**6,306**	**10,856**	**12,753**	**11,356**	**9,749**	**7,173**	**7,828**	**6,454**
Owned dwellings	6,543	1,245	5,581	8,832	8,093	7,149	4,838	5,802	3,781
Mortgage interest and charges	3,594	783	3,843	5,863	4,677	3,352	1,322	1,976	603
Property taxes	1,811	324	1,130	2,022	2,296	2,234	1,793	1,950	1,622
Maintenance, repair, insurance, other expenses	1,138	139	608	947	1,120	1,563	1,723	1,876	1,556
Rented dwellings	2,860	4,885	4,877	3,328	2,369	1,570	1,741	1,320	2,202
Other lodging	672	176	398	593	894	1,031	594	706	471
Utilities, fuels, and public services	**3,645**	**1,821**	**3,249**	**4,093**	**4,275**	**3,896**	**3,282**	**3,568**	**2,967**
Natural gas	483	188	405	524	552	530	494	485	504
Electricity	1,377	696	1,232	1,529	1,596	1,481	1,261	1,386	1,123
Fuel oil and other fuels	141	16	62	131	179	177	186	192	179
Telephone services	1,162	758	1,142	1,372	1,398	1,179	858	1,003	700
Water and other public services	481	163	409	537	550	528	483	503	461

	total consumer units	under 25	25 to 34	35 to 44	45 to 54	55 to 64	aged 65 or older total	65 to 74	75 or older
Household services	**$1,011**	**$370**	**$1,231**	**$1,377**	**$964**	**$871**	**$876**	**$801**	**$957**
Personal services	389	156	786	753	253	103	194	111	285
Other household services	622	214	445	623	711	767	681	690	672
Housekeeping supplies	**659**	**309**	**506**	**698**	**703**	**825**	**682**	**773**	**584**
Laundry and cleaning supplies	156	91	148	187	172	157	137	161	112
Other household products	360	168	247	372	380	490	377	443	306
Postage and stationery	143	49	111	139	152	178	167	169	166
Household furnishings and equipment	**1,506**	**929**	**1,416**	**1,786**	**1,705**	**1,651**	**1,184**	**1,491**	**850**
Household textiles	124	43	99	154	135	154	107	125	88
Furniture	343	336	432	391	375	330	209	252	163
Floor coverings	30	5	17	28	39	36	37	49	25
Major appliances	194	79	164	216	199	278	159	197	117
Small appliances, miscellaneous housewares	93	39	88	96	103	110	90	121	57
Miscellaneous household equipment	721	427	616	901	855	743	581	747	401
APPAREL AND RELATED SERVICES	**1,725**	**1,396**	**1,871**	**2,346**	**1,885**	**1,591**	**1,068**	**1,322**	**793**
Men and boys	**383**	**256**	**407**	**562**	**443**	**335**	**215**	**277**	**148**
Men, aged 16 or older	304	228	291	405	360	301	190	244	132
Boys, aged 2 to 15	79	28	116	156	83	34	25	33	16
Women and girls	**678**	**545**	**677**	**871**	**772**	**664**	**456**	**541**	**364**
Women, aged 16 or older	561	480	533	624	652	596	427	503	346
Girls, aged 2 to 15	118	65	144	248	120	69	29	38	18
Children under age 2	**91**	**153**	**198**	**109**	**50**	**66**	**26**	**39**	**12**
Footwear	**323**	**278**	**336**	**449**	**351**	**269**	**223**	**262**	**181**
Other apparel products and services	**249**	**163**	**253**	**355**	**270**	**256**	**149**	**204**	**88**
TRANSPORTATION	**7,658**	**5,334**	**7,671**	**8,364**	**9,409**	**8,323**	**5,409**	**7,033**	**3,631**
Vehicle purchases	**2,657**	**2,319**	**2,820**	**2,761**	**3,233**	**2,752**	**1,862**	**2,597**	**1,055**
Cars and trucks, new	1,297	542	1,063	1,199	1,618	1,623	1,210	1,604	778
Cars and trucks, used	1,304	1,760	1,682	1,523	1,532	1,064	619	932	277
Gasoline and motor oil	**1,986**	**1,483**	**2,071**	**2,359**	**2,398**	**2,074**	**1,241**	**1,573**	**877**
Other vehicle expenses	**2,536**	**1,298**	**2,293**	**2,694**	**3,199**	**2,962**	**1,968**	**2,488**	**1,402**
Vehicle finance charges	281	180	353	357	333	291	124	188	54
Maintenance and repairs	733	447	654	766	927	854	557	696	406
Vehicle insurance	1,075	465	837	1,055	1,406	1,307	972	1,214	712
Vehicle rentals, leases, licenses, other charges	447	206	450	516	534	510	314	390	230
Public transportation	**479**	**234**	**487**	**549**	**579**	**535**	**338**	**376**	**297**
HEALTH CARE	**3,126**	**676**	**1,805**	**2,520**	**3,173**	**3,895**	**4,846**	**4,906**	**4,779**
Health insurance	1,785	381	1,083	1,436	1,688	2,017	3,027	3,042	3,011
Medical services	736	167	466	650	862	1,054	821	818	824
Drugs	486	97	195	335	485	679	828	865	787
Medical supplies	119	30	61	100	139	144	170	181	158
ENTERTAINMENT	**2,693**	**1,233**	**2,504**	**3,317**	**3,176**	**2,906**	**2,062**	**2,498**	**1,587**
Fees and admissions	628	234	521	917	811	629	387	497	266
Audio and visual equipment and services	975	574	1,018	1,111	1,065	1,024	807	934	669
Pets, toys, hobbies, playground equipment	690	295	546	816	855	777	580	775	367
Other entertainment products and services	400	130	419	473	445	476	288	292	285
PERSONAL CARE PRODUCTS AND SERVICES	**596**	**360**	**555**	**685**	**666**	**617**	**531**	**600**	**456**
READING	**110**	**42**	**69**	**85**	**119**	**147**	**145**	**154**	**134**
EDUCATION	**1,068**	**1,910**	**808**	**935**	**2,055**	**1,003**	**162**	**181**	**141**

	total consumer units	under 25	25 to 34	35 to 44	45 to 54	55 to 64	aged 65 or older		
							total	65 to 74	75 or older
TOBACCO PRODUCTS AND SMOKING SUPPLIES	$380	$330	$368	$417	$513	$410	$207	$275	$133
MISCELLANEOUS	816	243	631	967	1,051	952	663	820	491
CASH CONTRIBUTIONS	1,723	349	1,001	1,581	2,056	2,092	2,226	2,087	2,378
PERSONAL INSURANCE AND PENSIONS	5,471	1,988	5,303	7,122	7,654	6,793	1,856	2,669	964
Life and other personal insurance	309	31	156	270	427	446	320	397	234
Pensions and Social Security	5,162	1,957	5,147	6,851	7,226	6,347	1,537	2,272	730
PERSONAL TAXES	2,104	173	1,707	2,105	3,515	3,023	807	1,140	443
Federal income taxes	1,404	25	1,063	1,306	2,510	2,090	490	761	194
State and local income taxes	524	144	550	658	779	673	113	183	37
Other taxes	177	5	94	143	229	261	205	197	214
GIFTS FOR PEOPLE IN OTHER HOUSEHOLDS	1,067	386	641	797	1,653	1,582	839	989	676

Note: Spending by category does not add to total spending because gift spending is also included in the preceding product and service categories and personal taxes are not included in the total.
Source: Bureau of Labor Statistics' 2009 Consumer Expenditure Survey, Internet site http://www.bls.gov/cex/

Table 9.3 Indexed Spending by Age of Householder, 2009

(indexed average annual spending of consumer units by product and service category and age of consumer unit reference person, 2009; index definition: an index of 100 is the average for all consumer units; an index of 125 means that spending by consumer units in that group is 25 percent above the average for all consumer units; an index of 75 indicates spending that is 25 percent below the average for all consumer units)

	total consumer units	under 25	25 to 34	35 to 44	45 to 54	55 to 64	aged 65 or older total	65 to 74	75 or older
Average spending of consumer units	$49,067	$28,119	$46,494	$57,301	$58,708	$52,463	$37,562	$42,957	$31,676
Indexed spending of consumer units	100	57	95	117	120	107	77	88	65
FOOD	100	66	97	122	117	99	77	87	66
Food at home	100	65	93	118	116	98	86	95	76
Cereals and bakery products	100	61	93	124	116	92	87	92	82
Cereals and cereal products	100	72	102	129	109	88	80	87	72
Bakery products	100	55	89	122	119	94	90	93	87
Meats, poultry, fish, and eggs	100	68	90	117	116	101	86	101	69
Beef	100	65	87	116	116	107	85	109	59
Pork	100	77	88	118	117	99	86	100	71
Other meats	100	60	89	122	113	96	89	100	76
Poultry	100	78	104	122	115	95	72	79	65
Fish and seafood	100	56	82	107	123	105	96	113	77
Eggs	100	75	91	114	107	98	95	109	84
Dairy products	100	69	93	122	115	95	85	94	76
Fresh milk and cream	100	76	100	124	108	88	87	94	78
Other dairy products	100	65	89	120	118	99	84	93	74
Fruits and vegetables	100	61	90	113	114	101	94	104	83
Fresh fruits	100	53	86	113	113	103	98	111	84
Fresh vegetables	100	62	88	110	118	105	92	105	77
Processed fruits	100	73	97	114	115	89	92	91	93
Processed vegetables	100	61	96	115	107	101	93	103	83
Other food at home	100	66	95	119	116	98	82	89	75
Sugar and other sweets	100	62	79	115	121	104	90	98	82
Fats and oils	100	62	92	114	115	104	89	102	75
Miscellaneous foods	100	69	102	122	113	93	81	82	79
Nonalcoholic beverages	100	69	93	119	120	98	78	92	64
Food prepared by consumer unit on trips	100	27	63	104	127	139	86	114	55
Food away from home	100	66	103	127	118	100	64	76	51
ALCOHOLIC BEVERAGES	100	79	111	114	115	101	67	89	43
HOUSING	100	58	102	123	112	101	78	86	70
Shelter	100	63	108	127	113	97	71	78	64
Owned dwellings	100	19	85	135	124	109	74	89	58
Mortgage interest and charges	100	22	107	163	130	93	37	55	17
Property taxes	100	18	62	112	127	123	99	108	90
Maintenance, repair, insurance, other expenses	100	12	53	83	98	137	151	165	137
Rented dwellings	100	171	171	116	83	55	61	46	77
Other lodging	100	26	59	88	133	153	88	105	70
Utilities, fuels, and public services	100	50	89	112	117	107	90	98	81
Natural gas	100	39	84	108	114	110	102	100	104
Electricity	100	51	89	111	116	108	92	101	82
Fuel oil and other fuels	100	11	44	93	127	126	132	136	127
Telephone services	100	65	98	118	120	101	74	86	60
Water and other public services	100	34	85	112	114	110	100	105	96

	total consumer units	under 25	25 to 34	35 to 44	45 to 54	55 to 64	aged 65 or older total	65 to 74	75 or older
Household services	100	37	122	136	95	86	87	79	95
Personal services	100	40	202	194	65	26	50	29	73
Other household services	100	34	72	100	114	123	109	111	108
Housekeeping supplies	100	47	77	106	107	125	103	117	89
Laundry and cleaning supplies	100	58	95	120	110	101	88	103	72
Other household products	100	47	69	103	106	136	105	123	85
Postage and stationery	100	34	78	97	106	124	117	118	116
Household furnishings and equipment	100	62	94	119	113	110	79	99	56
Household textiles	100	35	80	124	109	124	86	101	71
Furniture	100	98	126	114	109	96	61	73	48
Floor coverings	100	17	57	93	130	120	123	163	83
Major appliances	100	41	85	111	103	143	82	102	60
Small appliances, miscellaneous housewares	100	42	95	103	111	118	97	130	61
Miscellaneous household equipment	100	59	85	125	119	103	81	104	56
APPAREL AND RELATED SERVICES	100	81	108	136	109	92	62	77	46
Men and boys	100	67	106	147	116	87	56	72	39
Men, aged 16 or older	100	75	96	133	118	99	63	80	43
Boys, aged 2 to 15	100	35	147	197	105	43	32	42	20
Women and girls	100	80	100	128	114	98	67	80	54
Women, aged 16 or older	100	86	95	111	116	106	76	90	62
Girls, aged 2 to 15	100	55	122	210	102	58	25	32	15
Children under age 2	100	168	218	120	55	73	29	43	13
Footwear	100	86	104	139	109	83	69	81	56
Other apparel products and services	100	65	102	143	108	103	60	82	35
TRANSPORTATION	100	70	100	109	123	109	71	92	47
Vehicle purchases	100	87	106	104	122	104	70	98	40
Cars and trucks, new	100	42	82	92	125	125	93	124	60
Cars and trucks, used	100	135	129	117	117	82	47	71	21
Gasoline and motor oil	100	75	104	119	121	104	62	79	44
Other vehicle expenses	100	51	90	106	126	117	78	98	55
Vehicle finance charges	100	64	126	127	119	104	44	67	19
Maintenance and repairs	100	61	89	105	126	117	76	95	55
Vehicle insurance	100	43	78	98	131	122	90	113	66
Vehicle rentals, leases, licenses, other charges	100	46	101	115	119	114	70	87	51
Public transportation	100	49	102	115	121	112	71	78	62
HEALTH CARE	100	22	58	81	102	125	155	157	153
Health insurance	100	21	61	80	95	113	170	170	169
Medical services	100	23	63	88	117	143	112	111	112
Drugs	100	20	40	69	100	140	170	178	162
Medical supplies	100	25	51	84	117	121	143	152	133
ENTERTAINMENT	100	46	93	123	118	108	77	93	59
Fees and admissions	100	37	83	146	129	100	62	79	42
Audio and visual equipment and services	100	59	104	114	109	105	83	96	69
Pets, toys, hobbies, playground equipment	100	43	79	118	124	113	84	112	53
Other entertainment products and services	100	33	105	118	111	119	72	73	71
PERSONAL CARE PRODUCTS AND SERVICES	100	60	93	115	112	104	89	101	77
READING	100	38	63	77	108	134	132	140	122
EDUCATION	100	179	76	88	192	94	15	17	13

	total consumer units	under 25	25 to 34	35 to 44	45 to 54	55 to 64	aged 65 or older		
							total	65 to 74	75 or older
TOBACCO PRODUCTS AND SMOKING SUPPLIES	**100**	**87**	**97**	**110**	**135**	**108**	**54**	**72**	**35**
MISCELLANEOUS	**100**	**30**	**77**	**119**	**129**	**117**	**81**	**100**	**60**
CASH CONTRIBUTIONS	**100**	**20**	**58**	**92**	**119**	**121**	**129**	**121**	**138**
PERSONAL INSURANCE AND PENSIONS	**100**	**36**	**97**	**130**	**140**	**124**	**34**	**49**	**18**
Life and other personal insurance	100	10	50	87	138	144	104	128	76
Pensions and Social Security	100	38	100	133	140	123	30	44	14
PERSONAL TAXES	**100**	**8**	**81**	**100**	**167**	**144**	**38**	**54**	**21**
Federal income taxes	100	2	76	93	179	149	35	54	14
State and local income taxes	100	27	105	126	149	128	22	35	7
Other taxes	100	3	53	81	129	147	116	111	121
GIFTS FOR PEOPLE IN OTHER HOUSEHOLDS	**100**	**36**	**60**	**75**	**155**	**148**	**79**	**93**	**63**

Source: Calculations by New Strategist based on the Bureau of Labor Statistics 2009, Consumer Expenditure Survey, Internet site http://www.bls.gov/cex/home.htm

Table 9.4 Market Shares by Age of Householder, 2009

(share of total household spending accounted for by age group, 2009)

	total consumer units	under 25	25 to 34	35 to 44	45 to 54	55 to 64	aged 65 or older total	65 to 74	75 or older
Share of total consumer units	100.0%	6.5%	16.6%	18.4%	21.1%	17.2%	20.3%	10.6%	9.7%
Share of total spending	100.0	3.7	15.7	21.5	25.2	18.3	15.6	9.3	6.3
FOOD	100.0	4.3	16.1	22.4	24.6	17.0	15.6	9.3	6.4
Food at home	100.0	4.3	15.4	21.8	24.4	16.8	17.4	10.1	7.4
Cereals and bakery products	100.0	4.0	15.5	22.8	24.4	15.8	17.6	9.7	7.9
Cereals and cereal products	100.0	4.7	17.0	23.7	22.9	15.1	16.2	9.3	6.9
Bakery products	100.0	3.6	14.7	22.3	25.0	16.1	18.3	9.9	8.4
Meats, poultry, fish, and eggs	100.0	4.4	14.9	21.5	24.5	17.3	17.4	10.7	6.7
Beef	100.0	4.2	14.4	21.4	24.5	18.4	17.3	11.6	5.7
Pork	100.0	5.0	14.5	21.6	24.6	17.0	17.5	10.6	6.9
Other meats	100.0	3.9	14.8	22.4	23.8	16.6	18.0	10.6	7.4
Poultry	100.0	5.1	17.2	22.4	24.2	16.4	14.6	8.4	6.3
Fish and seafood	100.0	3.6	13.6	19.7	25.9	18.0	19.4	12.0	7.5
Eggs	100.0	4.9	15.1	20.9	22.5	16.8	19.4	11.6	8.1
Dairy products	100.0	4.5	15.4	22.4	24.1	16.3	17.3	10.0	7.4
Fresh milk and cream	100.0	5.0	16.6	22.8	22.7	15.1	17.6	10.0	7.6
Other dairy products	100.0	4.3	14.7	22.1	24.9	17.0	17.1	9.9	7.2
Fruits and vegetables	100.0	4.0	15.0	20.7	24.1	17.3	19.1	11.1	8.1
Fresh fruits	100.0	3.4	14.2	20.8	23.8	17.7	19.9	11.8	8.1
Fresh vegetables	100.0	4.1	14.6	20.1	24.9	18.0	18.7	11.2	7.5
Processed fruits	100.0	4.7	16.0	21.0	24.3	15.3	18.8	9.6	9.0
Processed vegetables	100.0	4.0	16.0	21.0	22.6	17.3	18.8	10.9	8.0
Other food at home	100.0	4.3	15.8	21.9	24.5	16.8	16.6	9.4	7.2
Sugar and other sweets	100.0	4.1	13.2	21.1	25.4	17.9	18.3	10.4	7.9
Fats and oils	100.0	4.0	15.3	20.9	24.1	17.8	18.1	10.8	7.3
Miscellaneous foods	100.0	4.5	16.9	22.3	23.8	15.9	16.4	8.7	7.7
Nonalcoholic beverages	100.0	4.5	15.5	21.9	25.3	16.7	15.9	9.7	6.2
Food prepared by consumer unit on trips	100.0	1.7	10.5	19.1	26.6	23.8	17.4	12.2	5.3
Food away from home	100.0	4.3	17.0	23.2	24.9	17.2	13.0	8.1	4.9
ALCOHOLIC BEVERAGES	100.0	5.2	18.3	21.0	24.3	17.4	13.6	9.5	4.2
HOUSING	100.0	3.8	16.9	22.5	23.7	17.3	15.9	9.1	6.8
Shelter	100.0	4.1	17.9	23.3	23.7	16.6	14.5	8.3	6.2
Owned dwellings	100.0	1.2	14.1	24.8	26.0	18.7	15.0	9.4	5.6
Mortgage interest and charges	100.0	1.4	17.7	30.0	27.4	16.0	7.5	5.8	1.6
Property taxes	100.0	1.2	10.3	20.5	26.7	21.2	20.1	11.4	8.7
Maintenance, repair, insurance, other expenses	100.0	0.8	8.9	15.3	20.7	23.6	30.8	17.5	13.2
Rented dwellings	100.0	11.1	28.3	21.4	17.4	9.4	12.4	4.9	7.5
Other lodging	100.0	1.7	9.8	16.2	28.0	26.3	18.0	11.2	6.8
Utilities, fuels, and public services	100.0	3.3	14.8	20.6	24.7	18.3	18.3	10.4	7.9
Natural gas	100.0	2.5	13.9	19.9	24.1	18.8	20.8	10.7	10.1
Electricity	100.0	3.3	14.8	20.4	24.4	18.5	18.6	10.7	7.9
Fuel oil and other fuels	100.0	0.7	7.3	17.1	26.7	21.5	26.8	14.5	12.3
Telephone services	100.0	4.3	16.3	21.7	25.3	17.4	15.0	9.2	5.8
Water and other public services	100.0	2.2	14.1	20.5	24.1	18.8	20.4	11.1	9.3

	total consumer units	under 25	25 to 34	35 to 44	45 to 54	55 to 64	aged 65 or older total	65 to 74	75 or older
Household services	100.0%	2.4%	20.2%	25.0%	20.1%	14.8%	17.6%	8.4%	9.2%
Personal services	100.0	2.6	33.5	35.6	13.7	4.5	10.1	3.0	7.1
Other household services	100.0	2.2	11.9	18.4	24.1	21.2	22.2	11.8	10.5
Housekeeping supplies	100.0	3.1	12.7	19.5	22.5	21.5	21.0	12.5	8.6
Laundry and cleaning supplies	100.0	3.8	15.7	22.0	23.2	17.3	17.8	11.0	7.0
Other household products	100.0	3.0	11.4	19.0	22.2	23.3	21.3	13.1	8.2
Postage and stationery	100.0	2.2	12.9	17.9	22.4	21.4	23.7	12.6	11.2
Household furnishings and equipment	100.0	4.0	15.6	21.8	23.8	18.8	16.0	10.5	5.5
Household textiles	100.0	2.3	13.2	22.8	22.9	21.3	17.5	10.7	6.9
Furniture	100.0	6.4	20.9	20.9	23.0	16.5	12.4	7.8	4.6
Floor coverings	100.0	1.1	9.4	17.1	27.4	20.6	25.1	17.4	8.1
Major appliances	100.0	2.7	14.0	20.5	21.6	24.6	16.7	10.8	5.8
Small appliances, misc. housewares	100.0	2.7	15.7	19.0	23.3	20.3	19.7	13.8	5.9
Miscellaneous household equipment	100.0	3.9	14.2	23.0	25.0	17.7	16.4	11.0	5.4
APPAREL AND RELATED SERVICES	100.0	5.3	18.0	25.0	23.0	15.8	12.6	8.1	4.5
Men and boys	100.0	4.4	17.6	27.0	24.3	15.0	11.4	7.7	3.7
Men, aged 16 or older	100.0	4.9	15.9	24.5	24.9	17.0	12.7	8.5	4.2
Boys, aged 2 to 15	100.0	2.3	24.4	36.3	22.1	7.4	6.4	4.4	2.0
Women and girls	100.0	5.2	16.6	23.6	24.0	16.8	13.7	8.5	5.2
Women, aged 16 or older	100.0	5.6	15.8	20.4	24.5	18.2	15.5	9.5	6.0
Girls, aged 2 to 15	100.0	3.6	20.2	38.6	21.4	10.0	5.0	3.4	1.5
Children under age 2	100.0	11.0	36.1	22.0	11.6	12.4	5.8	4.6	1.3
Footwear	100.0	5.6	17.3	25.5	22.9	14.3	14.0	8.6	5.4
Other apparel products and services	100.0	4.3	16.9	26.2	22.8	17.6	12.2	8.7	3.4
TRANSPORTATION	100.0	4.5	16.6	20.1	25.9	18.6	14.4	9.8	4.6
Vehicle purchases	100.0	5.7	17.6	19.1	25.6	17.8	14.2	10.4	3.8
Cars and trucks, new	100.0	2.7	13.6	17.0	26.3	21.5	19.0	13.1	5.8
Cars and trucks, used	100.0	8.8	21.4	21.5	24.7	14.0	9.6	7.6	2.1
Gasoline and motor oil	100.0	4.9	17.3	21.8	25.4	17.9	12.7	8.4	4.3
Other vehicle expenses	100.0	3.3	15.0	19.5	26.6	20.0	15.8	10.4	5.4
Vehicle finance charges	100.0	4.2	20.8	23.3	24.9	17.8	9.0	7.1	1.9
Maintenance and repairs	100.0	4.0	14.8	19.2	26.6	20.0	15.4	10.1	5.4
Vehicle insurance	100.0	2.8	12.9	18.0	27.5	20.9	18.4	12.0	6.4
Vehicle rentals, leases, licenses, other charges	100.0	3.0	16.7	21.2	25.1	19.6	14.3	9.3	5.0
Public transportation	100.0	3.2	16.9	21.1	25.4	19.2	14.3	8.3	6.0
HEALTH CARE	100.0	1.4	9.6	14.8	21.4	21.4	31.5	16.7	14.8
Health insurance	100.0	1.4	10.1	14.8	19.9	19.4	34.5	18.1	16.3
Medical services	100.0	1.5	10.5	16.2	24.7	24.6	22.7	11.8	10.8
Drugs	100.0	1.3	6.7	12.7	21.0	24.0	34.6	18.9	15.7
Medical supplies	100.0	1.6	8.5	15.4	24.6	20.8	29.0	16.2	12.9
ENTERTAINMENT	100.0	3.0	15.4	22.6	24.8	18.5	15.6	9.9	5.7
Fees and admissions	100.0	2.4	13.8	26.8	27.2	17.2	12.5	8.4	4.1
Audio and visual equipment and services	100.0	3.8	17.3	20.9	23.0	18.0	16.8	10.2	6.6
Pets, toys, hobbies, playground equipment	100.0	2.8	13.1	21.7	26.1	19.3	17.1	11.9	5.2
Other entertainment products and services	100.0	2.1	17.4	21.7	23.4	20.4	14.6	7.8	6.9
PERSONAL CARE PRODUCTS AND SERVICES	100.0	3.9	15.4	21.1	23.5	17.8	18.1	10.7	7.4
READING	100.0	2.5	10.4	14.2	22.8	22.9	26.8	14.9	11.8
EDUCATION	100.0	11.7	12.5	16.1	40.5	16.1	3.1	1.8	1.3

	total consumer units	under 25	25 to 34	35 to 44	45 to 54	55 to 64	aged 65 or older total	65 to 74	75 or older
TOBACCO PRODUCTS AND SMOKING SUPPLIES	**100.0%**	**5.7%**	**16.1%**	**20.2%**	**28.4%**	**18.5%**	**11.1%**	**7.7%**	**3.4%**
MISCELLANEOUS	**100.0**	**1.9**	**12.8**	**21.8**	**27.1**	**20.0**	**16.5**	**10.7**	**5.8**
CASH CONTRIBUTIONS	**100.0**	**1.3**	**9.6**	**16.9**	**25.1**	**20.8**	**26.3**	**12.9**	**13.4**
PERSONAL INSURANCE AND PENSIONS	**100.0**	**2.4**	**16.1**	**23.9**	**29.5**	**21.3**	**6.9**	**5.2**	**1.7**
Life and other personal insurance	100.0	0.7	8.4	16.1	29.1	24.8	21.0	13.7	7.3
Pensions and Social Security	100.0	2.5	16.5	24.4	29.5	21.1	6.1	4.7	1.4
PERSONAL TAXES	**100.0**	**0.5**	**13.5**	**18.4**	**35.2**	**24.6**	**7.8**	**5.8**	**2.0**
Federal income taxes	100.0	0.1	12.6	17.1	37.6	25.5	7.1	5.8	1.3
State and local income taxes	100.0	1.8	17.4	23.1	31.3	22.0	4.4	3.7	0.7
Other taxes	100.0	0.2	8.8	14.8	27.2	25.3	23.5	11.8	11.7
GIFTS FOR PEOPLE IN OTHER HOUSEHOLDS	**100.0**	**2.4**	**10.0**	**13.7**	**32.6**	**25.4**	**16.0**	**9.9**	**6.1**

Source: Calculations by New Strategist based on the Bureau of Labor Statistics 2009, Consumer Expenditure Survey, Internet site http://www.bls.gov/cex/home.htm

Spending Rises with Income

Households with incomes of $100,000 or more spend twice as much as the average household.

Households with incomes of $100,000 or more spent an average of $97,576 in 2009—about twice the $49,067 spent by the average household. The most affluent households are also the largest, with an average of 3.2 people according to the Bureau of Labor Statistics' Consumer Expenditure Survey, compared with 2.5 for the average household. Households with incomes of $150,000 or more (shown in the high-income tables) spent $124,306 in 2009. They are the only income group to spend more on restaurant meals than groceries.

Tables 9.6 and 9.9 show spending by household income in comparison with average household spending. An index of 100 means households in the income group spend an average amount on the item. An index above 100 indicates that households in the income group spend more than average on the item, while an index below 100 reveals below-average spending.

A look at tables 9.6 and 9.9 shows that spending is at or below average on most items for households with incomes below $50,000, about average for those with incomes between $50,000 and $70,000, and above average for households with incomes of $70,000 or more. There are some exceptions, however. Households with incomes below $50,000 spend more than average on rent. Households with incomes of $100,000 or more spend less than average on tobacco. The most affluent households—those with incomes of $150,000 or more—spend at least three times the average on items such as other lodging (which includes college dorm rooms as well as hotels and motels), household

High-income households account for a disproportionate share of spending

(share of spending accounted for by consumer unit income groups, 2009)

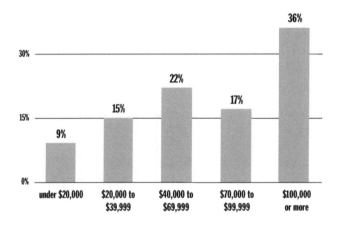

personal services (mostly day care), other household services (such as lawn care and housekeeping), furniture, floor coverings, new cars and trucks, public transportation (which is dominated by airfares), fees and admission to entertainment events, education, and cash contributions.

The Market Share tables show how much of total spending by category is accounted for by the various income groups. Table 9.10 shows how much high-income households dominate spending. While 18 percent of households have annual incomes of $100,000 or more, they control 36 percent of household spending. Households with incomes of $150,000 or more account for only 7 percent of households but control 18 percent of total household spending. These most affluent households control at least one-fourth of spending on other lodging, public transportation, fees and admissions to entertainment events, and education.

■ With the cost of necessities spiraling upward, high-income households are often the only ones able to devote a substantial sum to discretionary products and services.

Table 9.5 Average Spending by Household Income, 2009

(average annual spending of consumer units (CUs) by product and service category and before-tax income of consumer unit, 2009)

	total consumer units	under $10,000	$10,000–$19,999	$20,000–$29,999	$30,000–$39,999	$40,000–$49,999	$50,000–$69,999	$70,000 or more
Number of consumer units (in 000s)	120,847	9,952	15,395	15,022	13,053	11,444	17,799	38,181
Average number of persons per CU	2.5	1.6	1.8	2.2	2.4	2.5	2.7	3.1
Average annual spending	**$49,067**	**$20,274**	**$22,720**	**$29,397**	**$35,929**	**$39,553**	**$48,900**	**$82,060**
FOOD	**6,372**	**3,411**	**3,530**	**4,415**	**4,737**	**5,384**	**6,420**	**9,761**
Food at home	**3,753**	**2,302**	**2,541**	**2,996**	**2,959**	**3,362**	**3,755**	**5,236**
Cereals and bakery products	506	322	327	422	394	457	512	701
Cereals and cereal products	173	125	118	147	143	150	167	235
Bakery products	334	197	210	274	252	307	345	467
Meats, poultry, fish, and eggs	841	525	601	675	717	780	851	1,125
Beef	226	136	159	173	194	213	241	301
Pork	168	113	126	154	153	157	183	204
Other meats	114	68	77	97	92	102	109	158
Poultry	154	100	112	122	122	142	153	210
Fish and seafood	135	78	93	93	117	123	118	199
Eggs	44	31	35	37	39	43	48	53
Dairy products	406	265	266	313	308	363	402	577
Fresh milk and cream	144	107	104	120	121	131	144	189
Other dairy products	262	158	163	193	187	233	258	388
Fruits and vegetables	656	404	428	525	505	576	659	928
Fresh fruits	220	127	135	173	167	194	213	320
Fresh vegetables	209	119	128	171	154	184	206	304
Processed fruits	118	77	86	94	95	96	121	162
Processed vegetables	110	81	79	87	89	102	119	142
Other food at home	1,343	786	918	1,061	1,035	1,185	1,329	1,904
Sugar and other sweets	141	89	83	111	117	123	136	203
Fats and oils	102	64	70	88	90	94	98	138
Miscellaneous foods	715	399	516	561	543	633	701	1,014
Nonalcoholic beverages	337	222	236	279	262	306	344	455
Food prepared by consumer unit on trips	49	14	14	22	23	29	51	95
Food away from home	**2,619**	**1,109**	**989**	**1,419**	**1,778**	**2,022**	**2,666**	**4,525**
ALCOHOLIC BEVERAGES	**435**	**217**	**136**	**233**	**296**	**324**	**431**	**765**
HOUSING	**16,895**	**8,315**	**9,503**	**11,440**	**12,986**	**14,309**	**16,788**	**26,386**
Shelter	**10,075**	**5,165**	**5,582**	**6,575**	**7,579**	**8,477**	**9,989**	**15,916**
Owned dwellings	6,543	1,858	2,083	3,117	4,038	4,847	6,473	12,306
Mortgage interest and charges	3,594	996	768	1,315	1,928	2,631	3,579	7,171
Property taxes	1,811	526	729	1,023	1,233	1,398	1,776	3,231
Maintenance, repair, insurance, other expenses	1,138	336	586	780	878	818	1,118	1,904
Rented dwellings	2,860	3,175	3,360	3,228	3,296	3,295	2,977	2,098
Other lodging	672	131	139	229	245	336	539	1,511
Utilities, fuels, and public services	**3,645**	**1,969**	**2,449**	**3,028**	**3,289**	**3,513**	**3,899**	**4,849**
Natural gas	483	251	295	380	422	469	488	683
Electricity	1,377	836	1,028	1,218	1,293	1,338	1,445	1,729
Fuel oil and other fuels	141	56	91	109	116	115	172	199
Telephone services	1,162	585	744	936	1,048	1,136	1,290	1,556
Water and other public services	481	242	289	384	410	456	504	681

	total consumer units	under $10,000	$10,000– $19,999	$20,000– $29,999	$30,000– $39,999	$40,000– $49,999	$50,000– $69,999	$70,000 or more
Household services	$1,011	$364	$463	$587	$613	$706	$845	$1,873
Personal services	389	116	160	217	185	230	272	794
Other household services	622	248	303	370	428	476	573	1,079
Housekeeping supplies	659	295	377	499	494	540	632	1,018
Laundry and cleaning supplies	156	101	113	135	121	136	149	214
Other household products	360	134	170	263	276	293	337	583
Postage and stationery	143	61	94	101	96	111	146	221
Household furnishings and equipment	1,506	522	632	751	1,011	1,072	1,424	2,730
Household textiles	124	47	49	52	68	104	147	214
Furniture	343	94	164	193	242	234	331	611
Floor coverings	30	7	7	8	16	24	18	67
Major appliances	194	46	87	117	137	178	226	314
Small appliances, miscellaneous housewares	93	57	57	52	47	89	86	153
Miscellaneous household equipment	721	271	268	328	500	443	616	1,371
APPAREL AND RELATED SERVICES	1,725	799	928	1,080	1,225	1,336	1,608	2,850
Men and boys	383	163	231	204	278	293	345	644
Men, aged 16 or older	304	124	191	163	217	230	277	511
Boys, aged 2 to 15	79	40	40	41	61	63	69	133
Women and girls	678	294	311	425	447	515	641	1,156
Women, aged 16 or older	561	244	274	347	353	404	522	966
Girls, aged 2 to 15	118	50	37	78	95	111	119	189
Children under age 2	91	43	63	79	73	86	88	127
Footwear	323	197	193	241	265	284	336	460
Other apparel products and services	249	102	129	131	163	157	197	464
TRANSPORTATION	7,658	2,562	3,078	4,355	6,311	6,393	8,352	12,603
Vehicle purchases	2,657	785	812	1,201	2,112	2,099	2,742	4,775
Cars and trucks, new	1,297	59	262	514	717	823	1,242	2,712
Cars and trucks, used	1,304	726	549	675	1,367	1,231	1,423	1,953
Gasoline and motor oil	1,986	843	1,002	1,450	1,689	1,955	2,250	2,881
Other vehicle expenses	2,536	788	1,083	1,508	2,264	2,064	2,951	3,976
Vehicle finance charges	281	55	71	150	192	256	361	477
Maintenance and repairs	733	281	320	446	563	665	827	1,162
Vehicle insurance	1,075	308	541	701	1,239	796	1,328	1,503
Vehicle rentals, leases, licenses, other charges	447	144	150	210	270	347	434	833
Public transportation	479	146	182	196	246	275	409	971
HEALTH CARE	3,126	1,216	1,917	2,536	2,684	2,937	3,454	4,393
Health insurance	1,785	715	1,162	1,519	1,684	1,705	1,995	2,380
Medical services	736	261	362	468	476	607	806	1,212
Drugs	486	190	332	469	443	528	507	621
Medical supplies	119	51	61	81	80	97	147	180
ENTERTAINMENT	2,693	1,032	1,025	1,504	1,970	2,008	2,611	4,733
Fees and admissions	628	172	125	217	300	370	489	1,363
Audio and visual equipment and services	975	496	553	707	857	891	1,026	1,416
Pets, toys, hobbies, and playground equipment	690	263	287	481	580	512	642	1,146
Other entertainment products and services	400	101	61	100	233	235	453	809
PERSONAL CARE PRODUCTS AND SERVICES	596	248	282	372	438	476	578	991
READING	110	37	55	71	81	86	108	182
EDUCATION	1,068	965	311	303	557	441	654	2,257

	total consumer units	under $10,000	$10,000– $19,999	$20,000– $29,999	$30,000– $39,999	$40,000– $49,999	$50,000– $69,999	$70,000 or more
TOBACCO PRODUCTS AND SMOKING SUPPLIES	$380	$270	$328	$439	$405	$381	$436	$371
MISCELLANEOUS	816	269	343	438	668	738	853	1,351
CASH CONTRIBUTIONS	1,723	522	629	744	1,208	1,256	1,728	3,176
PERSONAL INSURANCE AND PENSIONS	5,471	411	654	1,466	2,362	3,485	4,881	12,241
Life and other personal insurance	309	99	109	123	177	212	275	607
Pensions and Social Security	5,162	311	545	1,343	2,185	3,273	4,605	11,634
PERSONAL TAXES	2,104	–35	–162	–201	289	793	1,399	5,823
Federal income taxes	1,404	–104	–207	–347	14	399	818	4,187
State and local income taxes	524	11	9	49	160	269	387	1,317
Other taxes	177	58	38	98	117	125	196	321
GIFTS FOR PEOPLE IN OTHER HOUSEHOLDS	1,067	365	492	418	688	603	803	2,119

Note: Spending by category does not add to total spending because gift spending is also included in the preceding product and service categories and personal taxes are not included in the total.
Source: Bureau of Labor Statistics' 2009 Consumer Expenditure Survey, Internet site http://www.bls.gov/cex/; calculations by New Strategist

Table 9.6 Indexed Spending by Household Income, 2009

(indexed average annual spending of consumer units by product and service category and before-tax income of consumer unit reference person, 2009; index definition: an index of 100 is the average for all consumer units; an index of 125 means that spending by consumer units in that group is 25 percent above the average for all consumer units; an index of 75 indicates spending that is 25 percent below the average for all consumer units)

	total consumer units	under $10,000	$10,000– $19,999	$20,000– $29,999	$30,000– $39,999	$40,000– $49,999	$50,000– $69,999	$70,000 or more
Average spending of consumer units	$49,067	$20,274	$22,720	$29,397	$35,929	$39,553	$48,900	$82,060
Indexed spending of consumer units	100	41	46	60	73	81	100	167
FOOD	100	54	55	69	74	84	101	153
Food at home	100	61	68	80	79	90	100	140
Cereals and bakery products	100	64	65	83	78	90	101	139
Cereals and cereal products	100	72	68	85	83	87	97	136
Bakery products	100	59	63	82	75	92	103	140
Meats, poultry, fish, and eggs	100	62	71	80	85	93	101	134
Beef	100	60	70	77	86	94	107	133
Pork	100	67	75	92	91	93	109	121
Other meats	100	59	68	85	81	89	96	139
Poultry	100	65	73	79	79	92	99	136
Fish and seafood	100	57	69	69	87	91	87	147
Eggs	100	71	78	84	89	98	109	120
Dairy products	100	65	66	77	76	89	99	142
Fresh milk and cream	100	74	72	83	84	91	100	131
Other dairy products	100	60	62	74	71	89	98	148
Fruits and vegetables	100	62	65	80	77	88	100	141
Fresh fruits	100	58	62	79	76	88	97	145
Fresh vegetables	100	57	61	82	74	88	99	145
Processed fruits	100	66	73	80	81	81	103	137
Processed vegetables	100	73	71	79	81	93	108	129
Other food at home	100	59	68	79	77	88	99	142
Sugar and other sweets	100	63	59	79	83	87	96	144
Fats and oils	100	62	69	86	88	92	96	135
Miscellaneous foods	100	56	72	78	76	89	98	142
Nonalcoholic beverages	100	66	70	83	78	91	102	135
Food prepared by consumer unit on trips	100	28	29	45	47	59	104	194
Food away from home	100	42	38	54	68	77	102	173
ALCOHOLIC BEVERAGES	100	50	31	54	68	74	99	176
HOUSING	100	49	56	68	77	85	99	156
Shelter	100	51	55	65	75	84	99	158
Owned dwellings	100	28	32	48	62	74	99	188
Mortgage interest and charges	100	28	21	37	54	73	100	200
Property taxes	100	29	40	56	68	77	98	178
Maintenance, repair, insurance, other expenses	100	30	51	69	77	72	98	167
Rented dwellings	100	111	117	113	115	115	104	73
Other lodging	100	19	21	34	36	50	80	225
Utilities, fuels, and public services	100	54	67	83	90	96	107	133
Natural gas	100	52	61	79	87	97	101	141
Electricity	100	61	75	88	94	97	105	126
Fuel oil and other fuels	100	40	65	77	82	82	122	141
Telephone services	100	50	64	81	90	98	111	134
Water and other public services	100	50	60	80	85	95	105	142

	total consumer units	under $10,000	$10,000–$19,999	$20,000–$29,999	$30,000–$39,999	$40,000–$49,999	$50,000–$69,999	$70,000 or more
Household services	100	36	46	58	61	70	84	185
Personal services	100	30	41	56	48	59	70	204
Other household services	100	40	49	59	69	77	92	173
Housekeeping supplies	100	45	57	76	75	82	96	154
Laundry and cleaning supplies	100	65	72	87	78	87	96	137
Other household products	100	37	47	73	77	81	94	162
Postage and stationery	100	43	66	71	67	78	102	155
Household furnishings and equipment	100	35	42	50	67	71	95	181
Household textiles	100	38	39	42	55	84	119	173
Furniture	100	27	48	56	71	68	97	178
Floor coverings	100	23	25	27	53	80	60	223
Major appliances	100	24	45	60	71	92	116	162
Small appliances, miscellaneous housewares	100	62	62	56	51	96	92	165
Miscellaneous household equipment	100	38	37	45	69	61	85	190
APPAREL AND RELATED SERVICES	100	46	54	63	71	77	93	165
Men and boys	100	43	60	53	73	77	90	168
Men, aged 16 or older	100	41	63	54	71	76	91	168
Boys, aged 2 to 15	100	50	51	52	77	80	87	168
Women and girls	100	43	46	63	66	76	95	171
Women, aged 16 or older	100	43	49	62	63	72	93	172
Girls, aged 2 to 15	100	42	32	66	81	94	101	160
Children under age 2	100	47	69	87	80	95	97	140
Footwear	100	61	60	75	82	88	104	142
Other apparel products and services	100	41	52	53	65	63	79	186
TRANSPORTATION	100	33	40	57	82	83	109	165
Vehicle purchases	100	30	31	45	79	79	103	180
Cars and trucks, new	100	5	20	40	55	63	96	209
Cars and trucks, used	100	56	42	52	105	94	109	150
Gasoline and motor oil	100	42	50	73	85	98	113	145
Other vehicle expenses	100	31	43	59	89	81	116	157
Vehicle finance charges	100	19	25	53	68	91	128	170
Maintenance and repairs	100	38	44	61	77	91	113	159
Vehicle insurance	100	29	50	65	115	74	124	140
Vehicle rentals, leases, licenses, other charges	100	32	34	47	60	78	97	186
Public transportation	100	30	38	41	51	57	85	203
HEALTH CARE	100	39	61	81	86	94	110	141
Health insurance	100	40	65	85	94	96	112	133
Medical services	100	35	49	64	65	82	110	165
Drugs	100	39	68	97	91	109	104	128
Medical supplies	100	43	52	68	67	82	124	151
ENTERTAINMENT	100	38	38	56	73	75	97	176
Fees and admissions	100	27	20	35	48	59	78	217
Audio and visual equipment and services	100	51	57	73	88	91	105	145
Pets, toys, hobbies, and playground equipment	100	38	42	70	84	74	93	166
Other entertainment products and services	100	25	15	25	58	59	113	202
PERSONAL CARE PRODUCTS AND SERVICES	100	42	47	62	73	80	97	166
READING	100	34	50	65	74	78	98	165
EDUCATION	100	90	29	28	52	41	61	211

	total consumer units	under $10,000	$10,000–$19,999	$20,000–$29,999	$30,000–$39,999	$40,000–$49,999	$50,000–$69,999	$70,000 or more
TOBACCO PRODUCTS AND SMOKING SUPPLIES	100	71	86	116	107	100	115	98
MISCELLANEOUS	100	33	42	54	82	90	105	166
CASH CONTRIBUTIONS	100	30	37	43	70	73	100	184
PERSONAL INSURANCE, PENSIONS	100	8	12	27	43	64	89	224
Life and other personal insurance	100	32	35	40	57	69	89	196
Pensions and Social Security	100	6	11	26	42	63	89	225
PERSONAL TAXES	100	–2	–8	–10	14	38	66	277
Federal income taxes	100	–7	–15	–25	1	28	58	298
State and local income taxes	100	2	2	9	31	51	74	251
Other taxes	100	33	21	55	66	71	111	181
GIFTS FOR PEOPLE IN OTHER HOUSEHOLDS	100	34	46	39	64	57	75	199

Source: Calculations by New Strategist based on the Bureau of Labor Statistics' 2009 Consumer Expenditure Survey, Internet site http://www.bls.gov/cex/home.htm

Table 9.7 Market Shares by Household Income, 2009

(share of total household spending accounted for by household income group, 2009)

	total consumer units	under $10,000	$10,000– $19,999	$20,000– $29,999	$30,000– $39,999	$40,000– $49,999	$50,000– $69,999	$70,000 or more
Share of total consumer units	100.0%	8.2%	12.7%	12.4%	10.8%	9.5%	14.7%	31.6%
Share of total spending	100.0	3.4	5.9	7.4	7.9	7.6	14.7	52.8
FOOD	100.0	4.4	7.1	8.6	8.0	8.0	14.8	48.4
Food at home	100.0	5.1	8.6	9.9	8.5	8.5	14.7	44.1
Cereals and bakery products	100.0	5.2	8.2	10.4	8.4	8.6	14.9	43.8
Cereals and cereal products	100.0	5.9	8.7	10.6	8.9	8.2	14.2	42.9
Bakery products	100.0	4.9	8.0	10.2	8.1	8.7	15.2	44.2
Meats, poultry, fish, and eggs	100.0	5.1	9.1	10.0	9.2	8.8	14.9	42.3
Beef	100.0	4.9	9.0	9.5	9.3	8.9	15.7	42.1
Pork	100.0	5.6	9.5	11.4	9.8	8.8	16.0	38.4
Other meats	100.0	4.9	8.6	10.6	8.7	8.5	14.1	43.8
Poultry	100.0	5.4	9.3	9.8	8.6	8.7	14.6	43.1
Fish and seafood	100.0	4.7	8.8	8.6	9.4	8.6	12.9	46.6
Eggs	100.0	5.8	10.0	10.5	9.6	9.3	16.1	38.1
Dairy products	100.0	5.4	8.3	9.6	8.2	8.5	14.6	44.9
Fresh milk and cream	100.0	6.1	9.2	10.4	9.1	8.6	14.7	41.5
Other dairy products	100.0	5.0	7.9	9.2	7.7	8.4	14.5	46.8
Fruits and vegetables	100.0	5.1	8.3	9.9	8.3	8.3	14.8	44.7
Fresh fruits	100.0	4.8	7.8	9.8	8.2	8.4	14.3	46.0
Fresh vegetables	100.0	4.7	7.8	10.2	8.0	8.3	14.5	46.0
Processed fruits	100.0	5.4	9.3	9.9	8.7	7.7	15.1	43.4
Processed vegetables	100.0	6.0	9.1	9.8	8.7	8.8	15.9	40.8
Other food at home	100.0	4.8	8.7	9.8	8.3	8.4	14.6	44.8
Sugar and other sweets	100.0	5.2	7.5	9.8	9.0	8.3	14.2	45.5
Fats and oils	100.0	5.1	8.7	10.7	9.5	8.7	14.2	42.7
Miscellaneous foods	100.0	4.6	9.2	9.8	8.2	8.4	14.4	44.8
Nonalcoholic beverages	100.0	5.4	8.9	10.3	8.4	8.6	15.0	42.7
Food prepared by consumer unit on trips	100.0	2.3	3.6	5.6	5.1	5.6	15.3	61.3
Food away from home	100.0	3.5	4.8	6.7	7.3	7.3	15.0	54.6
ALCOHOLIC BEVERAGES	100.0	4.1	4.0	6.7	7.3	7.1	14.6	55.6
HOUSING	100.0	4.1	7.2	8.4	8.3	8.0	14.6	49.3
Shelter	100.0	4.2	7.1	8.1	8.1	8.0	14.6	49.9
Owned dwellings	100.0	2.3	4.1	5.9	6.7	7.0	14.6	59.4
Mortgage interest and charges	100.0	2.3	2.7	4.5	5.8	6.9	14.7	63.0
Property taxes	100.0	2.4	5.1	7.0	7.4	7.3	14.4	56.4
Maintenance, repair, insurance, other expenses	100.0	2.4	6.6	8.5	8.3	6.8	14.5	52.9
Rented dwellings	100.0	9.1	15.0	14.0	12.4	10.9	15.3	23.2
Other lodging	100.0	1.6	2.6	4.2	3.9	4.7	11.8	71.0
Utilities, fuels, and public services	100.0	4.4	8.6	10.3	9.7	9.1	15.8	42.0
Natural gas	100.0	4.3	7.8	9.8	9.4	9.2	14.9	44.7
Electricity	100.0	5.0	9.5	11.0	10.1	9.2	15.5	39.7
Fuel oil and other fuels	100.0	3.3	8.3	9.6	8.9	7.7	18.0	44.6
Telephone services	100.0	4.1	8.2	10.0	9.7	9.3	16.4	42.3
Water and other public services	100.0	4.1	7.7	9.9	9.2	9.0	15.4	44.7

	total consumer units	under $10,000	$10,000– $19,999	$20,000– $29,999	$30,000– $39,999	$40,000– $49,999	$50,000– $69,999	$70,000 or more
Household services	100.0%	3.0%	5.8%	7.2%	6.5%	6.6%	12.3%	58.5%
Personal services	100.0	2.5	5.2	6.9	5.1	5.6	10.3	64.5
Other household services	100.0	3.3	6.2	7.4	7.4	7.2	13.6	54.8
Housekeeping supplies	100.0	3.7	7.3	9.4	8.1	7.8	14.1	48.8
Laundry and cleaning supplies	100.0	5.3	9.2	10.8	8.4	8.3	14.1	43.3
Other household products	100.0	3.1	6.0	9.1	8.3	7.7	13.8	51.2
Postage and stationery	100.0	3.5	8.4	8.8	7.3	7.4	15.0	48.8
Household furnishings and equipment	100.0	2.9	5.3	6.2	7.3	6.7	13.9	57.3
Household textiles	100.0	3.1	5.0	5.2	5.9	7.9	17.5	54.5
Furniture	100.0	2.3	6.1	7.0	7.6	6.5	14.2	56.3
Floor coverings	100.0	1.9	3.2	3.3	5.8	7.6	8.8	70.6
Major appliances	100.0	2.0	5.7	7.5	7.6	8.7	17.2	51.1
Small appliances, miscellaneous housewares	100.0	5.1	7.9	7.0	5.5	9.1	13.6	52.0
Miscellaneous household equipment	100.0	3.1	4.7	5.7	7.5	5.8	12.6	60.1
APPAREL AND RELATED SERVICES	100.0	3.8	6.9	7.8	7.7	7.3	13.7	52.2
Men and boys	100.0	3.5	7.7	6.6	7.8	7.2	13.3	53.1
Men, aged 16 or older	100.0	3.4	8.0	6.7	7.7	7.2	13.4	53.1
Boys, aged 2 to 15	100.0	4.1	6.5	6.5	8.3	7.6	12.9	53.2
Women and girls	100.0	3.6	5.9	7.8	7.1	7.2	13.9	53.9
Women, aged 16 or older	100.0	3.6	6.2	7.7	6.8	6.8	13.7	54.4
Girls, aged 2 to 15	100.0	3.5	4.0	8.2	8.7	8.9	14.9	50.6
Children under age 2	100.0	3.9	8.8	10.8	8.7	8.9	14.2	44.1
Footwear	100.0	5.0	7.6	9.3	8.9	8.3	15.3	45.0
Other apparel products and services	100.0	3.4	6.6	6.5	7.1	6.0	11.7	58.9
TRANSPORTATION	100.0	2.8	5.1	7.1	8.9	7.9	16.1	52.0
Vehicle purchases	100.0	2.4	3.9	5.6	8.6	7.5	15.2	56.8
Cars and trucks, new	100.0	0.4	2.6	4.9	6.0	6.0	14.1	66.1
Cars and trucks, used	100.0	4.6	5.4	6.4	11.3	8.9	16.1	47.3
Gasoline and motor oil	100.0	3.5	6.4	9.1	9.2	9.3	16.7	45.8
Other vehicle expenses	100.0	2.6	5.4	7.4	9.6	7.7	17.1	49.5
Vehicle finance charges	100.0	1.6	3.2	6.6	7.4	8.6	18.9	53.6
Maintenance and repairs	100.0	3.2	5.6	7.6	8.3	8.6	16.6	50.1
Vehicle insurance	100.0	2.4	6.4	8.1	12.4	7.0	18.2	44.2
Vehicle rentals, leases, licenses, other charges	100.0	2.7	4.3	5.8	6.5	7.4	14.3	58.9
Public transportation	100.0	2.5	4.8	5.1	5.5	5.4	12.6	64.0
HEALTH CARE	100.0	3.2	7.8	10.1	9.3	8.9	16.3	44.4
Health insurance	100.0	3.3	8.3	10.6	10.2	9.0	16.5	42.1
Medical services	100.0	2.9	6.3	7.9	7.0	7.8	16.1	52.0
Drugs	100.0	3.2	8.7	12.0	9.8	10.3	15.4	40.4
Medical supplies	100.0	3.5	6.6	8.5	7.3	7.7	18.2	47.8
ENTERTAINMENT	100.0	3.2	4.9	6.9	7.9	7.1	14.3	55.5
Fees and admissions	100.0	2.3	2.5	4.3	5.2	5.6	11.5	68.6
Audio and visual equipment and services	100.0	4.2	7.2	9.0	9.5	8.7	15.5	45.9
Pets, toys, hobbies, and playground equipment	100.0	3.1	5.3	8.7	9.1	7.0	13.7	52.5
Other entertainment products and services	100.0	2.1	1.9	3.1	6.3	5.6	16.7	63.9
PERSONAL CARE PRODUCTS AND SERVICES	100.0	3.4	6.0	7.8	7.9	7.6	14.3	52.5
READING	100.0	2.8	6.4	8.0	8.0	7.4	14.5	52.3
EDUCATION	100.0	7.4	3.7	3.5	5.6	3.9	9.0	66.8

	total consumer units	under $10,000	$10,000– $19,999	$20,000– $29,999	$30,000– $39,999	$40,000– $49,999	$50,000– $69,999	$70,000 or more
TOBACCO PRODUCTS AND SMOKING SUPPLIES	**100.0%**	**5.8%**	**11.0%**	**14.4%**	**11.5%**	**9.5%**	**16.9%**	**30.8%**
MISCELLANEOUS	**100.0**	**2.7**	**5.4**	**6.7**	**8.8**	**8.6**	**15.4**	**52.3**
CASH CONTRIBUTIONS	**100.0**	**2.5**	**4.7**	**5.4**	**7.6**	**6.9**	**14.8**	**58.2**
PERSONAL INSURANCE, PENSIONS	**100.0**	**0.6**	**1.5**	**3.3**	**4.7**	**6.0**	**13.1**	**70.7**
Life and other personal insurance	100.0	2.6	4.5	4.9	6.2	6.5	13.1	62.1
Pensions and Social Security	100.0	0.5	1.3	3.2	4.6	6.0	13.1	71.2
PERSONAL TAXES	**100.0**	**0.1**	**1.0**	**1.2**	**1.5**	**3.6**	**9.8**	**87.4**
Federal income taxes	100.0	0.6	1.9	3.1	0.1	2.7	8.6	94.2
State and local income taxes	100.0	0.2	0.2	1.2	3.3	4.9	10.9	79.4
Other taxes	100.0	2.7	2.7	6.9	7.1	6.7	16.3	57.3
GIFTS FOR PEOPLE IN OTHER HOUSEHOLDS	**100.0**	**2.8**	**5.9**	**4.9**	**7.0**	**5.4**	**11.1**	**62.7**

Source: Calculations by New Strategist based on the Bureau of Labor Statistics' 2009 Consumer Expenditure Survey, Internet site http://www.bls.gov/cex/home.htm

Table 9.8 Average Spending by High-Income Households, 2009

(average annual spending of consumer units (CUs) by product and service category and before-tax income of consumer unit, 2009)

| | total consumer units | less than $70,000 | $70,000–$79,999 | $80,000–$99,999 | $100,000 or more | | | |
					total	$100,000–$119,999	$120,000–$149,999	$150,000 or more
Number of consumer units (in 000s)	120,847	82,665	6,640	9,951	21,589	7,260	5,882	8,447
Average number of persons per CU	2.5	2.2	2.9	3.0	3.1	3.0	3.2	3.2
Average annual spending	$49,067	$33,810	$57,833	$65,027	$97,576	$76,140	$85,806	$124,306
FOOD	6,372	4,798	7,818	8,359	11,088	9,622	9,886	13,234
Food at home	3,753	3,064	4,471	4,713	5,752	5,319	5,201	6,529
Cereals and bakery products	506	416	607	636	765	700	714	860
Cereals and cereal products	173	144	205	221	252	225	224	295
Bakery products	334	272	401	416	514	475	490	566
Meats, poultry, fish, and eggs	841	709	963	1,040	1,221	1,134	1,080	1,401
Beef	226	191	261	289	321	310	264	372
Pork	168	152	179	201	215	217	213	213
Other meats	114	93	143	142	170	160	149	194
Poultry	154	128	176	193	230	200	206	274
Fish and seafood	135	105	156	163	231	194	197	288
Eggs	44	40	48	53	55	52	51	60
Dairy products	406	327	492	525	632	594	568	712
Fresh milk and cream	144	123	166	183	201	187	199	214
Other dairy products	262	204	326	342	431	407	369	497
Fruits and vegetables	656	530	772	808	1,041	934	954	1,197
Fresh fruits	220	173	256	268	368	330	336	424
Fresh vegetables	209	165	244	265	344	303	317	398
Processed fruits	118	97	144	141	179	161	159	209
Processed vegetables	110	95	129	133	151	141	143	165
Other food at home	1,343	1,082	1,637	1,704	2,092	1,957	1,885	2,359
Sugar and other sweets	141	112	167	178	227	209	208	257
Fats and oils	102	86	117	137	146	140	133	161
Miscellaneous foods	715	576	905	912	1,100	1,040	983	1,237
Nonalcoholic beverages	337	281	382	404	505	481	470	552
Food prepared by consumer unit on trips	49	27	65	73	114	87	91	153
Food away from home	2,619	1,734	3,347	3,646	5,336	4,303	4,685	6,704
ALCOHOLIC BEVERAGES	435	282	534	569	936	735	832	1,188
HOUSING	16,895	12,509	19,127	21,666	30,831	23,907	27,923	38,824
Shelter	10,075	7,377	11,393	12,815	18,736	14,190	16,872	23,941
Owned dwellings	6,543	3,880	8,296	9,663	14,759	11,090	13,496	18,790
Mortgage interest and charges	3,594	1,941	4,733	5,760	8,572	6,584	7,958	10,708
Property taxes	1,811	1,155	2,056	2,503	3,927	2,727	3,447	5,293
Maintenance, repair, insurance, other expenses	1,138	784	1,507	1,400	2,259	1,779	2,090	2,789
Rented dwellings	2,860	3,212	2,404	2,325	1,900	2,069	1,832	1,802
Other lodging	672	284	694	828	2,078	1,031	1,544	3,349
Utilities, fuels, and public services	3,645	3,089	4,188	4,470	5,226	4,618	5,100	5,837
Natural gas	483	391	580	601	752	615	736	882
Electricity	1,377	1,214	1,518	1,604	1,851	1,621	1,814	2,075
Fuel oil and other fuels	141	115	154	179	222	195	169	282
Telephone services	1,162	980	1,388	1,459	1,653	1,531	1,651	1,759
Water and other public services	481	389	548	626	748	657	730	838

	total consumer units	less than $70,000	$70,000– $79,999	$80,000– $99,999	$100,000 or more total	$100,000– $119,999	$120,000– $149,999	$150,000 or more
Household services	**$1,011**	**$613**	**$1,054**	**$1,309**	**$2,385**	**$1,587**	**$2,010**	**$3,330**
Personal services	389	203	409	604	999	673	907	1,344
Other household services	622	411	646	705	1,385	914	1,104	1,986
Housekeeping supplies	**659**	**492**	**776**	**824**	**1,195**	**944**	**1,044**	**1,526**
Laundry and cleaning supplies	156	129	186	203	228	217	193	265
Other household products	360	256	412	446	708	518	631	931
Postage and stationery	143	107	178	175	259	210	220	330
Household furnishings and equipment	**1,506**	**938**	**1,716**	**2,247**	**3,289**	**2,567**	**2,896**	**4,190**
Household textiles	124	82	146	191	249	236	198	296
Furniture	343	219	357	446	767	551	644	1,039
Floor coverings	30	13	30	39	91	59	68	135
Major appliances	194	138	217	296	353	223	332	480
Small appliances, miscellaneous housewares	93	66	107	128	180	135	124	261
Miscellaneous household equipment	721	419	859	1,148	1,648	1,364	1,530	1,979
APPAREL AND RELATED SERVICES	**1,725**	**1,203**	**1,795**	**2,388**	**3,428**	**2,595**	**2,934**	**4,508**
Men and boys	**383**	**262**	**338**	**670**	**738**	**666**	**597**	**902**
Men, aged 16 or older	304	208	224	573	581	527	446	726
Boys, aged 2 to 15	79	53	114	97	157	139	151	176
Women and girls	**678**	**457**	**768**	**908**	**1,408**	**1,092**	**1,140**	**1,877**
Women, aged 16 or older	561	373	634	739	1,189	904	944	1,616
Girls, aged 2 to 15	118	84	133	169	218	188	196	260
Children under age 2	**91**	**74**	**114**	**125**	**132**	**112**	**96**	**175**
Footwear	**323**	**260**	**325**	**399**	**536**	**416**	**482**	**682**
Other apparel products and services	**249**	**150**	**250**	**285**	**614**	**308**	**618**	**873**
TRANSPORTATION	**7,658**	**5,373**	**9,880**	**9,929**	**14,674**	**12,378**	**13,028**	**17,799**
Vehicle purchases	**2,657**	**1,679**	**3,410**	**3,386**	**5,835**	**4,800**	**4,713**	**7,506**
Cars and trucks, new	1,297	644	1,368	1,851	3,522	2,356	2,694	5,100
Cars and trucks, used	1,304	1,005	1,820	1,485	2,209	2,279	2,009	2,290
Gasoline and motor oil	**1,986**	**1,573**	**2,470**	**2,669**	**3,105**	**2,942**	**3,090**	**3,257**
Other vehicle expenses	**2,536**	**1,869**	**3,452**	**3,313**	**4,442**	**3,806**	**4,245**	**5,129**
Vehicle finance charges	281	191	452	455	494	486	508	492
Maintenance and repairs	733	534	890	929	1,356	1,202	1,316	1,515
Vehicle insurance	1,075	876	1,592	1,360	1,540	1,390	1,494	1,705
Vehicle rentals, leases, licenses, other charges	447	268	518	569	1,052	727	928	1,417
Public transportation	**479**	**252**	**547**	**560**	**1,292**	**830**	**980**	**1,907**
HEALTH CARE	**3,126**	**2,541**	**3,679**	**4,158**	**4,723**	**4,385**	**4,399**	**5,242**
Health insurance	1,785	1,510	2,019	2,264	2,544	2,408	2,442	2,732
Medical services	736	516	974	1,168	1,306	1,152	1,145	1,552
Drugs	486	424	555	573	665	632	636	715
Medical supplies	119	90	132	153	208	192	177	243
ENTERTAINMENT	**2,693**	**1,749**	**3,364**	**3,625**	**5,690**	**4,616**	**4,824**	**7,228**
Fees and admissions	628	288	672	809	1,837	1,282	1,370	2,643
Audio and visual equipment and services	975	771	1,096	1,289	1,575	1,317	1,529	1,829
Pets, toys, hobbies, playground equipment	690	478	857	882	1,368	1,262	1,102	1,650
Other entertainment products and services	400	211	739	645	910	755	823	1,105
PERSONAL CARE PRODUCTS AND SERVICES	**596**	**412**	**653**	**782**	**1,200**	**960**	**1,082**	**1,492**
READING	**110**	**76**	**118**	**130**	**226**	**174**	**198**	**292**
EDUCATION	**1,068**	**519**	**783**	**1,259**	**3,170**	**1,828**	**2,442**	**4,831**

| | total consumer units | less than $70,000 | $70,000– $79,999 | $80,000– $99,999 | $100,000 or more | | | |
					total	$100,000– $119,999	$120,000– $149,999	$150,000 or more
TOBACCO PRODUCTS AND SMOKING SUPPLIES	$380	$384	$449	$377	$344	$408	$307	$314
MISCELLANEOUS	816	569	979	1,005	1,630	1,327	1,396	2,054
CASH CONTRIBUTIONS	1,723	1,052	1,685	2,414	3,986	2,443	2,996	6,002
PERSONAL INSURANCE, PENSIONS	5,471	2,344	6,968	8,368	15,649	10,764	13,559	21,302
Life and other personal insurance	309	171	432	391	761	472	639	1,095
Pensions and Social Security	5,162	2,173	6,536	7,977	14,887	10,292	12,919	20,207
PERSONAL TAXES	2,104	386	2,470	2,966	8,172	3,862	5,535	13,711
Federal income taxes	1,404	119	1,666	1,958	5,989	2,516	3,969	10,381
State and local income taxes	524	158	628	826	1,756	1,053	1,287	2,685
Other taxes	177	110	176	181	430	297	284	646
GIFTS FOR PEOPLE IN OTHER HOUSEHOLDS	1,067	580	1,312	1,303	2,752	1,675	2,078	4,153

Note: Spending by category does not add to total spending because gift spending is also included in the preceding product and service categories and personal taxes are not included in the total.
Source: Bureau of Labor Statistics' 2009 Consumer Expenditure Survey, Internet site http://www.bls.gov/cex/

Table 9.9 Indexed Spending by High-Income Households, 2009

(indexed average annual spending of consumer units by product and service category and before-tax income of consumer unit reference person, 2009; index definition: an index of 100 is the average for all consumer units; an index of 125 means that spending by consumer units in that group is 25 percent above the average for all consumer units; an index of 75 indicates spending that is 25 percent below the average for all consumer units)

	total consumer units	less than $70,000	$70,000– $79,999	$80,000– $99,999	$100,000 or more total	$100,000– $119,999	$120,000– $149,999	$150,000 or more
Average spending of consumer units	$49,067	$33,810	$57,833	$65,027	$97,576	$76,140	$85,806	$124,306
Indexed spending of consumer units	100	69	118	133	199	155	175	253
FOOD	100	75	123	131	174	151	155	208
Food at home	100	82	119	126	153	142	139	174
Cereals and bakery products	100	82	120	126	151	138	141	170
Cereals and cereal products	100	83	118	128	146	130	129	171
Bakery products	100	81	120	125	154	142	147	169
Meats, poultry, fish, and eggs	100	84	115	124	145	135	128	167
Beef	100	85	115	128	142	137	117	165
Pork	100	90	107	120	128	129	127	127
Other meats	100	82	125	125	149	140	131	170
Poultry	100	83	114	125	149	130	134	178
Fish and seafood	100	78	116	121	171	144	146	213
Eggs	100	91	109	120	125	118	116	136
Dairy products	100	81	121	129	156	146	140	175
Fresh milk and cream	100	85	115	127	140	130	138	149
Other dairy products	100	78	124	131	165	155	141	190
Fruits and vegetables	100	81	118	123	159	142	145	182
Fresh fruits	100	79	116	122	167	150	153	193
Fresh vegetables	100	79	117	127	165	145	152	190
Processed fruits	100	82	122	119	152	136	135	177
Processed vegetables	100	86	117	121	137	128	130	150
Other food at home	100	81	122	127	156	146	140	176
Sugar and other sweets	100	79	118	126	161	148	148	182
Fats and oils	100	84	115	134	143	137	130	158
Miscellaneous foods	100	81	127	128	154	145	137	173
Nonalcoholic beverages	100	83	113	120	150	143	139	164
Food prepared by consumer unit on trips	100	55	133	149	233	178	186	312
Food away from home	100	66	128	139	204	164	179	256
ALCOHOLIC BEVERAGES	100	65	123	131	215	169	191	273
HOUSING	100	74	113	128	182	142	165	230
Shelter	100	73	113	127	186	141	167	238
Owned dwellings	100	59	127	148	226	169	206	287
Mortgage interest and charges	100	54	132	160	239	183	221	298
Property taxes	100	64	114	138	217	151	190	292
Maintenance, repair, insurance, other expenses	100	69	132	123	199	156	184	245
Rented dwellings	100	112	84	81	66	72	64	63
Other lodging	100	42	103	123	309	153	230	498
Utilities, fuels, and public services	100	85	115	123	143	127	140	160
Natural gas	100	81	120	124	156	127	152	183
Electricity	100	88	110	116	134	118	132	151
Fuel oil and other fuels	100	82	109	127	157	138	120	200
Telephone services	100	84	119	126	142	132	142	151
Water and other public services	100	81	114	130	156	137	152	174

	total consumer units	less than $70,000	$70,000– $79,999	$80,000– $99,999	$100,000 or more			
					total	$100,000– $119,999	$120,000– $149,999	$150,000 or more
Household services	100	61	104	129	236	157	199	329
Personal services	100	52	105	155	257	173	233	346
Other household services	100	66	104	113	223	147	177	319
Housekeeping supplies	100	75	118	125	181	143	158	232
Laundry and cleaning supplies	100	83	119	130	146	139	124	170
Other household products	100	71	114	124	197	144	175	259
Postage and stationery	100	75	124	122	181	147	154	231
Household furnishings and equipment	100	62	114	149	218	170	192	278
Household textiles	100	66	118	154	201	190	160	239
Furniture	100	64	104	130	224	161	188	303
Floor coverings	100	43	100	130	303	197	227	450
Major appliances	100	71	112	153	182	115	171	247
Small appliances, miscellaneous housewares	100	71	115	138	194	145	133	281
Miscellaneous household equipment	100	58	119	159	229	189	212	274
APPAREL AND RELATED SERVICES	100	70	104	138	199	150	170	261
Men and boys	100	68	88	175	193	174	156	236
Men, aged 16 or older	100	68	74	188	191	173	147	239
Boys, aged 2 to 15	100	67	144	123	199	176	191	223
Women and girls	100	67	113	134	208	161	168	277
Women, aged 16 or older	100	66	113	132	212	161	168	288
Girls, aged 2 to 15	100	71	113	143	185	159	166	220
Children under age 2	100	81	125	137	145	123	105	192
Footwear	100	80	101	124	166	129	149	211
Other apparel products and services	100	60	100	114	247	124	248	351
TRANSPORTATION	100	70	129	130	192	162	170	232
Vehicle purchases	100	63	128	127	220	181	177	282
Cars and trucks, new	100	50	105	143	272	182	208	393
Cars and trucks, used	100	77	140	114	169	175	154	176
Gasoline and motor oil	100	79	124	134	156	148	156	164
Other vehicle expenses	100	74	136	131	175	150	167	202
Vehicle finance charges	100	68	161	162	176	173	181	175
Maintenance and repairs	100	73	121	127	185	164	180	207
Vehicle insurance	100	81	148	127	143	129	139	159
Vehicle rentals, leases, licenses, other charges	100	60	116	127	235	163	208	317
Public transportation	100	53	114	117	270	173	205	398
HEALTH CARE	100	81	118	133	151	140	141	168
Health insurance	100	85	113	127	143	135	137	153
Medical services	100	70	132	159	177	157	156	211
Drugs	100	87	114	118	137	130	131	147
Medical supplies	100	76	111	129	175	161	149	204
ENTERTAINMENT	100	65	125	135	211	171	179	268
Fees and admissions	100	46	107	129	293	204	218	421
Audio and visual equipment and services	100	79	112	132	162	135	157	188
Pets, toys, hobbies, and playground equipment	100	69	124	128	198	183	160	239
Other entertainment products and services	100	53	185	161	228	189	206	276
PERSONAL CARE PRODUCTS AND SERVICES	100	69	110	131	201	161	182	250
READING	100	69	107	118	205	158	180	265
EDUCATION	100	49	73	118	297	171	229	452

	total consumer units	less than $70,000	$70,000–$79,999	$80,000–$99,999	$100,000 or more			
					total	$100,000–$119,999	$120,000–$149,999	$150,000 or more
TOBACCO PRODUCTS AND SMOKING SUPPLIES	**100**	**101**	**118**	**99**	**91**	**107**	**81**	**83**
MISCELLANEOUS	**100**	**70**	**120**	**123**	**200**	**163**	**171**	**252**
CASH CONTRIBUTIONS	**100**	**61**	**98**	**140**	**231**	**142**	**174**	**348**
PERSONAL INSURANCE AND PENSIONS	**100**	**43**	**127**	**153**	**286**	**197**	**248**	**389**
Life and other personal insurance	100	55	140	127	246	153	207	354
Pensions and Social Security	100	42	127	155	288	199	250	391
PERSONAL TAXES	**100**	**18**	**117**	**141**	**388**	**184**	**263**	**652**
Federal income taxes	100	8	119	139	427	179	283	739
State and local income taxes	100	30	120	158	335	201	246	512
Other taxes	100	62	99	102	243	168	160	365
GIFTS FOR PEOPLE IN OTHER HOUSEHOLDS	**100**	**54**	**123**	**122**	**258**	**157**	**195**	**389**

Source: Calculations by New Strategist based on the Bureau of Labor Statistics' 2009 Consumer Expenditure Survey, Internet site http://www.bls.gov/cex/home.htm

Table 9.10 Market Shares of High-Income Households, 2009

(share of total household spending accounted for by income groups, 2009)

	total consumer units	less than $70,000	$70,000–$79,999	$80,000–$99,999	$100,000 or more total	$100,000–$119,999	$120,000–$149,999	$150,000 or more
Share of total consumer units	100.0%	68.4%	5.5%	8.2%	17.9%	6.0%	4.9%	7.0%
Share of total spending	100.0	47.1	6.5	10.9	35.5	9.3	8.5	17.7
FOOD	100.0	51.5	6.7	10.8	31.1	9.1	7.6	14.5
Food at home	100.0	55.8	6.5	10.3	27.4	8.5	6.7	12.2
Cereals and bakery products	100.0	56.2	6.6	10.3	27.0	8.3	6.9	11.9
Cereals and cereal products	100.0	56.9	6.5	10.5	26.0	7.8	6.3	11.9
Bakery products	100.0	55.7	6.6	10.3	27.5	8.5	7.1	11.8
Meats, poultry, fish, and eggs	100.0	57.7	6.3	10.2	25.9	8.1	6.3	11.6
Beef	100.0	57.8	6.3	10.5	25.4	8.2	5.7	11.5
Pork	100.0	61.9	5.9	9.9	22.9	7.8	6.2	8.9
Other meats	100.0	55.8	6.9	10.3	26.6	8.4	6.4	11.9
Poultry	100.0	56.9	6.3	10.3	26.7	7.8	6.5	12.4
Fish and seafood	100.0	53.2	6.3	9.9	30.6	8.6	7.1	14.9
Eggs	100.0	62.2	6.0	9.9	22.3	7.1	5.6	9.5
Dairy products	100.0	55.1	6.7	10.6	27.8	8.8	6.8	12.3
Fresh milk and cream	100.0	58.4	6.3	10.5	24.9	7.8	6.7	10.4
Other dairy products	100.0	53.3	6.8	10.7	29.4	9.3	6.9	13.3
Fruits and vegetables	100.0	55.3	6.5	10.1	28.3	8.6	7.1	12.8
Fresh fruits	100.0	53.8	6.4	10.0	29.9	9.0	7.4	13.5
Fresh vegetables	100.0	54.0	6.4	10.4	29.4	8.7	7.4	13.3
Processed fruits	100.0	56.2	6.7	9.8	27.1	8.2	6.6	12.4
Processed vegetables	100.0	59.1	6.4	10.0	24.5	7.7	6.3	10.5
Other food at home	100.0	55.1	6.7	10.4	27.8	8.8	6.8	12.3
Sugar and other sweets	100.0	54.3	6.5	10.4	28.8	8.9	7.2	12.7
Fats and oils	100.0	57.7	6.3	11.1	25.6	8.2	6.3	11.0
Miscellaneous foods	100.0	55.1	7.0	10.5	27.5	8.7	6.7	12.1
Nonalcoholic beverages	100.0	57.0	6.2	9.9	26.8	8.6	6.8	11.4
Food prepared by consumer unit on trips	100.0	37.7	7.3	12.3	41.6	10.7	9.0	21.8
Food away from home	100.0	45.3	7.0	11.5	36.4	9.9	8.7	17.9
ALCOHOLIC BEVERAGES	100.0	44.3	6.7	10.8	38.4	10.2	9.3	19.1
HOUSING	100.0	50.6	6.2	10.6	32.6	8.5	8.0	16.1
Shelter	100.0	50.1	6.2	10.5	33.2	8.5	8.2	16.6
Owned dwellings	100.0	40.6	7.0	12.2	40.3	10.2	10.0	20.1
Mortgage interest and charges	100.0	36.9	7.2	13.2	42.6	11.0	10.8	20.8
Property taxes	100.0	43.6	6.2	11.4	38.7	9.0	9.3	20.4
Maintenance, repair, insurance, other expenses	100.0	47.1	7.3	10.1	35.5	9.4	8.9	17.1
Rented dwellings	100.0	76.8	4.6	6.7	11.9	4.3	3.1	4.4
Other lodging	100.0	28.9	5.7	10.1	55.2	9.2	11.2	34.8
Utilities, fuels, and public services	100.0	58.0	6.3	10.1	25.6	7.6	6.8	11.2
Natural gas	100.0	55.4	6.6	10.2	27.8	7.6	7.4	12.8
Electricity	100.0	60.3	6.1	9.6	24.0	7.1	6.4	10.5
Fuel oil and other fuels	100.0	55.8	6.0	10.5	28.1	8.3	5.8	14.0
Telephone services	100.0	57.7	6.6	10.3	25.4	7.9	6.9	10.6
Water and other public services	100.0	55.3	6.3	10.7	27.8	8.2	7.4	12.2

	total consumer units	less than $70,000	$70,000–$79,999	$80,000–$99,999	$100,000 or more total	$100,000–$119,999	$120,000–$149,999	$150,000 or more
Household services	100.0%	41.5%	5.7%	10.7%	42.1%	9.4%	9.7%	23.0%
Personal services	100.0	35.7	5.8	12.8	45.9	10.4	11.3	24.1
Other household services	100.0	45.2	5.7	9.3	39.8	8.8	8.6	22.3
Housekeeping supplies	100.0	51.1	6.5	10.3	32.4	8.6	7.7	16.2
Laundry and cleaning supplies	100.0	56.6	6.6	10.7	26.1	8.4	6.0	11.9
Other household products	100.0	48.6	6.3	10.2	35.1	8.6	8.5	18.1
Postage and stationery	100.0	51.2	6.8	10.1	32.4	8.8	7.5	16.1
Household furnishings and equipment	100.0	42.6	6.3	12.3	39.0	10.2	9.4	19.4
Household textiles	100.0	45.2	6.5	12.7	35.9	11.4	7.8	16.7
Furniture	100.0	43.7	5.7	10.7	39.9	9.7	9.1	21.2
Floor coverings	100.0	29.6	5.5	10.7	54.2	11.8	11.0	31.5
Major appliances	100.0	48.7	6.1	12.6	32.5	6.9	8.3	17.3
Small appliances, miscellaneous housewares	100.0	48.5	6.3	11.3	34.6	8.7	6.5	19.6
Miscellaneous household equipment	100.0	39.8	6.5	13.1	40.8	11.4	10.3	19.2
APPAREL AND RELATED SERVICES	100.0	47.7	5.7	11.4	35.5	9.0	8.3	18.3
Men and boys	100.0	46.8	4.8	14.4	34.4	10.4	7.6	16.5
Men, aged 16 or older	100.0	46.8	4.0	15.5	34.1	10.4	7.1	16.7
Boys, aged 2 to 15	100.0	45.9	7.9	10.1	35.5	10.6	9.3	15.6
Women and girls	100.0	46.1	6.2	11.0	37.1	9.7	8.2	19.4
Women, aged 16 or older	100.0	45.5	6.2	10.8	37.9	9.7	8.2	20.1
Girls, aged 2 to 15	100.0	48.7	6.2	11.8	33.0	9.6	8.1	15.4
Children under age 2	100.0	55.6	6.9	11.3	25.9	7.4	5.1	13.4
Footwear	100.0	55.1	5.5	10.2	29.6	7.7	7.3	14.8
Other apparel products and services	100.0	41.2	5.5	9.4	44.1	7.4	12.1	24.5
TRANSPORTATION	100.0	48.0	7.1	10.7	34.2	9.7	8.3	16.2
Vehicle purchases	100.0	43.2	7.1	10.5	39.2	10.9	8.6	19.7
Cars and trucks, new	100.0	34.0	5.8	11.8	48.5	10.9	10.1	27.5
Cars and trucks, used	100.0	52.7	7.7	9.4	30.3	10.5	7.5	12.3
Gasoline and motor oil	100.0	54.2	6.8	11.1	27.9	8.9	7.6	11.5
Other vehicle expenses	100.0	50.4	7.5	10.8	31.3	9.0	8.1	14.1
Vehicle finance charges	100.0	46.5	8.8	13.3	31.4	10.4	8.8	12.2
Maintenance and repairs	100.0	49.8	6.7	10.4	33.0	9.9	8.7	14.4
Vehicle insurance	100.0	55.7	8.1	10.4	25.6	7.8	6.8	11.1
Vehicle rentals, leases, licenses, other charges	100.0	41.0	6.4	10.5	42.0	9.8	10.1	22.2
Public transportation	100.0	36.0	6.3	9.6	48.2	10.4	10.0	27.8
HEALTH CARE	100.0	55.6	6.5	11.0	27.0	8.4	6.8	11.7
Health insurance	100.0	57.9	6.2	10.4	25.5	8.1	6.7	10.7
Medical services	100.0	48.0	7.3	13.1	31.7	9.4	7.6	14.7
Drugs	100.0	59.7	6.3	9.7	24.4	7.8	6.4	10.3
Medical supplies	100.0	51.7	6.1	10.6	31.2	9.7	7.2	14.3
ENTERTAINMENT	100.0	44.4	6.9	11.1	37.7	10.3	8.7	18.8
Fees and admissions	100.0	31.4	5.9	10.6	52.3	12.3	10.6	29.4
Audio and visual equipment and services	100.0	54.1	6.2	10.9	28.9	8.1	7.6	13.1
Pets, toys, hobbies, and playground equipment	100.0	47.4	6.8	10.5	35.4	11.0	7.8	16.7
Other entertainment products and services	100.0	36.1	10.2	13.3	40.6	11.3	10.0	19.3
PERSONAL CARE PRODUCTS AND SERVICES	100.0	47.3	6.0	10.8	36.0	9.7	8.8	17.5
READING	100.0	47.3	5.9	9.7	36.7	9.5	8.8	18.6
EDUCATION	100.0	33.2	4.0	9.7	53.0	10.3	11.1	31.6

	total consumer units	less than $70,000	$70,000–$79,999	$80,000–$99,999	$100,000 or more			
					total	$100,000–$119,999	$120,000–$149,999	$150,000 or more
TOBACCO PRODUCTS AND SMOKING SUPPLIES	**100.0%**	**69.1%**	**6.5%**	**8.2%**	**16.2%**	**6.5%**	**3.9%**	**5.8%**
MISCELLANEOUS	**100.0**	**47.7**	**6.6**	**10.1**	**35.7**	**9.8**	**8.3**	**17.6**
CASH CONTRIBUTIONS	**100.0**	**41.8**	**5.4**	**11.5**	**41.3**	**8.5**	**8.5**	**24.3**
PERSONAL INSURANCE AND PENSIONS	**100.0**	**29.3**	**7.0**	**12.6**	**51.1**	**11.8**	**12.1**	**27.2**
Life and other personal insurance	100.0	37.9	7.7	10.4	44.0	9.2	10.1	24.8
Pensions and Social Security	100.0	28.8	7.0	12.7	51.5	12.0	12.2	27.4
PERSONAL TAXES	**100.0**	**12.5**	**6.5**	**11.6**	**69.4**	**11.0**	**12.8**	**45.6**
Federal income taxes	100.0	5.8	6.5	11.5	76.2	10.8	13.8	51.7
State and local income taxes	100.0	20.6	6.6	13.0	59.9	12.1	12.0	35.8
Other taxes	100.0	42.5	5.5	8.4	43.4	10.1	7.8	25.5
GIFTS FOR PEOPLE IN OTHER HOUSEHOLDS	**100.0**	**37.2**	**6.8**	**10.1**	**46.1**	**9.4**	**9.5**	**27.2**

Source: Calculations by New Strategist based on the Bureau of Labor Statistics' 2009 Consumer Expenditure Survey, Internet site http://www.bls.gov/cex/home.htm

Couples with Children Spend the Most

Married couples with children spend 40 percent more than the average household.

Married couples with children spend much more than average because they have the highest incomes and the largest households. In 2009, couples with kids spent an average of $68,481 versus the $49,067 spent by the average household, according to the Bureau of Labor Statistics' Consumer Expenditure Survey.

Married couples without children at home spend 16 percent more than average. Most are empty-nesters whose grown children live elsewhere or young couples who have not yet had children. Single-parent households spent $36,763 in 2009, and single-person households spent the least—just $29,405.

The Indexed Spending table shows spending by household type in comparison with average household spending. An index of 100 means the household type spends an average amount on the item. An index above 100 indicates that the household type spends more than average on the item, while an index below 100 reveals below-average spending.

A look at Table 9.12 shows that spending is well below average for single-parent and single-person households, although single-parent households spend close to the average on most foods. Single-parent households spend 95 percent more than the average (with an index of 195) on household personal services, most of which is day care expenses. Married couples without children at home

Spending is below average for single parents

(average annual spending of consumer units by type, 2009)

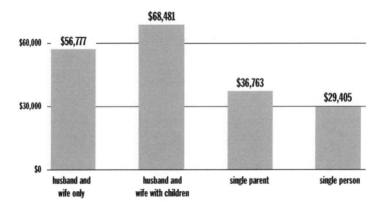

spend more than average on many items. But they spend less than average on household personal services, children's clothing, and education.

The Market Share table shows how much of total spending by category is accounted for by each household type. Married couples with children account for 24 percent of households and 34 percent of household spending. Single-person households account for 29 percent of households but only 17 percent of spending.

Married couples with children account for more than half of all household spending on some items such as household personal services (day care) and children's clothing. Married couples without children at home, who represent 22 percent of households, account for 39 percent of spending on other lodging (hotels and motels), 30 percent of spending on public transportation (mostly airline fares), 37 percent of spending on drugs, and 35 percent of spending on gifts for people in other households. Single parents, who represent 6 percent of households, account for less than 10 percent of spending on all but household personal services, and boys' and girls' clothing. Single-person households account for a larger than average share of spending on rent.

■ The spending of married couples without children at home is likely to grow in the years ahead as two-income baby-boom couples postpone retirement.

Table 9.11 Average Spending by Household Type, 2009

(average annual spending of consumer units (CUs) by product and service category and type of consumer unit, 2009)

	total consumer units	total married couples	married couples, no children	married couples with children total	oldest child under 6	oldest child 6 to 17	oldest child 18 or older	single parent, at least one child <18	single person
Number of CUs (in 000s)	120,847	61,271	26,852	29,480	5,154	14,983	9,342	6,810	34,770
Average number of persons per consumer unit	2.5	3.2	2.0	4.0	3.5	4.1	3.9	2.9	1.0
Average annual spending	**$49,067**	**$63,104**	**$56,777**	**$68,481**	**$62,138**	**$70,329**	**$69,089**	**$36,763**	**$29,405**
FOOD	**6,372**	**8,264**	**6,906**	**9,369**	**7,813**	**9,827**	**9,525**	**5,348**	**3,460**
Food at home	3,753	4,827	3,975	5,451	4,833	5,606	5,567	3,480	1,953
Cereals and bakery products	506	657	508	770	622	826	765	485	255
Cereals and cereal products	173	223	168	263	247	265	268	183	80
Bakery products	334	435	340	508	375	561	497	302	175
Meats, poultry, fish, and eggs	841	1,069	887	1,167	930	1,198	1,262	837	408
Beef	226	291	246	317	237	316	370	237	104
Pork	168	210	174	229	161	242	248	169	79
Other meats	114	148	125	166	139	178	163	115	53
Poultry	154	194	149	225	201	228	235	171	71
Fish and seafood	135	171	147	171	136	174	187	107	76
Eggs	44	54	46	59	56	59	59	39	24
Dairy products	406	530	427	615	599	637	587	350	214
Fresh milk and cream	144	183	136	220	232	226	201	135	75
Other dairy products	262	347	291	396	367	412	387	214	139
Fruits and vegetables	656	853	748	921	859	951	908	542	352
Fresh fruits	220	293	258	318	298	331	305	175	115
Fresh vegetables	209	274	252	280	270	287	272	147	112
Processed fruits	118	147	121	170	156	174	173	121	67
Processed vegetables	110	139	117	154	135	158	157	98	58
Other food at home	1,343	1,718	1,404	1,977	1,824	1,993	2,045	1,266	724
Sugar and other sweets	141	186	155	216	177	215	241	124	70
Fats and oils	102	134	123	141	133	141	148	87	50
Miscellaneous foods	715	908	704	1,076	1,048	1,099	1,053	708	391
Nonalcoholic beverages	337	421	349	476	416	468	530	324	186
Food prepared by CU on trips	49	69	74	67	50	70	73	22	26
Food away from home	**2,619**	**3,436**	**2,930**	**3,917**	**2,980**	**4,221**	**3,958**	**1,868**	**1,507**
ALCOHOLIC BEVERAGES	**435**	**511**	**582**	**470**	**507**	**485**	**422**	**177**	**355**
HOUSING	**16,895**	**20,654**	**18,140**	**22,858**	**24,503**	**23,906**	**20,258**	**14,836**	**11,388**
Shelter	**10,075**	**11,960**	**10,414**	**13,412**	**14,005**	**14,410**	**11,485**	**8,610**	**7,376**
Owned dwellings	6,543	9,049	7,835	10,226	10,279	10,796	9,284	3,711	3,495
Mortgage interest and charges	3,594	5,133	3,706	6,376	7,193	6,856	5,157	2,378	1,590
Property taxes	1,811	2,477	2,327	2,666	2,217	2,759	2,766	982	1,062
Maintenance, repair, insurance, other expenses	1,138	1,440	1,802	1,184	868	1,182	1,361	351	843
Rented dwellings	2,860	1,936	1,413	2,308	3,273	2,602	1,305	4,626	3,513
Other lodging	672	975	1,166	878	454	1,012	896	272	368
Utilities, fuels, public services	**3,645**	**4,403**	**3,937**	**4,708**	**3,853**	**4,731**	**5,144**	**3,438**	**2,298**
Natural gas	483	588	528	636	583	603	719	381	314
Electricity	1,377	1,653	1,487	1,747	1,390	1,794	1,870	1,409	868
Fuel oil and other fuels	141	189	216	169	108	176	193	57	84
Telephone services	1,162	1,379	1,174	1,527	1,260	1,511	1,701	1,190	722
Water and other public services	481	595	532	628	513	647	661	402	309

	total consumer units	total married couples	married couples, no children	married couples with children			single parent, at least one child <18	single person
				total	oldest child under 6	oldest child 6 to 17	oldest child 18 or older		
Household services	$1,011	$1,336	$873	$1,784	$3,537	$1,716	$928	$1,215	$548
Personal services	389	556	55	1,019	2,939	890	166	758	100
Other household services	622	780	818	766	598	826	762	456	448
Housekeeping supplies	659	886	916	851	796	867	858	583	345
Laundry and cleaning supplies	156	202	181	213	204	226	196	173	82
Other household products	360	492	520	458	445	459	465	300	179
Postage and stationery	143	192	214	180	147	183	197	111	83
Household furnishings, equip.	1,506	2,069	2,001	2,101	2,312	2,182	1,842	991	821
Household textiles	124	175	177	164	228	158	134	109	55
Furniture	343	467	440	480	739	477	343	268	185
Floor coverings	30	45	52	38	47	42	26	8	15
Major appliances	194	268	272	254	233	252	268	127	106
Small appliances, misc. housewares	93	126	119	126	107	114	158	68	53
Miscellaneous household equipment	721	989	941	1,040	958	1,141	914	411	407
APPAREL AND RELATED SERVICES	1,725	2,170	1,630	2,600	2,281	2,844	2,387	1,708	975
Men and boys	383	487	368	589	466	613	629	342	234
Men, aged 16 or older	304	377	339	408	331	359	544	174	225
Boys, aged 2 to 15	79	110	29	181	135	254	86	168	9
Women and girls	678	847	638	1,011	700	1,162	943	713	374
Women, aged 16 or older	561	681	596	732	532	750	827	460	356
Girls, aged 2 to 15	118	167	42	278	168	412	115	253	18
Children under age 2	91	126	56	182	592	106	59	115	22
Footwear	323	396	299	454	279	493	493	366	177
Other apparel products, services	249	314	269	365	243	469	262	172	168
TRANSPORTATION	7,658	10,021	9,202	10,487	9,889	9,988	11,673	5,337	4,182
Vehicle purchases	2,657	3,504	3,460	3,406	3,650	3,190	3,618	1,679	1,441
Cars and trucks, new	1,297	1,719	1,985	1,396	1,168	1,273	1,720	693	791
Cars and trucks, used	1,304	1,720	1,418	1,963	2,459	1,880	1,823	986	606
Gasoline and motor oil	1,986	2,572	2,139	2,868	2,417	2,838	3,166	1,573	1,022
Other vehicle expenses	2,536	3,315	2,962	3,557	3,191	3,293	4,241	1,801	1,417
Vehicle finance charges	281	387	323	432	385	419	479	225	109
Maintenance and repairs	733	915	882	932	812	907	1,040	587	470
Vehicle insurance	1,075	1,415	1,199	1,546	1,313	1,318	2,096	687	589
Vehicle rentals, leases, licenses, other charges	447	598	558	647	682	648	626	303	249
Public transportation	479	631	641	656	631	668	649	283	303
HEALTH CARE	3,126	4,182	4,852	3,556	2,884	3,460	4,082	1,381	2,007
Health insurance	1,785	2,365	2,802	1,975	1,669	1,941	2,200	743	1,169
Medical services	736	1,011	1,034	984	819	981	1,080	382	446
Drugs	486	642	820	465	302	408	647	194	326
Medical supplies	119	163	196	132	94	131	155	62	67
ENTERTAINMENT	2,693	3,606	3,259	4,030	2,894	4,532	3,852	1,907	1,510
Fees and admissions	628	900	733	1,096	658	1,406	835	409	307
Audio and visual equip., services	975	1,178	1,109	1,229	1,045	1,280	1,247	891	661
Pets, toys, hobbies, and playground equipment	690	911	872	976	670	976	1,163	420	407
Other entertainment products and services	400	617	546	728	521	870	606	188	134
PERSONAL CARE PRODUCTS AND SERVICES	596	758	708	798	779	800	802	552	345
READING	110	135	160	118	78	122	133	62	87
EDUCATION	1,068	1,478	840	2,105	378	2,096	3,071	874	492

	total consumer units	total married couples	married couples, no children	married couples with children				single parent, at least one child <18	single person
				total	oldest child under 6	oldest child 6 to 17	oldest child 18 or older		
TOBACCO PRODUCTS AND SMOKING SUPPLIES	$380	$375	$335	$357	$258	$326	$461	$345	$253
MISCELLANEOUS	816	1,016	923	1,014	860	1,091	971	613	565
CASH CONTRIBUTIONS	1,723	2,245	2,456	2,130	1,435	1,979	2,756	792	1,268
PERSONAL INSURANCE AND PENSIONS	5,471	7,689	6,785	8,590	7,580	8,873	8,695	2,830	2,518
Life and other personal insurance	309	481	512	464	292	488	521	123	118
Pensions and Social Security	5,162	7,208	6,273	8,126	7,288	8,384	8,174	2,707	2,399
PERSONAL TAXES	2,104	3,002	3,560	2,813	1,708	3,084	2,988	-148	1,395
Federal income taxes	1,404	2,035	2,558	1,799	951	1,952	2,023	-467	967
State and local income taxes	524	731	740	784	620	883	716	196	312
Other taxes	177	238	263	231	138	251	249	125	118
GIFTS FOR PEOPLE IN OTHER HOUSEHOLDS	1,067	1,424	1,666	1,232	709	1,207	1,569	517	778

Note: Spending by category does not add to total spending because gift spending is also included in the preceding product and service categories and personal taxes are not included in the total.
Source: Bureau of Labor Statistics' 2009 Consumer Expenditure Survey, Internet site http://www.bls.gov/cex/; calculations by New Strategist

Table 9.12 Indexed Spending by Household Type, 2009

(indexed average annual spending of consumer units (CUs) by product and service category and type of consumer unit, 2009; index definition: an index of 100 is the average for all consumer units; an index of 125 means that spending by consumer units in that group is 25 percent above the average for all consumer units; an index of 75 indicates spending that is 25 percent below the average for all consumer units)

	total consumer units	total married couples	married couples, no children	married couples with children total	oldest child under 6	oldest child 6 to 17	oldest child 18 or older	single parent, at least one child <18	single person
Average spending of CUs	$49,067	$63,104	$56,777	$68,481	$62,138	$70,329	$69,089	$36,763	$29,405
Indexed spending of CUs	100	129	116	140	127	143	141	75	60
FOOD	100	130	108	147	123	154	149	84	54
Food at home	100	129	106	145	129	149	148	93	52
Cereals and bakery products	100	130	100	152	123	163	151	96	50
Cereals and cereal products	100	129	97	152	143	153	155	106	46
Bakery products	100	130	102	152	112	168	149	90	52
Meats, poultry, fish, and eggs	100	127	105	139	111	142	150	100	49
Beef	100	129	109	140	105	140	164	105	46
Pork	100	125	104	136	96	144	148	101	47
Other meats	100	130	110	146	122	156	143	101	46
Poultry	100	126	97	146	131	148	153	111	46
Fish and seafood	100	127	109	127	101	129	139	79	56
Eggs	100	123	105	134	127	134	134	89	55
Dairy products	100	131	105	151	148	157	145	86	53
Fresh milk and cream	100	127	94	153	161	157	140	94	52
Other dairy products	100	132	111	151	140	157	148	82	53
Fruits and vegetables	100	130	114	140	131	145	138	83	54
Fresh fruits	100	133	117	145	135	150	139	80	52
Fresh vegetables	100	131	121	134	129	137	130	70	54
Processed fruits	100	125	103	144	132	147	147	103	57
Processed vegetables	100	126	106	140	123	144	143	89	53
Other food at home	100	128	105	147	136	148	152	94	54
Sugar and other sweets	100	132	110	153	126	152	171	88	50
Fats and oils	100	131	121	138	130	138	145	85	49
Miscellaneous foods	100	127	98	150	147	154	147	99	55
Nonalcoholic beverages	100	125	104	141	123	139	157	96	55
Food prepared by CU on trips	100	141	151	137	102	143	149	45	53
Food away from home	100	131	112	150	114	161	151	71	58
ALCOHOLIC BEVERAGES	100	117	134	108	117	111	97	41	82
HOUSING	100	122	107	135	145	141	120	88	67
Shelter	100	119	103	133	139	143	114	85	73
Owned dwellings	100	138	120	156	157	165	142	57	53
Mortgage interest and charges	100	143	103	177	200	191	143	66	44
Property taxes	100	137	128	147	122	152	153	54	59
Maintenance, repair, insurance, other expenses	100	127	158	104	76	104	120	31	74
Rented dwellings	100	68	49	81	114	91	46	162	123
Other lodging	100	145	174	131	68	151	133	40	55
Utilities, fuels, public services	100	121	108	129	106	130	141	94	63
Natural gas	100	122	109	132	121	125	149	79	65
Electricity	100	120	108	127	101	130	136	102	63
Fuel oil and other fuels	100	134	153	120	77	125	137	40	60
Telephone services	100	119	101	131	108	130	146	102	62
Water and other public services	100	124	111	131	107	135	137	84	64

	total consumer units	total married couples	married couples, no children	married couples with children total	oldest child under 6	oldest child 6 to 17	oldest child 18 or older	single parent, at least one child <18	single person
Household services	100	132	86	176	350	170	92	120	54
Personal services	100	143	14	262	756	229	43	195	26
Other household services	100	125	132	123	96	133	123	73	72
Housekeeping supplies	100	134	139	129	121	132	130	88	52
Laundry and cleaning supplies	100	129	116	137	131	145	126	111	53
Other household products	100	137	144	127	124	128	129	83	50
Postage and stationery	100	134	150	126	103	128	138	78	58
Household furnishings, equipment	100	137	133	140	154	145	122	66	55
Household textiles	100	141	143	132	184	127	108	88	44
Furniture	100	136	128	140	215	139	100	78	54
Floor coverings	100	150	173	127	157	140	87	27	50
Major appliances	100	138	140	131	120	130	138	65	55
Small appliances, misc. housewares	100	135	128	135	115	123	170	73	57
Miscellaneous household equipment	100	137	131	144	133	158	127	57	56
APPAREL AND RELATED SERVICES	100	126	94	151	132	165	138	99	57
Men and boys	100	127	96	154	122	160	164	89	61
Men, aged 16 or older	100	124	112	134	109	118	179	57	74
Boys, aged 2 to 15	100	139	37	229	171	322	109	213	11
Women and girls	100	125	94	149	103	171	139	105	55
Women, aged 16 or older	100	121	106	130	95	134	147	82	63
Girls, aged 2 to 15	100	142	36	236	142	349	97	214	15
Children under age 2	100	138	62	200	651	116	65	126	24
Footwear	100	123	93	141	86	153	153	113	55
Other apparel products, services	100	126	108	147	98	188	105	69	67
TRANSPORTATION	100	131	120	137	129	130	152	70	55
Vehicle purchases	100	132	130	128	137	120	136	63	54
Cars and trucks, new	100	133	153	108	90	98	133	53	61
Cars and trucks, used	100	132	109	151	189	144	140	76	46
Gasoline and motor oil	100	130	108	144	122	143	159	79	51
Other vehicle expenses	100	131	117	140	126	130	167	71	56
Vehicle finance charges	100	138	115	154	137	149	170	80	39
Maintenance and repairs	100	125	120	127	111	124	142	80	64
Vehicle insurance	100	132	112	144	122	123	195	64	55
Vehicle rentals, leases, licenses, other charges	100	134	125	145	153	145	140	68	56
Public transportation	100	132	134	137	132	139	135	59	63
HEALTH CARE	100	134	155	114	92	111	131	44	64
Health insurance	100	132	157	111	94	109	123	42	65
Medical services	100	137	140	134	111	133	147	52	61
Drugs	100	132	169	96	62	84	133	40	67
Medical supplies	100	137	165	111	79	110	130	52	56
ENTERTAINMENT	100	134	121	150	107	168	143	71	56
Fees and admissions	100	143	117	175	105	224	133	65	49
Audio and visual equip., services	100	121	114	126	107	131	128	91	68
Pets, toys, hobbies, and playground equipment	100	132	126	141	97	141	169	61	59
Other entertainment products and services	100	154	137	182	130	218	152	47	34
PERSONAL CARE PRODUCTS AND SERVICES	100	127	119	134	131	134	135	93	58
READING	100	123	145	107	71	111	121	56	79
EDUCATION	100	138	79	197	35	196	288	82	46

	total consumer units	total married couples	married couples, no children	married couples with children				single parent, at least one child <18	single person
				total	oldest child under 6	oldest child 6 to 17	oldest child 18 or older		
TOBACCO PRODUCTS AND SMOKING SUPPLIES	**100**	**99**	**88**	**94**	**68**	**86**	**121**	**91**	**67**
MISCELLANEOUS	**100**	**125**	**113**	**124**	**105**	**134**	**119**	**75**	**69**
CASH CONTRIBUTIONS	**100**	**130**	**143**	**124**	**83**	**115**	**160**	**46**	**74**
PERSONAL INSURANCE AND PENSIONS	**100**	**141**	**124**	**157**	**139**	**162**	**159**	**52**	**46**
Life and other personal insurance	100	156	166	150	94	158	169	40	38
Pensions and Social Security	100	140	122	157	141	162	158	52	46
PERSONAL TAXES	**100**	**143**	**169**	**134**	**81**	**147**	**142**	–	**66**
Federal income taxes	100	145	182	128	68	139	144	–	69
State and local income taxes	100	140	141	150	118	169	137	37	60
Other taxes	100	134	149	131	78	142	141	71	67
GIFTS FOR PEOPLE IN OTHER HOUSEHOLDS	**100**	**133**	**156**	**115**	**66**	**113**	**147**	**48**	**73**

Note: "–" means a refund was received.
Source: Calculations by New Strategist based on the Bureau of Labor Statistics' 2009 Consumer Expenditure Survey, Internet site http://www.bls.gov/cex/home.htm

Table 9.13 Market Shares by Household Type, 2009

(share of total household spending accounted for by household type, 2009)

	total consumer units	total married couples	married couples, no children	married couples with children total	married couples with children oldest child under 6	married couples with children oldest child 6 to 17	married couples with children oldest child 18 or older	single parent, at least one child <18	single person
Share of total consumer units	100.0%	50.7%	22.2%	24.4%	4.3%	12.4%	7.7%	5.6%	28.8%
Share of total spending	100.0	65.2	25.7	34.0	5.4	17.8	10.9	4.2	17.2
FOOD	100.0	65.8	24.1	35.9	5.2	19.1	11.6	4.7	15.6
Food at home	100.0	65.2	23.5	35.4	5.5	18.5	11.5	5.2	15.0
Cereals and bakery products	100.0	65.8	22.3	37.1	5.2	20.2	11.7	5.4	14.5
Cereals and cereal products	100.0	65.4	21.6	37.1	6.1	19.0	12.0	6.0	13.3
Bakery products	100.0	66.0	22.6	37.1	4.8	20.8	11.5	5.1	15.1
Meats, poultry, fish, and eggs	100.0	64.4	23.4	33.9	4.7	17.7	11.6	5.6	14.0
Beef	100.0	65.3	24.2	34.2	4.5	17.3	12.7	5.9	13.2
Pork	100.0	63.4	23.0	33.3	4.1	17.9	11.4	5.7	13.5
Other meats	100.0	65.8	24.4	35.5	5.2	19.4	11.1	5.7	13.4
Poultry	100.0	63.9	21.5	35.6	5.6	18.4	11.8	6.3	13.3
Fish and seafood	100.0	64.2	24.2	30.9	4.3	16.0	10.7	4.5	16.2
Eggs	100.0	62.2	23.2	32.7	5.4	16.6	10.4	5.0	15.7
Dairy products	100.0	66.2	23.4	37.0	6.3	19.5	11.2	4.9	15.2
Fresh milk and cream	100.0	64.4	21.0	37.3	6.9	19.5	10.8	5.3	15.0
Other dairy products	100.0	67.2	24.7	36.9	6.0	19.5	11.4	4.6	15.3
Fruits and vegetables	100.0	65.9	25.3	34.2	5.6	18.0	10.7	4.7	15.4
Fresh fruits	100.0	67.5	26.1	35.3	5.8	18.7	10.7	4.5	15.0
Fresh vegetables	100.0	66.5	26.8	32.7	5.5	17.0	10.1	4.0	15.4
Processed fruits	100.0	63.2	22.8	35.1	5.6	18.3	11.3	5.8	16.3
Processed vegetables	100.0	64.1	23.6	34.2	5.2	17.8	11.0	5.0	15.2
Other food at home	100.0	64.9	23.2	35.9	5.8	18.4	11.8	5.3	15.5
Sugar and other sweets	100.0	66.9	24.4	37.4	5.4	18.9	13.2	5.0	14.3
Fats and oils	100.0	66.6	26.8	33.7	5.6	17.1	11.2	4.8	14.1
Miscellaneous foods	100.0	64.4	21.9	36.7	6.3	19.1	11.4	5.6	15.7
Nonalcoholic beverages	100.0	63.3	23.0	34.5	5.3	17.2	12.2	5.4	15.9
Food prepared by consumer unit on trips	100.0	71.4	33.6	33.4	4.4	17.7	11.5	2.5	15.3
Food away from home	100.0	66.5	24.9	36.5	4.9	20.0	11.7	4.0	16.6
ALCOHOLIC BEVERAGES	100.0	59.6	29.7	26.4	5.0	13.8	7.5	2.3	23.5
HOUSING	100.0	62.0	23.9	33.0	6.2	17.5	9.3	4.9	19.4
Shelter	100.0	60.2	23.0	32.5	5.9	17.7	8.8	4.8	21.1
Owned dwellings	100.0	70.1	26.6	38.1	6.7	20.5	11.0	3.2	15.4
Mortgage interest and charges	100.0	72.4	22.9	43.3	8.5	23.7	11.1	3.7	12.7
Property taxes	100.0	69.3	28.6	35.9	5.2	18.9	11.8	3.1	16.9
Maintenance, repair, insurance, other expenses	100.0	64.2	35.2	25.4	3.3	12.9	9.2	1.7	21.3
Rented dwellings	100.0	34.3	11.0	19.7	4.9	11.3	3.5	9.1	35.3
Other lodging	100.0	73.6	38.6	31.9	2.9	18.7	10.3	2.3	15.8
Utilities, fuels, public services	100.0	61.2	24.0	31.5	4.5	16.1	10.9	5.3	18.1
Natural gas	100.0	61.7	24.3	32.1	5.1	15.5	11.5	4.4	18.7
Electricity	100.0	60.9	24.0	30.9	4.3	16.2	10.5	5.8	18.1
Fuel oil and other fuels	100.0	68.0	34.0	29.2	3.3	15.5	10.6	2.3	17.1
Telephone services	100.0	60.2	22.4	32.1	4.6	16.1	11.3	5.8	17.9
Water and other public services	100.0	62.7	24.6	31.8	4.5	16.7	10.6	4.7	18.5

	total consumer units	total married couples	married couples, no children	married couples with children				single parent, at least one child <18	single person
				total	oldest child under 6	oldest child 6 to 17	oldest child 18 or older		
Household services	100.0%	67.0%	19.2%	43.0%	14.9%	21.0%	7.1%	6.8%	15.6%
Personal services	100.0	72.5	3.1	63.9	32.2	28.4	3.3	11.0	7.4
Other household services	100.0	63.6	29.2	30.0	4.1	16.5	9.5	4.1	20.7
Housekeeping supplies	100.0	68.2	30.9	31.5	5.2	16.3	10.1	5.0	15.1
Laundry and cleaning supplies	100.0	65.7	25.8	33.3	5.6	18.0	9.7	6.2	15.1
Other household products	100.0	69.3	32.1	31.0	5.3	15.8	10.0	4.7	14.3
Postage and stationery	100.0	68.1	33.3	30.7	4.4	15.9	10.6	4.4	16.7
Household furnishings, equip.	100.0	69.7	29.5	34.0	6.5	18.0	9.5	3.7	15.7
Household textiles	100.0	71.6	31.7	32.3	7.8	15.8	8.4	5.0	12.8
Furniture	100.0	69.0	28.5	34.1	9.2	17.2	7.7	4.4	15.5
Floor coverings	100.0	76.1	38.5	30.9	6.7	17.4	6.7	1.5	14.4
Major appliances	100.0	70.0	31.2	31.9	5.1	16.1	10.7	3.7	15.7
Small appliances, misc. housewares	100.0	68.7	28.4	33.1	4.9	15.2	13.1	4.1	16.4
Misc. household equipment	100.0	69.5	29.0	35.2	5.7	19.6	9.8	3.2	16.2
APPAREL AND RELATED SERVICES	100.0	63.8	21.0	36.8	5.6	20.4	10.7	5.6	16.3
Men and boys	100.0	64.5	21.3	37.5	5.2	19.8	12.7	5.0	17.6
Men, aged 16 or older	100.0	62.9	24.8	32.7	4.6	14.6	13.8	3.2	21.3
Boys, aged 2 to 15	100.0	70.6	8.2	55.9	7.3	39.9	8.4	12.0	3.3
Women and girls	100.0	63.3	20.9	36.4	4.4	21.2	10.8	5.9	15.9
Women, aged 16 or older	100.0	61.5	23.6	31.8	4.0	16.6	11.4	4.6	18.3
Girls, aged 2 to 15	100.0	71.8	7.9	57.5	6.1	43.3	7.5	12.1	4.4
Children under age 2	100.0	70.2	13.7	48.8	27.7	14.4	5.0	7.1	7.0
Footwear	100.0	62.2	20.6	34.3	3.7	18.9	11.8	6.4	15.8
Other apparel products, and services	100.0	63.9	24.0	35.8	4.2	23.4	8.1	3.9	19.4
TRANSPORTATION	100.0	66.3	26.7	33.4	5.5	16.2	11.8	3.9	15.7
Vehicle purchases	100.0	66.9	28.9	31.3	5.9	14.9	10.5	3.6	15.6
Cars and trucks, new	100.0	67.2	34.0	26.3	3.8	12.2	10.3	3.0	17.5
Cars and trucks, used	100.0	66.9	24.2	36.7	8.0	17.9	10.8	4.3	13.4
Gasoline and motor oil	100.0	65.7	23.9	35.2	5.2	17.7	12.3	4.5	14.8
Other vehicle expenses	100.0	66.3	26.0	34.2	5.4	16.1	12.9	4.0	16.1
Vehicle finance charges	100.0	69.8	25.5	37.5	5.8	18.5	13.2	4.5	11.2
Maintenance and repairs	100.0	63.3	26.7	31.0	4.7	15.3	11.0	4.5	18.4
Vehicle insurance	100.0	66.7	24.8	35.1	5.2	15.2	15.1	3.6	15.8
Vehicle rentals, leases, licenses, other charges	100.0	67.8	27.7	35.3	6.5	18.0	10.8	3.8	16.0
Public transportation	100.0	66.8	29.7	33.4	5.6	17.3	10.5	3.3	18.2
HEALTH CARE	100.0	67.8	34.5	27.8	3.9	13.7	10.1	2.5	18.5
Health insurance	100.0	67.2	34.9	27.0	4.0	13.5	9.5	2.3	18.8
Medical services	100.0	69.6	31.2	32.6	4.7	16.5	11.3	2.9	17.4
Drugs	100.0	67.0	37.5	23.3	2.7	10.4	10.3	2.2	19.3
Medical supplies	100.0	69.4	36.6	27.1	3.4	13.6	10.1	2.9	16.2
ENTERTAINMENT	100.0	67.9	26.9	36.5	4.6	20.9	11.1	4.0	16.1
Fees and admissions	100.0	72.7	25.9	42.6	4.5	27.8	10.3	3.7	14.1
Audio, visual equip., services	100.0	61.3	25.3	30.7	4.6	16.3	9.9	5.1	19.5
Pets, toys, hobbies, and playground equipment	100.0	66.9	28.1	34.5	4.1	17.5	13.0	3.4	17.0
Other entertainment products and services	100.0	78.2	30.3	44.4	5.6	27.0	11.7	2.6	9.6
PERSONAL CARE PRODUCTS AND SERVICES	100.0	64.5	26.4	32.7	5.6	16.6	10.4	5.2	16.7
READING	100.0	62.2	32.3	26.2	3.0	13.8	9.3	3.2	22.8
EDUCATION	100.0	70.2	17.5	48.1	1.5	24.3	22.2	4.6	13.3

	total consumer units	total married couples	married couples, no children	married couples with children				single parent, at least one child <18	single person
				total	oldest child under 6	oldest child 6 to 17	oldest child 18 or older		
TOBACCO PRODUCTS AND SMOKING SUPPLIES	100.0%	50.0%	19.6%	22.9%	2.9%	10.6%	9.4%	5.1%	19.2%
MISCELLANEOUS	100.0	63.1	25.1	30.3	4.5	16.6	9.2	4.2	19.9
CASH CONTRIBUTIONS	100.0	66.1	31.7	30.2	3.6	14.2	12.4	2.6	21.2
PERSONAL INSURANCE AND PENSIONS	100.0	71.3	27.6	38.3	5.9	20.1	12.3	2.9	13.2
Life and other personal insurance	100.0	78.9	36.8	36.6	4.0	19.6	13.0	2.2	11.0
Pensions and Social Security	100.0	70.8	27.0	38.4	6.0	20.1	12.2	3.0	13.4
PERSONAL TAXES	100.0	72.3	37.6	32.6	3.5	18.2	11.0	–	19.1
Federal income taxes	100.0	73.5	40.5	31.3	2.9	17.2	11.1	–	19.8
State and local income taxes	100.0	70.7	31.4	36.5	5.0	20.9	10.6	2.1	17.1
Other taxes	100.0	68.2	33.0	31.8	3.3	17.6	10.9	4.0	19.2
GIFTS FOR PEOPLE IN OTHER HOUSEHOLDS	100.0	67.7	34.7	28.2	2.8	14.0	11.4	2.7	21.0

Note: "–" means a refund was received.
Source: Calculations by New Strategist based on the Bureau of Labor Statistics' 2009 Consumer Expenditure Survey, Internet site http://www.bls.gov/cex/home.htm

Asians Spend the Most

Blacks and Hispanics spend far less than the average household.

Asian households have the highest incomes and they spend the most—an average of $56,308 in 2009, or 15 percent more than the average household. Non-Hispanic whites and others (a category that also includes Asians and American Indians) spent 7 percent more than average. Hispanic households spent 14 percent less than average, and black households spent 28 percent less. There is great variation in spending by category, however.

The Indexed Spending table shows household spending for each racial and Hispanic origin group relative to what the average household spends. An index of 100 means households in the racial/Hispanic origin group spend an average amount on the item. An index above 100 means households in the racial/Hispanic origin group spend more than average on the item, while an index below 100 reveals below-average spending.

A look at Table 9.15 shows below-average spending on most items by black and Hispanic households, close-to-average spending by non-Hispanic white households, and above-average spending by Asian households. There are some important exceptions, however. Black households spend more than average on pork, poultry, and fish. They spend 9 percent more on boys' clothes and 33 percent more on shoes.

Hispanic households spend more than the average household on many foods, probably because their households are above average in size—3.3 people compared with 2.5 in the average household.

The spending of Asians and non-Hispanic whites is above average

(average annual spending of consumer units by race and Hispanic origin of householder, 2009)

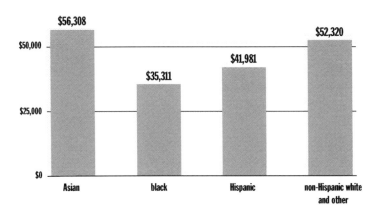

Hispanic households also spend 24 percent more than average on laundry and cleaning products, 62 percent more on infants' clothes, and 46 percent more on shoes.

Asian households spend 40 percent more than the average household on food away from home. They spend more than twice the average amount on public transportation—a category that includes airfares. They also spend more than twice the average on education.

Because Asian, black, and Hispanic households account for a small share of total households, they account for a small share of overall spending on most products and services. Blacks and Hispanics together, however, account for 33 percent of the footwear market. Asians account for a single-digit share of the market in every product and service category.

■ The spending of black households is likely to remain below average because few are headed by married couples—the most affluent household type. The spending of Hispanics will remain below average because many are recent immigrants with low incomes.

Table 9.14 Average Spending by Race and Hispanic Origin of Householder, 2009

(average annual spending of consumer units by product and service category and by race and Hispanic origin of consumer unit reference person, 2009)

	total consumer units	Asian	black	Hispanic	non-Hispanic white and other
Number of consumer units (in 000s)	120,847	4,584	14,659	14,295	92,119
Average number of persons per consumer unit	2.5	2.7	2.6	3.3	2.4
Average annual spending	**$49,067**	**$56,308**	**$35,311**	**$41,981**	**$52,320**
FOOD	**6,372**	**7,565**	**4,524**	**6,094**	**6,696**
Food at home	**3,753**	**3,905**	**2,880**	**3,784**	**3,882**
Cereals and bakery products	506	520	390	479	529
Cereals and cereal products	173	215	149	184	174
Bakery products	334	305	241	294	354
Meats, poultry, fish, and eggs	841	966	845	955	823
Beef	226	186	191	252	227
Pork	168	172	193	202	160
Other meats	114	82	91	110	118
Poultry	154	184	183	192	144
Fish and seafood	135	274	144	141	133
Eggs	44	67	42	58	42
Dairy products	406	346	258	403	429
Fresh milk and cream	144	152	105	171	146
Other dairy products	262	195	153	232	283
Fruits and vegetables	656	903	484	734	671
Fresh fruits	220	310	151	256	225
Fresh vegetables	209	385	136	240	216
Processed fruits	118	117	105	121	120
Processed vegetables	110	91	92	117	111
Other food at home	1,343	1,169	903	1,213	1,430
Sugar and other sweets	141	106	88	109	153
Fats and oils	102	99	82	105	105
Miscellaneous foods	715	646	462	617	768
Nonalcoholic beverages	337	267	253	348	348
Food prepared by consumer unit on trips	49	52	17	33	56
Food away from home	**2,619**	**3,660**	**1,645**	**2,310**	**2,814**
ALCOHOLIC BEVERAGES	**435**	**350**	**201**	**267**	**496**
HOUSING	**16,895**	**20,395**	**13,503**	**15,983**	**17,579**
Shelter	**10,075**	**13,571**	**7,919**	**10,043**	**10,429**
Owned dwellings	6,543	8,543	3,632	5,298	7,198
Mortgage interest and charges	3,594	5,349	2,220	3,454	3,837
Property taxes	1,811	2,334	912	1,368	2,021
Maintenance, repair, insurance, other expenses	1,138	860	500	476	1,340
Rented dwellings	2,860	4,411	4,046	4,415	2,437
Other lodging	672	616	241	330	794
Utilities, fuels, and public services	**3,645**	**3,270**	**3,668**	**3,532**	**3,660**
Natural gas	483	499	517	389	493
Electricity	1,377	1,056	1,462	1,339	1,369
Fuel oil and other fuels	141	48	50	47	171
Telephone services	1,162	1,123	1,224	1,272	1,135
Water and other public services	481	544	415	485	492

	total consumer units	Asian	black	Hispanic	non-Hispanic white and other
Household services	$1,011	$1,347	$633	$714	$1,119
Personal services	389	688	281	334	417
Other household services	622	659	352	380	702
Housekeeping supplies	659	536	429	517	714
Laundry and cleaning supplies	156	130	124	194	155
Other household products	360	292	224	233	399
Postage and stationery	143	113	81	91	160
Household furnishings and equipment	1,506	1,671	854	1,177	1,657
Household textiles	124	187	79	101	134
Furniture	343	304	271	331	357
Floor coverings	30	13	7	7	37
Major appliances	194	183	127	146	212
Small appliances, miscellaneous housewares	93	134	51	80	102
Miscellaneous household equipment	721	848	319	513	814
APPAREL AND RELATED SERVICES	1,725	2,150	1,755	2,002	1,678
Men and boys	383	427	388	432	375
Men, aged 16 or older	304	335	303	323	302
Boys, aged 2 to 15	79	91	86	109	73
Women and girls	678	913	629	693	682
Women, aged 16 or older	561	789	504	509	576
Girls, aged 2 to 15	118	124	126	185	106
Children under age 2	91	122	75	147	85
Footwear	323	344	430	472	285
Other apparel products and services	249	344	231	258	251
TRANSPORTATION	7,658	8,784	5,302	7,156	8,109
Vehicle purchases	2,657	2,582	1,489	2,333	2,897
Cars and trucks, new	1,297	1,131	568	1,010	1,460
Cars and trucks, used	1,304	1,451	910	1,293	1,371
Gasoline and motor oil	1,986	1,871	1,618	2,104	2,026
Other vehicle expenses	2,536	3,153	1,876	2,309	2,670
Vehicle finance charges	281	208	242	278	288
Maintenance and repairs	733	713	504	584	791
Vehicle insurance	1,075	1,610	859	1,049	1,109
Vehicle rentals, leases, licenses, other charges	447	623	270	398	482
Public transportation	479	1,178	319	410	516
HEALTH CARE	3,126	2,498	1,763	1,568	3,581
Health insurance	1,785	1,509	1,133	848	2,033
Medical services	736	575	294	418	855
Drugs	486	307	279	241	556
Medical supplies	119	107	57	61	137
ENTERTAINMENT	2,693	2,270	1,404	1,664	3,050
Fees and admissions	628	848	223	302	742
Audio and visual equipment and services	975	924	840	818	1,020
Pets, toys, hobbies, and playground equipment	690	295	242	391	804
Other entertainment products and services	400	202	99	153	485
PERSONAL CARE PRODUCTS AND SERVICES	596	557	536	532	614
READING	110	111	46	36	131
EDUCATION	1,068	2,327	591	707	1,197

	total consumer units	Asian	black	Hispanic	non-Hispanic white and other
TOBACCO PRODUCTS AND SMOKING SUPPLIES	$380	$122	$230	$182	$434
MISCELLANEOUS	816	611	626	544	887
CASH CONTRIBUTIONS	1,723	1,452	1,280	1,015	1,903
PERSONAL INSURANCE AND PENSIONS	5,471	7,117	3,550	4,230	5,966
Life and other personal insurance	309	283	235	119	350
Pensions and Social Security	5,162	6,834	3,315	4,111	5,616
PERSONAL TAXES	2,104	3,526	743	745	2,525
Federal income taxes	1,404	2,541	378	421	1,716
State and local income taxes	524	787	291	230	605
Other taxes	177	198	74	95	205
GIFTS FOR PEOPLE IN OTHER HOUSEHOLDS	1,067	1,153	570	743	1,193

Note: "Asian" and "black" include Hispanics and non-Hispanics who identify themselves as being of the respective race alone. "Hispanic" includes people of any race who identify themselves as being Hispanic. "Other" includes people who identify themselves as being non-Hispanic and as Alaska Native, American Indian, Asian (who are also included in the Asian column), Native Hawaiian or other Pacific Islander, as well as non-Hispanics reporting more than one race. Spending by category does not add to total spending because gift spending is also included in the preceding product and service categories and personal taxes are not included in the total.
Source: Bureau of Labor Statistics' 2009 Consumer Expenditure Survey, Internet site http://www.bls.gov/cex/

Table 9.15 Indexed Spending by Race and Hispanic Origin of Householder, 2009

(indexed average annual spending of consumer units by product and service category and by race and Hispanic origin of consumer unit reference person, 2009; index definition: an index of 100 is the average for all consumer units; an index of 125 means that spending by consumer units in that group is 25 percent above the average for all consumer units; an index of 75 indicates spending that is 25 percent below the average for all consumer units)

	total consumer units	Asian	black	Hispanic	non-Hispanic white and other
Average spending of consumer units	$49,067	$56,308	$35,311	$41,981	$52,320
Indexed spending of consumer units	100	115	72	86	107
FOOD	100	119	71	96	105
Food at home	100	104	77	101	103
Cereals and bakery products	100	103	77	95	105
Cereals and cereal products	100	124	86	106	101
Bakery products	100	91	72	88	106
Meats, poultry, fish, and eggs	100	115	100	114	98
Beef	100	82	85	112	100
Pork	100	102	115	120	95
Other meats	100	72	80	96	104
Poultry	100	119	119	125	94
Fish and seafood	100	203	107	104	99
Eggs	100	152	95	132	95
Dairy products	100	85	64	99	106
Fresh milk and cream	100	106	73	119	101
Other dairy products	100	74	58	89	108
Fruits and vegetables	100	138	74	112	102
Fresh fruits	100	141	69	116	102
Fresh vegetables	100	184	65	115	103
Processed fruits	100	99	89	103	102
Processed vegetables	100	83	84	106	101
Other food at home	100	87	67	90	106
Sugar and other sweets	100	75	62	77	109
Fats and oils	100	97	80	103	103
Miscellaneous foods	100	90	65	86	107
Nonalcoholic beverages	100	79	75	103	103
Food prepared by consumer unit on trips	100	106	35	67	114
Food away from home	100	140	63	88	107
ALCOHOLIC BEVERAGES	100	80	46	61	114
HOUSING	100	121	80	95	104
Shelter	100	135	79	100	104
Owned dwellings	100	131	56	81	110
Mortgage interest and charges	100	149	62	96	107
Property taxes	100	129	50	76	112
Maintenance, repair, insurance, other expenses	100	76	44	42	118
Rented dwellings	100	154	141	154	85
Other lodging	100	92	36	49	118
Utilities, fuels, and public services	100	90	101	97	100
Natural gas	100	103	107	81	102
Electricity	100	77	106	97	99
Fuel oil and other fuels	100	34	35	33	121
Telephone services	100	97	105	109	98
Water and other public services	100	113	86	101	102

	total consumer units	Asian	black	Hispanic	non-Hispanic white and other
Household services	100	133	63	71	111
Personal services	100	177	72	86	107
Other household services	100	106	57	61	113
Housekeeping supplies	100	81	65	78	108
Laundry and cleaning supplies	100	83	79	124	99
Other household products	100	81	62	65	111
Postage and stationery	100	79	57	64	112
Household furnishings and equipment	100	111	57	78	110
Household textiles	100	151	64	81	108
Furniture	100	89	79	97	104
Floor coverings	100	43	23	23	123
Major appliances	100	94	65	75	109
Small appliances, miscellaneous housewares	100	144	55	86	110
Miscellaneous household equipment	100	118	44	71	113
APPAREL AND RELATED SERVICES	100	125	102	116	97
Men and boys	100	111	101	113	98
Men, aged 16 or older	100	110	100	106	99
Boys, aged 2 to 15	100	115	109	138	92
Women and girls	100	135	93	102	101
Women, aged 16 or older	100	141	90	91	103
Girls, aged 2 to 15	100	105	107	157	90
Children under age 2	100	134	82	162	93
Footwear	100	107	133	146	88
Other apparel products and services	100	138	93	104	101
TRANSPORTATION	100	115	69	93	106
Vehicle purchases	100	97	56	88	109
Cars and trucks, new	100	87	44	78	113
Cars and trucks, used	100	111	70	99	105
Gasoline and motor oil	100	94	81	106	102
Other vehicle expenses	100	124	74	91	105
Vehicle finance charges	100	74	86	99	102
Maintenance and repairs	100	97	69	80	108
Vehicle insurance	100	150	80	98	103
Vehicle rentals, leases, licenses, other charges	100	139	60	89	108
Public transportation	100	246	67	86	108
HEALTH CARE	100	80	56	50	115
Health insurance	100	85	63	48	114
Medical services	100	78	40	57	116
Drugs	100	63	57	50	114
Medical supplies	100	90	48	51	115
ENTERTAINMENT	100	84	52	62	113
Fees and admissions	100	135	36	48	118
Audio and visual equipment and services	100	95	86	84	105
Pets, toys, hobbies, and playground equipment	100	43	35	57	117
Other entertainment products and services	100	51	25	38	121
PERSONAL CARE PRODUCTS AND SERVICES	100	93	90	89	103
READING	100	101	42	33	119
EDUCATION	100	218	55	66	112

	total consumer units	Asian	black	Hispanic	non-Hispanic white and other
TOBACCO PRODUCTS AND SMOKING SUPPLIES	**100**	**32**	**61**	**48**	**114**
MISCELLANEOUS	**100**	**75**	**77**	**67**	**109**
CASH CONTRIBUTIONS	**100**	**84**	**74**	**59**	**110**
PERSONAL INSURANCE AND PENSIONS	**100**	**130**	**65**	**77**	**109**
Life and other personal insurance	100	92	76	39	113
Pensions and Social Security	100	132	64	80	109
PERSONAL TAXES	**100**	**168**	**35**	**35**	**120**
Federal income taxes	100	181	27	30	122
State and local income taxes	100	150	56	44	115
Other taxes	100	112	42	54	116
GIFTS FOR PEOPLE IN OTHER HOUSEHOLDS	**100**	**108**	**53**	**70**	**112**

Note: "Asian" and "black" include Hispanics and non-Hispanics who identify themselves as being of the respective race alone. "Hispanic" includes people of any race who identify themselves as being Hispanic. "Other" includes people who identify themselves as being non-Hispanic and as Alaska Native, American Indian, Asian (who are also included in the Asian column), Native Hawaiian or other Pacific Islander, as well as non-Hispanics reporting more than one race.
Source: Calculations by New Strategist based on the Bureau of Labor Statistics' 2009 Consumer Expenditure Survey, Internet site http://www.bls.gov/cex/home.htm

Table 9.16 Market Shares by Race and Hispanic Origin of Householder, 2009

(share of total household spending accounted for by race and Hispanic origin group, 2009)

	total consumer units	Asian	black	Hispanic	non-Hispanic white and other
Share of total consumer units	100.0%	3.8%	12.1%	11.8%	76.2%
Share of total spending	100.0	4.4	8.7	10.1	81.3
FOOD	100.0	4.5	8.6	11.3	80.1
Food at home	100.0	3.9	9.3	11.9	78.8
Cereals and bakery products	100.0	3.9	9.3	11.2	79.7
Cereals and cereal products	100.0	4.7	10.4	12.6	76.7
Bakery products	100.0	3.5	8.8	10.4	80.8
Meats, poultry, fish, and eggs	100.0	4.4	12.2	13.4	74.6
Beef	100.0	3.1	10.3	13.2	76.6
Pork	100.0	3.9	13.9	14.2	72.6
Other meats	100.0	2.7	9.7	11.4	78.9
Poultry	100.0	4.5	14.4	14.7	71.3
Fish and seafood	100.0	7.7	12.9	12.4	75.1
Eggs	100.0	5.8	11.6	15.6	72.8
Dairy products	100.0	3.2	7.7	11.7	80.5
Fresh milk and cream	100.0	4.0	8.8	14.0	77.3
Other dairy products	100.0	2.8	7.1	10.5	82.3
Fruits and vegetables	100.0	5.2	8.9	13.2	78.0
Fresh fruits	100.0	5.3	8.3	13.8	78.0
Fresh vegetables	100.0	7.0	7.9	13.6	78.8
Processed fruits	100.0	3.8	10.8	12.1	77.5
Processed vegetables	100.0	3.1	10.1	12.6	76.9
Other food at home	100.0	3.3	8.2	10.7	81.2
Sugar and other sweets	100.0	2.9	7.6	9.1	82.7
Fats and oils	100.0	3.7	9.8	12.2	78.5
Miscellaneous foods	100.0	3.4	7.8	10.2	81.9
Nonalcoholic beverages	100.0	3.0	9.1	12.2	78.7
Food prepared by consumer unit on trips	100.0	4.0	4.2	8.0	87.1
Food away from home	100.0	5.3	7.6	10.4	81.9
ALCOHOLIC BEVERAGES	100.0	3.1	5.6	7.3	86.9
HOUSING	100.0	4.6	9.7	11.2	79.3
Shelter	100.0	5.1	9.5	11.8	78.9
Owned dwellings	100.0	5.0	6.7	9.6	83.9
Mortgage interest and charges	100.0	5.6	7.5	11.4	81.4
Property taxes	100.0	4.9	6.1	8.9	85.1
Maintenance, repair, insurance, other expenses	100.0	2.9	5.3	4.9	89.8
Rented dwellings	100.0	5.9	17.2	18.3	65.0
Other lodging	100.0	3.5	4.4	5.8	90.1
Utilities, fuels, and public services	100.0	3.4	12.2	11.5	76.5
Natural gas	100.0	3.9	13.0	9.5	77.8
Electricity	100.0	2.9	12.9	11.5	75.8
Fuel oil and other fuels	100.0	1.3	4.3	3.9	92.4
Telephone services	100.0	3.7	12.8	12.9	74.5
Water and other public services	100.0	4.3	10.5	11.9	78.0

	total consumer units	Asian	black	Hispanic	non-Hispanic white and other
Household services	**100.0%**	**5.1%**	**7.6%**	**8.4%**	**84.4%**
Personal services	100.0	6.7	8.8	10.2	81.7
Other household services	100.0	4.0	6.9	7.2	86.0
Housekeeping supplies	**100.0**	**3.1**	**7.9**	**9.3**	**82.6**
Laundry and cleaning supplies	100.0	3.2	9.6	14.7	75.7
Other household products	100.0	3.1	7.5	7.7	84.5
Postage and stationery	100.0	3.0	6.9	7.5	85.3
Household furnishings and equipment	**100.0**	**4.2**	**6.9**	**9.2**	**83.9**
Household textiles	100.0	5.7	7.7	9.6	82.4
Furniture	100.0	3.4	9.6	11.4	79.3
Floor coverings	100.0	1.6	2.8	2.8	94.0
Major appliances	100.0	3.6	7.9	8.9	83.3
Small appliances, miscellaneous housewares	100.0	5.5	6.7	10.2	83.6
Miscellaneous household equipment	100.0	4.5	5.4	8.4	86.1
APPAREL AND RELATED SERVICES	**100.0**	**4.7**	**12.3**	**13.7**	**74.2**
Men and boys	**100.0**	**4.2**	**12.3**	**13.3**	**74.6**
Men, aged 16 or older	100.0	4.2	12.1	12.6	75.7
Boys, aged 2 to 15	100.0	4.4	13.2	16.3	70.4
Women and girls	**100.0**	**5.1**	**11.3**	**12.1**	**76.7**
Women, aged 16 or older	100.0	5.3	10.9	10.7	78.3
Girls, aged 2 to 15	100.0	4.0	13.0	18.5	68.5
Children under age 2	**100.0**	**5.1**	**10.0**	**19.1**	**71.2**
Footwear	**100.0**	**4.0**	**16.1**	**17.3**	**67.3**
Other apparel products and services	**100.0**	**5.2**	**11.3**	**12.3**	**76.8**
TRANSPORTATION	**100.0**	**4.4**	**8.4**	**11.1**	**80.7**
Vehicle purchases	**100.0**	**3.7**	**6.8**	**10.4**	**83.1**
Cars and trucks, new	100.0	3.3	5.3	9.2	85.8
Cars and trucks, used	100.0	4.2	8.5	11.7	80.1
Gasoline and motor oil	**100.0**	**3.6**	**9.9**	**12.5**	**77.8**
Other vehicle expenses	**100.0**	**4.7**	**9.0**	**10.8**	**80.3**
Vehicle finance charges	100.0	2.8	10.4	11.7	78.1
Maintenance and repairs	100.0	3.7	8.3	9.4	82.3
Vehicle insurance	100.0	5.7	9.7	11.5	78.6
Vehicle rentals, leases, licenses, other charges	100.0	5.3	7.3	10.5	82.2
Public transportation	**100.0**	**9.3**	**8.1**	**10.1**	**82.1**
HEALTH CARE	**100.0**	**3.0**	**6.8**	**5.9**	**87.3**
Health insurance	100.0	3.2	7.7	5.6	86.8
Medical services	100.0	3.0	4.8	6.7	88.6
Drugs	100.0	2.4	7.0	5.9	87.2
Medical supplies	100.0	3.4	5.8	6.1	87.8
ENTERTAINMENT	**100.0**	**3.2**	**6.3**	**7.3**	**86.3**
Fees and admissions	100.0	5.1	4.3	5.7	90.1
Audio and visual equipment and services	100.0	3.6	10.5	9.9	79.7
Pets, toys, hobbies, and playground equipment	100.0	1.6	4.3	6.7	88.8
Other entertainment products and services	100.0	1.9	3.0	4.5	92.4
PERSONAL CARE PRODUCTS AND SERVICES	**100.0**	**3.5**	**10.9**	**10.6**	**78.5**
READING	**100.0**	**3.8**	**5.1**	**3.9**	**90.8**
EDUCATION	**100.0**	**8.3**	**6.7**	**7.8**	**85.4**

	total consumer units	Asian	black	Hispanic	non-Hispanic white and other
TOBACCO PRODUCTS AND SMOKING SUPPLIES	100.0%	1.2%	7.3%	5.7%	87.1%
MISCELLANEOUS	100.0	2.8	9.3	7.9	82.9
CASH CONTRIBUTIONS	100.0	3.2	9.0	7.0	84.2
PERSONAL INSURANCE AND PENSIONS	100.0	4.9	7.9	9.1	83.1
Life and other personal insurance	100.0	3.5	9.2	4.6	86.3
Pensions and Social Security	100.0	5.0	7.8	9.4	82.9
PERSONAL TAXES	100.0	6.4	4.3	4.2	91.5
Federal income taxes	100.0	6.9	3.3	3.5	93.2
State and local income taxes	100.0	5.7	6.7	5.2	88.0
Other taxes	100.0	4.2	5.1	6.3	88.3
GIFTS FOR PEOPLE IN OTHER HOUSEHOLDS	100.0	4.1	6.5	8.2	85.2

Note: "Asian" and "black" include Hispanics and non-Hispanics who identify themselves as being of the respective race alone. "Hispanic" includes people of any race who identify themselves as being Hispanic. "Other" includes people who identify themselves as being non-Hispanic and as Alaska Native, American Indian, Asian (who are also included in the Asian column), Native Hawaiian or other Pacific Islander, as well as non-Hispanics reporting more than one race.
Source: Calculations by New Strategist based on the Bureau of Labor Statistics' 2009 Consumer Expenditure Survey, Internet site http://www.bls.gov/cex/home.htm

Spending Is Highest in the Northeast

Households in the South spend the least.

The average household in the Northeast spent $53,868 in 2009, or 10 percent more than the average household. Households in the West spent 8 percent more than average—or $53,005 in 2009. In the Midwest, households spent 5 percent less than the all-household average. In the South, households spent 7 percent less than average. By product and service category, however, spending varies by region.

The Indexed Spending table shows spending by the average household in each region relative to average household spending. An index of 100 means households in the region spend an average amount on the item. An index above 100 indicates that households in the region spend more than average on the item, while an index below 100 reveals below-average spending.

Households in the West and Northeast spend more than the average household on most foods. Spending on housing is also above average in both regions. Households in the Northeast spend 58 percent more than the average household on property taxes and 42 percent more on public transportation. Households in the Midwest spend 8 percent more than average on tobacco, while those in the West spend 27 percent less than average on this item. Households in the South spend less than the average household on most items with some exceptions, such as electricity and vehicle finance charges.

Spending varies by region

(average annual spending of consumer units by region, 2009)

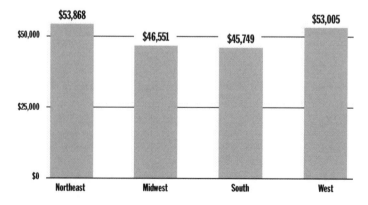

The Market Share table shows how much of total spending by category is accounted for by households in each region. In most categories, spending closely matches each region's share of total households. The South, which is home to 36 percent of households, accounts for 34 percent of household spending. With 22 percent of households, the West accounts for 24 percent of household spending. There are some exceptions, however. Households in the South, for example, account for a disproportionate share of spending on electricity (45 percent), while those in the West account for only 19 percent of spending on this item.

■ Because regional spending patterns are partly determined by climate, spending by region is not likely to change much in the years ahead.

Table 9.17 Average Spending by Region, 2009

(average annual spending of consumer units by product and service category and region of residence, 2009)

	total consumer units	Northeast	Midwest	South	West
Number of consumer units (in 000s)	120,847	22,411	27,536	43,819	27,080
Average number of persons per consumer unit	2.5	2.4	2.4	2.5	2.6
Average annual spending	**$49,067**	**$53,868**	**$46,551**	**$45,749**	**$53,005**
FOOD	6,372	6,975	6,031	5,944	6,903
Food at home	3,753	4,043	3,682	3,481	4,023
Cereals and bakery products	506	563	510	469	516
Cereals and cereal products	173	188	176	157	182
Bakery products	334	376	334	313	334
Meats, poultry, fish, and eggs	841	919	762	829	875
Beef	226	230	207	230	236
Pork	168	165	171	172	163
Other meats	114	133	123	101	108
Poultry	154	169	121	158	169
Fish and seafood	135	176	103	125	150
Eggs	44	46	37	43	50
Dairy products	406	435	419	367	432
Fresh milk and cream	144	152	140	140	148
Other dairy products	262	284	279	227	284
Fruits and vegetables	656	751	616	581	740
Fresh fruits	220	247	210	185	262
Fresh vegetables	209	247	186	180	249
Processed fruits	118	139	114	105	126
Processed vegetables	110	119	107	111	103
Other food at home	1,343	1,374	1,375	1,235	1,461
Sugar and other sweets	141	140	157	124	152
Fats and oils	102	109	105	98	101
Miscellaneous foods	715	731	742	649	782
Nonalcoholic beverages	337	334	323	329	365
Food prepared by consumer unit on trips	49	60	47	36	60
Food away from home	**2,619**	**2,932**	**2,349**	**2,463**	**2,880**
ALCOHOLIC BEVERAGES	**435**	**468**	**418**	**368**	**530**
HOUSING	**16,895**	**19,343**	**15,109**	**15,387**	**19,127**
Shelter	**10,075**	**11,944**	**8,756**	**8,524**	**12,378**
Owned dwellings	6,543	7,513	6,126	5,613	7,667
Mortgage interest and charges	3,594	3,434	2,970	3,147	5,084
Property taxes	1,811	2,865	1,962	1,309	1,599
Maintenance, repair, insurance, other expenses	1,138	1,214	1,195	1,158	984
Rented dwellings	2,860	3,507	1,986	2,361	4,021
Other lodging	672	924	643	550	690
Utilities, fuels, and public services	**3,645**	**4,095**	**3,421**	**3,741**	**3,343**
Natural gas	483	719	695	266	424
Electricity	1,377	1,306	1,119	1,719	1,143
Fuel oil and other fuels	141	434	114	62	57
Telephone services	1,162	1,241	1,080	1,191	1,133
Water and other public services	481	396	414	503	586

	total consumer units	Northeast	Midwest	South	West
Household services	**$1,011**	**$1,196**	**$780**	**$969**	**$1,164**
Personal services	389	551	258	339	472
Other household services	622	645	522	630	692
Housekeeping supplies	**659**	**640**	**682**	**667**	**638**
Laundry and cleaning supplies	156	142	163	159	155
Other household products	360	358	366	385	314
Postage and stationery	143	139	153	123	169
Household furnishings and equipment	**1,506**	**1,467**	**1,471**	**1,485**	**1,605**
Household textiles	124	126	116	122	134
Furniture	343	347	316	353	349
Floor coverings	30	30	39	30	22
Major appliances	194	175	189	202	201
Small appliances, miscellaneous housewares	93	90	100	80	112
Miscellaneous household equipment	721	700	711	697	786
APPAREL AND RELATED SERVICES	**1,725**	**1,782**	**1,461**	**1,786**	**1,844**
Men and boys	**383**	**412**	**339**	**371**	**422**
Men, aged 16 or older	304	331	264	294	340
Boys, aged 2 to 15	79	81	75	78	82
Women and girls	**678**	**662**	**590**	**727**	**702**
Women, aged 16 or older	561	564	476	599	581
Girls, aged 2 to 15	118	98	113	129	120
Children under age 2	**91**	**76**	**86**	**86**	**117**
Footwear	**323**	**343**	**251**	**349**	**336**
Other apparel products and services	**249**	**288**	**195**	**252**	**268**
TRANSPORTATION	**7,658**	**8,108**	**7,649**	**7,400**	**7,711**
Vehicle purchases	**2,657**	**2,754**	**2,921**	**2,612**	**2,380**
Cars and trucks, new	1,297	1,644	1,387	1,321	881
Cars and trucks, used	1,304	1,089	1,468	1,211	1,468
Gasoline and motor oil	**1,986**	**1,787**	**1,933**	**2,103**	**2,018**
Other vehicle expenses	**2,536**	**2,885**	**2,375**	**2,371**	**2,673**
Vehicle finance charges	281	218	252	336	274
Maintenance and repairs	733	762	706	646	876
Vehicle insurance	1,075	1,271	957	1,095	999
Vehicle rentals, leases, licenses, other charges	447	634	460	294	524
Public transportation	**479**	**682**	**420**	**314**	**640**
HEALTH CARE	**3,126**	**3,132**	**3,272**	**3,030**	**3,128**
Health insurance	1,785	1,916	1,845	1,730	1,703
Medical services	736	625	780	672	889
Drugs	486	481	508	521	414
Medical supplies	119	111	139	108	122
ENTERTAINMENT	**2,693**	**2,767**	**2,627**	**2,467**	**3,062**
Fees and admissions	628	780	573	508	751
Audio and visual equipment and services	975	1,003	927	993	970
Pets, toys, hobbies, and playground equipment	690	682	649	651	800
Other entertainment products and services	400	302	478	315	540
PERSONAL CARE PRODUCTS AND SERVICES	**596**	**601**	**538**	**593**	**653**
READING	**110**	**141**	**112**	**85**	**121**
EDUCATION	**1,068**	**1,710**	**1,103**	**820**	**902**

	total consumer units	Northeast	Midwest	South	West
TOBACCO PRODUCTS AND SMOKING SUPPLIES	**$380**	**$439**	**$409**	**$394**	**$278**
MISCELLANEOUS	**816**	**821**	**798**	**768**	**910**
CASH CONTRIBUTIONS	**1,723**	**1,568**	**1,684**	**1,692**	**1,941**
PERSONAL INSURANCE AND PENSIONS	**5,471**	**6,013**	**5,340**	**5,015**	**5,894**
Life and other personal insurance	309	350	340	298	262
Pensions and Social Security	5,162	5,662	5,000	4,717	5,633
PERSONAL TAXES	**2,104**	**2,745**	**2,042**	**1,846**	**2,053**
Federal income taxes	1,404	1,728	1,311	1,331	1,351
State and local income taxes	524	766	567	351	560
Other taxes	177	254	165	165	142
GIFTS FOR PEOPLE IN OTHER HOUSEHOLDS	**1,067**	**1,292**	**1,044**	**907**	**1,163**

Note: Spending by category does not add to total spending because gift spending is also included in the preceding product and service categories and personal taxes are not included in the total.
Source: Bureau of Labor Statistics' 2009 Consumer Expenditure Survey, Internet site http://www.bls.gov/cex/

Table 9.18 Indexed Spending by Region, 2009

(indexed average annual spending of consumer units by product and service category and region of residence, 2009; index definition: an index of 100 is the average for all consumer units; an index of 125 means that spending by consumer units in that group is 25 percent above the average for all consumer units; an index of 75 indicates spending that is 25 percent below the average for all consumer units)

	total consumer units	Northeast	Midwest	South	West
Average spending of consumer units	$49,067	$53,868	$46,551	$45,749	$53,005
Indexed spending of consumer units	100	110	95	93	108
FOOD	100	109	95	93	108
Food at home	100	108	98	93	107
Cereals and bakery products	100	111	101	93	102
Cereals and cereal products	100	109	102	91	105
Bakery products	100	113	100	94	100
Meats, poultry, fish, and eggs	100	109	91	99	104
Beef	100	102	92	102	104
Pork	100	98	102	102	97
Other meats	100	117	108	89	95
Poultry	100	110	79	103	110
Fish and seafood	100	130	76	93	111
Eggs	100	105	84	98	114
Dairy products	100	107	103	90	106
Fresh milk and cream	100	106	97	97	103
Other dairy products	100	108	106	87	108
Fruits and vegetables	100	114	94	89	113
Fresh fruits	100	112	95	84	119
Fresh vegetables	100	118	89	86	119
Processed fruits	100	118	97	89	107
Processed vegetables	100	108	97	101	94
Other food at home	100	102	102	92	109
Sugar and other sweets	100	99	111	88	108
Fats and oils	100	107	103	96	99
Miscellaneous foods	100	102	104	91	109
Nonalcoholic beverages	100	99	96	98	108
Food prepared by consumer unit on trips	100	122	96	73	122
Food away from home	100	112	90	94	110
ALCOHOLIC BEVERAGES	100	108	96	85	122
HOUSING	100	114	89	91	113
Shelter	100	119	87	85	123
Owned dwellings	100	115	94	86	117
Mortgage interest and charges	100	96	83	88	141
Property taxes	100	158	108	72	88
Maintenance, repair, insurance, other expenses	100	107	105	102	86
Rented dwellings	100	123	69	83	141
Other lodging	100	138	96	82	103
Utilities, fuels, and public services	100	112	94	103	92
Natural gas	100	149	144	55	88
Electricity	100	95	81	125	83
Fuel oil and other fuels	100	308	81	44	40
Telephone services	100	107	93	102	98
Water and other public services	100	82	86	105	122

	total consumer units	Northeast	Midwest	South	West
Household services	**100**	**118**	**77**	**96**	**115**
Personal services	100	142	66	87	121
Other household services	100	104	84	101	111
Housekeeping supplies	**100**	**97**	**103**	**101**	**97**
Laundry and cleaning supplies	100	91	104	102	99
Other household products	100	99	102	107	87
Postage and stationery	100	97	107	86	118
Household furnishings and equipment	**100**	**97**	**98**	**99**	**107**
Household textiles	100	102	94	98	108
Furniture	100	101	92	103	102
Floor coverings	100	100	130	100	73
Major appliances	100	90	97	104	104
Small appliances, miscellaneous housewares	100	97	108	86	120
Miscellaneous household equipment	100	97	99	97	109
APPAREL AND RELATED SERVICES	**100**	**103**	**85**	**104**	**107**
Men and boys	**100**	**108**	**89**	**97**	**110**
Men, aged 16 or older	100	109	87	97	112
Boys, aged 2 to 15	100	103	95	99	104
Women and girls	**100**	**98**	**87**	**107**	**104**
Women, aged 16 or older	100	101	85	107	104
Girls, aged 2 to 15	100	83	96	109	102
Children under age 2	**100**	**84**	**95**	**95**	**129**
Footwear	**100**	**106**	**78**	**108**	**104**
Other apparel products and services	**100**	**116**	**78**	**101**	**108**
TRANSPORTATION	**100**	**106**	**100**	**97**	**101**
Vehicle purchases	**100**	**104**	**110**	**98**	**90**
Cars and trucks, new	100	127	107	102	68
Cars and trucks, used	100	84	113	93	113
Gasoline and motor oil	**100**	**90**	**97**	**106**	**102**
Other vehicle expenses	**100**	**114**	**94**	**93**	**105**
Vehicle finance charges	100	78	90	120	98
Maintenance and repairs	100	104	96	88	120
Vehicle insurance	100	118	89	102	93
Vehicle rentals, leases, licenses, other charges	100	142	103	66	117
Public transportation	**100**	**142**	**88**	**66**	**134**
HEALTH CARE	**100**	**100**	**105**	**97**	**100**
Health insurance	100	107	103	97	95
Medical services	100	85	106	91	121
Drugs	100	99	105	107	85
Medical supplies	100	93	117	91	103
ENTERTAINMENT	**100**	**103**	**98**	**92**	**114**
Fees and admissions	100	124	91	81	120
Audio and visual equipment and services	100	103	95	102	99
Pets, toys, hobbies, and playground equipment	100	99	94	94	116
Other entertainment products and services	100	76	120	79	135
PERSONAL CARE PRODUCTS AND SERVICES	**100**	**101**	**90**	**99**	**110**
READING	**100**	**128**	**102**	**77**	**110**
EDUCATION	**100**	**160**	**103**	**77**	**84**

	total consumer units	Northeast	Midwest	South	West
TOBACCO PRODUCTS AND SMOKING SUPPLIES	**100**	**116**	**108**	**104**	**73**
MISCELLANEOUS	**100**	**101**	**98**	**94**	**112**
CASH CONTRIBUTIONS	**100**	**91**	**98**	**98**	**113**
PERSONAL INSURANCE AND PENSIONS	**100**	**110**	**98**	**92**	**108**
Life and other personal insurance	100	113	110	96	85
Pensions and Social Security	100	110	97	91	109
PERSONAL TAXES	**100**	**130**	**97**	**88**	**98**
Federal income taxes	100	123	93	95	96
State and local income taxes	100	146	108	67	107
Other taxes	100	144	93	93	80
GIFTS FOR PEOPLE IN OTHER HOUSEHOLDS	**100**	**121**	**98**	**85**	**109**

Source: Calculations by New Strategist based on the Bureau of Labor Statistics' 2009 Consumer Expenditure Survey, Internet site http://www.bls.gov/cex/home.htm

Table 9.19 Market Shares by Region, 2009

(share of total household spending accounted for by region of residence, 2009)

	total consumer units	Northeast	Midwest	South	West
Share of total consumer units	100.0%	18.5%	22.8%	36.3%	22.4%
Share of total spending	100.0	20.4	21.6	33.8	24.2
FOOD	100.0	20.3	21.6	33.8	24.3
Food at home	100.0	20.0	22.4	33.6	24.0
Cereals and bakery products	100.0	20.6	23.0	33.6	22.9
Cereals and cereal products	100.0	20.2	23.2	32.9	23.6
Bakery products	100.0	20.9	22.8	34.0	22.4
Meats, poultry, fish, and eggs	100.0	20.3	20.6	35.7	23.3
Beef	100.0	18.9	20.9	36.9	23.4
Pork	100.0	18.2	23.2	37.1	21.7
Other meats	100.0	21.6	24.6	32.1	21.2
Poultry	100.0	20.4	17.9	37.2	24.6
Fish and seafood	100.0	24.2	17.4	33.6	24.9
Eggs	100.0	19.4	19.2	35.4	25.5
Dairy products	100.0	19.9	23.5	32.8	23.8
Fresh milk and cream	100.0	19.6	22.2	35.3	23.0
Other dairy products	100.0	20.1	24.3	31.4	24.3
Fruits and vegetables	100.0	21.2	21.4	32.1	25.3
Fresh fruits	100.0	20.8	21.8	30.5	26.7
Fresh vegetables	100.0	21.9	20.3	31.2	26.7
Processed fruits	100.0	21.8	22.0	32.3	23.9
Processed vegetables	100.0	20.1	22.2	36.6	21.0
Other food at home	100.0	19.0	23.3	33.3	24.4
Sugar and other sweets	100.0	18.4	25.4	31.9	24.2
Fats and oils	100.0	19.8	23.5	34.8	22.2
Miscellaneous foods	100.0	19.0	23.6	32.9	24.5
Nonalcoholic beverages	100.0	18.4	21.8	35.4	24.3
Food prepared by consumer unit on trips	100.0	22.7	21.9	26.6	27.4
Food away from home	100.0	20.8	20.4	34.1	24.6
ALCOHOLIC BEVERAGES	100.0	20.0	21.9	30.7	27.3
HOUSING	100.0	21.2	20.4	33.0	25.4
Shelter	100.0	22.0	19.8	30.7	27.5
Owned dwellings	100.0	21.3	21.3	31.1	26.3
Mortgage interest and charges	100.0	17.7	18.8	31.8	31.7
Property taxes	100.0	29.3	24.7	26.2	19.8
Maintenance, repair, insurance, other expenses	100.0	19.8	23.9	36.9	19.4
Rented dwellings	100.0	22.7	15.8	29.9	31.5
Other lodging	100.0	25.5	21.8	29.7	23.0
Utilities, fuels, and public services	100.0	20.8	21.4	37.2	20.6
Natural gas	100.0	27.6	32.8	20.0	19.7
Electricity	100.0	17.6	18.5	45.3	18.6
Fuel oil and other fuels	100.0	57.1	18.4	15.9	9.1
Telephone services	100.0	19.8	21.2	37.2	21.8
Water and other public services	100.0	15.3	19.6	37.9	27.3

	total consumer units	Northeast	Midwest	South	West
Household services	**100.0%**	**21.9%**	**17.6%**	**34.8%**	**25.8%**
Personal services	100.0	26.3	15.1	31.6	27.2
Other household services	100.0	19.2	19.1	36.7	24.9
Housekeeping supplies	**100.0**	**18.0**	**23.6**	**36.7**	**21.7**
Laundry and cleaning supplies	100.0	16.9	23.8	37.0	22.3
Other household products	100.0	18.4	23.2	38.8	19.5
Postage and stationery	100.0	18.0	24.4	31.2	26.5
Household furnishings and equipment	**100.0**	**18.1**	**22.3**	**35.8**	**23.9**
Household textiles	100.0	18.8	21.3	35.7	24.2
Furniture	100.0	18.8	21.0	37.3	22.8
Floor coverings	100.0	18.5	29.6	36.3	16.4
Major appliances	100.0	16.7	22.2	37.8	23.2
Small appliances, miscellaneous housewares	100.0	17.9	24.5	31.2	27.0
Miscellaneous household equipment	100.0	18.0	22.5	35.1	24.4
APPAREL AND RELATED SERVICES	**100.0**	**19.2**	**19.3**	**37.5**	**24.0**
Men and boys	**100.0**	**19.9**	**20.2**	**35.1**	**24.7**
Men, aged 16 or older	100.0	20.2	19.8	35.1	25.1
Boys, aged 2 to 15	100.0	19.0	21.6	35.8	23.3
Women and girls	**100.0**	**18.1**	**19.8**	**38.9**	**23.2**
Women, aged 16 or older	100.0	18.6	19.3	38.7	23.2
Girls, aged 2 to 15	100.0	15.4	21.8	39.6	22.8
Children under age 2	**100.0**	**15.5**	**21.5**	**34.3**	**28.8**
Footwear	**100.0**	**19.7**	**17.7**	**39.2**	**23.3**
Other apparel products and services	**100.0**	**21.4**	**17.8**	**36.7**	**24.1**
TRANSPORTATION	**100.0**	**19.6**	**22.8**	**35.0**	**22.6**
Vehicle purchases	**100.0**	**19.2**	**25.0**	**35.6**	**20.1**
Cars and trucks, new	100.0	23.5	24.4	36.9	15.2
Cars and trucks, used	100.0	15.5	25.7	33.7	25.2
Gasoline and motor oil	**100.0**	**16.7**	**22.2**	**38.4**	**22.8**
Other vehicle expenses	**100.0**	**21.1**	**21.3**	**33.9**	**23.6**
Vehicle finance charges	100.0	14.4	20.4	43.4	21.9
Maintenance and repairs	100.0	19.3	21.9	32.0	26.8
Vehicle insurance	100.0	21.9	20.3	36.9	20.8
Vehicle rentals, leases, licenses, other charges	100.0	26.3	23.4	23.8	26.3
Public transportation	**100.0**	**26.4**	**20.0**	**23.8**	**29.9**
HEALTH CARE	**100.0**	**18.6**	**23.9**	**35.1**	**22.4**
Health insurance	100.0	19.9	23.6	35.1	21.4
Medical services	100.0	15.7	24.1	33.1	27.1
Drugs	100.0	18.4	23.8	38.9	19.1
Medical supplies	100.0	17.3	26.6	32.9	23.0
ENTERTAINMENT	**100.0**	**19.1**	**22.2**	**33.2**	**25.5**
Fees and admissions	100.0	23.0	20.8	29.3	26.8
Audio and visual equipment and services	100.0	19.1	21.7	36.9	22.3
Pets, toys, hobbies, and playground equipment	100.0	18.3	21.4	34.2	26.0
Other entertainment products and services	100.0	14.0	27.2	28.6	30.3
PERSONAL CARE PRODUCTS AND SERVICES	**100.0**	**18.7**	**20.6**	**36.1**	**24.6**
READING	**100.0**	**23.8**	**23.2**	**28.0**	**24.6**
EDUCATION	**100.0**	**29.7**	**23.5**	**27.8**	**18.9**

	total consumer units	Northeast	Midwest	South	West
TOBACCO PRODUCTS AND SMOKING SUPPLIES	**100.0%**	**21.4%**	**24.5%**	**37.6%**	**16.4%**
MISCELLANEOUS	**100.0**	**18.7**	**22.3**	**34.1**	**25.0**
CASH CONTRIBUTIONS	**100.0**	**16.9**	**22.3**	**35.6**	**25.2**
PERSONAL INSURANCE AND PENSIONS	**100.0**	**20.4**	**22.2**	**33.2**	**24.1**
Life and other personal insurance	100.0	21.0	25.1	35.0	19.0
Pensions and Social Security	100.0	20.3	22.1	33.1	24.5
PERSONAL TAXES	**100.0**	**24.2**	**22.1**	**31.8**	**21.9**
Federal income taxes	100.0	22.8	21.3	34.4	21.6
State and local income taxes	100.0	27.1	24.7	24.3	23.9
Other taxes	100.0	26.6	21.2	33.8	18.0
GIFTS FOR PEOPLE IN OTHER HOUSEHOLDS	**100.0**	**22.5**	**22.3**	**30.8**	**24.4**

Source: Calculations by New Strategist based on the Bureau of Labor Statistics' 2009 Consumer Expenditure Survey, Internet site http://www.bls.gov/cex/home.htm

College Graduates Spend More

The incomes of college graduates are much higher than average, and they spend more on most items.

College graduates have much higher incomes than those with less education. Consequently, they spend more. In 2009, households headed by people with at least a bachelor's degree spent $69,389—41 percent more than the average household. Householders who went no further than high school spent just $38,693, or 21 percent less than the average household.

The Indexed Spending table compares the spending of households by level of education with average household spending. An index of 100 means households in the educational group spend an average amount on the item. An index above 100 indicates that households in the educational group spend more than average on the item, while an index below 100 signifies below-average spending.

Households headed by people with at least a bachelor's degree spend like the more sophisticated consumers they are. They spend well above average on fish and seafood, fresh fruits and vegetables, restaurant meals (food away from home), and alcoholic beverages. They spend only slightly more than average on laundry and cleaning supplies, but much more than average on household textiles (bedroom and bathroom linens, for example) and floor coverings. They spend 88 percent more than average on fees and admissions to entertainment events, but less than half the average on tobacco.

The Market Share table shows how much of total household spending by category is accounted for by households in each educational group. College graduates spend disproportionately more than their share of households, while those who did not graduate from college spend less.

College graduates spend big on many items

(indexed average annual spending of consumer units headed by people with at least a bachelor's degree on selected items, 2009)

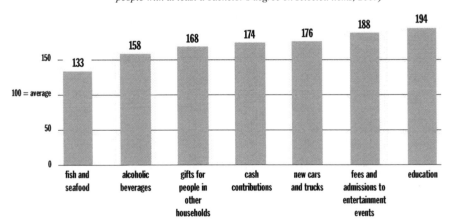

People with at least a bachelor's degree head 29 percent of households, but account for 42 percent of household spending. On some items their spending is even higher. They account for 60 percent of spending on other lodging, which includes dorm rooms, hotels, and motels. They account for 60 percent of spending on public transportation, which includes airline fares, for 55 percent of spending on fees and admission to entertainment events, and for 57 percent of education spending.

■ As the educational level of the population rises, college graduates will increasingly dominate spending on a growing number of products and services.

Table 9.20 Average Spending by Education of Householder, 2009

(average annual spending of consumer units by product and service category and educational attainment of consumer unit reference person, 2009)

	total consumer units	not a high school graduate	high school graduate	some college	associate's degree	bachelor's degree or more
Number of consumer units (in 000s)	120,847	16,692	31,015	25,512	12,051	35,576
Average number of persons per consumer unit	2.5	2.8	2.5	2.4	2.5	2.5
Average annual spending	**$49,067**	**$30,323**	**$38,693**	**$44,697**	**$50,446**	**$69,389**
FOOD	**6,372**	**4,735**	**5,426**	**5,977**	**6,588**	**8,097**
Food at home	**3,753**	**3,343**	**3,439**	**3,547**	**3,598**	**4,386**
Cereals and bakery products	506	454	468	470	493	590
Cereals and cereal products	173	167	158	161	166	198
Bakery products	334	287	310	310	327	392
Meats, poultry, fish, and eggs	841	856	826	797	728	912
Beef	226	228	239	212	193	233
Pork	168	203	177	160	152	158
Other meats	114	110	112	107	101	125
Poultry	154	149	141	155	138	171
Fish and seafood	135	116	114	122	105	179
Eggs	44	50	43	41	39	46
Dairy products	406	333	363	387	400	488
Fresh milk and cream	144	137	135	140	136	160
Other dairy products	262	197	229	246	264	328
Fruits and vegetables	656	570	568	596	590	831
Fresh fruits	220	185	183	192	194	293
Fresh vegetables	209	185	176	182	183	274
Processed fruits	118	96	105	114	111	144
Processed vegetables	110	104	104	108	101	120
Other food at home	1,343	1,129	1,213	1,297	1,387	1,565
Sugar and other sweets	141	122	125	134	162	161
Fats and oils	102	101	97	95	107	111
Miscellaneous foods	715	573	651	690	728	843
Nonalcoholic beverages	337	313	309	341	341	366
Food prepared by consumer unit on trips	49	20	31	38	49	84
Food away from home	**2,619**	**1,392**	**1,987**	**2,430**	**2,991**	**3,711**
ALCOHOLIC BEVERAGES	**435**	**213**	**298**	**384**	**424**	**686**
HOUSING	**16,895**	**11,181**	**13,261**	**15,142**	**17,702**	**23,695**
Shelter	**10,075**	**6,556**	**7,547**	**8,737**	**10,391**	**14,782**
Owned dwellings	6,543	3,263	4,556	5,259	6,876	10,621
Mortgage interest and charges	3,594	1,757	2,347	2,814	4,101	5,930
Property taxes	1,811	917	1,372	1,392	1,759	2,931
Maintenance, repair, insurance, other expenses	1,138	589	837	1,053	1,016	1,760
Rented dwellings	2,860	3,126	2,652	2,997	2,911	2,802
Other lodging	672	167	339	481	603	1,359
Utilities, fuels, and public services	**3,645**	**3,101**	**3,491**	**3,479**	**3,848**	**4,083**
Natural gas	483	396	447	439	458	595
Electricity	1,377	1,260	1,376	1,317	1,431	1,457
Fuel oil and other fuels	141	109	148	98	180	168
Telephone services	1,162	949	1,096	1,155	1,275	1,286
Water and other public services	481	386	423	470	504	577

	total consumer units	not a high school graduate	high school graduate	some college	associate's degree	bachelor's degree or more
Household services	$1,011	$346	$598	$889	$1,090	$1,745
Personal services	389	104	181	325	462	727
Other household services	622	242	417	564	628	1,018
Housekeeping supplies	659	414	568	607	723	854
Laundry and cleaning supplies	156	135	153	155	155	167
Other household products	360	221	295	330	406	480
Postage and stationery	143	58	120	122	163	207
Household furnishings and equipment	1,506	764	1,057	1,431	1,650	2,230
Household textiles	124	35	101	126	125	179
Furniture	343	197	244	312	370	510
Floor coverings	30	9	12	25	39	57
Major appliances	194	127	158	185	224	251
Small appliances, miscellaneous housewares	93	51	73	87	96	132
Miscellaneous household equipment	721	343	468	697	796	1,100
APPAREL AND RELATED SERVICES	1,725	1,454	1,369	1,432	1,742	2,358
Men and boys	383	365	317	319	471	469
Men, aged 16 or older	304	296	249	248	380	376
Boys, aged 2 to 15	79	70	68	71	92	93
Women and girls	678	436	511	527	656	1,038
Women, aged 16 or older	561	318	410	421	549	894
Girls, aged 2 to 15	118	118	101	106	107	144
Children under age 2	91	119	76	86	90	98
Footwear	323	354	320	299	290	340
Other apparel products and services	249	180	146	200	234	414
TRANSPORTATION	7,658	4,762	6,295	7,329	7,970	10,312
Vehicle purchases	2,657	1,430	2,017	2,477	2,714	3,901
Cars and trucks, new	1,297	389	928	951	1,347	2,277
Cars and trucks, used	1,304	1,022	1,020	1,474	1,206	1,596
Gasoline and motor oil	1,986	1,529	1,865	1,972	2,305	2,209
Other vehicle expenses	2,536	1,611	2,149	2,581	2,595	3,229
Vehicle finance charges	281	170	278	301	354	297
Maintenance and repairs	733	448	552	749	783	995
Vehicle insurance	1,075	783	1,027	1,120	981	1,230
Vehicle rentals, leases, licenses, other charges	447	209	292	411	477	708
Public transportation	479	193	264	299	356	972
HEALTH CARE	3,126	2,010	2,913	2,917	3,000	4,026
Health insurance	1,785	1,215	1,712	1,635	1,660	2,266
Medical services	736	364	624	691	729	1,044
Drugs	486	356	487	487	476	548
Medical supplies	119	76	90	105	135	169
ENTERTAINMENT	2,693	1,406	2,184	2,626	2,848	3,716
Fees and admissions	628	151	332	539	596	1,180
Audio and visual equipment and services	975	639	880	978	1,037	1,190
Pets, toys, hobbies, and playground equipment	690	426	637	678	779	827
Other entertainment products and services	400	190	336	431	436	518
PERSONAL CARE PRODUCTS AND SERVICES	596	361	459	555	602	845
READING	110	40	70	98	107	186
EDUCATION	1,068	236	447	1,039	907	2,074

	total consumer units	not a high school graduate	high school graduate	some college	associate's degree	bachelor's degree or more
TOBACCO PRODUCTS, SMOKING SUPPLIES	$380	$430	$531	$419	$418	$183
MISCELLANEOUS	816	437	596	843	957	1,122
CASH CONTRIBUTIONS	1,723	784	1,123	1,354	1,600	2,993
PERSONAL INSURANCE AND PENSIONS	5,471	2,275	3,721	4,580	5,580	9,098
Life and other personal insurance	309	151	239	248	298	492
Pensions and Social Security	5,162	2,124	3,482	4,332	5,282	8,607
PERSONAL TAXES	2,104	229	807	1,379	1,782	4,742
Federal income taxes	1,404	40	431	857	1,088	3,393
State and local income taxes	524	123	250	386	489	1,061
Other taxes	177	67	128	138	207	288
GIFTS FOR PEOPLE IN OTHER HOUSEHOLDS	1,067	522	682	904	1,004	1,790

Note: Spending by category does not add to total spending because gift spending is also included in the preceding product and service categories and personal taxes are not included in the total.
Source: Bureau of Labor Statistics' 2009 Consumer Expenditure Survey, Internet site http://www.bls.gov/cex/

Table 9.21 Indexed Spending by Education of Householder, 2009

(indexed average annual spending of consumer units by product and service category and educational attainment of consumer unit reference person, 2009; index definition: an index of 100 is the average for all consumer units; an index of 125 means that spending by consumer units in that group is 25 percent above the average for all consumer units; an index of 75 indicates spending that is 25 percent below the average for all consumer units)

	total consumer units	not a high school graduate	high school graduate	some college	associate's degree	bachelor's degree or more
Average spending of consumer units	$49,067	$30,323	$38,693	$44,697	$50,446	$69,389
Indexed spending of consumer units	100	62	79	91	103	141
FOOD	100	74	85	94	103	127
Food at home	100	89	92	95	96	117
Cereals and bakery products	100	90	92	93	97	117
Cereals and cereal products	100	97	91	93	96	114
Bakery products	100	86	93	93	98	117
Meats, poultry, fish, and eggs	100	102	98	95	87	108
Beef	100	101	106	94	85	103
Pork	100	121	105	95	90	94
Other meats	100	96	98	94	89	110
Poultry	100	97	92	101	90	111
Fish and seafood	100	86	84	90	78	133
Eggs	100	114	98	93	89	105
Dairy products	100	82	89	95	99	120
Fresh milk and cream	100	95	94	97	94	111
Other dairy products	100	75	87	94	101	125
Fruits and vegetables	100	87	87	91	90	127
Fresh fruits	100	84	83	87	88	133
Fresh vegetables	100	89	84	87	88	131
Processed fruits	100	81	89	97	94	122
Processed vegetables	100	95	95	98	92	109
Other food at home	100	84	90	97	103	117
Sugar and other sweets	100	87	89	95	115	114
Fats and oils	100	99	95	93	105	109
Miscellaneous foods	100	80	91	97	102	118
Nonalcoholic beverages	100	93	92	101	101	109
Food prepared by consumer unit on trips	100	41	63	78	100	171
Food away from home	100	53	76	93	114	142
ALCOHOLIC BEVERAGES	100	49	69	88	97	158
HOUSING	100	66	78	90	105	140
Shelter	100	65	75	87	103	147
Owned dwellings	100	50	70	80	105	162
Mortgage interest and charges	100	49	65	78	114	165
Property taxes	100	51	76	77	97	162
Maintenance, repair, insurance, other expenses	100	52	74	93	89	155
Rented dwellings	100	109	93	105	102	98
Other lodging	100	25	50	72	90	202
Utilities, fuels, and public services	100	85	96	95	106	112
Natural gas	100	82	93	91	95	123
Electricity	100	92	100	96	104	106
Fuel oil and other fuels	100	77	105	70	128	119
Telephone services	100	82	94	99	110	111
Water and other public services	100	80	88	98	105	120

	total consumer units	not a high school graduate	high school graduate	some college	associate's degree	bachelor's degree or more
Household services	100	34	59	88	108	173
Personal services	100	27	47	84	119	187
Other household services	100	39	67	91	101	164
Housekeeping supplies	100	63	86	92	110	130
Laundry and cleaning supplies	100	87	98	99	99	107
Other household products	100	61	82	92	113	133
Postage and stationery	100	41	84	85	114	145
Household furnishings and equipment	100	51	70	95	110	148
Household textiles	100	28	81	102	101	144
Furniture	100	57	71	91	108	149
Floor coverings	100	30	40	83	130	190
Major appliances	100	65	81	95	115	129
Small appliances, miscellaneous housewares	100	55	78	94	103	142
Miscellaneous household equipment	100	48	65	97	110	153
APPAREL AND RELATED SERVICES	100	84	79	83	101	137
Men and boys	100	95	83	83	123	122
Men, aged 16 or older	100	97	82	82	125	124
Boys, aged 2 to 15	100	89	86	90	116	118
Women and girls	100	64	75	78	97	153
Women, aged 16 or older	100	57	73	75	98	159
Girls, aged 2 to 15	100	100	86	90	91	122
Children under age 2	100	131	84	95	99	108
Footwear	100	110	99	93	90	105
Other apparel products and services	100	72	59	80	94	166
TRANSPORTATION	100	62	82	96	104	135
Vehicle purchases	100	54	76	93	102	147
Cars and trucks, new	100	30	72	73	104	176
Cars and trucks, used	100	78	78	113	92	122
Gasoline and motor oil	100	77	94	99	116	111
Other vehicle expenses	100	64	85	102	102	127
Vehicle finance charges	100	60	99	107	126	106
Maintenance and repairs	100	61	75	102	107	136
Vehicle insurance	100	73	96	104	91	114
Vehicle rentals, leases, licenses, other charges	100	47	65	92	107	158
Public transportation	100	40	55	62	74	203
HEALTH CARE	100	64	93	93	96	129
Health insurance	100	68	96	92	93	127
Medical services	100	49	85	94	99	142
Drugs	100	73	100	100	98	113
Medical supplies	100	64	76	88	113	142
ENTERTAINMENT	100	52	81	98	106	138
Fees and admissions	100	24	53	86	95	188
Audio and visual equipment and services	100	66	90	100	106	122
Pets, toys, hobbies, and playground equipment	100	62	92	98	113	120
Other entertainment products and services	100	48	84	108	109	130
PERSONAL CARE PRODUCTS AND SERVICES	100	61	77	93	101	142
READING	100	36	64	89	97	169
EDUCATION	100	22	42	97	85	194

	total consumer units	not a high school graduate	high school graduate	some college	associate's degree	bachelor's degree or more
TOBACCO PRODUCTS, SMOKING SUPPLIES	100	113	140	110	110	48
MISCELLANEOUS	100	54	73	103	117	138
CASH CONTRIBUTIONS	100	46	65	79	93	174
PERSONAL INSURANCE AND PENSIONS	100	42	68	84	102	166
Life and other personal insurance	100	49	77	80	96	159
Pensions and Social Security	100	41	67	84	102	167
PERSONAL TAXES	100	11	38	66	85	225
Federal income taxes	100	3	31	61	77	242
State and local income taxes	100	23	48	74	93	202
Other taxes	100	38	72	78	117	163
GIFTS FOR PEOPLE IN OTHER HOUSEHOLDS	100	49	64	85	94	168

Source: Calculations by New Strategist based on the Bureau of Labor Statistics' 2009 Consumer Expenditure Survey, Internet site http://www.bls.gov/cex/home.htm

Table 9.22 Market Shares by Education of Householder, 2009

(share of total household spending accounted for by educational group, 2009)

	total consumer units	not a high school graduate	high school graduate	some college	associate's degree	bachelor's degree or more
Share of total consumer units	100.0%	13.8%	25.7%	21.1%	10.0%	29.4%
Share of total spending	100.0	8.5	20.2	19.2	10.3	41.6
FOOD	100.0	10.3	21.9	19.8	10.3	37.4
Food at home	100.0	12.3	23.5	20.0	9.6	34.4
Cereals and bakery products	100.0	12.4	23.7	19.6	9.7	34.3
Cereals and cereal products	100.0	13.3	23.4	19.6	9.6	33.7
Bakery products	100.0	11.9	23.8	19.6	9.8	34.6
Meats, poultry, fish, and eggs	100.0	14.1	25.2	20.0	8.6	31.9
Beef	100.0	13.9	27.1	19.8	8.5	30.4
Pork	100.0	16.7	27.0	20.1	9.0	27.7
Other meats	100.0	13.3	25.2	19.8	8.8	32.3
Poultry	100.0	13.4	23.5	21.2	8.9	32.7
Fish and seafood	100.0	11.9	21.7	19.1	7.8	39.0
Eggs	100.0	15.7	25.1	19.7	8.8	30.8
Dairy products	100.0	11.3	22.9	20.1	9.8	35.4
Fresh milk and cream	100.0	13.1	24.1	20.5	9.4	32.7
Other dairy products	100.0	10.4	22.4	19.8	10.0	36.9
Fruits and vegetables	100.0	12.0	22.2	19.2	9.0	37.3
Fresh fruits	100.0	11.6	21.3	18.4	8.8	39.2
Fresh vegetables	100.0	12.2	21.6	18.4	8.7	38.6
Processed fruits	100.0	11.2	22.8	20.4	9.4	35.9
Processed vegetables	100.0	13.1	24.3	20.7	9.2	32.1
Other food at home	100.0	11.6	23.2	20.4	10.3	34.3
Sugar and other sweets	100.0	12.0	22.8	20.1	11.5	33.6
Fats and oils	100.0	13.7	24.4	19.7	10.5	32.0
Miscellaneous foods	100.0	11.1	23.4	20.4	10.2	34.7
Nonalcoholic beverages	100.0	12.8	23.5	21.4	10.1	32.0
Food prepared by consumer unit on trips	100.0	5.6	16.2	16.4	10.0	50.5
Food away from home	100.0	7.3	19.5	19.6	11.4	41.7
ALCOHOLIC BEVERAGES	100.0	6.8	17.6	18.6	9.7	46.4
HOUSING	100.0	9.1	20.1	18.9	10.4	41.3
Shelter	100.0	9.0	19.2	18.3	10.3	43.2
Owned dwellings	100.0	6.9	17.9	17.0	10.5	47.8
Mortgage interest and charges	100.0	6.8	16.8	16.5	11.4	48.6
Property taxes	100.0	7.0	19.4	16.2	9.7	47.6
Maintenance, repair, insurance, other expenses	100.0	7.1	18.9	19.5	8.9	45.5
Rented dwellings	100.0	15.1	23.8	22.1	10.1	28.8
Other lodging	100.0	3.4	12.9	15.1	8.9	59.5
Utilities, fuels, and public services	100.0	11.8	24.6	20.1	10.5	33.0
Natural gas	100.0	11.3	23.8	19.2	9.5	36.3
Electricity	100.0	12.6	25.6	20.2	10.4	31.1
Fuel oil and other fuels	100.0	10.7	26.9	14.7	12.7	35.1
Telephone services	100.0	11.3	24.2	21.0	10.9	32.6
Water and other public services	100.0	11.1	22.6	20.6	10.4	35.3

	total consumer units	not a high school graduate	high school graduate	some college	associate's degree	bachelor's degree or more
Household services	100.0%	4.7%	15.2%	18.6%	10.8%	50.8%
Personal services	100.0	3.7	11.9	17.6	11.8	55.0
Other household services	100.0	5.4	17.2	19.1	10.1	48.2
Housekeeping supplies	100.0	8.7	22.1	19.4	10.9	38.1
Laundry and cleaning supplies	100.0	12.0	25.2	21.0	9.9	31.5
Other household products	100.0	8.5	21.0	19.4	11.2	39.3
Postage and stationery	100.0	5.6	21.5	18.0	11.4	42.6
Household furnishings and equipment	100.0	7.0	18.0	20.1	10.9	43.6
Household textiles	100.0	3.9	20.9	21.5	10.1	42.5
Furniture	100.0	7.9	18.3	19.2	10.8	43.8
Floor coverings	100.0	4.1	10.3	17.6	13.0	55.9
Major appliances	100.0	9.0	20.9	20.1	11.5	38.1
Small appliances, miscellaneous housewares	100.0	7.6	20.1	19.7	10.3	41.8
Miscellaneous household equipment	100.0	6.6	16.7	20.4	11.0	44.9
APPAREL AND RELATED SERVICES	100.0	11.6	20.4	17.5	10.1	40.2
Men and boys	100.0	13.2	21.2	17.6	12.3	36.0
Men, aged 16 or older	100.0	13.4	21.0	17.2	12.5	36.4
Boys, aged 2 to 15	100.0	12.2	22.1	19.0	11.6	34.7
Women and girls	100.0	8.9	19.3	16.4	9.6	45.1
Women, aged 16 or older	100.0	7.8	18.8	15.8	9.8	46.9
Girls, aged 2 to 15	100.0	13.8	22.0	19.0	9.0	35.9
Children under age 2	100.0	18.1	21.4	20.0	9.9	31.7
Footwear	100.0	15.1	25.4	19.5	9.0	31.0
Other apparel products and services	100.0	10.0	15.0	17.0	9.4	48.9
TRANSPORTATION	100.0	8.6	21.1	20.2	10.4	39.6
Vehicle purchases	100.0	7.4	19.5	19.7	10.2	43.2
Cars and trucks, new	100.0	4.1	18.4	15.5	10.4	51.7
Cars and trucks, used	100.0	10.8	20.1	23.9	9.2	36.0
Gasoline and motor oil	100.0	10.6	24.1	21.0	11.6	32.7
Other vehicle expenses	100.0	8.8	21.7	21.5	10.2	37.5
Vehicle finance charges	100.0	8.4	25.4	22.6	12.6	31.1
Maintenance and repairs	100.0	8.4	19.3	21.6	10.7	40.0
Vehicle insurance	100.0	10.1	24.5	22.0	9.1	33.7
Vehicle rentals, leases, licenses, other charges	100.0	6.5	16.8	19.4	10.6	46.6
Public transportation	100.0	5.6	14.1	13.2	7.4	59.7
HEALTH CARE	100.0	8.9	23.9	19.7	9.6	37.9
Health insurance	100.0	9.4	24.6	19.3	9.3	37.4
Medical services	100.0	6.8	21.8	19.8	9.9	41.8
Drugs	100.0	10.1	25.7	21.2	9.8	33.2
Medical supplies	100.0	8.8	19.4	18.6	11.3	41.8
ENTERTAINMENT	100.0	7.2	20.8	20.6	10.5	40.6
Fees and admissions	100.0	3.3	13.6	18.1	9.5	55.3
Audio and visual equipment and services	100.0	9.1	23.2	21.2	10.6	35.9
Pets, toys, hobbies, and playground equipment	100.0	8.5	23.7	20.7	11.3	35.3
Other entertainment products and services	100.0	6.6	21.6	22.7	10.9	38.1
PERSONAL CARE PRODUCTS, SERVICES	100.0	8.4	19.8	19.7	10.1	41.7
READING	100.0	5.0	16.3	18.8	9.7	49.8
EDUCATION	100.0	3.1	10.7	20.5	8.5	57.2

	total consumer units	not a high school graduate	high school graduate	some college	associate's degree	bachelor's degree or more
TOBACCO PRODUCTS, SMOKING SUPPLIES	100.0%	15.6%	35.9%	23.3%	11.0%	14.2%
MISCELLANEOUS	100.0	7.4	18.7	21.8	11.7	40.5
CASH CONTRIBUTIONS	100.0	6.3	16.7	16.6	9.3	51.1
PERSONAL INSURANCE AND PENSIONS	100.0	5.7	17.5	17.7	10.2	49.0
Life and other personal insurance	100.0	6.7	19.9	16.9	9.6	46.9
Pensions and Social Security	100.0	5.7	17.3	17.7	10.2	49.1
PERSONAL TAXES	100.0	1.5	9.8	13.8	8.4	66.3
Federal income taxes	100.0	0.4	7.9	12.9	7.7	71.1
State and local income taxes	100.0	3.2	12.2	15.6	9.3	59.6
Other taxes	100.0	5.2	18.6	16.5	11.7	47.9
GIFTS FOR PEOPLE IN OTHER HOUSEHOLDS	100.0	6.8	16.4	17.9	9.4	49.4

Source: Calculations by New Strategist based on the Bureau of Labor Statistics' 2009 Consumer Expenditure Survey; Internet site http://www.bls.gov/cex/home.htm

Time Use Trends

■ Time use statistics show that traditional sex roles are still alive and well. On an average day, women spend much more time than men doing housework. Men spend more time than women working and watching television.

■ Time use varies by age, teenagers and older Americans having the most leisure time and the middle aged having the least. Women aged 25 to 44 have less leisure time than anyone else.

■ Asian men spend more time at work than black, Hispanic, or white men. On an average day in 2009, Asian men worked for 4.29 hours—13 percent more than the average man.

■ Hispanic women spend 22 percent more time than the average woman doing housework on an average day. Asian and Hispanic women spend 42 to 70 percent more time than the average woman caring for household children.

Americans Spend Nearly Three Hours a Day Watching Television

They spend about 23 minutes a day shopping, on average.

For the past few years, the Bureau of Labor Statistics has been asking Americans how they spend their time through the American Time Use Survey (ATUS). This annual survey collects data by asking a representative sample of the population about their activities during the past 24 hours. The diary data are combined and analyzed by type of activity and demographic characteristic.

Not surprisingly, sleep takes up the most time. The average person reported sleeping 8.67 hours per day in 2009. People work an average of 3.18 hours a day, a figure that includes both those who worked on diary day, those who had the day off, and those who had no job. Among the 43 percent of people who worked on diary day, work consumed an average of 7.44 hours.

Traditional sex roles are still abundantly evident in these statistics. On an average day, women spend much more time than men doing housework, tending children, and talking on the telephone. Men spend more time than women working, tending the lawn, and watching television.

■ Researchers and public policy makers use the results of the time use survey to determine how people balance work and family issues.

Women spend nearly one hour a day doing housework, on average

(average number of hours per day people spend on selected primary activities, by sex, 2009)

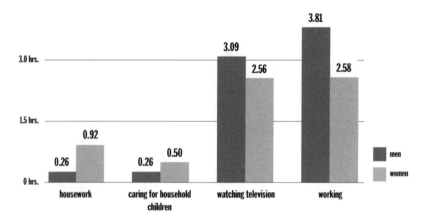

Table 10.1 Total Time Use and Percent Reporting Activity, 2009

(number and percent of total people aged 15 or older participating in primary activities on an average day, hours spent doing activity by the average person and by participants, 2009; number of people in thousands)

	total people participating		time spent in activity (hours)	
	number	percent	average person	participants
Total, all activities	**239,898**	**100.0%**	**24.00**	**24.00**
Personal care activities	239,856	100.0	9.43	9.43
Sleeping	239,635	99.9	8.67	8.68
Grooming	188,175	78.4	0.67	0.85
Household activities	187,518	78.2	1.83	2.34
Housework	87,006	36.3	0.60	1.65
Food preparation and cleanup	130,915	54.6	0.54	0.99
Lawn, garden, and houseplants	22,462	9.4	0.20	2.11
Animals and pets	35,693	14.9	0.09	0.62
Household management	69,369	28.9	0.21	0.73
Caring for and helping household members	60,426	25.2	0.46	1.83
Caring for and helping household children	50,519	21.1	0.38	1.82
Caring for and helping people in other households	31,938	13.3	0.14	1.07
Caring for and helping children in other households	12,662	5.3	0.07	1.26
Working and work-related activities	108,637	45.3	3.25	7.19
Working	102,370	42.7	3.18	7.44
Job search and interviewing	5,144	2.1	0.04	2.00
Education	19,566	8.2	0.44	5.34
Taking class	12,516	5.2	0.26	5.03
Research and homework	13,543	5.6	0.16	2.82
Shopping (store, telephone, Internet)	96,308	40.1	0.38	0.94
Grocery shopping	33,913	14.1	0.11	0.75
Shopping, except groceries, food, and gas	54,436	22.7	0.25	1.08
Eating and drinking	231,339	96.4	1.11	1.15
Socializing, relaxing, and leisure	228,253	95.1	4.69	4.93
Socializing and communicating	90,538	37.7	0.63	1.66
Relaxing and leisure	219,671	91.6	3.91	4.27
Watching television	196,168	81.8	2.82	3.44
Playing games (including computer)	24,980	10.4	0.22	2.13
Computer use for leisure (except games)	26,263	10.9	0.16	1.50
Reading for personal interest	58,016	24.2	0.34	1.42
Sports, exercise, and recreation	45,309	18.9	0.33	1.77
Religious and spiritual activities	21,510	9.0	0.15	1.62
Volunteering	16,911	7.0	0.15	2.14
Telephone calls	36,833	15.4	0.11	0.74
Traveling	208,635	87.0	1.20	1.38

Note: Primary activities are those respondents identified as their main activity. Other activities done simultaneously, such as eating while watching TV, are not included. Numbers may not add to total because not all categories are shown.
Source: Unpublished tables from the Bureau of Labor Statistics' 2009 American Time Use Survey, Internet site http://www.bls .gov/tus/home.htm

Table 10.2 Men's Time Use and Percent Reporting Activity, 2009

(number and percent of total men aged 15 or older participating in primary activities on an average day, hours spent doing activity by the average man and by male participants, 2009; number of men in thousands)

	total men participating		time spent in activity (hours)	
	number	percent	average man	male participants
Total, all activities	**116,135**	**100.0%**	**24.00**	**24.00**
Personal care activities	116,092	100.0	9.24	9.24
Sleeping	115,886	99.8	8.62	8.63
Grooming	86,603	74.6	0.54	0.73
Household activities	80,180	69.0	1.35	1.96
Housework	23,516	20.2	0.26	1.27
Food preparation and cleanup	46,364	39.9	0.29	0.73
Lawn, garden, and houseplants	13,313	11.5	0.28	2.42
Animals and pets	14,392	12.4	0.08	0.62
Household management	29,170	25.1	0.17	0.69
Caring for and helping household members	23,476	20.2	0.31	1.55
Caring for and helping household children	18,430	15.9	0.26	1.62
Caring for and helping people in other households	13,258	11.4	0.13	1.14
Caring for and helping children in other households	4,585	3.9	0.04	1.13
Working and work-related activities	60,148	51.8	3.90	7.54
Working	56,247	48.4	3.81	7.86
Job search and interviewing	3,300	2.8	0.06	1.97
Education	8,560	7.4	0.40	5.47
Taking class	5,934	5.1	0.26	5.01
Research and homework	5,744	4.9	0.14	2.84
Shopping (store, telephone, Internet)	41,524	35.8	0.29	0.82
Grocery shopping	12,904	11.1	0.08	0.71
Shopping, except groceries, food, and gas	22,080	19.0	0.19	1.01
Eating and drinking	111,609	96.1	1.13	1.18
Socializing, relaxing, and leisure	109,920	94.6	4.91	5.19
Socializing and communicating	38,745	33.4	0.56	1.68
Relaxing and leisure	106,700	91.9	4.21	4.58
Watching television	96,027	82.7	3.09	3.74
Playing games (including computer)	12,664	10.9	0.26	2.39
Computer use for leisure (except games)	13,812	11.9	0.20	1.66
Reading for personal interest	24,194	20.8	0.27	1.27
Sports, exercise, and recreation	25,155	21.7	0.44	2.05
Religious and spiritual activities	8,103	7.0	0.12	1.78
Volunteering	8,118	7.0	0.15	2.20
Telephone calls	12,070	10.4	0.07	0.69
Traveling	102,638	88.4	1.24	1.40

Note: Primary activities are those respondents identified as their main activity. Other activities done simultaneously, such as eating while watching TV, are not included. Numbers may not add to total because not all categories are shown.
Source: Unpublished tables from the Bureau of Labor Statistics' 2009 American Time Use Survey, Internet site http://www.bls .gov/tus/home.htm

Table 10.3 Women's Time Use and Percent Reporting Activity, 2009

(number and percent of total women aged 15 or older participating in primary activities on an average day, hours spent doing activity by the average woman and by female participants, 2009; number of women in thousands)

	total women participating		time spent in activity (hours)	
	number	percent	average woman	female participants
Total, all activities	**123,763**	**100.0%**	**24.00**	**24.00**
Personal care activities	123,763	100.0	9.61	9.61
Sleeping	123,749	100.0	8.73	8.73
Grooming	101,572	82.1	0.79	0.96
Household activities	107,339	86.7	2.28	2.63
Housework	63,489	51.3	0.92	1.79
Food preparation and cleanup	84,551	68.3	0.77	1.13
Lawn, garden, and houseplants	9,149	7.4	0.12	1.67
Animals and pets	21,302	17.2	0.11	0.62
Household management	40,199	32.5	0.25	0.76
Caring for and helping household members	36,951	29.9	0.60	2.01
Caring for and helping household children	32,089	25.9	0.50	1.94
Caring for and helping people in other households	18,680	15.1	0.15	1.02
Caring for and helping children in other households	8,076	6.5	0.09	1.32
Working and work-related activities	48,489	39.2	2.65	6.75
Working	46,123	37.3	2.58	6.93
Job search and interviewing	1,844	1.5	0.03	2.06
Education	11,006	8.9	0.47	5.23
Taking class	6,582	5.3	0.27	5.05
Research and homework	7,799	6.3	0.18	2.81
Shopping (store, telephone, Internet)	54,784	44.3	0.45	1.02
Grocery shopping	21,010	17.0	0.13	0.77
Shopping, except groceries, food, and gas	32,356	26.1	0.29	1.13
Eating and drinking	119,730	96.7	1.08	1.12
Socializing, relaxing, and leisure	118,333	95.6	4.48	4.68
Socializing and communicating	51,793	41.8	0.69	1.64
Relaxing and leisure	112,971	91.3	3.63	3.98
Watching television	100,141	80.9	2.56	3.16
Playing games (including computer)	12,316	10.0	0.19	1.87
Computer use for leisure (except games)	12,451	10.1	0.13	1.32
Reading for personal interest	33,822	27.3	0.42	1.53
Sports, exercise, and recreation	20,154	16.3	0.23	1.42
Religious and spiritual activities	13,407	10.8	0.17	1.53
Volunteering	8,793	7.1	0.15	2.09
Telephone calls	24,763	20.0	0.15	0.77
Traveling	105,997	85.6	1.17	1.36

Note: Primary activities are those respondents identified as their main activity. Other activities done simultaneously, such as eating while watching TV, are not included. Numbers may not add to total because not all categories are shown.
Source: Unpublished tables from the Bureau of Labor Statistics' 2009 American Time Use Survey, Internet site http://www.bls .gov/tus/home.htm

Table 10.4 Time Use by Sex, 2009

(hours per day spent in primary activities by people aged 15 or older by sex, and index of women's time to men's, 2009)

	hours per day		index, women's time to men's
	men	women	
Total, all activities	**24.00**	**24.00**	**100**
Personal care activities	9.24	9.61	104
Sleeping	8.62	8.73	101
Grooming	0.54	0.79	146
Household activities	1.35	2.28	169
Housework	0.26	0.92	354
Food preparation and cleanup	0.29	0.77	266
Lawn, garden, and houseplants	0.28	0.12	43
Animals and pets	0.08	0.11	138
Household management	0.17	0.25	147
Caring for and helping household members	0.31	0.60	194
Caring for and helping household children	0.26	0.50	192
Caring for and helping people in other households	0.13	0.15	115
Caring for and helping children in other households	0.04	0.09	225
Working and work-related activities	3.90	2.65	68
Working	3.81	2.58	68
Job search and interviewing	0.06	0.03	50
Education	0.40	0.47	118
Taking class	0.26	0.27	104
Research and homework	0.14	0.18	129
Shopping (store, telephone, Internet)	0.29	0.45	155
Grocery shopping	0.08	0.13	163
Shopping, except groceries, food, and gas	0.19	0.29	153
Eating and drinking	1.13	1.08	96
Socializing, relaxing, and leisure	4.91	4.48	91
Socializing and communicating	0.56	0.69	123
Relaxing and leisure	4.21	3.63	86
Watching television	3.09	2.56	83
Playing games (including computer)	0.26	0.19	73
Computer use for leisure (except games)	0.20	0.13	65
Reading for personal interest	0.27	0.42	156
Sports, exercise, and recreation	0.44	0.23	52
Religious and spiritual activities	0.12	0.17	142
Volunteering	0.15	0.15	100
Telephone calls	0.07	0.15	214
Traveling	1.24	1.17	94

Note: Primary activities are those respondents identified as their main activity. Other activities done simultaneously, such as eating while watching TV, are not included. Numbers may not add to total because not all categories are shown. The index is calculated by dividing women's time by men's time and multiplying by 100.
Source: Unpublished tables from the Bureau of Labor Statistics' 2009 American Time Use Survey, Internet site http://www.bls .gov/tus/home.htm; calculations by New Strategist

Women Aged 25 to 44 Have the Least Amount of Leisure Time

Men aged 25 to 44 spend the most time working.

Time use varies sharply by age, with teenagers and older Americans having the most leisure time and the middle aged having the least. Women aged 25 to 44 spend much more time than the average person caring for household children and men aged 25 to 44 spend much more time working.

Among men, leisure time is greatest for those aged 75 or older, with 7.83 hours of leisure a day—59 percent more than the average man. Men aged 25 to 44 spend 32 percent more time than the average man at work. Because many men in this age group are raising children, they spend twice as much time as the average man caring for household children. Among males, teenagers spend the most time on the telephone.

Women aged 25 to 44 spend more than twice as much time as the average woman caring for household children. They also spend 32 to 35 percent more time than the average woman at work. That explains why women aged 25 to 44 have 19 to 22 percent less leisure time than the average woman. Women aged 75 or older spend the most time reading. Girls aged 15 to 19 and women aged 75 or older spend the most time on the phone.

■ Women aged 25 to 44 spend only 2.04 to 2.08 hours a day watching television compared with a larger 2.68 hours a day watched by men in the age group.

Women have less leisure time than men

(average number of hours per day people spend in socializing, relaxing, and leisure as a primary activity, by sex, 2009)

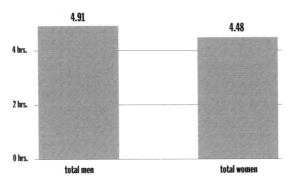

Table 10.5 Time Use by Age, 2009

(average hours per day spent in primary activities by people aged 15 or older by age, by type of activity, 2009)

	total people	15 to 19	20 to 24	25 to 34	35 to 44	45 to 54	55 to 64	65 to 74	75 or older
Total, all activities	**24.00**	**24.00**	**24.00**	**24.00**	**24.00**	**24.00**	**24.00**	**24.00**	**24.00**
Personal care	9.43	10.27	10.18	9.19	9.10	9.08	9.24	9.55	10.00
Sleeping	8.67	9.50	9.39	8.54	8.41	8.29	8.43	8.71	9.14
Grooming	0.67	0.77	0.73	0.62	0.65	0.67	0.67	0.66	0.66
Household activities	1.83	0.74	1.13	1.47	1.85	2.04	2.21	2.65	2.53
Housework	0.60	0.22	0.38	0.55	0.66	0.64	0.67	0.79	0.80
Food preparation and cleanup	0.54	0.14	0.30	0.50	0.62	0.59	0.60	0.68	0.76
Lawn, garden, and houseplants	0.20	0.06	0.10	0.09	0.13	0.21	0.32	0.39	0.39
Animals and pets	0.09	0.07	0.08	0.07	0.08	0.12	0.12	0.11	0.08
Household management	0.21	0.14	0.17	0.15	0.18	0.23	0.24	0.32	0.34
Caring for, helping household members	0.46	0.15	0.38	1.04	0.95	0.30	0.10	0.06	0.06
Caring for, helping household children	0.38	0.11	0.33	0.94	0.81	0.21	0.06	0.01	0.00
Caring for and helping people in other households	0.14	0.17	0.09	0.10	0.12	0.15	0.21	0.22	0.08
Caring for and helping children in other households	0.07	0.09	0.02	0.04	0.04	0.07	0.12	0.13	0.03
Work and work-related activities	3.25	0.95	3.50	4.35	4.30	4.30	3.41	1.15	0.28
Working	3.18	0.86	3.40	4.25	4.21	4.21	3.34	1.13	0.28
Job search and interviewing	0.04	0.01	0.06	0.05	0.06	0.07	0.04	0.00	0.00
Education	0.44	3.10	0.91	0.28	0.12	0.06	0.03	0.02	0.01
Taking class	0.26	2.29	0.37	0.09	0.03	0.02	0.01	0.02	0.00
Research and homework	0.16	0.71	0.52	0.18	0.08	0.03	0.01	0.01	0.00
Shopping (store, telephone, Internet)	0.38	0.32	0.36	0.35	0.39	0.38	0.44	0.41	0.32
Grocery shopping	0.11	0.04	0.08	0.09	0.11	0.12	0.12	0.13	0.14
Shopping, except groceries, food, gas	0.25	0.26	0.26	0.23	0.25	0.23	0.29	0.26	0.16
Eating and drinking	1.11	0.92	0.91	1.08	1.06	1.09	1.19	1.33	1.37
Socializing, relaxing, and leisure	4.69	4.68	4.25	4.00	3.80	4.32	5.01	6.25	7.36
Socializing and communicating	0.63	0.79	0.69	0.63	0.56	0.62	0.56	0.64	0.60
Relaxing and leisure	3.91	3.68	3.36	3.18	3.10	3.55	4.34	5.46	6.68
Watching television	2.82	2.32	2.45	2.38	2.36	2.67	3.22	3.75	4.40
Playing games (including computer)	0.22	0.55	0.31	0.23	0.14	0.13	0.15	0.22	0.28
Computer use for leisure (excluding games)	0.16	0.34	0.12	0.17	0.15	0.13	0.14	0.17	0.14
Reading for personal interest	0.34	0.15	0.18	0.16	0.19	0.29	0.47	0.70	1.03
Sports, exercise, recreation	0.33	0.73	0.39	0.32	0.29	0.30	0.25	0.31	0.23
Religious and spiritual activities	0.15	0.12	0.07	0.10	0.13	0.15	0.18	0.23	0.25
Volunteer activities	0.15	0.14	0.07	0.09	0.17	0.18	0.16	0.25	0.17
Telephone calls	0.11	0.23	0.10	0.08	0.09	0.09	0.11	0.12	0.17
Traveling	1.20	1.19	1.37	1.29	1.33	1.27	1.13	1.00	0.70

Note: Primary activities are those respondents identified as their main activity. Other activities done simultaneously, such as eating while watching TV, are not included. Numbers may not add to total because not all categories are shown.
Source: Unpublished tables from the Bureau of Labor Statistics' 2009 American Time Use Survey, Internet site http://www.bls.gov/tus/home.htm; calculations by New Strategist

Table 10.6 Index of Time Use by Age, 2009

(index of time use by age to average for total people, by type of activity, 2009)

	total people	15 to 19	20 to 24	25 to 34	35 to 44	45 to 54	55 to 64	65 to 74	75 or older
Total, all activities	**100**	**100**	**100**	**100**	**100**	**100**	**100**	**100**	**100**
Personal care	100	109	108	97	97	96	98	101	106
Sleeping	100	110	108	99	97	96	97	100	105
Grooming	100	115	109	93	97	100	100	99	99
Household activities	100	40	62	80	101	111	121	145	138
Housework	100	37	63	92	110	107	112	132	133
Food preparation and cleanup	100	26	56	93	115	109	111	126	141
Lawn, garden, and houseplants	100	30	50	45	65	105	160	195	195
Animals and pets	100	78	89	78	89	133	133	122	89
Household management	100	67	81	71	86	110	114	152	162
Caring for, helping household members	100	33	83	226	207	65	22	13	13
Caring for, helping household children	100	29	87	247	213	55	16	3	0
Caring for and helping people in other households	100	121	64	71	86	107	150	157	57
Caring for and helping children in other households	100	129	29	57	57	100	171	186	43
Work and work-related activities	100	29	108	134	132	132	105	35	9
Working	100	27	107	134	132	132	105	36	9
Job search and interviewing	100	25	150	125	150	175	100	0	0
Education	100	705	207	64	27	14	7	5	2
Taking class	100	881	142	35	12	8	4	8	0
Research and homework	100	444	325	113	50	19	6	6	0
Shopping (store, telephone, Internet)	100	84	95	92	103	100	116	108	84
Grocery shopping	100	36	73	82	100	109	109	118	127
Shopping, except groceries, food, gas	100	104	104	92	100	92	116	104	64
Eating and drinking	100	83	82	97	95	98	107	120	123
Socializing, relaxing, and leisure	100	100	91	85	81	92	107	133	157
Socializing and communicating	100	125	110	100	89	98	89	102	95
Relaxing and leisure	100	94	86	81	79	91	111	140	171
Watching television	100	82	87	84	84	95	114	133	156
Playing games (including computer)	100	250	141	105	64	59	68	100	127
Computer use for leisure (excluding games)	100	213	75	106	94	81	88	106	88
Reading for personal interest	100	44	53	47	56	85	138	206	303
Sports, exercise, recreation	100	221	118	97	88	91	76	94	70
Religious and spiritual activities	100	80	47	67	87	100	120	153	167
Volunteer activities	100	93	47	60	113	120	107	167	113
Telephone calls	100	209	91	73	82	82	100	109	155
Traveling	100	99	114	108	111	106	94	83	58

Note: Primary activities are those respondents identified as their main activity. Other activities done simultaneously, such as eating while watching TV, are not included. The index is calculated by dividing age groups' times by total people's time and multiplying by 100.
Source: Calculations by New Strategist based on unpublished tables from the Bureau of Labor Statistics' 2009 American Time Use Survey, Internet site http://www.bls.gov/tus/home.htm

Table 10.7 Men's Time Use by Age, 2009

(average hours per day spent in primary activities by men aged 15 or older by age; index of time use by age to average for total men, by type of activity, 2009)

	total men	15 to 19	20 to 24	25 to 34	35 to 44	45 to 54	55 to 64	65 to 74	75 or older
Total, all activities	**24.00**	**24.00**	**24.00**	**24.00**	**24.00**	**24.00**	**24.00**	**24.00**	**24.00**
Personal care	9.24	10.36	10.04	8.99	8.89	8.84	9.01	9.30	9.79
Sleeping	8.62	9.71	9.41	8.48	8.28	8.17	8.37	8.62	9.12
Grooming	0.54	0.64	0.60	0.49	0.54	0.53	0.54	0.52	0.51
Household activities	1.35	0.59	0.81	1.04	1.27	1.53	1.70	2.14	1.97
Housework	0.26	0.11	0.20	0.30	0.26	0.27	0.27	0.30	0.29
Food preparation and cleanup	0.29	0.10	0.18	0.26	0.37	0.32	0.34	0.32	0.35
Lawn, garden, and houseplants	0.28	0.10	0.18	0.13	0.17	0.30	0.43	0.52	0.67
Animals and pets	0.08	0.06	0.07	0.06	0.05	0.10	0.09	0.11	0.09
Household management	0.17	0.12	0.07	0.15	0.14	0.17	0.18	0.34	0.35
Caring for, helping household members	0.31	0.16	0.16	0.59	0.66	0.27	0.06	0.05	0.07
Caring for, helping household children	0.26	0.10	0.15	0.53	0.59	0.18	0.04	0.01	0.00
Caring for and helping people in other households	0.13	0.18	0.09	0.10	0.13	0.12	0.15	0.22	0.07
Caring for and helping children in other households	0.04	0.08	0.02	0.03	0.03	0.03	0.09	0.09	0.01
Work and work-related activities	3.90	0.99	4.06	5.12	5.16	5.00	4.09	1.44	0.45
Working	3.81	0.84	3.95	5.02	5.04	4.90	4.00	1.41	0.45
Job search and interviewing	0.06	0.02	0.10	0.05	0.08	0.08	0.06	0.00	0.00
Education	0.40	2.88	0.77	0.24	0.10	0.03	0.02	0.03	0.00
Taking class	0.26	2.26	0.31	0.06	0.03	0.01	0.01	0.02	0.00
Research and homework	0.14	0.56	0.46	0.18	0.08	0.01	0.01	0.00	0.00
Shopping (store, telephone, Internet)	0.29	0.23	0.27	0.27	0.30	0.29	0.36	0.31	0.32
Grocery shopping	0.08	0.04	0.06	0.07	0.08	0.08	0.10	0.09	0.13
Shopping, except groceries, food, gas	0.19	0.18	0.19	0.17	0.20	0.18	0.24	0.21	0.18
Eating and drinking	1.13	0.85	0.91	1.08	1.12	1.13	1.26	1.40	1.48
Socializing, relaxing, and leisure	4.91	4.87	4.44	4.36	4.11	4.48	5.20	6.72	7.83
Socializing and communicating	0.56	0.69	0.63	0.58	0.50	0.56	0.47	0.60	0.54
Relaxing and leisure	4.21	3.98	3.62	3.60	3.48	3.78	4.63	6.00	7.21
Watching television	3.09	2.32	2.51	2.68	2.68	2.98	3.65	4.24	4.97
Playing games (including computer)	0.26	0.81	0.47	0.32	0.18	0.08	0.08	0.19	0.25
Computer use for leisure (excluding games)	0.20	0.36	0.14	0.24	0.20	0.14	0.13	0.20	0.28
Reading for personal interest	0.27	0.11	0.14	0.10	0.12	0.21	0.40	0.63	0.95
Sports, exercise, recreation	0.44	1.01	0.52	0.43	0.35	0.36	0.34	0.43	0.32
Religious and spiritual activities	0.12	0.13	0.07	0.08	0.12	0.12	0.14	0.20	0.25
Volunteer activities	0.15	0.20	0.08	0.09	0.15	0.19	0.15	0.25	0.16
Telephone calls	0.07	0.19	0.08	0.05	0.07	0.04	0.04	0.07	0.07
Traveling	1.24	1.16	1.37	1.30	1.32	1.34	1.19	1.03	0.79

Note: Primary activities are those respondents identified as their main activity. Other activities done simultaneously, such as eating while watching TV, are not included. Numbers may not add to total because not all categories are shown.
Source: Unpublished tables from the Bureau of Labor Statistics' 2009 American Time Use Survey, Internet site http://www.bls .gov/tus/home.htm; calculations by New Strategist

Table 10.8 Index of Men's Time Use by Age, 2009

(index of time use by age to average for total men, by type of activity, 2009)

	total men	15 to 19	20 to 24	25 to 34	35 to 44	45 to 54	55 to 64	65 to 74	75 or older
Total, all activities	100	100	100	100	100	100	100	100	100
Personal care	100	112	109	97	96	96	98	101	106
Sleeping	100	113	109	98	96	95	97	100	106
Grooming	100	119	111	91	100	98	100	96	94
Household activities	100	44	60	77	94	113	126	159	146
Housework	100	42	77	115	100	104	104	115	112
Food preparation and cleanup	100	34	62	90	128	110	117	110	121
Lawn, garden, and houseplants	100	36	64	46	61	107	154	186	239
Animals and pets	100	75	88	75	63	125	113	138	113
Household management	100	71	41	88	82	100	106	200	206
Caring for, helping household members	100	52	52	190	213	87	19	16	23
Caring for, helping household children	100	38	58	204	227	69	15	4	0
Caring for and helping people in other households	100	138	69	77	100	92	115	169	54
Caring for and helping children in other households	100	200	50	75	75	75	225	225	25
Work and work-related activities	100	25	104	131	132	128	105	37	12
Working	100	22	104	132	132	129	105	37	12
Job search and interviewing	100	33	167	83	133	133	100	0	0
Education	100	720	193	60	25	8	5	8	0
Taking class	100	869	119	23	12	4	4	8	0
Research and homework	100	400	329	129	57	7	7	0	0
Shopping (store, telephone, Internet)	100	79	93	93	103	100	124	107	110
Grocery shopping	100	50	75	88	100	100	125	113	163
Shopping, except groceries, food, gas	100	95	100	89	105	95	126	111	95
Eating and drinking	100	75	81	96	99	100	112	124	131
Socializing, relaxing, and leisure	100	99	90	89	84	91	106	137	159
Socializing and communicating	100	123	113	104	89	100	84	107	96
Relaxing and leisure	100	95	86	86	83	90	110	143	171
Watching television	100	75	81	87	87	96	118	137	161
Playing games (including computer)	100	312	181	123	69	31	31	73	96
Computer use for leisure (excluding games)	100	180	70	120	100	70	65	100	140
Reading for personal interest	100	41	52	37	44	78	148	233	352
Sports, exercise, recreation	100	230	118	98	80	82	77	98	73
Religious and spiritual activities	100	108	58	67	100	100	117	167	208
Volunteer activities	100	133	53	60	100	127	100	167	107
Telephone calls	100	271	114	71	100	57	57	100	100
Traveling	100	94	110	105	106	108	96	83	64

Note: Primary activities are those respondents identified as their main activity. Other activities done simultaneously, such as eating while watching TV, are not included. The index is calculated by dividing age groups' times by total people's time and multiplying by 100.
Source: Calculations by New Strategist based on unpublished tables from the Bureau of Labor Statistics' 2009 American Time Use Survey, Internet site http://www.bls.gov/tus/home.htm

Table 10.9 Women's Time Use by Age, 2009

(average hours per day spent in primary activities by women aged 15 or older by age, by type of activity, 2009)

	total women	15 to 19	20 to 24	25 to 34	35 to 44	45 to 54	55 to 64	65 to 74	75 or older
Total, all activities	**24.00**	**24.00**	**24.00**	**24.00**	**24.00**	**24.00**	**24.00**	**24.00**	**24.00**
Personal care	9.61	10.19	10.32	9.39	9.31	9.31	9.46	9.76	10.13
Sleeping	8.73	9.28	9.38	8.61	8.53	8.42	8.49	8.79	9.15
Grooming	0.79	0.90	0.85	0.75	0.75	0.79	0.79	0.78	0.76
Household activities	2.28	0.89	1.45	1.90	2.42	2.52	2.68	3.09	2.89
Housework	0.92	0.33	0.57	0.80	1.06	1.00	1.04	1.22	1.13
Food preparation and cleanup	0.77	0.19	0.42	0.74	0.88	0.85	0.84	0.99	1.02
Lawn, garden, and houseplants	0.12	0.01	0.02	0.06	0.08	0.13	0.22	0.27	0.21
Animals and pets	0.11	0.07	0.09	0.08	0.10	0.14	0.15	0.11	0.07
Household management	0.25	0.16	0.27	0.16	0.21	0.29	0.29	0.31	0.34
Caring for, helping household members	0.60	0.15	0.59	1.49	1.24	0.34	0.13	0.07	0.05
Caring for, helping household children	0.50	0.12	0.52	1.35	1.03	0.23	0.09	0.02	0.01
Caring for and helping people in other households	0.15	0.18	0.08	0.10	0.11	0.19	0.26	0.23	0.08
Caring for and helping children in other households	0.09	0.08	0.02	0.05	0.04	0.11	0.14	0.17	0.04
Work and work-related activities	2.65	0.91	2.94	3.58	3.47	3.63	2.78	0.90	0.18
Working	2.58	0.87	2.85	3.48	3.40	3.55	2.72	0.89	0.17
Job search and interviewing	0.03	0.00	0.02	0.06	0.03	0.06	0.02	0.00	0.00
Education	0.47	3.33	1.04	0.32	0.13	0.09	0.04	0.02	0.01
Taking class	0.27	2.31	0.43	0.12	0.04	0.04	0.02	0.01	0.01
Research and homework	0.18	0.87	0.58	0.19	0.08	0.05	0.01	0.01	0.00
Shopping (store, telephone, Internet)	0.45	0.41	0.46	0.42	0.47	0.48	0.51	0.48	0.32
Grocery shopping	0.13	0.04	0.09	0.11	0.14	0.16	0.15	0.16	0.16
Shopping, except groceries, food, gas	0.29	0.35	0.34	0.28	0.30	0.28	0.34	0.30	0.15
Eating and drinking	1.08	0.98	0.92	1.09	1.00	1.05	1.13	1.27	1.30
Socializing, relaxing, and leisure	4.48	4.49	4.07	3.64	3.49	4.16	4.84	5.85	7.06
Socializing and communicating	0.69	0.89	0.74	0.68	0.63	0.69	0.65	0.67	0.64
Relaxing and leisure	3.63	3.37	3.10	2.76	2.72	3.33	4.06	5.01	6.33
Watching television	2.56	2.32	2.39	2.08	2.04	2.37	2.83	3.32	4.02
Playing games (including computer)	0.19	0.29	0.15	0.13	0.10	0.18	0.21	0.24	0.31
Computer use for leisure (excluding games)	0.13	0.32	0.10	0.10	0.11	0.13	0.16	0.14	0.05
Reading for personal interest	0.42	0.19	0.22	0.23	0.25	0.36	0.53	0.76	1.09
Sports, exercise, recreation	0.23	0.43	0.26	0.20	0.23	0.24	0.17	0.21	0.17
Religious and spiritual activities	0.17	0.11	0.07	0.12	0.14	0.18	0.21	0.25	0.25
Volunteer activities	0.15	0.09	0.05	0.08	0.18	0.17	0.16	0.25	0.18
Telephone calls	0.15	0.27	0.13	0.10	0.11	0.15	0.17	0.17	0.24
Traveling	1.17	1.22	1.38	1.28	1.34	1.20	1.07	0.96	0.64

Note: Primary activities are those respondents identified as their main activity. Other activities done simultaneously, such as eating while watching TV, are not included. Numbers may not add to total because not all categories are shown.
Source: Unpublished tables from the Bureau of Labor Statistics' 2009 American Time Use Survey, Internet site http://www.bls.gov/tus/home.htm; calculations by New Strategist

Table 10.10 Index of Women's Time Use by Age, 2009

(index of time use by age to average for total women, by type of activity, 2009)

	total women	15 to 19	20 to 24	25 to 34	35 to 44	45 to 54	55 to 64	65 to 74	75 or older
Total, all activities	**100**	**100**	**100**	**100**	**100**	**100**	**100**	**100**	**100**
Personal care	100	106	107	98	97	97	98	102	105
Sleeping	100	106	107	99	98	96	97	101	105
Grooming	100	114	108	95	95	100	100	99	96
Household activities	100	39	64	83	106	111	118	136	127
Housework	100	36	62	87	115	109	113	133	123
Food preparation and cleanup	100	25	55	96	114	110	109	129	132
Lawn, garden, and houseplants	100	8	17	50	67	108	183	225	175
Animals and pets	100	64	82	73	91	127	136	100	64
Household management	100	64	108	64	84	116	116	124	136
Caring for, helping household members	100	25	98	248	207	57	22	12	8
Caring for, helping household children	100	24	104	270	206	46	18	4	2
Caring for and helping people in other households	100	120	53	67	73	127	173	153	53
Caring for and helping children in other households	100	89	22	56	44	122	156	189	44
Work and work-related activities	100	34	111	135	131	137	105	34	7
Working	100	34	110	135	132	138	105	34	7
Job search and interviewing	100	0	67	200	100	200	67	0	0
Education	100	709	221	68	28	19	9	4	2
Taking class	100	856	159	44	15	15	7	4	4
Research and homework	100	483	322	106	44	28	6	6	0
Shopping (store, telephone, Internet)	100	91	102	93	104	107	113	107	71
Grocery shopping	100	31	69	85	108	123	115	123	123
Shopping, except groceries, food, gas	100	121	117	97	103	97	117	103	52
Eating and drinking	100	91	85	101	93	97	105	118	120
Socializing, relaxing, and leisure	100	100	91	81	78	93	108	131	158
Socializing and communicating	100	129	107	99	91	100	94	97	93
Relaxing and leisure	100	93	85	76	75	92	112	138	174
Watching television	100	91	93	81	80	93	111	130	157
Playing games (including computer)	100	153	79	68	53	95	111	126	163
Computer use for leisure (excluding games)	100	246	77	77	85	100	123	108	38
Reading for personal interest	100	45	52	55	60	86	126	181	260
Sports, exercise, recreation	100	187	113	87	100	104	74	91	74
Religious and spiritual activities	100	65	41	71	82	106	124	147	147
Volunteer activities	100	60	33	53	120	113	107	167	120
Telephone calls	100	180	87	67	73	100	113	113	160
Traveling	100	104	118	109	115	103	91	82	55

Note: Primary activities are those respondents identified as their main activity. Other activities done simultaneously, such as eating while watching TV, are not included. The index is calculated by dividing age groups' times by total people's time and multiplying by 100.
Source: Calculations by New Strategist based on unpublished tables from the Bureau of Labor Statistics' 2009 American Time Use Survey, Internet site http://www.bls.gov/tus/home.htm

Asian Men Spend the Most Time Working

Hispanic women spend the most time doing housework.

Time use varies by race and Hispanic origin, although not as much as it does by age. Asian men spend more time at work than either black, Hispanic, or white men. On an average day, Asian men work for 4.29 hours—13 percent more than the average man. Black men spend more time than the average man on religious activities. White men spend more time than Asian, black or Hispanic men taking care of animals and pets.

Among women, Asians and blacks spend more time at work than Hispanic or white women. Black women spend the most time participating in religious activities. Hispanic women spend 22 percent more time than the average woman doing housework. Asian and Hispanic women spend 42 to 70 percent more time than the average woman caring for household children. As is true among men, on an average day white women spend more time than Asian, black, or Hispanic women caring for animals and pets.

■ Because the Hispanic population is considerably younger than the black or white population, they spend more time in educational activities.

Time spent at work varies by race and Hispanic origin

(average number of hours per day people spend working as a primary activity, by sex, race, and Hispanic origin, 2009)

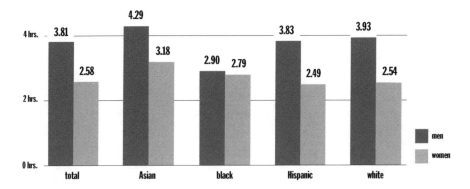

Table 10.11 Time Use by Race and Hispanic Origin, 2009

(average hours per day spent in primary activities by people aged 15 or older by race and Hispanic origin, by type of activity, 2009)

	total people	Asian	black	Hispanic	white
Total, all activities	**24.00**	**24.00**	**24.00**	**24.00**	**24.00**
Personal care	9.43	9.28	9.90	9.71	9.37
Sleeping	8.67	8.64	8.97	8.96	8.63
Grooming	0.67	0.60	0.83	0.70	0.65
Household activities	1.83	1.75	1.26	1.79	1.92
Housework	0.60	0.53	0.46	0.72	0.62
Food preparation and cleanup	0.54	0.78	0.47	0.61	0.54
Lawn, garden, and houseplants	0.20	0.17	0.12	0.13	0.21
Animals and pets	0.09	0.03	0.04	0.06	0.10
Household management	0.21	0.20	0.13	0.11	0.23
Caring for and helping household members	0.46	0.68	0.39	0.61	0.46
Caring for and helping household children	0.38	0.59	0.32	0.49	0.38
Caring for and helping people in other households	0.14	0.06	0.13	0.14	0.15
Caring for and helping children in other households	0.07	0.02	0.06	0.07	0.07
Work and work-related activities	3.25	3.75	2.94	3.27	3.30
Working	3.18	3.71	2.84	3.18	3.22
Job search and interviewing	0.04	0.02	0.06	0.04	0.04
Education	0.44	0.79	0.42	0.59	0.42
Taking class	0.26	0.32	0.29	0.42	0.25
Research and homework	0.16	0.47	0.11	0.15	0.15
Shopping (store, telephone, Internet)	0.38	0.41	0.31	0.42	0.39
Grocery shopping	0.11	0.14	0.09	0.12	0.11
Shopping, except groceries, food, and gas	0.25	0.25	0.19	0.29	0.25
Eating and drinking	1.11	1.32	0.84	1.05	1.14
Socializing, relaxing, and leisure	4.69	3.73	5.50	4.21	4.60
Socializing and communicating	0.63	0.42	0.68	0.71	0.63
Relaxing and leisure	3.91	3.16	4.69	3.37	3.82
Watching television	2.82	2.12	3.66	2.71	2.72
Playing games (including computer)	0.22	0.23	0.25	0.13	0.21
Computer use for leisure (excluding games)	0.16	0.24	0.13	0.08	0.17
Reading for personal interest	0.34	0.28	0.14	0.12	0.38
Sports, exercise, recreation	0.33	0.35	0.27	0.26	0.34
Religious and spiritual activities	0.15	0.17	0.28	0.16	0.12
Volunteer activities	0.15	0.11	0.13	0.08	0.15
Telephone calls	0.11	0.09	0.19	0.09	0.10
Traveling	1.20	1.20	1.14	1.25	1.21

Note: Primary activities are those respondents identified as their main activity. Other activities done simultaneously, such as eating while watching TV, are not included. Numbers may not add to total because not all categories are shown. Asians, blacks, and whites are those who identify themselves as being of the race alone. Hispanics may be of any race.
Source: Unpublished tables from the Bureau of Labor Statistics' 2009 American Time Use Survey, Internet site http://www.bls.gov/tus/home.htm; calculations by New Strategist

Table 10.12 Index of Time Use by Race and Hispanic Origin, 2009

(index of average hours per day people aged 15 or older spend doing primary activities by race and Hispanic origin, by type of activity, 2009)

	total people	Asian	black	Hispanic	white
INDEX OF TIME TO AVERAGE FOR TOTAL PEOPLE					
Total, all activities	**100**	**100**	**100**	**100**	**100**
Personal care	100	98	105	103	99
Sleeping	100	100	103	103	100
Grooming	100	90	124	104	97
Household activities	100	96	69	98	105
Housework	100	88	77	120	103
Food preparation and cleanup	100	144	87	113	100
Lawn, garden, and houseplants	100	85	60	65	105
Animals and pets	100	33	44	67	111
Household management	100	95	62	52	110
Caring for and helping household members	100	148	85	133	100
Caring for and helping household children	100	155	84	129	100
Caring for and helping people in other households	100	43	93	100	107
Caring for and helping children in other households	100	29	86	100	100
Work and work-related activities	100	115	90	101	102
Working	100	117	89	100	101
Job search and interviewing	100	50	150	100	100
Education	100	180	95	134	95
Taking class	100	123	112	162	96
Research and homework	100	294	69	94	94
Shopping (store, telephone, Internet)	100	108	82	111	103
Grocery shopping	100	127	82	109	100
Shopping, except groceries, food, and gas	100	100	76	116	100
Eating and drinking	100	119	76	95	103
Socializing, relaxing, and leisure	100	80	117	90	98
Socializing and communicating	100	67	108	113	100
Relaxing and leisure	100	81	120	86	98
Watching television	100	75	130	96	96
Playing games (including computer)	100	105	114	59	95
Computer use for leisure (excluding games)	100	150	81	50	106
Reading for personal interest	100	82	41	35	112
Sports, exercise, recreation	100	106	82	79	103
Religious and spiritual activities	100	113	187	107	80
Volunteer activities	100	73	87	53	100
Telephone calls	100	82	173	82	91
Traveling	100	100	95	104	101

Note: Primary activities are those respondents identified as their main activity. Other activities done simultaneously, such as eating while watching TV, are not included. Asians, blacks, and whites are those who identify themselves as being of the race alone. Hispanics may be of any race. The index is calculated by dividing time use in each race/Hispanic origin group by time use of the average person and multiplying by 100.
Source: Calculations by New Strategist based on unpublished tables from the Bureau of Labor Statistics' 2009 American Time Use Survey, Internet site http://www.bls.gov/tus/home.htm

Table 10.13 Time Use of Men by Race and Hispanic Origin, 2009

(average hours per day spent in primary activities by men aged 15 or older by race and Hispanic origin, by type of activity, 2009)

	total men	Asian	black	Hispanic	white
Total, all activities	24.00	24.00	24.00	24.00	24.00
Personal care	9.24	9.23	9.86	9.56	9.16
Sleeping	8.62	8.63	9.10	8.88	8.55
Grooming	0.54	0.54	0.69	0.64	0.52
Household activities	1.35	1.02	1.05	1.20	1.40
Housework	0.26	0.23	0.30	0.35	0.25
Food preparation and cleanup	0.29	0.31	0.31	0.24	0.29
Lawn, garden, and houseplants	0.28	0.20	0.20	0.19	0.29
Animals and pets	0.08	0.01	0.05	0.06	0.08
Household management	0.17	0.21	0.11	0.09	0.18
Caring for and helping household members	0.31	0.35	0.25	0.39	0.32
Caring for and helping household children	0.26	0.30	0.19	0.28	0.27
Caring for and helping people in other households	0.13	0.05	0.12	0.14	0.13
Caring for and helping children in other households	0.04	0.01	0.06	0.04	0.04
Work and work-related activities	3.90	4.34	3.01	3.93	4.02
Working	3.81	4.29	2.90	3.83	3.93
Job search and interviewing	0.06	0.03	0.06	0.08	0.05
Education	0.40	0.87	0.35	0.57	0.39
Taking class	0.26	0.34	0.27	0.43	0.25
Research and homework	0.14	0.53	0.08	0.13	0.13
Shopping (store, telephone, Internet)	0.29	0.27	0.24	0.36	0.30
Grocery shopping	0.08	0.08	0.08	0.08	0.08
Shopping, except groceries, food, and gas	0.19	0.17	0.13	0.26	0.20
Eating and drinking	1.13	1.33	0.81	1.03	1.17
Socializing, relaxing, and leisure	4.91	4.35	5.94	4.58	4.78
Socializing and communicating	0.56	0.42	0.64	0.73	0.56
Relaxing and leisure	4.21	3.78	5.17	3.74	4.08
Watching television	3.09	2.49	3.97	2.93	2.99
Playing games (including computer)	0.26	0.37	0.40	0.19	0.23
Computer use for leisure (excluding games)	0.20	0.32	0.15	0.09	0.20
Reading for personal interest	0.27	0.24	0.11	0.12	0.29
Sports, exercise, recreation	0.44	0.43	0.40	0.36	0.45
Religious and spiritual activities	0.12	0.12	0.25	0.13	0.11
Volunteer activities	0.15	0.13	0.14	0.08	0.16
Telephone calls	0.07	0.10	0.15	0.07	0.06
Traveling	1.24	1.22	1.14	1.27	1.25

Note: Primary activities are those respondents identified as their main activity. Other activities done simultaneously, such as eating while watching TV, are not included. Numbers may not add to total because not all categories are shown. Asians, blacks, and whites are those who identify themselves as being of the race alone. Hispanics may be of any race.
Source: Unpublished tables from the Bureau of Labor Statistics' 2009 American Time Use Survey, Internet site http://www.bls .gov/tus/home.htm; calculations by New Strategist

Table 10.14 Index of Men's Time Use by Race and Hispanic Origin, 2009

(index of average hours per day men aged 15 or older spend doing primary activities by race and Hispanic origin, by type of activity, 2009)

	total men	Asian	black	Hispanic	white
INDEX OF TIME TO AVERAGE FOR TOTAL MEN					
Total, all activities	**100**	**100**	**100**	**100**	**100**
Personal care	100	100	107	103	99
Sleeping	100	100	106	103	99
Grooming	100	100	128	119	96
Household activities	100	76	78	89	104
Housework	100	88	115	135	96
Food preparation and cleanup	100	107	107	83	100
Lawn, garden, and houseplants	100	71	71	68	104
Animals and pets	100	13	63	75	100
Household management	100	124	65	53	106
Caring for and helping household members	100	113	81	126	103
Caring for and helping household children	100	115	73	108	104
Caring for and helping people in other households	100	38	92	108	100
Caring for and helping children in other households	100	25	150	100	100
Work and work-related activities	100	111	77	101	103
Working	100	113	76	101	103
Job search and interviewing	100	50	100	133	83
Education	100	218	88	143	98
Taking class	100	131	104	165	96
Research and homework	100	379	57	93	93
Shopping (store, telephone, Internet)	100	93	83	124	103
Grocery shopping	100	100	100	100	100
Shopping, except groceries, food, and gas	100	89	68	137	105
Eating and drinking	100	118	72	91	104
Socializing, relaxing, and leisure	100	89	121	93	97
Socializing and communicating	100	75	114	130	100
Relaxing and leisure	100	90	123	89	97
Watching television	100	81	128	95	97
Playing games (including computer)	100	142	154	73	88
Computer use for leisure (excluding games)	100	160	75	45	100
Reading for personal interest	100	89	41	44	107
Sports, exercise, recreation	100	98	91	82	102
Religious and spiritual activities	100	100	208	108	92
Volunteer activities	100	87	93	53	107
Telephone calls	100	143	214	100	86
Traveling	100	98	92	102	101

Note: Primary activities are those respondents identified as their main activity. Other activities done simultaneously, such as eating while watching TV, are not included. Asians, blacks, and whites are those who identify themselves as being of the race alone. Hispanics may be of any race. The index is calculated by dividing time use of men in each race/Hispanic origin group by time use of the average man and multiplying by 100.
Source: Calculations by New Strategist based on unpublished tables from the Bureau of Labor Statistics' 2009 American Time Use Survey, Internet site http://www.bls.gov/tus/home.htm

Table 10.15 Time Use of Women by Race and Hispanic Origin, 2009

(average hours per day spent in primary activities by women aged 15 or older by race and Hispanic origin, by type of activity, 2009)

	total women	Asian	black	Hispanic	white
Total, all activities	**24.00**	**24.00**	**24.00**	**24.00**	**24.00**
Personal care	9.61	9.33	9.93	9.86	9.57
Sleeping	8.73	8.64	8.87	9.04	8.70
Grooming	0.79	0.67	0.95	0.77	0.77
Household activities	2.28	2.43	1.44	2.42	2.41
Housework	0.92	0.81	0.60	1.12	0.98
Food preparation and cleanup	0.77	1.21	0.61	1.00	0.78
Lawn, garden, and houseplants	0.12	0.14	0.05	0.06	0.14
Animals and pets	0.11	0.06	0.03	0.05	0.12
Household management	0.25	0.20	0.15	0.13	0.27
Caring for and helping household members	0.60	0.99	0.51	0.84	0.59
Caring for and helping household children	0.50	0.85	0.43	0.71	0.49
Caring for and helping people in other households	0.15	0.07	0.13	0.14	0.16
Caring for and helping children in other households	0.09	0.03	0.06	0.09	0.09
Work and work-related activities	2.65	3.19	2.88	2.58	2.60
Working	2.58	3.18	2.79	2.49	2.54
Job search and interviewing	0.03	0.01	0.05	0.01	0.03
Education	0.47	0.72	0.48	0.60	0.44
Taking class	0.27	0.30	0.31	0.41	0.25
Research and homework	0.18	0.42	0.13	0.17	0.18
Shopping (store, telephone, Internet)	0.45	0.54	0.37	0.48	0.46
Grocery shopping	0.13	0.20	0.10	0.15	0.13
Shopping, except groceries, food, and gas	0.29	0.32	0.24	0.31	0.30
Eating and drinking	1.08	1.31	0.86	1.07	1.11
Socializing, relaxing, and leisure	4.48	3.15	5.13	3.83	4.43
Socializing and communicating	0.69	0.42	0.71	0.69	0.69
Relaxing and leisure	3.63	2.57	4.29	2.97	3.57
Watching television	2.56	1.77	3.39	2.47	2.46
Playing games (including computer)	0.19	0.09	0.13	0.06	0.19
Computer use for leisure (excluding games)	0.13	0.18	0.12	0.07	0.13
Reading for personal interest	0.42	0.32	0.16	0.12	0.47
Sports, exercise, recreation	0.23	0.26	0.16	0.16	0.24
Religious and spiritual activities	0.17	0.22	0.31	0.19	0.14
Volunteer activities	0.15	0.09	0.13	0.09	0.15
Telephone calls	0.15	0.08	0.23	0.11	0.14
Traveling	1.17	1.18	1.14	1.23	1.17

Note: Primary activities are those respondents identified as their main activity. Other activities done simultaneously, such as eating while watching TV, are not included. Numbers may not add to total because not all categories are shown. Asians, blacks, and whites are those who identify themselves as being of the race alone. Hispanics may be of any race.
Source: Unpublished tables from the Bureau of Labor Statistics' 2009 American Time Use Survey, Internet site http://www.bls.gov/tus/home.htm; calculations by New Strategist

Table 10.16 Index of Women's Time Use by Race and Hispanic Origin, 2009

(index of average hours per day women aged 15 or older spend doing primary activities by race and Hispanic origin, by type of activity, 2009)

	total women	Asian	black	Hispanic	white
INDEX OF TIME TO AVERAGE FOR TOTAL WOMEN					
Total, all activities	**100**	**100**	**100**	**100**	**100**
Personal care	100	97	103	103	100
Sleeping	100	99	102	104	100
Grooming	100	85	120	97	97
Household activities	100	107	63	106	106
Housework	100	88	65	122	107
Food preparation and cleanup	100	157	79	130	101
Lawn, garden, and houseplants	100	117	42	50	117
Animals and pets	100	55	27	45	109
Household management	100	80	60	52	108
Caring for and helping household members	100	165	85	140	98
Caring for and helping household children	100	170	86	142	98
Caring for and helping people in other households	100	47	87	93	107
Caring for and helping children in other households	100	33	67	100	100
Work and work-related activities	100	120	109	97	98
Working	100	123	108	97	98
Job search and interviewing	100	33	167	33	100
Education	100	153	102	128	94
Taking class	100	111	115	152	93
Research and homework	100	233	72	94	100
Shopping (store, telephone, Internet)	100	120	82	107	102
Grocery shopping	100	154	77	115	100
Shopping, except groceries, food, and gas	100	110	83	107	103
Eating and drinking	100	121	80	99	103
Socializing, relaxing, and leisure	100	70	115	85	99
Socializing and communicating	100	61	103	100	100
Relaxing and leisure	100	71	118	82	98
Watching television	100	69	132	96	96
Playing games (including computer)	100	47	68	32	100
Computer use for leisure (excluding games)	100	138	92	54	100
Reading for personal interest	100	76	38	29	112
Sports, exercise, recreation	100	113	70	70	104
Religious and spiritual activities	100	129	182	112	82
Volunteer activities	100	60	87	60	100
Telephone calls	100	53	153	73	93
Traveling	100	101	97	105	100

Note: Primary activities are those respondents identified as their main activity. Other activities done simultaneously, such as eating while watchin TV, are not included. Asians, blacks, and whites are those who identify themselves as being of the race alone. Hispanics may be of any race. The index is calculated by dividing time use of women in each race/Hispanic origin group by time use of the average woman and multiplying by 100.
Source: Calculations by New Strategist based on unpublished tables from the Bureau of Labor Statistics' 2009 American Time Use Survey, Internet site http://www.bls.gov/tus/home.htm

11

Wealth Trends

■ Net worth has decreased.

Median household net worth peaked in 2007 at $125,400, but fell sharply during the Great Recession. By 2009, median net worth was just $96,000.

■ The value of financial assets has fallen.

The median value of the financial assets owned by the average household fell 5 percent between 2007 and 2009, after adjusting for inflation. Among households owning stock directly, the median value of their holdings fell 35 percent during those years.

■ Home values have declined.

The median value of the average owned home was just $176,000 in 2009, fully 15 percent below the $207,100 of 2007.

■ Most households are in debt.

In 2009, nearly 78 percent of households were in debt, owing a median of $75,600. Mortgage loans account for most of the debt.

■ Many workers do not have access to a retirement plan at work.

Sixty-nine percent of workers have access to a retirement plan at work. Among service workers, the proportion is just 49 percent.

■ The expected age of retirement is climbing.

Only 13 percent of workers are "very confident" in their ability to afford a comfortable retirement, according to the 2011 Retirement Confidence Survey.

Net Worth Fell Sharply during the Great Recession

Every demographic segment lost ground during the economic downturn.

Net worth is what remains when a household's debts are subtracted from its assets. During the Great Recession, which officially lasted from December 2007 until June 2009, the value of houses, stocks, and retirement accounts fell sharply. At the same time, debt increased. Consequently, net worth fell 23 percent between 2007 and 2009, after adjusting for inflation. These data come from a unique follow-up to the 2007 Survey of Consumer Finances. The survey is taken only every three years. Because of the severity of the Great Recession, however, the Federal Reserve Board arranged for the 2007 respondents to be re-interviewed in 2009 to determine the impact of the Great Recession on household assets, debt, and net worth.

The impact was severe. Net worth fell in every region and in all demographic segments. Median net worth tumbled 32 percent in the West, where housing prices had increased the most, and fell a smaller 16 percent in the Northeast. It declined 37 percent among householders under age 35— many of them recent homebuyers who bought at the peak—and fell by a smaller 12 percent among householders aged 65 to 74, many of whom bought their house decades ago. It diminished 29 percent among nonwhites and Hispanics, and fell by a smaller 16 percent among non-Hispanic whites.

Net worth typically rises with age as people pay off their debts. That pattern has not changed. In 2009, median net worth peaked in the 55-to-64 age group at $222,300.

■ Net worth will continue to decline until home values stabilize.

Net worth has fallen since reaching a peak in 2007

(median household net worth, 2007 and 2009; in 2009 dollars)

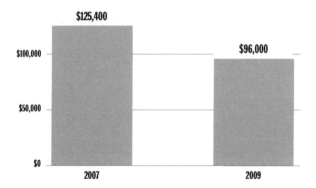

Table 11.1 Net Worth of Households, 2007 and 2009

(median net worth of households by selected characteristics, 2007 and 2009; percent change, 2007–09; in 2009 dollars)

	2009	2007	percent change
Total households	$96,000	$125,400	–23.4%
Household income percentile			
Below 20 percent	7,200	10,100	–28.7
20 to 39.9 percent	32,900	39,100	–15.9
40 to 59.9 percent	72,600	95,400	–23.9
60 to 79.9 percent	167,500	216,700	–22.7
80 to 89.9 percent	302,500	373,500	–19.0
90 percent or higher	894,500	1,205,100	–25.8
Age of householder			
Under age 35	9,000	14,200	–36.6
Aged 35 to 44	69,400	97,100	–28.5
Aged 45 to 54	150,400	203,000	–25.9
Aged 55 to 64	222,300	257,700	–13.7
Aged 65 to 74	205,500	232,700	–11.7
Aged 75 or older	191,000	228,900	–16.6
Education of householder			
No high school diploma	21,200	34,400	–38.4
High school diploma	64,200	80,900	–20.6
Some college	66,800	81,300	–17.8
College degree	244,000	294,600	–17.2
Race and Hispanic origin of householder			
Non-Hispanic white	149,900	178,800	–16.2
Nonwhite or Hispanic	23,300	32,800	–29.0
Region			
Northeast	141,400	168,900	–16.3
Midwest	92,200	121,000	–23.8
South	83,500	102,700	–18.7
West	103,200	151,000	–31.7
Housing status			
Owner	192,600	244,800	–21.3
Renter or other	3,600	5,500	–34.5

Source: Federal Reserve Board, Surveying the Aftermath of the Storm: Changes in Family Finances from 2007 to 2009, Jesse Bricker, Brian Bucks, Arthur Kennickell, Traci Mach, and Kevin Moore, Finance and Economics Discussion Series, 2011-17, Appendix tables, Internet site http://www.federalreserve.gov/pubs/oss/oss2/2009p/scf2009phome.html; calculations by New Strategist

Table 11.2 Distribution of Household Assets and Debts by Type, 2007 and 2009

(percent distribution of household assets and debts by type, 2007 and 2009; percentage point change, 2007–09)

	2009	2007	percentage point change
Financial assets, total	**100.0%**	**100.0%**	–
Transaction accounts	12.7	9.9	2.8
Certificates of deposit	5.0	3.6	1.4
Savings bonds	0.5	0.4	0.1
Bonds	6.1	4.0	2.1
Stocks	13.6	18.1	–4.5
Pooled investment funds	11.7	15.1	–3.4
Retirement accounts	38.2	37.7	0.5
Cash value of life insurance	3.1	3.1	0.0
Other managed assets	6.7	5.8	0.9
Other	2.4	2.2	0.2
Nonfinancial assets, total	**100.0**	**100.0**	–
Vehicles	4.6	4.4	0.2
Primary residence	48.5	47.6	0.9
Business equity	11.6	10.3	1.3
Other residential real estate	5.7	6.2	–0.5
Equity in nonresidential property	27.9	30.2	–2.3
Other	1.7	1.3	0.4
Debt, total	**100.0**	**100.0**	–
Secured by primary residence	72.9	75.0	–2.1
Secured by other residential property	10.0	9.5	0.5
Installment loans (education, vehicle, etc.)	11.7	10.3	1.4
Lines of credit, not secured by residential property	0.8	0.5	0.3
Credit card balances	3.5	3.5	0.0
Other	1.1	1.2	–0.1

Note: Pooled investment funds exclude money market funds and indirectly held mutual funds. They include open-end and closed-end mutual funds, real estate investment trusts, and hedge funds. "–" means not applicable.
Source: Federal Reserve Board, Surveying the Aftermath of the Storm: Changes in Family Finances from 2007 to 2009, Jesse Bricker, Brian Bucks, Arthur Kennickell, Traci Mach, and Kevin Moore, Finance and Economics Discussion Series, 2011-17, Appendix tables, Internet site http://www.federalreserve.gov/pubs/oss/oss2/2009p/scf2009phome.html; calculations by New Strategist

Financial Asset Values Fell between 2007 and 2009

Some demographic segments saw the median value of their financial assets increase, however.

Most households own financial assets, which range from transaction accounts (checking and saving) to stocks, mutual funds, retirement accounts, and life insurance. The median value of the financial assets owned by the average household stood at $29,600 in 2009, down 5 percent since 2007 after adjusting for inflation. The Great Recession greatly reduced the value of the stocks, bonds, and mutual funds.

Transaction accounts, the most commonly owned financial asset, are held by 92 percent of households. Their median value was just $4,000 in 2009—slightly lower than the $4,100 of 2007. Retirement accounts are the second most commonly owned financial asset, with 56 percent of households having one. Most retirement accounts are not large, however, with an overall median value of just $48,000 in 2009. This figure is 5 percent lower than the $50,600 of 2007, after adjusting for inflation.

Only 18.5 percent of households owned stock directly in 2009 (outside of a retirement account). The median value of stock owned by stockholding households was just $12,000 in 2009, 35 percent less than the value in 2007, after adjusting for inflation.

■ The median value of financial assets peaked in the 55-to-64 age group in 2009, at $72,500.

Retirement accounts were modest in 2009 and their median value has declined since then

(median value of retirement accounts owned by households, by age of householder, 2009)

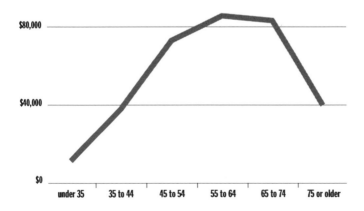

Table 11.3 Ownership and Value of Household Financial Assets, 2007 and 2009

(percentage of households owning any financial asset and median value of financial assets for owners, by selected characteristics, 2007 and 2009; percentage point change in ownership and percent change in value, 2007–09; in 2009 dollars)

	percent owning any financial asset			median value of financial assets		
	2009	2007	percentage point change	2009	2007	percent change
Total households	**94.6%**	**94.3%**	**0.3**	**$29,600**	**$31,300**	**–5.4%**
Household income percentile						
Below 20 percent	82.7	80.9	1.8	2,100	1,800	16.7
20 to 39.9 percent	94.3	93.7	0.6	8,800	8,500	3.5
40 to 59.9 percent	96.6	97.8	–1.2	21,600	19,000	13.7
60 to 79.9 percent	99.6	99.7	–0.1	63,900	68,600	–6.9
80 to 89.9 percent	100.0	100.0	0.0	134,100	149,000	–10.0
90 percent or higher	100.0	100.0	0.0	398,000	497,100	–19.9
Age of householder						
Under age 35	91.4	90.2	1.2	7,400	7,400	0.0
Aged 35 to 44	92.3	93.5	–1.2	27,500	25,500	7.8
Aged 45 to 54	96.0	94.1	1.9	58,500	64,300	–9.0
Aged 55 to 64	97.0	97.9	–0.9	72,500	78,200	–7.3
Aged 65 to 74	97.8	96.1	1.7	48,000	63,900	–24.9
Aged 75 or older	95.8	98.1	–2.3	39,000	41,400	–5.8
Education of householder						
No high school diploma	83.5	80.9	2.6	3,900	3,100	25.8
High school diploma	93.2	93.3	–0.1	15,800	15,300	3.3
Some college	96.4	96.0	0.4	16,700	20,100	–16.9
College degree	98.7	99.1	–0.4	101,100	107,500	–6.0
Race and Hispanic origin of householder						
Non-Hispanic white	96.9	97.3	–0.4	47,700	50,100	–4.8
Nonwhite or Hispanic	89.2	87.3	1.9	8,500	10,200	–16.7
Region						
Northeast	94.5	93.2	1.3	40,000	49,100	–18.5
Midwest	95.6	95.7	–0.1	34,000	34,200	–0.6
South	94.6	94.2	0.4	22,000	25,500	–13.7
West	93.6	94.2	–0.6	27,000	27,500	–1.8
Housing status						
Owner	97.9	98.5	–0.6	57,900	63,000	–8.1
Renter or other	87.3	85.2	2.1	4,000	4,200	–4.8

Source: Federal Reserve Board, Surveying the Aftermath of the Storm: Changes in Family Finances from 2007 to 2009, Jesse Bricker, Brian Bucks, Arthur Kennickell, Traci Mach, and Kevin Moore, Finance and Economics Discussion Series, 2011-17, Appendix tables, Internet site http://www.federalreserve.gov/pubs/oss/oss2/2009p/scf2009phome.html; calculations by New Strategist

Table 11.4 Percent of Households Owning Transaction Accounts, Life Insurance, and CDs, 2007 and 2009

(percent of households owning transaction accounts, cash value life insurance, and certificates of deposit by selected characteristics of households, 2007 and 2009; percentage point change, 2007–09)

	transaction accounts			cash value life insurance			certificates of deposit		
	2009	2007	percentage point change	2009	2007	percentage point change	2009	2007	percentage point change
Total households	**92.3%**	**92.6%**	**–0.3**	**24.3%**	**23.2%**	**1.1**	**15.9%**	**15.4%**	**0.5**
Household income percentile									
Below 20 percent	77.4	76.6	0.8	15.0	12.5	2.5	9.4	9.1	0.3
20 to 39.9 percent	91.2	90.5	0.7	22.1	18.2	3.9	13.7	12.9	0.8
40 to 59.9 percent	94.5	96.9	–2.4	21.8	21.3	0.5	13.8	13.3	0.5
60 to 79.9 percent	99.5	99.3	0.2	26.4	28.3	–1.9	18.8	19.0	–0.2
80 to 89.9 percent	98.8	100.0	–1.2	31.6	33.0	–1.4	20.8	19.3	1.5
90 percent or higher	100.0	100.0	0.0	40.9	39.3	1.6	26.4	26.8	–0.4
Age of householder									
Under age 35	88.5	88.0	0.5	13.1	12.4	0.7	7.9	6.5	1.4
Aged 35 to 44	89.8	91.8	–2.0	16.8	17.1	–0.3	9.4	8.9	0.5
Aged 45 to 54	94.1	92.8	1.3	25.3	22.0	3.3	13.9	14.5	–0.6
Aged 55 to 64	95.3	96.5	–1.2	33.4	35.7	–2.3	20.2	19.5	0.7
Aged 65 to 74	95.0	95.0	0.0	36.3	34.6	1.7	24.8	23.0	1.8
Aged 75 or older	94.2	95.1	–0.9	34.2	29.2	5.0	35.2	36.8	–1.6
Education of householder									
No high school diploma	79.3	76.8	2.5	14.3	12.7	1.6	11.8	8.3	3.5
High school diploma	90.5	90.7	–0.2	24.3	22.2	2.1	14.8	13.4	1.4
Some college	93.2	94.2	–1.0	23.3	23.9	–0.6	11.3	12.5	–1.2
College degree	98.0	98.9	–0.9	28.2	27.5	0.7	20.6	21.2	–0.6
Race and Hispanic origin of householder									
Non-Hispanic white	95.5	96.0	–0.5	25.8	25.4	0.4	19.4	18.7	0.7
Nonwhite or Hispanic	84.9	84.7	0.2	20.8	18.1	2.7	7.4	7.7	–0.3
Region									
Northeast	92.7	91.7	1.0	25.8	24.1	1.7	20.1	17.4	2.7
Midwest	93.0	93.7	–0.7	27.9	26.3	1.6	16.2	16.3	–0.1
South	91.7	91.9	–0.2	24.6	24.1	0.5	14.9	14.5	0.4
West	92.3	93.2	–0.9	18.7	17.9	0.8	13.5	14.4	–0.9
Housing status									
Owner	96.4	97.4	–1.0	30.2	29.0	1.2	20.0	19.1	0.9
Renter or other	83.4	82.0	1.4	11.1	10.4	0.7	6.7	7.3	–0.6

Source: Federal Reserve Board, Surveying the Aftermath of the Storm: Changes in Family Finances from 2007 to 2009, Jesse Bricker, Brian Bucks, Arthur Kennickell, Traci Mach, and Kevin Moore, Finance and Economics Discussion Series, 2011-17, Appendix tables, Internet site http://www.federalreserve.gov/pubs/oss/oss2/2009p/scf2009phome.html; calculations by New Strategist

Table 11.5 Percent of Households Owning Retirement Accounts and Stocks, 2007 and 2009

(percent of households owning retirement accounts and stocks by selected characteristics of households, 2007 and 2009; percentage point change, 2007–09)

	retirement accounts			stocks		
	2009	**2007**	**percentage point change**	**2009**	**2007**	**percentage point change**
Total households	**56.2%**	**55.6%**	**0.6**	**18.5%**	**18.4%**	**0.1**
Household income percentile						
Below 20 percent	14.7	12.7	2.0	4.8	5.6	–0.8
20 to 39.9 percent	41.5	39.5	2.0	9.8	8.9	0.9
40 to 59.9 percent	57.6	58.1	–0.5	14.0	13.4	0.6
60 to 79.9 percent	78.3	78.6	–0.3	24.2	25.1	–0.9
80 to 89.9 percent	87.9	89.3	–1.4	29.3	29.2	0.1
90 percent or higher	91.7	91.3	0.4	50.8	49.6	1.2
Age of householder						
Under age 35	48.4	44.9	3.5	12.6	14.6	–2.0
Aged 35 to 44	61.2	59.4	1.8	18.9	17.0	1.9
Aged 45 to 54	68.2	68.0	0.2	20.3	18.4	1.9
Aged 55 to 64	62.7	64.3	–1.6	21.3	21.2	0.1
Aged 65 to 74	51.8	53.3	–1.5	21.9	21.0	0.9
Aged 75 or older	29.5	31.3	–1.8	18.6	22.8	–4.2
Education of householder						
No high school diploma	23.3	23.2	0.1	3.5	3.8	–0.3
High school diploma	46.6	45.7	0.9	9.1	9.6	–0.5
Some college	56.7	56.2	0.5	17.8	17.8	0.0
College degree	75.6	75.2	0.4	32.4	31.6	0.8
Race and Hispanic origin of householder						
Non-Hispanic white	62.0	61.6	0.4	22.5	22.1	0.4
Nonwhite or Hispanic	42.3	41.5	0.8	9.1	9.7	–0.6
Region						
Northeast	59.3	56.9	2.4	20.2	22.2	–2.0
Midwest	59.9	60.1	–0.2	17.9	18.1	–0.2
South	52.0	52.3	–0.3	17.2	16.2	1.0
West	56.4	55.2	1.2	20.0	19.2	0.8
Housing status						
Owner	65.9	66.0	–0.1	23.1	23.0	0.1
Renter or other	34.6	32.5	2.1	8.4	8.3	0.1

Note: Stock ownership is direct ownership outside of a retirement account or mutual fund.
Source: Federal Reserve Board, Surveying the Aftermath of the Storm: Changes in Family Finances from 2007 to 2009, Jesse Bricker, Brian Bucks, Arthur Kennickell, Traci Mach, and Kevin Moore, Finance and Economics Discussion Series, 2011-17, Appendix tables, Internet site http://www.federalreserve.gov/pubs/oss/oss2/2009p/scf2009phome.html; calculations by New Strategist

Table 11.6 Percent of Households Owning Pooled Investment Funds and Bonds, 2007 and 2009

(percent of households owning pooled investment funds and bonds by selected characteristics of households, 2007 and 2009; percentage point change, 2007–09)

	pooled investment funds			bonds		
	2009	2007	percentage point change	2009	2007	percentage point change
Total households	**10.8%**	**11.5%**	**–0.7**	**2.6%**	**1.7%**	**0.9**
Household income percentile						
Below 20 percent	3.6	4.1	–0.5	0.7	0.4	0.3
20 to 39.9 percent	5.3	5.1	0.2	1.0	0.4	0.6
40 to 59.9 percent	6.8	6.6	0.2	1.8	0.6	1.2
60 to 79.9 percent	11.6	14.6	–3.0	2.0	1.4	0.6
80 to 89.9 percent	15.9	18.4	–2.5	3.8	1.6	2.2
90 percent or higher	38.0	36.6	1.4	11.4	9.5	1.9
Age of householder						
Under age 35	5.4	5.8	–0.4	0.5	0.2	0.3
Aged 35 to 44	10.0	11.7	–1.7	1.3	0.7	0.6
Aged 45 to 54	13.2	12.6	0.6	2.4	1.1	1.3
Aged 55 to 64	14.5	14.1	0.4	3.3	2.4	0.9
Aged 65 to 74	11.5	13.8	–2.3	6.2	4.5	1.7
Aged 75 or older	12.6	15.1	–2.5	5.5	3.9	1.6
Education of householder						
No high school diploma	2.0	1.9	0.1	0.6	0.2	0.4
High school diploma	4.7	5.6	–0.9	1.1	0.7	0.4
Some college	8.0	9.1	–1.1	2.2	1.1	1.1
College degree	20.7	21.4	–0.7	4.9	3.3	1.6
Race and Hispanic origin of householder						
Non-Hispanic white	13.1	14.0	–0.9	3.4	2.2	1.2
Nonwhite or Hispanic	5.4	5.8	–0.4	0.8	0.4	0.4
Region						
Northeast	13.1	16.0	–2.9	3.3	2.0	1.3
Midwest	10.3	10.6	–0.3	2.3	1.1	1.2
South	10.0	10.1	–0.1	2.8	1.9	0.9
West	10.9	11.3	–0.4	2.1	1.6	0.5
Housing status						
Owner	13.8	15.3	–1.5	3.5	2.2	1.3
Renter or other	4.3	3.3	1.0	0.8	0.4	0.4

Note: Pooled investment funds exclude money market funds and indirectly held mutual funds. They include open-end and closed-end mutual funds, real estate investment trusts, and hedge funds.
Source: Federal Reserve Board, Surveying the Aftermath of the Storm: Changes in Family Finances from 2007 to 2009, Jesse Bricker, Brian Bucks, Arthur Kennickell, Traci Mach, and Kevin Moore, Finance and Economics Discussion Series, 2011-17, Appendix tables, Internet site http://www.federalreserve.gov/pubs/oss/oss2/2009p/scf2009phome.html; calculations by New Strategist

Table 11.7 Median Value of Transaction Accounts, Life Insurance, and CDs, 2007 and 2009

(median value of transaction accounts, cash value life insurance, and certificates of deposit for households owning asset, by selected characteristics of households, 2007 and 2009; percent change, 2007–09; in 2009 dollars)

	transaction accounts			cash value life insurance			certificates of deposit		
	2009	2007	percent change	2009	2007	percent change	2009	2007	percent change
Total households	**$4,000**	**$4,100**	**−2.4%**	**$7,300**	**$8,300**	**−12.0%**	**$20,000**	**$20,700**	**−3.4%**
Household income percentile									
Below 20 percent	1,000	800	25.0	5,000	2,600	92.3	10,000	23,800	−58.0
20 to 39.9 percent	2,000	1,800	11.1	4,100	4,700	−12.8	20,000	18,600	7.5
40 to 59.9 percent	3,000	2,900	3.4	7,200	5,200	38.5	20,000	14,000	42.9
60 to 79.9 percent	5,700	6,200	−8.1	8,000	9,300	−14.0	20,000	13,000	53.8
80 to 89.9 percent	10,400	12,900	−19.4	8,000	9,300	−14.0	20,000	15,500	29.0
90 percent or higher	32,000	36,200	−11.6	20,000	29,100	−31.3	40,000	46,400	−13.8
Age of householder									
Under age 35	2,300	2,600	−11.5	2,500	3,600	−30.6	9,000	4,900	83.7
Aged 35 to 44	3,000	3,500	−14.3	7,000	8,300	−15.7	10,000	5,200	92.3
Aged 45 to 54	5,000	4,800	4.2	8,000	10,400	−23.1	18,000	18,600	−3.2
Aged 55 to 64	5,500	5,600	−1.8	10,000	10,400	−3.8	25,000	20,700	20.8
Aged 65 to 74	5,500	7,000	−21.4	10,000	10,600	−5.7	27,700	22,800	21.5
Aged 75 or older	7,000	6,200	12.9	8,000	5,200	53.8	31,400	31,100	1.0
Education of householder									
No high school diploma	1,200	1,300	−7.7	3,200	2,600	23.1	11,000	12,400	−11.3
High school diploma	2,500	2,600	−3.8	5,600	5,200	7.7	20,000	18,400	8.7
Some college	2,700	3,000	−10.0	8,700	8,100	7.4	14,000	15,500	−9.7
College degree	9,500	10,400	−8.7	10,000	14,500	−31.0	25,000	20,700	20.8
Race and Hispanic origin of householder									
Non-Hispanic white	5,300	5,200	1.9	8,000	9,300	−14.0	22,000	20,700	6.3
Nonwhite or Hispanic	1,800	2,100	−14.3	5,000	5,200	−3.8	11,300	10,400	8.7
Region									
Northeast	4,600	4,900	−6.1	7,500	9,300	−19.4	25,000	20,700	20.8
Midwest	3,800	3,900	−2.6	10,000	8,300	20.5	20,000	15,500	29.0
South	3,500	3,800	−7.9	6,800	8,300	−18.1	20,000	22,800	−12.3
West	5,000	4,200	19.0	7,500	7,800	−3.8	26,000	20,700	25.6
Housing status									
Owner	6,000	6,300	−4.8	8,400	10,100	−16.8	22,000	20,700	6.3
Renter or other	1,400	1,200	16.7	2,500	2,100	19.0	10,000	8,300	20.5

Source: Federal Reserve Board, Surveying the Aftermath of the Storm: Changes in Family Finances from 2007 to 2009, Jesse Bricker, Brian Bucks, Arthur Kennickell, Traci Mach, and Kevin Moore, Finance and Economics Discussion Series, 2011-17, Appendix tables, Internet site http://www.federalreserve.gov/pubs/oss/oss2/2009p/scf2009phome.html; calculations by New Strategist

Table 11.8 Median Value of Retirement Accounts and Stocks, 2007 and 2009

(median value of retirement accounts and stocks for households owning asset, by selected characteristics of households, 2007 and 2009; percent change, 2007–09; in 2009 dollars)

	retirement accounts			stocks		
	2009	2007	percent change	2009	2007	percent change
Total households	$48,000	$50,600	−5.1%	$12,000	$18,500	−35.1%
Household income percentile						
Below 20 percent	6,100	6,200	−1.6	6,000	4,100	46.3
20 to 39.9 percent	12,500	12,400	0.8	4,500	9,100	−50.5
40 to 59.9 percent	25,800	26,300	−1.9	4,400	6,900	−36.2
60 to 79.9 percent	50,000	51,800	−3.5	10,000	12,400	−19.4
80 to 89.9 percent	91,400	102,000	−10.4	10,000	16,100	−37.9
90 percent or higher	213,800	238,200	−10.2	55,300	72,500	−23.7
Age of householder						
Under age 35	11,400	10,400	9.6	3,000	3,100	−3.2
Aged 35 to 44	38,000	38,300	−0.8	12,000	15,500	−22.6
Aged 45 to 54	73,000	81,400	−10.3	11,700	19,700	−40.6
Aged 55 to 64	85,600	103,600	−17.4	16,000	24,900	−35.7
Aged 65 to 74	83,200	79,700	4.4	25,000	36,200	−30.9
Aged 75 or older	40,000	36,200	10.5	35,000	101,500	−65.5
Education of householder						
No high school diploma	17,000	17,600	−3.4	4,100	2,300	78.3
High school diploma	30,000	28,400	5.6	8,800	10,400	−15.4
Some college	28,600	33,100	−13.6	4,000	6,200	−35.5
College degree	80,000	88,000	−9.1	20,000	28,100	−28.8
Race and Hispanic origin of householder						
Non-Hispanic white	58,500	61,800	−5.3	14,000	20,700	−32.4
Nonwhite or Hispanic	26,000	29,500	−11.9	5,500	7,100	−22.5
Region						
Northeast	50,000	62,100	−19.5	26,000	18,200	42.9
Midwest	41,000	39,700	3.3	13,000	16,100	−19.3
South	50,000	49,100	1.8	9,400	18,500	−49.2
West	45,000	49,700	−9.5	9,000	18,600	−51.6
Housing status						
Owner	63,700	65,600	−2.9	15,000	20,700	−27.5
Renter or other	12,000	9,800	22.4	5,000	5,200	−3.8

Note: Stock ownership is direct ownership outside of a retirement account or mutual fund.
Source: Federal Reserve Board, Surveying the Aftermath of the Storm: Changes in Family Finances from 2007 to 2009, Jesse Bricker, Brian Bucks, Arthur Kennickell, Traci Mach, and Kevin Moore, Finance and Economics Discussion Series, 2011-17, Appendix tables, Internet site http://www.federalreserve.gov/pubs/oss/oss2/2009p/scf2009phome.html; calculations by New Strategist

Table 11.9 Median Value of Pooled Investment Funds and Bonds, 2007 and 2009

(median value of pooled investment funds and bonds for households owning asset, by selected characteristics of households, 2007 and 2009; percent change, 2007–09; in 2009 dollars)

	pooled investment funds			bonds		
	2009	2007	percent change	2009	2007	percent change
Total households	$47,000	$58,700	–19.9%	$50,000	$62,100	–19.5%
Household income percentile						
Below 20 percent	50,000	39,700	25.9	–	–	–
20 to 39.9 percent	30,000	31,100	–3.5	–	–	–
40 to 59.9 percent	35,000	44,700	–21.7	10,000	–	–
60 to 79.9 percent	19,000	35,400	–46.3	15,000	18,300	–18.0
80 to 89.9 percent	34,000	48,400	–29.8	25,000	–	–
90 percent or higher	104,000	207,100	–49.8	250,000	186,400	34.1
Age of householder						
Under age 35	10,000	15,000	–33.3	–	–	–
Aged 35 to 44	35,000	27,300	28.2	5,000	103,600	–95.2
Aged 45 to 54	35,000	51,800	–32.4	27,000	127,600	–78.8
Aged 55 to 64	70,400	115,000	–38.8	65,000	82,800	–21.5
Aged 65 to 74	100,000	155,300	–35.6	86,000	51,600	66.7
Aged 75 or older	70,000	77,700	–9.9	37,400	96,500	–61.2
Education of householder						
No high school diploma	–	22,300	–	–	–	–
High school diploma	30,000	31,100	–3.5	18,000	41,400	–56.5
Some college	25,100	28,400	–11.6	1,700	51,800	–96.7
College degree	60,000	80,800	–25.7	95,000	103,600	–8.3
Race and Hispanic origin of householder						
Non-Hispanic white	50,000	67,300	–25.7	50,000	70,400	–29.0
Nonwhite or Hispanic	20,000	30,800	–35.1	25,000	18,300	36.6
Region						
Northeast	39,400	51,800	–23.9	100,000	103,600	–3.5
Midwest	50,000	41,400	20.8	57,600	51,800	11.2
South	60,000	89,100	–32.7	30,000	82,800	–63.8
West	35,000	51,800	–32.4	25,000	51,800	–51.7
Housing status						
Owner	50,000	62,100	–19.5	58,700	72,500	–19.0
Renter or other	18,000	41,400	–56.5	10,000	–	–

Note: Pooled investment funds exclude money market funds and indirectly held mutual funds. They include open-end and closed-end mutual funds, real estate investment trusts, and hedge funds. "–" means sample is too small to make a reliable estimate.
Source: Federal Reserve Board, Surveying the Aftermath of the Storm: Changes in Family Finances from 2007 to 2009, Jesse Bricker, Brian Bucks, Arthur Kennickell, Traci Mach, and Kevin Moore, Finance and Economics Discussion Series, 2011-17, Appendix tables, Internet site http://www.federalreserve.gov/pubs/oss/oss2/2009p/scf2009phome.html; calculations by New Strategist

Nonfinancial Assets Are the Foundation of Household Wealth

The average household saw the value of its nonfinancial assets fall during the Great Recession.

The median value of the nonfinancial assets owned by the average American household stood at $204,000 in 2009, far surpassing the $29,600 median in financial assets. Between 2007 and 2009, the value of the nonfinancial assets owned by the average household fell 13 percent, after adjusting for inflation. Nearly every demographic segment saw its nonfinancial assets decline in value, primarily because of the decline in housing values.

Eighty-seven percent of households own a vehicle, the most commonly held nonfinancial asset. The value of the vehicles owned by the average household fell steeply (down 26 percent) between 2007 and 2009, after adjusting for inflation. Behind the decline was the reluctance of households to buy new vehicles during the Great Recession.

The second most commonly owned nonfinancial asset is a home, owned by 70 percent. Homes are by far the most valuable asset owned by Americans, and they account for the largest share of net worth. In 2009, the median value of the average owned home was $176,000, 15 percent below the median of $207,100 in 2007 (in 2009 dollars). Housing prices have continued to decline since 2009, driving median home values even lower than the numbers shown here.

■ The continuing decline in housing values has probably reduced average household net worth below the 2009 figure.

Median housing value peaks in the 45-to-54 age group

(median value of the primary residence among homeowners, by age of householder, 2009)

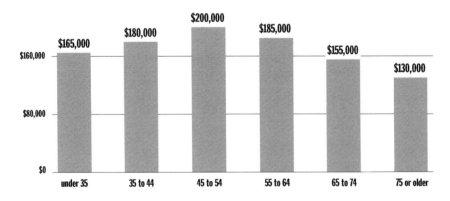

Table 11.10 Ownership and Value of Nonfinancial Assets, 2007 and 2009

(percentage of households owning any nonfinancial asset and median value of nonfinancial assets for owners, by selected characteristics, 2007 and 2009; percentage point change in ownership and percent change in value, 2007–09; in 2009 dollars)

	percent owning any nonfinancial asset			median value of nonfinancial assets		
	2009	2007	percentage point change	2009	2007	percent change
Total households	**92.6%**	**92.7%**	**–0.1**	**$204,000**	**$234,800**	**–13.1%**
Household income percentile						
Below 20 percent	77.7	76.2	1.5	20,400	26,400	–22.7
20 to 39.9 percent	92.0	91.8	0.2	85,200	89,600	–4.9
40 to 59.9 percent	95.5	97.5	–2.0	180,000	201,800	–10.8
60 to 79.9 percent	98.9	98.8	0.1	316,000	369,600	–14.5
80 to 89.9 percent	99.0	99.1	–0.1	503,000	608,700	–17.4
90 percent or higher	99.9	99.8	0.1	1,225,000	1,473,000	–16.8
Age of householder						
Under age 35	89.5	88.1	1.4	52,800	44,400	18.9
Aged 35 to 44	92.3	91.8	0.5	196,500	232,000	–15.3
Aged 45 to 54	95.0	95.2	–0.2	289,500	326,600	–11.4
Aged 55 to 64	95.5	96.1	–0.6	308,000	361,900	–14.9
Aged 65 to 74	96.0	95.3	0.7	253,000	306,200	–17.4
Aged 75 or older	86.2	90.4	–4.2	193,100	238,900	–19.2
Education of householder						
No high school diploma	82.9	82.8	0.1	60,100	71,500	–15.9
High school diploma	91.1	92.3	–1.2	152,900	167,800	–8.9
Some college	92.5	91.9	0.6	175,000	187,300	–6.6
College degree	97.3	96.7	0.6	397,800	455,800	–12.7
Race and Hispanic origin of householder						
Non-Hispanic white	95.4	95.1	0.3	259,800	287,700	–9.7
Nonwhite or Hispanic	86.0	86.9	–0.9	90,200	100,200	–10.0
Region						
Northeast	84.7	83.9	0.8	275,200	312,300	–11.9
Midwest	92.8	93.9	–1.1	192,300	226,000	–14.9
South	95.7	95.1	0.6	177,200	192,000	–7.7
West	93.9	94.5	–0.6	240,500	301,700	–20.3
Housing status						
Owner	99.6	100.0	–0.4	315,100	361,500	–12.8
Renter or other	77.2	76.4	0.8	14,100	15,200	–7.2

Source: Federal Reserve Board, Surveying the Aftermath of the Storm: Changes in Family Finances from 2007 to 2009, Jesse Bricker, Brian Bucks, Arthur Kennickell, Traci Mach, and Kevin Moore, Finance and Economics Discussion Series, 2011-17, Appendix tables, Internet site http://www.federalreserve.gov/pubs/oss/oss2/2009p/scf2009phome.html; calculations by New Strategist

Table 11.11 Percent of Households Owning Primary Residence, Other Residential Property, and Nonresidential Property, 2007 and 2009

(percent of households owning primary residence, other residential property, and nonresidential property by selected characteristics of households, 2007 and 2009; percentage point change, 2007–09)

	primary residence			other residential property			nonresidential property		
	2009	2007	percentage point change	2009	2007	percentage point change	2009	2007	percentage point change
Total households	70.3%	68.9%	1.4	13.%0	13.9%	−0.9	7.6%	8.3%	−0.7
Household income percentile									
Below 20 percent	42.6	42.0	0.6	3.3	5.7	−2.4	2.3	2.3	0.0
20 to 39.9 percent	57.5	55.3	2.2	7.9	8.0	−0.1	4.6	4.4	0.2
40 to 59.9 percent	72.4	70.3	2.1	10.4	9.5	0.9	5.9	7.6	−1.7
60 to 79.9 percent	86.6	84.7	1.9	13.7	16.0	−2.3	9.3	10.3	−1.0
80 to 89.9 percent	92.7	92.1	0.6	18.7	19.8	−1.1	12.3	12.3	0.0
90 percent or higher	94.3	94.2	0.1	40.5	40.6	−0.1	20.2	22.0	−1.8
Age of householder									
Under age 35	44.6	40.5	4.1	7.1	5.3	1.8	3.1	3.1	0.0
Aged 35 to 44	68.9	66.6	2.3	11.4	12.5	−1.1	7.0	7.9	−0.9
Aged 45 to 54	78.1	77.3	0.8	14.4	15.5	−1.1	9.5	10.0	−0.5
Aged 55 to 64	81.9	82.2	−0.3	18.6	21.0	−2.4	10.9	11.5	−0.6
Aged 65 to 74	86.8	85.5	1.3	17.9	19.2	−1.3	11.1	10.9	0.2
Aged 75 or older	77.2	79.2	−2.0	11.2	14.3	−3.1	5.7	9.0	−3.3
Education of householder									
No high school diploma	55.1	53.3	1.8	6.2	7.1	−0.9	3.0	3.8	−0.8
High school diploma	69.0	69.4	−0.4	8.5	9.5	−1.0	6.6	7.2	−0.6
Some college	63.8	61.9	1.9	12.2	13.6	−1.4	6.4	6.1	0.3
College degree	80.1	77.4	2.7	19.6	20.2	−0.6	10.8	12.0	−1.2
Race and Hispanic origin of householder									
Non-Hispanic white	77.3	75.8	1.5	15.0	15.6	−0.6	8.7	9.4	−0.7
Nonwhite or Hispanic	54.0	52.7	1.3	8.3	9.7	−1.4	5.2	5.7	−0.5
Region									
Northeast	66.5	65.1	1.4	12.3	12.5	−0.2	5.1	5.8	−0.7
Midwest	72.3	71.6	0.7	13.5	14.9	−1.4	8.0	8.4	−0.4
South	73.6	71.5	2.1	12.2	11.9	0.3	9.1	9.3	−0.2
West	66.0	65.0	1.0	14.3	17.3	−3.0	7.0	8.7	−1.7
Housing status									
Owner	96.4	100.0	−3.6	16.9	17.3	−0.4	10.0	11.1	−1.1
Renter or other	12.6	0.0	12.6	4.2	6.1	−1.9	2.3	2.1	0.2

Note: Renters were classified in the 2007 survey and when reinterviewed in 2009 some (12.6 percent) had bought a home.
Source: Federal Reserve Board, Surveying the Aftermath of the Storm: Changes in Family Finances from 2007 to 2009, Jesse Bricker, Brian Bucks, Arthur Kennickell, Traci Mach, and Kevin Moore, Finance and Economics Discussion Series, 2011-17, Appendix tables, Internet site http://www.federalreserve.gov/pubs/oss/oss2/2009p/scf2009phome.html; calculations by New Strategist

Table 11.12 Percent of Households Owning Vehicles and Business Equity, 2007 and 2009

(percent of households owning vehicles and business equity by selected characteristics of households, 2007 and 2009; percentage point change, 2007–09)

	vehicles			business equity		
	2009	2007	percentage point change	2009	2007	percentage point change
Total households	**86.8%**	**87.9%**	**−1.1**	**11.9%**	**12.4%**	**−0.5**
Household income percentile						
Below 20 percent	67.1	67.5	−0.4	2.5	3.1	−0.6
20 to 39.9 percent	86.0	87.2	−1.2	4.8	4.4	0.4
40 to 59.9 percent	91.7	94.9	−3.2	9.7	10.0	−0.3
60 to 79.9 percent	95.1	95.5	−0.4	14.9	16.2	−1.3
80 to 89.9 percent	94.5	95.0	−0.5	17.6	18.7	−1.1
90 percent or higher	95.0	95.1	−0.1	38.4	37.9	0.5
Age of householder						
Under age 35	87.2	85.8	1.4	7.7	7.1	0.6
Aged 35 to 44	87.6	87.9	−0.3	15.4	15.8	−0.4
Aged 45 to 54	90.6	91.1	−0.5	15.0	15.1	−0.1
Aged 55 to 64	90.5	92.5	−2.0	15.9	17.2	−1.3
Aged 65 to 74	88.3	90.8	−2.5	9.1	10.1	−1.0
Aged 75 or older	67.6	74.3	−6.7	3.8	5.4	−1.6
Education of householder						
No high school diploma	74.4	76.9	−2.5	5.9	6.0	−0.1
High school diploma	84.8	87.5	−2.7	8.4	8.7	−0.3
Some college	88.9	88.5	0.4	10.2	10.6	−0.4
College degree	91.8	91.8	0.0	18.1	18.8	−0.7
Race and Hispanic origin of householder						
Non-Hispanic white	90.0	90.3	−0.3	13.8	14.3	−0.5
Nonwhite or Hispanic	79.5	82.3	−2.8	7.5	7.8	−0.3
Region						
Northeast	76.4	76.3	0.1	8.3	8.5	−0.2
Midwest	87.8	90.4	−2.6	12.9	12.9	0.0
South	89.7	90.4	−0.7	11.5	12.1	−0.6
West	89.7	90.9	−1.2	14.7	15.6	−0.9
Housing status						
Owner	92.3	94.2	−1.9	15.3	15.9	−0.6
Renter or other	74.8	74.2	0.6	4.5	4.7	−0.2

Source: Federal Reserve Board, Surveying the Aftermath of the Storm: Changes in Family Finances from 2007 to 2009, Jesse Bricker, Brian Bucks, Arthur Kennickell, Traci Mach, and Kevin Moore, Finance and Economics Discussion Series, 2011-17, Appendix tables, Internet site http://www.federalreserve.gov/pubs/oss/oss2/2009p/scf2009phome.html; calculations by New Strategist

Table 11.13 Median Value of Primary Residence, Other Residential Property, and Nonresidential Property, 2007 and 2009

(median value of primary residence, other residential property, and nonresidential property for households owning asset, by selected characteristics of households, 2007 and 2009; percent change, 2007–09; in 2009 dollars)

	primary residence			other residential property			nonresidential property		
	2009	2007	percent change	2009	2007	percent change	2009	2007	percent change
Total households	$176,000	$207,100	–15.0	$150,000	$141,700	5.9	$69,000	$78,800	–12.4
Household income percentile									
Below 20 percent	90,000	103,600	–13.1	75,800	62,100	22.1	30,000	39,400	–23.9
20 to 39.9 percent	103,300	124,300	–16.9	45,000	62,100	–27.5	40,000	77,700	–48.5
40 to 59.9 percent	145,000	165,700	–12.5	95,100	77,700	22.4	50,000	41,400	20.8
60 to 79.9 percent	190,000	220,000	–13.6	137,400	134,600	2.1	90,000	82,800	8.7
80 to 89.9 percent	262,000	310,700	–15.7	225,000	186,400	20.7	60,000	82,800	–27.5
90 percent or higher	450,000	517,800	–13.1	350,000	346,900	0.9	200,000	181,200	10.4
Age of householder									
Under age 35	165,000	186,400	–11.5	100,000	62,100	61.0	30,000	51,800	–42.1
Aged 35 to 44	180,000	212,300	–15.2	155,700	155,300	0.3	28,600	59,000	–51.5
Aged 45 to 54	200,000	238,200	–16.0	176,000	163,800	7.4	90,000	79,000	13.9
Aged 55 to 64	185,000	207,100	–10.7	150,000	155,300	–3.4	100,000	103,600	–3.5
Aged 65 to 74	155,000	191,600	–19.1	149,500	139,800	6.9	100,000	103,600	–3.5
Aged 75 or older	130,000	155,300	–16.3	160,000	103,600	54.4	60,000	103,600	–42.1
Education of householder									
No high school diploma	100,000	129,400	–22.7	60,000	63,700	–5.8	45,000	77,700	–42.1
High school diploma	135,000	155,300	–13.1	100,000	77,700	28.7	50,000	51,800	–3.5
Some college	160,000	196,800	–18.7	136,100	103,600	31.4	60,000	53,900	11.3
College degree	250,000	284,800	–12.2	200,000	207,100	–3.4	109,100	99,400	9.8
Race and Hispanic origin of householder									
Non-Hispanic white	180,000	207,100	–13.1	150,000	141,400	6.1	80,000	79,000	1.3
Nonwhite or Hispanic	150,000	186,400	–19.5	130,000	170,900	–23.9	45,000	67,300	–33.1
Region									
Northeast	250,000	290,000	–13.8	200,000	207,100	–3.4	100,000	103,800	–3.7
Midwest	145,000	160,500	–9.7	110,000	116,000	–5.2	60,000	61,000	–1.6
South	150,000	165,700	–9.5	150,000	133,600	12.3	61,000	77,700	–21.5
West	230,000	293,100	–21.5	175,000	196,800	–11.1	103,600	93,200	11.2
Housing status									
Owner	180,000	207,100	–13.1	160,000	155,300	3.0	80,000	82,800	–3.4
Renter or other	152,000	0	–	50,000	103,600	–51.7	20,000	51,800	–61.4

Note: Renters were classified in the 2007 survey and when reinterviewed in 2009 some had bought a home and had equity in a primary residence. "–" means not applicable
Source: Federal Reserve Board, Surveying the Aftermath of the Storm: Changes in Family Finances from 2007 to 2009, Jesse Bricker, Brian Bucks, Arthur Kennickell, Traci Mach, and Kevin Moore, Finance and Economics Discussion Series, 2011-17, Appendix tables, Internet site http://www.federalreserve.gov/pubs/oss/oss2/2009p/scf2009phome.html; calculations by New Strategist

Table 11.14 Median Value of Vehicles and Business Equity, 2007 and 2009

(median value of vehicles and business equity for households owning asset, by selected characteristics of house-holds, 2007 and 2009; percent change, 2007–09; in 2009 dollars)

	vehicles			business equity		
	2009	2007	percent change	2009	2007	percent change
Total households	**$12,000**	**$16,200**	**−25.9%**	**$94,500**	**$103,600**	**−8.8%**
Household income percentile						
Below 20 percent	4,200	5,800	−27.6	35,000	93,200	−62.4
20 to 39.9 percent	8,000	10,500	−23.8	50,000	46,600	7.3
40 to 59.9 percent	12,000	15,100	−20.5	46,700	51,800	−9.8
60 to 79.9 percent	17,000	21,400	−20.6	60,000	82,600	−27.4
80 to 89.9 percent	25,000	26,700	−6.4	85,000	103,600	−18.0
90 percent or higher	30,000	34,900	−14.0	259,900	517,800	−49.8
Age of householder						
Under age 35	10,500	14,500	−27.6	41,300	46,600	−11.4
Aged 35 to 44	15,000	18,100	−17.1	70,000	98,700	−29.1
Aged 45 to 54	15,000	18,600	−19.4	80,000	103,600	−22.8
Aged 55 to 64	15,000	17,800	−15.7	150,000	152,500	−1.6
Aged 65 to 74	12,000	15,200	−21.1	500,000	517,800	−3.4
Aged 75 or older	7,900	9,700	−18.6	250,000	258,900	−3.4
Education of householder						
No high school diploma	6,000	10,500	−42.9	50,000	68,300	−26.8
High school diploma	11,000	13,700	−19.7	80,000	94,600	−15.4
Some college	11,000	15,100	−27.2	50,000	93,200	−46.4
College degree	17,000	20,600	−17.5	120,000	124,300	−3.5
Race and Hispanic origin of householder						
Non-Hispanic white	15,000	17,900	−16.2	100,000	108,700	−8.0
Nonwhite or Hispanic	9,000	12,400	−27.4	46,700	73,300	−36.3
Region						
Northeast	12,000	14,800	−18.9	125,000	120,800	3.5
Midwest	12,000	15,200	−21.1	100,000	103,600	−3.5
South	12,000	16,400	−26.8	75,000	103,600	−27.6
West	15,000	18,000	−16.7	87,200	103,600	−15.8
Housing status						
Owner	15,000	19,100	−21.5	100,000	109,300	−8.5
Renter or other	7,000	9,000	−22.2	50,000	61,100	−18.2

Source: Federal Reserve Board, Surveying the Aftermath of the Storm: Changes in Family Finances from 2007 to 2009, Jesse Bricker, Brian Bucks, Arthur Kennickell, Traci Mach, and Kevin Moore, Finance and Economics Discussion Series, 2011-17, Appendix tables, Internet site http://www.federalreserve.gov/pubs/oss/oss2/2009p/scf2009phome.html; calculations by New Strategist

Most Households Are in Debt

Among households with debt, the amount owed increased between 2007 and 2009.

Seventy-eight percent of households have debt, owing a median of $75,600 in 2009. The median amount of debt owed by the average debtor household increased by 7.5 percent between 2007 and 2009, after adjusting for inflation. The percentage of households in debt fell slightly, however.

Householders aged 35 to 54 are most likely to be in debt, with 87 to 88 percent owing money. Debt declines with age, falling to a low of 35 percent among householders aged 75 or older.

Four types of debt are most common—debt secured by the primary residence (mortgages), held by 47 percent of households; credit card debt (43 percent); vehicle loans (34 percent); and education loans (18 percent). Mortgages account for the largest share of debt. The median amount owed by the average homeowner for the primary residence stood at $113,500 in 2009. Education loans are second in size, the average household with this type of debt owing a median of $15,000—more than the $12,400 owed by (the more numerous) households with vehicle loans. Credit card debt is tiny by comparison, the average household with a credit card balance owing only $3,300.

■ Americans are attempting to pay down their debts because of the Great Recession, reducing consumer demand.

Home-secured debt accounts for the largest amount owed

(median amount of debt for debtors, for the four most common types of debt, 2009)

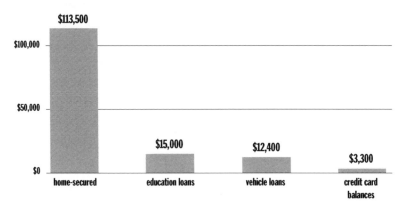

Table 11.15 Debt of Households, 2007 and 2009

(percentage of households with debts and median amount of debt for debtors, by selected characteristics of households, 2007 and 2009; percentage point change in households with debt and percent change in amount of debt, 2007–09; in 2009 dollars)

	percent with debt			median amount of debt		
	2009	2007	percentage point change	2009	2007	percent change
Total households	77.5%	79.7%	−2.2	$75,600	$70,300	7.5%
Household income percentile						
Below 20 percent	55.8	56.3	−0.5	10,000	9,000	11.1
20 to 39.9 percent	73.1	75.1	−2.0	23,000	19,200	19.8
40 to 59.9 percent	84.0	86.0	−2.0	69,300	63,900	8.5
60 to 79.9 percent	88.2	92.2	−4.0	130,000	122,200	6.4
80 to 89.9 percent	89.2	91.2	−2.0	192,500	188,700	2.0
90 percent or higher	84.4	87.5	−3.1	260,000	245,400	5.9
Age of householder						
Under age 35	84.6	85.4	−0.8	51,000	37,800	34.9
Aged 35 to 44	87.7	87.3	0.4	109,500	113,700	−3.7
Aged 45 to 54	86.6	88.1	−1.5	100,200	103,500	−3.2
Aged 55 to 64	77.7	83.4	−5.7	62,000	64,300	−3.6
Aged 65 to 74	62.1	68.5	−6.4	48,100	41,800	15.1
Aged 75 or older	35.0	36.2	−1.2	8,200	20,000	−59.0
Education of householder						
No high school diploma	59.9	60.4	−0.5	20,000	20,700	−3.4
High school diploma	75.8	77.7	−1.9	42,300	41,400	2.2
Some college	84.3	83.1	1.2	61,000	60,200	1.3
College degree	81.5	86.2	−4.7	141,300	131,500	7.5
Race and Hispanic origin of householder						
Non-Hispanic white	76.5	79.7	−3.2	89,000	82,800	7.5
Nonwhite or Hispanic	79.7	79.6	0.1	44,000	45,300	−2.9
Region						
Northeast	72.7	75.6	−2.9	76,800	64,500	19.1
Midwest	76.5	79.7	−3.2	65,000	65,300	−0.5
South	79.4	78.8	0.6	64,800	65,100	−0.5
West	79.2	84.5	−5.3	106,500	100,500	6.0
Housing status						
Owner	81.7	84.3	−2.6	111,000	117,000	−5.1
Renter or other	68.1	69.3	−1.2	13,000	9,400	38.3

Source: Federal Reserve Board, Surveying the Aftermath of the Storm: Changes in Family Finances from 2007 to 2009, Jesse Bricker, Brian Bucks, Arthur Kennickell, Traci Mach, and Kevin Moore, Finance and Economics Discussion Series, 2011-17, Appendix tables, Internet site http://www.federalreserve.gov/pubs/oss/oss2/2009p/scf2009phome.html; calculations by New Strategist

Table 11.16 Percent of Households with Residential Debt, 2007 and 2009

(percentage of households with residential debt by selected characteristics, 2007 and 2009; percentage point change, 2007–09)

	secured by residential property								
	secured by primary residence			home equity line of credit			other residential debt		
	2009	2007	percentage point change	2009	2007	percentage point change	2009	2007	percentage point change
Total households	46.6%	47.8%	−1.2	10.5%	8.7%	1.8	5.1%	5.7%	−0.6
Household income percentile									
Below 20 percent	12.6	14.3	−1.7	2.5	1.8	0.7	1.1	1.5	−0.4
20 to 39.9 percent	28.5	28.0	0.5	6.7	6.5	0.2	2.1	2.6	−0.5
40 to 59.9 percent	53.2	52.7	0.5	8.7	7.3	1.4	2.9	2.5	0.4
60 to 79.9 percent	67.4	69.9	−2.5	15.4	10.8	4.6	5.3	7.6	−2.3
80 to 89.9 percent	75.9	77.5	−1.6	16.2	16.1	0.1	7.7	7.3	0.4
90 percent or higher	68.9	73.1	−4.2	22.6	19.0	3.6	20.1	20.9	−0.8
Age of householder									
Under age 35	39.8	37.4	2.4	4.3	3.7	0.6	3.3	3.2	0.1
Aged 35 to 44	60.0	60.0	0.0	10.2	8.5	1.7	6.0	7.0	−1.0
Aged 45 to 54	62.2	64.3	−2.1	14.0	12.3	1.7	6.7	7.7	−1.0
Aged 55 to 64	46.8	51.9	−5.1	17.1	12.8	4.3	6.6	8.3	−1.7
Aged 65 to 74	34.9	37.4	−2.5	11.9	10.3	1.6	4.7	4.3	0.4
Aged 75 or older	11.5	13.4	−1.9	4.3	3.8	0.5	0.9	0.6	0.3
Education of householder									
No high school diploma	26.3	27.3	−1.0	4.2	3.5	0.7	1.4	2.5	−1.1
High school diploma	41.1	43.8	−2.7	8.8	7.8	1.0	3.1	3.2	−0.1
Some college	45.0	44.8	0.2	11.1	8.1	3.0	4.4	6.4	−2.0
College degree	59.3	60.0	−0.7	13.8	11.7	2.1	8.4	8.5	−0.1
Race and Hispanic origin of householder									
Non-Hispanic white	49.7	51.2	−1.5	12.2	10.2	2.0	5.5	6.0	−0.5
Nonwhite or Hispanic	39.3	39.9	−0.6	6.4	5.4	1.0	3.9	4.8	−0.9
Region									
Northeast	44.0	46.1	−2.1	12.6	10.8	1.8	3.5	5.0	−1.5
Midwest	47.9	48.9	−1.0	12.2	9.3	2.9	4.7	5.8	−1.1
South	46.4	47.4	−1.0	7.6	5.9	1.7	5.9	5.1	0.8
West	47.7	49.0	−1.3	11.7	11.2	0.5	5.4	7.0	−1.6
Housing status									
Owner	63.0	69.4	−6.4	15.1	12.7	2.4	6.7	6.8	−0.1
Renter or other	10.2	0.0	10.2	0.3	0.0	0.3	1.5	3.2	−1.7

Note: Renters were classified in the 2007 survey and when reinterviewed in 2009 some had bought a home and had residential debt.
Source: Federal Reserve Board, Surveying the Aftermath of the Storm: Changes in Family Finances from 2007 to 2009, Jesse Bricker, Brian Bucks, Arthur Kennickell, Traci Mach, and Kevin Moore, Finance and Economics Discussion Series, 2011-17, Internet site http://www.federalreserve.gov/pubs/oss/oss2/2009p/scf2009phome.html; calculations by New Strategist

Table 11.17 Percent of Households with Credit Card Debt, Vehicle Loans, and Education Loans, 2007 and 2009

(percentage of households with credit card, vehicle, and education debt by selected characteristics, 2007 and 2009; percentage point change, 2007–09)

	credit card balances			vehicle loans			education loans		
	2009	2007	percentage point change	2009	2007	percentage point change	2009	2007	percentage point change
Total households	**43.2%**	**47.8%**	**−4.6**	**33.9%**	**36.0%**	**−2.1**	**17.7%**	**16.3%**	**1.4**
Household income percentile									
Below 20 percent	28.4	28.3	0.1	14.1	14.5	−0.4	12.3	12.6	−0.3
20 to 39.9 percent	38.2	42.1	−3.9	32.0	30.9	1.1	16.2	13.7	2.5
40 to 59.9 percent	50.7	56.5	−5.8	40.2	41.2	−1.0	20.2	17.3	2.9
60 to 79.9 percent	56.9	63.3	−6.4	46.1	51.8	−5.7	22.2	20.1	2.1
80 to 89.9 percent	51.9	58.4	−6.5	43.4	48.7	−5.3	23.2	22.3	0.9
90 percent or higher	32.4	40.1	−7.7	31.9	36.6	−4.7	12.5	13.3	−0.8
Age of householder									
Under age 35	42.8	50.6	−7.8	43.1	46.0	−2.9	36.8	35.7	1.1
Aged 35 to 44	49.6	52.6	−3.0	44.7	44.1	0.6	19.7	15.7	4.0
Aged 45 to 54	50.5	54.1	−3.6	35.5	38.3	−2.8	18.0	14.8	3.2
Aged 55 to 64	44.6	50.4	−5.8	30.8	35.5	−4.7	9.9	11.3	−1.4
Aged 65 to 74	35.0	38.7	−3.7	21.3	21.9	−0.6	1.9	1.9	0.0
Aged 75 or older	20.2	21.8	−1.6	5.5	7.2	−1.7	0.0	0.5	−0.5
Education of householder									
No high school diploma	29.0	29.9	−0.9	19.1	25.1	−6.0	6.0	6.3	−0.3
High school diploma	45.4	47.9	−2.5	36.5	36.2	0.3	12.1	9.5	2.6
Some college	48.2	52.8	−4.6	38.6	39.7	−1.1	21.4	19.2	2.2
College degree	43.5	51.2	−7.7	34.3	37.8	−3.5	24.8	24.2	0.6
Race and Hispanic origin of householder									
Non-Hispanic white	42.2	46.7	−4.5	34.7	36.7	−2.0	15.9	15.2	0.7
Nonwhite or Hispanic	45.5	50.3	−4.8	32.1	34.6	−2.5	21.9	18.7	3.2
Region									
Northeast	36.1	45.7	−9.6	26.1	27.1	−1.0	18.6	18.7	−0.1
Midwest	41.1	46.2	−5.1	31.8	36.6	−4.8	19.6	15.5	4.1
South	43.3	45.8	−2.5	38.7	38.3	0.4	15.9	15.1	0.8
West	51.1	54.5	−3.4	34.6	39.2	−4.6	18.1	17.0	1.1
Housing status									
Owner	46.1	51.2	−5.1	36.2	38.5	−2.3	14.9	13.5	1.4
Renter or other	36.6	40.1	−3.5	28.9	30.7	−1.8	24.0	22.4	1.6

Source: Federal Reserve Board, Surveying the Aftermath of the Storm: Changes in Family Finances from 2007 to 2009, Jesse Bricker, Brian Bucks, Arthur Kennickell, Traci Mach, and Kevin Moore, Finance and Economics Discussion Series, 2011-17, Appendix tables, Internet site http://www.federalreserve.gov/pubs/oss/oss2/2009p/scf2009phome.html; calculations by New Strategist

Table 11.18 Median Value of Residential Debt Owed by Households, 2007 and 2009

(median value of residential debt owed by households with debt, by selected characteristics of households, 2007 and 2009; percent change, 2007–09; in 2009 dollars)

	secured by residential property								
	secured by primary residence			home equity line of credit			other residential debt		
	2009	2007	percent change	2009	2007	percent change	2009	2007	percent change
Total households	**$113,500**	**$113,900**	**–0.4**	**$21,500**	**$22,800**	**–5.7**	**$130,000**	**$98,400**	**32.1**
Household income percentile									
Below 20 percent	47,900	35,300	35.7	22,000	–	–	–	63,700	–
20 to 39.9 percent	68,700	62,100	10.6	14,500	15,500	–6.5	43,000	60,800	–29.3
40 to 59.9 percent	91,500	92,700	–1.3	18,000	16,100	11.8	44,000	62,100	–29.1
60 to 79.9 percent	128,000	120,100	6.6	20,000	21,500	–7.0	70,000	87,000	–19.5
80 to 89.9 percent	169,200	169,800	–0.4	30,000	35,200	–14.8	150,000	129,200	16.1
90 percent or higher	215,000	207,100	3.8	51,000	49,700	2.6	190,000	152,800	24.3
Age of householder									
Under age 35	144,600	140,100	3.2	20,000	20,300	–1.5	118,000	80,800	46.0
Aged 35 to 44	127,800	128,300	–0.4	20,000	24,900	–19.7	150,000	110,600	35.6
Aged 45 to 54	111,600	113,900	–2.0	30,000	25,900	15.8	115,000	86,000	33.7
Aged 55 to 64	95,000	93,200	1.9	20,000	21,900	–8.7	155,000	110,900	39.8
Aged 65 to 74	80,000	81,800	–2.2	28,000	15,500	80.6	115,000	116,000	–0.9
Aged 75 or older	49,000	33,900	44.5	13,000	25,900	–49.8	23,000	51,800	–55.6
Education of householder									
No high school diploma	66,000	51,800	27.4	20,000	13,500	48.1	–	62,100	–
High school diploma	87,000	87,000	0.0	18,500	18,300	1.1	75,000	77,700	–3.5
Some college	113,100	103,700	9.1	25,000	20,700	20.8	118,000	82,800	42.5
College degree	140,500	145,000	–3.1	26,400	31,100	–15.1	150,000	116,000	29.3
Race and Hispanic origin of householder									
Non-Hispanic white	112,000	112,900	–0.8	20,000	20,700	–3.4	130,000	94,200	38.0
Nonwhite or Hispanic	120,000	119,100	0.8	30,000	25,900	15.8	150,000	103,600	44.8
Region									
Northeast	122,500	106,700	14.8	26,000	25,900	0.4	160,000	104,600	53.0
Midwest	96,000	100,500	–4.5	18,000	18,600	–3.2	100,000	86,000	16.3
South	100,100	104,400	–4.1	20,800	20,700	0.5	92,400	82,800	11.6
West	159,100	152,200	4.5	40,000	38,300	4.4	200,000	126,900	57.6
Housing status									
Owner	110,400	113,900	–3.1	21,000	22,800	–7.9	149,100	103,600	43.9
Renter or other	147,000	0	–	–	–	–	13,400	82,800	–83.8

Note: Renters were classified in the 2007 survey and when reinterviewed in 2009 some had bought a home and had debt secured by their primary residence. "–" means sample is too small to make a reliable estimate or not applicable.
Source: Federal Reserve Board, Surveying the Aftermath of the Storm: Changes in Family Finances from 2007 to 2009, Jesse Bricker, Brian Bucks, Arthur Kennickell, Traci Mach, and Kevin Moore, Finance and Economics Discussion Series, 2011-17, Internet site http://www.federalreserve.gov/pubs/oss/oss2/2009p/scf2009phome.html; calculations by New Strategist

Table 11.19 Median Amount of Credit Card Debt, Vehicle Loans, and Education Loans Owed by Households, 2007 and 2009

(median amount of credit card, vehicle, and education debt owed by households with debt, by selected characteristics of households, 2007 and 2009; percent change, 2007–09; in 2009 dollars)

	credit card balances			vehicle loans			education loans		
	2009	2007	percent change	2009	2007	percent change	2009	2007	percent change
Total households	$3,300	$3,100	6.5%	$12,400	$11,200	10.7%	$15,000	$12,400	21.0%
Household income percentile									
Below 20 percent	1,100	1,000	10.0	8,000	5,200	53.8	13,800	7,200	91.7
20 to 39.9 percent	2,100	1,800	16.7	9,000	9,500	–5.3	12,000	11,400	5.3
40 to 59.9 percent	3,000	2,600	15.4	12,000	11,500	4.3	12,100	11,100	9.0
60 to 79.9 percent	4,700	4,000	17.5	14,000	11,900	17.6	20,000	17,600	13.6
80 to 89.9 percent	7,500	6,200	21.0	17,000	14,500	17.2	19,000	11,200	69.6
90 percent or higher	9,300	7,200	29.2	18,000	17,700	1.7	17,200	16,700	3.0
Age of householder									
Under age 35	3,000	1,900	57.9	12,200	11,300	8.0	15,000	14,500	3.4
Aged 35 to 44	3,000	3,600	–16.7	13,000	12,300	5.7	16,000	12,400	29.0
Aged 45 to 54	4,000	3,700	8.1	13,000	10,900	19.3	15,000	10,700	40.2
Aged 55 to 64	4,500	4,100	9.8	12,000	9,600	25.0	12,000	7,300	64.4
Aged 65 to 74	2,900	3,200	–9.4	10,000	12,500	–20.0	–	–	–
Aged 75 or older	2,000	800	150.0	9,500	7,600	25.0	–	–	–
Education of householder									
No high school diploma	1,500	1,900	–21.1	11,000	11,400	–3.5	6,000	6,200	–3.2
High school diploma	3,000	2,400	25.0	11,000	10,600	3.8	10,000	6,700	49.3
Some college	3,000	2,900	3.4	12,000	10,500	14.3	13,000	9,900	31.3
College degree	5,500	4,100	34.1	14,300	12,100	18.2	20,300	19,200	5.7
Race and Hispanic origin of householder									
Non-Hispanic white	4,300	3,500	22.9	12,400	11,400	8.8	16,000	13,500	18.5
Nonwhite or Hispanic	2,000	2,100	–4.8	12,000	10,500	14.3	13,800	9,500	45.3
Region									
Northeast	2,700	2,600	3.8	12,000	9,700	23.7	15,000	13,100	14.5
Midwest	3,000	3,100	–3.2	10,000	9,700	3.1	16,000	13,500	18.5
South	4,000	3,100	29.0	13,000	11,500	13.0	16,000	11,400	40.4
West	3,600	3,100	16.1	13,000	12,300	5.7	15,000	13,500	11.1
Housing status									
Owner	4,000	3,800	5.3	13,000	11,800	10.2	17,300	15,300	13.1
Renter or other	1,900	1,300	46.2	9,500	9,300	2.2	12,000	10,400	15.4

Note: "–" means sample is too small to make a reliable estimate.
Source: Federal Reserve Board, Surveying the Aftermath of the Storm: Changes in Family Finances from 2007 to 2009, Jesse Bricker, Brian Bucks, Arthur Kennickell, Traci Mach, and Kevin Moore, Finance and Economics Discussion Series, 2011-17, Appendix tables, Internet site http://www.federalreserve.gov/pubs/oss/oss2/2009p/scf2009phome.html; calculations by New Strategist

Many Workers Do Not Have a Retirement Plan

Fewer than half of service workers have access to a retirement plan through work.

Retirement benefits have changed over the past few decades as the number of companies that offer defined-benefit pension plans has declined. Among workers with a retirement plan in 2009, only 39 percent said that a defined-benefit pension was their primary plan, down from 57 percent in 1988. (This figure was higher than the 31 percent of 2006 largely because of changes in methodology, according to the Employee Benefit Research Institute.) The 60 percent majority of workers with a plan in 2009 reported that their primary type of plan was defined-contribution (such as a 401k), up from 26 percent in 1988.

Sixty-nine percent of the nation's workers have access to a retirement plan at work, according to the Bureau of Labor Statistics' Employee Benefits Survey. The percentage of workers with access to a retirement plan varies widely from a low of 49 percent among service workers to a high of 86 percent among management and business workers. Only 31 percent of the lowest-paid workers have access to a retirement plan compared with 90 percent of the highest paid workers. Unionized workers are more likely to have a retirement plan (92 percent) than those not in unions (65 percent). Most teachers, protective service workers, and union workers have defined-benefit retirement plans.

■ The Great Recession depleted savings in defined-contribution retirement plans and raises the question of whether these plans will be adequate to support the nation's retirees.

Highly paid workers are more likely to have access to a retirement plan at work

(percent of workers with access to a retirement plan, by average wage percentile, 2010)

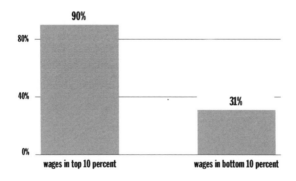

Table 11.20 Workers with a Retirement Plan by Type, 1988 to 2009

(percent distribution of nonagricultural wage and salary workers aged 16 or older who participate in a retirement plan at work, by type of plan considered primary, selected years, 1988 to 2009)

	total workers with a retirement plan	primary type of plan	
		defined benefit	defined contribution
2009	100.0%	39.1%	60.0%
2006	100.0	30.9	67.1
2003	100.0	40.5	57.7
1998	100.0	46.3	51.5
1993	100.0	38.2	49.8
1988	100.0	56.7	25.8

Note: Figures do not sum to 100 because "other/don't know" is not shown.
Source: Employee Benefit Research Institute, Retirement Plan Participation: Survey of Income and Program Participation (SIPP) Data, 2009, Notes, November 2010, Internet site http://www.ebri.org/publications/notes/index .cfm?fa=notesDisp&content_id=4702

Table 11.21 Workers with Retirement Benefits, 2010

(percent of workers with access to and who participate in a retirement plan, and percent with access who participate (take-up rate), by selected characteristics, 2010)

	all retirement benefits			defined benefit			defined contribution		
	access	participation	take-up rate	access	participation	take-up rate	access	participation	take-up rate
Total workers	**69%**	**55%**	**80%**	**31%**	**28%**	**92%**	**54%**	**37%**	**69%**
Worker characteristics									
Management, business, and financial	86	78	90	43	40	93	74	59	81
Professional and related	82	73	88	47	44	93	56	42	74
Teachers	86	81	95	73	69	94	31	20	64
Registered nurses	82	69	85	38	35	94	66	48	72
Service	49	32	66	19	18	94	36	18	50
Protective service	75	63	84	55	51	94	38	20	53
Sales and office	71	56	78	25	22	86	62	44	71
Natural resources, construction, maintenance	67	55	81	32	31	97	54	38	70
Production, transportation, and material moving	67	52	78	28	26	94	54	37	68
Full time	78	65	84	36	34	94	61	45	72
Part time	39	23	58	14	11	80	30	14	47
Union	92	87	94	82	78	96	41	29	71
Nonunion	65	49	77	21	19	90	57	39	69
Average wage within the following percentiles									
Lowest 10 percent	31	12	39	5	3	61	28	9	34
Lowest 25 percent	43	24	56	10	8	77	37	18	49
Second 25 percent	70	54	78	26	23	91	57	38	67
Third 25 percent	80	68	86	37	35	94	62	46	75
Highest 25 percent	88	81	92	54	51	95	64	51	79
Highest 10 percent	90	83	92	54	50	94	67	54	80

Note: "Total workers" includes all workers in the private, nonfarm economy except private household workers and includes all workers in the public sector except those working for the federal government.
Source: Bureau of Labor Statistics, Employee Benefits Survey, Internet site http://www.bls.gov/ncs/ebs/benefits/2010/ownership_civilian.htm

Retirement Worries Are Growing

A record share of workers lack confidence in having enough money for a comfortable retirement.

Only 13 percent of workers are "very confident" in their ability to afford a comfortable retirement, according to the 2011 Retirement Confidence Survey. The 13 percent figure is less than half of the 27 percent who felt very confident in 2007—just before the start of the Great Recession.

Reality may be dawning on many workers. Since 2007, the expected age of retirement has climbed sharply. The percentage of workers expecting to retire at age 65 or older increased from 51 to 70 percent between 2000 and 2011. At the same time, the percentage expecting to retire before age 65 fell from 44 to 23 percent.

■ Only 22 percent of workers are very confident that they are doing a good job of saving for retirement, down from 30 percent who felt that way in 2000.

Most workers are not planning on an early retirement

(percent of workers who expect to retire at age 65 or older, 2000 and 2011)

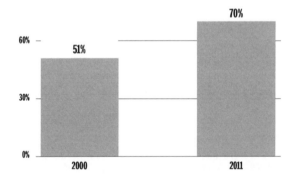

Table 11.22 Retirement Outlook, 2000 to 2011

(responses of workers aged 25 or older to selected questions about retirement, 2000 to 2011; percentage point change, 2000–07 and 2007–11)

	2011	2007	2000	percentage point change 2000–07	2007–11
Confidence in having enough money to live comfortably in retirement:					
Very confident	13%	27%	26%	1	–14
Somewhat confident	36	43	47	–4	–7
Not too confident	23	19	18	1	4
Not at all confident	27	10	8	2	17
Confident that they are doing a good job of preparing financially for retirement					
Very confident	22	26	30	–4	–4
Somewhat confident	41	45	49	–4	–4
Not too confident	19	15	13	2	4
Not at all confident	17	13	8	5	4
Confident that the Social Security system will continue to provide benefits of at least equal value to the benefits received by retirees today					
Very confident	5	7	7	0	–2
Somewhat confident	24	24	21	3	0
Not too confident	31	34	39	–5	–3
Not at all confident	39	34	32	2	5
Confident that the Medicare system will continue to provide benefits of at least equal value to the benefits received by retirees today:					
Very confident	5	6	6	0	–1
Somewhat confident	25	30	29	1	–5
Not too confident	36	33	38	–5	3
Not at all confident	34	28	26	2	6
Expected age of retirement					
Before age 60	7	17	22	–5	–10
Aged 60 to 64	16	21	22	–1	–5
Age 65	26	27	28	–1	–1
Aged 66 or older	36	24	19	5	12
Never retire	8	6	4	2	2

Note: Figures may not sum to total because "don't know/refused" is not shown.
Source: Employee Benefit Research Institute, Retirement Confidence Surveys, Internet site http://www.ebri.org/surveys/rcs/

Glossary

adjusted for inflation Income or a change in income that has been adjusted for the rise in the cost of living, or the consumer price index (CPI-U-RS).

American Community Survey The ACS is an on-going nationwide survey of 250,000 households per month, providing detailed demographic data at the community level. Designed to replace the census long-form questionnaire, the ACS includes more than 60 questions that formerly appeared on the long form, such as language spoken at home, income, and education. ACS data are available for areas as small as census tracts.

American Housing Survey The AHS collects national and metropolitan-level data on the nation's housing, including apartments, single-family homes, and mobile homes. The nationally representative survey, with a sample of 60,000 homes, is conducted by the Census Bureau for the Department of Housing and Urban Development every other year.

American Indians Includes Alaska Natives (Eskimos and Aleuts) unless those groups are shown separately.

American Time Use Survey Under contract with the Bureau of Labor Statistics, the Census Bureau collects ATUS information, revealing how people spend their time. The ATUS sample is drawn from U.S. households completing their final month of interviews for the Current Population Survey. One individual from each selected household is chosen to participate in ATUS. Respondents are interviewed by telephone about their time use during the previous 24 hours. About 40,000 households are included in the sample each year.

Asian Includes Native Hawaiians and other Pacific Islanders unless those groups are shown separately.

average hours per day In the time use tables, the average number of hours spent in a 24-hour day (between 4 a.m. on the diary day and 4 a.m. on the interview day) doing a specified activity. Estimates are adjusted for variability in response rates across days of the week. Average hours per day are shown in decimals. To convert decimal portions of an hour into minutes, multiply 60 by the decimal. For example, if the average is 1.2 hours, multiply 60 by 0.2 to get 12 minutes, so the average is 1 hour and 12 minutes. If the average is 0.05 hours, multiply 60 by .05 to get 3 minutes. If the average is 5.36 hours, multiply 60 by 0.36 to get 21.6, so the average is 5 hours and about 22 minutes.

baby boom U.S. residents born between 1946 and 1964.

baby bust U.S. residents born between 1965 and 1976, also known as Generation X.

Behavioral Risk Factor Surveillance System The BRFSS is a collaborative project of the Centers for Disease Control and Prevention and U.S. states and territories. It is an ongoing data collection program designed to measure behavioral risk factors in the adult population aged 18 or older. All 50 states, three territories, and the District of Columbia take part in the survey, making the BRFSS the primary source of information on the health-related behaviors of Americans.

black A racial category that includes those who identified themselves as "black" or "African American."

Consumer Expenditure Survey The CEX is an ongoing study of the day-to-day spending of American households administered by the Bureau of Labor Statistics. The CEX includes an interview survey and a diary survey. The average spending figures shown are the integrated data from both the diary and interview components of the survey. Two separate, nationally representative samples are used for the interview and diary surveys. For the interview survey, about 7,500 consumer units are interviewed on a rotating panel basis each quarter for five consecutive quarters. For the diary survey, 7,500 consumer units keep weekly diaries of spending for two consecutive weeks.

consumer unit *(on spending tables only)* For convenience, the term consumer unit and household are used interchangeably in the Spending chapter of this book, although consumer units are somewhat different from the Census Bureau's households. Consumer units are all related members of a household, or financially independent members of a household. A household may include more than one consumer unit.

Current Population Survey The CPS is a nationally representative survey of the civilian noninstitutional population aged 15 or older. It is taken monthly by the Census Bureau for the Bureau of Labor Statistics, collecting information from more than 50,000 households on employment and unemployment. In March of each year, the survey includes the Annual Social and Economic Supplement (formerly called the Annual Demographic Survey), which is the source of most national data on the characteristics of Americans, such as educational attainment, living arrangements, and incomes.

disability The National Health Interview Survey estimates the number of people aged 18 or older who have difficulty in physical functioning, probing whether respondents could perform nine activities by themselves without using special equipment. The categories are walking a quarter mile; standing for two hours; sitting for two hours; walking up ten steps without resting; stooping, bending, kneeling; reaching over one's head; grasping or handling small objects; carrying a ten-pound object; and pushing/pulling a large object. Adults who reported that any of these activities was very difficult or they could not do it at all were defined as having physical difficulties.

dual-earner couple A married couple in which both the husband and wife are in the labor force.

earnings A type of income, it is the amount of money a person receives from his or her job. *See also* Income.

employed All civilians who did any work as a paid employee or farmer/self-employed worker, or who worked 15 hours or more as an unpaid farm worker or in a family-owned business, during the reference period. All those who have jobs but who are temporarily absent from their jobs due to illness, bad weather, vacation, labor management dispute, or personal reasons are considered employed.

expenditure The transaction cost including excise and sales taxes of goods and services acquired during the survey period. The full cost of each purchase is recorded even though full payment may not have been made at the date of purchase. Average expenditure figures may be artificially low for infrequently purchased items such as cars because figures are calculated using all consumer units within a demographic segment rather than just purchasers. Expenditure estimates include money spent on gifts for others.

family A group of two or more people (one of whom is the householder) related by birth, marriage, or adoption and living in the same household.

family household A household maintained by a householder who lives with one or more people related to him or her by blood, marriage, or adoption.

female/male householder A woman or man who maintains a household without a spouse present. May head family or nonfamily households.

foreign-born population People who are not U.S. citizens at birth.

full-time employment Thirty-five or more hours of work per week during a majority of the weeks worked.

full-time, year-round Fifty or more weeks of full-time employment during the previous calendar year.

General Social Survey The GSS is a biennial survey of the attitudes of Americans taken by the University of Chicago's National Opinion Research Center. NORC conducts the GSS through face-to-face interviews with an independently drawn, representative sample of 1,500 to 3,000 noninstitutionalized people aged 18 or older who live in the United States.

generation X U.S. residents born between 1965 and 1976, also known as the baby-bust generation.

Hispanic Because Hispanic is an ethnic origin rather than a race, Hispanics may be of any race. While most Hispanics are white, there are black, Asian, American Indian, and even Native Hawaiian Hispanics.

household All the persons who occupy a housing unit. A household includes the related family members and all the unrelated persons, if any, such as lodgers, foster children, wards, or employees who share the housing unit. A person living alone is counted as a household. A group of unrelated people who share a housing unit as roommates or unmarried partners is also counted as a household. Households do not include group quarters such as college dormitories, prisons, or nursing homes.

household, race/ethnicity of Households are categorized according to the race or ethnicity of the householder only.

householder The person (or one of the persons) in whose name the housing unit is owned or rented or, if there is no such person, any adult member. With married couples, the householder may be either the husband or wife. The householder is the reference person for the household.

householder, age of Used to categorize households into age groups such as those used in this book. Married couples, for example, are classified according to the age of either the husband or wife, depending on which one identified him or herself as the householder.

housing unit A house, apartment, group of rooms, or single room occupied or intended for occupancy as separate living quarters. Separate living quarters are those in which the occupants do not live and eat with any other persons in the structure and that have direct access from the outside of the building or through a common hall that is used or intended for use by the occupants of another unit or by the general public. The occupants may be a single family, one person living alone, two or more families living together, or any other group of related or unrelated persons who share living arrangements.

Housing Vacancy Survey The HVS is a supplement to the Current Population Survey, providing quarterly and annual data on rental and homeowner vacancy rates, characteristics of units available for occupancy, and homeownership rates by age, household type, region, state, and metropolitan area. The Current Population Survey sample includes 51,000 occupied housing units and 9,000 vacant units.

housing value The respondent's estimate of how much his or her house and lot would sell for if it were for sale.

iGeneration U.S. residents born in 1995 or later.

immigration The relatively permanent movement (change of residence) of people into the country of reference.

in-migration The relatively permanent movement (change of residence) of people into a subnational geographic entity, such as a region, division, state, metropolitan area, or county.

income Money received in the preceding calendar year by each person aged 15 or older from each of the following sources: (1) earnings from longest job (or self-employment); (2) earnings from jobs other than longest job; (3) unemployment compensation; (4) workers' compensation; (5) Social Security; (6) Supplemental Security income; (7) public assistance; (8) veterans' payments; (9) survivor benefits; (10) disability benefits; (11) retirement pensions; (12) interest; (13) dividends; (14) rents and royalties or estates and trusts; (15) educational assistance; (16) alimony; (17) child support; (18) financial assistance from outside the household, and other periodic income. Income is reported in several ways in this book. Household income is the combined income of all household members. Income of persons is all income accruing to a person from all sources. Earnings are the money a person receives from his or her job.

industry The industry in which a person worked longest in the preceding calendar year.

job tenure The length of time a person has been employed continuously by the same employer.

labor force The labor force tables in this book show the civilian labor force only. The labor force includes both the employed and the unemployed (people who are looking for work). People are counted as in the labor force if they were working or looking for work during the reference week in which the Census Bureau fields the Current Population Survey.

labor force participation rate The percent of the civilian noninstitutional population that is in the civilian labor force, which includes both the employed and the unemployed.

married couples with or without children under age 18 Married couples with or without own children under age 18 living in the same household. Couples without children under age 18 may be parents of grown children who live elsewhere, or they could be childless couples.

median The amount that divides the population or households into two equal portions: one below and one above the median. Medians can be calculated for income, age, and many other characteristics.

median income The amount that divides the income distribution into two equal groups, half having incomes above the median, half having incomes below the median. The medians for households or families are based on all households or families. The median for persons are based on all persons aged 15 or older with income.

metropolitan statistical area The general concept of a metropolitan area is a large population nucleus with adjacent communities having a high degree of social and economic integration with the core. The Office of Management and Budget defines the nation's metropolitan statistical areas. In general, they must include a city or urbanized area with 50,000 or more inhabitants and a total population of 100,000 or more. The county (or counties) that contains the largest city is the "central county" (counties), along with any adjacent counties that are socially and economically integrated with the central county (or counties). In New England, MSAs are defined in terms of cities and towns rather than counties.

millennial generation U.S. residents born between 1977 and 1994.

mobility status People are classified according to their mobility status on the basis of a comparison between their place of residence at the time of the March Current Population Survey and their place of residence in March of the previous year. Nonmovers are people living in the same house at the end of the period as at the beginning of the period. Movers are people living in a different house at the end of the period than at the beginning of the period. Movers from abroad are either citizens or aliens whose place of residence is outside the United States at the beginning of the period, that is, in an outlying area under the jurisdiction of the United States or in a foreign country. The mobility status of children is fully allocated from the mother if she is in the household; otherwise it is allocated from the householder.

National Ambulatory Medical Care Survey The NAMCS is an annual survey of visits to nonfederally employed office-based physicians who are primarily engaged in direct patient care. Data are collected from physicians rather than patients, with each physician assigned a one-week reporting period. During the week, the physician or office staff record a systematic random sample of visit characteristics.

National Compensation Survey The Bureau of Labor Statistics' NCS examines the incidence and detailed provisions of selected employee benefit plans in small, medium, and large private establishments, and state and local governments. Each year BLS economists visit a representative sample of establishments across the country, asking questions about the establishment, its employees, and their benefits.

National Health and Nutrition Examination Survey The NHANES is a continuous survey of a representative sample of the U.S. civilian noninstitutionalized population. Respondents are interviewed at home about their health and nutrition, and the interview is followed up by a physical examination that measures such things as height and weight in mobile examination centers.

National Health Interview Survey The NHIS is a continuing nationwide sample survey of the civilian noninstitutional population of the U.S. conducted by the Census Bureau for the National Center for Health Statistics. In interviews each year, data are collected from more than 100,000 people about their illnesses, injuries, impairments, chronic and acute conditions, activity limitations, and use of health services.

National Hospital Ambulatory Medical Care Survey The NHAMCS, sponsored by the National Center for Health Statistics, is an annual national probability sample survey of visits to emergency departments and outpatient departments at non-Federal, short stay and general hospitals. Hospital staff collect data from patient records.

National Household Education Survey The NHES, sponsored by the National Center for Education Statistics, provides descriptive data on the educational activities of the U.S. population, including after-school care and adult education. The NHES is a system of telephone surveys of a representative sample of 45,000 to 60,000 households in the U.S.

Native Hawaiian and other Pacific Islander The 2000 census identified this group for the first time as a separate racial category from Asians. In most survey data, however, the population is included with Asians.

net migration The result of subtracting out-migration from in-migration for an area. Another way to derive net migration is to subtract natural increase (births minus deaths) from total population change in an area.

nonfamily household A household maintained by a householder who lives alone or who lives with people to whom he or she is not related.

nonfamily householder A householder who lives alone or with nonrelatives.

non-Hispanic People who do not identify themselves as Hispanic are classified as non-Hispanic. Non-Hispanics may be of any race.

non-Hispanic white People who identify their race as white alone and who do not indicate an Hispanic origin.

nonmetropolitan area Counties that are not classified as metropolitan areas.

occupation Occupational classification is based on the kind of work a person did at his or her job during the previous calendar year. If a person changed jobs during the year, the data refer to the occupation of the job held the longest during that year.

occupied housing units A housing unit in which a person or group of people are living in it or the occupants are only temporarily absent—on vacation, example. By definition, the count of occupied housing units is the same as the count of households.

outside principal cities The portion of a metropolitan county or counties that falls outside of the principal city or cities; generally regarded as the suburbs.

own children Sons and daughters, including stepchildren and adopted children, of the householder. The totals include never-married children living away from home in college dormitories.

owner occupied A housing unit in which the owner lives in the unit, even if it is mortgaged or not fully paid for. A cooperative or condominium unit is "owner occupied" only if the owner lives in it. All other occupied units are classified as "renter occupied."

part-time employment Less than 35 hours of work per week in a majority of the weeks worked during the year.

percent change The change (either positive or negative) in a measure that is expressed as a proportion of the starting measure. When median income changes from $20,000 to $25,000, for example, this is a 25 percent increase.

percentage point change The change (either positive or negative) in a value which is already expressed as a percentage. When a labor force participation rate changes from 70 percent of 75 percent, for example, this is a 5 percentage point increase.

population versus participant measures On the time use tables, average time spent doing an activity is shown for either the population as a whole (such as all 25-to-34-year-olds) or only for those participating in an activity in the previous 24-hours, or diary day. Data referring to the population as a whole include every respondent, even those who did not engage in the activity on diary day. This type of calculation allows researchers to see how Americans prioritize the entire range of daily activities, but it results in artificially short amounts of time devoted to activities done infrequently (such as volunteering). Data referring to participant time show only the time spent on specific activities by respondents who reported doing the activity on diary day. They more accurately reflect the amount of time people spend doing specific activities when they do them.

poverty level The official income threshold below which families and people are classified as living in poverty. The threshold rises each year with inflation and varies depending on family size and age of householder. For more on poverty thresholds, go to Internet site http://www.census.gov/hhes/www/poverty/data/threshld/index.html.

primary activity On the time use tables, primary activity is the main activity a respondent was doing at a specified time.

principal cities The largest cities in a metropolitan area are called the principal cities. The balance of a metropolitan area outside the principal cities is regarded as the "suburbs."

proportion or share The value of a part expressed as a percentage of the whole. If there are 4 million people aged 25 and 3 million of them are white, then the white proportion is 75 percent.

race Race is self-reported and can be defined in three ways. The "race alone" population comprises people who identify themselves as only one race. The "race in combination" population comprises people who identify themselves as more than one race, such as white and black. The "race, alone or in combination" population includes both those who identify themselves as one race and those who identify themselves as more than one race.

regions The four major regions and nine census divisions of the United States are the state groupings as shown below:

Northeast:
—New England: Connecticut, Maine, Massachusetts, New Hampshire, Rhode Island, and Vermont
—Middle Atlantic: New Jersey, New York, and Pennsylvania

Midwest:
—East North Central: Illinois, Indiana, Michigan, Ohio, and Wisconsin
—West North Central: Iowa, Kansas, Minnesota, Missouri, Nebraska, North Dakota, and South Dakota

South:
—South Atlantic: Delaware, District of Columbia, Florida, Georgia, Maryland, North Carolina, South Carolina, Virginia, and West Virginia
—East South Central: Alabama, Kentucky, Mississippi, and Tennessee
—West South Central: Arkansas, Louisiana, Oklahoma, and Texas

West:
—Mountain: Arizona, Colorado, Idaho, Montana, Nevada, New Mexico, Utah, and Wyoming
—Pacific: Alaska, California, Hawaii, Oregon, and Washington

renter occupied *See* Owner Occupied.

Retirement Confidence Survey The RCS, sponsored by the Employee Benefit Research Institute, the American Savings Education Council, and Mathew Greenwald & Associates, is an annual survey of a nationally representative sample of 1,000 people aged 25 or older. Respondents are asked a core set of questions that have been asked since 1996, measuring attitudes and behavior towards retirement. Additional questions are also asked about current retirement issues.

rounding Percentages are rounded to the nearest tenth of a percent; therefore, the percentages in a distribution do not always add exactly to 100.0 percent. The totals, however, are always shown as 100.0. Moreover, individual figures are rounded to the nearest thousand without being adjusted to group totals, which are independently rounded; percentages are based on the unrounded numbers.

self-employment A person is categorized as self-employed if he or she was self-employed in the job held longest during the reference period. Persons who report self-employment from a second job are excluded, but those who report wage-and-salary income from a second job are included. Unpaid workers in family businesses are excluded. Self-employment statistics include only nonagricultural workers and exclude people who work for themselves in incorporated business.

sex ratio The number of men per 100 women.

suburbs *See* Outside principal city.

Survey of Consumer Finances A triennial survey taken by the Federal Reserve Board. It collects data on the assets, debts, and net worth of American households. For the 2007 survey, the Federal Reserve Board interviewed a representative sample of 4,422 households. To capture the effect of the Great Recession on household wealth, the Federal Reserve re-interviewed in 2009 the households that participated in the 2007 survey.

unemployed People who, during the survey period, had no employment but were available and looking for work. Those who were laid off from their jobs and were waiting to be recalled are also classified as unemployed.

white A racial category that includes many Hispanics (who may be of any race) unless the term "non-Hispanic white" is used.

Bibliography

Bureau of Labor Statistics

Internet site http://www.bls.gov

—2000, 2006, and 2009 Consumer Expenditure Surveys, Internet site http://www.bls.gov/cex/

—2009 American Time Use Survey, Internet site http://www.bls.gov/tus/home.htm

—Economic and Employment Projections, Internet site http://www.bls.gov/news.release/ecopro.toc.htm

—Employee Benefits Survey, Internet site http://www.bls.gov/ncs/ebs/benefits/2010/ownership_civilian.htm

—Employee Tenure, Internet site http://www.bls.gov/news.release/tenure.toc.htm

—Employment Characteristics of Families, Internet site http://www.bls.gov/news.release/famee.toc.htm

—Labor Force Statistics from the Current Population Survey, Internet site http://www.bls.gov/cps/tables.htm#empstat

—Monthly Labor Review, "Labor Force Projections to 2018: Older Workers Staying More Active," November 2009, Internet site http://www.bls.gov/opub/mlr/2009/11/home.htm

Bureau of the Census

Internet site http://www.census.gov/

—2000 Census, American FactFinder, Internet site http://factfinder.census.gov/servlet/BasicFactsServlet

—2000 Census, Table DP-1: Profile of General Demographic Characteristics: 2000, Internet site http://www.census.gov/Press-Release/www/2001/demoprofile.html

—2009 American Community Survey, Internet site http://factfinder.census.gov/servlet/DatasetMainPageServlet?_program=ACS&_submenuId=&_lang=en&_ts=

—2010 Census Factfinder, Internet site http://factfinder2.census.gov/faces/nav/jsf/pages/index
.xhtml

—2010 Census, State Population Distribution and Change: 2000 to 2010, 2010 Census Briefs, Internet site http://2010.census.gov/2010census/data/

—American Housing Survey for the United States, Internet site http://www.census.gov/hhes/www/housing/ahs/ahs.html

—America's Families and Living Arrangements, 2010 Current Population Survey Annual Social and Economic Supplement, Internet site http://www.census.gov/population/www/socdemo/hh-fam/cps2010.html

—Families and Living Arrangements, Historical Time Series, Current Population Survey Annual Social and Economic Supplements, Internet site http://www.census.gov/population/www/socdemo/hh-fam.html

—Geographic Mobility: 2008 to 2009, Detailed Tables, Current Population Survey Annual Social and Economic Supplement, Internet site http://www.census.gov/population/www/socdemo/migrate/cps2009.html

—Geographical Mobility/Migration, Current Population Survey Annual Social and Economic Supplements, Internet site http://www.census.gov/population/www/socdemo/migrate.html

—Health Insurance, Internet site http://www.census.gov/hhes/www/cpstables/032010/health/toc.htm

—Historical Health Insurance Tables, Internet site http://www.census.gov/hhes/www/hlthins/historic/index.html

—Historical Income Tables, Current Population Survey Annual Social and Economic Supplements, Internet site http://www.census.gov/hhes/www/income/histinc/histinctb.html

—Historical Poverty Tables, Current Population Survey Annual Social and Economic Supplements, Internet site http://www.census.gov/hhes/www/poverty/histpov/histpovtb.html

—Historical Statistics of the United States, Colonial Times to 1970, Part 1, 1975

—Housing Vacancy Surveys, Internet site http://www.census.gov/hhes/www/housing/hvs/hvs.html

—Income, Poverty, and Health Insurance Coverage in the United States: 2009, Current Population Report, P60-238, 2010; Internet site http://www.census.gov/hhes/www/income/data/incpovhlth/2009/index.htm

—Metropolitan Areas and Cities, 1990 Census Profile, No. 3, 1991

—National Population Estimates, Internet site http://www.census.gov/popest/national/asrh/

—Number, Timing, and Duration of Marriages and Divorces: 2004, Detailed Tables, Internet site http://www.census.gov/population/www/socdemo/marr-div/2004detailed_tables.html

—School Enrollment, Historical Tables, Internet site http://www.census.gov/population/www/socdemo/school.html

—School Enrollment—Social and Economic Characteristics of Students: October 2009, detailed tables, Internet site http://www.census.gov/population/www/socdemo/school/cps2009.html

—What's It Worth: Field of Training and Economic Status in 2004, Detailed Tables, Internet site http://www.census.gov/population/www/socdemo/education/sipp2004w2.html

Centers for Disease Control and Prevention

Internet site http://www.cdc.gov

—Behavioral Risk Factor Surveillance System, Prevalence Data, Internet site http://apps.nccd.cdc.gov/brfss/

—HIV/AIDS, Internet site http://www.cdc.gov/hiv/surveillance/resources/reports/2008report/table2a.htm

Department of Homeland Security

Internet site http://www.dhs.gov/index.shtm

—Immigration, 2010 Yearbook of Immigration Statistics, Internet site http://www.uscis.gov/graphics/shared/statistics/yearbook/index.htm

—Estimates of the Unauthorized Immigrant Population Residing in the United States: January 2010, Internet site http://www.uscis.gov/graphics/shared/statistics/yearbook/index.htm

Employee Benefit Research Institute

Internet site http://www.ebri.org/

—2011 Retirement Confidence Survey, Internet site http://www.ebri.org/surveys/rcs/2011/

—"Retirement Plan Participation: Survey of Income and Program Participation (SIPP) Data, 2009," Notes, February 2010, Internet site http://www.ebri.org/publications/notes/index.cfm?fa=notesDisp&content_id=4702

Federal Interagency Forum on Child and Family Statistics
Internet site http://childstats.gov
—America's Children in Brief: Key National Indicators of Well-Being, 2010, Internet site http://childstats.gov/americaschildren/tables.asp

Federal Reserve Board
Internet site http://www.federalreserve.gov/pubs/oss/oss2/scfindex.html
—"Surveying the Aftermath of the Storm: Changes in Family Finances from 2007 to 2009," Appendix tables, Internet site http://www.federalreserve.gov/pubs/oss/oss2/2009p/scf2009phome.html

National Center for Education Statistics
Internet site http://nces.ed.gov
—The Condition of Education, Internet site http://nces.ed.gov/programs/coe/
—Digest of Education Statistics: 2010, Internet site http://nces.ed.gov/programs/digest/
—National Household Education Surveys Program, Parent and Family Involvement in Education, 2006–07 School Year, Internet site http://nces.ed.gov/pubsearch/pubsinfo.asp?pubid=2008050
—Projections of Education Statistics to 2019, Internet site http://nces.ed.gov/programs/projections/projections2019/tables.asp

National Center for Health Statistics
Internet site http://www.cdc.gov/nchs
—Anthropometric Reference Data for Children and Adults: United States, 2003–2006, National Health Statistics Reports, Number 10, 2008, Internet site http://www.cdc.gov/nchs/products/pubs/pubd/nhsr/nhsr.htm
—Births: Preliminary Data for 2009, National Vital Statistics Reports, Vol. 59, No. 3, 2010, Internet site http://www.cdc.gov/nchs/births.htm
—Complementary and Alternative Medicine Use Among Adults and Children: United States, 2007, National Health Statistics Report, No. 12, 2008, Internet site http://nccam.nih.gov/news/camstats/2007/index.htm
—Deaths: Preliminary Data for 2009, National Vital Statistics Reports, Vol. 59, No. 4, 2011, Internet site http://www.cdc.gov/nchs/deaths.htm
—Fertility, Contraception, and Fatherhood: Data on Men and Women from Cycle 6 of the 2002 National Survey of Family Growth, Vital and Health Statistics, Series 23, No. 26, 2006; Internet site http://www.cdc.gov/nchs/nsfg.htm
—Fertility, Family Planning, and Reproductive Health of U.S. Women: Data from the 2002 National Survey of Family Growth, Vital and Health Statistics, Series 23, No. 25, 2005; Internet site http://www.cdc.gov/nchs/nsfg.htm

—Health, United States, 2010, Internet site http://www.cdc.gov/nchs/hus.htm

—Summary Health Statistics for U.S. Adults: National Health Interview Survey, 2009, Series 10, No. 249, 2010, Internet site http://www.cdc.gov/nchs/nhis.htm

—Summary Health Statistics for U.S. Children: National Health Interview Survey, 2009, Series 10, No. 247, 2010, Internet site http://www.cdc.gov/nchs/nhis.htm

—Summary Health Statistics for the U.S. Population: National Health Interview Survey, 2009, Series 10, No. 248, 2010, Internet site http://www.cdc.gov/nchs/nhis.htm

National Sporting Goods Association

Internet site http://www.nsga.org

—Sports Participation, Internet site http://www.nsga.org

Substance Abuse and Mental Health Services Administration

Internet site http://www.samhsa.gov

—National Survey on Drug Use and Health, 2009, Internet site http://oas.samhsa.gov/NSDUH/2k9NSDUH/2k9Results.htm

Survey Documentation and Analysis, Computer-assisted Survey Methods Program, University of California, Berkeley

Internet site http://sda.berkeley.edu/

—General Social Surveys, 1972-2010 Cumulative Data Files, Internet site http://sda.berkeley.edu/cgi-bin/hsda?harcsda+gss10

Index

disposal in sink, 186
dividends, as a source of income, 284
divorce, 400, 402–403
doctor visits. *See* Health care visits.
drinking. *See* Alcohol use.
drug use, illicit, 125, 128
drugs, prescription, 135–137
dual-earners. *See* Households, married-couple.

earners, household income by number of, 210–212
earnings. *See also* Income.
    as source of income, 271–272
    by educational attainment, 270–272
    by occupation, 270–279
    by sex, 271–279
    of husbands and wives, 396, 398
eating and drinking, time spent, 545–562
education, spending on
    by age of householder, 470, 473, 476
    by educational attainment, 531, 534, 537, 540
    by high-income households, 490, 493, 496
    by household income, 481, 484, 487
    by household type, 501, 504, 507
    by race and Hispanic origin, 512, 515, 518
    by region, 523, 526, 529
    trends in, 462, 465
educational activities, time spent, 545–562
educational assistance loans for college, 90
educational attainment. *See also* College enrollment and
    School enrollment.
    abortion, attitudes toward, 43, 46
    alcohol use by, 125, 127
    alternative medicine use by, 148, 150–152
    assets by, 567–586
    by age, 50–53
    by race and Hispanic origin, 54–57
    by region, 58–59
    by sex, 50, 52–53, 56–57
    by state, 58, 60
    childrens' SAT scores by parents', 83–84
    cigarette smoking by, 125–126
    day care use by mother's, 307
    death penalty, attitudes toward, 43–44
    divorce by, 402–403
    earnings by, 254–255
    evolution, attitudes toward, 30
    excitement in life by, 7
    gay marriage, attitudes toward, 38
    gun permits, attitudes toward, 43, 45
    happiness by, 5–8
    health care visits by, 146
    health conditions of children by parental,
      135–137
    health insurance, reason for no coverage by, 133
    health status by, 111
    high school dropouts, 78–79
    high school graduates, projections of, 80–82
    homeownership by, 167, 170
    homeschooling, 66–67
    hospital stays by, 154
    ideal number of children, 22–23
    income by, 219–220, 254–255, 270–272

marital status by, 394–395
mobility by, 11
net worth by, 565
news sources by, 39–40
of husbands and wives, 396–397
of parents by involvement in children's school
    activities, 64–66
of same-sex couples, 405
parents satisfaction with schools, 72–73
perception of income by, 15–17
political attitudes by, 39, 41–42
premarital sex, attitudes toward, 35–36
religion, attitudes toward, 28, 31–34
religious preferences by, 28, 31
right to die, attitudes toward, 43, 47
satisfaction with financial situation by, 17
science, attitudes toward, 29
sex roles by, 25–26
should government help the sick, 27
social class by, 15
spanking children, attitudes toward, 24
spending by, 461, 463
standard of living by, 19–21
tolerance of same-sex relationships, 35, 37, 38
trust in others by, 8
weight status by, 113
working at home by, 336–337
educational enrichment activities, children's participation
    in, 64–66
electricity. *See also* Utilities, fuels, and public services,
    spending on.
    cost, 199, 463–464, 469, 472, 475, 480, 483, 486,
      489, 492, 495, 503, 506, 509, 511, 514, 517, 522,
      525, 528, 533, 536, 539
    use, 179, 183–184
emphysema, 138–141
employee benefits, 341
employment. *See* Labor force.
English, ability to speak, 458–459
entertainment, spending on
    by age of householder, 470, 473, 476
    by educational attainment, 531, 534, 537, 540
    by high-income households, 490, 493, 496
    by household income, 481, 484, 487
    by household type, 501, 504, 507
    by race and Hispanic origin, 512, 515, 518
    by region, 523, 526, 529
    trends in, 465
environment versus economy, 13
evolution, attitudes toward, 3, 30
excitement in life, 3–4, 7
exercise. *See also* Recreational activities.
    time spent in, 545–555

family type
    divorce by, 402–403
    health conditions of children by, 134–137
fireplace, in home, 187
food, spending on
    by age of householder, 469, 472, 475
    by educational attainment, 533, 536, 539
    by high-income households, 489, 492, 495